Readings in Applied Microeconomic Theory

BLACKWELL READINGS FOR CONTEMPORARY ECONOMICS

This series presents collections of writings by some of the world's foremost economists on core issues in the discipline. Each volume dovetails with a variety of existing economics courses at the advanced undergraduate, graduate, and MBA levels. The readings, gleaned from a wide variety of classic and contemporary sources, are placed in context by a comprehensive introduction from the editor. In addition, a thorough index facilitates research.

Readings in Urban Economics: Issues and Public Policy edited by Robert W. Wassmer
Readings in Industrial Organization edited by Luís M. B. Cabral
Readings in Applied Microeconomic Theory: Market Forces and Solutions edited by Robert E. Kuenne
Readings in Social Welfare: Theory and Policy edited by Robert E. Kuenne
Readings in the Theory of Economic Development edited by Dilip Mookherjee and Debraj Ray
Readings in Games and Information edited by Eric Rasmusen

Readings in Applied Microeconomic Theory

Market Forces and Solutions

Edited by

Robert E. Kuenne
Princeton University

Copyright © Blackwell Publishers Ltd 2000
Editorial matter and organization copyright © Robert E. Kuenne 2000

First published 2000

2 4 6 8 10 9 7 5 3 1

Blackwell Publishers Inc.
350 Main Street
Malden, Massachusetts 02148
USA

Blackwell Publishers Ltd
108 Cowley Road
Oxford OX4 1JF
UK

Library of Congress Cataloging-in-Publication Data

Readings in applied microeconomic theory : market forces and solutions / edited by Robert E. Kuenne.
    p. cm.
  Includes bibliographical references and index.
  ISBN 0–631–22069–0 (hb : alk. paper)—ISBN 0–631–22070–4 (pb : alk. paper)
  1. Microeconomics. I. Kuenne, Robert E.

HB172.R328 2000
338.5—dc21

                                                                    99–086005

British Library Cataloguing in Publication Data
A CIP catalogue record for this book is available from the British Library.

Typeset in 10pt on 11.5pt Ehrhardt
by Kolam Information Services Pvt. Ltd., Pondicherry, India
Printed in Great Britain by MPG Books, Bodmin, Cornwall.

This book is printed on acid-free paper.

Commemorating the fiftieth anniversary of the founding of
The Liquidity Preference Marching and Chowder Society
and dedicated to its founding members
graduate students, Department of Economics
Harvard University
1949

Contents

Notes on Editor and Authors

Robert E. Kuenne is director of the General Economic Systems Company (*GENESYS*), Princeton, New Jersey.

Gary S. Becker, Nobel Laureate in Economics, 1992, is University Professor in Economics and Sociology, University of Chicago, a senior fellow of the Hoover Institution, and editor of *The Journal of Political Economy*.

Severin Borenstein is a professor at the Haas School of Business, University of California at Berkeley, and editor of *The Journal of Industrial Economics*.

Steven N. S. Cheung is a professor and chairman of the school of economics, University of Hong Kong, and president of the Western Economic Association International.

Charles T. Clotfelter is the Z. Smith Reynolds Professor of Public Policy Studies, professor of economics and law, director of the Center for the Study of Philanthropy and Voluntarism, and associate director of the Terry Sanford Institute of Public Policy, Duke University.

Philip J. Cook is ITT/Terry Sanford Distinguished Professor of Public Policy Studies, director of the Terry Sanford Institute of Public Policy, and chairman of the department of public policy studies, Duke University.

Robert S. Gibbons is Sloan Distinguished Professor of Management at the Sloan School of Management, Massachusetts Institute of Technology.

Richard J. Gilbert is professor of economics and director of the Universitywide Energy Research Group, University of California at Berkeley.

Daniel M. Hausman is professor of philosophy and chairman of the department of philosophy, University of Wisconsin.

Harvey Leibenstein, deceased, was professor of economics, emeritus, Harvard University.

Mark J. Machina is professor of economics, University of California at San Diego, a fellow of the Center for Advanced Study in the Behavioral Sciences, 1987–88, and a fellow of the Econometric Society.

Paul R. Milgrom is a professor of economics and the Shirley R. and Leonard W. Ely, Jr., Professor of Humanities and Sciences, Graduate School of Business, Stanford University, and a fellow of the American Academy of Arts and Sciences and of the Econometric Society.

Mark V. Pauly is a professor of economics, professor of public management, Bendheim Professor of Health Care Systems, professor of insurance, and director of the Center for Research, Leonard Davis Institute of Health Economics, University of Pennsylvania.

R. A. Radford was a prisoner of war in a German Stalag during a portion of World War II.

John Roberts is the Jonathan B. Lovelace Professor of Economics and Strategic Management and director of the Global Management Program, Stanford Graduate Business School, and a fellow of the Econometric Society.

Paul M. Romer is the STANCO 25 Professor of Economics and Ralph Landau Senior Fellow of the Institute for Economic Policy Research, Stanford Graduate Business School, a senior fellow of the Hoover Institution and fellow of the Econometric Society.

Stephen A. Ross, the inventor of the economic theory of agency, is a principal of Roll & Ross Asset Management Corporation, and a fellow of the American Academy of Arts and Sciences. He is currently a visiting professor at the Sloan School of Management, Massachusetts Institute of Technology.

Herbert A. Simon, Nobel Laureate in Economics, 1978, is the Richard King Mellon University Professor of Computer Science and Psychology, Carnegie Mellon University, and recipient of the National Medal of Science, 1986.

A. Michael Spence is dean emeritus and Philip H. Knight Professor, Graduate Business School, and professor of economics, Stanford University. He is the recipient of the John Bates Clark Medal, 1981, and is a fellow of the Econometric Society, the American Academy of Arts and Sciences, and the American Economic Association.

George J. Stigler, deceased, was a Nobel Laureate in Economics, 1982, and the Charles R. Walgreen Distinguished Service Professor, University of Chicago.

Robert J. Weber is Frederic E. Nemmers Distinguished Professor of Decision Sciences, Kellogg School of Management, Northwestern University.

Preface

The articles in this collection have been chosen with the needs of students in upper class microeconomic theory courses and first-year graduate school in mind. Because of the richness of materials and breadth of the field, practical size limitations to keep the price of the book within reasonable bounds, and the large variance in student preparation for mathematical methodology, some care was exercised to obtain constrained maximum usefulness.

The guidelines for substantive choices were the following. First, we sought an admixture of classic articles that were innovations of concepts and methods that are still of current importance in microeconomic analysis, as well as modern treatments of the frontier issues in applied microeconomic theory. For both types of article, the emphasis in choice was on the relevance and importance of the topics treated. Virtuoso performances in arcane irrelevance, however fashionable, were systematically, nay, zealously, shunned.

Second, when selections contained mathematical treatments that demanded more than the standard advanced mathematics studied by today's students (for example, variational methods or algorithms to solve nonconvex models), we required that the literary presentations be able to stand alone in making the major contributions accessible to students without such preparation. We felt that instructors who wished to explicate such methods could refer students to materials that were beyond the reach of our goals for them. The selections generally contain bibliographic references for such greater study in depth.

Third, lucid presentations of overviews of important new fields (for example, game theory, decision making under uncertainty theory, auction theory) were preferred to narrow-gauged presentations. Of necessity, microeconomic theory courses can pursue only a few topics in nonsurvey depth, and the choice of those topics is best left to the instructor. The survey selections in this collection take the student well beyond textbook treatments, without introducing him or her to the minutiae of the subfields. The bibliographies of the selections, again in this instance, provide pathways for more detailed study.

Last, the book concentrates on the forces generated by the market economy and the nature of the solutions they bring about, without heavy emphasis on the social welfare aspects of those solutions. Such consideration is not entirely excluded, as in the discussion of the excess capacity theorem and X-efficiency, but it is not a consistent concern in the book. Initially, we had hoped to include theoretical and policy issues in the area of social welfare in the volume, but concluded that, to do a creditable job of coverage, it would have to be twice its present size. It was decided, therefore, to gather an integrated selection bearing upon these important topics in a second volume, *Readings in Social Welfare: Theory and Policy*, published simultaneously with the present book, which complements and completes the latter's coverage.

R. E. K.
Genequil
Charlotte, Vermont

Acknowledgments

The editor and publisher wish to thank the following who have kindly given permission for the use of copyright material.

The American Economic Association and the authors for articles:

- Severin Borenstein, The evolution of U.S. airline competition, *Journal of Economic Perspectives*, 6 (2), (1991), 45–73.
- Charles T. Clotfelter and Philip J. Cook, On the economics of state lotteries, *Journal of Economic Perspectives*, 4 (4), (1990), 105–19.
- Robert S. Gibbons, An introduction to applicable game theory, *Journal of Economic Perspectives*, 11 (1), (1997), 127–49.
- Richard J. Gilbert, The role of potential competition in industrial organization, *Journal of Economic Perspectives*, 3 (3), (1989), 107–27.
- Daniel M. Hausman, Economic methodology in a nutshell, *Journal of Economic Perspectives*, 3 (2), (1989), 115–27.
- Harvey Leibenstein, Allocative efficiency vs. X-efficiency, *American Economic Review*, 56, (1966), 392–415.
- Mark J. Machina, Choice under uncertainty: Problems solved and unsolved, *Journal of Economic Perspectives*, 1 (1), (1987), 121–54.
- Paul R. Milgrom and John Roberts, The economics of modern manufacturing: Technology, strategy, and organization, *American Economic Review*, 80, (1990), 511–28.
- Mark V. Pauly, The economics of moral hazard: Comment, *American Economic Review*, 58, (1968), 531–7.
- Paul M. Romer, Why, indeed, in America? Theory, history and the origins of modern economic growth, *American Economic Review, Papers and Proceedings*, 86, (1996), 202–6.
- Stephen A. Ross, The economic theory of agency: The principal's problem, *American Economic Review, Papers and Proceedings*, 63, (1973), 134–9.
- Herbert A. Simon, Theories of decision-making in economics and behavioral science, *American Economic Review*, 49, (1959), 253–83.

The Econometric Society for article:

- Paul R. Milgrom and Robert J. Weber, A theory of auctions and competitive bidding, *Econometrica*, 50, (1982), 1089–122.

The London School of Economics & Political Science for article:

- R. A. Radford, The economic organization of a P.O.W. camp, *Economica*, 12, (1945), 189–210.

The MIT Press for article:

- A. Michael Spence, Job market signaling, *Quarterly Journal of Economics*, 87, (1973), 355–74.

The Review of Economic Studies Ltd. for article:

- A. Michael Spence, Product selection, fixed costs, and monopolistic competition, *Review of Economic Studies*, 43, (1976), 217–35.

The Royal Economic Society for article:

- Gary S. Becker, A theory of the allocation of time, *Economic Journal*, 75, (1965), 493–517.

The University of Chicago Law School and the author for article:

- Steven N. S. Cheung, The fable of the bees: An economic investigation, *Journal of Law and Economics*, 16, (1973), 11–33.

The University of Chicago Press for article:

- George J. Stigler, Perfect competition, historically contemplated, *Journal of Political Economy*, 65, (1957), 1–17.

Every attempt has been made to trace copyright holders. The editor and publisher would like to apologize in advance for any inadvertent use of copyright material, and thank the individuals and organizations acknowledged above who have kindly given their permission to reproduce the selections noted.

Introduction

Methodologies are the frameworks used in a field of scholarship to gain insights into the causal forces that determine the values of variables and the states of attributes that are the data of explanatory concern to that field. Chapter 1 presents, in a formal manner, the neoclassical methodology that constitutes the most widely used framework in microeconomic analysis. It is grounded in the basic assumption that economic agents act in informed, egoistic self-interest to maximize benefits or minimize costs in making their choices. Insights into the causation of the models constructed by usage of the methodology are gained by parametric displacements.

Although, as we shall see, there are a variety of methodologies ranging from the formal to the informal in microeconomics, an understanding of this dominant form is most important for the student. It is necessary to understand the analytical procedures he or she will encounter typically, as well as to understand the arguments of their critics. Such understanding provides the student with an understanding of the framework of thought of the microeconomist, and to perceive the thread of continuity that underlies their work, however different the subjects may be. One application of the model in a much more sophisticated form, given the nature of the functions in the model and the interdependence among the parametric variables employed is found in chapter 7; nonetheless, the methodology will be recognized by the student as a variant of the methodology discussed in chapter 1.

Different methodologies arise from a variety of considerations. One such consideration is the set of variables and attributes that it is the goal of the methodology to explain. Are they the prices, quantities and qualities of goods and services at a given time in an economy? Or, is the researcher interested in the innovations that change the structure of product and goods availabilities over time? More abstractly, do they center about the defining economic laws and institutions of an era?

The choice among methodologies is also affected by what scholars perceive to be the potentials and limitations of the human agents acting within given constraints to make their economic choices. In chapter 2, Simon issues his seminal challenge to the assumption of informed optimization employed in the neoclassical model of chapter 1. His objections are based on the complexity of realistic choice environments and the limitations of the human mind in processing a wealth of information in the presence of uncertainty. The economic agent, he argues, should be depicted as making choices under a motivation of "satisficing" rather than optimizing. In these and other dimensions of decision making. Simon urges that economists include the findings of social psychologists in formulating the assumptions of their models. His paper was instrumental in inspiring economists' interests in the investigations discussed at length in chapter 17, for example.

Methodologies are also shaped by the standards of judgment different investigators accept as relevant in validating the results of such approaches. In chapter 3, Hausman asks whether, to be useful, the projected states of the variables and attributes of a methodology must pass repeated tests that rely only on the evidence of the senses (the criterion adopted by the exact sciences). Alternatively, can they be judged worthwhile even though they are not testable if they are judged plausible to most experts in the relevant subject? Or, should the results of the models specific to a given methodology be judged by the realism of the assumptions whose mutual implications imply those results?

Finally, in chapter 20, Romer proposes that, in adopting a methodology that seeks to explain historical reality with theoretical modeling, one should follow *historical reductionism*, which moves in Hegelian manner from models whose component variables progress from less to the more detailed specifications, each such model seeking more detailed explanations of the components of the model that precedes it.

CHAPTER ONE

On Methodologies in Modern Microeconomics

ROBERT E. KUENNE

1. The Structure of a Microeconomic Model

Methodologies are the frameworks employed by workers in a field of scholarship to gain insights into the causal forces that determine the values of variables and the states of attributes of explanatory concern to that field. Different methodologies arise from different perceptions of what those variables and attributes are; for example, are they the prices and quantities of goods and services at a given time in an economy, the innovations that change the structure of production and goods availabilities over time, the defining economic institutions of an era, or the processes of changes over time in these and other potential economic variables and attributes? They are also affected by what researchers perceive to be the potentials and limitations of the human agents acting within given constraints to energize those forces of change. Finally, they are shaped by the standards of judgment different investigators perceive to be relevant in validating the results of such approaches (e.g., to be useful, must the projected states of the variables and attributes of a methodology pass repeated tests that rely only on the evidence of the senses, can they be judged worthwhile if they are plausible to most experts in the relevant subject even though they are not testable, or must the results of the methodology be judged by the realism of the assumptions that underlie its results?).

Despite the multiplicity of methodologies that characterizes modern microeconomics, one analytical approach has been dominant for the last 130 years, and we may safely term it the "orthodox" framework of analysis employed in the field currently. As such, it shapes the "vision" of economic causation possessed by the modern microeconomist and, thereby, defines his or her manner of approaching causation problems. It is important for the student, approaching the subject as a neophyte, to understand it as the way in which the microeconomist thinks, because the methodology provides the thread of continuity which knits analyses in the quite different subfields within microeconomics into a unified field of expertise.

1.1. An overview

The relevant methodology is *deductive* in approach, which is to say that it seeks to determine the *state* of a *model* of economic causation by deriving the mutual implications of a set of *assumptions* constrained by certain given variable values called *parameters* and given functions termed *exogenous relations*. The method is borrowed from the fields of mathematics, physics and engineering which gave rise to models of static and dynamic mechanics, and pioneered the study of optimum decision making and equilibrium states. That is a large platterful, and we must now seek to make it more understandable.

A deductive approach to understanding the causal patterns of a group of variables is frequently resorted to when the number of variables involved is quite large; as noted above, it tries to isolate a manageable body of plausible assumptions concerning the causation and, then, deduces their mutual implications to determine a set of "causal paths" along which the variables under study impact one another. Those variables, the determination of whose values is the goal of the analysis, are called the *endogenous* (i.e., internal) variables and, taken together, their values constitute the state of the system or model. However, in addition to the assumptions of the model, their values are determined:

1 by a set of variables (the *exogenous*, or external, variables, frequently called the *parameters* of the model) which are assumed to be unchanged in value and given before the modeling begins; and
2 by a set of mathematical functions linking the exogenous and endogenous variables in manners prescribed before the analyst starts his or her modeling.

The state of the system, therefore, is determined by the mutual implications of the assumptions acting within the constraints set by the parameters and prescribed functions.

1.2. The contents of a model

The models of which we speak consist of four structural modules which, taken together, define their content. Presenting and discussing the contents and significance of each module will permit a better understanding of the microeconomist's manner of analysis. After discussing the more abstract contents of the modules and their roles, we will illustrate them with the relevant counterpart in a model with which you are familiar: the model of individual consumer choice.

THE VARIABLE SET   When the economist begins to formalize his interest in the causation of a given economic phenomenon, he or she will have preliminary hypotheses and intuitions about the variables that are included in the relationships that contribute to the causation of the phenomenon. Let us specify this body as the set V for the variables the analyst thinks relevant in this causation. For example, in the model of the consumer's choice of quantities of goods to consume, Q, our notional analyst believes that the prices of goods P, the income of the consumer I, the state of the weather during the period of analysis W, the amount of advertising and other marketing activity devoted to each good A, the sex of the consumer S, and perhaps many more such variables or attributes are involved in the consumer's choice.

A first important step in the construction of the model is to determine its *ambition*: how many variables' values is the model going to determine (i.e., how many variables' values are to comprise the *state* of the model) and, therefore, which will remain in the set V as variables whose values will not be captured in the state? The first subset of variables V

selected for inclusion as state variables we shall denote X, and term them the *endogenous* variables. We will refer to them as state or endogenous variables interchangeably hereafter, and their values as determined by the model under construction are the goals of the analyst.

The remaining set $(V\text{-}X)$ are those variables believed to be significantly influential in their relation to X, but are excluded from the state variables. Let us designate these the subset Y, and refer to them as the *exogenous* variables, or interchangeably as the *parameters* of the model. Their values will be held constant in the analysis in any particular determination of a state of the model, but may be changed arbitrarily by the modeler to see how the state of the system reacts to such changes. That is, the parameters of the model aid in the determination of X but are not affected by changes in the values of X: variables Y do not react to any feedbacks from X, but exercise causal impacts on X.

Let us illustrate with the consumer model. Our analyst asks: "Given my state of knowledge about consumer choice, given my research budget and given the time I have available, how ambitious should my model be in its explanatory domain? How shall I divide $V = (Q, P, I, W, A, S, \ldots)$ into state variables X and parameters Y? The more I include in the endogenous category, the more complicated my model will be, since I will be determining a larger domain of variation. The more complicated my model is in this sense, the greater the grasp of my preliminary knowledge must be, the more resources will be consumed in the model's construction, and (as we shall see) the more difficult will be the manipulation of the model to gain insights from it. On the other hand, if I include too few variables in the endogenous category, I run the danger of constructing a trivial model which yields little useful information. How shall I divide V into subsets X and Y?"

Let us place the question in the context of consumer choice theory. First, to attempt to build a model in which the quantities of *all* consumer goods in the purview of the consumer, Q, would be determined is, on the face of it, too ambitious. Therefore, the analyst might decide to divide all goods in the consumer's purview into two groups: one real good, say bread, and one virtual good which consists of the aggregate of all other goods except bread. Thus the consumer's quantity of bread, q_B and the quantity of all other goods, q_I, are chosen as the two endogenous or state variables to be determined.

Because the analysis will focus on the amounts of the two goods purchased, it would be an inappropriate and costly endeavor to determine prices P, and so they will be placed in the exogenous category. All of them are assumed to be given and unchanged for each run of the model, but they are capable of being changed at the will of the analyst for separate runs. Indeed, to gain insights from the model, it will be necessary to make such changes to study how they affect q_B and q_I. The analyst can conveniently set the price of the virtual good, what we might call "the income good," at $p_I = 1$, or "one dollar's worth," and hold it constant through all runs of the model, and most of the other prices can also be assumed to remain unchanged on the assumption that they have a negligible impact on q_B.

Obviously, however, this cannot be assumed for p_B, which must be deemed to be an influential cause of change in q_B, so the analyst will designate it a *strategic* parameter of the model and a candidate for controlled changes. Also, certain substitutes for bread such as pasta, with price p_P, must be placed in this category, as well as important complements of bread, such as margarine with price p_M, on the basis of their presumed impact on q_B. The set of prices P is placed in the exogenous or parameter category, with a small number, p_B, p_P, p_M (and perhaps others the reader might designate) placed in the strategic parameter category for alterations in value if the analyst desires. The remainder are relegated to the nonstrategic catetory and assumed to be unchanged at values that are implicit but not explicitly specified.

The consumer's income, I, is also assumed by the modeler to be a strategic parameter, but the weather is obviously exogenous and believed to have negligible impacts on bread consumption, as is the sex, S, of the consumer. They are nonstrategic parameters. Finally, advertising expended upon bread, A, may impact particular brands of bread, but when the purchase of that good in the aggregate is under analysis, the analyst might judge it to have only a slight impact, and consign it, as well, to the nonstrategic parameters.

The variable set, then, has been divided into the endogenous and the exogenous subsets, and the latter into strategic and nonstrategic parameters. Note that the quantity of the income good, q_I has not be set as a parameter, but will change in value as an endogenous variable, but one that is derivative from q_B, p_B and I, given the implication (see below) that the consumer will spend all of his or her income.

THE ASSUMPTION SET　The core of the deductive model is the set of assumptions adopted whose mutual implications, constrained by the strategic parameters, will determine the state of the model as defined by the values of the endogenous variables. The assumptions define the paths of causation that link the endogenous variables to each other in a mutually interdependent fashion, and to the strategic parameters in a dependent fashion. This is to say, that, in such paths, endogenous variable x_1 affects x_2 which impacts x_3 which, in turn, acts upon x_1 and x_2 and so forth; and on the other hand, strategic parameter y_1 may impact x_1 and x_3, but will not be affected by them. The causation is unidirectional from Y to X, without feedbacks from X to Y; and it is the assumption set that defines these paths of causation.

In economic models, we can identify certain frequently occurring subsets of assumptions:

- Exogenous functions
- Environmental assumptions
- Behavioral assumptions
- Instrumental assumptions

These we will discuss below and exemplify with our consumer choice problem.

Certain relevant characteristics of the actor or his or her environment, which specify relations among the endogenous variables of importance to the modeling and which are not deemed to be the task of the economist to isolate are assumed given in *functional form*. For example, the firm is assumed to face a given technology, defined as a function relating inputs, z_j, to the maximum amount of output of good i, o_i, derivable from their combination:

$$o_i = t_i(z_1, z_2, \ldots, z_m) \tag{1}$$

The isolation of this relation is the task of the engineer or technologist, and the economist begins a modeling of the firm's economic decision making with it in hand.

The counterpart for the consumer, of course, is the *preference function*, which relates the index of satisfaction of the consumer to the market baskets of goods under analysis. In the present example, this function is symbolized

$$u = u(q_B, q_I) \tag{2}$$

which can be depicted as a three-dimensional figure with height u and base plane axes q_B and q_I. More simply, its height contours can be depicted in the two-dimensional base plane as the familiar indifference curves of consumer theory. The derivation of this relationship is assumed by the economist to be the task of the psychologist, and the former takes it as given when he or she begins the analysis of the consumer's decision making.

The group of *environmental assumptions* specifies the important features of the decision-making environment within which agents act and which conditions their choices. For example, our modeler makes five assumptions:

1 The consumer is such a small portion of total demand for bread that he or she cannot affect its price, no matter how large or small q_B. The consumer is a *price taker*.

2 The consumer's choices among goods depend wholly upon the satisfactions derived from the goods chosen by the consumer. He or she gets no satisfactions from goods consumed by others, nor does the consumer take into decision-making account such satisfactions as others may derive from the goods taken by him or her. The consumer's actions are wholly egoistic and non-envious of others' welfare.

3 The consumer is constrained in his or her choices by the amount of income, I, that he or she has to spend. The consumer cannot spend more than I on goods consumed, but may spend less than I.

4 Within the consumer's field of choice he or she is never *satiated* in goods: the consumer never prefers a basket containing less of every good in the utility function to more of every good, nor does he or she prefer a basket that has the same amounts of one or more goods as another but less of one or more others to one that has more of the latter set of goods. More of any one or more goods is always welcome. This assumption assures that the indifference curves are negatively sloped.

5 As the consumer obtains more of any good or group of goods, he or she will be willing to give up fewer of other goods not in the specified group to obtain the former. He or she always welcomes more of one or more goods, but as the amount of them he or she gains grows larger, he or she values them less in terms of what he or she would give up of the excluded goods to obtain them. That is, the consumer has a diminishing marginal rate of substitution as he or she receives more of a good. This assures that the negatively sloped indifference curves bow in toward the origin (i.e., they are *convex*).

Behavioral assumptions are an important group of assumptions to be found in economic models; these assumptions concern the motivations of economic agents in making their decisions. They are assumed to be goal-oriented in such actions and "rational" in their search for attainment of their goals. That is, they are assumed to act in manners that maximize their achievement or minimize the cost of such achievement. In this regard, one generally finds, in microeconomic models, the assumption that the economic agent acts to maximize or to minimize some performance index subject to constraints: he or she seeks a constrained maximum or minimum, or, equivalently, *optimizes*. The reason for this near-universal behavioral assumption will be shown in the discussion of the next component of models, but now let us illustrate it in terms of the consumer choice model.

The consumer is assumed to choose goods baskets to maximize his or her satisfactions, subject to the constraints of income, prices, and such other strategic parameters as the modeler has specified. More formally, the consumer seeks to maximize his or her utility or preference function subject to

1   spending no more than his or her income, I, and
2   choosing only nonnegative q_B and q_I.

Mathematically, we may state this as

$$\max_{q_B, q_I} u = u(q_B, q_I) \tag{3}$$

subject to:

$$q_B \cdot p_B + q_I \leq I \tag{4}$$

$$q_B, q_I \geq 0 \tag{5}$$

Note that one of the implications of the consumer's desire to maximize satisfactions is that, because q_I includes all goods other than bread, if the consumer consumes less than his or her income, he or she cannot be maximizing utility. This is because we have assumed that the consumer is not satiated in any good, and because the budget inequality includes all possible goods that can be purchased, not spending all of one's income amounts to wasting it. Hence, the force of the assumptions effectively makes the budget inequality an equality: the consumer cannot spend more than the budget and will not, as a satisfaction maximizer, spend less.

A final group of assumptions – *instrumental assumptions* – consists of those the analyst may introduce to make the model more amenable to solution or manipulation. They frequently introduce unrealistic characteristics into the model, but the analyst judges that these distortions do not seriously jeopardize the derivation of useful insights into the causation of the model compared with the facility they provide in such derivation.

For example, in the consumer choice model, the analyst would probably add two assumptions:

1   The endogenous variables, q_B and q_I, are divisible into arbitrarily small amounts: thus, the consumer may buy 2.345678 loaves of bread, for instance, or spend $105.987654 on all other goods. Introducing this continuity is obviously unreal, but it permits us to employ certain techniques for maximizing utility which would not be permitted if the domain of the utility function consisted of only integer values of the endogenous variables. Given this advantage in solving and manipulat-

ing the model and the close approximation to integer values that can be obtained if desired by rounding the decimal answers, the price in terms of foregone reality is not great. Besides, as we shall see, we are frequently only interested in *qualitative* movements of the endogenous variables, rather than *quantitative*, and noninteger values provide no distortions in yielding these.

2   Another distorting assumption the analyst would almost certainly introduce is that the utility function $u = u(q_B, q_I)$ is smooth and continuous, which is to say that first and second derivatives exist everywhere over the relevant domain of the function. The reason for such an assumption is once more that it makes the solution and manipulation of the model easier without a major distortion, and hence the motivation for its inclusion is explained in the same terms as the first instrumental assumption above.

THE ISOLATION OF THE INTERRELATIONSHIPS   The *interrelationships* are the paths of causation among the variables that are implied by the assumptions as constrained by the parameters. They detail, taken individually, the interdependence among the endogenous variables and the dependence of the endogenous variables on the exogenous variables along one path of causation. Taken together, they constitute all such paths that are implied by the assumptions and parameters. In general, but in rare cases not necessarily, we must have one such independent interrelationship for each endogenous variable, where independence means that no interrelationship can be derived from any set of the remaining interrelationships.

Given the limitations of the mind in dealing simultaneously with a potentially large group of assumptions, how can we derive such causal implications? The answer explains why the economist is anxious to include maximization or minimization in the subset of motivational assumptions. If he or she can view the economic agent as acting to maximize (e.g., utility) or minimize (e.g., costs) some measure, subject to the constraints enforced by the assumptions and parameters, it is possible to derive the interrelationships by employing the mathematical tools to obtain a constrained maximum or minimum. In so doing, an infeasible task becomes feasible, in that the interrelationships are derived as precisely defined functions and, by solving them simultaneously, the values of the state variables are determined.

Return to the problem of consumer choice as stated formally in expressions (3)–(5). With our instrumental assumptions that (3) is smooth and continuous, and with our insight that at a maximum (4) will hold as an equation by virtue of nonsatiation, we may use standard mathematical procedures to obtain the values of q_B and q_I that maximize utility subject to the income and nonnegativity constraints. When this is done, we obtain two conditions for the maximum:

$$\frac{\frac{\partial u}{\partial q_B}}{\frac{\partial u}{\partial q_I}} = \frac{p_B}{p_I} = p_B \tag{6.1}$$

$$q_B p_B + q_I = I \tag{6.2}$$

Condition (6.1) says that, at the constrained optimum, the ratio of the partial derivatives of $u = u(q_B, q_I)$ with respect to q_B and q_I must equal the ratio of prices p_B and p_I; but

$p_I = 1$, so that the ratio of partials must equal p_B. If we interpret the partials as the marginal utilities of bread and "income," (6.1) says that the marginal utility of bread per dollar spent on it must equal the marginal utility of a dollar of income. Another way of stating this requirement is that the marginal rate of substitution (MRS) of good B for good I must equal the ratio of their prices, for the ratio of partial derivatives is the marginal rate of substitution of the goods in terms of the consumer's preferences. The ratio of the prices of the goods is the rate at which the goods can be substituted in the markets for them. So, the first condition says that, in the optimum, the psychologically determined rate at which the consumer trades off the goods at the margin of preference must equal the rate at which prices dictate they can be traded at the market. The MRS is the slope of the optimal indifference curve at the optimal values of q_B and q_I, and this slope must equal the ratio of prices, which is the slope of the budget equation (6.2).

This equality of slopes condition, however, while a necessary condition is not sufficient, for such equalities can exist at many places on the indifference map: think of a line parallel to the budget line on the graph – hence reflecting the same slope as that of the budget line – and points on the indifference curves that happen to have the same slope (MRS). That is, the equality of (6.1) need not occur at a tangency point between the budget line and an indifference curve. This would imply that the consumer was spending less or more than the total income he or she possesses. However, we have seen that elementary maximization conditions require that he or she spend all of it, and is constrained to spend no more than all of it. Hence, (6.2) requires that the consumer be on the budget line at the optimum. Hence, the equality of the MRS and the slope of the budget line must occur at the tangency of the budget line with an indifference curve.

Conditions (6.1) and (6.2) are the interrelationships that yield the exact relationships among the endogenous variables, q_B and q_I and the exogenous variables, p_B, p_I, and I. They yield two paths of causation along which the state variables must move and to which, in the optimum, they must conform. They summarize the mutual implications of the assumption set interacting with the fixed parameters and, for every feasible set of parameter values, they may be solved to obtain the optimal values of the state variables.

This set of interrelationships constitutes the core of the model. If a parameter changes, we must revert back to them to resolve the equations for the new state of the system. They are frequently called the *structural forms* of the model, for they do indeed constitute the anatomy of the system the analyst has synthesized. If the model is to be capable of yielding insights into the relationships of the endogenous variables among themselves and with the exogenous variables, these interrelationships must be capable of manipulation, and we shall address this requirement below.

At this point, let us recall that we are dealing with interrelationships that have not been numerically specified. Microeconomic theory deals with such models, in which the variables have been given symbols but not numerical values, and the functional relations among them are also specified only symbolically. Therefore, when we change parameter values, we can only speak of increasing or decreasing their values, and we can hope to solve only for *qualitative* changes in the endogenous variables. If the analyst raises the price of bread, will the quantity of bread rise, fall or remain unchanged? If the consumer's income falls, will the quantity of bread rise, fall or remain unchanged? The analyst, in the absence of quantitative values of the parameters and numerically specified exogenous functions, is constrained by manipulations of the model to seek insights only in qualitative terms.

THE REDUCED FORMS   A final component of the typical microeconomic model is not always capable of determination. Moreover, even when it is capable of isolation, it is not as vital to the usefulness of the model as the three components already discussed. It consists of functions which define each of the endogenous variables as functions of the exogenous variables alone. We have seen that the interrelationships are functions that reveal:

1   the manner in which the endogenous variables are related to each other, and
2   the manner in which the endogenous variables are related to the exogenous variables or parameters.

In the last analysis, though, the exogenous variables are the agents of all of the causation in the interrelationships (given the assumptions). Even when one state variable impacts another state variable, this interaction is ultimately caused by the parameters, directly or indirectly.

Under certain conditions, it may be possible to disentangle this complex of dependence and relate all of the variation in the state variables to their ultimate agents of causation in the parameters. If this is possible, it is convenient, because, as we have noted, we will seek to manipulate the model by changing the values of the parameters. When we do so, if we have the interrelationships only, it is necessary to resolve them each time we change one or more parameters. However, if we have this new set of functions – we will call them the *reduced forms* to distinguish them from the *structural forms* – we need only substitute the new parameters into each expression for a state variable and obtain the new answers immediately.

In the example of consumer choice, the reduced forms will be immediately recognized by you: they are the demand functions for q_B and q_I

$$q_B = q_B(p_B, I) \tag{7.1}$$

$$q_I = q_I(p_B, I) \tag{7.2}$$

whose advantages in terms of solution with parameter changes are readily perceived. The truth is, though, that when these reduced forms are not numerically specified (so that we must work with them as symbolic functions only), they are of little use. To compute the qualitative changes in state variables incumbent on parameter changes, it is necessary to revert to the interrelationships of (6). To the theorist, this last set of components, if obtainable, is generally of secondary interest in the employment of the model to obtain insights into the causation under study.

2. Defining Varieties of the Typical Model

Before we discuss the manner in which the microeconomist derives insights into the qualitative features of variation with which the model deals, it will be helpful to use our presentation of the model and its components as a means of defining the various types of models that will be discussed in the selections to follow.

A first distinction among model types is that between a *static* and a *dynamic* model. A static model is one in which time plays no part in the determination of the state variables. If a parameter changes and causes changes in them via solutions to system (6) or (7), the changes are assumed to occur instantaneously. The system moves from the prior solution to the new without time lag, and can yield no information on the time path followed by the endogenous variables between the solutions. The manner in which one determines that a model is static is to see whether the interrelationships of (6) contain *time forms* of the state variables. That is, are there such expressions as x_t or dx/dt, or $\int x dt$, or $\sum_t x_t$, and so forth, where t is time? If not, the model is static. If the exogenous variables or parameters are dated, such as y_t, but the state variables are not, the model remains a static model, with the state variables changing instantaneously as the parameters vary through time. This type of model is one of *intermporal statics*.

On the other hand, if time forms of the state variables are found in the interrelationships, the model is *dynamic*. The state variables move through time in paths that are determined internally by the relationships among them; that is, the laws of their temporal change inhere in the interrelationship functions (6) that determine how $x_{1,t}$ relates to $x_{1,t-1}$, as well as to other state variable time forms. The distinctive feature of the solution functions (7) in a dynamic model is that they must be expressed as trajectories through time for given sets of parameters.

For example, let us model the phenomenon of compound interest, where x_t is the value of principal in period t, and i is the interest rate (a parameter) at which the money is invested. The interrelationship in this simple model is

$$x_t = x_{t-1}(1 + i)$$

which relates principal value today to principal value yesterday and the rate of compound interest. The reduced form is

$$x_t = x_0(1 + i)^t$$

where x_0 is the principal originally invested in period 0 (a parameter) and t is the number of periods for which it is invested (also a parameter). The state variable is expressed wholly in terms of parameters x_0, i, and t. Note that if one wished to graph the movement of x_t it would be necessary to construct a graph with time t (say) on the horizontal axis and x_t on the vertical axis.

Another distinction among models can be readily made: that between *stochastic* and *nonstochastic* models. These terms refer to the existence, respectively, of random variables or nonexistence of such variables. Such variables are specified as a distribution of values from which random draws are made in each run. Let us denote this variable ε and, if it is present in the interrelationships or the reduced forms, the system is stochastic, and the state variables will be affected not only by systematic variation in the model but by random variables with values subject to chance as well. Nonstochastic, or *determinate* models, do not have such variables, as exemplified in the consumer choice model we have been employing. Stochastic models are used by econometricians to fit interrelationship or reduced forms to empirical data. By assuming that a random error variable exists, and by specifying the form of the distribution, its mean and its variance, they draw from a set of data the estimated values of parameters and state variables in manners that permit them to infer the reliability of the estimates.

3. Manipulation of the Model for Qualitative Insights into Variation of the State Variables

Suppose, now, the microeconomic theorist confronts a policy person whose interest in economics inheres wholly in the insights it can yield in the formation of social policy. The theorist takes pride of creation in his or her completed model, and explains it to the sponsor of the research – say a business executive or government policy maker – in great detail, pointing out the significance of the interrelationships or the reduced forms. The economist is somewhat taken aback by the sponsor's yawning reception of the model with an "if so, so what?" response. Using the illustration of the consumer choice model, we can see the basis of the unenthusiastic response: after all, both sets of relations merely say that the consumption of bread is a function of its price and the consumer's income level. These are trivial insights that the economist's audience was quite aware of, without the help of the model.

The sponsor demands that the economist tell him or her deeper theorems about the behavior of the consumer's choices. What happens if the price of bread falls: does the consumer buy more, less or the same quantity of bread? Suppose his or her income rises – how does this affect the consumer's purchase of bread? And, if the prices of all other goods fall relative to the price of bread – what happens to bread consumption then? These insights give the business executive or the policy maker the kinds of information needed to formulate their strategies.

The point is that the model is relatively sterile unless the theorist can manipulate it to derive insights of this sort. To do so, the theorist conducts *parametric displacements* of the solutions to the model, increasing or decreasing the value of the exogenous variables to study the qualitative nature of the movements of the endogenous or state variables. A change in a parameter displaces a prior solution of the model to a new solution, and a comparison of old and new variables yields the valuable insights the sponsor is seeking. In a static model, this method of manipulation is called *comparative statics*, and on the ability to derive *theorems* or *propositions* about qualitative movements of the state variables hinges the usefulness of the modeling.

The ability to obtain the information necessary to evaluate such displacements comes in large part from what the instrumental and other assumptions tell the theorist about the shape of the functions involved in the analysis. We will not discuss these techniques here, except to say that they are another dividend of casting the motivation of the agents in a maximization or minimization mold. The important point is this: *the construction of a theoretical model with unspecified functions is unrewarding unless it is capable of being manipulated to yield interesting insights concerning the qualitative movements of state variables in response to parametric changes.*

The technique for doing this in dynamic models is termed *comparative dynamics*, and is wholly analogous to its static counterpart. The parameter that is most frequently changed is the initial position of the model, and the question posed after such a change is whether the state variables reattain their previous values with the passage of time, whether they reach a new solution set, or whether they do not reach a new stationary solution. In general, dynamic models in the sense of our definition are much more complicated in their construction, solution and manipulation, and are met with much less frequently than static. In the selections to follow, almost all of the material will concern static models and the use of comparative statics.

4. Conclusion

The methodological material presented above provides a thread of continuity linking many of the selections to follow. It also familiarizes you with the manner in which the authors approach their problems, the analytical frameworks within which they have been taught to think, and, in general, their derivations of the pathways through the economic domain.

Static and dynamic models; parametric displacements and comparative statics and dynamics; the use of constrained maximization and minimization to obtain interrelationships and, additionally, to evaluate the movements of state variable solutions after displacements; and the use of the notion of equilibrium as a balance of opposing economic forces (e.g., supply and demand) as a means of obtaining state variable solutions are tools that the economist has borrowed from the mathematician, the engineer, and the physicist. They have become, over the past 130 years, the basics of microeconomic theory, and knowledge of them is necessary to perform and understand the results of current economic analysis. However, their applicability and usefulness in economic analysis, at least to the degree they have come to dominate it, have not been accepted universally. Rival, or complementary, frameworks of analysis have been developed or recommended, and it is important to become aware of them on the modern scene and the criticisms of the standard model that lead to them. Some of the more important challenges to that standard model are presented in the remaining chapters in this section.

CHAPTER TWO

Theories of Decision-Making in Economics and Behavioral Science

HERBERT A. SIMON

Source: *American Economic Review*, 49 (1959), pp. 253–83. Reprinted with the permission of the author and the American Economic Association. © American Economic Association.

Recent years have seen important new explorations along the boundaries between economics and psychology. For the economist, the immediate question about these developments is whether they include new advances in psychology that can fruitfully be applied to economics. But the psychologist will also raise the converse question – whether there are developments in economic theory and observation that have implications for the central core of psychology. If economics is able to find verifiable and verified generalizations about human economic behavior, then these generalizations must have a place in the more general theories of human behavior to which psychology and sociology aspire. Influence will run both ways.[1]

1. How Much Psychology Does Economics Need?

How have psychology and economics gotten along with little relation in the past? The explanation rests on an understanding of the goals toward which economics, viewed as a science and a discipline, has usually aimed.

Broadly speaking, economics can be defined as the science that describes and predicts the behavior of several kinds of economic man – notably the consumer and the entrepreneur. While perhaps literally correct, this definition does not reflect the principal focus in the literature of economics. We usually classify work in economics along two dimensions:

(a)   whether it is concerned with industries and the whole economy (macroeconomics) or with individual economic actors (microeconomics); and

(b)   whether it strives to describe and explain economic behavior (descriptive economics), or to guide decisions either at the level of public policy (normative macroeconomics) or at the level of the individual consumer or businessman (normative microeconomics).

The profession and literature of economics have been largely preoccupied with normative macroeconomics. Although descriptive macroeconomics provides the scientific base for policy prescription, research emphases have been determined in large part by relevance to policy (e.g., business cycle theory). Normative microeconomics, carried forward under such labels as "management science," "engineering economics," and "operations research," is now a flourishing area of work having an uneasy and ill-defined relation with the profession of economics, traditionally defined. Much of the work is being done by mathematicians, statisticians, engineers, and physical scientists (although many mathematical economists have also been active in it).[2]

This new area, like the old, is normative in orientation. Economists have been relatively uninterested in descriptive microeconomics – understanding the behavior of individual economic agents – except as this is necessary to provide a foundation for macroeconomics. The normative microeconomist "obviously" doesn't need a theory of human behavior: he wants to know how people *ought* to behave, not how they *do* behave. On the other hand, the macroeconomist's lack of concern with individual behavior stems from different considerations. First, he assumes that the economic actor is rational, and hence he makes strong predictions about human behavior without performing the hard work of observing people. Second, he often assumes competition, which carries with it the implication that only the rational survive. Thus, the classical economic theory of markets with perfect competition and rational agents is deductive theory that requires almost no contact with empirical data once its assumptions are accepted.[3]

Undoubtedly there is an area of human behavior that fits these assumptions to a reasonable approximation, where the classical theory with its assumptions of rationality is a powerful and useful tool. Without denying the existence of this area, or its importance, I may observe that it fails to include some of the central problems of conflict and dynamics with which economics has become more and more concerned. A metaphor will help to show the reason for this failure.

Suppose we were pouring some viscous liquid – molasses – into a bowl of very irregular shape. What would we need in order to make a theory of the form the molasses would take in the bowl? How much would we have to know about the properties of molasses to predict its behavior under the circumstances? If the bowl were held motionless, and if we wanted only to predict behavior in equilibrium, we would have to know little, indeed, about molasses. The single essential assumption would be that the molasses, under the force of gravity, would minimize the height of its center of gravity. With this assumption, which would apply as well to any other liquid, and a complete knowledge of the environment – in this case the shape of the bowl – the equilibrium is completely determined. Just so, the equilibrium behavior of a perfectly adapting organism depends only on its goal and its environment; it is otherwise completely independent of the internal properties of the organism.

If the bowl into which we were pouring the molasses were jiggled rapidly, or if we wanted to know about the behavior before equilibrium was reached, prediction would require much more information. It would require, in particular, more information about the properties of molasses: its viscosity, the rapidity with which it "adapted" itself to the containing vessel and moved towards its "goal" of lowering its center of gravity. Likewise, to predict the short-run behavior of an adaptive organism, or its behavior in a complex and rapidly changing environment, it is not enough to know its goals. We must know also a great deal about its internal structure and particularly its mechanisms of adaptation.

If, to carry the metaphor a step farther, new forces, in addition to gravitational force, were brought to bear on the liquid, we would have to know still more about it even to predict behavior in equilibrium. Now its tendency to lower its center of gravity might be countered by a force to minimize an electrical or magnetic potential operating in some lateral direction. We would have to know its relative susceptibility to gravitational and electrical or magnetic force to determine its equilibrium position. Similarly, in an organism having a multiplicity of goals, or afflicted with some kind of internal goal conflict, behavior could be predicted only from information about the relative strengths of the several goals and the ways in which the adaptive processes responded to them.

Economics has been moving steadily into new areas where the power of the classical equilibrium model has never been demonstrated, and where its adequacy must be considered anew. Labor economics is such an area, oligopoly or imperfect competition theory another, decision making under uncertainty a third, and the theory of economic development a fourth. In all of these areas the complexity and instability of his environment becomes a central feature of the choices that economic man faces. To explain his behavior in the face of this complexity, the theory must describe him as something more than a featureless, adaptive organism; it must incorporate at least some description of the processes and mechanisms through which the adaptation takes place. Let us list a little more concretely some specific problems of this kind:

(a) The classical theory postulates that the consumer maximizes utility. Recent advances in the theory of rational consumer choice have shown that the existence of a utility function, and its characteristics, if it exists, can be studied empirically.

(b) The growing separation between ownership and management has directed attention to the motivations of managers and the adequacy of the profit-maximization assumption for business firms. So-called human relations research has raised a variety of issues about the motivation of both executives and employees.

(c) When, in extending the classical theory, the assumptions of perfect competition were removed, even the definition of rationality became ambiguous. New definitions had to be constructed, by no means as "obvious" intuitively as simple maximization, to extend the theory of rational behavior to bilateral monopoly and to other bargaining and outguessing situations.

(d) When the assumptions of perfect foresight were removed, to handle uncertainty about the environment, the definition of rationality had to be extended in another direction to take into account prediction and the formation of expectations.

(e) Broadening the definition of rationality to encompass goal conflict and uncertainty made it hard to ignore the distinction between the objective environment in which the economic actor "really" lives and the subjective environment that he perceives and to which he responds. When this distinction is made, we can no longer predict his behavior – even if he behaves rationally – from the characteristics of the objective environment; we also need to know something about his perceptual and cognitive processes.

We shall use these five problem areas as a basis for sorting out some recent explorations in theory, model building, and empirical testing. In section 2, we will examine developments in the theory of utility and consumer choice. In section 3, we will consider somewhat parallel issues relating to the motivation of managers. In section 4, we will deal with conflict of goals and the phenomena of bargaining. In section 5, we will survey some of the work that has been done on uncertainty and the formation of expectations. In section 6, we will explore recent developments in the theory of human problem solving and other higher mental processes, and see what implications these have for economic decision making.

2. The Utility Function

The story of the re-establishment of cardinal utility, as a consequence of the introduction of uncertainty into the theory of choice, is well known.[4] When Pareto and Slutsky had shown that the theory of consumer demand could be derived from the properties of indifference curves, without postulating a cardinal utility function underlying these curves, it became fashionable to regard utility as an ordinal measure – a ranking of alternatives by preference. Indeed, it could be shown that only ordinal utility had operational status – that the experiments that had been proposed, and even tried in a couple of instances, to measure an individual's utilities by asking him to choose among alternatives could never distinguish between two cardinal utility functions that were ordinally equivalent – that differed only by stretchings and contractions of the unit of measurement.

It was shown by von Neumann and Morgenstern, as a byproduct of their development of the theory of games, that if the choice situation were extended to include choices among uncertain prospects – among lottery tickets, say – cardinal utilities could be assigned to the outcomes in an unequivocal way.[5] Under these conditions, if the subject's behavior was consistent, it was possible to measure cardinally the utilities that different outcomes had for him.

A person who behaved in a manner consistent with the axioms of choice of von Neumann and Morgenstern would act so as to maximize the expected value – the average, weighted by the probabilities of the alternative outcomes of a choice – of his utility. The theory could be tested empirically, however, only on the assumption that the probabilities assigned to the alternatives by the subject were identical with the "objective" probabilities of these events as known to the experimenter. For example, if a subject believed in the gamblers' fallacy, that after a run of heads an unbiased coin would be more likely to fall tails, his choices might appear inconsistent with his utility function, while the real difficulty would lie in his method of assigning probabilities. This difficulty of "subjective" versus "objective" probability soon came to light when attempts were made to test experimentally whether people behaved in accordance with the predictions of the new utility theory. At the same time, it was discovered that the problem had been raised and solved thirty years earlier by the English philosopher and mathematician Frank Ramsey.[6] Ramsey had shown that, by an appropriate series of experiments, the utilities and subjective probabilities assigned by a subject to a set of uncertain alternatives could be measured simultaneously.

2.1. Empirical studies

The new axiomatic foundations of the theory of utility, which show that it is possible at least in principle to determine empirically whether people "have" utility functions of the appropriate kind, have led to a rash of choice experiments. An experimenter who wants to measure utilities, not merely in principle but in fact, faces innumerable difficulties. Because of these difficulties, most experiments have been limited to confronting the subjects with alternative lottery tickets, at various odds, for small amounts of money. The weight of evidence is that, under these conditions, most persons choose in a way that is reasonably consistent with the axioms of the theory – they behave as though they were maximizing the expected value of utility and as though the utilities of the several alternatives can be measured.[7]

When these experiments are extended to more "realistic" choices – choices that are more obviously relevant to real-life situations – difficulties multiply. In the few extensions that have been made, it is not at all clear that the subjects behave in accordance with the utility axioms. There is some indication that when the situation is very simple and transparent, so that the subject can easily see and remember when he is being consistent, he behaves like a utility maximizer. But as the choices become a little more complicated – choices, for example, among phonograph records instead of sums of money – he becomes much less consistent [21, Ch. 3] [47].[8]

We can interpret these results in either of two ways. We can say that consumers "want" to maximize utility, and that if we present them with clear and simple choices that they understand they will do so. Or we can say that the real world is so complicated that the theory of utility maximization has little relevance to real choices. The former interpretation has generally appeared more attractive to economists trained in classical utility theory and to management scientists seeking rules of behavior for normative microeconomics; the latter to behavioral scientists interested in the description of behavior.

2.2. Normative applications

The new utility theory has provided the formal framework for much recent work in mathematical statistics – i.e., statistical decision theory.[9] Similarly (it would be accurate to say "synonymously"), this framework provides the basis for most of the normative models of management science and operations research designed for actual application to the decision-making problems of the firm.[10] Except for some very recent developments, linear programming has been limited to decision making under certainty, but there have been far-reaching developments of dynamic programming dealing with the maximization of expected values of outcomes (usually monetary outcomes) in situations where future events can be predicted only in terms of probability distributions.[11]

Again, there are at least two distinct interpretations that can be placed on these developments. On the one hand, it can be argued: "Firms would like to maximize profits if they could. They have been limited in doing so by the conceptual and computational difficulties of finding the optimal courses of action. By providing powerful new mathematical tools and computing machines, we now enable them to behave in the manner predicted by Alfred Marshall, even if they haven't been able to in the past." Nature will imitate art and economic man will become as real (and as artificial) as radios and atomic piles.

The alternative interpretation rests on the observation that, even with the powerful new tools and machines, most real-life choices still lie beyond the reach of maximizing techniques – unless the situations are heroically simplified by drastic approximations. If man, according to this interpretation, makes decisions and choices that have some appearance of rationality, rationality in real life must involve something simpler than maximization of utility or profit. In section 6, we will see where this alternative interpretation leads.

2.3. The binary choice experiment

Much recent discussion about utility has centered around a particularly simple choice experiment. This experiment, in numerous variants, has been used by both economists and psychologists to test the most diverse kinds of hypotheses. We will describe it so that we can use it as a common standard of comparison for a whole range of theories and empirical studies.[12]

We will call the situation we are about to describe the *binary choice* experiment. It is better known to most game theorists – particularly those located not far from Nevada – as a two-armed bandit; and to most psychologists as a partial reinforcement experiment. The subject is required, in each of a series of trials, to choose one or the other of two symbols – say, plus or minus. When he has chosen, he is told whether his choice was "right" or "wrong," and he may also receive a reward (in psychologist's language, a reinforcement) for "right" choices. The experimenter can arrange the schedule of correct responses in a variety of ways. There may be a definite pattern, or they may be randomized. It is not essential that one and only one response be correct on a given trial: the experimenter may determine that both or neither will be correct. In the latter case the subject may or may not be informed whether the response he did not choose would have been correct.

How would a utility-maximizing subject behave in the binary choice experiment? Suppose that the experimenter rewarded "plus" on one-third of the trials, determined at random, and "minus" on the remaining two-thirds. Then a subject, provided that he believed the sequence was random and observed that minus was rewarded twice as often as plus, should always, rationally, choose minus. He would find the correct answer two-thirds of the time, and more often than with any other strategy.

Unfortunately for the classical theory of utility in its simplest form, few subjects behave in this way. The most commonly observed behavior is what is called *event matching*.[13] The subject chooses the two alternatives (not necessarily at random) with relative frequencies roughly proportional to the relative frequencies with which they are rewarded. Thus, in the example given, two-thirds of the time he would choose minus, and as a result would make a correct response, on the average, in 5 trials out of 9 (on two-thirds of the trials in which he chooses minus, and one-third of those in which he chooses plus).[14]

All sorts of explanations have been offered for the event-matching behavior. The simplest is that the subject just doesn't understand what strategy would maximize his expected utility; but with adult subjects in a situation as transparent as this one, this explanation seems farfetched. The alternative explanations imply either that the subject regards himself as being engaged in a competitive game with the experimenter (or with "nature" if he accepts the experimenter's explanation that the stimulus is random), or that his responses are the outcome of certain kinds of learning processes. We will examine these two types of explanation further in sections 4 and 5 respectively. The important conclusion at this point is that even in an extremely simple situation, subjects do not behave in the way predicted by a straightforward application of utility theory.

2.4. Probabilistic preferences

Before we leave the subject of utility, we should mention one recent important development. In the formalizations mentioned up to this point, probabilities enter only into the estimation of the consequences that will follow one alternative or another. Given any two alternatives, the first is definitely preferable to the second (in terms of expected utility), or the second to the first, or they are strictly indifferent. If the same pair of alternatives is presented to the subject more than once, he should always prefer the same member of the pair.

One might think this requirement too strict – that, particularly if the utility attached to one alternative were only slightly greater or less than that attached to the other, the subject might vacillate in his choice. An empirical precedent for such vacillation comes not only from casual observation of indecision but from analogous phenomena in the psychophysical laboratory. When subjects are asked to decide which of two weights is heavier, the objectively heavier one is chosen more often than the lighter one, but the relative frequency of choosing the heavier approaches one-half as the two weights approach equality. The probability that a subject will choose the objectively heavier weight depends, in general, on the ratio of the two weights.

Following several earlier attempts, a rigorous and complete axiom system for a utility theory incorporating probabilistic preferences has been constructed recently by Duncan Luce [cf. 43, App. 1]. Although the theory weakens the requirements of consistency in preference, it is empirically testable, at least in principle. Conceptually, it provides a more plausible interpretation of the notion of "indifference" than does the classical theory.

3. The Goals of Firms

Just as the central assumption in the theory of consumption is that the consumer strives to maximize his utility, so the crucial assumption in the theory of the firm is that the entrepreneur strives to maximize his residual share – his profit. Attacks on this hypothesis have been frequent.[15] We may classify the most important of these as follows:

(a) The theory leaves ambiguous whether it is short-run or long-run profit that is to be maximized.

(b) The entrepreneur may obtain all kinds of "psychic income" from the firm, quite apart from monetary rewards. If he is to maximize his utility, then he will sometimes balance a loss of profits against an increase in psychic income. But if we allow "psychic income," the criterion of profit maximization loses all of its definiteness.

(c) The entrepreneur may not care to maximize, but may simply want to earn a return that he regards as satisfactory. By sophistry and and adept use of the concept of psychic income, the notion of seeking a satisfactory return can be translated into utility maximizing but not in any operational way. We shall see in a moment that "satisfactory profits" is a concept more meaningfully related to the psychological notion of aspiration levels than to maximization.

(d)   It is often observed that under modern conditions the equity owners and the active managers of an enterprise are separate and distinct groups of people, so that the latter may not be motivated to maximize profits.
(e)   Where there is imperfect competition among firms, maximizing is an ambiguous goal, for what action is optimal for one firm depends on the actions of the other firms.

In the present section we shall deal only with the third of these five issues. The fifth will be treated in the following section; the first, second, and fourth are purely empirical questions that have been discussed at length in the literature; they will be considered here only for their bearing on the question of satisfactory profits.

3.1. Satisficing versus maximizing

The notion of satiation plays no role in classical economic theory, while it enters rather prominently into the treatment of motivation in psychology. In most psychological theories the motive to act stems from *drives*, and action terminates when the drive is satisfied. Moreover, the conditions for satisfying a drive are not necessarily fixed, but may be specified by an aspiration level that itself adjusts upward or downward on the basis of experience.

If we seek to explain business behavior in the terms of this theory, we must expect the firm's goals to be not maximizing profit, but attaining a certain level or rate of profit, holding a certain share of the market or a certain level of sales. Firms would try to "satisfice" rather than to maximize.[16]

It has sometimes been argued that the distinction between satisficing and maximizing is not important to economic theory. For in the first place, the psychological evidence on individual behavior shows that aspirations tend to adjust to the attainable. Hence in the long run, the argument runs, the level of aspiration and the attainable maximum will be very close together. Second, even if some firms satisficed, they would gradually lose out to the maximizing firms, which would make larger profits and grow more rapidly than the others.

These are, of course, precisely the arguments of our molasses metaphor, and we may answer them in the same way that we answered them earlier. The economic environment of the firm is complex, and it changes rapidly; there is no *a priori* reason to assume the attainment of long-run equilibrium. Indeed, the empirical evidence on the distribution of firms by size suggests that the observed regularities in size distribution stem from the statistical equilibrium of a population of adaptive systems rather than the static equilibrium of a population of maximizers.[17]

Models of satisficing behavior are richer than models of maximizing behavior, because they treat not only of equilibrium but of the method of reaching it as well. Psychological studies of the formation and change of aspiration levels support propositions of the following kinds.[18]

(a)   When performance falls short of the level of aspiration, search behavior (particularly search for new alternatives of action) is induced
(b)   At the same time, the level of aspiration begins to adjust itself downward until goals reach levels that are practically attainable.

(c)   If the two mechanisms just listed operate too slowly to adapt aspirations to performance, emotional behavior – apathy or aggression, for example – will replace rational adaptive behavior.

The aspiration level defines a natural zero point in the scale of utility – whereas in most classical theories the zero point is arbitrary. When the firm has alternatives open to it that are at or above its aspiration level, the theory predicts that it will choose the best of those known to be available. When none of the available alternatives satisfies current aspirations, the theory predicts qualitatively different behavior: in the short run, search behavior and the revision of targets; in the longer run, what we have called above emotional behavior, and what the psychologist would be inclined to call neurosis.[19]

3.2. Studies of business behavior

There is some empirical evidence that business goals are, in fact, stated in satisficing terms.[20] First, there is the series of studies stemming from the pioneering work of Hall and Hitch that indicates that businessmen often set prices by applying a standard markup to costs. Some economists have sought to refute this fact, others to reconcile it – if it is a fact – with marginalist principles. The study of Earley [22a, pp. 44–70] belongs to the former category, but its evidence is suspect because the questions asked of businessmen are leading ones – no one likes to admit that he would accept less profit if he could have more. Earley did not ask his respondents how they determined marginal cost and marginal revenue, how, for example, they estimated demand elasticities.

Another series of studies derived from the debate over the Keynesian doctrine that the amount of investment was insensitive to changes in the rate of interest. The general finding in these studies has been that the rate of interest is not an important factor in investment decisions [24] [39, Ch. 11] [71].

More recently, my colleagues Cyert and March, have attempted to test the satisficing model in a more direct way [19]. They found in one industry some evidence that firms with a declining share of market strove more vigorously to increase their sales than firms whose shares of the market were steady or increasing.

3.3. Aspirations in the binary choice experiment

Although to my knowledge this has not been done, it would be easy to look for aspiration-level phenomena in the binary choice experiment. By changing the probabilities of reward in different ways for different groups of subjects, we could measure the effects of these changes on search behavior – where amount of search would be measured by changes in the pattern of responses.

3.4. Economic implications

It has sometimes been argued that, however realistic the classical theory of the firm as a profit maximizer, it is an adequate theory for purposes of normative macroeconomics. Mason, for example, in commenting on Papandreou's essay on "Problems in the Theory of the Firm" [55, pp. 183–222] says, "The writer of this critique must confess a lack of confidence in the marked superiority, *for purposes of economic analysis*, of this newer concept of the firm over the older conception of the entrepreneur." The italics are Mason's.

The theory of the firm is important for welfare economics – e.g., for determining under what circumstances the behavior of the firm will lead to efficient allocation of resources. The satisficing model vitiates all the conclusions about resource allocation that are derivable from the maximizing model when perfect competition is assumed. Similarly, a dynamic theory of firm sizes, like that mentioned above, has quite different implications for public policies dealing with concentration than a theory that assumes firms to be in static equilibrium. Hence, welfare economists are justified in adhering to the classical theory only if:

(a) the theory is empirically correct as a description of the decision-making process; or

(b) it is safe to assume that the system operates in the neighborhood of the static equilibrium.

What evidence we have mostly contradicts both assumptions.

4. Conflict of Interest

Leaving aside the problem of the motivations of hired managers, conflict of interest among economic actors creates no difficulty for classical economic theory – indeed, it lies at the very core of the theory – so long as each actor treats the other actors as parts of his "given" environment, and doesn't try to predict their behavior and anticipate it. But when this restriction is removed, when it is assumed that a seller takes into account the reactions of buyers to his actions, or that each manufacturer predicts the behaviors of his competitors – all the familiar difficulties of imperfect competition and oligopoly arise.[21]

The very assumptions of omniscient rationality that provide the basis for deductive prediction in economics when competition is present lead to ambiguity when they are applied to competition among the few. The central difficulty is that rationality requires one to outguess one's opponents, but not to be outguessed by them, and this is clearly not a consistent requirement if applied to all the actors.

4.1. Game theory

Modern game theory is a vigorous and extensive exploration of ways of extending the concept of rational behavior to situations involving struggle, outguessing, and bargaining. Since Luce and Raiffa [43] have recently provided us with an excellent survey and evaluation of game theory, I shall not cover the same ground here.[22] I concur in their general evaluation that, while game theory has greatly clarified the issues involved, it has not provided satisfactory solutions. Not only does it leave the definition of rational conduct ambiguous in all cases save the zero-sum two-person game, but it requires of economic man even more fantastic reasoning powers than does classical economic theory.[23]

4.2. Power and bargaining

A number of exploratory proposals have been put forth as alternatives to game theory – among them Galbraith's notion of countervailing power [30] and Schelling's bargaining theory [59] [60]. These analyses draw at least as heavily upon theories of power and bargaining developed initially to explain political phenomena as upon economic theory. They do not lead to any more specific predictions of behavior than do game-theoretic approaches, but place a greater emphasis upon description and actual observation, and are modest in their attempt to derive predictions by deductive reasoning from a few "plausible" premises about human behavior.

At least four important areas of social science and social policy, two of them in economics and two more closely related to political science, have as their central concern the phenomena of power and the processes of bargaining: the theory of political parties, labor-management relations, international politics, and oligopoly theory. Any progress in the basic theory applicable to one of these is certain to be of almost equal importance to the others. A growing recognition of their common concern is evidenced by the initiation of a new cross-disciplinary journal, *Journal of Conflict Resolution*.

4.3. Games against nature

While the binary choice experiment is basically a one-person game, it is possible to interpret it as a "game against nature," and hence to try to explain it in game-theoretic terms. According to game theory, the subject, if he believes in a malevolent nature that manipulates the dice against him, should minimax his expected utility instead of maximizing it. That is, he should adopt the course of action that will maximize his expected utility under the assumption that nature will do her worst to him.

Minimaxing expected utility would lead the subject to call plus or minus at random and with equal probability, regardless of what the history of rewards has been. This is something that subjects demonstrably do not do.

However, it has been suggested by Savage [58] and others that people are not as interested in maximizing utility as they are in minimizing regret. "Regret" means the difference between the reward actually obtained and the reward that could have been obtained with perfect foresight (actually, with perfect hindsight!). It turns out that minimaxing regret in the binary choice experiment leads to event-matching behavior [64, Ch. 16]. Hence, the empirical evidence is at least crudely consistent with the hypothesis that people play against nature by minimaxing regret. We shall see, however, that event-matching is also consistent with a number of other rules of behavior that seem more plausible on their face; hence we need not take the present explanation too seriously – at least I am not inclined to do so.

5. The Formation of Expectations

While the future cannot enter into the determination of the present, expectations about the future can and do. In trying to gain an understanding of the saving, spending, and investment behavior of both consumers and firms, and to make short-term predictions of this behavior for purposes of policy making, economists have done substantial empirical work as well as theorizing on the formation of expectations.

5.1. Empirical studies

A considerable body of data has been accumulated on consumers' plans and expectations from the Survey of Consumer Finances, conducted for the Board of Governors of the Federal Reserve System by the Survey Research Center of the University of Michigan [39, Ch. 5]. These data, and similar data obtained by others, begin to give us some information on the expectations of consumers about their own incomes, and the predictive value of their expenditure plans for their actual subsequent behavior. Some large-scale attempts have been made, notably by Modigliani and Brumberg [48, pp. 388–436] and, a little later, by Friedman [28] to relate these empirical findings to classical utility theory. The current empirical research on businessmen's expectations is of two main kinds:

1   Surveys of businessmen's own forecasts of business and business conditions in the economy and in their own industries [24, pp. 165–88] [29, pp. 189–98]. These are obtained by straightforward questionnaire methods that assume, implicitly, that businessmen can and do make such forecasts. In some uses to which the data are put, it is also assumed that the forecasts are used as one basis for businessmen's actions.

2   Studies of business decisions and the role of expectations in these decisions – particularly investment and pricing decisions. We have already referred to studies of business decisions in our discussion of the goals of the firm.[24]

5.2. Expectations and probability

The classical way to incorporate expectations into economic theory is to assume that the decision maker estimates the joint probability distribution of future events.[25] He can then act so as to maximize the expected value of utility or profit, as the case may be. However satisfying this approach may be conceptually, it poses awkward problems when we ask how the decision maker actually estimates the parameters of the joint probability distribution. Common sense tells us that people don't make such estimates, nor can we find evidence that they do by examining actual business forecasting methods. The surveys of businessmen's expectations have never attempted to secure such estimates, but have contented themselves with asking for point predictions – which, at best, might be interpreted as predictions of the means of the distributions.

It has been shown that under certain special circumstances the mean of the probability distribution is the only parameter that is relevant for decision – that even if the variance and higher moments were known to the rational decision maker, he would have no use for them.[26] In these cases, the arithmetic mean is actually a certainty equivalent, the optimal decision turns out to be the same as if the future were known with certainty. But the situations where the mean is a certainty equivalent are, as we have said, very special ones, and there is no indication that businessmen ever ask whether the necessary conditions for this equivalence are actually met in practice. They somehow make forecasts in the form of point predictions and act upon them in one way or another.

The "somehow" poses questions that are important for business cycle theory, and perhaps for other problems in economics. The way in which expectations are formed may affect the dynamic stability of the economy, and the extent to which cycles will be amplified or damped. Some light, both empirical and theoretical, has recently been cast on these questions. On the empirical side, attempts have been made:

(a) to compare businessmen's forecasts with various "naïve" models that assume the future will be some simple function of the recent past, and

(b) to use such naïve models themselves as forecasting devices.

The simplest naïve model is one that assumes the next period will be exactly like the present. Another assumes that the change from present to next period will equal the change from last period to present; a third, somewhat more general, assumes that the next period will be a weighted average of recent past periods. The term "naïve model" has been applied loosely to various forecasting formulae of these general kinds. There is some affirmative evidence that business forecasts fit such models. There is also evidence that elaboration of the models beyond the first few steps of refinement does not much improve prediction; see, for example, [20]. Arrow and his colleagues [4] have explored some of the conditions under which forecasting formulae will, and will not, introduce dynamic instability into an economic system that is otherwise stable. They have shown, for example, that if a system of multiple markets is stable under static expectations, it is stable when expectations are based on a moving average of past values.

The work on the formation of expectations represents a significant extension of classical theory. For, instead of taking the environment as a "given," known to the economic decision maker, it incorporates in the theory the process of acquiring knowledge about that environment. In doing so, it forces us to include in our model of economic man some of his properties as a learning, estimating, searching, information processing organism [65].

5.3. The cost of information

There is one way in which the formation of expectations might be reincorporated in the body of economic theory: by treating information-gathering as one of the processes of production, so to speak, and applying to it the usual rules of marginal analysis. Information, says price theory, should be gathered up to the point where the incremental cost of additional information is equal to the incremental profit that can be earned by having it. Such an approach can lead to propositions about optimal amounts of information-gathering activity and about the relative merits of alternative information-gathering and estimating schemes.[27]

This line of investigation has, in fact, been followed in statistical decision theory. In sampling theory we are concerned with the optimal size of sample (and in the special and ingenious case of sequential sampling theory, with knowing when to stop sampling), and we wish to evaluate the efficiencies of alternative sampling procedures. The latter problem is the simpler, since it is possible to compare the relative costs of alternative schemes that have the same sampling error, and hence to avoid estimating the value of the information.[28] However, some progress has been made also toward estimating the value of improved forecast accuracy in situations where the forecasts are to be used in applying formal decision rules to choice situations.[29]

The theory of teams developed by Marschak and Radner is concerned with the same problem (see, e.g., [46]) It considers situations involving decentralized and interdependent decision making by two or more persons who share a common goal and who, at a cost, can transmit information to each other about their own actions or about the parts of the environment with which they are in contact. The problem then is to discover the optimal communication strategy under specified assumptions about communication costs and payoffs.

The cost of communication in the theory of teams, like the cost of observations in sampling theory, is a parameter that characterizes the economic actor, or the relation of the actor to his environment. Hence, while these theories retain, in one sense, a classical picture of economic man as a maximizer, they clearly require considerable information about the characteristics of the actor, and not merely about his environment. They take a long stride toward bridging the gap between the traditional concerns of economics and the concerns of psychology.

5.4. Expections in the binary choice experiment

I should like to return again to the binary choice experiment, to see what light it casts on the formation of expectations. If the subject is told by the experimenter that the rewards are assigned at random, if he is told what the odds are for each alternative, *and if he believes the experimenter*, the situation poses no forecasting problem. We have seen, however, that the behavior of most subjects is not consistent with these assumptions.

How would sequential sampling theory handle the problem? Each choice the subject makes now has two consequences: the immediate reward he obtains from it, and the increment of information it provides for predicting the future rewards. If he thinks only of the latter consequences, he is faced with the classical problem of induction: to estimate the probability that an event will occur in the future on the basis of its frequency of occurrence in the past. Almost any rule of induction would require a rational (maximizing) subject to behave in the following general manner: to sample the two alternatives in some proportion to estimate the probability of reward associated with each; after the error of estimate had been reduced below some bound, always to choose the alternative with the higher probability of reward. Unfortunately, this does not appear to be what most subjects do.

If we give up the idea of maximization, we can make the weaker assumption that the subject is adaptive – or learns – but not necessarily in any optimal fashion. What do we mean by adaptation or learning? We mean, gradually and on the basis of experience responding more frequently with the choice that, in the past, has been most frequently rewarded. There is a whole host of rules of behavior possessing this characteristic. Postulate, for example, that at each trial the subject has a certain probability of responding "plus," and the complementary probability of responding "minus." Postulate further that when he makes a particular response the probability of making the same response on the next trial is increased if the response is rewarded and decreased if the response is not rewarded. The amount of increment in the response probability is a parameter character-izing the learning rate of the particular subject. Almost all schemes of this kind produce asymptotic behaviors, as the number of trials increases, that are approximately event matching in character.

Stochastic learning models, as the processes just described are usually called, were introduced into psychology in the early 1950s by W. K. Estes and Bush and Mosteller [15] and have been investigated extensively since that time. The models fit some of the gross features of the observed behaviors – most strikingly the asymptotic probabilities – but do not explain very satisfactorily the fine structure of the observations.

Observation of subjects in the binary choice experiment reveals that usually they not only refuse to believe that (or even to act as if) the reward series were random, but in fact persist over many trials in searching for systematic patterns in the series. To account for such behavior, we might again postulate a learning model, but in this case a model in which the subject does not react probabilistically to his environment, but forms and tests definite hypotheses about systematic patterns in it. Man, in this view, is not only a learning animal; he is a pattern-finding and concept-forming animal. Julian Feldman [25] has constructed theories of this kind to explain the behavior of subjects in the binary choice experiment, and while the tests of the theories are not yet completed, his findings look exceedingly promising.

As we move from maximizing theories, through simple stochastic learning theories, to theories involving pattern recognition our model of the expectation-forming processes and the organism that performs it increases in complexity. If we follow this route, we reach a point where a theory of behavior requires a rather elaborate and detailed picture of the rational actor's cognitive processes.

6. Human Cognition and Economics

All the developments we have examined in the preceding four sections have a common theme: they all involve important modifications in the concept of economic man and, for the reasons we have stated, modifications in the direction of providing a fuller description of his characteristics. The classical theory is a theory of a man choosing among fixed and known alternatives, to each of which is attached known consequences. But when perception and cognition intervene between the decision maker and his objective environment, this model no longer proves adequate. We need a description of the choice process that recognizes that alternatives are not given but must be sought; and a description that takes into account the arduous task of determining what consequences will follow on each alternative [63, Ch. 5] [64, Part 4] [14].

The decision maker's information about his environment is much less than an approximation to the real environment. The term "approximation" implies that the subjective world of the decision maker resembles the external environment closely, but lacks, perhaps, some fineness of detail. In actual fact the perceived world is fantastically different from the "real" world. The differences involve both omissions and distortions, and arise in both perception and inference. The sins of omission in perception are more important than the sins of commission. The decision maker's model of the world encompasses only a minute fraction of all the relevant characteristics of the real environment, and his inferences extract only a minute fraction of all the information that is present even in his model.

Perception is sometimes referred to as a "filter." This term is as misleading as "approximation," and for the same reason: it implies that what comes through into the central nervous system is really quite a bit like what is "out there." In fact, the filtering is not merely a passive selection of some part of a presented whole, but an active process involving attention to a very small part of the whole and exclusion, from the outset, of almost all that is not within the scope of attention.

Every human organism lives in an environment that generates millions of bits of new information each second, but the bottleneck of the perceptual apparatus certainly does not admit more than 1,000 bits per second, and probably much less. Equally significant omissions occur in the processing that takes place when information reaches the brain. As every mathematician knows, it is one thing to have a set of differential equations, and another thing to have their solutions. Yet the solutions are logically implied by the equations – they are "all there," if we only knew how to get to them! By the same token, there are hosts of inferences that *might* be drawn from the information stored in the brain that are not in fact drawn. The consequences implied by information in the memory become known only through active information-processing, and hence through active selection of particular problem-solving paths from the myriad that might have been followed.

In this section we shall examine some theories of decision making that take the limitations of the decision maker and the complexity of the environment as central concerns. These theories incorporate some mechanisms we have already discussed – for example, aspiration levels and forecasting processes – but go beyond them in providing a detailed picture of the choice process.

A real-life decision involves some goals or values, some facts about the environment, and some inferences drawn from the values and facts. The goals and values may be simple or complex, consistent or contradictory; the facts may be real or supposed, based on observation or the reports of others; the inferences may be valid or spurious. The whole process may be viewed, metaphorically, as a process of "reasoning," where the values and facts serve as premises, and the decision that is finally reached is inferred from these premises [63]. The resemblance of decision making to logical reasoning is only metaphorical, because there are quite different rules in the two cases to determine what constitute "valid" premises and admissible modes of inference. The metaphor is useful because it leads us to take the individual *decision premise* as the unit of description, hence to deal with the whole interwoven fabric of influences that bear on a single decision – but without being bound by the assumptions of rationality that limit the classical theory of choice.

6.1. Rational behavior and role theory

We can find common ground to relate the economist's theory of decision making with that of the social psychologist. The latter is particularly interested, of course, in social influences on choice, which determine the *role* of the actor. In our present terms, a role is a social prescription of some, but not all, of the premises that enter into an individual's choices of behavior. Any particular concrete behavior is the resultant of a large number of premises, only some of which are prescribed by the role. In addition to role premises there will be premises about the state of the environment based directly on perception, premises representing beliefs and knowledge, and idiosyncratic premises that characterize the personality. Within this framework we can accommodate both the rational elements in choice, so much emphasized by economics, and the nonrational elements to which psychologists and sociologists often prefer to call attention.

6.2. Decision premises and computer programs

The analysis of choice in terms of decision premises gives us a conceptual framework for describing and explaining the process of deciding. But so complex is the process that our explanations of it would have remained schematic and hypothetical for a long time to come had not the modern digital computer appeared on the scene. The notion of decision premise can be translated into computer terminology, and when this translation has been accomplished, the digital computer provides us with an instrument for simulating human decision processes – even very complex ones – and hence for testing empirically our explanations of those processes [53].

A fanciful (but only slightly fanciful) example will illustrate how this might be done. Some actual examples will be cited presently. Suppose we were to construct a robot incorporating a modern digital computer, and to program (i.e., to instruct) the robot to take the role of a business executive in a specified company. What would the program look like? Since no one has yet done this, we cannot say with certainty, but several points are fairly clear. The program would not consist of a list of prescribed and proscribed behaviors, since what an executive does is highly contingent on information about a wide variety of circumstances. Instead, the program would consist of a large number of *criteria* to be applied to possible and proposed courses of action, of routines for *generating* possible courses of action, of computational procedures for *assessing* the state of the environment and its implications for action, and the like. Hence, the program – in fact, a role prescription – would interact with information to produce concrete behavior adapted to the situation. The elements of such a program take the form of what we have called decision premises, and what the computer specialists would call instructions.

The promise of constructing actual detailed descriptions of concrete roles and decision processes is no longer, with the computer, a mere prospectus to be realized at some undefined future date. We can already provide actual examples, some of them in the area of economics.

MANAGEMENT SCIENCE   In the paragraphs on normative applications in section 2, we have already referred to the use of such mathematical techniques as linear programming and dynamic programming to construct formal decision processes for actual situations. The relevance of these decision models to the present discussion is that they are not merely abstract "theories" of the firm, but actual decision-making devices. We can think of any such device as a simulation of the corresponding human decision maker, in which the equations and other assumptions that enter into the formal decision-making procedure correspond to the decision premises – including the role prescription – of the decision maker.

The actual application of such models to concrete business situations brings to light the information-processing tasks that are concealed in the assumptions of the more abstract classical models [65, pp. 51–2]:

1 The models must be formulated so as to require for their application only data that are obtainable. If one of the penalties, for example, of holding too small inventories is the loss of sales, a decision model that proposes to determine optimal inventory levels must incorporate a procedure for putting a dollar value on this loss.

2 The models must call only for practicable computations. For example, several proposals for applying linear programming to certain factory scheduling problems have been shown to be impracticable because, even with computers, the computation time is too great. The task of decision theory (whether normative or descriptive) is to find alternative techniques – probably only approximate – that demand much less computation.

3 The models must not demand unobtainable forecast information. A procedure that would require a sales department to estimate the third moment of next month's sales distribution would not have wide application, as either description or prescription, to business decision making.

These models, then, provide us with concrete examples of roles for a decision maker described in terms of the premises he is expected to apply to the decision – the data and the rules of computation.

ENGINEERING DESIGN   Computers have been used for some years to carry out some of the analytic computations required in engineering design – computing the stresses, for example, in a proposed bridge design. Within the past two years, ways have been found to program computers to carry out synthesis as well as analysis – to evolve the design itself.[30] A number of companies in the electrical industry now use computers to design electric motors, transformers, and generators, going from customer specifications to factory design without human intervention. The significance of this for our purpose here is that the synthesis programs appear to simulate rather closely the processes that had previously been used by college-trained engineers in the same design work. It has proved possible to write down the engineers' decision premises and inference processes in sufficient detail to produce workable computer programs.

HUMAN PROBLEM SOLVING   The management science and engineering design programs already provide examples of simulation of human decision making by computer. It may be thought that, since in both instances the processes are highly arithmetical, these examples are relevant to only a very narrow range of human problem-solving activity. We generally think of a digital computer as a device which, if instructed in painful detail by its operator, can be induced to perform rather complicated and tedious arithmetical operations. More recent developments require us to revise these conceptions of the computer, for they enable it to carry out tasks that, if performed by humans, we would certainly call "thinking" and "learning."

Discovering the proof of a theorem of Euclid – a task we all remember from our high school geometry course – requires thinking and usually insight and imagination. A computer is now being programmed to perform this task (in a manner closely simulating the human geometer), and another computer has been successfully performing a highly similar task in symbolic logic for the past two years.[31] The latter computer is programmed to learn – that is to improve its performance on the basis of successful problem-solving experience – to use something akin to imagery or metaphor in planning its proofs, and to transfer some of its skills to other tasks – for example, solving trigonometric identities – involving completely distinct subject matter. These programs, it should be observed, do not involve the computer in rapid arithmetic – or any arithmetic for that matter. They are basically non-numerical, involving the manipulation of all kinds of symbolic material, including words.

Still other computer programs have been written to enable a computer to play chess.[32] Not all of these programs, or those previously mentioned, are close simulations of the processes humans use. However, in some direct attempts to investigate the human processes by thinking-aloud techniques and to reproduce in computer programs the processes observed in human subjects, several striking simulations have been achieved.[33] These experiments have been described elsewhere and can't be reviewed here in detail.

BUSINESS GAMES   Business games, like those developed by the American Management Association, International Business Machines Corporation, and several universities, represent a parallel development.[34] In the business game, the decisions of the business firms are still made by the human players, but the economic environment of these firms, including their markets, are represented by computer programs that calculate the environment's responses to the actions of the players. As the games develop in detail and realism, their programs will represent more and more concrete descriptions of the decision processes of various economic actors – for example, consumers.

The games that have been developed so far are restricted to numerical magnitudes like prices and quantities of goods, and hence resemble the management science and engineering design programs more closely than they do those we have described under the heading of human problem solving. There is no reason, however, to expect this restriction to remain very long.

6.3. *Implications for economics*

Apart from normative applications (e.g., substituting computers for humans in certain decision-making tasks) we are not interested so much in the detailed descriptions of roles as in broader questions:

1   What general characteristics do the roles of economic actors have?
2   How do roles come to be structured in the particular ways they do?
3   What bearing does this version of role theory have for macroeconomics and other large-scale social phenomena?

CHARACTERIZING ROLE STRUCTURE   Here we are concerned with generalizations about thought processes, particularly those generalizations that are relatively independent of the substantive content of the role. A classical example is Dewey's description of stages in the problem-solving process. Another example, of particular interest to economics, is the hypothesis we have already discussed at length: that economic man is a *satisficing* animal whose problem solving is based on search activity to meet certain aspiration levels rather than a *maximizing* animal whose problem solving involves finding the best alternatives in terms of specified criteria [64]. A third hypothesis is that operative goals (those associated with an observable criterion of success, and relatively definite means of attainment) play a much larger part in governing choice than nonoperative goals (those lacking a concrete measure of success or a program for attainment) [45, p. 156].

UNDERSTANDING HOW ROLES EMERGE   Within almost any single business firm, certain characteristic types of roles will be represented: selling roles, production roles, accounting roles, and so on [22]. Partly, this consistency may be explained in functional terms – that a model that views the firm as producing a product, selling it, and accounting for its assets and liabilities is an effective simplification of the real world, and provides the members of the organization with a workable frame of reference. Imitation within the culture provides an alternative explanation. It is exceedingly difficult to test hypotheses as to the origins and causal conditions for roles as universal in the society as these, but the underlying mechanisms could probably be explored effectively by the study of less common roles – safety director, quality control inspector, or the like – that are to be found in some firms, but not in all.

With our present definition of role, we can also speak meaningfully of the role of an entire business firm – of decision premises that underlie its basic policies. In a particular industry we find some firms that specialize in adapting the product to individual customer's specifications; others that specialize in product innovation. The common interest of economics and psychology includes not only the study of individual roles, but also the explanation of organizational roles of these sorts.

TRACING THE IMPLICATIONS FOR MACROECONOMICS   If basic professional goals remain as they are, the interest of the psychologist and the economist in role theory will stem from somewhat different ultimate aims. The former will use various economic and organizational phenomena as data for the study of the structure and determinants of roles; the latter will be primarily interested in the implications of role theory for the model of economic man, and indirectly, for macroeconomics.

The first applications will be to those topics in economics where the assumption of static equilibrium is least tenable. Innovation, technological change, and economic development are examples of areas to which a good empirically tested theory of the processes of human adaptation and problem solving could make a major contribution. For instance, we know very little at present about how the rate of innovation depends on the amounts of resources allocated to various kinds of research and development activity [34]. Nor do we understand very well the nature of "know how," the costs of transferring technology from one firm or economy to another, or the effects of various kinds and amounts of education upon national product. These are difficult questions to answer from aggregative data and gross observation, with the result that our views have been formed more by arm-chair theorizing than by testing hypotheses with solid facts.

7. Conclusion

In exploring the areas in which economics has common interests with the other behavioral sciences, we have been guided by the metaphor we elaborated in section 1. In simple, slow-moving situations, where the actor has a single, operational goal, the assumption of maximization relieves us of any need to construct a detailed picture of economic man or his processes of adaptation. As the complexity of the environment increases, or its speed of change, we need to know more and more about the mechanisms and processes that economic man uses to relate himself to that environment and achieve his goals.

How closely we wish to interweave economics with psychology depends, then, both on the range of questions we wish to answer and on our assessment of how far we may trust the assumptions of static equilibrium as approximations. In considerable part, the demand for a fuller picture of economic man has been coming from the profession of economics itself, as new areas of theory and application have emerged in which complexity and change are central facts. The revived interest in the theory of utility, and its application to choice under uncertainty, and to consumer saving and spending is one such area. The needs of normative macroeconomics and management science for a fuller theory of the firm have led to a number of attempts to understand the actual processes of making business decisions. In both these areas, notions of adaptive and satisficing behavior, drawn largely from psychology, are challenging sharply the classical picture of the maximizing entrepreneur.

The area of imperfect competition and oligopoly has been equally active, although the activity has thus far perhaps raised more problems than it has solved. On the positive side, it has revealed a community of interest among a variety of social scientists concerned with bargaining as a part of political and economic processes. Prediction of the future is another element common to many decision processes, and particularly important to explaining business cycle phenomena. Psychologists and economists have been applying a wide variety of approaches, empirical and theoretical, to the study of the formation of expectations. Surveys of consumer and business behavior, theories of statistical induction, stochastic learning theories, and theories of concept formation have all been converging on this problem area.

The very complexity that has made a theory of the decision-making process essential has made its construction exceedingly difficult. Most approaches have been piecemeal – now focused on the criteria of choice, now on conflict of interest, now on the formation of expectations. It seemed almost utopian to suppose that we could put together a model of adaptive man that would compare in completeness with the simple model of classical economic man. The sketchiness and incompleteness of the newer proposals has been urged as a compelling reason for clinging to the older theories, however inadequate they are admitted to be.

The modern digital computer has changed the situation radically. It provides us with a tool of research – for formulating and testing theories – whose power is commensurate with the complexity of the phenomena we seek to understand. Although the use of computers to build theories of human behavior is very recent, it has already led to concrete results in the simulation of higher mental processes. As economics finds it more and more necessary to understand and explain disequilibrium as well as equilibrium, it will find an increasing use for this new tool and for communication with its sister sciences of psychology and sociology.

Notes

1   The influence of economics upon recent work in the psychology of higher mental processes is well illustrated by Bruner, Goodnow and Austin [14, Ch. 3 and 4]. In this work, game theory is used to throw light on the processes of concept formation.

2   The models of rational decision making employed in operations research are surveyed in Churchman, Ackoff, and Arnoff [16], Bowman and Fetter [11]; and Vazsonyi [69]

3   As an example of what passes for empirical "evidence" in this literature, I cite pp. 22–23 of Friedman's *Essays in Positive Economics* [27], which will amaze anyone brought up in the empirical tradition of psychology and sociology, although it has apparently excited little adverse comment among economists.

4   Ward Edwards [23] provides an account of these developments from the psychologist's point of view; Chapter 2 of Luce and Raiffa [43] is an excellent introduction to the "new" utility theory. Arrow [5] contains a nonmathematical survey of this and related topics.

5   The second edition of von Neumann and Morgenstern [50] contains the first rigorous axiomatic demonstration of this point.

6   Ramsey's important essay [57] was sufficiently obscure that it was overlooked until the ideas were rediscovered independently by de Finetti [26]. Valuable notes on the history of the topic together with a thorough formal treatment will be found in the first five chapters of Savage [58].

7   Some of the empirical evidence is reviewed in [23]. A series of more recent empirical studies is reported in Davidson and Suppes [21].

8   Some more recent experiments [57a], show a relatively high degree of transitivity. A. G. Papandreou, in a publication I have not yet seen (University of California Publications in Economics) also reports a high degree of transitivity.

9   The systematic development of statistics as decision theory is due largely to A. Wald [70] on the basis of the earlier work of J. Neyman and E. Pearson. Savage [58] carries the development further, erecting the foundations of statistics solidly on utility and probability theory.

10   This work relates, of course, to profit maximization and cost minimization rather than utility maximization, but it is convenient to mention it at this point. See [11] [16] [69].

11   Arrow, Harris and Marschak [3] were among the first to treat inventory decisions dynamically. A general treatment of the theory of dynamic programming will be found in Bellman [9].

12   My understanding of the implications of the binary choice experiment owes much to conversations with Julian Feldman, and to his unpublished work on the experiment. See also, Bush and Mosteller [15] particularly Chapter 13.

13   An example of data consistent with event-matching behavior is given on page 283 of [15].

14   Subjects tend to choose the more highly rewarded alternative slightly more frequently than is called for by event matching. Hence, the actual behavior tends to be some kind of average between event matching and the optimal behavior. See [15, Ch. 13].

15   For a survey of recent discussions see Papandreou [55].

16   A comparison of satisficing with maximizing models of decision making can be found in [64, Ch. 14]. Katona [40] has independently made similar comparisons of economic and psychological theories of decision.

17   Simon and Bonini [66] have constructed a stochastic model that explains the observed data on the size distributions of business firms.

18   A standard psychological reference on aspiration levels is [42]. For applications to economics, see [61] and [45] (in the latter, consult the index under "aspiration levels").

19   Lest this last term appear fanciful I should like to call attention to the phenomena of panic and broken morale, which are well known to observers of the stock market and of organizations but which have no reasonable interpretation in classical utility theory. I may also mention that

psychologists use the theory described here in a straightforward way to produce experimental neurosis in animal and human subjects.

20 A comprehensive bibliography of empirical work prior to 1950 will be found in [37]. Some of the more recent work is [19] [24] [39, Ch. 11].

21 There is by now a voluminous literature on the problem. The difficulties in defining rationality in competitive situations are well stated in the first chapter of von Neumann and Morgenstern [50].

22 Chapters 5 and 6 of [43] provide an excellent survey of the attempts that have been made to extend the theory of games to the kinds of situations most relevant to economics.

23 In *Strategy and Market Structure*, Martin Shubik [60A] approaches the topics of imperfect competition and oligopoly from the standpoint of the theory of games.

24 See the references cited [12, p. 160].

25 A general survey of approaches to decision making under uncertainty will be found in [2] and in [43, Ch. 13].

26 The special case in which mean expectations constitute a certainty equivalent is treated in [62]. An alternative derivation, and fuller discussion is given by Theil [67, Ch. 8, sect. 6].

27 Fundamental and applied research are examples of economically significant information-gathering activities. Griliches [34] has recently made an attempt to estimate the economic return from research on hybrid corn.

28 Modern treatments of sampling theory, like Cochran [17] are based on the idea of minimizing the cost of obtaining a fixed amount of information.

29 For the theory and an application to macroeconomics, see Theil [67, Ch. 8, sects. 5 and 6].

30 A nontechnical description of such a program will be found in [33].

31 The program for proving theorems in logic is discussed in [51] and [52], Gelernter and Rochester's geometry program in [31].

32 A survey of computer chess programs can be found in [54].

33 Much of this work is still unpublished, but see [53] and [54].

34 Two business games are described by Andlinger [1].

References and Further Reading

1 Andlinger, G. R. (1958): "Business Games – Play One," *Harvard Business Review*, 36, April, 115–25.

2 Arrow, K. J. (1951): "Alternative Approaches to the Theory of Choice in Risk-Taking Situations," *Econometrica*, 19, October, 404–37.

3 Arrow, K. J., Harris, T. E. and Marschak, J. (1951): "Optimal Inventory Policy," *Econometrica*, 19, July, 250–72.

4 Arrow, K. J. and Nerlove, M. (1958): "A Note on Expectations and Stability," *Econometrica*, 26, April, 297–305.

5 Arrow, K. J. (1958): "Utilities, Attitudes, Choices," *Econometrica*, 26, January, 1–23.

6 Bakan, D. (1953): "Learning and the Principle of Inverse Probability," *Psychology Review*, 60, September, 360–70.

7 Bavelas, A. (1948): "A Mathematical Model for Group Structures," *Applied Anthropology*, 7, Summer 16–30.

8 Beckmann, M. (1958): "Decision and Team Problems in Airline Reservations," *Econometrica* 26, January, 134–45.

9 Bellman, R. (1957): *Dynamic Programming*, Princeton: Princeton University Press.

10 Bowen, H. R. (1955): *The Business Enterprise as a Subject for Research*. New York: Committee on Business Enterprise.

11 Bowman, E. H. and Fetter, R. B. (1957): *Analysis for Production Management*. Homewood, Ill: Irwin.

12 Bowman, M. J. (ed.) (1958): *Expectations, Uncertainty, and Business Behavior*. New York: Social Sciences Research Center.

13 Brems, H. (1958): "Response Lags and Nonprice Competition," in M. J. Bowman (ed.) [12], 134–43.

14 Bruner, J., Goodnow J. J. and Austin, G. A. (1956): *A Study of Thinking*. New York: Wiley.

15 Bush, R. R. and Mosteller, F. (1955): *Stochastic Models for Learning*. New York: Wiley.

16 Churchman, C. W., Ackoff, R. L. and Arnoff, E. L. (1957): *Introduction to Operations Research*. New York: Wiley.

17 Cochran, W. G. (1953): *Sampling Techniques*. New York: Wiley.

18 Cyert, R. M. and March, J. G. (1955): "Organizational Structure and Pricing Behavior in an Oligopolistic Market," *American Economic Review*, 45, March, 129–39.

19 —— (1956): "Organizational Factors in the Theory of Oligopoly," *Quarterly Journal of Economics*, 70, February, 44–64.

20 Darcovich, W. (1958): "Evaluation of Some Naive Expectations Models for Agricultural Yields and Prices," in M. J. Bowman (ed.) [12], 199–202.

21 Davidson, D. and Suppes, P. (1957): *Decision Making: An Experimental Approach*. Stanford: Stanford University Press.

22 Dearborn, D. C. and Simon, H. A. (1958): "Selective Perception: A Note on the Departmental Identification of Executives," *Sociometry*, 21, June, 140–4.

22a Earley, J. S. (1956): "Marginal Policies of 'Excellently Managed' Companies," *American Economic Review*, 66, March, 44–70.

23 Edwards, W. (1954): "The Theory of Decision Making," *Psychological Bulletin*, 51, September, 380–417.

24 Eisner, R. (1958): "Expectations, Plans, and Capital Expenditures," in M. J. Bowman (ed.) [12], 165–88.

25 Feldman, J. (1958): "A Theory of Binary Choice Behavior," Carnegie Institute of Technology Graduate School of Industry Administration, Complex information processing working paper No. 12, revised, May 5. Unpublished.

26 de Finetti B. (1937): "La prevision: Ses lois Logiques, ses Sources Subjectives," *Annales Institute Henri Poincare*, 7, 1–68.

27 Friedman, M. (1953): *Essays in Positive Economics*. Chicago: University of Chicago Press.

28 —— (1957): *A Theory of the Consumption Function*. New York: Princeton University Press.

29 Friend, I. (1958): "Critical Evaluation of Surveys of Expectations, Plans, and Investment Behavior," in M. J. Bowman (ed.) [12], 189–98.

30 Galbraith, J. K. (1952): *American Capitalism: The Concept of Countervailing Power*. Boston: Houghton Mifflin.

31 Gelernter, H. L. and Rochester, N. (1958): "Intelligent Behavior in Problem-Solving Machines," *IBM Journal of Research and Development*, 2, October, 336–45.

32 Georgescu-Roegen, N. (1958): "The Nature of Expectation and Uncertainty" in M. J. Bowman (ed.) [12], 11–29.

33 Godwin, G. L. (1958): "Digital Computers Tap Out Designs for Large Motors – Fast," *Power*, April.

34 Griliches, Z. (1957): "Hybrid Corn: An Exploration in the Economics of Technological Change," *Econometrica*, 25, October, 501–22.

35 Guetzkow, H. and Simon, H. A. (1955): "The Impact of Certain Communication Nets in Task Oriented Groups," *Management Science*, 1, July, 233–50.

36 Haley, B. F. (ed.) (1952): *A Survey of Contemporary Economics, II*. Homewood, Ill: Irwin, for the American Economic Association.

37 Hayes, S. P. (1950): "Some Psychological Problems of Economics," *Psychological Bulletin*, 47, July, 289–330.

38 Holt, C. C., Modigliani, F. and Simon, H. A. (1955): "A Linear Decision Rule for Production and Employment Scheduling," *Management Science*, 2, October, 1–30.
39 Katona, G. (1951): *Psychological Analysis of Economic Behavior*, New York: McGraw Hill.
40 —— (1953): "Rational Behavior and Economic Behavior," *Psychological Review*, 60, July 307–18.
41 Leavitt, H. J. (1951): "Some Effects of Certain Communication Patterns on Group Performance," *Journal of Abnormal and Social Psychology*, 46, February, 38–50.
42 Lewin, K. et al. (1944): "Level of Aspiration," in J. McV. Hunt (ed.), *Personality and the Behavior Disorders*, New York: Wiley, 333–78.
43 Luce, R. D. and Raiffa, H. (1957): *Games and Decisions*. New York: Wiley.
44 Mack, R. (1958): "Business Expectations and the Buying of Materials," in M. J. Bowman [12], 106–18.
45 March, J. G. and Simon, H. A. (1958): *Organizations*. New York: Wiley.
46 Marschak, J. (1955): "Elements for a Theory of Teams," *Management Science*, 1, January, 127–37.
47 May, K. O. (1954): "Intransitivity, Utility, and the Aggregation of Preference Patterns," *Econometrica*, 22, January, 1–13.
48 Modigliani, F. and Brumberg, R. E. (1954): "Utility Analysis and the Consumption Function," in K. K. Kurihara (ed.) *Post Keynesian Economics*, New Brunswick, NJ: 388–436.
49 Mosteller, F. and Nogee, P. (1951): "An Experimental Measurement of Utility," *Journal of Political Economy*, 59, October, 371–404.
50 von Neumann, J. and Morgenstern, O. (1947): *Theory of Games and Economic Behavior*. Princeton: Princeton University Press.
51 Newell, A. and Simon, H. A. (1956): "The Logic Theory Machine," *IRE Transactions of Information Theory*, IT–2, September, 61–79.
52 Newell, A., Shaw, J. C. and Simon, H. A. (1957): "Empirical Explorations of the Logic Theory Machine," *Proceedings of the Western Joint Computer Conference*, 26–28, February, 218–30.
53 —— (1958): "Elements of a Theory of Human Problem Solving," *Psychological Review*, 65, May, 151–66.
54 —— (1958): "Chess-Playing Programs and the Problem of Complexity," *IBM Journal of Research and Development*, 2, October, 320–35.
55 Papandreou, A. G. (1952): "Some Basic Problems in the Theory of the Firm," in B. F. Haley [36], 183–222.
56 Peck, M. J. (1958): "Marginal Analysis and the Explanation of Business Behavior Under Uncertainty," in M. J. Bowman [12], 119–33.
57 Ramsey, F. P. (1931): "Truth and Probability," in R. B. Braithewaite (ed.), *Foundations of Mathematics and Other Logical Essays*, London: Routledge & Kegan Paul, 156–98.
57a Rose, A. M. (1957): "A Study of Irrational Judgments," *Journal of Political Economy*, 65, October, 394–402.
58 Savage, L. J. (1954): *The Foundations of Statistics*. New York: Wiley.
59 Schelling, T. C. (1957): "Bargaining, Communication, and Limited War," *Journal of Conflict Resolution*, 1, March, 19–36.
60 —— (1956): "An Essay on Bargaining," *American Economic Review*, 46, June, 281–306.
60a Shubik, M. (1959): *Strategy and Market Structure*. New York: Wiley.
61 Siegel, S. (1957): "Level of Aspiration and Decision Making," *Psychological Review*, 64, July, 253–62.
62 Simon, H. A. (1956): "Dynamic Programming Under Uncertainty with a Quadratic Criterion Function," *Econometrica*, 24, January, 74–81.
63 —— (1957): *Administrative Behavior*, 2nd edn. New York: Macmillan.
64 —— (1957): *Models of Man*. New York: Wiley.

65 —— (1958): "The Role of Expectations in an Adaptive or Behavioristic Model," in M. J. Bowman [12], 49–58.

66 Simon, H. A. and Bonini, C. P. (1958): "The Size Distribution of Business Firms," *American Economic Review*, 48, September, 607–17.

67 Theil, H. (1958): *Economic Forecasts and Policy*. Amsterdam: North-Holland.

68 Thurstone, L. L. (1931): "The Indifference Function," *Journal of Social Psychology*, 2, May, 139–67.

69 Vazsonyi, A. (1958): *Scientific Programming in Business and Industry*. New York: Wiley.

70 Wald, A. (1950): *Statistical Decision Functions*. New York: Wiley.

71 Wilson, B. T. and Andrews, P. W. S. (eds) (1951): *Oxford Studies in the Price Mechanism*. Oxford: Clarendon Press.

CHAPTER THREE

Economic Methodology in a Nutshell

Daniel M. Hausman

Source: *Journal of Economic Perspectives*, 3, 2, (1989), pp. 115–27.
Reprinted with the permission of the author and the American
Economic Association. © American Economic Association.

The literature on economic methodology is concerned mainly with questions of theory confirmation or disconfirmation or empirical theory choice. The central question is usually, "How one can tell whether a particular bit of economics is good science?" Economists would like methodologists to provide the algorithm for doing good economic science – and they want the algorithm to vindicate their own practice and to reveal the foolishness of those who do economics differently. For example, Milton Friedman (1953) tells economists that good theories are those that provide correct and useful predictions, while Paul Samuelson (1947, 1963) tells economists to formulate theories with "operational" concepts that are, ideally, logically equivalent to their descriptive consequences.

In my view, not only are these (and most other) specific views on theory appraisal mistaken, but the concern with problems of empirical appraisal is exaggerated, for there are also interesting methodological questions to consider – both normative and descriptive – concerning the structure, strategy, goals and heuristics of various economic theories. For example, few writers on economic methodology recognize that the activities of formulating economic models and investigating their implications are a sort of conceptual exploration. Instead, most mistakenly regard these activities as offering empirical hypotheses and assess them in terms of some philosophical model of confirmation or falsification.

As a tendentious survey of standard methodological literature, this essay will, however, share its preoccupation with the empirical appraisal of theory, microeconomic theory in particular. I shall in particular discuss four approaches to praising or damning microeconomic theory that have dominated methodological discussions. They might be called the deductivist, the positivist or Popperian, the predictionist, and the eclectic. Or to assign representative or striking figures to positions, these are John Stuart Mill's, Mark Blaug's, Milton Friedman's, and Donald McCloskey's views. I shall sketch and assess each position and defend aspects of the deductivist and eclectic views. Along the way I shall have something to say not only about how to do economics, but also about how to philosophize about economic methodology.

1. Deductivism

John Stuart Mill was both a Ricardian economist and a staunch empiricist, yet his economics seems not to measure up to empiricist standards for knowledge. After all, the implications of Ricardian economics appeared to be disconfirmed (de Marchi, 1970); for example, the share of national income paid as rent did not increase. How could Mill reconcile his confidence in Ricardian economics and his empiricism?

In Mill's view (1836, 1843, bk. 6), a complex subject matter like political economy can only be studied scientifically by means of the deductive method. Since so many causal factors influence economic phenomena, and experimentation is generally not possible, there is no way to employ the methods of induction directly. The only solution is first inductively to establish basic psychological or technical laws – such as "people seek more wealth," or the law of diminishing returns – and then to deduce their economic implications given specifications of relevant circumstances. Empirical confirmation or verification has an important role in determining whether the deductively derived conclusions are applicable, in checking the correctness of the deductions and in determining whether significant causal factors have been left out, but such testing does not bear on one's commitment to the basic "laws." They have already been established by introspection or experimentation. Political economy is in this regard similar to the science of tides, which applies independently established laws.

Mill believed that these established premises state accurately how specific causal factors operate. They are obviously not universal laws; for example, everyone does not always seek more wealth. These basic generalizations are instead statements of tendencies. Since these tendencies are subject to various "disturbances" or "interfering causes," which cannot all be specified in advance, vague *ceteris paribus* (other things being equal) clauses that allow for these disturbances will be unavoidable in formulating them. Economics explores the consequences of these established, but inexact, premises. Since much is left out of the theory, these consequences will not always obtain.

In Mill's view economics is a science, for economists do know the basic causes of economic phenomena. But it is an inexact science, for there are myriad interferences or disturbing causes. Mill's views are almost the opposite of Milton Friedman's, for Mill holds that the confidence of economists in the science of political economy is based on direct and rather casual confirmation of its assumptions, not on serious tests of their implications. Not only were Mill's views adopted by followers such as Cairnes (1888) and early neoclassical methodologists such as John Neville Keynes (1890), but if one updates the language and the economic theory, one has the view to which, I suggest, most orthodox economists (regardless of what they may say in methodological discussion) still subscribe (see also Stewart, 1979).

The transition from classical to neoclassical economics brought not only changes in economic theory, but methodological changes as well, for neoclassical theory focuses much more on individual preferences and decision making than did classical economics. Despite this difference, which was much emphasized by authors such as Frank Knight (1935, 1940), Ludwig von Mises (1981), and Lionel Robbins (1935), early neoclassical economists agreed with Mill that the basic premises of economics are well- justified, and that empirical failures do not cast them into doubt. In defending this view, Lionel Robbins

(1935, p. 121) explicitly notes his intellectual debts to Mill, and, by exaggerating the obviousness of the basic assumptions of neoclassical microeconomics, he provides a particularly persuasive formulation of what is essentially Mill's view (pp. 78–9):

> The propositions of economic theory, like all scientific theory, are obviously deductions from a series of postulates. . . . The main postulate of the theory of value is the fact that individuals can arrange their preferences in an order, and in fact do so. The main postulate of the theory of production is the fact that there are [sic] more than one factor of production. The main postulate of the theory of dynamics is the fact that we are not certain regarding future scarcities. These are not postulates the existence of whose counterpart in reality admits of extensive dispute once their nature is fully realised. We do not need controlled experiments to establish their validity: they are so much the stuff of our everyday experience that they have only to be stated to be recognized as obvious.

Although Robbins overstates his case, I think that he is basically right.

2. Positivist or Popperian Views

To anyone familiar with the methodological literature of the last half-century, such a complacent view of the deductive method must seem perverse. For the theme which has dominated this period is that claims that are hedged with qualifications and *ceteris paribus* clauses are untestable and uninformative. What Mill or Robbins called "tendencies" or "inexact laws" are qualified claims such as, "In the absence of disturbances or interferences, people prefer more wealth," or "*Ceteris paribus* returns to variable inputs will diminish." Since the content of the *ceteris paribus* clause is not fully specified, it seems that these statements are unfalsifiable and lack definite empirical meaning. Either things are as claimed by the tendency, or there is some disturbance. No outcomes are prohibited, and new evidence never requires economists to alter their beliefs about the basic tendencies.

Fifty years ago, under the influence of logical positivism, Terence Hutchison made essentially just this charge. The statements of "pure theory" in economics are empty definitional or logical truths, he argued, and even applied claims are so hedged that they lack content (1938, esp. ch. 2). Hutchison insisted that economists should start behaving like responsible empirical scientists. Thus, under the guiding star of logical positivism, and later on of Karl Popper (1959), began the first and only major change in economists' official position on the appraisal of microeconomics.

As Hutchison himself partly recognized (1938, ch. 2), this critique can be answered from within the Millian tradition. For one need not regard or employ *ceteris paribus* clauses as blanket excuses (Hausman, 1981a, ch. 7; 1981b). *Ceteris paribus* clauses are part of almost all of science. Rather than condemning them all, one needs to distinguish when one may legitimately employ them and to recognize that rough generalizations can have worth and content despite their vagueness and imprecision. I learned something useful when I was taught that aspirin cures headaches, even though (alas!) this generalization is not a universal law.[1]

Hutchison's attack was still disquieting. Did neoclassical microeconomic theory measure up to the standards for science defended by contemporary (positivist) philosophers of science? Those who first rose to answer Hutchinson's challenge, such as Frank

Knight (1940), may have aggravated rather than allayed this disquiet, for Knight explicitly repudiated the empiricist or positivist philosophy of science upon which Hutchison's challenge relied. Knight accuses the positivists of overlooking the complexity and uncertainty of testing in all sciences (1940, p. 153) and argues at length that positivist views of science are particularly inappropriate to economics, which, like all sciences of human action, must concern itself with reasons, motives, values and errors, not just causes and regularities. Younger and less philosophically ambitious economists might well have wondered whether there was any way to respond to Hutchison without thus repudiating up-to-date philosophy of science. Indeed, in his review, Knight worries about the pernicious effect Hutchison's book may have on the young (1940, pp. 151, 152). Positivistic recastings of economic theory, such as Samuelson's (1947) "operationalism" and particularly his revealed preference theory, which appeared to provide a behaviorist reduction of talk about preference and utility to observable claims about actions, were beginning to appear. Were they the way of the future? Did logical positivism make traditional neoclassical theory untenable?

Indeed, similar challenges to contemporary economic practice continue in works such as Mark Blaug's *The Methodology of Economics* (1980), which argue that neoclassical economics does not meet Popperian or positivist standards for science. Could the profession's high regard for microeconomic theory be squared with the demand that good science be well- confirmed by empirical data?[2]

After World War II, qualms about the empirical standing of microeconomic theory grew, when economists such as Richard Lester attempted to test fundamental propositions of the neoclassical theory of the firm (1946, 1947). Lester's tests, which consisted of surveys sent to various businesses, were not well-designed. But they attracted attention and provoked fierce responses (especially Machlup, 1946, 1947; Stigler, 1947), partly because everybody knew that Lester was right about one thing: Firms do not behave precisely as marginal productivity theory maintains they do. Indeed one of Lester's sharpest critics, Fritz Machlup, conceded (1956, p. 488), "But we would certainly not find that all of the businessmen do so [maximize profits] all of the time. Hence, the assumption of consistently profit-maximizing conduct is contrary to fact." But does it not follow immediately that neoclassical theory makes false statements and is thus on positivist and Popperian standards inadequate?

Although some, such as Knight and the Austrians, were prepared to deny that the standards of the natural sciences apply to economics, most tried to show that economics satisfies all reasonable demands that one may make of a science. Fritz Machlup's essays (1955, 1960) give some idea of such attempts. Machlup argues that microeconomic theory is compatible with later and more sophisticated logical positivist (or "logical empiricist") accounts of the nature of science, which considerably loosen the connection that is required between theory and observation. Machlup argues that both instrumentalists and defenders of "partial interpretation" views recognize that one need not be concerned about the truth of a theoretical claim such as profit maximization. But the philosophers who defended instrumentalism and "partial interpretation" views were concerned to show how theories that make claims about unobservable entities and properties and thus cannot be directly empirically tested might nevertheless be meaningful and indirectly testable. They never suggested that one should ignore the falsity of a claim – such as "all firms attempt to maximize profits" – on the grounds that such a claim is "theoretical."

3. Predictionism

The most influential way of reconciling economics and up-to-date philosophy of science was, however, not Machlup's, but Milton Friedman's. In his famous essay, "The Methodology of Positive Economics" (1953), Friedman offered the apparent way out of the empirical difficulties raised by Lester and others that has proven most popular with economists. It is that apparent way out, not the possible intricacies of Friedman's views, with which I shall be concerned. Although Friedman does not refer to contemporary philosophy of science, he too attempts to show that economics satisfies sophisticated positivist standards.

After distinguishing between positive and normative economics, Friedman begins by asserting that the goals of a positive science are predictive, not at all explanatory (1953, p. 7). Economists seek significant and usable predictions, not understanding or explanation. The view that science, or at least economic science, aims only at prediction is a contentious one, and one for which Friedman offers no argument. It might reasonably be challenged. But in holding this instrumentalist view of the goals of science, Friedman is in good philosophical company and not obviously mistaken (see Morgenbesser, 1969). Since Friedman's methodological views are untenable even if one grants his claim that the goals of economics are exclusively predictive, let us not contest it here.

In Friedman's usage, any implication of a theory whose truth is not yet known counts as a prediction of a theory, even if it is not concerned with the future. Since the goals of science are exclusively predictive, a theory which enables one to make reliable predictions is a good theory. In case of a tie on the criterion of predictive success, simpler theories or theories of wider scope (that apply to a wider range of phenomena) are to be preferred (p. 10).

Friedman stresses that there is no other test of a theory in terms of whether its "assumptions" are "unrealistic" (p. 14). When Friedman speaks of the "assumptions" of a theory, he includes both fundamental assertions (such as the claim that consumers are utility maximizers) and additional premises needed in particular applications (for example, the claim that different brands of cigarettes are perfect substitutes for one another). Although Friedman equivocates with the term "unrealistic," usually he means (as he must if he is to respond to Lester's challenge) that an assumption is unrealistic if it is not true, perhaps not even approximately true, of the phenomena to which the theory is applied.

Friedman can then argue that researchers such as Lester mistakenly attempt to assess the "assumptions" of neoclassical theory instead of its predictions. In dismissing any assessment of assumptions, Friedman is also responding to a critical tradition which extends back to the German Historical School via American Institutionalists, such as Veblen. This critical tradition questions the worth of abstract theorizing and objects to the purportedly unreasonably unrealistic assumptions of neoclassical theory. Friedman apparently enables one to reject all such criticism as fundamentally confused.

But Lester's case cannot be dismissed so easily, for Lester apparently showed that neoclassical theory makes false predictions concerning, for instance, the results of his surveys. The distinction between assumptions and implications is, indeed, a shallow one that rests on nothing but the particular formulation of a theory. Assumptions trivially imply themselves, and theories can be reformulated with different sets of assumptions that have the same implications. Unrealistic assumptions (in the sense of false assumptions) will always result in false predictions, except, perhaps, in the case of assumptions concerning unobservables.

Friedman notices the problem (pp. 26–7) and responds to it by insisting that all that matters is how well a theory predicts the phenomena in which economists are (at least on the particular occasion) interested (pp. 20, 27–8). This odd instrumentalism suggests that falsity of assumptions or of predictions is unimportant unless it detracts from a theory's performance in predicting the phenomena in which one is interested. A theory of the distribution of leaves on trees that states that it is as if leaves had the ability to move instantaneously from branch to branch is thus regarded by Friedman as perfectly "plausible" (p. 20), although of narrower scope than accepted theory. If a theory predicts accurately what one wants to know, it is a good theory, otherwise it is not.

When Friedman says that it is as if leaves move or as if expert billiard players solve complicated equations (p. 21), he means that attributing movement to leaves or calculating power to billiard players leads to correct predictions concerning the phenomena in which one is interested. And a theory which accomplishes this is a good theory, for a "theory is to be judged by its predictive power for the class of phenomena which it is intended to explain" (p. 8). Friedman is not just saying that if a theory "works," then one should use it, but that all one wants of science are theories that work for particular purposes. The realism of the assumptions of microeconomics or the truth of its uninteresting or irrelevant implications is unimportant, except insofar as either restricts the theory's scope. Since economists are not interested in what business people say, but in the consequences of what they do, Lester's surveys are irrelevant.

Yet even if one fully grants Friedman's view of the goals of science, one should still be concerned about the realism of assumptions. For there is no good way to know what to try when a prediction fails or whether to employ a theory in a new application without judging one's assumptions. Without assessments of realism (approximate truth) of assumptions, the process of theory modification would be hopelessly inefficient and the application of theories to new circumstances nothing but arbitrary guesswork. The point is simple: if one wants to use a machine in a new application or to build a new machine out of its components or to diagnose a malfunction, it helps to know something about the reliability of the components of which it is made. Even if all one wants of theories are valid predictions concerning particular phenomena, one needs to judge whether the needed assumptions are reasonable approximations, and one thus needs to be concerned about incorrect predictions, no matter how irrelevant.

I have dwelled on Friedman's views because of their influence and because they illustrate a paradox. Friedman's confidence in "the maximization-of-returns hypothesis" and in neoclassical theory in general purportedly rests entirely on "the repeated failure of its implications to be contradicted" (p. 22; but see pp. 26–30 on indirect testing). On this, Friedman is at one with Popperian methodologists such as Blaug. But the implications of neoclassical theory have certainly been contradicted on many occasions. This would be so even if the theory lived up to its highest praises. All it takes is some disturbance, such as a change in tastes, a new invention or a real or imagined invasion from Mars.[3] Does any economist really accept neoclassical theory on the basis of "the repeated failure of its implications to be contradicted"? Is this not rather a doctrine piously enunciated in the presence of philosophers or of their economist fellow travellers and conveniently forgotten when there is serious work to do?

Those who have noticed that economists do not practice what they preach have most often attacked the practice. Instead of attempting to discover what methodology neoclassical economists actually practice and to think seriously about how that methodology might be justified, these critics (with some notable exceptions, such as Simon, 1976) have usually relied on indefensible philosophical theories of science to support broad condemnations (for example, Blaug, 1980). There is, of course, nothing mistaken about judging the work of economists – normative concerns are central to economic methodology. But most of these judgments have relied on unreasonable standards that were supposedly vindicated by up-to-date philosophical insight. Philosophers have, however, little to offer by way of informative well-supported systematic theories of the scientific enterprise and that little does not lend itself to mechanical application.

4. Eclecticism

Many have by now recognized that there are few good philosophical authorities on matters of theory assessment. Although there is still a great deal to be learned from the judicious study of contemporary philosophy of science, those interested in economic methodology must use their own judgment and their knowledge of the practice of economists to formulate and to defend rational standards for the practice of economics. The situation of a methodologist concerned about understanding and improving economic practice is similar to that of an economist concerned with understanding and improving business practice. Although both may find some of the practices they study mistaken or irrational, both had better show some sense and caution in applying general theories and had better understand thoroughly the actual problems and procedures of the object they study.

Attempts to carry out such a delicate task have varied. Alexander Rosenberg's *Microeconomic Laws: A Philosophical Analysis* (1976) is something of a watershed. In the decade since publishing this book Rosenberg's own views have shifted drastically; he denied at one point (1983) that economics is an empirical science at all. But in publishing his first book, and especially in his discussion there of particular aspects of economics, such as the relations between micro-and macroeconomics or the sense in which explanations in economics involve both reasons and causes (chapter 5), Rosenberg is responsible for a growing literature on economic methodology by philosophers of science. This literature is distinctive in its attention to the details of methodological practice and in its cautious use of philosophical models of science.

Among economists the best-known authors in this more eclectic and empirical vein are probably Bruce Caldwell (1982) with his "methodological pluralism" and Donald McCloskey (1985) with his "rhetoric of economics." I do not yet find Caldwell's methodological pluralism to be a clear philosophical position. Sometimes it seems to be intended as the thesis that different economic methodologies must be assessed entirely in their own terms and that no more than internal coherence is to be demanded. But I think that Caldwell should be interpreted more charitably, not as abandoning the normative tasks of economic methodology, but as recognizing that they cannot come first. Since philosophers of science have no gospel for scientific practice, economic methodologists have no prepared sermons. Cast among the heathen, bereft of revealed truth, methodologists must face the bewildering task of attempting to understand and to assess the practices and products of economists. Before judging competing methodological views, one must make a serious attempt to understand and to appreciate them.

Donald McCloskey with his "rhetoric of economics" (1985) also points out that systematic philosophy provides no well-justified code of scientific practice. He proposes that the tools of classical rhetoric and literary criticism are better suited to understanding what economists do. Thus, for example, in discussing a couple of pages from Samuelson's *Foundations of Economic Analysis*, McCloskey (1985, pp. 70–2) finds that Samuelson uses a variety of "rhetorical devices:" analogy, appeals to authority, relaxation of assumptions, and hypothetical "toy" economies. Whether any of these may also be construed as good arguments that ought rationally to persuade the reader to accept Samuelson's conclusions is not McCloskey's concern, because he is skeptical about whether there are any detailed standards for what counts as a good argument in economics apart from whatever in fact persuades economists. Like Rosenberg and others, McCloskey encourages careful study of economic argumentation, and in his striking discussions of works by John Muth (Ch. 6) and Robert Fogel (Ch. 7) he provides memorable models of such study.

But McCloskey offers little solid argument for employing his favored literary tools, and he has a hard time explaining how his proposed successor to economic methodology is supposed to retain any normative role. And the normative role of methodology is unavoidable; whether methodological rules are garnered from imitation, methodological asides, or systematic methodological treatises, there is no doing economics without some standards or norms. Furthermore, if economics is to make any rational claim to guide policy, these standards or norms cannot be arbitrary.

The current literature on theory appraisal in economics and on economic methodology in general is quite eclectic, and I find this development healthy. One finds work as diverse as Neil deMarchi's and Abraham Hirsch's (1986) analysis of how Friedman employs monetary history to argue for his monetary theory, Cristina Bicchieri's (1987) treatment of the epistemological complications of the rational expectations hypothesis, Philip Mirowski's (1989) detailed account of the analogy between classical physics and neoclassical economic theory, or Alan Nelson's (1986) argument that microeconomics is a theory of individual choice. One moral of the past decade of philosophy of science is that the most interesting and substantive methodological work will usually turn on the details of the particular discipline discussed. A dispassionate look at recent methodological studies of economics strongly supports this view.

5. Conclusions

Methodological writing is pouring out at an increasing rate. Over the past decade there have been scores of books, hundreds of articles, and even a new journal, *Economics and Philosophy*. This literature is still preoccupied with problems of theory appraisal, although other questions are attracting growing attention. All of the main streams discussed above are represented.

So, first, one still finds positivist or Popperian complaints that neoclassical economists refuse to put microeconomic theory to the test or to heed its disconfirmation. Many of these are from an institutionalist perspective (Eichner, 1983; Samuels, 1980). Since the models of science upon which these criticisms are based are unacceptable, I am skeptical about the value of these criticisms.

Second, one finds more refutations or rehabilitations of Milton Friedman. It will be a step forward when economists come to regard Friedman's essay only as an historically interesting document.

Third, one finds applications of current trends in philosophy of science – especially work by Thomas Kuhn (1970), Imre Lakatos (1970), and Paul Feyerabend (1975). This literature is almost as disappointing as is positivist or Popperian grumbling or rehashing Friedman. Apart from philosophical difficulties with their views, Kuhn, Lakatos, and Feyerabend have been hard to apply, for they are evasive on questions of theory appraisal, which still interest most of those writing on economic methodology. The most valuable work here (such as E. Roy Weintraub's 1985 Lakatosian account of the structure and history of general equilibrium theorizing) has little to say about issues of appraisal (see also Latsis, 1976). There is also a separate technical literature on econometric methods that overlaps too infrequently with the methodological mainstream.[4]

Not surprisingly, I think that the best way forward concerning both theory appraisal and economic methodology more generally is the fourth (eclectic) way, the path I have taken: to focus on the methodology economists practice, making use of whatever tools philosophers of science have had to offer that appear to be well-made and apt for the job (Hausman, 1981a, ch. 12). Although methodologists may find much to criticize, they had better begin by understanding as thoroughly as they can how economists go about their business and why they do what they do. The Popperian/positivist and predictionist interludes in economic methodology have been largely unenlightening. With some restatement and toning down of the overly optimistic conviction that economics starts with the central truths concerning its domain, I think that Mill's views still stand.

The most promising and interesting methodological issues to tackle now are not directly concerned with theory appraisal. The role and significance of general equilibrium theory are still not entirely clear. The implications of rational expectations for the objectivity and logic of economics remain to be explored. The notion of rationality in strategic and uncertain circumstances presents difficult open questions. In tackling problems such as these, I look forward to profitable collaboration between economists and philosophers.

Notes

1 I owe this example to Sidney Morgenbesser. Although rough generalizations have statistical implications, they are also not well constructed as statistical laws.

2 Given positivist or Popperian standards, the answer is "no." But no science meets these unreasonable standards. In contrast to Samuelson (1963), the early positivists, and (to a lesser extent) Popper, neither the truth nor falsity of theoretical claims can be inferred directly from observation reports. Contrary to Popper's views, intelligent testing requires (inductive) knowledge of how well supported statements are by evidence. Given how poorly supported are the various auxiliary statements needed to derive predictions from economic theories, it is usually not sensible or responsible to follow Blaug's Popperian advice and to regard predictive failures as falsifying economic theories. For a more comprehensive and accurate critique of Popperian economic methodology than is possible here see my 1988(a).

3   Objections that readers have voiced to these examples instructively support my point. One
    objected that neoclassical theory obviously allows for "shocks." But, unless it does so by
    means of a not-fully-specified *ceteris paribus* clause, there will still be refutations of the kind
    cited. And if not-fully-specified *ceteris paribus* clauses are permitted, the "repeated failure of its
    implications to be contradicted" is a cheap triumph. Another reader objected that better
    examples are those in which the assumptions involved in the particular application of the theory
    are satisfied. I agree, but this is certainly not a line that Friedman or others who rest everything
    on the success of predictions can follow. For we are not supposed to pay any attention to whether
    the assumptions are satisfied – that is, to whether the assumptions are "realistic" for the situation
    at hand. There are examples in which predictive failures are more puzzling and disturbing than
    in the cases cited in the text. Consider the fact that even in inflationary circumstances many
    firms evaluate their inventories on a first in, first out basis or the fact that shares in closed-end
    mutual funds sometimes sell for less than the value of the assets of the funds (Stiglitz, 1982).
4   Although less familiar, there have also been a number of attempted applications of the views of
    Joseph Sneed (1971) and Wolfgang Stegmueller (1979). Many of these are to be found in Steg-
    mueller, Balzer and Spohn (1982). For further references and well-taken criticism, see Hands
    (1985). There is also a good deal of methodological discussion written from a specifically "Aus-
    trian" perspective. Much of this is concerned with the interpretation of the views of major Austrian
    figures such as Mises and Hayek and with the defense of views of theory appraisal in economics
    similar to those of Mill and of Robbins. Caldwell (1982) provides a good discussion of the
    methodological views of the Austrians. For a fairly recent collection of essays, see Dolan (1976).

References and Further Reading

Bicchieri, C. (1987): "Rationality and Predictability in Economics," *British Journal for the Philosophy
    of Science*, 38 (4), 501–13.
Blaug, M. (1980): *The Methodology of Economics: Or How Economists Explain*. Cambridge: Cam-
    bridge University Press.
Cairnes, J. (1888): *The Character and Logical Method of Political Economy*, 2nd edn, reprinted 1965.
    New York: A. M. Kelley.
Caldwell, B. (1982): *Beyond Positivism: Economic Methodology in the Twentieth Century*. New York:
    Allen and Unwin.
Caldwell, B. (ed.), (1984): *Appraisal and Criticism in Economics*. London: Allen and Unwin.
De Marchi, N. (1970): "The Empirical Content and Longevity of Ricardian Economics," *Economica*,
    37, August, 257–76.
De Marchi, N. and Hirsch, A. (1986): "Making a Case When Theory is Unfalsifiable: Friedman's
    Monetary History," *Economics and Philosophy*, 2, April, 1–22.
Dolan, E. (ed.) (1976): *The Foundations of Modern Austrian Economics*, Kansas City: Sheed and Ward.
Eichner, A. (1983): "Why Economics is not yet a Science," in Eichner, A. (ed.), *Why Economics is
    Not Yet a Science*. Armonk, N.Y.: M. E. Sharpe, 205–41.
Feyerabend, P. (1975): *Against Method: Outline of an Anarchistic Theory of Knowledge*. London:
    Verso Books.
Friedman, M. (1953): "The Methodology of Positive Economics," in *The Methodology of Positive
    Economics*, Chicago: University of Chicago Press 3–43.
Hands, D. W. (1985): "The Structuralist View of Economic Theories: The Case of General
    Equilibrium in Particular," *Economics and Philosophy*, 1, October, 303–36.
Hausman, D. (1981a): *Capital, Profits and Prices: An Essay in the Philosophy of Economics*. New York:
    Columbia University Press.
Hausman, D. (1981b): "John Stuart Mill's Philosophy of Economics," *Philosophy of Science*, 48,
    September, 363–85.

Hausman, D. (ed.) (1984): *The Philosophy of Economics: An Anthology*. Cambridge: Cambridge University Press.

Hausman, D. (1986): "Philosophy and Economic Methodology," in P. Asquith and P. Kitcher (eds), *PSA 1984*, Vol. 2, East Lansing: Philosophy of Science Association, 231–49.

Hausman, D. (1988a): "An Appraisal of Popperian Economic Methodology," in N. de Marchi (eds.) *The Popperian Legacy in Economics*, Cambridge: Cambridge University Press, 65–84.

Hausman, D. (1988b): "Philosophy of Science and Economic Methodology," in R. Teichgraeber and G. Winston (eds), *The Boundaries of Economics*, Cambridge: Cambridge University Press, 88–116.

Hutchison, T. (1938): *The Significance and Basic Postulates of Economic Theory*. Reprinted 1960. New York: A. M. Kelley.

Keynes, J. N. (1890): *Scope and Method of Political Economy*, 4th edn. reprinted 1955. New York: Kelley and Millman, Inc.

Knight, F. (1935): *The Ethics of Competition and Other Essays*. New York and London: Harper and Brothers.

Knight, F. (1940): "What is 'Truth' in Economics?" *Journal of Political Economy*, 48, February, 1–32. Reprinted 1956 in F. H. Knight (ed.), *On the History and Method of Economics*, Chicago: University of Chicago Press. 151–78.

Kuhn, T. (1970): *The Structure of Scientific Revolutions*, 2nd edn. Chicago: University of Chicago Press.

Lakatos, I. (1970): "Falsification and the Methodology of Scientific Research Programmes," in I. Lakatos and A. Musgrave (eds), *Criticism and the Growth of Knowledge*, Cambridge: Cambridge University Press 91–196.

Latsis, S. (ed.) (1976): *Method and Appraisal in Economics*, Cambridge: Cambridge University Press.

Lester, R. (1946): "Shortcomings of Marginal Analysis for Wage-Employment Problems." *American Economic Review*, 36, March, 62–82.

Lester, R. (1947): "Marginalism, Minimum Wages, and Labor Markets," *American Economic Review*, 37, March, 135–48.

Machlup, F. (1946): "Marginal Analysis and Empirical Research," *American Economic Review*, 36, September, 519–54.

Machlup, F. (1947): "Rejoinder to an Antimarginalist," *American Economic Review*, 37, March, 148–54.

Machlup, F. (1955): "The Problem of Verification in Economics," *Southern Economic Journal*, 22, July, 1–21.

Machlup, F. (1956): "Rejoinder to a Reluctant Ultra-Empiricist," *Southern Economic Journal*, 22, April, 483–93.

Machlup, F. (1960): "Operational Concepts and Mental Constructs in Model and Theory Formation," *Giornale Degli Economisti*, 19, September–October, 553–82.

McCloskey, D. (1985): *The Rhetoric of Economics*. Madison: University of Wisconsin Press.

Mill, J. S. (1836): "On the Definition of Political Economy and the Method of Investigation Proper to It," in (1967) *Collected Works of John Stuart Mill*, vol. 4, Toronto: University of Toronto Press.

Mill, J. S. (1843): *A System of Logic* Reprinted 1949. London: Longmans Green.

Mirowski, P. (1989): *More Heat Than Light*. Cambridge: Cambridge University Press.

Morgenbesser, S. (1969): "The Realist-Instrumentalist Controversy," in S. Morgenbesser, P. Suppes and M. White (eds), *Philosophy, Science and Method*, New York: Harcourt, Brace & World, 200–18.

Nelson, A. (1986): "New Individualistic Foundations for Economics," *Nous*, 20, December, 469–90.

Popper, Sir K. (1959): *The Logic of Scientific Discovery*. London: Hutchinson.

Robbins, L. (1935): *An Essay on the Nature and Significance of Economic Science*, 2nd edn. London: Macmillan.

Rosenberg, A. (1976): *Microeconomic Laws: A Philosophical Analysis*. Pittsburgh: University of Pittsburgh Press.

Rosenberg, A. (1983): "If Economics Isn't Science, What Is It?" *The Philosophical Form*, 14, Spring-Summer, 296–314.

Samuels, W. (ed.) (1980): *The Methodology of Economic Thought: Critical Papers from the Journal of Economic Thought* [*Issues*]. New Brunswick: Transaction Books.

Samuelson, P. (1947): *Foundations of Economic Analysis*. Cambridge, Mass: Harvard University Press.

Samuelson, P. (1963): "Problems of Methodology – Discussion," *American Economic Review*, 54, May, 232–6.

Simon, H. (1976): "From Substantive to Procedural Rationality," in S. Latsis (ed.), *Method and Appraisal in Economics*, Cambridge: Cambridge University Press, 129–48.

Sneed, J. (1971): *The Logical Structure of Mathematical Physics*. Dordrecht: Reidel.

Stegmueller, W. (1979): *The Structuralist View of Theories*. New York: Springer-Verlag.

Stegmueller, W., Balzer, W. and Spohn, W. (eds) (1982): *Philosophy of Economics: Proceedings, Munich, July 1981*. New York: Springer-Verlag.

Stewart, I. (1979): *Reasoning and Method in Economics: An Introduction to Economic Methodology*. London: McGraw-Hill.

Stigler, G. (1947): "Professor Lester and the Marginalists," *American Economic Review*, 37, March, 154–7.

Stiglitz, J. (1982): "Ownership, Control, and Efficient Markets: Some Paradoxes in the Theory of Capital Markets," in K. D. Boyer and W. G. Shepherd (eds), *Economic Regulation: Essays in Honor of James R. Nelson*. Ann Arbor: University of Michigan Press, 311–40.

von Mises, L. (1981): *Epistemological Problems of Economics*. Trans. G. Reisman. New York: New York University Press.

Weintraub, E. R. (1985): *General Equilibrium Analysis: Studies in Appraisal*, Cambridge: Cambridge University Press.

PART II

Consumer Behavior

Introduction

Instead of the usual treatment of nonwork time as "leisure," Professor Becker in chapter 4 introduces time as a coordinate input into the consumer's production of utility via consumption of products and services. The effective prices of consumer goods consist of market prices enhanced by the imputed opportunity cost of the time devoted to obtaining and consuming such goods. The relevant values of the goods, therefore, vary with the wage rate that determines the opportunity cost of the time involved in the consumption. Commodities may then be classified as goods-intensive or earnings-intensive, and different consumers confront different total prices for goods with identical market prices.

One interesting application explains the smaller families of large income earners as reflecting the high opportunity cost of the intensive time dedication necessary for child rearing. The source of income, as well as its total value, will impact consumer choice, depending on whether it is work- or nonwork-related. Innovative progress in productivity includes not only the resources necessary in their production, but also a reduction in the time necessary for their consumption. The cost of commuting time is integrated into decisions about consumer residence. These analyses employ interesting extensions of substitution-income effect analysis of price changes in explaining consumer behavior. More broadly in these respects, wealthy nations tend to substitute resources to conserve time. From the examples cited, Becker's insights can be seen to increase the explanatory power of conventional consumer theory in conditions of certainty.

No commodity permits so pure a study of consumer behavior under risk as state lottery tickets. The consumer of these products faces long odds but, typically, commits small amounts of income to their purchase. However, viewed as transfers of an excise tax from consumers to states, the average profit rate of 40 percent implies a 60 percent tax rate. Clotfelter and Cook in chapter 5 pose the question: Why do persons who exhibit risk aversion in other pursuits voluntarily submit to such punishing rates? Postulating that the dominant motivation of the consumer must be the hope of monetary reward, the authors' explanations range from the Friedman–Savage hypothesis of a von Neumann–Morgenstern utility function with a convex segment to misleading advertising and the insights of cognitive psychology. The authors make interesting attempts to derive "prices" of "units" of the various products of the lotteries and to estimate demand elasticities. They conclude by considering the normative aspects of state gambling operations with payoffs so far below other forms of legal wagering.

This paper should be read in conjunction with chapter 17 of part III. It deals generally with choices under risk, and we have placed it somewhat arbitrarily in our treatment of firms' decisions. However, in employing expected utility and discussing the arguments of its critics, and in dealing with choices involving lotteries in a broader sense, it has a direct relevance to consumer behavior in this environment.

II A
Under Conditions of Certainty

CHAPTER FOUR

A Theory of the Allocation of Time

GARY S. BECKER

Source: *Economic Journal*, 75 (1965), pp. 493–517. Reprinted with the permission of the Royal Economic Society. © The Royal Economic Society.

1. Introduction

Throughout history the amount of time spent at work has never consistently been much greater than that spent at other activities. Even a work week of fourteen hours a day for six days still leaves half the total time for sleeping, eating and other activities. Economic development has led to a large secular decline in the work week, so that whatever may have been true of the past, today it is below fifty hours in most countries, less than a third of the total time available. Consequently the allocation and efficiency of non-working time may now be more important to economic welfare than that of working time; yet the attention paid by economists to the latter dwarfs any paid to the former.

Fortunately, there is a movement under way to redress the balance. The time spent at work declined secularly, partly because young persons increasingly delayed entering the labour market by lengthening their period of schooling. In recent years many economists have stressed that the time of students is one of the inputs into the educational process, that this time could be used to participate more fully in the labour market and therefore that one of the costs of education is the forgone earnings of students. Indeed, various estimates clearly indicate that forgone earnings is the dominant private and an important social cost of both high-school and college education in the United States.[1] The increased awareness of the importance of forgone earnings has resulted in several attempts to economise on students' time, as manifested, say, by the spread of the quarterly and trimester systems.[2]

Most economists have now fully grasped the importance of forgone earnings in the educational process and, more generally, in all investments in human capital, and criticise educationalists and others for neglecting them. In the light of this it is perhaps surprising that economists have not been equally sophisticated about other non-working uses of time. For example, the cost of a service like the theatre or a good like meat is generally simply said to equal their market prices, yet everyone would agree that the theatre and even dining take time, just as schooling does, time that often could have been used productively. If so, the full costs of these activities would equal the sum of market prices and the forgone value of the time used up. In other words, indirect costs should be treated on the same footing when discussing all non-work uses of time, as they are now in discussions of schooling.

In the last few years a group of us at Columbia University have been occupied, perhaps initially independently but then increasingly less so, with introducing the cost of time systematically into decisions about non-work activities. J. Mincer has shown with several empirical examples how estimates of the income elasticity of demand for different commodities are biased when the cost of time is ignored;[3] J. Owen (1964) has analysed how the demand for leisure can be affected; E. Dean (1963) has considered the allocation of time between subsistence work and market participation in some African economies; while, as already mentioned, I have been concerned with the use of time in education, training and other kinds of human capital. Here I attempt to develop a general treatment of the allocation of time in all other non-work activities. Although under my name alone, much of any credit it merits belongs to the stimulus received from Mincer, Owen, Dean and other past and present participants in the Labor Workshop at Columbia.[4]

The plan of the discussion is as follows. The first section sets out a basic theoretical analysis of choice that includes the cost of time on the same footing as the cost of market goods, while the remaining sections treat various empirical implications of the theory. These include a new approach to changes in hours of work and "leisure," the full integration of so-called "productive" consumption into economic analysis, a new analysis of the effect of income on the quantity and "quality" of commodities consumed, some suggestions on the measurement of productivity, an economic analysis of queues and a few others as well. Although I refer to relevant empirical work that has come to my attention, little systematic testing of the theory has been attempted.

2. A Revised Theory of Choice

According to traditional theory, households maximise utility functions of the form

$$U = U(y_1, y_2, \ldots, y_n) \tag{1}$$

subject to the resource constraint

$$\sum p'_i y_i = I = W + V \tag{2}$$

where y_i are goods purchased on the market, p'_i are their prices, I is money income, W is earnings and V is other income. As the introduction suggests, the point of departure here is the systematic incorporation of non-working time. Households will be assumed to combine time and market goods to produce more basic commodities that directly enter their utility functions. One such commodity is the seeing of a play, which depends on the input of actors, script, theatre and the playgoer's time; another is sleeping, which depends on the input of a bed, house (pills?) and time. These commodities will be called Z_i and written as

$$Z_i = f_i(x_i, T_i) \tag{3}$$

where x_i is a vector of market goods and T_i a vector of time inputs used in producing the ith commodity.[5] Note that, when capital goods such as refrigerators or automobiles are used, x refers to the services yielded by the goods. Also note that T_i is a vector because, e.g., the hours used during the day or on weekdays may be distinguished from those used at night or on week-ends. Each dimension of T_i refers to a different aspect of time. Generally, the partial derivatives of Z_i with respect to both x_i and T_i are non-negative.[6]

In this formulation households are both producing units and utility maximisers. They combine time and market goods via the "production functions" f_i to produce the basic commodities Z_i, and they choose the best combination of these commodities in the conventional way by maximising a utility function

$$U = U(Z_i, \ldots, Z_m) \equiv U(f_1, \ldots, f_m) \equiv U(x_1, \ldots, x_m; T_1, \ldots, T_m) \tag{4}$$

subject to a budget constraint

$$g(Z_i, \ldots, Z_m) = Z \tag{5}$$

where g is an expenditure function of Z_i and Z is the bound on resources. The integration of production and consumption is at odds with the tendency for economists to separate them sharply, production occurring in firms and consumption in households. It should be pointed out, however, that in recent years economists increasingly recognise that a household is truly a "small factory" see, for example, (Cairncross, 1958): it combines capital goods, raw materials and labour to clean, feed, procreate and otherwise produce useful commodities. Undoubtedly the fundamental reason for the traditional separation is that firms are usually given control over working time in exchange for market goods, while "discretionary" control over market goods and consumption time is retained by households as they create their own utility. If (presumably different) firms were also given control over market goods and consumption time in exchange for providing utility the separation would quickly fade away in analysis as well as in fact.

The basic goal of the analysis is to find measures of g and Z which facilitate the development of empirical implications. The most direct approach is to assume that the utility function in equation (4) is maximised subject to separate constraints on the expenditure of market goods and time, and to the production functions in equation (3). The goods constraint can be written as

$$\sum_{1}^{m} p_i x_i = I = V + T_w \bar{w} \tag{6}$$

where p_i is a vector giving the unit prices of x_i, T_w is a vector giving the hours spent at work and $\bar{w}$ is a vector giving the earnings per unit of T_w. The time constraints can be written as

$$\sum_{1}^{m} T_i = T_c = T - T_w \tag{7}$$

where T_c is a vector giving the total time spent at consumption and T is a vector giving the total time available. The production functions (3) can be written in the equivalent form

$$T_i \equiv t_i Z_i$$
$$x_i \equiv b_i Z_i \tag{8}$$

where t_i is a vector giving the input of time per unit of Z_i and b_i is a similar vector for market goods.

The problem would appear to be to maximise the utility function (4) subject to the multiple constraints (6) and (7) and to the production relations (8). There is, however, really only one basic constraint: (6) is not independent of (7) because time can be converted into goods by using less time at consumption and more at work. Thus, substituting for T_w in (6) its equivalent in (7) gives the single constraint.[7]

$$\sum p_i x_i + \sum T_i \bar{w} = V + T\bar{w} \tag{9}$$

By using (8), (9) can be written as

$$\sum (p_i b_i + t_i \bar{w}) Z_i = V + T\bar{w} \tag{10}$$

with

$$\pi_i \equiv p_i b_i + t_i \bar{w}$$
$$S' \equiv V + T\bar{w} \tag{11}$$

The full price of a unit of $Z_i(\pi_i)$ is the sum of the prices of the goods and of the time used per unit of Z_i. That is, the full price of consumption is the sum of direct and indirect prices in the same way that the full cost of investing in human capital is the sum of direct and indirect costs (Becker, 1964). These direct and indirect prices are symmetrical determinants of total price, and there is no analytical reason to stress one rather than the other.

The resource constraint on the right side of equation (10), S', is easy to interpret if $\bar{w}$ were a constant, independent of the Z_i. For then S' gives the money income achieved if all the time available were devoted to work. This achievable income is "spent" on the commodities Z_i either directly through expenditures on goods, $\sum p_i b_i Z_i$, or indirectly through the forgoing of income, $\sum t_i \bar{w} Z_i$, i.e., by using time at consumption rather than at work. As long as $\bar{w}$ were constant, and if there were constant returns in producing Z_i so that b_i and t_i were fixed for given p_i and $\bar{w}$ the equilibrium condition resulting from maximising (4) subject to (10) takes a very simple form:

$$U_i = \frac{\partial U}{\partial Z_i} = \lambda \pi_i \qquad i = 1, \ldots, m \tag{12}$$

where λ is the marginal utility of money income. If $\bar{w}$ were not constant the resource constraint in equation (10) would not have any particularly useful interpretation: $S' = V + T\bar{w}$ would overstate the money income achievable as long as marginal wage-rates were below average ones. Moreover, the equilibrium conditions would become more complicated than (12) because marginal would have to replace average prices.

The total resource constraint could be given the sensible interpretation of the maximum money income achievable only in the special and unlikely case when average earnings were constant. This suggests dropping the approach based on explicitly considering separate goods and time constraints and substituting one in which the total resource constraint necessarily equalled the maximum money income achievable, which will be simply called "full income."[8] This income could in general be obtained by devoting all the time and other resources of a household to earning income, with no regard for consumption. Of course, all the time would not usually be spent "at" a job: sleep, food, even leisure are required for efficiency, and some time (and other resources) would have to be spent on these activities in order to maximise money income. The amount spent would, however, be determined solely by the effect on income and not by any effect on utility. Slaves, for example, might be permitted time "off" from work only in so far as that maximised their output, or free persons in poor environments might have to maximise money income simply to survive.[9]

Households in richer countries do, however, forfeit money income in order to obtain additional utility, i.e., they exchange money income for a greater amount of psychic income. For example, they might increase their leisure time, take a pleasant job in preference to a better-paying unpleasant one, employ unproductive nephews or eat more than is warranted by considerations of productivity. In these and other situations the amount of money income forfeited measures the cost of obtaining additional utility.

Thus the full income approach provides a meaningful resource constraint and one firmly based on the fact that goods and time can be combined into a single overall constraint because time can be converted into goods through money income. It also incorporates a unified treatment of all substitutions of non-pecuniary for pecuniary income, regardless of their nature or whether they occur on the job or in the household. The advantages of this will become clear as the analysis proceeds.

If full income is denoted by S, and if the total earnings forgone or "lost" by the interest in utility is denoted by L, the identity relating L to S and I is simply

$$L(Z_1, \ldots, Z_m) \equiv S - I(Z_1, \ldots, Z_m) \tag{13}$$

I and L are functions of the Z_i because how much is earned or forgone depends on the consumption set chosen; for example, up to a point, the less leisure chosen the larger the money income and the smaller the amount forgone.[10] Using equations (6) and (8), equation (13) can be written as

$$\sum p_i b_i Z_i + L(Z_1, \ldots, Z_m) \equiv S \tag{14}$$

This basic resource constraint states that full income is spent either directly on market goods or indirectly through the forgoing of money income. Unfortunately, there is no simple expression for the average price of Z_i as there is in equation (10). However, marginal, not average, prices are relevant for behaviour, and these would be identical for the constraint in (10) only when average earnings, $\bar{w}$, was constant. But, if so, the expression for the loss function simplifies to

$$L = \bar{w}T_c = \bar{w}\sum t_i Z_i \qquad (15)$$

and (14) reduces to (10). Moreover, even in the general case the total marginal prices resulting from (14) can always be divided into direct and indirect components: the equilibrium conditions resulting from maximising the utility function subject to (14)[11] are

$$U_i = T(p_i b_i + L_i) \qquad i = 1,\ldots,m \qquad (16)$$

where $p_i b_i$ is the direct and L_i the indirect component of the total marginal price $p_i b_i + L_i$.[12]

Behind the division into direct and indirect costs is the allocation of time and goods between work-orientated and consumption-orientated activities. This suggests an alternative division of costs; namely, into those resulting from the allocation of goods and those resulting from the allocation of time. Write $L_i = \partial L/\partial Z_i$ as

$$L_i = \frac{\partial L}{\partial T_i}\frac{\partial T_i}{\partial Z_i} + \frac{\partial L}{\partial x_i}\frac{\partial x_i}{\partial Z_i} \qquad (17)$$

$$= l_i t_i + c_i b_i \qquad (18)$$

where $l_i = \partial L/\partial T_i$ and $c_i = \partial L/\partial x_i$ are the marginal forgone earnings of using more, time and goods respectively on Z_i. Equation (16) can then be written as

$$U_i = T[b_i(p_i + c_i) + t_i l_i] \qquad (19)$$

The total marginal cost of Z_i is the sum of $b_i(p_i + c_i)$, the marginal cost of using goods in producing Z_i, and $t_i l_i$, the marginal cost of using time. This division would be equivalent to that between direct and indirect costs only if $c_i = 0$ or if there were no indirect costs of using goods.

Figure 1 shows the equilibrium given by equation (16) for a two-commodity world. In equilibrium the slope of the full income opportunity curve, which equals the ratio of marginal prices, would equal the slope of an indifference curve, which equals the ratio of marginal utilities. Equilibrium occurs at p and p' for the opportunity curves S and S' respectively.

The rest of the paper is concerned with developing numerous empirical implications of this theory, starting with determinants of hours worked and concluding with an economic interpretation of various queueing systems. To simplify the presentation, it is assumed that the distinction between direct and indirect costs is equivalent to that between goods and time costs; in other words, the marginal forgone cost of the use of goods, c_i, is set equal to zero. The discussion would not be much changed, but would be

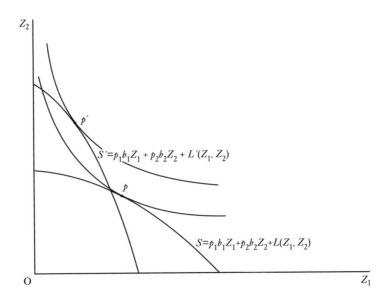

Figure 1

more cumbersome were this not assumed.[13] Finally, until section 4 goods and time are assumed to be used in fixed proportions in producing commodities; that is, the coefficients b_i and t_i in equation (8) are treated as constants.

3. Applications

3.1. Hours of work

If the effects of various changes on the time used on consumption, T_c, could be determined their effects on hours worked, T_w, could be found residually from equation (7). This section considers, among other things, the effects of changes in income, earnings and market prices on T_c, and thus on T_w, using as the major tool of analysis differences among commodities in the importance of forgone earnings.

The relative marginal importance of forgone earnings is defined as

$$\alpha_i = \frac{l_i t_i}{p_i b_i + l_i t_i} \tag{20}$$

The importance of forgone earnings would be greater the larger l_i and t_i, the forgone earnings per hour of time and the number of hours used per unit of Z_i respectively, while it would be smaller the larger p_i and b_i, the market price of goods and the number of goods used per unit of Z_i respectively. Similarly, the relative marginal importance of time is defined as

$$\gamma_i = \frac{t_i}{p_i b_i + l_i t_i} \tag{21}$$

If full income increased solely because of an increase in V (other money income) there would simply be a parallel shift of the opportunity curve to the right with no change in relative commodity prices. The consumption of most commodities would have to increase; if all did, hours worked would decrease, for the total time spent on consumption must increase if the output of all commodities did, and by equation (7) the time spent at work is inversely related to that spent on consumption. Hours worked could increase only if relatively time intensive commodities, those with large γ, were sufficiently inferior.[14]

A uniform percentage increase in earnings for all allocations of time would increase the cost per hour used in consumption by the same percentage for all commodities.[15] The relative prices of different commodities would, however, change as long as forgone earnings were not equally important for all; in particular, the prices of commodities having relatively important forgone earnings would rise more. Now the fundamental theorem of demand theory states that a compensated change in relative prices would induce households to consume less of commodities rising in price. The figure shows the effect of a rise in earnings fully compensated by a decline in other income: the opportunity curve would be rotated clockwise through the initial position p if Z_1 were the more earnings-intensive commodity. In the figure the new equilibrium p' must be to the left and above p, or less Z_1 and more Z_2 would be consumed.

Therefore a compensated uniform rise in earnings would lead to a shift away from earnings-intensive commodities and towards goods-intensive ones. Since earnings and time intensiveness tend to be positively correlated,[16] consumption would be shifted from time-intensive commodities. A shift away from such commodities would, however, result in a reduction in the total time spent in consumption, and thus an increase in the time spent at work.[17]

The effect of an uncompensated increase in earnings on hours worked would depend on the relative strength of the substitution and income effects. The former would increase hours, the latter reduce them; which dominates cannot be determined *a priori*.

The conclusion that a pure rise in earnings increases and a pure rise in income reduces hours of work must sound very familiar, for they are traditional results of the well-known labour–leisure analysis. What, then, is the relation between our analysis, which treats all commodities symmetrically and stresses only their differences in relative time and earning intensities, and the usual analysis, which distinguishes a commodity having special properties called "leisure" from other more commonplace commodities? It is easily shown that the usual labour–leisure analysis can be looked upon as a special case of ours in which the cost of the commodity called leisure consists entirely of forgone earnings and the cost of other commodities entirely of goods.[18]

As a description of reality such an approach, of course, is not tenable, since virtually all activities use both time and goods. Perhaps it would be defended either as an analytically necessary or extremely insightful approximation to reality. Yet the usual substitution and income effects of a change in resources on hours worked have easily been derived from a more general analysis which stresses only that the relative importance of time varies among commodities. The rest of the paper tries to go further and demonstrate that the traditional approach, with its stress on the demand for "leisure," apparently has seriously impeded the development of insights about the economy, since the more direct and general approach presented here naturally leads to a variety of implications never yet obtained.

The two determinants of the importance of forgone earnings are the amount of time used per dollar of goods and the cost per unit of time. Reading a book, taking a haircut or commuting use more time per dollar of goods than eating dinner, frequenting a night-club or sending children to private summer camps. Other things the same, forgone earnings would be more important for the former set of commodities than the latter.

The importance of forgone earnings would be determined solely by time intensity only if the cost of time was the same for all commodities. Presumably, however, it varies considerably among commodities and at different periods. For example, the cost of time is often less on week-ends and in the evenings because many firms are closed then,[19] which explains why a famous liner intentionally includes a week-end in each voyage between the United States and Europe.[20] The cost of time would also tend to be less for commodities that contribute to productive effort, traditionally called "productive consumption." A considerable amount of sleep, food and even "play" fall under this heading. The opportunity cost of the time is less because these commodities indirectly contribute to earnings. Productive consumption has had a long but bandit-like existence in economic thought; our analysis does systematically incorporate it into household decision making.

Although the formal specification of leisure in economic models has ignored expenditures on goods, cannot one argue that a more correct specification would simply associate leisure with relatively important forgone earnings? Most conceptions of leisure do imply that it is time intensive and does not indirectly contribute to earnings,[21] two of the important characteristics of earnings-intensive commodities. On the other hand, not all of what are usually considered leisure activities do have relatively important forgone earnings: night-clubbing is generally considered leisure, and yet, at least in its more expensive forms, has a large expenditure component. Conversely, some activities have relatively large forgone earnings and are not considered leisure: haircuts or child care are examples. Consequently, the distinction between earnings-intensive and other commodities corresponds only partly to the usual distinction between leisure and other commodities. Since it has been shown that the relative importance of forgone earnings rather than any concept of leisure is more relevant for economic analysis, less attention should be paid to the latter. Indeed, although the social philosopher might have to define precisely the concept of leisure,[22] the economist can reach all his traditional results as well as many more without introducing it at all!

Not only is it difficult to distinguish leisure from other non-work[23] but also even work from non-work. Is commuting work, non-work or both? How about a business lunch, a good diet or relaxation? Indeed, the notion of productive consumption was introduced precisely to cover those commodities that contribute to work as well as to consumption. Cannot pure work then be considered simply as a limiting commodity of such joint commodities in which the contribution to consumption was nil? Similarly, pure consumption would be a limiting commodity in the opposite direction in which the contribution to work was nil, and intermediate commodities would contribute to both consumption and work. The more important the contribution to work relative to consumption, the smaller would tend to be the relative importance of forgone earnings. Consequently, the effects of changes in earnings, other income, etc., on hours worked then become assimilated to and essentially a special case of their effects on the consumption of less earnings-intensive commodities. For example, a pure rise in earnings would reduce the relative price, and thus increase the time spent on these commodities, *including the time spent at work*;

similarly, for changes in income and other variables. The generalisation wrought by our approach is even greater than may have appeared at first.

Before concluding this section a few other relevant implications of our theory might be briefly mentioned. Just as a (compensated) rise in earnings would increase the prices of commodities with relatively large forgone earnings, induce a substitution away from them and increase the hours worked, so a (compensated) fall in market prices would also induce a substitution away from them and increase the hours worked: the effects of changes in direct and indirect costs are symmetrical. Indeed, Owen presents some evidence indicating that hours of work in the United States fell somewhat more in the first thirty years of this century than in the second thirty years, not because wages rose more during the first period, but because the market prices of recreation commodities fell more then.[24]

A well-known result of the traditional labour–leisure approach is that a rise in the income tax induces at least a substitution effect away from work and towards "leisure." Our approach reaches the same result only via a substitution towards time-intensive consumption rather than leisure. A simple additional implication of our approach, however, is that if a rise in the income tax were combined with an appropriate excise on the goods used in time-intensive commodities or subsidy to the goods used in other commodities there need be no change in full relative prices, and thus no substitution away from work. The traditional approach has recently reached the same conclusion, although in a much more involved way.[25]

There is no exception in the traditional approach to the rule that a pure rise in earnings would not induce a decrease in hours worked. An exception does occur in ours, for if the time and earnings intensities (i.e., $l_i t_i$ and t_i) were negatively correlated a pure rise in earnings would induce a substitution towards time-intensive commodities, and thus away from work.[26] Although this exception does illustrate the greater power of our approach, there is no reason to believe that it is any more important empirically than the exception to the rule on income effects.

3.2. The productivity of time

Most of the large secular increase in earnings, which stimulated the development of the labour–leisure analysis, resulted from an increase in the productivity of working time due to the growth in human and physical capital, technological progress and other factors. Since a rise in earnings resulting from an increase in productivity has both income and substitution effects, the secular decline in hours worked appeared to be evidence that the income effect was sufficiently strong to swamp the substitution effect.

The secular growth in capital and technology also improved the productivity of consumption time: supermarkets, automobiles, sleeping pills, safety and electric razors, and telephones are a few familiar and important examples of such developments. An improvement in the productivity of consumption time would change relative commodity prices and increase full income, which in turn would produce substitution and income effects. The interesting point is that a very different interpretation of the observed decline in hours of work is suggested because these effects are precisely the opposite of those produced by improvements in the productivity of working time.

Assume a uniform increase only in the productivity of consumption time, which is taken to mean a decline in all t_i, time required to produce a unit of Z_i, by a common percentage. The relative prices of commodities with large forgone earnings would fall, and substitution would be induced towards these and away from other commodities, causing hours of work also to fall. Since the increase in productivity would also produce an income effect,[27] the demand for commodities would increase, which, in turn, would induce an increased demand for goods. But since the productivity of working time is assumed not to change, more goods could be obtained only by an increase in work. That is, the higher real income resulting from an advance in the productivity of consumption time would cause hours of work to *increase*.

Consequently, an emphasis on the secular increase in the productivity of consumption time would lead to a very different interpretation of the secular decline in hours worked. Instead of claiming that a powerful income effect swamped a weaker substitution effect, the claim would have to be that a powerful substitution effect swamped a weaker income effect.

Of course, the productivity of both working and consumption time increased secularly, and the true interpretation is somewhere between these extremes. If both increased at the same rate there would be no change in relative prices, and thus no substitution effect, because the rise in l_i induced by one would exactly offset the decline in t_i induced by the other, marginal forgone earnings $(i_i t_i)$ remaining unchanged. Although the income effects would tend to offset each other too, they would do so completely only if the income elasticity of demand for time-intensive commodities was equal to unity. Hours worked would decline if it was above and increase if it was below unity.[28] Since these commodities have probably on the whole been luxuries, such an increase in income would tend to reduce hours worked.

The productivity of working time has probably advanced more than that of consumption time, if only because of familiar reasons associated with the division of labour and economies of scale.[29] Consequently, there probably has been the traditional substitution effect towards and income effect away from work, as well as an income effect away from work because time-intensive commodities were luxuries. The secular decline in hours worked would only imply therefore that the combined income effects swamped the substitution effect, not that the income effect of an advance in the productivity of working time alone swamped its substitution effect.

Cross-sectionally, the hours worked of males have generally declined less as incomes increased than they have over time. Some of the difference between these relations is explained by the distinction between relevant and reported incomes, or by interdependencies among the hours worked by different employees;[30] some is probably also explained by the distinction between working and consumption productivity. There is a presumption that persons distinguished cross-sectionally by money incomes or earnings differ more in working than consumption productivity because they are essentially distinguished by the former. This argument does not apply to time series because persons are distinguished there by calendar time, which in principle is neutral between these productivities. Consequently, the traditional substitution effect towards work is apt to be greater cross-sectionally, which would help to explain why the relation between the income and hours worked of men is less negatively sloped there, and be additional evidence that the substitution effect for men is not weak.[31]

Productivity in the service sector in the United States appears to have advanced more slowly, at least since 1929, than productivity in the goods sector (Fuchs, 1964). Service industries like retailing, transportation, education and health, use a good deal of the time of households that never enter into input, output and price series, or therefore into measures of productivity. Incorporation of such time into the series and consideration of changes in its productivity would contribute, I believe, to an understanding of the apparent differences in productivity advance between these sectors.

An excellent example can be found in a recent study of productivity trends in the barbering industry in the United States (Wilburn, 1964). Conventional productivity measures show relatively little advance in barbers' shops since 1929, yet a revolution has occurred in the activities performed by these shops. In the 1920s shaves still accounted for an important part of their sales, but declined to a negligible part by the 1950s because of the spread of home safety and electric razors. Instead of travelling to a shop, waiting in line, receiving a shave and continuing to another destination, men now shave themselves at home, saving travelling, waiting and even some shaving time. This considerable advance in the productivity of shaving nowhere enters measures for barbers' shops. If, however, a productivity measure for general barbering activities, including shaving, was constructed, I suspect that it would show an advance since 1929 comparable to most goods.[32]

3.3. Income elasticities

Income elasticities of demand are often estimated cross-sectionally from the behaviour of families or other units with different incomes. When these units buy in the same market-place it is natural to assume that they face the same prices of goods. If, however, incomes differ because earnings do, and cross-sectional income differences are usually dominated by earnings differences, commodities prices would differ systematically. All commodities prices would be higher to higher-income units because their forgone earnings would be higher (which means, incidentally, that differences in real income would be less than those in money income), and the prices of earnings-intensive commodities would be unusually so.

Cross-sectional relations between consumption and income would not therefore measure the effect of income alone, because they would be affected by differences in relative prices as well as in incomes.[33] The effect of income would be underestimated for earnings-intensive and overestimated for other commodities, because the higher relative prices of the former would cause a substitution away from them and towards the latter. Accordingly, the income elasticities of demand for "leisure," unproductive and time-intensive commodities would be under-stated, and for "work," productive and other goods-intensive commodities over-stated by cross-sectional estimates. Low apparent income elasticities of earnings-intensive commodities and high apparent elasticities of other commodities may simply be illusions resulting from substitution effects.[34]

Moreover, according to our theory demand depends also on the importance of earnings as a source of income. For if total income were held constant an increase in earnings would create only substitution effects: away from earnings-intensive and towards goods-intensive commodities. So one unusual implication of the analysis that can and should be tested with available budget data is that the source of income may have a significant effect on consumption patterns. An important special case is found in comparisons of the consumption of employed and unemployed workers. Unemployed workers not only have lower incomes but also lower forgone costs, and thus lower relative prices of time and other earnings-intensive commodities. The propensity of unemployed workers to go fishing, watch television, attend school and so on are simply vivid illustrations of the incentives they have to substitute such commodities for others.

One interesting application of the analysis is to the relation between family size and income.[35] The traditional view, based usually on simple correlations, has been that an increase in income leads to a reduction in the number of children per family. If, however, birth-control knowledge and other variables were held constant economic theory suggests a positive relation between family size and income, and therefore that the traditional negative correlation resulted from positive correlations between income, knowledge and some other variables. The data I put together supported this interpretation, as did those found in several subsequent studies.[36]

Although positive, the elasticity of family size with respect to income is apparently quite low, even when birth-control knowledge is held constant. Some persons have interpreted this (and other evidence) to indicate that family-size formation cannot usefully be fitted into traditional economic analysis.[37] It was pointed out, however, that the small elasticity found for children is not so inconsistent with what is found for goods as soon as quantity and quality income elasticities are distinguished.[38] Increased expenditures on many goods largely take the form of increased quality – expenditure per pound, per car, etc. – and the increase in quantity is modest. Similarly, increased expenditures on children largely take the form of increased expenditures per child, while the increase in number of children is very modest.

Nevertheless, the elasticity of demand for number of children does seem somewhat smaller than the quantity elasticities found for many goods. Perhaps the explanation is simply the shape of indifference curves; one other factor that may be more important, however, is the increase in forgone costs with income.[39] Child care would seem to be a time-intensive activity that is not "productive" (in terms of earnings) and uses many hours that could be used at work. Consequently, it would be an earnings-intensive activity, and our analysis predicts that its relative price would be higher to higher-income families.[40] There is already some evidence suggesting that the positive relation between forgone costs and income explains why the apparent quantity income elasticity of demand for children is relatively small. Mincer (1963) found that cross-sectional differences in the forgone price of children have an important effect on the number of children.[41]

3.4. Transportation

Transportation is one of the few activities where the cost of time has been explicitly incorporated into economic discussions. In most benefit-cost evaluations of new transportation networks the value of the savings in transportation time has tended to overshadow other benefits; see, for example, Mohring (1961). The importance of the value placed on time has encouraged experiment with different methods of determination: from the simple view that the value of an hour equals average hourly earnings to sophisticated considerations of the distinction between standard and overtime hours, the internal and external margins, etc.

The transport field offers considerable opportunity to estimate the marginal productivity or value of time from actual behaviour. One could, for example, relate the ratio of the number of persons travelling by aeroplane to those travelling by slower mediums to the distance travelled (and, of course, also to market prices and incomes). Since relatively more people use faster mediums for longer distances, presumably largely because of the greater importance of the saving in time, one should be able to estimate a marginal value of time from the relation between medium and distance travelled.[42]

Another transportation problem extensively studied is the length and mode of commuting to work (Moses and Williamson 1963; Muth 1961; Kain 1965). It is usually assumed that direct commuting costs, such as train fare, vary positively and that living costs, such as space, vary negatively with the distance commuted. These assumptions alone would imply that a rise in incomes would result in longer commutes as long as space ("housing") were a superior good (Muth, 1961).

A rise in income resulting at least in part from a rise in earnings would, however, increase the cost of commuting a given distance because the forgone value of the time involved would increase. This increase in commuting costs would discourage commuting in the same way that the increased demand for space would encourage it. The outcome depends on the relative strengths of these conflicting forces: one can show with a few assumptions that the distance commuted would increase as income increased if, and only if, space had an income elasticity greater than unity.

For let Z_1 refer to the commuting commodity, Z_2 to other commodities, and let

$$Z_1 = f_1(x, t) \tag{22}$$

where t is the time spent commuting and x is the quantity of space used. Commuting costs are assumed to have the simple form $a + l_1 t$, where a is a constant and l_1 is the marginal forgone cost per hour spent commuting. In other words, the cost of time is the only variable commuting cost. The cost per unit of space is $p(t)$, where by assumption $p' < 0$. The problem is to maximise the utility function

$$U = U(x, t, Z_2) \tag{23}$$

subject to the resource constraint

$$a + l_1 t + px + h(Z_2) = S \tag{24}$$

If it were assumed that $U_t = 0$ – commuting was neither enjoyable nor irksome – the main equilibrium condition would reduce to

$$l_1 + p'x = 0 \tag{25}$$

which would be the equilibrium condition if households simply attempt to minimise the sum of transportation and space costs (Kain, 1963, pp. 6–12).[43] If $l_1 = kS$, where k is a constant, the effect of a change in full income on the time spent commuting can be found by differentiating equation (25) to be

$$\frac{\partial t}{\partial S} = \frac{k(\varepsilon_x - 1)}{p''x} \tag{26}$$

where ε_x is the income elasticity of demand for space. Since stability requires that $p'' > 0$, an increase in income increases the time spent commuting if, and only if, $\varepsilon_x > 1$.

In metropolitan areas of the United States higher-income families tend to live further from the central city,[44] which contradicts our analysis if one accepts the traditional view that the income elasticity of demand for housing is less than unity. In a definitive study of the demand for housing in the United States, however, Margaret Reid (1962, p. 6) found income elasticities greater than unity. Moreover, the analysis of distance commuted incorporates only a few dimensions of the demand for housing; principally the demand for outdoor space. The evidence on distances commuted would then only imply that outdoor space is a "luxury," which is rather plausible[45] and not even inconsistent with the traditional view about the total elasticity of demand for housing.

3.5. The division of labour within families

Space is too limited to do more than summarise the main implications of the theory concerning the division of labour among members of the same household. Instead of simply allocating time efficiently among commodities, multi-person households also allocate the time of different members. Members who are relatively more efficient at market activities would use less of their time at consumption activities than would other members. Moreover, an increase in the relative market efficiency of any member would effect a reallocation of the time of all other members towards consumption activities in order to permit the former to spend more time at market activities. In short, the allocation of the time of any member is greatly influenced by the opportunities open to other members.

4. Substitution Between Time and Goods

Although time and goods have been assumed to be used in fixed proportions in producing commodities, substitution could take place because different commodities used them in different proportions. The assumption of fixed proportions is now dropped in order to include many additional implications of the theory.

It is well known from the theory of variable proportions that households would minimise costs by setting the ratio of the marginal product of goods to that of time equal to the ratio of their marginal costs.[46] A rise in the cost of time relative to goods would induce a reduction in the amount of time and an increase in the amount of goods used per unit of each commodity. Thus, not only would a rise in earnings induce a substitution away from earnings-intensive commodities but also a substitution away from time and towards goods in the production of each commodity. Only the first is (implicitly) recognised in the labour–leisure analysis, although the second may well be of considerable importance. It increases one's confidence that the substitution effect of a rise in earnings is more important than is commonly believed.

The change in the input coefficients of time and goods resulting from a change in their relative costs is defined by the elasticity of substitution between them, which presumably varies from commodity to commodity. The only empirical study of this elasticity assumes that recreation goods and "leisure" time are used to produce a recreation commodity

(Owen, 1964, ch. x). Definite evidence of substitution is found, since the ratio of leisure time to recreation goods is negatively related to the ratio of their prices. The elasticity of substitution appears to be less than unity, however, since the share of leisure in total factor costs is apparently positively related to its relative price.

The incentive to economise on time as its relative cost increases goes a long way towards explaining certain broad aspects of behaviour that have puzzled and often disturbed observers of contemporary life. Since hours worked have declined secularly in most advanced countries, and so-called "leisure" has presumably increased, a natural expectation has been that "free" time would become more abundant, and be used more "leisurely" and "luxuriously." Yet, if anything, time is used more carefully today than a century ago; see, for example, de Grazia (1962, ch. iv). If there was a secular increase in the productivity of working time relative to consumption time (see section 3.3) there would be an increasing incentive to economise on the latter because of its greater expense (our theory emphatically cautions against calling such time "free"). Not surprisingly, therefore, it is now kept track of and used more carefully than in the past.

Americans are supposed to be much more wasteful of food and other goods than persons in poorer countries, and much more conscious of time: they keep track of it continuously, make (and keep) appointments for specific minutes, rush about more, cook steaks and chops rather than time-consuming stews and so forth.[47] They are simultaneously supposed to be wasteful – of material goods – and overly economical – of immaterial time. Yet both allegations may be correct and not simply indicative of a strange American temperament because the market value of time is higher relative to the price of goods there than elsewhere. That is, the tendency to be economical about time and lavish about goods may be no paradox, but in part simply a reaction to a difference in relative costs.

The substitution towards goods induced by an increase in the relative cost of time would often include a substitution towards more expensive goods. For example, an increase in the value of a mother's time may induce her to enter the labour force and spend less time cooking by using pre-cooked foods and less time on child-care by using nurseries, camps or baby-sitters. Or barbers' shops in wealthier sections of town charge more and provide quicker service than those in poorer sections, because waiting by barbers is substituted for waiting by customers. These examples illustrate that a change in the quality of goods[48] resulting from a change in the relative cost of goods may simply reflect a change in the methods used to produce given commodities, and not any corresponding change in *their* quality.

Consequently, a rise in income due to a rise in earnings would increase the quality of goods purchased not only because of the effect of income on quality but also because of a substitution of goods for time; a rise in income due to a rise in property income would not cause any substitution, and should have less effect on the quality of goods. Put more dramatically, with total income held constant, a rise in earnings should increase while a rise in property income should decrease the quality chosen. Once again, the composition of income is important and provides testable implications of the theory.

One analytically interesting application of these conclusions is to the recent study by Margaret Reid (1963) of the substitution between store-bought and home-delivered milk. According to our approach, the cost of inputs into the commodity "milk consumption at home" is either the sum of the price of milk in the store and the forgone value of the time used to carry it home or simply the price of delivered milk. A reduction in the price of store relative to delivered milk, the value of time remaining constant, would reduce the cost of the first method relatively to the second, and shift production towards the first. For the same reason a reduction in the value of time, market prices of milk remaining constant, would also shift production towards the first method.

Reid's finding of a very large negative relation between the ratio of store to delivered milk and the ratio of their prices, income and some other variables held constant, would be evidence both that milk costs are a large part of total production costs and that there is easy substitution between these alternative methods of production. The large, but not quite as large, negative relation with income simply confirms the easy substitution between methods, and indicates that the cost of time is less important than the cost of milk. In other words, instead of conveying separate information, her price and income elasticities both measure substitution between the two methods of producing the same commodity, and are consistent and plausible.

The importance of forgone earnings and the substitution between time and goods may be quite relevant in interpreting observed price elasticities. A given percentage increase in the price of goods would be less of an increase in commodity prices the more important forgone earnings are. Consequently, even if all commodities had the same true price elasticity, those having relatively important forgone earnings would show lower apparent elasticities in the typical analysis that relates quantities and prices of goods alone.

The importance of forgone earnings differs not only among commodities but also among households for a given commodity because of differences in income. Its importance would change in the same or opposite direction as income, depending on whether the elasticity of substitution between time and goods was less or greater than unity. Thus, even when the true price elasticity of a commodity did not vary with income, the observed price elasticity of goods would be negatively or positively related to income as the elasticity of substitution was less or greater than unity.

The importance of substitution between time and goods can be illustrated in a still different way. Suppose, for simplicity, that only good x and no time was initially required to produce commodity Z. A price ceiling is placed on x, it nominally becomes a free good, and the production of x is subsidised sufficiently to maintain the same output. The increased quantity of x and Z demanded due to the decline in the price of x has to be rationed because the output of x has not increased. Suppose that the system of rationing made the quantity obtained a positive function of the time and effort expended. For example, the quantity of price-controlled bread or medical attention obtained might depend on the time spent in a queue outside a bakery or in a physician's office. Or if an appointment system were used a literal queue would be replaced by a figurative one, in which the waiting was done at "home," as in the Broadway theatre, admissions to hospitals or air travel during peak seasons. Again, even in depressed times the likelihood of obtaining a job is positively related to the time put into job hunting.

Although x became nominally a free good, Z would not be free, because the time now required as an input into Z is not free. The demand for Z would be greater than the supply (fixed by assumption) if the cost of this time was less than the equilibrium price of Z before the price control. The scrambling by households for the limited supply would increase the time required to get a unit of Z, and thus its cost. Both would continue to increase until the average cost of time tended to the equilibrium price before price control.

At that point equilibrium would be achieved because the supply and demand for Z would be equal.

Equilibrium would take different forms depending on the method of rationing. With a literal "first come first served" system the size of the queue (say outside the bakery or in the doctor's office) would grow until the expected cost of standing in line discouraged any excess demand;[49] with the figurative queues of appointment systems, the "waiting" time (say to see a play) would grow until demand was sufficiently curtailed. If the system of rationing was less formal, as in the labour market during recessions, the expected time required to ferret out a scarce job would grow until the demand for jobs was curtailed to the limited supply.

Therefore, price control of x combined with a subsidy that kept its amount constant would not change the average private equilibrium price of Z,[50] but would substitute indirect time costs for direct goods costs.[51] Since, however, indirect costs are positively related to income, the price of Z would be raised to higher-income persons and reduced to lower-income ones, thereby redistributing consumption from the former to the latter. That is, women, the poor, children, the unemployed, etc., would be more willing to spend their time in a queue or otherwise ferreting out rationed goods than would high-earning males.

5. Summary and Conclusions

This paper has presented a theory of the allocation of time between different activities. At the heart of the theory is an assumption that households are producers as well as consumers; they produce commodities by combining inputs of goods and time according to the cost-minimisation rules of the traditional theory of the firm. Commodities are produced in quantities determined by maximising a utility function of the commodity set subject to prices and a constraint on resources. Resources are measured by what is called full income, which is the sum of money income and that forgone or "lost" by the use of time and goods to obtain utility, while commodity prices are measured by the sum of the costs of their goods and time inputs.

The effect of changes in earnings, other income, goods prices and the productivity of working and consumption time on the allocation of time and the commodity set produced has been analysed. For example, a rise in earnings, compensated by a decline in other income so that full income would be unchanged, would induce a decline in the amount of time used at consumption activities, because time would become more expensive. Partly goods would be substituted for the more expensive time in the production of each commodity, and partly goods-intensive commodities would be substituted for the more expensive time-intensive ones. Both substitutions require less time to be used at consumption, and permit more to be used at work. Since the reallocation of time involves simultaneously a reallocation of goods and commodities, all three decisions become intimately related.

The theory has many interesting and even novel interpretations of, and implications about, empirical phenomena. A few will be summarised here.

A traditional "economic" interpretation of the secular decline in hours worked has stressed the growth in productivity of working time and the resulting income and substitution effects, with the former supposedly dominating. Ours stresses that the substitution effects of the growth in productivity of working and consumption time tended to offset each other, and that hours worked declined secularly primarily because time-intensive commodities have been luxuries. A contributing influence has been the secular decline in the relative prices of goods used in time-intensive commodities.

Since an increase in income partly due to an increase in earnings would raise the relative cost of time and of time-intensive commodities, traditional cross-sectional estimates of income elasticities do not hold either factor or commodity prices constant. Consequently, they would, among other things, be biased downward for time-intensive commodities, and give a misleading impression of the effect of income on the quality of commodities consumed. The composition of income also affects demand, for an increase in earnings, total income held constant, would shift demand away from time-intensive commodities and input combinations.

Rough estimates suggest that forgone earnings are quantitatively important and there-fore that full income is substantially above money income. Since forgone earnings are primarily determined by the use of time, considerably more attention should be paid to its efficiency and allocation. In particular, agencies that collect information on the expenditure of money income might simultaneously collect information on the "expenditure" of time. The resulting time budgets, which have not been seriously investigated in most countries, including the United States and Great Britain, should be integrated with the money budgets in order to give a more accurate picture of the size and allocation of full income.

Notes

1 See T. W. Schultz (1960), and Becker (1964, Ch. IV). I argue there that the importance of forgone earnings can be directly seen, e.g., from the failure of free tuition to eliminate impediments to college attendance or the increased enrolments that sometimes occur in depressed areas or time periods.
2 On the cause of the secular trend towards an increased school year see my comments (Becker, 1964, p. 103).
3 See Mincer (1963). In his well-known earlier study Mincer (1962) considered the allocation of married women between "housework" and labour force participation.
4 Let me emphasise, however, that I alone am responsible for any errors.
5 There are several empirical as well as conceptual advantages in assuming that households combine goods and time to produce commodities instead of simply assuming that the amount of time used at an activity is a direct function of the amount of goods consumed. For example, a change in the cost of goods relative to time could cause a significant substitution away from the one rising in relative cost. This, as well as other applications, are treated in the following sections.
6 If a good or time period was used in producing several commodities I assume that these "joint costs" could be fully and uniquely allocated among the commodities. The problems here are no different from those usually arising in the analysis of multi-product firms.
7 The dependency among constraints distinguishes this problem from many other multiple constraint situations in economic analysis, such as those arising in the usual theory of rationing Tobin (1952). Rationing would reduce to a formally identical single-constraint situation if rations were saleable and fully convertible into money income.

8   This term emerged from a conversation with Milton Friedman.
9   Any utility received would only be an incidental by-product of the pursuit of money income. Perhaps this explains why utility analysis was not clearly formulated and accepted until economic development had raised incomes well above the subsistence level.
10 Full income is achieved by maximising the earnings function

$$W = W(Z_1, \ldots, Z_m) \tag{1'}$$

subject to the expenditure constraint in equation (6), to the inequality

$$\sum_i^m T_i \leq T \tag{2'}$$

and to the restrictions in (8). I assume for simplicity that the amount of each dimension of time used in producing commodities is less than the total available, so that (2') can be ignored; it is not difficult to incorporate this constraint. Maximising (1') subject to (6) and (8) yields the following conditions

$$\frac{\partial W}{\partial Z_i} = \frac{p_i b_i \sigma}{1 + \sigma} \tag{3'}$$

where σ is the marginal productivity of money income. Since the loss function $L = (S - V) - W$, the equilibrium conditions to minimise the loss is the same as (3') except for a change in sign.
11 Households maximise their utility subject only to the single total resource constraint given by (14), for once the full income constraint is satisfied, there is no other restriction on the set of Z_i that can be chosen. By introducing the concept of full income the problem of maximising utility subject to the time and goods constraints is solved in two stages: first, full income is determined from the goods and time constraints, and then utility is maximised subject only to the constraint imposed by full income.
12 It can easily be shown that the equilibrium conditions of (16) are in fact precisely the same as those following in general from equation (10).
13 Elsewhere I have discussed some effects of the allocation of goods on productivity (Becker, 1962b), section 2); essentially the same discussion can be found in (Becker, 1964, ch. II).
14 The problem is: under what conditions would

$$-\frac{\partial T_w}{\partial V} = \frac{\partial T_c}{\partial V} = \sum_i t_i \frac{\partial Z_i}{\partial V} < 0 \tag{1'}$$

when

$$\sum (p_i b_i + l_i t_i) \frac{\partial Z_i}{\partial V} = 1 \tag{2'}$$

If the analysis were limited to a two-commodity world where Z_1 was more time intensive, then it can easily be shown that (1') would hold if, and only if,

$$\frac{\partial Z_1}{\partial V} < \frac{-\gamma_2}{(\gamma_1 - \gamma_2)(p_1 b_1 + l_1 t_1)} < 0 \tag{3'}$$

15 By a uniform change of β is meant

$$W_1 = (1 + \beta) W_0 (Z_1, \ldots Z_n)$$

where W_0 represents the earnings function before the change and W_1 represents it afterwards. Since the loss function is defined as

$$L = S - W - V$$
$$= W(\hat{Z}) - W(Z)$$

then

$$L_1 = W_1(\hat{Z}) - W_1(Z)$$
$$= (1 + \beta)[W_0(\hat{Z}) - W_0(Z)] = (1 + \beta)L_0$$

Consequently, all opportunities costs also change by β.

16   According to the definitions of earning and time intensity in equations (20) and (21), they would be positively correlated unless l_i and t_i were sufficiently negatively correlated. See the further discussion later on.

17   Let it be stressed that this conclusion usually holds, even when households are irrational; sophisticated calculations about the value of time at work or in consumption, or substantial knowledge about the amount of time used by different commodities is not required. Changes in the hours of work, even of non-maximising, impulsive, habitual, etc., households would tend to be positively related to compensated changes in earnings because demand curves tend to be negatively inclined even for such households (Becker, 1962a).

18   Suppose there were two commodities Z_1 and Z_2 where the cost of Z_1 depended only on the cost of market goods, while the cost of Z_2 depended only on the cost of time. The goods-budget constraint would then simply be

$$p_1 b_1 Z_1 = I = V + T_\omega \bar{\omega}$$

and the constraint on time would be

$$t_2 Z_2 = T - T_\omega$$

This is essentially the algebra of the analysis presented by Henderson and Quandt (1958, p. 23), and their treatment is representative. They call Z_2 "leisure," and Z_1 an average of different commodities. Their equilibrium condition that the rate of substitution between goods and leisure equals the real wage-rate is just a special case of our equation (19).

19   For workers receiving premium pay on the week-ends and in the evenings, however, the cost of time may be considerably greater then.

20   See the advertisement by United States Lines in various issues of the *New Yorker* magazine: "The S.S. *United States* regularly includes a week-end in its 5 days to Europe, saving [economic] time for businessmen" (my insertion).

21   For example, *Webster's Collegiate Dictionary* defines leisurely as "characterized by leisure, taking *abundant time*" (my italics); or S. de Grazia (1962, p. 15) says, "Leisure is a state of being in which activity is performed for its own sake or as its own end."

22   S. de Grazia (1962, chs III and IV) has recently entertainingly shown the many difficulties in even reaching a reliable definition, and *a fortiori*, in quantitatively estimating the amount of leisure. Also see Moore, (1963, Chapter II); Morgan et al. (1962, p. 322), and Owen (1964, Ch. II).

23   Sometimes true leisure is defined as the amount of discretionary time available (Moore, 1963, p. 18). It is always difficult to attach a rigorous meaning to the word "discretionary" when referring to economic resources. One might say that in the short run consumption time is and working time is not discretionary, because the latter is partially subject to the authoritarian control of employers. (Even this distinction would vanish if households gave certain firms

authoritarian control over their consumption time; see the discussion in section 2.) In the long run this definition of discretionary time is suspect too because the availability of alternative sources of employment would make working time also discretionary.

24   See (Owen, 1964, ch. VIII). Recreation commodities presumably have relatively large forgone earnings.

25   See Corbett and Hague (1953–54); also Harberger, (1964).

26   The effect on earnings is more difficult to determine because, by assumption, time intensive commodities have smaller costs per unit time than other commodities. A shift towards the former would, therefore, raise hourly earnings, which would partially and perhaps more than entirely offset the reduction in hours worked. Incidentally, this illustrates how the productivity of hours worked is influenced by the consumption set chosen.

27   Full money income would be unaffected if it were achieved by using all time at pure work activities. If other uses of time were also required it would tend to increase. Even if full money income were unaffected, however, full real income would increase because prices of the Z_i would fall.

28   So the "Knight" view that an increase in income would increase "leisure" is not necessarily true, even if leisure were a superior good and even aside from Robbins' emphasis on the substitution effect (Robbins, 1930).

29   Wesley Mitchell's (1932) justly famous essay spells out some of these reasons.

30   A. Finnegan (1962) does find steeper cross-sectional relations when the average incomes and hours of different occupations are used (1962).

31   Note that Mincer (1962) has found a very strong substitution effect for women.

32   The movement of shaving from barbers' shops to households illustrates how and why even in urban areas households have become "small factories." Under the impetus of a general growth in the value of time they have been encouraged to find ways of saving on travelling and waiting time by performing more activities themselves.

33   More appropriate income elasticities for several commodities are estimated in Mincer (1963).

34   In this connection note that cross-sectional data are often preferred to time-series data in estimating income elasticities precisely because they are supposed to be largely free of co-linearity between prices and incomes; see, e.g., Tobin (1950).

35   Biases in cross-sectional estimates of the demand for work and leisure were considered in the last section.

36   See Becker (1960), Easterlin (1961), Adelman (1963), Weintraub, (1962), Silver (1964), and several other studies; for an apparent exception, see the note by Freedman (1963).

37   See, for example, Duesenberry's (1960) comment on Becker.

38   See Becker (1960).

39   In Becker (1960, p. 214 fn. 8), the relation between forgone costs and income was mentioned but not elaborated.

40   Other arguments suggesting that higher-income families face a higher price of children have generally confused price with quality (Becker, 1960, pp. 214–15).

41   Mincer measures the price of children by the wife's potential wage-rate, and fits regressions to various cross-sectional data, where number of children is the dependent variable, and family income and the wife's potential wage-rate are among the independent variables.

42   The only quantitative estimate of the marginal value of time that I am familiar with uses the relation between the value of land and its commuting distance from employment; see Mohring (1961). With many assumptions I have estimated the marginal value of time of those commuting at about 40% of their average hourly earnings. It is not clear whether this value is so low because of errors in these assumptions or because of severe kinks in the supply and demand functions for hours of work.

43   If $U_t \neq 0$, the main equilibrium condition would be

$$\frac{U_t}{U_x} = \frac{l_1 + p'x}{p}$$

Probably the most plausible assumption is that $U_t < 0$, which would imply that $l_1 + p'x < 0$.

44   For a discussion, including many qualifications, of this proposition see Schnore (1963).

45   According to Reid (1962, ch. 12), the elasticity of demand for indoor space is less than unity. If her total elasticity is accepted this suggests that outdoor space has an elasticity exceeding unity.

46   The cost of producing a given amount of commodity Z_i would be minimised if

$$\frac{\partial f_i / \partial x_i}{\partial f_i / \partial T_i} = \frac{P_i}{\partial L / \partial T_i}$$

If utility were considered an indirect function of goods and time rather than simply a direct function of commodities the following conditions, among others, would be required to maximise utility:

$$\frac{\partial U / \partial x_i}{\partial U / \partial T_i} = \frac{\partial Z_i / \partial x_i}{\partial Z_i / \partial T_i} = \frac{p_i}{\partial L / \partial T}$$

which are exactly the same conditions as above. The ratio of the marginal utility of x_i to that of T_i depends only on f_i, x_i and T_i, and is thus independent of other production functions, goods and time. In other words, the indirect utility function is what has been called "weakly separable" (Muth).

47   For a comparison of the American concept of time with others see Hall (1959, ch. 9).

48   Quality is usually defined empirically by the amount spent per physical unit, such as pound of food, car or child. See especially Prais and Houthakker. (1971); also Becker (1962).

49   In queueing language the cost of waiting in line is a "discouragement" factor that stabilises the queueing scheme; see, for example, Cox and Smith (1961).

50   The social price, on the other hand, would double, for it is the sum of private indirect costs and subsidised direct costs.

51   Time costs can be criticised from a Pareto optimality point of view because they often result in external diseconomies: e.g., a person joining a queue would impose costs on subsequent joiners. The diseconomies are real, not simply pecuniary, because time is a cost to demanders, but is not revenue to suppliers.

References

Adelman, I. (1963): "An Econometric Analysis of Population Growth," *American Economic Review*, 53 (3), June, 314–39.

Becker, G. S. (1960): "An Economic Analysis of Fertility," in *Demographic and Economic Change in Developed Countries*, National Bureau Committee for Economic Research Conference Volume, Princeton: Princeton University Press.

Becker, G. S. (1962a): "Irrational Behavior and Economic Theory," *Journal of Political Economy*, 70 (1), February, 1–13.

Becker, G. S. (1962b): "Investment in Human Capital: A Theoretical Analysis," *Journal of Political Economy*, 70 (5), special supplement, October, section 2, 9–49.

Becker, G. S. (1964): *Human Capital: A Theoretical and Empirical Analysis*. New York: Columbia University Press for the National Bureau of Economic Analysis.

Cairncross, A. K. (1958): "Economic Schizophrenia," *Scottish Journal of Political Economy*, 5 (1), February, 15–21.

Corbett, W. J. and Hague, D. C. (1953–4): "Complementarity and the Excess Burden of Taxation," *Review of Economic Studies*, 21 (1)–30.

Cox, D. R. and Smith, W. L. (1961): *Queues*. New York: Wiley.

de Grazia, S. (1962): *Of Time, Work and Leisure*. New York: The Twentieth Century Fund.

Dean, E. (1963): Economic Analysis and African Response to Price. Unpublished Ph.D. dissertation, Columbia University.

Duesenberry, J. (1960): "Comment on Becker," in NBER's Demographic and Economic Change in Developed Countries, Princeton: Princeton University Press, 231–4.

Easterlin, R. A. (1961): "The American Baby Boom in Historical Perspective," *American Economic Review*, 51 (5), December, 869–911.

Finnegan, A. (1962): "A Cross-sectional Analysis of Hours of Work," *Journal of Political Economy*, 70 (5), October, 452–70.

Freedman, D. (1963): "The Relation of Economic Status to Fertility," *American Economic Review*, 53 (3), June, 414–26.

Fuchs, V. (1964): *Productivity Trends in the Goods and Service Sectors, 1929–61: A Preliminary Survey*. NBER Occasional Paper, October.

Hall, E. T. (1959): *The Silent Language*. New York: Doubleday.

Harberger, A. C. (1964): "Taxation, Resource Allocation and Welfare," in NBER's *Role of Direct and Indirect Taxes in the Federal Revenue System*, Princeton: Princeton University Press, 25–70.

Henderson, J. M. and Quandt, R. E. (1958): *Microeconomic Theory*. New York: McGraw-Hill

Kain, J. F. (1965): "Commuting and the Residential Decisions of Chicago and Detroit Central Business District Workers," in *National Bureau Committee for Economic Research Transporation Economics*, New York: Columbia University, 245–74.

Mincer, J. (1962): "Labor Force Participation of Married Women," in NBER's *Aspects of Labor Economics*, Princeton: Princeton University Press, 63–97.

——, (1963): "Market Prices, Opportunity Costs, and Income Effects," in Carl F. Christ et al. (eds), *Measurement in Economics: Studies in Mathematical Economics and Econometrics: In Memory of Yehuda Grunfeld*, Stanford: Stanford University Press, 67–82.

Mitchell, W. (1932): "The Backward Art of Spending Money," in W. Mitchell (ed.), *The Backward Art of Spending Money and Other Essays*, New York: McGraw-Hill, 3–19.

Mohring, H. (1961): "Land Values and the Measurement of Highway Benefits," *Journal of Political Economy*, 69 (3), June, 236–49.

Moore, W. (1963): *Man, Time and Society*. New York: Wiley.

Morgan, J. N., David, M. H., Cohen, W. J. and Brazer, H. E. (1962): *Income and Welfare in the United States*. New York: McGraw-Hill.

Moses, L. N. and Williamson, H. F. (1963): "Value of Time, Choice of Mode, and the Subsidy Issue in Urban Transportation," *Journal of Political Economy*, 71 (3), June, 247–64.

Muth, R. (nd): Household Production and Consumer Demand Functions. Unpublished manuscript.

——, (1961): "Economic Change and Rural–Urban Conversion," *Econometrica*, 29 (1), January, 1–23.

Owen, J. (1964): The Supply of Labor and the Demand for Recreation. Unpublished PhD dissertation, Columbia University.

Prais, S. J. and Houthakker, H. (1971): *The Analysis of Family Budgets*. Cambridge: Cambridge University Press.

Reid, M. (1962): *Housing and Income*. Chicago: University of Chicago Press.

Reid, M. (1963): "Consumer Response to the Relative Price of Store versus Delivered Milk," *Journal of Political Economy*, 71 (2), April, 180–6.

Robbins, L. (1930): "On the Elasticity of Demand for Income in Terms of Effort," *Economica*, X, June, 123–9.

Schnore, L. F. (1963): "The Socio-economic Status of Cities and Suburbs," *American Sociological Review*, 28 (1), February, 76–85.

Schultz, T. W. (1960): "The Formation of Human Capital by Education," *Journal of Political Economy*, 68 (6), December, 571–83.

Silver, M. (1964): Birth Rates, Marriages and Business Cycles. Unpublished PhD dissertation, Columbia University.

Tobin, J. (1950): "A Statistical Demand Function for Food in the U.S.A.," *Journal of the Royal Statistical Society*, Series A.

——, (1952): "A Survey of the Theory of Rationing," *Econometrica*, 20 (4), October, 521–53.

Weintraub, R. (1962): "The Birth Rate and Economic Development: An Empirical Study,". *Econometrica*, 40 (4), October, 812–17.

Wilburn, J. (1964): Productivity Trends in Barber and Beauty Shops. Mimeographed report, NBER, September.

II B

Under Conditions of Uncertainty

CHAPTER FIVE

On the Economics of State Lotteries

CHARLES T. CLOTFELTER AND PHILIP J. COOK

Source: *Journal of Economic Perspectives*, 4, 4, (1990), pp. 105–19. Reprinted with the permission of the authors and the American Economic Association. © American Economic Association.

State lotteries can be evaluated from either of two perspectives familiar to economists: as a consumer commodity or as a source of public revenue. As a commodity, the lottery is notable for its broad market penetration and rapid growth. Sixty percent of the adults in lottery states play at least once in a year. The annual growth in real per capita sales in lottery states has averaged 12 percent, rising in 1989 dollars from $22 in 1975 to $108 in 1989. As a source of public revenue, lotteries account for a rather modest fraction of revenue in states that run them (3.3 percent in 1986), but they are nonetheless one of the most visible state government activities. Lottery sales exceed those of all other products sold directly by state governments to the public and are larger than all but three major activities of state government: education, public welfare and highways (Clotfelter and Cook, 1989, Table 2.5).

Moreover, lotteries are a qualitatively new activity for state governments, in that they are a business operated, in effect, for profit. State liquor stores are perhaps the closest analog, but they were created to encourage temperate drinking practices and do not engage in the sales promotion and marketing activities that are characteristic of the lotteries.

Lotteries enjoy an honored place in American history as a device for raising funds for public purposes. Funding for such institutions as the Jamestown settlement, Harvard College, and the Continental Army, as well as hundreds of bridges, fire houses and schools came from lotteries. But after the notorious Louisiana lottery of the post-Civil War era,[1] lotteries were prohibited by every state in this century until 1963, when New Hampshire adopted one. Thus, modern lotteries are a restoration of a device for exploiting the widespread interest in gambling at long odds for the sake of funding worthy activities. Since 1963, 32 states and the District of Columbia have created lotteries, and it is a good bet that other states will follow in the next few years.

This article examines several aspects of the economics of state lotteries, focusing primarily on the demand for lottery products. We begin by giving a descriptive overview. The succeeding sections examine the motivations for playing lottery games and evidence on the determinants of lottery demand. The final section considers the welfare economics of the apparent objective of lotteries – to maximize profits for the state.

1. An Overview of State Lottery Operations

Table 1 provides summary information on the 32 American state lotteries in operation during 1989.[2] States are arranged in decreasing order of gross sales for 1988, and data are

Table 1 U.S. lottery sales and distribution of revenues

State	Year began	1989 sales (millions)	1989 sales per capita	Payout prizes, from FY 1989 (percent)	Operation costs from FY 1989 (percent)	Net revenue from FY 1989 (percent)	Games offered[a]
California	1985	$2595	$89	50%	11%	39%	I, L
New York	1967	2034	113	47	7	46	I, L, N
Florida	1988	1982	156	50	12	38	I, L, N
Pennsylvania	1972	1653	137	51	8	42	I, L, N
Massachusetts	1972	1551	262	60	10	30	I, L, N
Ohio	1974	1540	141	49	12	39	I, L, N
Illinois	1974	1521	130	55	7	38	I, L, N
New Jersey	1970	1250	161	49	9	43	I, L, N
Michigan	1972	1171	126	48	10	42	I, L, N
Maryland	1973	765	163	47	8	45	I, L, N
Connecticut	1972	494	152	49	6	44	I, L, N
Virginia	1988	375	61	50	15	34	I, L, N
Arizona	1981	295	83	48	13	40	I, L
Wisconsin	1988	262	54	52	11	37	I, L
Washington	1982	255	54	46	13	41	I, L, N
Missouri	1986	223	43	50	16	34	I, L, N
Kentucky	1989	217	58	51	16	33	I, L
Iowa	1985	170	60	54	18	29	I, L
Oregon	1985	164	58	52	15	33	I, L, N
District of Columbia	1982	144	240	47	16	37	I, L, N
Indiana[b]	1989	143	26				I
Maine	1974	105	86	51	17	32	I, L, N
Colorado	1983	105	32	51	25	23	I, L
New Hampshire	1964	86	77	53	11	36	I, L, N
Kansas	1988	76	30	49	19	32	I, L
Delaware	1975	64	96	53	10	38	I, L, N
West Virginia	1986	62	33	45	25	30	I, L, N
Rhode Island[c]	1974	61	61	47	14	39	I, L, N
Vermont	1978	39	68	52	16	32	I, L, N
Idaho[b]	1989	33	33				I
South Dakota	1988	20	28	46	24	30	I
Montana	1988	13	16	46	30	24	I, L
United States		$19468	$108	51%	10%	40%	

[a] L = Lotto, N = Numbers, I = Instant
[b] Began operation after July 1, 1989.
[c] Sales are for fiscal year ending June 30.
Sources: Gaming and Wagering Business 11 (February 15, 1990), 30; (May 15, 1990), 47; U.S. Bureau of the Census, *Current Population Reports*, Series P-25, No. 1058, *State Population and Household Estimates: July 1, 1989*, March 1990. Table 1: unpublished information obtained from state lottery agencies.

provided on the year the lottery began operation, the per capita sales, the distribution of revenues, and the types of games offered. Table 1 displays an interestingly high variation between states in sales per capita. For example, Massachusetts outsells neighboring Vermont by a factor of three, despite the fact that they both have well-established lotteries offering very similar products. These interstate differences suggest that tastes for lottery gambling differ widely across population groups.

The next three columns of Table 1 show how each state distributes its lottery revenues. On average, half of all lottery revenues are returned in the form of prizes, a ratio that is much lower than that offered by other forms of commercial gambling such as bingo (74 percent), horseracing (81 percent), or slot machines (89 percent) (Clotfelter and Cook, 1989, Table 2.1). In 1989 the payout rate for lotteries ranged from a low of 45 percent in West Virginia to a high of 60 percent in Massachusetts. Operating expenses, which include the roughly 5 percent of sales paid as commissions to retail sales agents, average 10 percent of gross revenues. The states at the top of the list have lower operating costs per dollar of sales than states with lower sales figures at the bottom of the list, which provides some evidence of increasing returns to scale in the provision of lottery products.[3] From Table 1, it appears that scale economies in provision are exhausted at about $300 million in annual sales.

The "profit" or net revenue remaining after prizes and operating expenses are deducted goes to the state treasury. These transfers can be thought of as implicit taxes levied on the purchase of lottery tickets. Expressed in a form comparable to excise tax rates these implicit taxes are extraordinarily high: the average profit rate of 40 percent (of gross revenues) is equivalent to an excise tax rate of 66 percent (of expenditures net of this tax).[4] By virtue of the evident economies of scale in lottery operation, the large states enjoy the highest rates of profit.

The product line offered by state lotteries today bears little resemblance to the games available in the early 1970s. As late as 1973, the only significant lottery product was a sweepstakes game conducted in much the same way as colonial lotteries; it was essentially a raffle in which bettors bought tickets and waited days or weeks to see if their ticket was drawn. Today this old-fashioned game is virtually extinct, having been replaced by games with quicker payoffs, bigger prizes, and greater intrinsic "play value." The lotteries' first major innovation was the instant game ticket, offering players a chance to discover immediately if they had won a prize. The second new lottery product was a daily numbers game, a computerized imitation of the illegal game that has long been popular in many cities. Designed to appeal largely to this pre-existing market, this game (like its illegal counterpart) lets players choose their own numbers, thus providing an opportunity to become actively involved in the gambling process.

The on-line computer network that supports the numbers game also made it possible to offer a third major lottery product in the early 1980s: lotto. This game features long odds and huge jackpots that build from one drawing to the next if there are no winners. One typical format is a 6/44 game, in which players select six out of 44 numbers, with a probability of 1 in 7.1 million of picking all six numbers correctly. With jackpots (typically stated as the undiscounted sum of 20 annual payments) reaching as high as $100 million, lotto has garnered enormous public interest. As shown in Table 1, most lottery states now offer all three of these games – instant, numbers and lotto – and there is every indication that the states will continue to develop new products in the quest for increased sales.

Oregon introduced sports betting in 1989, and a number of states are considering video game slot machines.[5]

2. Why People Play

Setting aside its game-playing aspects for a moment, a lottery ticket is a sort of risky financial asset, offering a prospect of prizes in return for an investment of 50 cents or a dollar. Since the expected value of the prizes is typically only half the ticket price, the question naturally arises as to why so many adults consider this investment worthwhile. It is true that well-informed players who schedule their bets carefully can improve on the standard 50 percent payout rate. When a lotto jackpot grows sufficiently large through rollovers accumulating from a series of drawings in which no one wins, it may even be possible to place a favorable bet, that is, one with an expected return greater than the cost of the ticket (Thaler and Ziemba, 1988; Chernoff, 1981). But such occasions are rare indeed, and it is safe to say that normally this asset has no place in the portfolio of a prudent investor. Nonetheless, it has very broad appeal.

For some, playing the lottery is an amusing pastime, one that offers the modest pleasures of discovering whether an instant ticket is a winner or discussing lotto strategy with workmates. When players in California were asked whether they played the lottery more for fun or the money, the respondents were about evenly divided. However, of those with incomes below $30,000, 25 percent more respondents cited money than fun, while the reverse was true at upper incomes (*Los Angeles Times* Poll, 1986). In addition to promoting the idea that it is fun to play, lotteries encourage people to think of playing as a public-spirited activity, with the proceeds going to support education or other public services, and that thought may indeed strengthen some citizens' motivation to play.[6] But surely, the hope of private gain is what sells the bulk of lottery tickets.

The challenge to the analyst is understanding why the risky prospects offered by lottery games appeal to people who exhibit some aversion to risk in other circumstances. As a simple example of risk aversion, it has been shown that most people, when given a choice between a 50 percent chance of receiving $1000 and a sure thing of $400, prefer the latter (Kahneman and Tversky, 1979). The propensity to gamble at unfavorable odds was the subject of the classic article by Milton Friedman and L. J. Savage (1948). They suggested that people may perceive a disproportionate benefit to a prize that is large enough to elevate their social standing, and be willing to pay a premium for that sort of chance.

The Friedman–Savage explanation for why otherwise risk-averse people may buy unfavourable chances at large prizes is intuitively appealing. Among other things, it helps explain why lottery games with a relatively modest top prize appeal primarily to low-income players (for whom $500 may be enough to buy a quantum improvement in standard of living, at least temporarily), whereas games with comparatively large jackpots attract more middle-class players (Clotfelter and Cook, 1987, p. 538).

A quite different line of explanation for why rational people would accept unfair bets at long odds is offered by the cognitive psychology literature. In the usual lotto format, the odds against hitting the jackpot are several million to one. Such probabilities are well beyond the realm of experience gained from playing the game, and as a result players cannot be expected to have much intuition about their chances. For example, someone who spends $20 per week on a 6/49 lotto game for his or her adult lifetime would have less than 1 in 200 chance of winning the jackpot. Faced with such a remote chance, people tend to assess the prospect on the basis of rough heuristics like what Tversky and Kahneman (1974) called "availability," defined as the ease with which instances of the event can be brought to mind. In the case of lotteries, the ability to visualize such instances is aided by the steady stream of winners, who are announced each week with considerable fanfare, and by the advertising of lottery agencies.

We documented how lottery advertising emphasizes the chance of winning big with a sample of over 151 television and radio ads from 13 of the largest state lotteries. These ads included very little objective information on the probability of winning. Only 12 percent of our sample ads provided any information about the odds of winning, and none of them stated the probability of winning one of the large prizes. On the other hand the dollar amounts of prizes were mentioned in fully half the ads, and in most cases the reference was to the largest prize.

These ads accentuated the possibility of winning. Out of the 52 television ads in the sample that portrayed a lottery player, two-thirds showed at least one person winning a prize. Some ads debunked pessimists who claimed it was unlikely to win big, or offered themes like: "Somebody's going to win. Why not you?" Such messages, implicit or explicit, help make the dream of wealth credible. By aiding "availability," such ads may tend to produce an exaggerated sense of the likelihood of winning. A gamble which is objectively unfair may thus be perceived as attractive by people who normally are averse to risk.

Tversky and Kahneman's explanation may appeal to economists because it preserves a view of the lottery player as an objective, albeit poorly informed, assessor of the risky prospect offered by a game. However, a more fundamental departure from the economist's expected utility framework may be necessary to explain the existence of an apparently profitable business of providing advice to players on how to choose their numbers. Although every possible play in numbers or lotto has the same chance of winning, many players are willing to pay for advice in the form of "dream books," consultations with astrologers, tabloids offering numerology columns, and computer software that facilitates the analysis of patterns in recent drawings of winning numbers. There is a common tendency to deny the operation of chance even in situations that are entirely chance-determined: an "illusion of control," to use psychologist Ellen Langer's term. She has demonstrated in several gambling experiments that this illusion is heightened if subjects are asked to make choices, even if their efforts have no effect on the probability of winning (Langer 1975, 1978). Thus the success of the lottery may in part reflect the widespread illusion that choosing winning numbers is partly a matter of skill.

3. Who Plays the Lottery?

Most adults who live in lottery states have played the lottery at least once, but a small percentage of lottery customers are so active as to account for the bulk of all sales. In any given week about one-third of all adults play; over the course of a year participation broadens to encompass 60 percent of the adult public.[7] Among those who do play, the most active 10 percent of players account for 50 percent of the total amount wagered, while the top 20 percent wager about 65 percent of the total.

Interestingly, the degree of concentration among players (as indicated by these percentages) does not depend on the time interval under consideration.[8] This pattern of concentration of sales is typical of consumer products. One rule of thumb in marketing, the "law of the heavy half," holds that the top 20 percent of consumers of any commodity account for about 80 percent of total purchases.[9] Unless heavy players are appreciably less responsive to advertising than occasional players, this concentration implies that the "typical" (median) consumer is of little relevance in marketing the lottery, since it is the atypical, relatively heavy player who accounts for most of the sales. It appears that the primary instrument for converting moderate or inactive players into active players is product innovation, rather than advertising.

Socioeconomic patterns of lottery expenditures have received considerable attention from social scientists as well as lottery marketing directors. We obtained information on the characteristics of players from a number of sources, including several household surveys. Whether measured by participation rate, average expenditure, or the prevalence of heavy players, certain consistent generalizations emerged from our analysis of these sources. Men play somewhat more than women. Adults play more in their middle years than when young (18 to 25) or old (65 and over). Catholics play more than Protestants, approximately half again as much. And lottery play is systematically related to social class, although perhaps not always as strongly as the conventional wisdom would suggest in this regard.

The pattern is clear with respect to one indicator of social class: lottery play falls with formal education. For example, a survey in California found that the proportion of adults who participated during one week in July 1986 ranged from 49 percent for those with less than a high school education to 30 percent for those with a college degree. With respect to occupation, in the California survey lottery play was most common among laborers (including both skilled and unskilled) at 46 percent, and least among advanced professionals (25 percent). Retired people and students played least of all. With respect to race, survey evidence suggests that Hispanics in the west and blacks in the east play more than non-Hispanic whites.

Remarkably, the same sources of data do not demonstrate any consistent relationship between lottery play and household income over the broad middle range; the average expenditure in dollars for households making $10,000 is about the same as for those making $60,000. One implication of this pattern of demand is that the tax implicit in lottery finance is regressive, in the sense that as a percentage of income, tax payments decline as income increases.

It is interesting to note that even when all these socioeconomic factors are taken into account, there remain certain individuals who simply display a strong propensity toward gambling that is strongly predictive of lottery play. The most complete survey of gambling participation ever conducted in the United States was the National Study of Gambling, a national survey conducted in 1975 involving 1,735 respondents (Commission on the Review of the National Policy toward Gambling, 1976). Questions were asked concerning participation in all forms of commercial gambling, both legal and illegal. For the respondents from lottery states, lottery participation was twice as high among gamblers as among those who did not participate in other commercial gambling (74 percent as opposed to 36 percent), and that association remained strong in a multivariate analysis.

However, the majority of lottery players were not otherwise involved in commercial gambling, and would not have been in the absence of the lottery. For example, a person

with the socioeconomic characteristics associated with a 27 percent likelihood of participating in some form of commercial gambling if living in a non-lottery state had a
participation probability of 52 percent in a lottery state. In sum, the lottery has an
especially strong appeal to established gamblers, but it also recruits many people who
would not otherwise become involved in commercial gambling.

4. The Effect of Changing Prices and Payoffs

An appropriate definition of price is not obvious in the case of lottery products because
there is no single best definition of quantity. One reasonable definition of the quantity unit
is "one dollar's worth of expected prize value." Price would then be the cost of buying
that unit, or the reciprocal of the payout rate. Consider, for example, the straight three-
digit numbers game, in which the probability of winning is 1 in 1000. Most states pay off
at a rate of 500 to 1, for an average payout rate of 50 percent and a price, by this definition,
of $2.00. In Massachusetts, which is unique in paying 700 to 1 on a straight three-digit bet
in its numbers game, the price would be $1.43. Although quantities of different lottery
games cannot be added together – one "unit" of the numbers game cannot be added to one
"unit" of lotto to get a meaningful total – total expenditures may be.

It would be surprising indeed if a reduction in price (an increase in the payout rate) did not
increase expenditures somewhat. One common pattern of lottery play is for players to
"reinvest" small prizes in additional tickets (Clotfelter and Cook, 1989, p. 111), which
virtually ensures an expenditure increase from a hike in the payout rate, even if players'
evaluation of the game does not change.[10] If it is true that total expenditures are stimulated by
an increase in the payout rate, then by definition the demand for lottery products is elastic.
But knowing that would not be sufficient for a lottery designer who requires assurance that
an increase in the payout rate will increase the lottery's profitability, a result that would
require under current payout rates a price elasticity greater than 2 in absolute value.[11]

This issue cannot be resolved with available data, simply because payout rates over time
and across states are too uniform to create the necessary contrast. For example, as of 1986
numbers games in all states except for Massachusetts offered a payout rate of 50 percent.
Lotto exhibits slightly more interstate variation in payout rates, but it also differs across
states in format and the size of the betting pool, which may also influence sales and make
specifying a demand equation difficult. Our regression analyses suggested that sales were
quite sensitive to price, but the coefficient estimate was not very stable with respect to
alternative specifications for cross-section data on states.[12]

Much more clearcut is the evidence that lotto sales are responsive to rollovers in the
jackpot. Under typical lotto rules, if a drawing fails to produce a winner the money in that
jackpot is "rolled over" to the subsequent drawing. If several consecutive drawings
produce no winners, the jackpot continues to accumulate and the expected value of a
bet grows accordingly.[13] This form of price reduction stimulates sales.[14] We estimated an
equation using data on 170 consecutive drawings in the Massachusetts lotto game, covering the period from July 18, 1984 to March 1, 1986. For each thousand dollars of
"rollover" added to the jackpot, we estimated an increase of sales of $418, with a standard
error of $19.[15] The stimulus to betting is insufficient in this case to make it worthwhile for
the state to augment the jackpot "artificially," in the absence of a rollover.

There is also intriguing evidence on the cross-price elasticity of demand for closely related lottery products. Although each number in the numbers game has the same probability of winning, some players choosing the numbers do not view them as perfect substitutes. They see some numbers as "luckier" than others; 777 and 333 are perennial favorites. In most states, there is a fixed payout (500 to 1), so that every number has the same price. But a few states calculate payoffs on a parimutuel basis, so that popular numbers have a lower payout and higher price than unpopular numbers. A comparison of patterns of play in two states suggests that players are responsive to differences in price for specific numbers. In Maryland, where numbers have equal payout rates, players concentrate their bets on popular numbers. Players in the parimutuel state of New Jersey, on the other hand, tend to spread their bets out, placing fewer bets on the most popular numbers and more on the least popular numbers.

5. Are Lottery Products Substitutes for Each Other or Other Games?

Most lotteries added lotto to their existing product line during the 1980s, and in the majority of states it soon became the sales leader. It is natural to suppose that lotto sales would to some extent come at the expense of reducing the sales of the numbers and instant games.[16] But surprisingly, the evidence indicates that the sales of existing games have not been hurt by the introduction of lotto. We compared the average growth rates in sales for numbers and instant games during the two-year periods before and after the introduction of lotto for a sample of 13 states. In only four states did the growth rate decrease, as would be expected if lotto were a substitute for the other games. The growth rate of the other games *increased* in the other nine states.

Another type of evidence supports this conclusion, too. Lotto sales tend to vary widely from drawing to drawing, depending on the size of the jackpot (as determined by the rollovers from previous drawings). If lotto were a substitute for other games, then the run-up in lotto sales when there is a large jackpot would depress sales of other games. An analysis of Massachusetts numbers sales data for 85 consecutive weeks was conducted to test for this possibility; it revealed that the size of the lotto jackpot, which had an enormous effect on lotto sales, had *no* discernible effect on sales of the numbers game. The additional betting on lotto was "new" money.

It would be of great interest to know whether this result extends to illegal gambling, and especially the illegal numbers game of which the state numbers games are a direct imitation. Not surprisingly, there is no reliable evidence on the illegal game's profitability or sales, although it has clearly survived the introduction of the legal game. Whatever their effect on the illegal numbers game, we do know that the state lotteries have greatly broadened participation in commercial gambling, legal and illegal included.

6. The Peculiar Economies of Scale of Lotto

For the game of lotto, bigger is better. Small states appear to be unable to mount a lotto game that attracts much public interest because the jackpots are inevitably small compared to the multimillion-dollar bonanzas generated in California and New York. As a result, multistate lottery consortiums have formed to offer a lotto game that, by combining the populations of several small states, rivals the games of the largest states. The first such consortium was the Tri-State (Maine, New Hampshire, and Vermont). The second was LottoAmerica, initiated in 1988, with the District of Columbia and five widely scattered states with a combined population of about 12 million.

Lotto is a game with peculiar economies of scale. It is a parimutuel game, with the jackpot set equal to a percentage of the amount bet (typically about 25 percent). If a drawing has no jackpot winner, the money in the jackpot rolls over into the jackpot for the next drawing. When several players win, the jackpot is divided among them. The reason that the population base is important to lotto sales, but not sales of other lottery games, hinges on the role of the jackpot in attracting lotto action. An example may help explain how this works.

Suppose state A has an adult population of 10 million and state B has only 100,000. Given equally attractive games, we assume that lotto purchases in both states will average $1 per capita at each drawing. In state A the initial jackpot is then worth $2.5 million, compared with only $25,000 in state B. If both states set the probability of winning at 1 in 100,000 with the average price per winner the same in both states, then state A will have an average of 100 winners while state B will have one winner. Given these rules, the games in the two states do not appear to differ much. However, state A has the option of reducing the probability of winning to, say, 1 in 10 million, in which case each state has only one winner on the average.

Under these rules, state A offers one hundred times the jackpot of state B and only 1 percent of state B's probability of winning. For reasons discussed above, most players prefer state A's game to state B's. The prize in state A is the stuff that dreams are made of, and in case anyone is not paying attention, the lottery agency will focus its advertising on the magnitude of this jackpot. Yet the offsetting large difference in probabilities between the two states has little influence on potential players. As long as most drawings produce a winner, the prospect of winning will be credible in both states.

7. The Government's Business

As they are presently constituted, state lotteries are guided by one objective: to raise as much revenue as possible for state treasuries. This objective is sometimes stated explicitly in state law and often in the annual reports of lottery agencies and in state government studies.[17] It is also evident in the lotteries' high price (implied by the 50 percent average payout rate) and the vigorous style of marketing. By focusing on net revenue, the lotteries are behaving as if the public are shareholders in this state enterprise, and hence that the "bottom line" is a valid guide to the public interest.[18]

However, the normative perspective guiding this revenue maximization objective is incomplete. It ignores the fact that the lottery is a commodity as well as a revenue source. This fact opens the door to a consideration of alternative objectives for government. If the commodity were seen as a more or less harmless form of entertainment, reducing the markup over cost would be welfare-enhancing. Alternatively, the government might believe that lottery games are harmful, perhaps creating negative externalities for nonplayers. After all, gambling has long been viewed as a vice that justifies public concern and government regulation. In that case, high prices would be justified as a means for discouraging consumption, either on efficiency grounds, to reflect negative externalities, or on sumptuary grounds, to signal society's disapproval.

However, two aspects of existing lotteries make it very clear that revenue maximization, and not a desire to curtail consumption, motivate the high price of lotteries. First, the percentage of lottery sales going to the state treasury exceeds the comparable tax rates on alcoholic beverages and on cigarettes, both of which are more harmful commodities by any metric. Although we lack the necessary knowledge about parameters of demand to apply formulas of optimal taxation, it seems very likely that the implicit tax rate on lottery purchases is too high relative to taxes on other commodities.[19] The high price/low payout strategy may serve the public well in their role as "stockholders," but it shortchanges the majority of the public in their dual role as consumers.

The other reason the sumptuary pricing argument fails to explain lottery prices becomes obvious when one examines the second important characteristic of supply – the active marketing of the product. The agencies seek to recruit new players by improving distribution networks and offering coupons and tie-in sales to encourage novices to try playing. To increase sales to regular players they have increased the frequency of drawings, offered some bets on a subscription basis, and (in one state) packaged instant game tickets together in groups of five. Advertising, publicity, and product innovations boost sales by recruiting new players and increasing the activity of existing players. In short, the lottery agencies are clearly *not* interested in discouraging sales of their products. The low payout rate is motivated by revenue rather than sumptuary concerns.

A lottery could be operated in other ways. A state could license one or more private firms to take the place of its lottery agency. This would allow the state to distance itself from the promotion of gambling, but it would also lessen the state's control over operations, which to date has been effective in keeping the games free of corruption. Furthermore, the lottery agencies could increase payout rates to levels typical of other forms of commercial gambling, increasing consumer surplus at the expense of state revenue collections. Another option would be to require lottery agencies to disclose more information on the probability distribution of prizes, and to be more candid in characterizing the value of jackpots paid out in the form of annuities. Restrictions on advertising, of the sort currently in effect in Virginia and Wisconsin, could be adopted in other states.[20] However, states appear to have little enthusiasm for making any major changes in what has become a popular and profitable formula for raising revenue.

Notes

1 From 1878 until 1894, the Louisiana Lottery Company offered the only legal game in the country. Most of its sales were to residents of other states, where lotteries were outlawed. In response to increasing demands for federal intervention, Congress enacted a series of restrictions on the use of the mails to conduct lotteries, and finally in 1895 barred all lottery activity in interstate commerce. The Lottery Company earned its reputation of corruption by routinely bribing Louisiana legislators to continue its monopoly charter in the state.

2 Minnesota's lottery began selling tickets in April 1990.

3   The differences among state lotteries with respect to operating expenses are in part the result of differences in advertising budgets. Collectively lotteries spent 1.4 percent of sales revenue on advertising during fiscal year 1989. At the high end of the distribution, five states spent more than 4 percent: Colorado, Kansas, South Dakota, Virginia, and West Virginia. All of these states had sales below a half billion dollars. Of the nine states with sales above $1 billion, California spent the largest percentage on advertising, at 2.2 percent. Thus part of the scale economies in producing lotteries may be in connection with advertising. (Data from *Gaming & Wagering Business*, March 15, 1990.)

4   These figures refer to implicit tax rates and do not relate to the administrative costs of lottery finance. Some have suggested that lotteries are an especially inefficient form of taxation since it "costs," say, 11 cents to raise 40 cents, which is much higher than the ratio of administrative costs per dollar of revenue raised for most taxes. This comparison is flawed because the 11 cents per dollar of operating costs for lotteries pays for the provision of a product, not just the collection of revenue. The lottery is not simply a tax.

5   South Dakota has such devices in place at lottery outlets. Its video lottery terminals offer an electronic version of poker and several other games. West Virginia lottery has recently introduced video keno at racetracks.

6   Stephen Crocker (1986), a marketing strategist for one of the largest lottery suppliers, Scientific Games, Inc., argued that the Colorado lottery's decision to earmark revenues for parks and recreation made it possible to sell tickets to many citizens who would otherwise not have played.

7   Personal communication from Irving Piliavin, estimated from a national telephone survey conducted by the University of Wisconsin Letters & Science Survey Center between June and August, 1989 ($n = 733$). Results from this survey also show that 20 percent of adults living in states without a lottery played at least once in the preceding year, yielding an overall national participation rate of 47.5 percent.

8   The figures cited are based on *Los Angeles Times* Poll 104, March 1986. Measures of concentration are virtually identical for three surveys that asked respondents to report lottery expenditures for some period preceding the interview: a one-week period (Maryland, 1984), a two-month period (California, 1985), and a twelve-month period (all lottery states combined, 1974). For a discussion of these surveys, see Clotfelter and Cook (1989).

9   This is also referred to as Pareto's law of the "80/20 rule." See Buell (1986, pp. 8–10).

10 This behavior could be understood as an effort by players to limit their net expenditures on lottery products, staying within a self-imposed budget that allocated a certain amount to lottery play each week.

11 Let $C(Q)$ represent operating costs as a function of quantity units, where one quantity unit is defined as one dollar in expected value of prizes. The lottery agency's net profits are given by $N = PQ - Q - C(Q)$, where P is the price charged for a quantity unit. The first-order condition for profit maximization can be written

$$-E_{PQ} = \frac{P(1 - C')}{[P(1 - C') - 1]}$$

If marginal operating costs are 6 percent of sales and the payout rate is 50 percent, we have $P = 2$ and $C' = .12$, implying that the price elasticity of demand at maximum profit is -2.3. For an increase in the payout rate to increase profits, E_{PQ} must exceed 2.3 in absolute value.

12 Log-linear equations were estimated for per capita numbers and lotto sales, where independent variables were population, income, percent black, percent urban, and payout rate. The estimated elasticities of sales with respect to the payout rate (with *t*-statistics in parentheses) were 3.05 (0.7) for numbers and 2.55 (2.3) for lotto. The equations were estimated with 15

and 16 observations, respectively. For the complete equations, see Clotfelter and Cook (1989, Table A.4).

13   If players play randomly, it can be shown that the expected value of a lotto bet increases monotonically with the total amount bet, assuming there is no rollover in the jackpot. The expected value of a lotto bet for a given number of bettors is of course increased if a rollover is added to the pot. Thus the addition of a rollover to the jackpot increases the jackpot both directly, by increasing the available prize money, and indirectly, by attracting more action which also increases the amount of available prize money.

14   The prospect offered by a lotto bet when the jackpot has been augmented by rollovers is qualitatively different than when there are no rollovers; the probability of winning remains the same, but the probability distribution for the amount won (which depends on the number of other winners, since the jackpot is divided among them) is transformed by the increase in the number of players. Thus, strictly speaking, the difference between a lotto drawing with and without rollovers present is not just a difference in "price," as we have defined that term. But the qualitative difference in the two products is slight enough that we believe our regression results can sustain the interpretation offered above.

15   We extended the analysis to take account of the fact that the rollover generates more action and hence a still larger jackpot than the rollover itself would produce. In this "rational expectations" formulation, each $1000 of increase in predicted jackpot size increases play by $333 (S.E. = $15) (Cook and Clotfelter, 1989).

16   This intuition follows from the presumption that players will view lotto as a substitute for other lottery games. Alternatively, a transactions cost argument suggests one basis for complementarity. The introduction of lotto broadens participation in the lottery, and some of these new bettors may not limit themselves to lotto tickets when they make a lottery purchase.

17   Of course, this objective is constrained in various ways. In some states the enabling legislation specifies revenue as the primary objective subject to preservation of "the dignity of the state" (Arizona), "the general welfare of the people" (Michigan), or "the public good" (West Virginia). Every state bans sales to minors, and two states have placed limits on the content of advertising.

18   This bottom line ignores the fact that lottery expenditures affect other sources of tax revenues. Clotfelter and Cook (1989, Chap. 11, App.) offer a general equilibrium model suggesting that the lottery reduces other tax collections by a few percentage points. More important is the question of how lottery promotion affects the public's propensity to work, save, invest, and otherwise engage in productive economic activity. If the image of easy wealth undermines productive activity, the effect on public revenues over the long run could be considerable.

19   The optimal excise tax rate on a commodity depends on its price elasticity, whether it produces externalities, and the distribution of its consumption over income. Ignoring externalities and distribution, the efficient assignment of excise tax rates requires minimization of deadweight loss by taxing those items with elastic demand less heavily than those with inelastic demand. If it is indeed true that the price elasticity of demand for lottery tickets exceeds one in absolute value, as argued above, then lottery taxation generates proportionately greater deadweight loss than taxation of items with inelastic demand. One natural comparison is between the implicit tax rates on lottery products to excise tax rates on alcohol and tobacco. The implicit lottery tax rate in the U.S. exceeds the others, yet on the basis of externality and distributional considerations, and perhaps price elasticity as well, lotteries should probably be taxed less rather than more heavily relative to those commodities. For a discussion of this point, see Clotfelter and Cook (1987).

20   For a discussion of alternative models of lottery operations, see Clotfelter and Cook (1990).

References

Buell, V. P. (ed.) (1986): *Handbook of Modern Marketing*, 2nd edn. New York: McGraw-Hill.

Chernoff, H. (1981): "How to Beat the Massachusetts Numbers Game: An Application of Some Basic Ideas in Probability and Statistics," *Mathematical Intelligencer*, 3, 166–72.

Clotfelter, C. T. and Cook, P. J. (1987): "Implicit Taxation in Lottery Finance," *National Tax Journal*, 40, December, 533–546.

Clotfelter, C. T. and Cook, P. J. (1989): *Selling Hope: State Lotteries in America*. National Bureau of Economic Research monograph. Cambridge: Harvard University Press.

Clotfelter, C. T. and Cook, P. J. (1990): "Redefining 'Success' in the State Lottery Business," *Journal of Policy Analysis and Management*, 9, Winter 99–104.

Commission on the Review of the National Policy toward Gambling (1976): *Gambling in America*. Washington, DC: Government Printing Office.

Cook, P. J. and Clotfelter, C. T. (1989): The Economics of Lotto Duke University, unpublished.

Crocker, S. (1986): "Scientific Games Lure Lifestyles," *American Demographics*, 8, October, 26–7.

Friedman, M. and Savage, L. J. (1948): "The Utility Analysis of Choices Involving Risk," *Journal of Political Economy*, 56, August, 279–304.

Kahneman, D. and Tversky, A. (1979): "Prospect Theory: An Analysis of Decision Under Risk," *Econometrica*, 47, March, 263–91.

Langer, E. J. (1975): "The Illusion of Control," *Journal of Personality and Social Psychology*, 32, 311–28.

Langer, E. J. (1978): "The Psychology of Chance," *Journal for the Theory of Social Behavior*, 7, 185–207.

Los Angeles Times (1986): Poll 104, March.

Thaler, R. H. and Ziemba, W. T. (1988): "Anomalies: Parimutuel Betting Markets: Racetracks and Lotteries," *Journal of Economic Perspectives*, 2, Spring 161–74.

Tversky, A. and Kahneman, D. (1974): "Judgement under Uncertainty: Heuristics and Biases," *Science* 185, 1124–31.

PART III

The Firm's Decision Making in Differing Market Structures

Introduction

Leibenstein in chapter 6 distinguishes between two types of inefficiency that concern microeconomics. The first is *allocative* inefficiency, which arises when firms are assumed to be operating using state-of-the-art techniques most efficiently but are reducing social welfare by exercising pricing power to create deadweight loss. This is the typical social concern with monopoly and oligopoly market structures. The second is *nonallocative* or X-inefficiency, which occurs when lax or incompetent management fails to employ up-to-date technology, when labor is not motivated to perform efficiently, or when inputs are employed in wasteful amounts. The result is lower productivity of factor usage and higher costs.

The paper presents the results of empirical investigations to argue that X-inefficiency is far more costly in social welfare than allocative inefficiency, but that microeconomists give excessive attention to the latter. More deeply, he argues that the qualitative variances of management skills and labor motivation, the imperfect perception of existing or innovative technology by firms, and the inertia which continues to use defective inputs makes the notion of a well-defined production function employing well-defined inputs a questionable concept for realistic analysis.

Chapter 7 complements the arguments of chapter 6 by updating the latter. The modern firm differs fundamentally from the firm of a few decades ago. Instead of the sequenced production line with its specialized capital equipment using narrowly focused labor to produce large quantities of standardized products, computerization of all aspects of product design, manufacture and marketing has created a new prototype. The firm now employs rapidly programmable, flexible equipment permitting quick resetting of lines to produce small batches of product, closely tailored to varying consumer demands. Instead of sequenced production, the firm employs teams of workers enjoying substantial decision-making freedom in radically redesigned floor layouts and using outsourced components frequently modularized in assembly. Close contact is retained with the firm's suppliers, frequently in the design and quality control of its purchased components, and in its drive for "just in time" deliveries of such components to minimize inventories. The net result is a competitively driven attention to the costs of X-inefficiency, with a greater technological capability to reduce or eliminate it.

A new emphasis on product quality and variety is often found in management's approach, and a team concept is used in the design, production planning and marketing strategy for the product. Instead of the design department independently evolving a product, passing it on to production engineers who pass on its feasibility after perhaps months of contemplating complicated blueprints and engaging in compromise bargaining with designers, only to throw the result over the wall to marketing specialists who again pass on its likely salability, the representatives of these departments sit together from the beginning of the design phase.

Milgrom and Roberts present the new firm paradigm in a lucid description, but their unique contribution is to discern intimate interconnections among these developments. The new technology, largely centered in the information revolution, requires that the firm change its manner of decision making in all of the dimensions of management, design, production and marketing simultaneously rather than selectively. The activities are *complements* by virtue of the indirect impacts that changes in one sector require in others. They develop a model that deals with optimal decision making under these conditions.

In terms of the orthodox methodology discussed in chapter 1, important departures are required in the assumption sets noted there, although the underlying methodology is the same. A change in activity A cannot be treated in a marginal way – changing slightly without impacting activities B, C, D, ... Rather, such activities must be changed as a group. The profit function can no longer be viewed as continuous in all state (choice) variables, nor can other instrumental assumptions be made that permit the methodology to obtain realistic solutions in simple ways. Nonconvexities arise – changes in variables do not necessarily give rise to diminishing profit returns. Milgrom and Roberts resort to a lattice methodology to obtain their optima and to perform comparative statics.

The formal model and the explanation of its structure and manipulation are interesting. However, they are not really necessary to understanding the important points that the authors are making about the nature of the new firm and the obsolescence of much of the microeconomic analysis that explicitly or implicitly was based on the mass production technologies of decades ago. The student whose mathematical background does not permit rapid absorption of these portions of the chapter may skip them and concentrate upon the lucid literary explanation of the concepts involved.

Is it possible ever to define a concept in economics in such manner as to include all conditions that must hold in any conceivable environment in which it may be called upon for usage? In chapter 8, Stigler asserts that the answer is no, and uses the notion of perfect competition to illustrate his point. He traces the evolution of its definition from the inexact usage of Adam Smith and the classical economists, through the improvements but still imperfect concepts of the mathematical economists, Marshall, John Bates Clark and finally to Frank H. Knight. Its history is meticulously examined to discern the confusions with other concepts (like the stationary state and uniqueness of equilibrium) that were introduced into its definition until Knight gave it the definition accepted today. Stigler shows how Chamberlin's attempt to soften perfect competition to "pure" competition is unacceptable, and concludes that, in the future, it may have to be altered or extended to meet the conditions of markets not envisaged when he wrote (e.g., the internet markets).

The non-collusive auction market may depart in some respects from the perfectly or purely competitive definition discussed by Stigler in chapter 8, especially in sealed tender auctions where bidders are not aware of prices offered, but they are intensely competitive markets nonetheless. In chapter 9, Milgrom and Weber discuss four auction mechanisms: the *English auction*, with announced bids going from lowest to highest; the *Dutch auction*, where the auctioneer announces descending prices; the *first-price sealed tender*, in which the highest bidder wins the object at his or her bid price; and the *second-price sealed tender*, in which the highest bidder wins the object at the price of the second-highest bidder, so that the size of each bid affects only the probability of winning, not the price paid.

The authors show that the outcomes of these mechanisms depend on whether one or more objects are offered, valuations are private or common to all bidders, such common valuations are known with certainty or not, bidders are risk-averse or risk-neutral, the seller releases information about the object and, if so, whether it is true, and whether reservation prices are placed.

The authors present a general model for risk-neutral bidders that includes the cases of independent and common values. One surprising result is that, with risk-neutral bidders acting with independent valuations, all four auction mechanisms yield Pareto-optimal solutions, and, moreover, it pays sellers to be honest in revealing information. Risk-neutrality is a special case, and probably the exception, but the result is somewhat counterintuitive and, therefore, interesting.

The field of auction bidding and the design of game theoretic optimal bidding strategies is an active one in microeconomics, and this paper is a valuable introduction to it.

One of the controversies that arose with the definitions and analyses of the monopolistic and imperfect competition market structures by Chamberlin and Robinson was the "excess capacity" hypothesis. It asserted that, because the long-run solution in that market structure occurred at a higher average cost than perfect competition brought about, and because products were only slightly differentiated, consumers were penalized by higher prices because of "too many" product brands. Instead of being allowed to buy generic corn flakes at lowest average cost, they were confronted with essentially the same product selling under various brand names at prices reflecting higher average costs: Social inefficiency with firms operating at less than optimal capacity was the result if the consumer had no choice among branded and unbranded products.

In a lucidly written analysis, Spence develops a broader framework in chapter 10 within which to discuss this hypothesis, arguing that production and marketing costs are active restrictions on the number of products produced in this market structure. In terms of social optimality, any potential product whose incremental social surplus (i.e., profits plus consumer surplus) is positive should be produced. In the market economy, however, the decision as to production is made according to the sign of profits alone: expected profits may be negative but consumer surplus positive and sufficiently large to outweigh the negative profits to yield a positive social surplus. Hence, a type of market failure may occur when profits alone dictate brand introduction. Too few, rather than too many, brands may be produced from the viewpoint of social optimality. Large fixed costs and highly inelastic demand functions lead to a bias against the good's introduction. On the other hand, elastic demand functions for products with strong cross-elasticities with other products in the group may lead to socially excessive proliferation. Finally, yet another potential warping of product introductions from the ideal occurs because firms treat the impact of their introduction decisions on other firms' profits as externalities, myopically focusing only on their own.

One of the ongoing debates presently in oligopoly and monopoly theory, reinvigorated recently by the introduction of contestable market theory, is the relative importance of actual versus potential market entry in restraining the pricing power of incumbent firms in an industry, in chapter 11, Gilbert introduces the four most important hypotheses about incumbent firm behavior in the face of potential entrants: limit pricing theory, dynamic limit pricing theory, contestable market theory and strategic behavior among incumbents. What are the assumptions that lie at the base of these theories, and to what extent can they be substantiated on the basis of experimental economics and empirical studies of concentrated industries? The author's discussion presents a lucent presentation of the theories and their limitations, in the face of the difficulties surrounding the research efforts to support or undermine them. Because the airline industry and its recent deregulation are most conformant to the assumptions of contestable market theory, this hypothesis receives the greatest attention in Gilbert's selection. His discussion serves as a useful introduction to chapter 12, which deals with the history of airline industry competition and its recent deregulation in more detail and in broader terms of oligopoly behavior.

The deregulation of the airline industry in the US in 1977–78 gave microeconomists the rare opportunity of observing a major industry, freed from strict government regulation in every aspect of its operation, struggle to achieve a free market equilibrium. Hypotheses abounded: contestability would move the industry to a competitive equilibrium because the sunk costs of entering the industry were thought to be low; the industry would move toward a "natural oligopoly" structure given the economies of density as more seats are filled and the expected constant costs as networks are expanded proportionally; and, in view of these varied expectations, fares would rise or fall.

Not foreseen, however, was the emergence of hub-and-spoke network development, the cooperative arrangements or mergers of large airlines with commuter airlines, the ownership and exploitation of computer reservation systems, the travel agency commission overrides, and the loyalty creating frequent flyer programs. Borenstein, in chapter 12, reveals the direct and more subtle indirect impacts these institutions have had on the structure and strategic functioning of the industry as it continues to move toward a new equilibrium as yet but dimly seen. One broader lesson that emerges from the reading of this paper is the extreme complexity of judging the structure, performance and conduct of modern industries in the many dimensions of firms' decision making. With this difficulty, emerges the controversial choosing of government policies to improve social welfare.

In chapter 13, Gibbons provides a concise introduction to game theoretic concepts and frameworks for readers who are unfamiliar with their basics and usage in microeconomic analysis. It discusses both static and dynamic games with complete and incomplete information, and incorporates strategic equilibrium concepts of Nash equilibrium, subgame perfect Nash equilibrium, and Bayesian Nash equilibrium. The reinterpretation of mixed strategies in static games with incomplete information is noteworthy, and the discussion of subgame perfect equilibrium as a refinement of Nash equilibrium to rule out noncredible threats at each stage of a sequential game, while not new, is extremely clear. The tour of this broad and burgeoning subject is, of necessity, of whirlwind velocity, but the author provides a critical review of existing textbooks for those who wish to examine the subject in greater depth.

In chapter 14, Pauly extends the simpler notion of *moral hazard* into a more complex phenomenon than normally indicated by the term. Generally, this impediment to the insurance principle arises when the fact or extent of insurance alters the probability of occurrence of the undesirable event against which it is written. A fire insurance policy may make the insured more careless in the use of fire than he or she would be absent the policy, health insurance may lead to more carelessness in avoiding unhealthy situations, or collision insurance make may insured drivers more careless behind the wheel.

Pauly deals with health insurance which does not affect the probability of disease but rather where the nonzero elasticity of demand for medical services whose cost is fully covered by (generally government issued) insurance leads individuals to consume such services at levels appropriate to free goods. Although each individual realizes that society must pay for such services at marginal cost, the benefit each receives from the over-indulgence exceeds the cost he or she must pay in taxes for them, since such costs are spread over the host of taxpayers. It is not the probability of suffering disease that is affected by insurance but the likelihood of excessive or unnecessary treatment in this instance of moral hazard.

It follows that establishment by government of such an insurance "market" is not socially optimal without some restrictions upon usage (e.g., deductibles and coinsurance) which would substitute for pricing services at marginal costs. Additional inefficiency arises from failure to design insurance policies to meet the individual needs of consumers.

In a separate argument, the author argues that the derogatory implication of the word "moral" in such individual behavior is misplaced, for the consumer is simply acting "rationally" in treating the service as a free good. While one may properly indict the arsonist exploiting the overinsurance of a building, the individual enjoying unlimited access to medical care at a zero price is simply acting egoistically as market theory preaches. The burden falls on social policy to correct this "market failure" as in other instances of the "tragedy of the commons" where the individual is not forced to face up to the true social costs of his or her consumption.

Spence's seminal article, reproduced in chapter 15, introduced the microeconomics profession to the concepts of *signaling* and *market signaling equilibrium*. Sellers of a commodity (in Spence's example, workers selling their labor services) possess certain characteristics of interest to buyers (potential employers). Some of these characteristics are unchangeable (sex, race, past criminal records), but others (in the example, education level) can be altered by the seller at a cost. Spence terms the unalterable characteristics *indices* and the alterable *signals*. Employers enter negotiations with potential employees with conditional probabilities (whose arguments are these characteristics) of the productivity of the individual. The seller attempts to maximize the difference between the wage offered and the cost of the level of education attained, that characteristic being used as a signal by the seller to the potential buyer of his or her productivity. The buyer is in the position of purchasing a lottery, absent certain knowledge of the potential employee's usefulness, and must base a judgment on such signals (and indices). The conditional probability distributions in the mind of the employer change with feedback from experience with the employment process, until those distributions attain stability in the feedback process. Spence illustrates the private and social implications of such negotiations with simple models.

One helpful hint in reading the paper: when Spence speaks of a negative correlation between productivity and cost of education, he is not speaking of the productivity that may result from the educational spending. Individuals are assumed to have certain native productive capabilities in terms of specific jobs, and the assumption is made that those with lower native capabilities must pay a higher cost (in money, time, psychological travail) to acquire a given educational enhancement than those with higher native capabilities.

In the mathematically demanding chapter 16, Ross analyses the "principal–agent" problem, which arises when one partly gives another the power to act on his or her behalf to confront uncertainty under well-defined circumstances in return for a fee. This type of arrangement arises in a wide variety of circumstances. It is especially interesting under conditions of uncertainty when the payoff to the agent's action is dependent on Nature's choice of contingency state. The principal's problem is to devise an incentivizing fee schedule over the agent's action set that maximizes the principal's expected utility over the contingency states, when utility is a function of the gross payoff less fee paid to the agent.

Ross analyzes this variational problem when such maximization is constrained by (a) the agent's maximization of his or her own expected utility, which is a function of the fee, and (b) the agent's attainment of at least a minimum level of utility reflecting his or her opportunity cost. In simplified conditions, where principal and agent have the same subjective probability distributions over contingency states, Ross investigates the types of utility functions over risky alternatives that would lead to solutions to the principal's problem that are Pareto optimal. When the opportunity cost constraint binds, Ross isolates a family of utility functions that will lead to this result and concludes that they can occur with some frequency. In general, however, the optimal fee schedule will not be Pareto optimal. A primary virtue of this paper is the demonstration of the variational methods used to derive the fee schedule and the necessary conditions that must hold to maximize the Hamiltonian involved.

In chapter 17, Machina begins with a discussion of received microeconomic theory of decision making under risk which evolved from the expected value valuation of "lotteries" to the expected utility valuation using von Neumann–Morgenstern cardinal utility indices under risk to classify agents as risk-averse, risk-neutral or risk-loving. Such valuations, however, are linear in the probabilities of the lotteries, which implies that the probability combinations yielding equal expected utility lie along parallel straight lines (for lotteries with three outcomes) in probability space. So also, under the same conditions, will isocontour lines for expected value. Finally, the common slope for expected utility isocontours will be greater than that for expected value contours for risk-averse agents and less for risk-loving agents.

However, such empirically based challenges as Allais' Paradox reveal that decision-making agents frequently do not reveal such monotonic relations between the slopes of these isocontours, which violates the axiom of linearity in the probabilities. Machina skillfully leads the reader through the implications of such challenges to the received theory and suggests explanations for them. In addition, he deals with such puzzles as why agents frequently choose between two lotteries in one way, yet value them for sale or purchase in another. This violates consistency (transitivity) which, in the received theory, is unacceptable. Psychologists suggest that agents may follow independent modes in choice and valuation – a position that economists generally do not accept. The author deals skillfully with this paradox as well.

To conclude his presentation, Machina discusses the impact of different framing modes on agents' choices, as well as problems arising with subjective probabilities when objective probabilities do not exist. Do subjects consistently overestimate the importance of posterior outcomes in altering prior values? Indeed, do subjective probabilities exist in the minds of agents in making decisions under uncertainty?

In dealing with these matters, the paper provides a concise introduction to the major problems confronting the economist seeking consistent theories of decision making under risk and uncertainty.

III A

The Firm's Decision Making Under Certainty: All Market Structures

CHAPTER SIX

Allocative Efficiency vs. "X-Efficiency"

Harvey Leibenstein

Source: *American Economic Review*, 56 (1966), pp. 392–415. Reprinted with the permission of Mrs. M. Leibenstein and the American Economic Association. © American Economic Association.

At the core of economics is the concept of efficiency. Microeconomic theory is concerned with allocative efficiency. Empirical evidence has been accumulating that suggests that the problem of allocative efficiency is trivial. Yet it is hard to escape the notion that efficiency in some broad sense is significant. In this paper I want to review the empirical evidence briefly and to consider some of the possible implications of the findings, especially as they relate to the theory of the firm and to the explanation of economic growth. The essence of the argument is that microeconomic theory focuses on allocative efficiency to the exclusion of other types of efficiencies that, in fact, are much more significant in many instances. Furthermore, improvement in "nonallocative efficiency" is an important aspect of the process of growth.

In section 1 the empirical evidence on allocative efficiency is presented. In this section we also consider the reasons why allocation inefficiency is frequently of small magnitude. Most of the evidence on allocative inefficiency deals with either monopoly or international trade. However, monopoly and trade are not the focus of this paper. Our primary concern is with the broader issue of allocative efficiency versus an initially undefined type of efficiency that we shall refer to as "X-efficiency." The magnitude and nature of this type of efficiency is examined in sections 2 and 3. Although a major element of "X-efficiency" is motivation, it is not the only element, and hence the terms "motivation efficiency" or "incentive efficiency" have not been employed.

As he proceeds, the reader is especially invited to keep in mind the sharp contrast in the magnitudes involved between Tables 1 and 2.

1. Allocative Inefficiency: Empirical Evidence

The studies that are of interest in assessing the importance of allocative efficiency are summarized in Table 1. These are of two types. On the one side we have the studies of Harberger and Schwartzman on the "social welfare cost" of monopoly. On the other side we have a number of studies, among them those by Johnson, Scitovsky, Wemelsfelder, Janssen, and others, on the benefits of reducing or eliminating restrictions to trade. In

Table 1   Calculated "welfare loss" as percentage of gross or net national product attributed to misallocation of resources

Study	Source	Country	Cause	Loss (%)
A. C. Harberger	*A.E.R.* 1954	U.S.A. 1929	Monopoly	.07
D. Schwartzman	*J.P.E.* 1960	U.S.A. 1954	Monopoly	.01
T. Scitovsky	(1)	Common Market 1952	Tariffs	.05
J. Wemelsfelder	*E.J.* 1960	Germany 1958	Tariffs	.18
L. H. Janssen	(2)	Italy 1960	Tariffs	max. .1
H. G. Johnson	*Manchester School* 1958	U. K. 1970	Tariffs	max. 1.0
A. Singh	(3)	Montevideo Treaty Countries	Tariffs	max. .0075

Sources:
(1) [29].
(2) [16].
(3) Unpublished calculation made by A. Singh based on data found in A. A. Faraq, *Economic Integration: A Theoretical, Empirical Study*, University of Michigan, Ph.D. Thesis, 1963.

both cases the computed benefits attributed to the reallocation of resources turn out to be exceedingly small.

Let us look at some of the findings. In the original Harberger study [14] the benefits for eliminating monopoly in the United States would raise income no more than 1/13 of 1 per cent. Schwartzman's [28] study which recomputes the benefits of eliminating monopoly by comparing Canadian monopolized industries as against counterpart competitive U.S. industries, and vice versa in order to determine the excess price attributable to monopoly, ends up with a similar result. Similarly, the benefits attributed to superior resource allocation as a consequence of the Common Market or a European Free Trade Area are also minute – usually much less than 1 per cent.

The calculations made by Scitovsky of the benefits to the Common Market (based on Verdoorn's data) led him to the conclusion that "the most striking feature of these estimates is their smallness. The one that is really important (for reasons to appear presently), the gain from increased specialization . . . which is less than one-twentieth of one per cent of the gross social product of the countries involved. This is ridiculously small . . ." [29, p. 64]. J. Wemelsfelder [33, p. 100] has calculated that the welfare gain of reducing import duties and increasing imports and exports accordingly amounts to .18 of 1 per cent of national income. Harry Johnson in an article on England's gain in joining a Free Trade Area [17, pp. 247 ff.] calculates the net gain from trade at less than 1 per cent. That is, Johnson arrives at the conclusion that 1 per cent of the national income would be the absolute maximum gain for Britain from entering the European Free Trade Area.

A recent study by L. H. Janssen [16, p. 132] calculates that the gains from increased specialization for the different countries of the European Economic Community would be largest for Italy, but even here the amount is only 1/10 of 1 per cent of total production.[1] Janssen points out that, if the production gain for Italy due to specialization were calculated by Scitovsky's method, which he believes involves an overestimation, "the production gain in the most extreme case is still less than .4 per cent." Janssen concludes, as have others, that the welfare effects of a customs union based on the superior allocation of resources are likely to be trivial. He does, however, point to the possibility "that the mere prospect of the frontiers opening would infuse fresh energy into entrepreneurs." He recognizes that certain qualitative factors may be highly important and that the consequences of growth are certainly more significant than those of allocative welfare.

My research assistant, A. Singh, has calculated the gains from trade (following the Scitovsky method) for the Montevideo Treaty Countries[2] (Argentina, Brazil, Chile, Mexico, Paraguay, Peru, and Uruguay) and found it to be less than 1/150 of 1 per cent of their combined GNP. Even if we double or triple this result to allow for such factors as the effect of failing to take account of quantitative restrictions in the analysis, the outcome is still trivial.

Harberger's study on Chile [14] which involves the reallocation of both labor and capital yields a relatively large estimate. Harberger intends to obtain as large an estimate as possible of the consequences of reallocating resources by using what I believe to be (and what he admits to be) rather extreme assumptions in order to obtain maximum outer bounds. Despite this he comes up with a number that is between 9 and 15 per cent. However, no actual data are employed. What are used are outer-bound estimates based on personal impressions. I expect that a careful study similar to the Verdoorn–Scitovsky study would probably come up with numbers that would be no larger than 1 or 2 per cent.

The empirical evidence, while far from exhaustive, certainly suggests that the welfare gains that can be achieved by increasing *only* allocative efficiency are usually exceedingly small, at least in capitalist economies. In all but one of the cases considered all of the gains are likely to be made up in one month's growth. They hardly seem worth worrying about.

Let us see briefly why these gains are usually small. We cannot prove that we would expect them to be small on purely theoretical grounds. If we combine our theory with what we could agree are probably reasonable estimates of some of the basic magnitudes, then it appears likely that in many cases (but certainly not all *possible* cases) the welfare loss of allocative inefficiency is of trivial significance. The idea could be developed with the aid of the diagram employed by Harberger. (See Figure 1.) In Figure 1 we assume that costs are constant within the relevant range. D is the demand function. Under competition price and quantity are determined at the intersection C. The monopoly price is above the competitive price equal to AB in the figure. The monopoly output is determined at the point A. The welfare loss due to monopoly, which is the same as the welfare gain if we shifted to competition, is equal to the triangle ABC. We obtain an approximation to this amount by multiplying the price differential AB by the quantity differential BC by one-half and multiplying this by the proportion of national income in industries involving the misallocation.

Let us play around with some numbers and see the kind of results we get as a consequence of this formulation. Suppose that half of the national output is produced in monopolized industries and that the price differential is 20 per cent and that the average elasticity of demand is 1.5. Now the outcome will turn out to be $1\frac{1}{2}$ per cent. But we really used enormous figures for the misallocation. And yet the result is small. Monopoly prices, according to estimates, appear to be only about 8 per cent on the average above competitive prices. We can substitute some reason other than monopoly for the misallocation and still come out with similar results.[3]

Consider the cases of subsidized industries under some sort of governmental inducements to growth; and that of governmentally run industries. In the subsidy case the

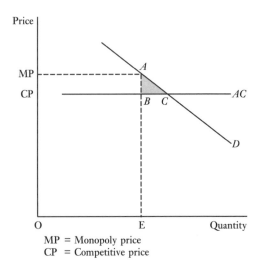

MP = Monopoly price
CP = Competitive price

Figure 1

calculation would be similar. Suppose that as much as 50 per cent of the industries are subsidized to the extent of a 20 per cent difference in cost and that the output point on the demand function is where elasticity is unity. This last point may be reasonable since the operators of subsidized industries might want gross revenue to be as large as possible. If, on the other hand, we assume that they are profit maximizers and restrict output to a greater extent, then we might assume a price elasticity of two. This latter, however, is unlikely because monopoly profits are inconsistent with subsidized industries. Those who receive the subsidy would have the legitimate fear that the subsidy would be lowered if unusual profits were earned. Hence, behavior in the direction of revenue maximization appears reasonable and the calculated welfare loss is less than 2 per cent.

A similar result could be achieved in the case in which the government runs industries that affect 50 per cent of the national income of an economy. In all the cases we have considered, the magnitudes chosen appear to be on the large side and the outcome is on the small side.

Of course, it is possible that the magnitude of allocative inefficiency would be large if there are large discontinuities in productivity between those industries where inputs are located and those industries to which the same inputs could be moved. This, in effect. is the basic assumption that Harberger made in his study of Chile [14]. But if it turns out that there is a reasonable degree of continuity in productivity, and that the only way shifts could be made is by simultaneously increasing either social overhead capital or direct capital in order to make the shifts involved, then, of course, a great deal of the presumed gains would be eaten up by the capital costs and the net marginal gains would turn out to be rather small. My general impression is that this is likely to be the case in a great many underdeveloped countries where differential productivities appear to exist between the agricultural sector and the industrial sector. One cannot go beyond stating vague impressions since there is a lack of hard statistical evidence on this matter.

Why are the welfare effects of reallocation so small? Allocational inefficiency involves only the net marginal effects. The basic assumption is that every firm *purchases and utilizes* all of its inputs "efficiently." Thus, what is left is simply the consequences of price and quantity distortions. While some specific price distortions might be large it seems unlikely that all relative price distortions are exceptionally large. This implies that most quantity distortions must also be relatively small since for a given aggregate output a significant distortion in one commodity will be counterbalanced by a large number of small distortions in the opposite direction in quantities elsewhere. While it is possible to *assume* relative price distortions and quantity distortions that would be exceedingly high, it would be difficult to believe that, without intent, the sum of such distortions should be high. However, it is not *necessarily* so on purely *a priori* grounds.

There is one important type of distortion that cannot easily be handled by existing microeconomic theory. This has to do with the allocation of managers. It is conceivable that in practice a situation would arise in which managers are exceedingly poor, that is, others are available who do not obtain management posts, and who would be very much superior. Managers determine not only their own productivity but the productivity of all cooperating units in the organization. It is therefore possible that the actual loss due to such a misallocation might be large. But the theory does not allow us to examine this matter because firms are presumed to exist as entities that make optimal input decisions, apart from the decisions of its managers. This is obviously a contradiction and therefore cannot be handled.

2. X-Efficiency: The Empirical Evidence

We have seen that the welfare loss due to allocational inefficiency is frequently no more than 1/10 of 1 per cent. Is it conceivable that the value of X-inefficiency would be larger than that? One way of looking at it is to return to the problem of the welfare loss due to monopoly. Suppose that one-third of the industries are in the monopolized sector. Is it possible that the lack of competitive pressure of operating in monopolized industries would lead to cost 3/10 of a per cent higher than would be the case under competition? This magnitude seems to be very small, and hence it certainly seems to be a possibility. The question essentially, is whether we can visualize managers bestirring themselves sufficiently, if the environment forced them to do so, in order to reduce costs by more than 3/10 of 1 per cent. Some of the empirical evidence available suggests that not only is this a possibility, but that the magnitudes involved are very much larger. As we shall see, the spotty evidence on this subject does not prove the case but it does seem to be sufficiently persuasive to suggest the possibility that X-efficiency exists, and that it frequently is much more significant than allocational efficiency.

Professor Eric Lundberg in his studies of Swedish industries points to the case of the steel plant at Horndal that was left to operate without any new capital investment or *technological change*, and furthermore maintenance and replacement were kept at a minimum, and yet output per man hour rose by 2 per cent per annum. Professor Lundberg asserts that according to his interviews with industrialists and technicians "sub-optimal disequilibrium in regard to technology and utilization of existing capital stock is a profoundly important aspect of the situation at any time." (This according to Gorin Ohlin's summary of Lundberg's findings [24].) If a suboptimal disequilibrium exists at any time, then it would seem reasonable that under the proper motivations managers and workers could bestir themselves to produce closer to optimality, and that under other conditions they may be motivated to move farther away from optimality.

Frederick Harbison reports visiting two petroleum refineries in Egypt less than one-half mile apart. "The labor productivity of one had been nearly double that in the other for many years. But recently, under completely new management, the inefficient refinery was beginning to make quite spectacular improvements in efficiency with the same labor force" [15, p. 373]. We may inquire why the management was changed only recently whereas the difference in labor productivity existed for many years. It is quite possible that had the motivation existed in sufficient strength, this change could have taken place earlier.

In a recent book on the firm, Neil Chamberlain [5, p. 341] visualizes his firms reacting to variances between forecasted revenues and expenditures and actual. He quotes from the president of a corporation: "Actual sales revenue for the fiscal year varied one per cent from the original forecast. Expenditures varied 30 per cent. The reasons were practically entirely due to manufacturing problems of inefficiency and quality.... The only actions specifically taken were in attempted changes in methods of production ... [and] the use of an engineering consulting firm...."One would have thought that the cost-reducing activities mentioned could be carried out irrespective of the variance. Nevertheless, the quotation clearly implies that, in fact, they would not have been motivated to attempt the changes were it not that they were stimulated by the variance.

Before proceeding to present more empirical evidence on the possible magnitude of X-efficiency it is of importance to say something about the nature of the data. The empirical evidence does not present many unambiguous cases. Most of the evidence has to do with specific firms or, at best, industries, and not for the economy as a whole. In the evidence presented on allocative efficiency the entire economy was considered. It is quite possible that the cases considered are entirely atypical and could not be duplicated in large segments of the economy. In addition, the cases do not always deal with X-efficiency in a pure sense. Some additional inputs or reallocations are sometimes involved. Also uncertainty elements and accidental variations play a role. Nevertheless, it seems that the magnitudes involved are so large that they suggest that the conjecture that X-efficiency is frequently more significant than allocative efficiency must be taken seriously.

Now let us turn to Tables 1 and 2. In contrast to Table 1 where the misallocation effects are small, we see in Table 2 that the X-efficiency effects, at least for specific firms, are usually large. Table 2 abstracts (in the interest of conserving space) from a much more comprehensive table developed by Kilby [19] that summarizes the results of a number of ILO productivity missions. (I usually picked for each country the first three and the last items contained in Kilby's table.) It is to be observed that the cost-reducing methods used do not involve additional capital nor, as far as one can tell, any increase in depreciation or obsolescence of existing capital. The methods usually involve some simple reorganizations of the production process, e.g., plant-layout reorganization, materials handling, waste controls, work methods, and payments by results. It is of interest that the cost reductions are frequently above 25 per cent and that this result is true for a technically advanced country such as Israel as well as for the developing countries considered in other parts of the table. If the firms and/or operations considered are representative, then it would appear that the contrast in significance between X-efficiency and allocative efficiency is indeed startling. Representativeness has not been established. However, the reports of the

Table 2 ILO productivity mission results

Factory or operation	Method[a]	Increase in labor productivity (%)	Impact on the firm (Unit cost reduction)	
			Labor savings (%)	Capital[b] savings (%)
India				
Seven textile mills	n.a.	5-to-250	5–71	5–71
Engineering firms				
All operations	F, B	102	50	50
One operation	F	385	79	79
One operation	F	500	83	83
Burma				
Molding railroad brake shoes	A, F, B	100	50	50
Smithy	A	40	29	29
Chair assembly	A, B	100	50	50
Match manufacture	A, F	24	19	–
Indonesia				
Knitting	A, B	15	13	–
Radio assembly	A, F	40	29	29
Printing	A, F	30	23	–
Enamel ware	F	30	23	–
Malaya				
Furniture	A, D	10	9	9
Engineering workshop	A, D	10	9	9
Pottery	A, B	20	17	17
Thailand				
Locomotive maintenance	A, F	44	31	31
Saucepan polishing	E, D	50	33	–
Saucepan assembly	B, F	42	30	–
Cigarettes	A, B	5	5	–
Pakistan				
Textile plants	C, H, G			
Weaving		50	33	33
Weaving		10	9	9
Bleaching		59	37	37
Weaving		141	29	29
Israel				
Locomotive repair	F, B, G	30	23	23
Diamond cutting and polishing	C, B, G	45	31	–
Refrigerator assembly	F, B, G	75	43	43
Orange picking	F	91	47	–

[a] A = plant layout reorganized; B = machine utilization and flow; C = simple technical alterations; D = materials handling; E = waste control; F = work method; G = payment by results; H = workers training and supervision
[b] Limited to plant and equipment, excluding increased depreciation costs.
Source: P. Kilby [19, p. 305].

productivity missions do not suggest that they went out of their way to work only on cases where large savings in costs could be obtained. By comparative standards (with other productivity missions) some of the results were modest, and in some cases Kilby reports that when some members of the missions returned to some of the firms they had worked on previously (e.g., in Pakistan) they found a reversion to previous methods and productivities.

There are of course a number of other studies, in addition to those by Lundberg and Harbison just mentioned which present results similar to the ILO reports. L. Rostas in his study of comparative productivity in British and American industry [26] points to the finding that differences in amount and quality of machinery per worker and the rates of utilization and replacement do not account for the entire difference in output per worker in the two countries. He further states that "in a number of industries (or firms) where the equipment is very largely identical in the U.S. and U.K., eggs, boots and shoes, tobacco, strip steel (or in firms producing both in the U.K. and U.S....), there are still substantial differences in output per worker in the U.K. and the U.S." Clearly there is more to the determination of output than the obviously observable inputs. The nature of the management, the environment in which it operates, and the incentives employed are significant.

That changes in incentives will change productivity per man (and cost per unit of output) is demonstrated clearly by a wide variety of studies on the effects of introducing payments by results schemes. Davison, Florence, Gray, and Ross [7, p. 203] review the literature in this area for British industry, survey the results for a number of manufacturing operations, and present illustrative examples of their findings from a number of firms. The summary of their findings follows: "The change in output per worker was found to vary among the different operations all the way from an increase of 7.5 per cent to one of 291 per cent, about half the cases falling between 43 per cent and 76 per cent. Such increases in output, most of them large, from our 'first-line' case histories, and from additional evidence, were found not to be just a 'flash in the pan' but were sustained over the whole period of study."

Roughly similar findings were obtained for the consequences of introducing payments by results in Australia, Belgium, India, the Netherlands, and the United States [36]. In Victoria it was found that "soundly designed and properly operated incentive plans have in practice increased production rate in the reporting firms from 20 to 50 per cent." In the Netherlands labor efficiency increases of 36.5 per cent were reported. It seems clear that with the same type of equipment the working tempo varies considerably both between different workers and different departments. Appropriate incentives can obviously change such tempos considerably and reduce costs, without any changes in purchasable inputs per unit.

The now-famous Hawthorne Studies [25] suggest that the mere fact that management shows a special interest in a certain group of workers can increase output. That is, management's greater interest in the group on whom the experiments were tried, both when working conditions were improved and when they were worsened, created a positive motivation among the workers. (The magnitudes were from 13 to 30 per cent [20].) In one of the ILO missions to Pakistan an improvement in labor relations in a textile mill in Lyallpur resulted in a productivity increase of 30 per cent. Nothing else was changed except that labor turnover was reduced by one-fifth [37] [38].

Individual variations in worker proficiency are probably larger than plant differences. Frequently the variation between the best to poorest worker is as much as four to one.

Certainly improved worker selection could improve productivity at the plant level. To the extent that people are not working at what they are most proficient at, productivity should rise as a consequence of superior selection methods [13, p. 147].

Although there is a large literature on the importance of psychological factors on productivity, it is usually quite difficult to assess this literature because many psychologists work on the basis of high- and low-productivity groups but do not report the actual numerical differences. In general, it seems that some of the psychological factors studied in terms of small-group theory can account for differences in productivity of from 7 to 18 per cent. The discoveries include such findings as:

1   up to a point smaller working units are more productive than larger ones;
2   working units made up of friends are more productive than those made up of nonfriends;
3   units that are generally supervised are more efficient than those that are closely supervised [1], and
4   units that are given more information about the importance of their work are more proficient than those given less information [32].

A partial reason for these observed differences is probably the likelihood that individual motivation towards work is differently affected under the different circumstances mentioned.

The shorter-hours movement in Western Europe and in the United States, especially up to World War I, has some interesting lessons for productivity differentials without capital changes. Economists frequently assume that for a given capital stock and quality of work force, output will be proportional to number of hours worked. Experiments during World War I and later showed that not only was the proportionality law untrue, but that frequently *absolute* output actually increased with reductions in hours – say from a ten-hour day to an eight-hour day.[4] It was also found that with longer hours a disproportionate amount of time was lost from increased absenteeism, industrial accidents, and so on. In many cases it would obviously have been to a firm's interest to reduce hours below that of the rest of the industry. Firms could have investigated these relations and taken advantage of the findings. For the most part, governments sponsored the necessary research on the economics of fatigue and unrest under the stimulus of the war effort, when productivity in some sectors of the economy was believed to be crucial. The actual reduction of hours that took place was a consequence of the pressure of labor unions and national legislation.

In this connection it is of interest to note that Carter and Williams [4, pp. 57ff.] in their study of investment in innovations found that a high proportion (over 40 per cent) was of a "passive" character – i.e., either in response to the "direct pressure of competition" or "force of example of firms (etc.) other than immediate rivals." Unfortunately it is difficult to find data that would represent the obverse side of the coin; namely, data that would suggest the degree to which firms do not innovate for lack of a sufficient motivating force, such as a lack of competitive pressure. However, there is a great deal of evidence that the delay time between invention and innovation is often exceedingly long (sometimes more than 50 years) [9, pp. 305–6], and the lag time between the use of new methods in the "best practice" firms in an industry and other firms is also often a matter of years. Salter in his study on *Productivity and Technical Change* [27, p. 98] points to the following striking example. "In the United States copper mines, electric locomotives allow a cost saving of 67 per cent yet although first used in the mid-twenties, by 1940 less than a third of locomotives in use were electric."[5] Other similar examples are mentioned by Salter and others. A survey of industrial research undertaken by 77 companies showed that one-third were carrying on research for "aggressive purposes," but that two-thirds were "forced into research for defensive purposes." [3]

The relation between the "cost" of advice or consulting services and the return obtained has not been worked out for the ILO productivity missions as a whole. In one case (in Pakistan) the savings affected in three textile mills as a consequence of the work of the mission during the year that the mission was there "represented about 20 times the entire cost of the mission in that year." While the study does not indicate how representative this result was, the impression one gets is that rates of return of rather large magnitudes are not entirely unusual.

J. Johnston studied the return to consulting services in Great Britain. For the class of jobs where it was possible to make a quantitative assessment of the results (600 jobs were involved), it was found that on the average the rate of return was about 200 per cent on consulting fees [18, p. 248]. Johnston's study is of special interest for our purposes because (a) it is a very careful study, and (b) the magnitudes of increases in productivity are of the same order (although the variations are less extreme) as those obtained in underdeveloped countries. The nature of the consulting work was not too dissimilar to that carried out by the ILO teams. On the whole they involved improvements in general management, plant layout, personnel, production procedures, selling organization, management and budgeting and accounting systems. For the consulting jobs whose consequences were quantitatively assessed, the average increase in productivity was 53 per cent, the lowest quartile showed an increase of 30 per cent, and the highest quartile 70 per cent [18, p. 273].

The studies mentioned deal with examples that are more or less of a microeconomic nature. In recent years we have had a number of studies that are their *macro*economic complements. The work of Solow, Aukrust, Denison, and others show that only a small proportion of increase in GNP is accounted for by increases in inputs of labor or capital. The "unexplained residual" covers about 50 per cent to 80 per cent of growth in advanced countries [2] [10] [23] [30] [31]. The residual comprehends a greater range of "noninput" growth factors (e.g., technological change, education of the labor force) than was covered in the examples we considered, but the motivational efficiency elements may account for some fraction of the residual. (For example, Johnston estimates that one quarter of the annual increase in product is accounted for by consulting services.)

What conclusions can we draw from all of this? First, the data suggest that there is a great deal of possible variation in output for similar amounts of capital and labor and for similar techniques, in the broad sense, to the extent that technique is determined by similar types of equipment. However, in most of the studies the nature of the influences involved are mixed, and in some cases not all of them are clear to the analyst. In many instances there appears to have been an attempt to impart knowledge, at least of a managerial variety, which accounts for *some* of the increase in output. But should this knowledge be looked upon as an increase in inputs of production in all instances? Although the first reaction might be that such attempts involve inputs similar to inputs of capital or labor, I will want to argue that in many instances this is not the case.

It is obvious that not every change in technique implies a change in knowledge. The knowledge may have been there already, and a change in circumstances induced the change in technique. In addition, knowledge may not be used to capacity just as capital or labor may be underutilized. More important, a good deal of our knowledge is vague. A man may have nothing more than a sense of its existence, and yet this may be the critical element. Given a sufficient inducement, he can then search out its nature in detail and get it to a stage where he can use it. People normally operate within the bounds of a great deal of intellectual slack. Unlike underutilized capital, this is an element that is very difficult to observe. As a result, occasions of genuine additions to knowledge become rather difficult to distinguish from those circumstances in which no new knowledge has been added, but in which existing knowledge is being utilized to greater capacity.

Experience in U.S. industry suggests that adversity frequently stimulates cost-reducing attempts, some of which are successful, within the bounds of existing knowledge [12]. In any event, some of the studies suggest that motivational aspects are involved entirely apart from additional knowledge. The difficulty of assessment arises because these elements are frequently so intertwined that it is difficult to separate them.

Let us now consider types of instances in which the motivational aspect appears fairly clearly to play a role. The ILO studies discuss a number of cases in which there had been reversion to previous less efficient techniques when demonstration projects were revisited after a year or more. This seems to have occurred both in India and in Pakistan [38, p. 157]. Clearly, the new knowledge, if there were such knowledge, was given to the management by the productivity mission at the outset, and the new management methods were installed at least for the period during which the productivity mission was on hand, but there was not a sufficient motivational force for the management to maintain the new methods. The "Hawthorne effects" are of a more clear-cut nature. Here an intentional reversion to previous methods still led to some increases in output simply because the motivational aspects were more important than the changes in the work methods. The ILO mission reports also mention with regret the fact that techniques applied in one portion of a plant, which led to fairly large increases in productivity, were not taken over by the management and applied to other aspects of the production process, although they could quite easily have done so [38, p. 157]. In a sense we may argue that the knowledge was available to the management, but that somehow it was not motivated to transfer techniques from one portion of a plant to another.

Studies which showed increases in output as a consequence of introducing payment by results clearly involve motivational elements. For the men subjected to the new payment scheme economic motivations are involved. For the management the situation is less clear. It is possible that in many instances the firms were not aware of the possible advantages of payment by results until they obtained the new knowledge that led to the introduction of the scheme. However, it seems most likely that this scheme is so well known that this is not the case in all, or in many instances. Management quite likely had to be motivated to introduce the scheme by some factors either within the firm or within the industry. In any event, these studies clearly suggest that for some aspects of production, motivational elements are significant.

Both the ILO studies and the Johnston study speak of the need to get the acceptance of top management for the idea of obtaining and implementing consulting advice. In addition, the ILO studies make the point that low productivity is frequently caused by top management's concern with the commercial and financial affairs of the firm rather than with the running of the factory. The latter was frequently treated as a very subordinate task. Whether this last aspect involves a lack of knowledge or a lack of motivation is difficult to determine. However, it seems hard to believe that if some top-management people in some of the firms in a given industry were to become concerned with factory management and achieve desirable results thereby, some of the others would not follow suit. Johnston makes the point that, "without the willing cooperation of management the consultant is unlikely to be called in the first instance or to stay for long if he does come in" [18, p. 237]. The ILO missions make similar remarks.

It is quite clear that consulting services are not only profitable to consultants but also highly profitable to many of the firms that employ them. But it is rather surprising that more of these services are not called for. Part of the answer may be that managements of firms are not motivated to hire consultants if things appear to be going "in any reasonably satisfactory rate." There are, of course, numerous personal resistances to calling for outside advice. If the motivation is strong enough, e.g., the threat of the failure of the firm, then it is likely that such resistances would be overcome. But these are simply different aspects of the motivational elements involved.

3. The Residual and X-Efficiency: An Interpretation

The main burden of these findings is that X-inefficiency exists, and that improvement in X-efficiency is a significant source of increased output. In general, we may specify three elements as significant in determining what we have called X-efficiency:

1   intra-plant motivational efficiency,
2   external motivational efficiency, and
3   nonmarket input efficiency.

The simple fact is that neither individuals nor firms work as hard, nor do they search for information as effectively, as they could. The importance of motivation and its association with degree of effort and search arises because the relation between inputs and outputs is *not* a determinate one. There are four reasons why given inputs cannot be transformed into predetermined outputs:

(a)   contracts for labor are incomplete,
(b)   not all factors of production are marketed,
(c)   the production function is not completely specified or known, and
(d)   interdependence and uncertainty lead competing firms to cooperate tacitly with each other in some respects, and to imitate each other with respect to technique, to some degree.

The conventional theoretical assumption, although it is rarely stated, is that inputs have a fixed specification and yield a fixed performance. This ignores other likely possibilities. Inputs may have a fixed specification that yields a variable performance, or they may be of a variable specification and yield a variable performance. Some types of complex machinery may have fixed specifications, but their performance may be variable depending on the exact nature of their employment. The most common case is that of labor services of various kinds that have variable specifications and variable performance – although markets sometimes operate as if much of the labor of a given class has a fixed specification. Moreover, it is exceedingly rare for all elements of performance in a labor contract to be spelled out. A good deal is left to custom, authority, and whatever motivational techniques are available to management as well as to individual discretion and judgment.

Similarly, the production function is neither completely specified nor known. There is always an experimental element involved so that something may be known about the current state; say the existing relation between inputs and outputs, but not what will happen given changes in the input ratios. In addition, important inputs are frequently not marketed or, if they are traded, they are not equally accessible (or accessible on equal terms) to all potential buyers. This is especially true of management knowledge. In many areas of the world managers may not be available in well-organized markets. But even when they are available, their capacities may not be known. One of the important capacities of management may be the degree to which managers can obtain factors of production that in fact are not marketed in well-organized markets or on a universalistic basis. In underdeveloped countries the capacity to obtain finance may depend on family connections. Trustworthiness may be similarly determined. Some types of market information may be available to some individuals but not purchasable in the market. For these and other reasons it seems clear that it is one thing to purchase or hire inputs in a given combination; it is something else to get a a predetermined output out of them.

Another possible interpretation of the data presented is in connection with the "residual" in economic growth analysis. The residual manifests itself in three basic ways:

1 through cost reduction in the production of existing commodities without inventions or innovations;
2 the introduction of innovations in processes of production; and
3 the introduction of new commodities or, what is the same thing, quality improvements in consumer goods or inputs.

We have ignored the introduction of new commodities, but the other two elements are pertinent here. The data suggest that cost reduction that is essentially a result of improvement in X-efficiency is likely to be an important component of the observed residual in economic growth. In addition, there is no doubt that, in some of the cases of reduced cost, new knowledge was conveyed to the firms involved, and this too is part of the residual. It is of special interest that such new knowledge involves knowledge dissemination rather than invention. The detailed studies suggest that the magnitudes are large, and hence a significant part of the residual does not depend on the types of considerations that have been prominent in the literature in recent years, such as those that are *embodied* in capital accumulation or in invention. We have considered the problem in terms of decreasing real costs per unit of output. It is clear that for a given set of resources, if real costs per unit of output are decreased, then total output will grow, and output per unit of input will also rise. Such efforts to reduce cost are part of the contribution of the residual to economic growth.

Both competition and adversity create some pressure for change. Even if knowledge is vague, if the incentive is strong enough there will be an attempt to augment information so that it becomes less vague and possibly useful. Where consulting advice is available it is significant that relatively few firms buy it. Clearly, motivations play a role in determining the degree that consulting advice is sought. The other side of the coin is that, where the motivation is weak, firm managements will permit a considerable degree of slack in their operations and will not seek cost-improving methods. Cyert and March [6, pp. 37, 38, 242] point to cases in which costs per unit are allowed to rise when profits are high. In the previous sections we have cited cases in which there was a reversion to less efficient methods after the consultants left the scene. Thus we have instances where competitive pressures from other firms or adversity lead to efforts toward cost reduction, and the absence of such pressures tends to cause costs to rise.

Some of the essential points made in the previous paragraphs can be illustrated diagramatically, if (in the interest of simplicity) we allow for abstraction from some of the realities of the situation. The main ideas to be illustrated are as follows:

1   Some firms operate under conditions of nonminimum costs, and it is possible for an industry to have a nonminimal cost equilibrium.
2   Improvements in X-efficiency are part of the process of development, and probably a significant proportion of the "residual."

In what follows we assume that there are many firms, and that each firm's output is sufficiently small so as not to affect the output, costs, or prices set by other firms. For simplicity we also assume that for each firm there is an average total unit cost (ATUC) curve that has a significant horizontal segment at its trough, and that the output selected will be on that segment. When we visualize a firm's costs reacting to competitive conditions in the industry we imply that the entire ATUC curve moves up or down. Some firms are presumed to react to changes in the unit cost of production of the industry as a whole, i.e., to the weighted average of the unit costs of all the firms, in which each firm's weight is in proportion to its contribution to the output of the industry. Here we posit a one-period lag relation. Each firm's expectations of current industry units costs depend on actual industry unit cost in the previous period. If we choose sufficiently small periods, then this seems to be reasonable relation.

In Figure 2 each curve represents the "reaction cost line" of a firm. The ordinate shows the actual unit cost of any firm determined by that firm's reaction to what it believes or expects to be the unit cost performance of the industry as a whole. The alternate expected unit cost performance of the industry is shown on the abscissa. Thus each point on line C_t^i associates the unit cost for firm i in period t, given the average unit cost in the industry in period $t-1$. The lines are drawn in such a way that they reflect the idea that if the unit cost that is the average for the industry is higher, then the firm's unit cost will also be higher. As average industry unit costs fall, some firms are motivated to reduce their unit costs accordingly. The higher the industry unit cost, the easier it is for any firm to search and successfully *find* means for reducing its own cost. Therefore, for a given incentive toward cost reduction, the firm is likely to find more successful ways of reducing its cost

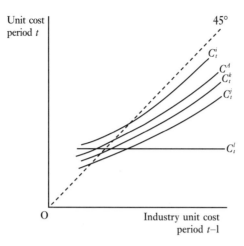

Figure 2

when industry costs are high compared to what they might find when they are low. As a consequence the typical reaction unit cost lines are more steeply sloped where industry unit costs are high compared to when they are low. Indeed, at very low industry unit costs the firm reaction cost lines approach an asymptote. It is not necessary for our analysis to assume that all firms are nonminimizers. Therefore some firms may have reaction cost lines that are horizontal.

The curve C^A is the average of the unit costs of all the firms in question, where the weight for any firm's cost is the proportion of its output to the total industry output. C^A is the average reaction cost line for all the firms. The basic assumption is that a firm's costs will be higher if the average industry costs are expected to be higher, and vice versa. Beyond some point, where expected average industry costs are very low, every reaction cost line will be above the 45° line.

In Figure 3 the line P is a locus of equilibrium prices. Each point on the line associates an equilibrium price with a level of industry unit cost in the previous period, which in turn determines the unit costs level of the various firms in the current period. Thus, given the industry unit cost in period $t-1$, this determines the unit cost level for each firm in period t. Each firm in turn will pick that output that maximizes its profits. The sum of all the outputs determines the industry output, and given the demand function for the product, the industry output determines the price. The price will be an equilibrium price if at that price no additional firms are induced to enter the industry or to withdraw from it. Thus the price for each industry unit cost is determined in accordance with conventional price theory considerations. If the price at the outset is above equilibrium price, then the entry of firms will bring that price down toward equilibrium, and if the price is below equilibrium, marginal firms will be forced to leave the industry, which in turn will cause the price to rise. Thus at every level of industry unit cost in period $t-1$ there is a determinate number of firms, that number consistent with the associated equilibrium price.

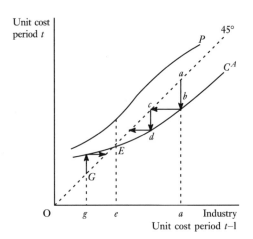

Figure 3

The point E in Figure 3, the intersection between curve C^A and the 45° line, is an equilibrium point for all the firms. The process envisioned is that each firm sets its cost in period t in accordance with its expectation of the industry cost, which by assumption is what the industry cost was in period $t-1$. This is a one-period lag relation. Each firm finds out what all of its competitors were doing as a group in terms of cost and reacts accordingly in the next period. If the industry cost is equal to Oe then in the subsequent period each firm would set its cost so that the weighted average unit cost of all the firms would be equal to Oe. Hence E is an equilibrium point.[6]

But suppose that the initial industry costs were equal to Oa. We want to show that this sets up a movement that leads eventually to the point E. The firms' unit costs will average out at ab, which generates a process shown by the set of arrows $abcd$, etc., toward the point E. In a similar fashion, if we start with an industry cost of Og, a process is set in motion so that costs move from G toward the point E. Clearly E is a stable equilibrium point. It is to be noted that every point on curve C^A need not presume that the same number of firms exist in the industry. At higher costs more firms exist, but as costs decline, some firms are forced out and fewer firms exist. In terms of the weighted average indicated by the points on the curve C^A, this simply means that some of the outputs will be zero for some of the firms as we get to lower and lower industry costs.

Figure 4 is intended to illustrate the cost reduction aspect of the residual in growth. When we begin the process the average reaction cost line is C_1^A. Firms start at point a and reduce costs along the arrow shown by ab. At this point additional information is introduced into the industry which is reflected in the diagram by the shift in the reaction cost line from C_1^A to C_2^A. Once firms are on C_2^A they then proceed with the cost reduction process as shown by the arrow cd. This illustrates two basic elements involved in the residual, the process of cost reduction in response to the motivation created by competitive pressures, as well as that part of cost reduction that is reflected in actual innovations, and is illustrated by downward shifts in the reaction cost lines.

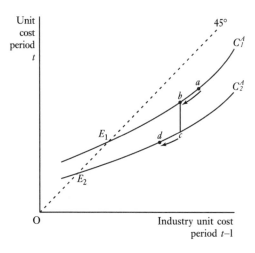

Figure 4

4. Conclusions

We have suggested three reasons for X-inefficiency connected with the possibility of variable performance for given units of the inputs. These are:

(a) contracts for labor are incomplete,
(b) the production function is not completely specified or known, and
(c) not all inputs are marketed or, if marketed, are not available on equal terms to all buyers.

These facts lead us to suggest an approach to the theory of the firm that does not depend on the assumption of cost-minimization by all firms. The level of unit cost depends in some measure on the degree of X-efficiency, which in turn depends on the degree of competitive pressure, as well as on other motivational factors. The responses to such pressures, whether in the nature of effort, search, or the utilization of new information, is a significant part of the residual in economic growth.

One idea that emerges from this study is that firms and economies do not operate on an outer-bound production possibility surface consistent with their resources. Rather they actually work on a production surface that is well within that outer bound. This means that for a variety of reasons people and organizations normally work neither as hard nor as effectively as they could. In situations where competitive pressure is light, many people will trade the disutility of greater effort, of search, and the control of other peoples' activities for the utility of feeling less pressure and of better interpersonal relations. But in situations where competitive pressures are high, and hence the costs of such trades are also high, they will exchange less of the disutility of effort for the utility of freedom from pressure, etc. Two general types of movements are possible. One is along a production surface towards greater allocative efficiency and the other is from a lower surface to a higher one that involves greater degrees of X-efficiency. The data suggest that in a great many instances the amount to be gained by increasing allocative efficiency is trivial while the amount to be gained by increasing X-efficiency is frequently significant.

Notes

1 R. A. Mundell in a review of Janssen's book appears to reach a similar conclusion to the point made in this paper when he speculates that:

> there have appeared in recent years studies purporting to demonstrate that the welfare loss due to monopoly is small, that the welfare importance of efficiency and production is exaggerated, and that gains from trade and the welfare gains from tariff reduction are almost negligible. Unless there is a thorough theoretical re-examination of the validity of the tools on which these studies are founded, and especially of the revitalized concepts of producers' and consumers' surplus, some one inevitably will draw the conclusion that economics has ceased to be important! [22, p. 622].

2 Based on data found in [11].
3 For the sake of completeness we should take the income effect into account in our estimation of consumer surplus. It may readily be seen that this magnitude is likely to be exceedingly small. Suppose that the initial effect of a superior allocation is 1 per cent; then the income effect for a noninferior good will be to shift the demand function to the right by 1 per cent on the average. Thus, the addition to consumers' surplus will be 1 per cent, and the consumers' surplus foregone will be roughly 1 per cent of 1 per cent. If we consider all consequent effects in a similar vein, then the estimated welfare loss will be $.010101 \ldots < .0102$. The actual magnitude will, of course, be smaller because the demand will shift to the left in the case of inferior goods. For an excellent discussion of these matters see A. P. Lerner [21].
4 The empirical findings and experimental literature are reviewed in a number of places. For a brief review of the literature see [37]. See page 5 for bibliography of major works in the area.
5 [27]. See especially Appendix to Chapter 7, "Evidence Relating to the Delay in the Utilization of New Techniques." It seems to me that Salter did not quite draw the only possible conclusion from his Table 11. Plants with no significant changes in equipment, method, and plant layout had quite startling changes in output per man-hour, especially if we consider the fact demonstrated in the table that output per man-hour frequently falls under such circumstances. The range of variation in the changes (24 per cent) is larger for the plants without significant changes in equipment, etc., than for those with significant improvements. This is not to argue against the thesis that changes in techniques are important, but to suggest that significant variations in production can and do occur without such changes.
6 In essence the existence of an equilibrium can be shown on the basis of Brouwer's fixed-point theorem. (Point E in Figure 3 can be interpreted as a fixed point.) It would be possible to develop a much more general theory along the same lines based on less restrictive assumptions and achieve essentially the same result. For instance the one-period lag in the reaction unit cost relation can readily be eliminated. Similarly, the unique relation between the firm's unit cost and the industry unit cost level can be relaxed. See G. Debreu [8, pp. 17–18 and p. 26]. However the essence of the theory would remain the same. To conserve space and in the interest of simplicity I present the more restrictive version.

References and Further Reading

1 Argyle, M., Gardner, G. and Cioffi, F. (1958): "Supervisory Methods Related to Productivity, Absenteeism, and Labor Turnover," *Human Relations*, 10, 23–9.

2 Aukrust, O. (1959): "Investment and Economic Growth," *Productivity Measurement Review*, 16, February, 35–53.

3 Brozen, Y. (1951): "Research, Technology, and Productivity," *Industrial Productivity*, December, Industrial Relations Research Association paper 7, 30.

4 Carter, C. F. and Williams, B. R. (1958): *Investment in Innovations*. London: Oxford University Press.

5 Chamberlain, N. (1962): *The Firm: Micro Economic Planning and Action*. New York: McGraw Hill.

6 Cyert, R. M. and March, J. G. (1963): *A Behavioral Theory of the Firm*, Englewood Cliffs, N.J: 36–38, and Ch. 9, by Williamson, O. E. 237–52.

7 Davison, J. P. Florence, P. S. Gray, B. and Ross, N. (1958): *Productivity and Economic Incentives*. London: Allen & Unwin.

8 Debreu, G. (1959): *Theory of Value*. New York: Wiley.

9 Enos, J. L. (1962) "Invention and Innovation in the Petroleum Refining Industry," in *Rate and Direction of Inventive Activity*, Princeton: Princeton University Press for the NBER, 299–321.

10 Fabricant, S. (1959): *Basic Facts on Productivity*. New York, NBER.

11 Faraq, A. A. (1963): *Economic Integration: A Theoretical Empirical Study*. Unpublished doctoral dissertation, University of Michigan.

12 Friedman, J. J. (1961): "Top Management Faces the Cost Challenge," *Dun's Review and Modern Industry*, 77, January, 34–6.

13 Ghiselli E. E. and Brown, C. W. (1948): *Personnel and Industrial Psychology*. New York: McCraw Hill.

14 Harberger, A. (1959): "Using the Resources at Hand More Effectively," *American Economic Review Proceedings*, 59 May, 134–47.

15 Harbison, F. (1956): "Entrepreneurial Organization as a Factor in Economic Development," *Quarterly Journal of Economics*, 70, August, 364–79.

16 Janssen, L. H. (1961): *Free Trade, Protection and Customs Union*. Leiden: H. E. Stentest Kroese, 132.

17 Johnson, H. (1958): "The Gains from Freer Trade with Europe: An Estimate," *Manchester School of Economics Social Studies*, 26, September, 247–55.

18 Johnston, J. (1963): "The Productivity of Management Consultants," *Journal of the Royal Statistical Society* Series A. 126 (2), 237–49.

19 Kilby, P. (1962): "Organization and Productivity in Backward Economies," *Quarterly Journal Economics* 76, May, 303–10.

20 Landsberger, H. A. (1958): *Hawthorne Revisited*. Ithaca: Cornell University Press, 13.

21 Lerner, A. P. (1963): "Consumer Surplus and Micro-Macro," *Journal of Political Economy*, 71, February, 76.

22 Mundell, R. A. (1962): "Review of L. H. Janssen, *Free Trade, Protection and Customs Union*," *American Economic Review*, 52, June, 621–2.

23 Niitamo, O. (1958): "Development of Productivity in Finnish Industry, 1925–1952," *Productivity Measurement Review*, 15, November, 30–41.

24 Ohlin, G. (1962): Review of E. Lundberg, "Productivity and Profitability: Studies of the Role of Capital in the Swedish Economy," *American Economic Review*, 52, September, 827–9.

25 Roethlisberger, F. T. and Dickson, W. J. (1947): *Management and the Worker*. Cambridge MA: Harvard University Press.

26 Rostas, L. (1964): *Comparative Productivity in British and American Industry*. National Institute of Economics Society research paper 13, Cambridge, England: 64.

27 Salter, W. E. G. (1960): *Productivity and Technical Change*. Cambridge, England: Cambridge University Press.

28 Schwartzman, D. (1960): "The Burden of Monopoly," *Journal of Political Economy*, 68, December, 727–9.

29 Scitovsky, T. (1958): *Economic Theory and Western European Integration*. Stanford: Stanford University Press.

30 Solow, R. (1957): "Technical Progress and the Aggregate Production Function," *Review of Economics and Statitics*, August, 39, 312–20.

31 —— (1959): "Investment and Economic Growth," *Productivity Measurement Review*, 16, November, 62–8.

32 Tomekovic, T. (1962): "Levels of Knowledge of Requirements as a Motivational Factor in the Work Situation," *Human Relations*, 15, 197–216.

33 Wemelsfelder, J. (1960): "The Short-Term Effect of Lowering Import Duties in Germany," *Economic Journal*, 60, March, 94–104.

34 Winter, Jr., S. G. (1963): "Economic Natural Selection and the Theory of the Firm." Unpublished doctoral dissertation, mimeo, Yale University, 83–5.

35 Anglo-American Council on Productivity, (1950): *Productivity Measurement in British Industry*. New York.

36 International Labor Organization, (1951): "Payment by Results," *ILO Studies and Reports*, New Series, 27, Geneva.

37 —— (1957): "ILO Productivity Missions to Underdeveloped Countries, Part 1," *International Labor Review*, 76, July, 1–29.

38 —— (1957): "ILO Productivity Missions to Underdeveloped Countries, Part 2," *International Labor Review*, 76, August, 139–66.

39 —— (1956): "Repercussions of a Reduction in Hours of Work," *International Labor Review*, 74, July, 23–45.

CHAPTER SEVEN

The Economics of Modern Manufacturing: Technology, Strategy, and Organization

PAUL R. MILGROM AND JOHN ROBERTS

Source: *American Economic Review*, 80 (1990), pp. 511–28. Reprinted with the permission of the authors and the American Economic Association. © American Economic Association.

Manufacturing is undergoing a revolution. The mass production model is being replaced by a vision of a flexible multiproduct firm that emphasizes quality and speedy response to market conditions while utilizing technologically advanced equipment and new forms of organization. Our optimizing model of the firm generates many of the observed patterns that mark modern manufacturing. Central to our results is a method of handling optimization and comparative statics problems that requires neither differentiability nor convexity.

In the early twentieth century, Henry Ford revolutionized manufacturing with the introduction of his "transfer line" technology for mass production, in which basic inputs are processed in a fixed sequence of steps using equipment specifically designed to produce a single standardized product in extremely large quantities for extended periods of time. Although the specialization of Ford's factories was extreme – the plants had to be shut down and redesigned when production of the Model T was ended – the transfer line approach influenced generations of industrialists and changed the face of manufacturing (see David A. Hounshell, 1984).

In the late twentieth century, the face of manufacturing is changing again.[1] First, the specialized, single-purpose equipment for mass production which had characterized Ford's factories is being replaced by flexible machine tools and programmable, multitask production equipment. Because these new machines can be quickly and cheaply switched from one task to another, their use permits the firm to produce a variety of outputs efficiently in very small batches,[2] especially in comparison to the usual image of mass production (Nicholas Valery, 1987). Kenneth Wright and David Bourne (1988) report that in a recent survey of aerospace and other high precision industries 8.2 percent of all batches were of size one and 38 percent were sixteen or less. An Allen-Bradley Company plant making electric controls is reported to be able to switch production among its 725 products and variations with an average changeover time for resetting equipment of six seconds, enabling it to schedule batches of size one with relative efficiency (Tracy O'Rourke, 1988). Even in the automobile industry, flexible equipment has become much more common. Recently, General Motors' engineers were able, for the first time in company history, to use a regular, producing facility to make pilots of the next year's model cars. The engineers set the equipment to make 1989 models after workers left the factory on Friday afternoon, ran the equipment to manufacture the new models over the weekend, and then reset the equipment to produce 1988 model cars so that regular production could be resumed on Monday morning (Thomas Moore, 1988). In contrast, with the older, less flexible technologies that have been the norm in the industry, changing over to produce the new year's models typically involved shutting down production for weeks.

Flexible equipment and small batch sizes have been accompanied by other changes. Smaller batch sizes are directly associated with a shortening of production cycles and with reductions in work-in-process and finished goods inventories. Shorter product cycles in turn support speedier responses to demand fluctuations and lead to lower back orders. Indeed, a general strategic emphasis on speeding up all aspects of the firm's operations is becoming common (Brian Dumaine, 1989). This is manifested in shorter product-development times, quicker order-processing, and speedier delivery, as well as in producing products faster. Examples abound. General Electric has reduced the design and production time it takes to fill an order for a circuit-breaker box from three weeks to three days, in the process reducing back orders from sixty days to two (Dumaine). The Allen-Bradley plant mentioned above fills orders the day after they are received, then ships them that same day by air express (O'Rourke). Building on early development by Toyota, many manufacturers now plan production jointly with their suppliers and maintain constant communication with them. This allows the downstream firms to replace inventories of components and supplies with "just-in-time" deliveries of needed inputs (James Abegglen and George Stalk, Jr., 1985, Nicholas Valery, 1987). Combining flexible production and low finished goods inventories with reliance on electronic data communications, Benetton maintains inventories of undyed clothing (shirts, scarves, pullovers) and uses nightly sales data gathered at its automated distribution center from terminals in individual stores to determine the colors it should make and where to ship its output (Tom Peters, 1987). Strategies like this one require not only flexible equipment to produce the right products, but short production cycles so that products are available at the right time. The extreme of this line of development is production of previously mass-produced items on a make-to-order basis: Moore reports a widespread rumor that the GM Saturn project will involve cars being custom-built within days of receipt of customers' computer-transmitted individual orders.

The manufacturing firms that adopt these new technologies and methods appear to differ from traditional firms in their product strategies as well. Many firms are broadening product lines, and there is a widespread increased emphasis on quality, both through frequent product improvements and new product introductions, and through reductions in defects in manufacturing. Caterpillar Corporation's $1.2 billion "Plant with a Future" modernization program has been accompanied by a doubling of the size of its product line (Ronald Henkoff, 1988). Rubbermaid insists that 30 percent of its sales should come from the products introduced in the preceding five years, and 3M Company has a similar 25 percent rule for each of its 42 divisions, with 32 percent of its $10.6 billion in 1988 sales actually coming from products less than five years old (Russell Mitchell, 1989). Meanwhile, reports of order-of-magnitude reductions in percentage defects are becoming commonplace.

New organizational strategies and workforce management policies are also part of this complex of changes. Ford has adopted a parallel, team (rather than sequential) approach to design and manufacturing engineering that, in conjunction with CAD/CAM (*computer aided design/computer aided manufacturing*) techniques, has cut development time on new models by one third (Alex Taylor, III, 1988). AT&T successfully used a similar, multi-departmental team approach in developing its new 4200 cordless phone (Dumaine), as did NCR with its recently introduced 2760 electronic cash register (Otis Port, 1989b). Lock-heed Corp.'s Aeronautical Systems Group has managed to reduce the time for designing and manufacturing sheet-metal parts by 96 percent, from 52 days to 2; the project manager credits organizational changes (including the arrangement of workstations, redefinition of worker responsibilities, and adoption of team approaches) with 80 percent of the productivity gain (Port, 1989a, p. 143; Warren Hausman, 1988). Motorola's adoption of a pay scheme based on the skills employees acquire (rather than on their job assignments), its elimination of segmented pay categories among production workers, and its giving workers multiple responsibilities (including having production workers do quality inspections) is credited with major improvements in quality (Norm Alster, 1989). A further auto industry example comes from GM's massive investments in new technology, which have gone hand-in-hand with new supplier relations and more flexible work arrangements, as well as a broadened product line (General Motors Corporation, 1988).

More generally, Michael J. Piore (1986) provides survey evidence from firms around Route 128 in Boston of wider product lines, shorter product life cycles, greater emphasis on product quality, increased reliance on independent suppliers and subcontractors, and a more flexible organization of work that is supported by new compensation policies. Banri Asanuma, (1989), has found similar trends among Japanese firms, Valery provides more anecdotal evidence drawn from a wide variety of industries internationally, and earlier Piore and Charles F. Sabel (1984) described related developments among small businesses in Italy and Austria.

A striking feature of the discussions of flexible manufacturing found in the business press is the frequency with which it is asserted that successful moves toward "the factory of the future" are not a matter of small adjustments made independently at each of several margins, but rather have involved substantial and closely coordinated changes in a whole range of the firm's activities. Even though these changes are implemented over time, perhaps beginning with "islands of automation," the full benefits are achieved only by an ultimately radical restructuring. Henkoff (p. 74) noted that one of the lessons of Cater-pillar's program was "Don't just change selected parts of your factory, as many manu-facturers have done. To truly boost efficiency . . . it's necessary to change the layout of the entire plant." The first lesson that Dumaine drew from studying successful adoption of speed-based strategies was to "start from scratch." In discussing the adoption of "com-puter integrated manufacturing" (CIM), Valery (p. 15) stated that "nothing short of a total overhaul of the company's strategy has first to be undertaken." And in a parallel fashion, Walter Kiechel III (1988, p. 42) noted: "To get these benefits (of more timely operations), you probably have to totally redesign the way you do business, changing everything from procurement to quality control."

This paper seeks to provide a coherent framework within which to understand the changes that are occurring in modern manufacturing. We ask, Why are these changes taking place? Is it mere coincidence that these various changes appear to be grouped together; or is there instead some necessary interconnection between them and common driving force behind them? What are the implications of the changes in manufacturing technology for inventory policy, product market strategy, and supplier and customer relations? What are the implications for the "make or buy" and vertical integration decisions and for the structure of business organization more generally?

Our approach to these questions is a price-theoretic, supply-side one involving three elements: exogenous input price changes, complementarities among the elements of the firm's strategy, and non-convexities. The first element is the effect of technological change in reducing a set of costs. The particular ones on which we focus include:

- the costs of collecting, organizing, and communicating data, which have been reduced over time by the development of computer networks and electronic data transmission systems;
- the cost of product design and development, which have fallen with the emergence of computer-aided design; and
- the costs of flexible manufacturing, which have declined with the introduction of robots and other programmable production equipment.

We take these relative price reductions, whose existence is well documented, to be exogenous.

The direct effect of any of these price changes individually would be to increase use of the corresponding factor: for example, the emergence (i.e., falling cost) of CAD/CAM encourages its adoption, and the reduced cost of designing and beginning production of new products directly increases the attractiveness of expanded product lines and frequent product improvements. However, with several relative prices falling, there are multiple interactions, both among the corresponding technological factors and between them and marketing and organizational variables. These interactions give rise to indirect effects that might in principle be as large as the direct effects, and opposite in sign. Here, the second element of our analysis appears: These indirect effects tend, in the main, to reinforce the direct effects because the corresponding relationships are ones of "complementarity." Here, we use the term "complements" not only in its traditional sense of a relation between *pairs of inputs*, but also in a broader sense as a relation among *groups of activities*. The defining characteristic of these groups of complements is that if the levels of any subset of the activities are increased, then the marginal return to increases in any or all of the remaining activities rises. It then follows that if the marginal costs associated with some activities fall, it will be optimal to increase the level of all of the activities in the grouping.

As an illustration, let us trace some of the indirect effects of a fall in the cost of computer-aided design (CAD) equipment and software that leads to the equipment being purchased. Some CAD programs prepare actual coded instructions that can be used by programmable manufacturing equipment, so one effect of the adoption of CAD may be to reduce the cost of adopting and using programmable manufacturing equipment. Since the prices of that equipment are also falling, the effects of the two price changes on the adoption of that equipment are mutually reinforcing. Of course, CAD also makes it cheaper for the firm to adopt a broader product line and to update its products more frequently. If the firm does so, then an indirect effect is to make it more profitable to switch to more flexible manufacturing equipment that is cheaper to change over. So, this indirect effect reinforces the direct effects of the changing input prices. With short production runs, the firm can economize on inventory costs (such as interest, storage, and obsolescence) by scheduling production in a way that is quickly responsive to customer demand. Such a scheduling strategy increases the profitability of technologies that enable quicker and more accurate order processing, such as modern data communications technologies. So, another indirect effect of falling CAD prices coincides with the falling price of data communication equipment. Thus, CAD equipment, flexible manufacturing technologies, shorter production runs, lower inventories, increased data communications, and more frequent product redesigns are complementary. However, the complementarities do not stop at the level of manufacturing, but extend to marketing, engineering, and organization.

The marketing side of the analysis involves two additional elements besides those already mentioned. First, more frequent setups lower the inventory necessary to support a unit of sales and thus also the marginal cost of output. This encourages lower prices. The second element arises because buyers value fast delivery. If most customers have good alternative sources of supply and only a few are "locked in," then the resulting relationship between delivery time and demand is convex. In that case, reducing or eliminating production delays makes it profitable to reduce other sources of delay as well. Then, computerized order processing and a fast means of delivery are complementary to the quick responsiveness of the modern factory to new orders.

On the engineering side, as product life cycles become much shorter than the life of the production equipment, it becomes increasingly important to account for the characteristics of existing equipment in designing new products. At the same time, the emergence of computer-aided design has made it less costly to modify initial designs, to estimate the cost of producing various designs with existing equipment, and to evaluate a broader range of potential designs. These changes have contributed to the growing popularity among U.S. firms of "design for manufacturability," in which products are developed by teams composed of designers, process engineers, and manufacturing managers (Robert Hayes, Steven Wheelwright, and Kim Clark, 1988), and the corresponding practice among Japanese automakers of providing preliminary specifications to suppliers who comment on the proposed design and supply drawings of parts (Asanuma, 1988b) – innovations in engineering organization that contribute to a more efficient use of existing production equipment and manufacturing know-how. Moreover, taking account of the limits and capabilities of production equipment in the design phase makes it easier to ensure that quality standards can be met, and so is complementary to a marketing strategy based on high quality.

The firm's problem in deciding whether to adopt any or all of these changes is marked by important *non-convexities*. These are first of the familiar sorts associated with indivisibilities: product line sizes are naturally integer-valued. A form of increasing returns also figures in the model, because the marginal impact of increasing the speed with which customers are served increases the service speed. Beyond these, however, the complementarities noted above can be a further source of non-convexities that are associated with the need to coordinate choices among several decision variables. For example, purchase of CAD/CAM technology makes it less costly for a firm to increase its frequency of product improvements, and more frequent product introductions raise the return to investments in CAD/CAM technology. Thus, it may be unprofitable for a firm to purchase a flexible CAD/CAM system without changing its marketing strategy, or to alter its marketing approach without adopting a flexible manufacturing system, and yet it may be highly profitable to do both together. (In contrast, if the value of a smooth concave function at some point in the interior of its domain cannot be increased by a small change in the value of any single variable, then the function achieves a global maximum at that point.) These non-convexities then explain why the successful adoption of modern manufacturing methods may not be a marginal decision.

It is natural to expect the characteristics of the modern manufacturing firm to be reflected in the way the firm is managed and the way it structures its relations with customers, employees, and suppliers. Exploiting such an extensive system of complementarities requires coordinated action between the traditionally separate functions of design, engineering, manufacturing, and marketing. Also, according to transaction costs theories, the increasing use of flexible, general purpose equipment in place of specialized, single purpose equipment ought to improve the investment incentives of independent suppliers (Oliver Williamson, 1986; Benjamin Klein, Robert Crawford, and Armen Alchian, 1978; Jean Tirole, 1986) and to reduce cost of the negotiating short-term contracts (Milgrom and Roberts, 1987) and so to favor short-term contracting with independent suppliers over alternatives like vertical integration or long-term contracting. The supplier relations that mark modern manufacturing firms – involving close coordination between the firm and its independently owned contractors and suppliers – appear to be consistent with these theories, and inconsistent with theories in which joint planning can only take place in integrated firms.

In this essay, we develop a theoretical model of the firm that allows us to explore many of the complementarities in modern manufacturing firms. The non-convexities inherent in our problem makes it inappropriate to use differential techniques to study the effects of changing parameters. Instead, we utilize purely algebraic (lattice-theoretic) methods first introduced by Donald M. Topkis (1978), which provide an exact formalization of the idea of groups of complementary activities. In problems with complementarities among the choice variables this approach easily handles both indivisibilities and non-concave maximands while allowing sharp comparative statics results. In particular, we give conditions under which the set of maximizers moves monotonically with changes in a (possibly multidimensional) parameter. Because these methods are quite straightforward and would seem to be of broad applicability in economics, but are not well known among economists, we describe them in some detail in section 1.

Our model and its basic analysis are provided in section 2. The firm in our model chooses its price; the length of the product life cycle or frequency of product improvements (a surrogate for quality); its order-receipt, processing, and delivery technologies; various characteristics of its manufacturing and design technologies as reflected in its marginal cost of production and its costs of setups and new product development; its manufacturing plan, including the length of the production cycle (and, implicitly, its inventory and back-order levels); and aspects of its quality control policy, all with the aim of maximizing its expected profits. Using reasonable assumptions about the nature and equipment costs, we find that the complementarities in the system are pervasive. We use the firm's optimizing response to assumed trends in input prices (the falling costs of communication, computer-aided design, and flexible manufacturing) in the presence of these complementarities to explain both the clustering of characteristics and the trends in manufacturing.

In section 3, we turn our attention to the organizational problems associated with the new technologies. We summarize and review the predictions of the model in the concluding section 4.

1. The Mathematics of Complementarities

Here we review some basic definitions and results in the mathematics of complementarities. The results permit us to make definite statements about the nature of the optimal solution to the firm's problem and how it depends on various parameters, even though the domain of the objective function may be non-convex (for example, some variables may be integer-valued) and the objective function itself may be non-concave, non-differentiable, and even discontinuous at some points. For additional developments and missing proofs, see Topkis.

We first introduce our notation. Let $x, x' \in \mathbb{R}^n$. We say that $x \geq x'$ if $x_i \geq x'_i$ for all i. Define max (x, x') to be the point in $\mathbb{R}^n$ whose ith component is max (x_i, x'_i), and min (x, x') to be the point whose ith component is min (x_i, x'_i). This notation is used below to define the two key notions of the theory. The first notion is that of a supermodular function, which is a function that exhibits complementarities among its arguments. The second is that of a sublattice of $\mathbb{R}^n$, a subset of $\mathbb{R}^n$ that is closed under the max and min operations and whose structure lets us characterize the set of optima of a supermodular function.

Definition 1: A function $f: \mathbb{R}^n \to \mathbb{R}$ is *supermodular* if for all $x, x' \in \mathbb{R}^n$,

$$f(x) + f(x') \leq f(\min(x, x')) + f(\max(x, x')) \tag{1}$$

The function f is *submodular* if $-f$ is supermodular.

Inequality (1) is clearly equivalent to

$$[f(x) - f(\min(x, x'))] + [f(x') - f(\min(x, x'))] \leq f(\max(x, x')) - f(\min(x, x'))$$

the sum of the changes in the function when several arguments are increased separately is less than the change resulting from increasing all the arguments together. The inequality is also equivalent to

$$f(\max(x, x')) - f(x') \geq f(x) - f(\min(x, x'))$$

increasing one or more variables raises the return to increasing other variables. These reformulations of the defining inequality make clear the sense in which the supermodularity of a function corresponds to complementarity among its arguments.

Note that any function of a single variable is trivially supermodular. This observation serves to resolve various questions about possible relationships between supermodularity and other concepts. However, even in a multidimensional context, supermodularity is distinct from, but related to, a number of more familiar notions. First, supermodularity has no necessary relation to the concavity or convexity of the function: consider

$$f(x_1, x_2) = x_1^a + x_2^b$$

which is supermodular for all values of a and b but may be either concave or convex (or both or neither). Nor, in the context of production functions, does supermodularity carry implications for returns to scale. For example, the CobbDouglas functions

$$f(x_1, x_2) = x_1^a x_2^b$$

may show increasing or decreasing returns to scale but are supermodular for all positive values of a and b. This is most easily checked using Theorem 2, below, which states that a smooth function f is supermodular if and only if

$$\frac{\partial^2 f}{\partial x_i \partial x_j} \geq 0 \qquad \text{for } i \neq j$$

Thus, if f is supermodular and smooth, then the smooth supermodular function $-f$ shows weak cost complementarities as defined by William Baumol, John Panzar, and Robert Willig (1982, pp. 74–5). Even without smoothness, it is easily shown that a submodular function that is zero at the origin shows economies of scope as defined by Baumol et al. More generally, submodularity is related to, but distinct from, the notion of subadditivity that figures centrally in the study of cost functions.[3] For example, any function of a single variable is submodular, but obviously not all such functions are subadditive. Meanwhile, the functions on $[0, 1] \times [0, 1]$ given by

$$f(x_1, x_2) = 1 + x_1 + x_2 + \varepsilon x_1 x_2$$

are submodular for $\varepsilon > 0$, supermodular for $\varepsilon \geq 0$, and subadditive for all ε sufficiently close to zero in absolute value.

Six theorems about supermodular functions are provided here. The first four together provide a relatively easy way to check whether a given function is supermodular. Theorem 5 indicates how, in a parameterized maximization problem, the maximizer changes with changing parameters, while Theorem 6 characterizes the set of maximizers of a supermodular function. It is Theorem 5 that makes our comparative statics exercises possible.

Let $x_{\backslash i}$ denote the vector x with the ith component removed and let $x_{\backslash ij}$ denote x with the ith and jth components removed. Let subscripts on f denote partial derivatives, for example,

$$f_i = \frac{\partial f}{\partial x_i} \qquad f_{ij} = \frac{\partial^2 f}{\partial x_i \partial x_j}$$

Theorem 1: Suppose $f: \mathbb{R}^n \to \mathbb{R}$. If for all i, j, and $x_{\backslash ij}, f\left(x_i, x_j, x_{\backslash ij}\right)$ is supermodular when regarded as a function of the arguments $\left(x_i, x_j\right)$ only, then f is supermodular.

Theorem 2:   Let $I = [a_1, b_1] \times \cdots \times [a_n, b_n]$ be an interval in $\mathbb{R}^n$ with nonempty interior and suppose that f: $I \to \mathbb{R}$ is continuous and twice continuously differentiable on the interior of I. Then f is supermodular on I if and only if for all $i \neq j$, $f_{ij} \geq 0$.

Theorem 2 is stated above in the form given in Topkis. For our application, we will need a slightly stronger theorem in which the condition that f is twice continuously differen-tiable is weakened to the condition that it can be written as an indefinite double integral with a nonnegative integrand. The precise extension is stated and proved in the Appendix.

Theorem 3: Suppose that $f, g: \mathbb{R}^n \to \mathbb{R}$ are supermodular functions. Then $f + g$ is super-modular. If, in addition, f and g are nonnegative and nondecreasing, then fg is supermodular.

Theorem 4: Suppose that $f: \mathbb{R}^{1+n} \to \mathbb{R}$ is supermodular and continuous in its first argu-ment. Then for all $a, b \in \mathbb{R}$, the function $g: \mathbb{R}^n \to \mathbb{R}$ defined by

$$g(x) = \max_{y \in [a, b]} f(y, x)$$

is supermodular.

Proof: Since f is continuous in its first argument, the function g is well defined. For all x and x', there exist y and y' with $g(x) = f(y, x)$ and $g(x') = f(y', x')$. Then,

$$g(x) + g(x') = f(y, x) + f(y', x')$$
$$\leq f(\max(y, y'), \max(x, x')) + f(\min(y, y'), \min(x, x'))$$
$$\leq g(\max(x, x')) + g(\min(x, x'))$$

In what follows we will be particularly concerned with constrained optimization of super-modular functions, and our results will depend on the constraint set having the right structure or shape, namely, that of a sublattice of $\mathbb{R}^n$.

Definition 2: A set T is a *sublattice* of $\mathbb{R}^n$ if for all $x, x' \in T$, $\min(x, x') \in T$ and $\max(x, x') \in T$.

In our application, the definition of a sublattice represents the idea that if it is possible to engage in high (respectively, low) levels of each of several activities separately, then it is possible to engage in equally high (resp., low) levels of all of the activities simultaneously. Thus, for example, if $S_1, \ldots, S_n$ are arbitrary subsets of $\mathbb{R}$, then $S_1 \times \cdots \times S_n$ is a sublattice of $\mathbb{R}^n$. However, the product sets are not the only sublattices. The sublattice structure also permits the possibility that some activities can be engaged in at a high level *only if* the others are also carried out at a high level. For example, if $x \geq x'$, then $\{x, x'\}$ is a sublattice.

Definition 3:　Given two sets $S, S' \subset \mathbb{R}^n$, we say that S is *higher than* S' and write $S \geq S'$ if for all $x \in S$ and $x' \in S'$, $\max(x, x') \in S$ and $\min(x, x') \in S'$.

Theorem 5: Suppose $f: \mathbb{R}^{n+k} \to \mathbb{R}$ is supermodular and suppose $T(y)$ and $T(y')$ are sublattices of $\mathbb{R}^n$. *Let*

$$S(y) \equiv \operatorname{argmax}\{f(z, y) | z \in T(y)\}$$

and define $S(y')$ analogously. Then $y \geq y'$ *and* $T(y) \geq T(y')$ imply that $S(y) \geq S(y')$.
Proof: Let $x \in S(y)$ and $x' \in S(y')$ and $y \geq y'$ so that $y = \max(y, y')$ and $y' = \min(y, y')$. Since $T(y) \geq T(y')$, $\max(x, x') \in T(y)$ and $\min(x, x') \in T(y')$. From the definitions,

$$f(x, y') \geq f(\max(x, x'), y)$$

and

$$f(x', y') \geq f(\min(x, x'), y')$$

but since f is supermodular,

$$f(x, y) + f(x', y') \leq f(\max(x, x'), y) + f(\min(x, x'), y')$$

from which the conclusion is immediate.

Theorem 6: Suppose f: $\mathbb{R}^n \to \mathbb{R}$ is supermodular and suppose T is a sublattice of $\mathbb{R}^n$. Then the set of maximizers of f over T is also a sublattice.
Proof: Apply Theorem 5 with $y = y'$.

Theorem 5 is particularly important for our application. When its conclusion holds, we shall say that the set of optimizers "rises" as the parameter values increase. What justifies this language? The theorem implies, for example, that if $x^*(y)$ and $x^*(y')$ are the unique maximizers given their respective parameter vectors y and y' and if $y \geq y'$, then $x^*(y) \geq x^*(y')$. (For uniqueness implies that $x^*(y) = \max(x^*(y), x^*(y'))$, from which $x^*(y) \geq x^*(y')$ follows.) Alternatively, suppose we assume that f is a *continuous* supermodular function that T is a *compact* sublattice, so that the set of maximizers corresponding to any parameter vector y is compact. Then, by Theorem 5, there are greatest and least elements $\bar{x}(y)$ and $\underline{x}(y)$ in the set of maximizers S. One can show that both $\bar{x}(y)$ and $\underline{x}(y)$ are nondecreasing functions of y. (Using Theorem 6 and the definitions, $\bar{x}(y') \leq \max(\bar{x}(y), \bar{x}(y')) \leq \bar{x}(y)$ and similarly $\underline{x}(y) \geq \min(\underline{x}(y), \underline{x}(y')) \geq \underline{x}(y')$.)

2. Complementarities in Production

We study a model of a multiproduct firm facing a downward sloping demand curve. The firm may be a monopoly or monopolistic competitor. Alternatively, our model may be viewed as a building block for a model of oligopolistic markets.

In the formal model, the firm chooses the levels of the decision variables shown in the table.

Variable	Interpretation
p	Price of each product
q	(Expected) number of improvements per product per period
a	Order receipt and processing time
b	Delivery time
c	Direct marginal costs of production
d	Design cost per product improvement
e	Extra set-up costs on newly changed products
m	Number of setups per period
r	Probability of a defective batch
s	Direct cost of a setup
w	Wastage costs per setup

In addition, we denote the number of products by n.

The functional relationships and parameters that complete the model include the demand specification, the specification of the capital costs of different levels of the technological variables, the functional relation linking the average delay between receipt of an order and its being filled to the number of products and of setups, the marginal cost of production, the marginal cost of reworking defectives, the cost of holding inventories, and a time parameter that will proxy for the state of technology and demand. More specifically, we have parameters as shown in the table.

Parameter	Interpretation
ρ	Marginal cost of reworking a defective unit
τ	Calendar time
ι	Cost of holding inventory per unit
κ	Capital costs ($\kappa = \kappa(a, b, c, d, e, r, s, w, \tau)$)
μ	Base demand per product ($\mu = \mu(p, q, n, \tau)$)
δ	Demand shrinkage with delay time ($\delta = \delta(t, \tau)$)
ω	Expected wait for a processed order to be filled ($\omega = \omega(m, r, n)$)

The total expected wait for an order to be received, processed, filled, and shipped, which determines the value of the shrinkage factor (δ) on demand, is $t = a + w + b$, and realized demand is then $\mu(p, q, n, \tau)\delta(a + w + b, \tau)$. Thus, the firm's payoff function Π is

$$\Pi(p, q, m, a, b, c, d, e, r, s, w, \tau) = (p - c - r\rho - \iota/m)n\mu(p, q, n, \tau)$$

$$\times \; \delta(a + \omega(m, r, n) + b, \tau) - m(s + w) - nq(d + e) - \kappa(a, b, c, d, e, r, s, w, \tau)$$

The total profit Π is the operating profit minus the fixed costs associated with machine setups, product redesign, and the purchase of capital equipment.

The first term $(p - c - r\rho - 1/m)n\mu\delta$ is the operating profit. For each unit sold, the firm receives the price p and pays direct production costs, expected rework costs, and inventory holding and handling costs. In line with the Economic Order Quantity models commonly used for inventory analysis, we treat the average levels of work-in-process and finished goods inventories as being directly proportional to demand and inversely proportional to the number of setups. Similarly, back orders are directly proportional to demand and decreasing in the number of setups. We have used the function δ, which we take to be uniform across products, to model the cost of back orders; this takes the form of lost demand when delivery is delayed. We have also modeled the firm as setting a uniform price (p) across the product line, which is reasonable given the symmetry of the products in the model.

The second term $m(s + w)$ is the cost of the setups, which, as suggested above, consists of the number of setups times the sum of the direct costs plus wastage per setup. The term $nq(d + e)$ is the cost of redesign over the period, including the extra setup costs on newly altered products. In this term nq is the total number of redesigns or improvements.

The last term is κ, which is the capital cost of selecting the various technological variables, a, b, c, d, e, r, s, and w, at any date τ. Among these technology variables, the order receipt and processing time (a) is determined by the technology used for communicating orders (mail, express courier, FAX, electronic data communications networks, etc.) and by the means used to handle orders once received (manual entry, computerized order entry systems). Whichever choices are made, there are capital costs involved in setting up the corresponding systems. Similarly, different options exist that determine the speed of delivery (b) from inventory, and these too have differing capital costs.

Our model allows us to represent many aspects and tradeoffs in the firm's choice of manufacturing strategy. For example, the flexibility of design technology is modeled by the variable d. The introduction of computer aided design (CAD) lowers these marginal costs of redesigning and improving products, but it also involves significant capital expenditures on training, hardware, and software. Both of these effects are captured in our profit function.

Flexibility of manufacturing equipment has a number of aspects, several of which are represented in our model. First, flexibility is often associated with low costs of routinely changing over from producing one good to another. Here, this effect is represented first through the variable s: more flexible equipment means lower setup costs in terms of the downtime and direct labor costs involved in resetting the machines, switching dies, etc. Also, more flexible equipment might involve less wastage (lower w) per setup. This wastage might be in the form of extra inspection, scrap, rework, and repair costs that are necessary when a changeover is made. The precision of computer aided equipment, "design for manufacturability" (facilitated by CAD-CAM), and similar investments lower these costs. Finally, flexibility might involve costs of changing machinery over to produce new or redesigned products (low values of e).

The technological quality variable (r) captures a somewhat different feature of modern manufacturing methods. Improving quality on this dimension may involve investing in more precisely controlled machinery which may even constantly monitor and adjust itself. It may also improve more prosaic but possibly more significant efforts aimed at changing attitudes toward quality, such as giving workers the ability to stop the production line when a problem arises.

Although we do not explicitly model labor force decisions here, an element of the flexibility of modern manufacturing is associated with broadly trained workers and with work rules that facilitate frequent changes in activities. In this context we may interpret investments in flexibility in terms of worker education and industrial relations efforts, as well as the purchase of physical capital. Certainly, flexibility in the labor force and in the capital equipment are mutually complementary.

Finally, the choice of c, the marginal costs of production, has capital cost implications, if only through investing in learning how to control costs.

Even before we make any assumptions about the form of the unspecified functions κ, μ, δ, and ω, certain complementarities are evident in the model. For example, with more frequent changeovers (higher q), the returns to more efficient technologies for redesigning products and changing over equipment (higher values of $-d$ and $-e$) will naturally rise and, conversely, more efficient changeover and redesign technologies raise the marginal returns to increasing q. Similarly, an increase in the number of setups per period (m) and the concomitant reduction in inventories and back orders is complementary with a reduction in the components of set-up costs (increases in $-s$ and $-w$). Technologically, one expects that reduced set-up and changeover costs are bundled together in the new equipment. However, conclusions such as that one require that we make an assumption about the properties of the unspecified function κ. To make further statements, we need to make assumptions about properties of all the unspecified functions.

Our assumption about the form of δ is the following:

Assumption A1: δ is twice continuously differentiable, nonnegative, decreasing and convex in t, nondecreasing in τ and submodular in (t, τ).

The assumption that δ is decreasing in t simply means that increased delay reduces sales, while convexity says that the larger is the delay, the smaller is the marginal impact of additional delay. Inclusion of τ allows for a time trend in demand through δ. This trend must be nonnegative for our results, but it could be trivial. The submodularity assumption means that, as time passes, δ_t becomes weakly more negative or, equivalently, the returns to reducing waiting time, $-t$, increase weakly. This might come about because the adoption of more modern manufacturing methods by the firm's customers raises the importance of speedy service to them.

An immediate implication of the convexity assumption in Assumption A1 is that activities that reduce the several components of delay time (a, b, and ω) are mutually complementary, as can be easily verified by checking that the corresponding mixed partial derivatives of the profit function are positive. These complementarities may seem surprising, since the three components of waiting time are perfect substitutes for one another in determining the total delay. However, as our analysis shows, the possibility of substituting these elements to achieve a fixed time delay is irrelevant to their assessment as potential complements within the corporate strategy.

To complete our evaluation of the complementarities associated with speed, we must take an assumption about the ω function. Generally, we would expect ω to be increasing in the probability of a batch requiring reworking (r) and decreasing in the number of setups (m). The one nonobvious element in Assumption A2 below is that r and m are complements in determining ω: an increase in the number of setups (or decrease in batch size) is assumed to raise the impact on delay time of an increase in the probability of a batch being defective. This complementarity may be caused by the more frequent changeovers in the rework facility being required by more frequent changeovers in the main facility. Otherwise, it seems natural to expect the effect to be zero, which is also consistent with our assumption.

Assumption A2: $\omega = \omega(m, r, n)$ is twice continuously differentiable, decreasing in m, increasing in r and supermodular in m and r, given n. That is, $\omega_m \leq 0$, $\omega_r \geq 0$, and $\omega_{mr} \geq 0$.

As a consequence of (A1) and (A2), $-a$, $-b$, m and $-r$ are mutually complementary in increasing demand.

To complete our analysis of the marketing aspects of strategy, the form of the demand function μ must be restricted. We make two assumptions. The first is a standard one:

Assumption A3: μ is twice continuously differentiable, increasing in q, and decreasing in p, while operating profits, defined by

$$\left(\frac{p - c - r\rho - \iota}{m}\right) n\mu(p, q, n, \tau)\delta(a + \omega + b, \tau)$$

are a strictly quasi-concave function of p.

The first part asserts innocuously that consumers prefer lower prices and higher quality. Since we will hold n fixed, we need make no assumptions on its effect, although it would be natural to assume that $n\mu$ is increasing in n. The assumption that demand is quasi-concave in prices is standard. The nonstandard part of our assumption about demand is contained in Assumption A4:

Assumption A4: $\mu(p, q, n, \tau)$ is non-decreasing in τ and supermodular when regarded as a function of $-p, q$ and τ, for given n.

A4 is a complicated assumption. It would be satisfied, for example, by a multiplicatively separable specification of demand,

$$\mu = A(p)B(q)C(\tau)$$

as well as by additively separable demand

$$A(p) + B(q) + C(\tau)$$

and $A' < 0, B' \geq 0$, and $C' \geq 0$ in both cases. It asserts that the quantity demanded becomes (weakly) more sensitive to price and quality with passing time, and that at higher quality levels the quantity demanded is more sensitive to price changes. Again, we emphasize that we allow demand to be independent of τ, but if a dependence exists, it should not be such as to offset the supply-side effects of technological progress embodied in the effect of τ in the κ function.

Our final assumption is the following one, on the κ function. It is key because it embodies the presumed technological changes in the capital goods industries supplying the firm that are the basis for our arguments.

Assumption A5: $\kappa(-a,-b,-c,-d,-e,-r,-s,-w,\tau)$ is submodular.

This assumption is stated in terms of the negatives of the natural decision variables because a and b decrease with improved communication systems, better data transmission, entry, storage, manipulation, and retrieval systems, and speedier delivery methods, and the other choice variables decrease with improved design, manufacturing, quality, and cost-control technologies, that is, with increases in τ.

Conceptually, A5 has two parts. The first is our assumption about the time path of exogenous technological change: the incremental capital costs of modern technologies for communication, delivery, design, and flexible production are falling over time. Assuming differentiability of κ, so that Theorem 2 applies, these trends are captured in the inequalities

$$\frac{\partial^2 \kappa}{\partial x \partial \tau} \leq 0 \qquad x = -a,-b,-c,-d,-e,-r,-s,-w$$

Technological change among capital equipment suppliers lowers the costs over time of the firm's increasing delivery speeds, using more flexible manufacturing methods, reducing the probability of defects, reducing costs of redesign and controlling production costs. Notice that we require no assumptions about the relative rates at which these prices are falling, because all these price changes will turn out to have mutually reinforcing effects.

The second part of A5 concerns the inter-relationships among investments in the new technologies. For example, assuming that the mixed partial derivative of κ with respect to $-d$ and $-e$ is positive means that the level of investment in flexible equipment necessary to reduce extra set-up costs by a given amount is reduced by investments in flexible design equipment. Of course, if the technologies were completely separable, the condition would be met but, as we argued in the introduction, separability is not a realistic assumption. The cost of instituting both computer-aided design and flexible machining systems (FMS) to achieve given levels of design and set-up costs is generally less than the sum of the costs of instituting the two separately because the CAD equipment may provide set-up instructions readable by the FMS machinery, eliminating the costly step of encoding (possibly with error) the design instructions into a form readable by the flexible machine. Other complementarities in the physical equipment are similarly represented in κ. Thus, CAD makes it less costly to reduce defects by making it much cheaper to design products that are easily manufactured, while a computerized order-entry system can eliminate the need to transcribe order information into a form readable by the manufacturing computers, saving costs and reducing errors.

Other interactions, based on substitute uses of resources, could work against our complementary assumptions. For example, if the firm faces a fixed capital budget or a rising cost of capital with increased levels of investment, or if there are constraints on space or personnel and computer based systems for communication and design compete for these resources, then an investment in lowering a would raise the cost of investments to lower d. The second part of A5 is the hypothesis that the technological complementarities we have identified are larger than the effects of any constraints on the resources that the systems must share.

Note that throughout the analysis, we are holding the rework cost parameter ρ and the inventory holding cost parameter ι fixed.

The problem of maximizing Π is not amenable to standard, calculus-based techniques. First, although demand is assumed to be a quasi-concave in price, we have made no other concavity assumptions. Indeed, the assumed convexity of δ means that profit, exclusive of capital costs, is actually *convex* in the total delay between placing an order and receiving shipment, and since A5 places no restrictions on the concavity or convexity of κ, Π may well be convex in $-a$, $-b$, m and $-r$ over some ranges. In this case, satisfaction of a first-order condition identifies a (local) minimum with respect to the variable in question. Moreover, it is natural to take m to be integer-valued of the form, nk, where k is the number of production cycles per period and n is the number of products. However, the methods developed in the previous section are applicable here, once we have the necessary complementarities. In this, A5 plays a major role.

We are now ready to state and prove our main results. The idea is to use Theorem 2 to show that the firm's objective function is supermodular in the firm's (sign-adjusted) decision variables and that consequently, by Theorems 5 and 6, the set of optimizers forms a sublattice that moves up over time. However, it is not true that Π is a supermodular function of all its arguments, because the mixed partial derivatives of that function involving the price can have the wrong sign. To avoid that difficulty, we consider the optimized value of profit with respect to the price and show that this indirect profit function is supermodular. Further, the optimal price is monotone in the other decision variables. [Our originally published treatment included only A4 as a restriction on the demand function, omitting the restriction on elasticities that is in the version of Theorem 7 stated below. The need for such restrictions was subsequently shown by Bushnell and Shepard (1995) and by Topkis (1995).]

Theorem 7: Assume A1 through A5, and assume as well that the absolute price elasticity $-\partial ln\mu/\partial ln p$ is nondecreasing in q and τ. Then the function

$$\pi(q, m, -a, -b, -c, -d, -e, -r, -s, -w, \tau)$$
$$= max_p \Pi(p, q, m, a, b, c, d, e, r, s, w, \tau)$$

is supermodular on the sublattice of $\mathbb{R}^n$ defined by the restrictions that all the decision variables be non-negative. In addition, the optimum function $p * (q, m, -a, -b, -c, -r, \tau)$ is nonincreasing.

Proof: See Bushnell and Shepard (1995, pp. 987–90), and Topkis, (1995, pp. 991–6) for the arguments. See also Milgrom and Roberts, (1995, pp. 997–9).

Theorem 8: Assume A1 through A5 and that κ is continuous. Let the individual decision variables each be constrained to lie in a compact set consistent with the nonnegativity requirement, so that together they lie in a compact set that is a sublattice. Then the set of maximizers of π is a compact sublattice which rises with τ.

Proof: Apply Theorems 6 and 7. Note that this result allows us to restrict the decision variables to be integer valued and to limit the number of available technologies to some finite set. The supermodularity of the functional form $\pi + \kappa$ is verified by investigating its derivatives on continuous intervals, and the restriction to a compact sublattice is imposed later in a way that permits a restriction to discrete choices.

The key conclusion is that the sign-adjusted decision variables all rise over time. Thus, as time passes, one expects to see a pattern of the following sort linking changes in a wide range of variables:

- Lower prices
- Lower marginal costs
- More frequent product redesigns and improvements
- Higher quality in production, marked by fewer defects
- Speedier communication with customers and processing of orders
- More frequent setups and smaller batch sizes, with correspondingly lower levels of finished-goods and work-in-process inventories and of back orders per unit demand
- Speedier delivery from inventory
- Lower setup, wastage, and changeover costs
- Lower marginal costs of product redesign

The conclusion in Theorem 6 that the set of optimizers forms a sublattice implies that if at any time there are multiple solutions to the optimization problem, then there is a highest and a lowest optimal solution in the vector inequality sense. Further, comparing any two firm's choices, if these differ, then the choice of selecting the higher, "more modern" level for each decision variable is also optimal, as is the vector made up of the term-by-term minimal values of the two firm's choices. More typically, however, we might expect a unique solution.

In any case, the chosen levels move up together over time in response to the falling costs of faster communications, more flexible production, and more frequent redesign.

The model we have presented is a static one, but it is nevertheless suggestive about the nature of the path to the modern manufacturing strategy. Specifically, it suggests that even if the changes that take place in the environment – especially the falling cost of the equipment used under the modern manufacturing strategy – happen gradually, the adoption process may be much more erratic, for two reasons. First, there are non-convexities, which mean that the optimum may shift discontinuously, with the profit-maximizing levels of the whole complex of variables moving sharply upward. This makes it relatively unprofitable to be stuck with a mixture of highly flexible and highly specialized production equipment. One does not necessarily expect to find that the adoption of the new equipment is sudden; it may still be desirable to iron out the wrinkles in the new technology with an initial small-scale adoption. What the theory suggests we should not see is an extended period of time during which there are substantial volumes of both highly flexible and highly specialized equipment being used side-by-side. Then, once the adoption is well underway, it should proceed rapidly, with increasing momentum.

Second, there are the complementarities, which make it relatively unprofitable to adopt only one part of the modern manufacturing strategy. The theory suggests that we should not see an extended period of time during which one component of the strategy is in place and the other components have barely begun to be put into place. For example, we should not see flexible equipment used for a long period with unchanging product lines.

The conclusion of Theorem 8 that firms will increase quality in the sense of reducing the probability r of a defective batch is worth further comment. Many observers have noted a focus on increased quality of output among modern manufacturing firms. One would expect that design for manufacturability would result directly in lower defect rates. However, the complementarities displayed in the model provide a second, less obvious incentive for increased quality. Decreases in the probability of defects are strictly complementary with increases in m through the effect on operating profit: demand grows with increases in m, and this increases the return to lowering costs by reducing the probability of reworking.[4]

Recall that we have held n, the number of products, fixed throughout this analysis. Inspection of the profit function in light of the arguments in Theorem 7 should make the necessity of doing this clear: neither n nor its negative are naturally complementary with the other decision variables. This shows up most clearly in the cost of redesign term, $-nq(d + e)$, where increases in n make decreases in d and e more attractive but increases in q less attractive. There are further potential complications through the demand term, and so without very special assumptions we cannot include n in the cluster of complements.

That we cannot include the number of products is somewhat surprising: surely broader product lines would seem to be complementary with reduced set-up costs, and this intuition has in fact been verified in simpler models (see Xavier de Groote, 1988). However, the ambiguity surrounding n in richer models appear to reflect something real. On the one side, there are numerous examples of firms massively broadening their product lines with the adoption of modern manufacturing methods, and some of these were cited above. On the other, anecdotal evidence (for example, James B. Treece, 1989) as well as both the discussions of the "focused factory" found in the literature on manufacturing strategy (for example, David A. Garvin, 1988, especially Ch. 8) and some formal statistical analysis (Mikhel Tombak and Arnoud De Meyer, 1988) point to firms having reason to narrow their product lines when shifting to more modern manufacturing patterns and of their acting to do so.

3. Manufacturing and Organization

How is a manufacturing firm most efficiently organized and managed? Several of the trends analyzed in section 2 have a direct bearing on this question. First, consider the complementarities that exist between the various functions in the firm: marketing, order-processing, shipping, engineering, and manufacturing. If the firm's problem were smooth and concave (despite the complementarities) and its environment were stationary and if the optimum is not on the boundary of the feasible set, the complementarities would not pose a serious organizational problem: if none of the managers controlling the individual functions can find a small change that raises the firm's expected profits, then there is no coordinated change – large or small – that can raise profits. However, in our non-concave problem, it is possible that only coordinated changes among all the variables will allow the firm to achieve its optimum. Non-convexities and significant complementarities provide a reason for explicit coordination between functions such as marketing and production.[5]

(Extension of the methods in this paper to a game-theoretic context can be used to model this coordination problem and the role of the central coordinator: see Milgrom and Roberts, 1989.)

Even without non-convexities, significant complementarities in a rapidly changing environment provide another reason for close coordination between functions. Think of the managerial planning process as an algorithm to seek the maximum of the profit function. Successful performance in the face of rapid environmental change-requires the use of fast algorithms (for example, Newton's method), and these require a coordinated choice of the decision variables that recognizes the interactions among these variables in the profit function.

Second, suppose that the organization being modeled is one where sales are made through several different stores. If the optimal speed of order-processing (a) jumps down, it may be desirable that all the stores install computerized systems linked to the manufacturing facility to track orders and sales. If there are fixed costs or other economies of scale in the computer system, then it is important that all, or nearly all, of the stores participate. However, unless all the costs and benefits of the change accrue to one agent, there arises a standard public goods, free-rider problem. Eliciting efficient cooperation from the store owners could be expensive and may provide a reason for vertical ownership of the distribution channel.

Third, Oliver Williamson (1986) and Klein, Crawford, and Alchian (1978) have argued that the advantages of increased vertical governance grow as assets become increasingly specialized. This occurs, it is argued, because the returns from specialized investments are vulnerable to appropriation. Then, as Williamson (1986) and Jean Tirole (1986) have argued, fear of appropriation causes insufficient investment to be made or, as we have argued (Milgrom and Roberts, 1987), it encourages the parties to waste resources by investing in bargaining positions. Following this line of argument, let us equate "specialization" of assets with inflexibility of retooling to produce different products, so that it may be measured by e. The net costs of governance, bargaining, and deterred or distorted incentives are $\gamma(-v, -e)$, where v is a vector measure of the extent or complexity of vertical governance. We formalize a version of the hypothesis that increased flexibility of assets reduces the marginal value of governance activities with:

Assumption A6: The function $\gamma(-v, -e)$ is sub-modular.

Theorem 9: Assume that *A1–A6* hold and consider the profit function:

$$\pi(-p, m, q, -a, -b, -c, -d, -e, -r, -s, -w, \tau) - \gamma(-v, -e)$$

Let each decision variable be constrained as in Theorem 8. Then the set of optimizers of $\pi - \gamma$ is a sublattice and rises with τ.
Proof: A direct consequence of Theorems 3, 5, 6, and 7, and A6.

Thus, given Assumptions A1–A6 another predicted attribute in the characteristic cluster for flexible manufacturing companies is low vertical governance, for example, the extensive use of independently owned suppliers and subcontractors. This characteristic is an especially interesting one, given the usual conception of the difference between internal and market organization. Although uncertainty is not formally part of our model,[6] running this sort of "tight," low inventory operation with frequent redesigning of products in a world of uncertainties would surely require close coordination and communications with suppliers.[7] Yet according to our theory, the modern firm – despite its close relationships with suppliers and customers – will have little formal vertical governance.

Economists sometimes emphasize the need for close communication in the presence of supply or demand uncertainty as a reason for vertical integration (for example, Kenneth Arrow, 1975). If we were to formulate this alternative hypothesis using a submodular governance cost function $\lambda(m, v)$, we would arrive at the conclusion that v increases over time and that more extensive vertical governance is part of the cluster of characteristics of a modern manufacturing firm. The anecdotal evidence contained in press reports suggests to us that this conclusion is wrong, and that the former hypothesis A6 is the better one.

4. Conclusion

The cluster of characteristics that are often found in manufacturing firms that are technologically advanced encompasses marketing, production, engineering, and organization variables. On the marketing side, these firms hold down prices while emphasizing high quality supported by frequent product improvements. Customers orders are filled increasingly quickly, with back-order levels being systematically reduced. In terms of technology, modern manufacturing firms exploit rapid mass data communications, production equipment with low setup, wastage, and retooling costs, flexible design technologies, product designs that use common inputs, very low levels of inventories (of both work in process and finished goods), and short production cycle times. They also seem to push differentially to increase manufacturing quality and simultaneously, to control variable production costs. At the engineering and organizational levels, there is an integration of the product and process engineering functions and an extensive use of independently owned suppliers linked with the buying firm by close communications and joint planning.

We have argued in this paper that this clustering is no accident. Rather, it is a result of the adoption by profit-maximizing firms of a coherent business strategy that exploits complementarities, and the trend to adopt this strategy is the result of identifiable changes in technology and demand. Our formal model includes eleven decision variables from the claimed cluster of complements plus a parameter to account for the passage of time. There are thus 66 potential cross effects among the twelve variables, and all of these are nonnegative: there are extensive complementarities in marketing, manufacturing, engineering, design, and organization that make it profitable for a firm that adopts some of these characteristics to adopt more. We have also argued that the non-convexities in the problem mitigate against any smooth distribution of these characteristics among firms. For this reason, we are hopeful that empirical work will provide evidence of distinctly separated clusters of firm characteristics as support for our theory. Given our assumptions about time trends in prices, we also expect to find an increasing proportion of manufacturing firms adopting the modern manufacturing strategic cluster that we have described.

Appendix

Theorem 2*: Let $I = [a_1, b_1] \times \ldots \times [a_n, b_n]$ be an interval in $\mathbb{R}^n$ with nonempty interior and let $f\colon I \to \mathbb{R}$. Suppose that for every pair of arguments ij, there exists a function $f_{ij}; I \to \mathbb{R}$ such that f is the indefinite integral of f_{ij}. That is, for fixed $x_{\setminus ij}$ and for $x_i' > x_i$ and $x_j' > x_j$,

$$f\left(x_i', x_j', x_{\setminus ij}\right) + f\left(x_i, x_j, x_{\setminus ij}\right) - f\left(x_i', x_j, x_{\setminus ij}\right) - f\left(x_i, x_j', x_{\setminus ij}\right)$$

$$= \int_{x_i}^{x_i'} \int_{x_j}^{x_j'} f_{ij}\left(s, t, x_{\setminus ij}\right) ds dt$$

If each f_{ij} is nonnegative, then f is supermodular on I.

Remark 1: In our application, f is continuous on I and twice continuously differentiable on a set S with $\partial^2 f / \partial x_i \partial x_j \geq 0$ on S. Moreover, for all $\bar{x}_{\setminus ij}$ the set $(I - S) \cap \{x | x_{\setminus ij} = \bar{x}_{\setminus ij}\}$ is a curve. So, taking $f_{ij} = \partial^2 f / \partial x_i \partial x_j$ where defined and $f_{ij} = 0$ elsewhere, Theorem 2* implies that f is supermodular.

Proof: In view of Theorem 1, it suffices to establish the conclusion for the case $n = 2$. Given any two unordered points x and x' with, say, $x_1 > x_1'$ and $x_2' > x_2$,

$$f(\max(x, x')) + f(\min(x, x')) - f(x) - f(x') = \int_{x_1'}^{x_1} \int_{x_2}^{x_2'} f_{12}(s, t) ds dt$$

$$\geq 0$$

from which it follows that

$$f(x) + f(x') \leq f(\max(x, x')) + f(\min(x, x'))$$

Notes

1 Probably no single firm is involved in all the changes we will describe. Nevertheless, there is a definite, discernible pattern of change in technology, manufacturing, marketing, and organizational strategy that characterizes successful "modern manufacturing." For a description of the technologies involved, see U.S. Congress Office of Technology Assessment, 1984.

2 Optimal batch size can be determined via a standard Economic Order Quantity model, in which the setup costs of switching from making one product to making another are traded off against the costs of holding the larger average inventories of finished goods that go with longer runs and less frequent changeovers. Optimal batch size is a decreasing function of setup costs and so batch sizes optimally decrease as more flexible machines are introduced.

3   A function f is subadditive if

$$f(x) + f(y) \geq f(x+y)$$

for all x and y.

4   Note too that decreases in r are also strictly complementary with increases in the other quality variable, q, as well as with decreases in the delay in communicating with customers and processing their orders (a) and in the time to deliver the inventory (b).

5   A similar point is made by de Groote, (1988) who investigates a different model of complementarities between marketing and manufacturing.

6   However, introducing uncertainty would cause no difficulties because the expectation of a supermodular function is supermodular. See Milgrom and Roberts (1989).

7   For a model of some aspects of this issue, see Milgrom and Roberts (1988). In that model, inventories play a buffering role whose importance is reduced when communication is increased.

References

Abegglen, J. and Stalk, Jr. G. (1985): *Kaisha: The Japanese Corporation*, New York: Basic Books.

Alster, N. (1989): "What Flexible Workers Can Do," *Fortune*, February 13, 62–6.

Arrow, K. (1985) "Vertical Integration and Communication," *Bell Journal of Economics*, 6, Spring, 173–83.

Asanuma, B. (1989): "Manufacturer–Supplier Relationships in Japan and the Concept of Relation-Specific Skill," *Journal of the Japanese and International Economies*, 3 (1), 1–30.

——(1988b) "Japanese Manufacturer-Supplier Relationships in International Perspective," Kyoto University Economics working paper 8, September.

Baumol, W. J., Panzar, J. C. and Willig, R. D. (1982): *Contestable Markets and the Theory of Industry Structure*, New York: Harcourt Brace Jovanovich.

Bushnell, P. T. and Shepard, A. P. (1995): "The Economics of Modern Manufacture: Comment," *American Economic Review*, 85, 987–90.

de Groote, X. (1988): The Strategic Choice of Production Processes. Unpublished doctoral dissertation, Stanford University.

Dumaine, B. (1989): "How Managers can Succeed through Speed," *Fortune*, February 13, 54–9.

Garvin, D. A. (1988): *Managing Quality: The Strategic and Competitive Edge*. New York: Free Press.

General Motors Corporation (1988): "First a Vision, Now the Payoff," *General Motors Public Interest Report 1988*, Detroit, 2–15.

Hausman, W. (1988): Computer-Integrated Manufacturing: Lessons from Ten Plant Visits. Seminar presented at the Graduate School of Business, Stanford University, Stanford, CA, November.

Hayes, R. H., Wheelwright, S. C. and Clark, K. B. (1988): *Dynamic Manufacturing: Creating the Learning Organization*. New York: Free Press.

Henkoff, R. (1988): "This Cat is Acting like a Tiger," *Fortune*, December 19, 69–76.

Hounshell, D. A. (1984): *From the American System to Mass Production: 1800–1932*, Baltimore: Johns Hopkins University Press.

Kiechel, W. III (1988): "Corporate Strategy for the 1990s," *Fortune*, February 29, 34–42.

Klein, B., Crawford, R. and Alchian, A. (1978): "Vertical Integration, Appropriable Rents, and the Competitive Contracting Process," *Journal of Law and Economics*, 26, October, 297–326.

Milgrom, P. and Roberts, J. (1987): "Bargaining and Influence Costs and the Organization of Economic Activity," discussion paper, Graduate School of Business, Stanford University.

Republished 1990 in J. Alt and K. Shepsle (eds), *Perspectives on Positive Political Economy*, Cambridge: Cambridge University Press, 57–89.

——(1988): "Communication and Inventories as Substitutes in Organizing Production," *Scandinavian Journal of Economics*, 90 (3), 275–89.

——(1989): "Rationalizability, Learning and Equilibrium in Games with Strategic Complementarities," discussion paper, Graduate School of Business, Stanford University.

——(1995): "The Economics of Modern Manufacturing: Reply," *American Economic Review*, 85, 997–9.

Mitchell, R. (1989): "Masters of Innovation: How 3M Keeps Its New Products Coming," *Business Week*, April 10, 58–63.

Moore, T. (1988): "Make or Break Time for General Motors," *Fortune*, February 15, 32–50.

O'Rourke, T. (1988): "A Case for CIM," lecture delivered at the Conference on Manufacturing, Stanford University, Stanford, CA, May.

Peters, T. (1987): "Hats off to Benetton's Apparel Network," *Palo Alto Times-Tribune*, November 18, E1.

Piore, M. J. (1986): *Corporate Reform in American Manufacturing and the Challenge to Economic Theory*, mimeo, Massachusetts Institute of Technology.

——and Sabel, C. F. (1984): *The Second Industrial Divide: Prospects for Prosperity*. New York: Basic Books.

Port, O. (1989a) "Smart Factories: America's Turn?" *Business Week*, May 8, 142–8.

——(1989b) "The Best-Engineered Part is no Part at All," *Business Week*, May 8, 150.

Taylor, A. III (1988): "Why Fords sell like Big Macs," *Fortune*, November 21, 122–8.

Tirole, J. (1986): "Procurement and Renegotiation," *Journal of Political Economy*, 94, April, 235–59.

Tombak, M. and De Meyer, A. (1988): "Flexibility and FMS: An Empirical Appraisal," *IEEE Transactions on Engineering Management*, 35, May, 101–7.

Topkis, D. M. (1978): "Minimizing a Submodular Function on a Lattice," *Operations Research*, 26, March–April, 305–21.

——(1995): "The Economics of Modern Manufacturing: Comment," *American Economic Review*, 85, 991–6.

Treece, J. B. (1989): "GM's Bumpy Ride on the Long Road Back," *Business Week*, February 13, 74–8.

U.S. Congress (1984): Office of Technology Assessment, *Computerized Manufacturing Automation: Employment, Education and the Workplace*, Washington.

Valery, N. (1987): "Factory of the Future: Survey," *The Economist*, May 30, 3–18.

Williamson, O. (1986): *Economic Institutions of Capitalism*. New York: Free Press.

Wright, K. and Bourn, D. (1988): *Manufacturing Intelligence*. Reading, MA: Addison Wesley.

III B

The Firm's Decision Making Under Certainty: Perfectly Competitive Markets

CHAPTER EIGHT

Perfect Competition, Historically Contemplated

GeoRGe J. Stigler

Source: *Journal of Political Economy*, 65 (1957), pp. 1–17. Reprinted with the permission of the University of Chicago. © University of Chicago.

No concept in economics – or elsewhere – is ever defined fully, in the sense that its meaning under every conceivable circumstance is clear. Even a word with a wholly arbitrary meaning in economics, like "elasticity," raises questions which the person who defined it (in this case, Marshall) never faced: for example, how does the concept apply to finite changes or to discontinuous or stochastic or multiple-valued functions? And of course a word like "competition," which is shared with the whole population, is even less likely to be loaded with restrictions or elaborations to forestall unfelt ambiguities.

Still, it is a remarkable fact that the concept of competition did not begin to receive explicit and systematic attention in the main stream of economics until 1871. This concept – as pervasive and fundamental as any in the whole structure of classical and neoclassical economic theory – was long treated with the kindly casualness with which one treats the intuitively obvious. Only slowly did the elaborate and complex concept of perfect competition evolve, and it was not until after the first World War that it was finally received into general theoretical literature. The evolution of the concept and the steps by which it became confused with a perfect market, uniqueness of equilibrium, and stationary conditions are the subject of this essay.

1. The Classical Economists

"Competition" entered economics from common discourse, and for long it connoted only the independent rivalry of two or more persons. When Adam Smith wished to explain why a reduced supply led to a higher price, he referred (Smith, 1937, pp. 56–7) to the "competition [which] will immediately begin" among buyers; when the supply is excessive, the price will sink more, the greater "the competition of the sellers, or according as it happens to be more or less important to them to get immediately rid of the commodity." It will be noticed that "competition" is here (and usually) used in the sense of rivalry in a race – a race to get limited supplies or a race to be rid of excess supplies. Competition is a process of responding to a new force and a method of reaching a new equilibrium.

Smith (1937, pp. 126, 342) observed that economic rivals were more likely to strive for gain by under-or overbidding one another, the more numerous they were:

> The trades which employ but a small number of hands, run most easily into such combinations.
>   If this capital [sufficient to trade in a town] is divided between two different grocers, their competition will tend to make both of them sell cheaper, than if it were in the hands of one only; and if it were divided among twenty, their competition would be just so much the greater, and the chance of their combining together, in order to raise the price, just so much the less.

This is all that Smith has to say of the number of rivals.

Of course something more is implicit, and partially explicit, in Smith's treatment of competition, but this "something more" is not easy to state precisely, for it was not precise in Smith's mind. But the concept of competition seemed to embrace also several other elements:

1 The economic units must possess tolerable knowledge of the conditions of employment of their resources in various industries. "This equality [of remuneration] can take place only in those employments which are well known, and have been long established in the neighbourhood" (Smith, 1937, p. 114). But the necessary information was usually available: "Secrets..., it must be acknowledged, can seldom be long kept; and the extraordinary profit can last very little longer than they are kept" (Smith, 1937, p. 60).
2 Competition achieved its results only in the long run: "This equality in the whole of the advantages and disadvantages of the different employments of labour and stock, can take place only in the ordinary, or what may be called the natural state of those employments" (Smith, 1937, p. 115).
3 There must be freedom of trade; the economic unit must be free to enter or leave any trade. The exclusive privileges or corporations which exclude men from trades, and the restrictions imposed on mobility by the settlement provisions of the poor law, are examples of such interferences with "free competition."

In sum, then, Smith had five conditions of competition:

1 The rivals must act independently, not collusively.
2 The number of rivals, potential as well as present, must be sufficient to eliminate extraordinary gains.
3 The economic units must possess tolerable knowledge of the market opportunities.
4 There must be freedom (from social restraints) to act on this knowledge.
5 Sufficient time must elapse for resources to flow in the directions and quantities desired by their owners.

The modern economist has a strong tendency to read more into such statements than they meant to Smith and his contemporaries. The fact that he (and many successors) was willing to call the ownership of land a monopoly – although the market in agricultural land met all these conditions – simply because the total supply of land was believed to be fixed is sufficient testimony to the fact that he was not punctilious in his language.[1]

Smith did not state how he was led to these elements of a concept of competition. We may reasonably infer that the conditions of numerous rivals and of independence of action of these rivals were matters of direct observation. Every informed person knew, at least in a general way, what competition was, and the essence of this knowledge was the striving of rivals to gain advantages relative to one another.

The other elements of competition, on the contrary, appear to be the necessary conditions for the validity of a proposition which was to be associated with competition: the equalization of returns in various directions open to an entrepreneur or investor or laborer. If one postulates equality of returns as the equilibrium state under competition, then adequacy of numbers and independence of rivals are not enough for equilibrium. The entrepreneur (or other agents) must know what returns are obtainable in various fields, he must be allowed to enter the fields promising high rates of return, and he must be given time to make his presence felt in these fields. These conditions were thus prerequisites of an analytical theorem, although their reasonableness was no doubt enhanced by the fact that they corresponded more or less closely to observable conditions.

This sketch of a concept of competition was not amplified or challenged in any significant respect for the next three-quarters of a century by any important member of the English school. A close study of the literature, such as I have not made, would no doubt reveal many isolated passages on the formal properties or realism of the concept, especially when the theory was applied to concrete problems. For example, Senior was more interested in methodology than most of his contemporaries, and he commented (Senior, 1854, p. 102):

> But though, under free competition, cost of production is the regulator of price, its influence is subject to much occasional interruption. Its operation can be supposed to be perfect only if we suppose that there are no disturbing causes, that capital and labour can be at once transferred, and without loss, from one employment to another, and that every producer has full information of the profit to be derived from every mode of production. But it is obvious that these suppositions have no resemblance to the truth. A large portion of the capital essential to production consists of buildings, machinery, and other implements, the results of much time and labour, and of little service for any except their existing pur- poses. . . . Few capitalists can estimate, except upon an average of some years, the amounts of their own profits, and still fewer can estimate those of their neighbours.

Senior made no use of the concept of perfect competition hinted at in this passage, and he was wholly promiscuous in his use of the concept of monopoly.

Cairnes, the last important English economist to write in the classical tradition, did break away from the Smithian concept of competition. He defined a state of free competition as one in which commodities exchanged in proportion to the sacrifices (of labor and capital) in their production (Cairnes, 1874, p. 79). This condition was amply fulfilled, he believed, so far as capital was concerned, for there was a large stock of disposable capital which quickly flowed into unusually remunerative fields (p. 68). The condition was only partly fulfilled in the case of labor, however, for there existed a hierarchy of occupational classes ("non-competing industrial groups") which the laborer found it most difficult to ascend (p. 72). Even the extra rewards of skill beyond those which paid for the sacrifices in obtaining training were a monopoly return.[2] This approach was not analytically rigorous – Cairnes did not tell how to equate the sacrifices of capitalists and laborers – nor was it empirically fruitful.

Cairnes labeled as "industrial competition" the force which effects the proportioning of prices to psychological costs which takes place to the extent that the products are made in one non-competing group, and he called on the reciprocal demand theory of international trade to explain exchanges of products between non-competing groups. Hence we might call industrial competition the competition within non-competing groups, and commercial competition that between non-competing groups. But Sidgwick and Edgeworth attribute the opposite concepts to Cairnes: commercial competition is competition within an industry, and industrial competition requires the ability of resources to flow between industries (Sidgwick, 1883, p. 182; Edgeworth, 1925, II, pp. 280, 311). Their nomenclature seems more appropriate; I have not been able to find Cairnes's discussion of commercial competition and doubt that it exists.[3]

2. The Critics of Private Enterprise

The main claims for a private-enterprise system rest upon the workings of competition, and it would not have been unnatural for critics of this system to focus much attention on the competitive concept. They might have argued that Smith's assumptions were not strong enough to insure optimum results or that, even if perfect competition were formulated as the basis of the theory, certain deviations from optimum results (such as those associated with external economies) could occur. The critics did not make this type of criticism, however, possibly simply because they were not first-class analysts; and for this type of development we must return to the main line of theorists, consisting mostly of politically conservative economists.

Or, at another pole, the critics might simply have denied that competition was the basic form of market organization. In the nineteenth century, however, this was only a minor and sporadic charge.[4] The Marxists did not press this point: both the labor theory of value and the doctrine of equalization of profit rates require competition.[5] The early Fabian essayists were also prepared to make their charges rest upon the deficiencies in the workings of competition rather than its absence.[6] The charge that competition was non-existent or vanishing did not become commonplace until the end of the nineteenth century.

The critics, to the extent that they took account of competition at all, emphasized the evil tendencies which they believed flowed from its workings. It would be interesting to examine their criticisms systematically with a view to their treatment of competition; it is my impression that their most common, and most influential, charge was that competition led to a highly objectionable, and perhaps continuously deteriorating, distribution of income by size.[7] In their explanations of the workings of a competitive economy the most striking deficiency of the classical economists was their failure to work out the theory of the effects of competition on the distribution of income.

3. The Mathematical School

The first steps in the analytical refinement of the concept of competition were made by the mathematical economists. This stage in the history of the concept is of special interest because it reveals both the types of advances that were achieved by this approach and the manner in which alien elements were introduced into the concept.

When an algebraically inclined economist seeks to maximize the profits of a producer, he is led to write the equation

$$\text{Profits} = \text{Revenue} - \text{Cost}$$

and then to maximize this expression; that is, to set the derivative of profits with respect to output equal to zero. He then faces the question: How does revenue (say, pq) vary with output (q)? The natural answer is to *define* competition as that situation in which p does not vary with q – in which the demand curve facing the firm is horizontal. This is precisely what Cournot (1927, p. 90) did:

> The effects of competition have reached their limit, when each of the partial productions D_k [the output of producer k] is *inappreciable*, not only with reference to the total production $D = F(p)$, but also with reference to the derivative $F'(p)$, so that the partial production D_k could be substracted from D without any appreciable variation resulting in the price of the commodity.[8]

This definition of competition was especially appropriate in Cournot's system because, according to his theory of oligopoly, the excess of price over marginal cost approached zero as the number of like producers became large.[9] Cournot believed that this condition of competition was fulfilled "for a multitude of products, and, among them, for the most important products" (Cournot, 1927, p. 90).

Cournot's definition was enormously more precise and elegant than Smith's so far as the treatment of numbers was concerned. A market departed from unlimited competition to the extent that price exceeded the marginal cost of the firm, and the difference approached zero as the number of rivals approached infinity.

But the refinement was one-sided: Cournot paid no attention to conditions of entry and so his definition of competition held also for industries with numerous firms even though no more firms could enter.

The role of knowledge was made somewhat more prominent in Jevons' exposition. His concept of competition was a part of his concept of a market, and a perfect market was characterized by two conditions (Jevons, 1871, pp. 87 and 86).

1 A market, then, is theoretically perfect only when all traders have perfect knowledge of the conditions of supply and demand, and the consequent ratio of exchange...
2 ...there must be perfectly free competition, so that anyone will exchange with any one else upon the slightest advantage appearing. There must be no conspiracies for absorbing and holding supplies to produce unnatural ratios of exchange.

One might interpret this ambiguous second condition in several ways, for the pursuit of advantages is not inconsistent with conspiracies. At a minimum, Jevons assumes complete independence of action by every trader for a corollary of the perfect market in that "in the same market, at any moment, there cannot be two prices for the same kind of article."[10] This rule of a single price (it is called the "law of indifference" in the second edition) excludes price discrimination and probably requires that the market have numerous buyers and sellers, but the condition is not made explicit. The presence of large numbers is clearly implied, however, when we are told that "a single trader... must buy and sell at the current prices, which he cannot in an appreciable degree affect."[11]

The merging of the concepts of competition and the market was unfortunate, for each deserved a full and separate treatment. A market is an institution for the consummation of transactions. It performs this function efficiently when every buyer who will pay more than the minimum realized price for any class of commodities succeeds in buying the commodity, and every seller who will sell for less than the maximum realized price succeeds in selling the commodity. A market performs these tasks more efficiently if the commodities are well specified and if buyers and sellers are fully informed of their properties and prices. Possibly also a perfect market allows buyers and sellers to act on differing expectations of future prices. A market may be perfect and monopolistic or imperfect and competitive. Jevons' mixture of the two has been widely imitated by successors, of course, so that even today a market is commonly treated as a concept subsidiary to competition.

Edgeworth was the first to attempt a systematic and rigorous definition of perfect competition. His exposition deserves the closest scrutiny in spite of the fact that few economists of his time or ours have attempted to disentangle and uncover the theorems and conjectures of the *Mathematical Psychics*, probably the most elusively written book of importance in the history of economics. For his allegations and demonstrations seem to be the parents of widespread beliefs on the nature of perfect competition.

The conditions of perfect competition are stated as follows (Edgeworth, 1881, pp. 17–19):

> The *field of competition* with reference to a contract, or contracts, under consideration consists of all individuals who are willing and able to recontract about the articles under consideration....
>
> There is free communication throughout a *normal* competitive field. You might suppose the constituent individuals collected at a point, or connected by telephones – an ideal supposition [1881], but sufficiently approximate to existence or tendency for the purposes of abstract science.
>
> A *perfect* field of competition professes in addition certain properties peculiarly favourable to mathematical calculation;... The conditions of a *perfect* field are four; the first pair referrible to the heading *multiplicity* or continuity, the second *dividedness* or fluidity.

> I.   An individual is free to *recontract* with any out of an indefinite number,...
> II. Any individual is free to *contract* (at the same time) with an indefinite number;... This condition combined with the first appears to involve the indefinite divisibility of each *article* of contract (if any X deal with an indefinite number of Ys he must give each an indefinitely small portion of x); which might be erected into a separate condition.
> III. Any individual is free to *recontract* with another independently of, *without the consent being required of*, any third party,...
> IV. Any individual is free to *contract* with another independently of a third party;...

> The failure of the first [condition] involves the failure of the second, but not *vice versa*; and the third and fourth are similarly related.

The natural question to put to such a list of conditions of competition is: Are the conditions necessary and sufficient to achieve what intuitively or pragmatically seems to be a useful concept of competition? Edgeworth replies, in effect that the conditions are both necessary and sufficient. More specifically, competition requires

1 indefinitely large numbers of participants on both sides of the market;
2 complete absence of limitations upon individual self-seeking behavior; and
3 complete divisibility of the commodities traded.[12]

The rationale of the requirement of indefinite numbers is as follows. With bilateral monopoly, the transaction will be indeterminate – equilibrium can be anywhere on the contract curve. If we add a second buyer and seller, it is shown that the range of permissible equilibriums (the length of the tenable contract curve) will shrink (p. 35). By intuitive induction, with infinitely many traders it will shrink to a single point; a single price must rule in the market (pp. 37–9).

Before we discuss this argument, we may take account also of the condition that individual traders are free to act independently. Edgeworth shows that combinations reduce the effective number of traders and that "combiners *stand to gain*" (p. 43). In effect, then, he must assume that the individual trader not only is free to act independently but will in fact do so.

The proof of the need for indefinite numbers has serious weaknesses. The range of indeterminacy shrinks only because one seller or buyer tries to cut out the other by offering better terms.[13] Edgeworth fails to show that such price competition (which is palpably self-defeating) will occur or that, if it does occur, why the process should stop before the parties reach a unique (competitive) equilibrium. Like all his descendants, he treated the small-numbers case unsatisfactorily.

It is intuitively plausible that with infinite numbers all monopoly power (and indeterminacy) will vanish, and Edgeworth essentially postulates rather than proves this. But a simple demonstration, in case of sellers of equal size, would amount only to showing that

$$\text{Marginal revenue} = \text{Price} + \frac{\text{Price}}{\text{Number of sellers} \times \text{Market elasticity}}$$

and that this last term goes to zero as the number of sellers increases indefinitely.[14] This was implicitly Cournot's argument.

But why do we require divisibility of the traded commodity?

> Suppose a market, consisting of an equal number of masters and servants, offering respectively wages and service; subject to the condition that no man can serve two masters, no master employ more than one man; or suppose equilibrium already established between such parties to be disturbed by any sudden influx of wealth into the hands of the masters. Then there is no *determinate*, and very generally *unique*, arrangement towards which the system tends under the operation of, may we say, a law of Nature, and which would be predictable if we knew beforehand the real requirements of each, or of the average, dealer; ... (p. 46).

Consider the simple example: a thousand masters will each employ a man at any wage below 100; a thousand laborers will each work for any wage above 50. There will be a single wage rate: knowledge and numbers are sufficient to lead a worker to seek a master paying more than the going rate or a master to seek out a worker receiving less than the market rate. But any rate between 50 and 100 is a possible equilibrium.[15]

It is not the lack of uniqueness that is troublesome, however, for a market can be perfectly competitive even though there be a dozen possible stable equilibrium positions.[16] Rather, the difficulty arises because the demand (or supply) functions do not possess continuous derivatives: the withdrawal of even one unit will lead to a large change in price, so that the individual trader – even though he has numerous independent rivals – can exert a perceptible influence upon price.

The element of market control arising out of the non-continuity is easily eliminated, of course. If the article which is traded is divisible, then equalities replace inequalities in the conditions of equilibrium: the individual trader can no longer influence the market price. A master may employ a variable amount of labor, and he will therefore bid for additional units so long as the wage rate is below his marginal demand price. A worker may have several employers, and he will therefore supply additional labor so long as any employer will pay more than his marginal supply price. "If the labour of the assistants can be sold by the hour, or other sort of differential dose, the phenomenon of determinate equilibrium will reappear."[17] Divisibility was introduced to achieve determinateness, which it fails to do, but it is required to eliminate monopoly power.

Divisibility had a possible second role in the assumptions, which, however, was never made explicit. If there are infinitely many possessors of a commodity, presumably each must have only an infinitesimal quantity of it if the existing total stock is to be finite. But no economist placed emphasis upon the strict mathematical implications of concepts like infinity, and this word was used to convey only the notion of an indefinitely large number of traders.

The remainder of the mathematical economists of the period did not extend, or for that matter even reach, the level of precision of Edgeworth. Walras (1954, pp. 83, 185) gave no adequate definition of competition.[18] Pareto noticed the possible effects of social controls over purchases and sales.[19] Henry Moore (1905–6), in what may have been the first article on the formal definition of competition,[20] listed five "implicit hypotheses" of competition:

I.   Each economic factor seeks a maximum net income.
II. There is but one price for commodities of the same quality in the same market.
III. The influence of the product of any one producer upon the price per unit of the total product is negligible.
IV. The output of any one producer is negligible as compared with the total output.
V.   Each producer orders the amount of his product without regard to the effect of his act upon the conduct of his competitors.[21]

This list of conditions is noteworthy chiefly because it marked an unsuccessful attempt to revert to the narrower competitive concept of Jevons.

4. Marshall

Marshall as usual refused to float on the tide of theory, and his treatment of competition was much closer to Adam Smith's than to that of his contemporaries. Indeed, Marshall's exposition was almost as informal and unsystematic as Smith's in this area. His main statement (Marshall, 1890, p. 402) was:

> We are investigating the equilibrium of normal demand and normal supply in their most general form: we are neglecting those features which are special to particular parts of economic science, and are confining our attention to those broad relations which are common to nearly the whole of it. Thus we assume that the forces of demand and supply have free play in a perfect market; there is no combination among dealers on either side, but each acts for himself: and there is *free competition*; that is, buyers compete freely with buyers, and sellers compete freely with sellers. But though everyone acts for himself, his knowledge of what others are doing is supposed to be sufficient to prevent him from taking a lower price or paying a higher price than others are doing; ... [22]

If this quotation suggests that Marshall was invoking a strict concept of competition, we must remember that he discussed the "fear of spoiling the market" and the firms with negatively sloping demand curves in the main chapters on competition (8th edn, pp. 374, 458) and that the only time perfect competition was mentioned was when it was expressly spurned (p. 540).

Soon he yielded a bit to the trend toward refinement of the concept. Beginning with the third (1895) edition, he explicitly introduced the horizontal demand curve for the individual firm as the normal case and gave it the same mathematical formulation as did Cournot (1927, pp. 517, 849–50). But these were patchwork revisions, and they were not carried over into the many passages where looser concepts of competition had been employed.

Marshall's most significant contribution was indirect: he gave the most powerful analysis up to his time of the relationship of competition to optimum economic organization (Book V, chap. xiii, on the doctrine of maximum satisfaction). There he found the competitive results to have not only the well-known qualification that the distribution of resources must be taken as a datum, and the precious exception that only one of several multiple stable equilibriums could be the maximum,[23] but also a new and possibly extremely important exception, arising out of external economies and diseconomies. The doctrine of external economies in effect asserts that in important areas the choices of an individual are governed by only part of the consequences, and inevitably the doctrine opens up a wide range of competitive equilibriums which depart from conventional criteria of optimum arrangement. It was left for Pigou (1912) to elaborate, and exaggerate, the importance of this source of disharmonies.

5. The Complete Formulation Clark and Knight

Only two new elements were needed to be added to the Edgeworth conditions for competition in order to reach the modern concept of perfect competition. They pertained to the mobility of resources and the model of the stationary economy, and both were presented, not first,[24] but most influentially, by John Bates Clark.

Clark, in his well-known development of the concept of a static economy (Clark, 1899) ascribed all dynamic disturbances to five forces (p. 56):

1   Population is increasing.
2   Capital is increasing.
3   Methods of production are improving.
4   The forms of industrial establishments are changing: . . .
5   The wants of consumers are multiplying.

The main purpose of his treatise was to analyze the stationary economy in which these forces were suppressed, and for this analysis the assumption of competition was basic (pp. 68, 71):

> There is an ideal arrangement of the elements of society, to which the force of competition, acting on individual men, would make the society conform. The producing mechanism actually shapes itself about this model, and at no time does it vary greatly from it.
>
> We must use assumptions boldly and advisedly, making labor and capital absolutely mobile, and letting competition work in ideal perfection.

Although the concepts of a stationary economy and of competition are completely independent of each other, Clark somehow believed that competition was an element of static analysis (p. 76; see also p. 78):

> The statement made in the foregoing chapter that a static state excludes true entrepreneurs' profits does not deny that a legal monopoly might secure to an entrepreneur a profit that would be permanent as the law that should create it – and that, too, in a social condition which, at first glance, might appear to be static. The agents, labor and capital, would be prevented from moving into the favored industry, though economic forces, if they had been left unhindered, would have caused them to move in. This condition, however, is not a true static state, as it has been defined . . . Industrial groups are in a truly static state when the industrial agents, labor and capital, show a *perfect mobility, but no motion*. A legal monopoly destroys at a certain point this mobility. . . .

I shall return to this identification of competition with stationary equilibrium at a later point.

The introduction of perfect mobility of resources as an assumption of competition was new, and Clark offers no real explanation for the assumption. One could simply eliminate his five dynamic influences, and then equilibrium would be reached after a time even with "friction" (or less than instantaneous mobility). Clark was aware of this possible approach but merely said that "it is best to assume" that there is no friction (p. 81). The only gain in his subsequent work, of course, is the avoidance of an occasional "in the long run."

Mobility of resources had always been an implicit assumption of competition, and in fact the conditions of adequate knowledge of earning opportunities and absence of contrived barriers to movement were believed to be adequate to insure mobility. But there exist also technological limitations to the rate at which resources can move from one place or industry to another, and these limitations were in fact the basis of Marshall's concept of the short-run normal period. Once this fact was generally recognized, it became inevitable that mobility of resources be given an explicit time dimension, although of course it was highly accidental that instantaneous mobility was postulated.

The concept of perfect competition received its complete formulation in Frank Knight's. *Risk, Uncertainty and Profit* (1921). It was the meticulous discussion in this work that did most to drive home to economists generally the austere nature of the rigorously defined concept[25] and so prepared the way for the widespread reaction against it in the 1930s.

Knight sought to establish the precise nature of an economy with complete knowledge as a preliminary step in the analysis of the impact of uncertainty. Clark's procedure of eliminating historical changes was shown to be neither necessary nor sufficient: a stationary economy was not necessary to achieve complete competitive equilibrium if men had complete foresight; and it was not sufficient to achieve this equilibrium, because there might still be non-historical fluctuations, owing, for example, to drought or flood, which were imperfectly anticipated (Knight, 1921, pp. 35–8). Complete, errorless adjustments required full knowledge of all relevant circumstances, which realistically can be possessed only when these circumstances do not change; that is, when the economy is stationary.

The assumptions necessary to competition are presented as part of a list that describes the pure enterprise economy, and I quote those that are especially germane to competition (Knight, 1921, pp. 76–9; cf also p. 648):

2. We assume that the members of the society act with complete "rationality." By this we do not mean that they are to be "as angels, knowing good from evil;" we assume ordinary human motives ...; but they are supposed to "know what they want" and to seek it "intelligently." ... They are supposed to know absolutely the consequence of their acts when they are performed, and to perform them in the light of the consequences. ...

4. We must also assume complete absence of physical obstacles to the making, execution, and changing of plans at will; that is, there must be "perfect mobility" in all economic adjustments, no cost involved in movements or changes. To realize this ideal all the elements entering into economic calculations – effort, commodities, etc. – must be continuously variable, divisible without limit. ... The exchange of commodities must be virtually instantaneous and costless.

5. It follows as a corollary from number 4 that there is perfect competition. There must be perfect, continuous, costless intercommunication between all individual members of the society. Every potential buyer of a good constantly knows and chooses among the offers of all potential sellers, and conversely. Every commodity, it will be recalled, is divisible into an indefinite number of units which must be separately owned and compete effectually with each other.

6. Every member of the society is to act as an individual only, in entire independence of all other persons. ... And in exchanges between individuals, no interests of persons not parties to the exchange are to be concerned, either for good or for ill. Individual independence in action excludes all forms of collusion, all degrees of monopoly or tendency to monopoly ...

9. All given factors and conditions are for the purposes of this and the following chapter
    and until notice to the contrary is expressly given, to remain absolutely unchanged.
    They must be free from periodic or progressive modification as well as irregular
    fluctuation. The connection between this specification and number 2 (perfect knowledge)
    is clear. Under static conditions every person would soon find out, if he did not
    already know, everything in his situation and surroundings which affected his
    conduct. . . .
        The above assumptions, especially the first eight, are idealizations or purifications of
    tendencies which hold good more or less in reality. They are the conditions necessary to
    perfect competition. The ninth, as we shall see, is on a somewhat different footing. Only
    its corollary of perfect knowledge (specification number 2) which may be present even
    when change takes place is necessary for perfect competition.

This list of requirements of perfect competition is by no means a statement of
the *minimum* requirements, and in fact no one is able to state the minimum requirements.

Consider first complete knowledge. If each seller in a market knows any *n* buyers, and
each seller knows a different (but overlapping) set of buyers, then there will be perfect
competition if the set of *n* buyers is large enough to exclude joint action. Or let there be
indefinitely many brokers in any market, and let each broker know many buyers and
sellers, and also let each buyer or seller know many brokers – again we have perfect
competition. Since entrepreneurs in a stationary economy are essentially brokers between
resource owners and consumers, it is sufficient for competition if they meet this condition.
That is, resource owners and consumers could dwell in complete ignorance of all save the
bids of many entrepreneurs. Hence knowledge possessed by any one trader need not be
complete; it is sufficient if the knowledge possessed by the ensemble of individuals in the
market is in a sense comprehensive.

And now, mobility. Rigid immobility of every trader is compatible with perfect
competition if we wish to have this concept denote only equilibrium which is not affected
by the actions of individual traders: large numbers (in any market) and comprehensive
knowledge are sufficient to eliminate monopoly power. If we wish perfect competition to
denote also that a resource will obtain equal returns in all possible uses, mobility becomes
essential, but not for all resources. If one resource were immobile and all others mobile,
clearly the returns of all resources in all uses could be equalized. Even if all resources were
immobile, under certain conditions free transport of consumers' goods would lead to
equalization of returns (Samuelson, 1949; James and Pierce, 1951–52). Even in the general
case in which mobility of resources is required, not all the units of a resource need be
mobile. If some units of each resource are mobile, the economic system will display
complete mobility for all displacements up to a limit that depends upon the proportion
of mobile units and the nature of the displacement.

The condition that there be no costs of movement of resources is not necessary in order
to reach maximum output for an economy; under competition only those movements of
resources will take place for which the additional return equals or exceeds the cost of
movement. But costless movement is necessary if equality is to obtain in the return to a
resource in all uses: if the movement between *A* and *B* costs $1.00 (per unit of time), the
return to a resource at *A* can vary within $1.00 of either direction of its return at *B*.
Equilibrium could be reached anywhere within these limits (but would be uniquely

determined), and this equilibrium would depend upon the historical distribution of resources and consumers.

Next, divisibility. It is not enough to have a large number of informed traders in a market: price must change continuously with quantity if an individual trader is to have only an imperceptible influence upon the market rate, and this will generally require divisibility of the commodity traded. Infinite divisibility, however, is not necessary to eliminate significant control over price by the individual trader, and divisibility of time in the use of a resource is a substitute for divisibility in its quantity. Divisibility, however, is not sufficient to insure uniqueness of equilibriums; even in the simpler problems one must also require that the relevant economic functions display strict monotonicity, but this has nothing to do with competition.

And homogeneity. The formal condition that there be many producers of *a* commodity assumes homogeneity of this commodity (Knight's assumption 5). Certain forms of heterogeneity are of course unimportant because they are superficial: potatoes need not be of the same size if they are sold by the pound; laborers do not have to be equally efficient if the differences in their productivity are measurable. As these examples may suggest, heterogeneity can be a substitute for divisibility.

The final assumption, concerning collusion, is especially troublesome. If one merely postulates the absence of collusion, then why not postulate also that even two rivals can behave in such a way as to reach competitive equilibrium? Instead, one usually requires that the number of traders be large enough so that collusion will not appear. To determine this number, one must have a theory of the conditions under which collusion occurs. Economists have generally emphasized two barriers to collusion. The first is imperfect knowledge, especially of the consequences of rivalry and of the policy which would maximize profits for the group, and of course neither of these difficulties would arise in the stationary economy with perfect knowledge. The second barrier is the difficulty of determining the division of profits among colluders, and we simply do not know whether this difficulty would increase with the number of traders under the conditions we are examining. Hence it seems essential to assume the absence of collusion as a supplement to the presence of large numbers: one of the assumptions of perfect competition is the existence of a Sherman Act.

It is therefore no occasion for complaint that Knight did not state the minimum requirements for perfect competition; this statement was impossible in 1921, and it is impossible today. The minimum assumptions for a theoretical model can be stated with precision only when the complete theory of that model is known. The complete theory of competition cannot be known because it is an open-ended theory; it is always possible that a new range of problems will be posed in this framework, and then, no matter how well developed the theory was with respect to the earlier range of problems, it may require extensive elaboration in respects which previously it glossed over or ignored.

The analytical appeal of a definition of competition does not depend upon its economy of assumptions, although gratuitously wide assumptions are objectionable.[26] We wish the definition to specify with tolerable clarity – with such clarity as the state of the science affords – a model which can be used by practitioners in a great variety of theoretical researches, so that the foundations of the science need not be debated in every extension or application of theory. We wish the definition to capture the essential general content of important markets, so the predictions drawn from the theory will have wide empirical reliability. And we wish a concept with normative properties that will allow us to judge the efficiency of policies. That the concept of perfect competition has served these varied needs as well as it has is providential.

6. Concluding Reflections

If we were free to redefine competition at this late date, a persuasive case could be made that it should be restricted to meaning the absence of monopoly power in a market. This is an important concept that deserves a name, and "competition" would be the appropriate name. But it would be idle to propose such a restricted signification for a word which has so long been used in a wide sense, and at best we may hope to denote the narrower concept by a suggestive phrase. I propose that we call this narrower concept *market competition*.

Perfect market competition will prevail when there are indefinitely many traders (no one of which controls an appreciable share of demand or supply) acting independently in a perfect market. A perfect market is one in which the traders have full knowledge of all offer and bid prices. I have already remarked that it was unfortunate that a perfect market was made a subsidiary characteristic of competition, for a perfect market may also exist under monopoly. Indeed, in realistic cases a perfect market may be more likely to exist under monopoly, since complete knowledge is easier to achieve under monopoly.

Market competition can exist even though resources or traders cannot enter or leave the market in question. Hence market competition can rule in an industry which is not in long-run competitive equilibrium and is compatible with the existence of large profits or losses.

It is interesting to note that Chamberlin's (1933, p. 6) definition of "pure" competition is identical with my definition of market competition: "competition unalloyed with monopoly elements" But Chamberlin implied that pure competition could rule in an imperfect market; the only conditions he postulated were large numbers of traders and a standardized commodity. The conditions are incomplete: if one million buyers dealt with one million sellers of a homogeneous product, each pair dealing in ignorance of all others, we should simply have one million instances of bilateral monopoly. Hence pure competition cannot be contrasted with perfect competition, for the former also requires "perfect" knowledge (subject to qualifications I have previously discussed), and for this reason I prefer the term "market competition."

The broad concept of perfect competition is defined by the condition that the rate of return (value of the marginal product) of each resource be equal in all uses. If we wish to distinguish this concept from market competition, we may call it (after the terminology attributed to Cairnes) *industrial competition*. Industrial competition requires

1   that there be market competition within each industry;
2   that owners of resources be informed of the returns obtainable in each industry; and
3   that they be free to enter or leave any industry.

In addition, the resources must be infinitely divisible if there is to be strict equality in the rate of return on a resource in all uses.

An industrial competitive equilibrium will obtain continuously if resources are instantaneously mobile or in the long run if they move at a finite time rate. Since the concept of long-run competitive equilibrium is deeply imbedded in modern economic theory, it seems most desirable that we interpret industrial competition as a long-run concept. It may be noticed that a time period did not have to figure explicitly in the pre-Marshallian theory because that theory did not separate and devote special attention to a short-run normal period in which only a portion of the resources were mobile: the basic classical theory was a long-run theory.

The concept of industrial competition has a natural affinity to the static economy even though our definition does not pay any explicit attention to this problem. Rates of return on resources will be equalized only if their owners have complete knowledge of future returns (in the case of durable resources), and it seems improper to assume complete knowledge of the future in a changing economy. Not only is it misleading to endow the population with this gift of prophecy but also it would often be inconsistent to have people foresee a future event and still have that event remain in the future.

One method by which we might seek to adapt the definition to a historically evolving economy is to replace the equalization of rates of return by *expected* rates of return. But it is not an irresistably attractive method. There are troublesome questions of what entrepreneurs seek to maximize under these conditions and of whether risk or uncertainty premiums also enter into their calculations. A more important difficulty is that this formulation implies that the historically evolving industry is in equilibrium in long-run normal periods, and there is no strong reason to believe that such long-run normal periods can be defined for the historically evolving industry. If all economic progress took the form of a secularly smooth development, we could continue to use the Marshallian long-run normal period, and indeed much progress does take this form. But often, and sooner or later always, the historical changes come in vast surges, followed by quiescent periods or worse, and it is harder to assume that the fits and starts can be foreseen with tolerable confidence or that they will come frequently enough to average out within economically relevant time periods.

It seems preferable, therefore, to adapt the concept of competition to changing conditions by another method: to insist only upon the absence of barriers to entry and exit from an industry in the long-run normal period; that is, in the period long enough to allow substantial changes in the quantities of even the most durable and specialized resources. Then we may still expect that some sort of expected return will tend to be equalized under conditions of reasonably steady change, although much work remains to be done before we can specify exactly what this return will be.[27]

The way in which the competitive concept loses precision when historically changing conditions are taken into account is apparent. It is also easily explained: the competitive concept can be no better than the economic theory with which it is used, and until we have a much better theory of economic development we shall not have a much better theory of competition under conditions of non-repetitive change.

The normative role of the competitive concept arises from the fact that the equality of rate of return on each resource in all uses which defines competition is also the condition for maximum output from given resources. The outputs are measured in market prices, and the maximum is relative to the distribution of ownership of resources. This well-known restriction of the competitive optimum to production, it may be remarked, should be qualified by the fact that the effects of competition on distribution have not been studied. A competitive system affects the distribution of the ownership of resources, and –

given a stable distribution of human abilities – a competitive system would probably lead eventually to a stable income distribution whose characteristics are unknown. The theory of this distribution might have substantial normative value.

The vitality of the competitive concept in its normative role has been remarkable. One might have expected that, as economic analysis became more precise and as the range of problems to which it was applied widened, a growing list of disparities between the competitive allocation of resources and the maximum-output allocation would develop. Yet to date there have been only two major criticisms of the norm.[28] The first is that the competitive individual ignores external economies and diseconomies, which – rightly or wrongly – most economists are still content to treat as an exception to be dealt with in individual cases. The second, and more recent, criticism is that the competitive system will not provide the right amount (and possibly not the right types) of economic progress, and this is still an undocumented charge. The time may well come when the competitive concept suitable to positive analysis is not suitable to normative analysis, but it is still in the future.

Finally, we should notice the most common and the most important criticism of the concept of perfect competition – that it is unrealistic. This criticism has been widespread since the concept was completely formulated and underlies the warm reception which the profession gave to the doctrines of imperfect and monopolistic competition in the 1930s. One could reply to this criticism that all concepts sufficiently general and sufficiently precise to be useful in scientific analysis must be abstract: that, if a science is to deal with a large class of phenomena, clearly it cannot work with concepts that are faithfully descriptive of even one phenomenon, for then they will be grotesquely undescriptive of others. This conventional line of defense for all abstract concepts is completely valid, but there is another defense, or rather another form of this defense, that may be more persuasive.

This second defense is that the concept of perfect competition has defeated its newer rivals in the decisive area: the day-to-day work of the economic theorist. Since the 1930s, when the rival doctrines of imperfect and monopolistic competition were in their heyday, economists have increasingly reverted to the use of the concept of perfect competition as their standard model for analysis. Today the concept of perfect competition is being used more widely by the profession in its theoretical work than at any time in the past. The vitality of the concept is strongly spoken for by this triumph.

Of course, this is not counsel of complacency. I have cited areas in which much work must be done before important aspects of the definition of competition can be clarified. My fundamental thesis, in fact, is that hardly any important improvement in general economic theory can fail to affect the concept of competition. But it has proved to be a tough and resilient concept, and it will stay with us in recognizable form for a long time to come.

Notes

1   Smith, 1937, p. 145. Perhaps this is not the ideal illustration of the laxness of the period in the use of the competitive concept, for several readers of this paper have sympathized with this usage. But, to repeat, competition is consistent with a zero elasticity of supply: the fact of windfall gains from unexpected increases in demand is characteristic of all commodities with less than infinitely elastic supplies.

2 Cairnes (1874, p. 85). Thus Cairnes tacitly labeled all differences in native ability as "monopolistic."

3 Karl Marx (1905, II, Part 2, 14 n) once distinguished interindustry from intraindustry competition.

4 For example, Leslie repeatedly denied that resource owners possessed sufficient knowledge to effect an equalization of the rates of return (Leslie, 1879, pp. 47, 48, 81, 158–9, 184–5).

5 See especially Marx (1962) and also Engels (1962, p. 109). The Marxian theory of the increasing concentration of capital was a minor and inconsistent dissent from the main position (Marx, 1906, p. 684).

6 See Shaw and Webb. (1948). But the attention devoted to monopoly was increasing, and the essay by Clarke (1948, p. 84) argued that "combination is absorbing commerce." A few years later the Webbs used a competitive model in their celebrated discussion of "higgling in the market" and then went on to describe the formation of monopolistic structures as defences erected against the competitive pressures the Webbs did not quite understand (Webb and Webb 1920, III, ch. ii).

7 A second main criticism became increasingly more prominent in the second half of the nineteenth century: that a private-enterprise system allowed or compelled large fluctuations in employment. For some critics (e.g., Engels), competition was an important cause of these fluctuations.

8 It is sufficient to assume that D_k is small relative to D if one assumes that the demand function is continuous, for then "the variations of the demand will be sensibly proportional to the variations in price so long as these last are small fractions of the original price" (Cournot, 1927, p. 50).

9 Let the revenue of the firm be $q_i p$, and let all firms have the same marginal costs, MC. Then the equation for maximum profits for one firm would be

$$p + q_i \frac{dp}{dq} = MC$$

The sum of n such equations would be

$$np + q \frac{dp}{dq} = nMC$$

for $nq_i = q$. This last equation may be written,

$$p = MC - \frac{p}{nE}$$

where E is the elasticity of market demand (Cournot, 1927, p. 84).

10 Jevons, 1871, p. 92. This is restated as the proposition that the last increments of an act of exchange (i.e., the last exchange in a competitive market) must be proportional to the total quantities exchanged, or that dy exchanges for dx in the same proportion that y exchanges for x, or

$$\frac{dy}{dx} = \frac{y}{x}$$

It would have been better for Jevons simply to assert that, if x_i exchanges for y_i, then for all i

$$\frac{x_i}{y_i} = \frac{P_y}{P_x}$$

11 Jevons, 1871, p. 111. In the Preface to the second edition, where on most subjects Jevons was farseeing, the conceptual treatment of competition deteriorated: "Property is only another name for monopoly ... Thus monopoly is limited by competition ... " (pp. xlvi–xlvii).

12 Edgeworth's emphasis upon recontract, the institution which allows tentative contracts to be broken without penalty, is motivated by a desire to assure that equilibrium will be achieved and will not be affected by the route by which it is achieved. It will not be examined here.

13 " ... It will in general be possible for *one* of the *Y*s (without the consent of the other) to *recontract* with the two *X*s, so that for all those three parties the recontract is more advantageous than the previously existing contract" (Edgeworth, 1881, p. 35).

14 Let one seller dispose of q_i, the other sellers each disposing of q. Then the seller's marginal revenue is

$$\frac{d(pq_i)}{dq_i} = p + qi\frac{dp}{dQ}\frac{dQ}{dq_i}$$

where Q is total sales, and $dQ/dq_i = 1$. Letting $Q = nq_i = nq$, and writing E for

$$\frac{dQ}{dp}\frac{p}{Q}$$

we obtain the expression in the text.

15 Of course, let there be one extra worker, and the wage will be 50; one extra master, and it will be 100.

16 Since chance should operate in the choice of the equilibrium actually attained, it is not proper to say, as Edgeworth (p. 50) does (in a wider context), that the dice will be "loaded with villainy."

17 Edgeworth (1925, I, p. 36). One might also seek to eliminate the indeterminateness by appeal to the varying demand-and-supply prices of individual traders; this is the path chosen by Hicks (1930). This, however, is a complicated solution; one must make special hypotheses about the distribution of these demand and-supply prices.

18 It is indicative that the word "competition" is not indexed.

19 Pareto (1897, §§ 46, 87, 705, 814); cf. also Pareto (1927), pp. 163, 210, 230).

20 Most of the article is concerned with duopoly.

21 Moore, 1905–6, pp. 213–14. The fifth statement is held to be a corollary of III and IV; but see p. 165.

22 A comparison with the corresponding passage in the eighth edition (p. 341) will reveal the curious changes which were later made in the description of competition.

23 Both of these qualifications were of course recognized by predecessors such as Walras and Edgeworth.

24 In the mathematical exposition of theory it was natural to postulate stable supply and demand functions, and therefore stable technologies and tastes, so one could trace a gradually expanding concept of the stationary economy in Walras, Auspitz and Lieben, and Irving Fisher.

25 Although Pigou was not concerned with the formal definition of competition, he must also be accounted an influential figure in the popularization of the concept of perfect competition. In his *Wealth and Welfare* (1912), he devoted individual chapters to the effects of immobility (with incorrect knowledge as one component) and indivisibility upon the ability of a resource to receive an equal rate of return in all uses (Pigou, 1912, II, ch. iv and v).

26 They are objectionable chiefly because they mislead some user or abusers of the concept as to its domain of applicability. That dreadful list of assumptions of perfect competition which textbooks in labor economics so often employ to dismiss the marginal productivity theory is a case in point.

27 It is worth noticing that even under static conditions the definition of the return is modified to suit the facts and that mobility of resources is the basic competitive requirement. Thus we say that laborers move so that the net advantages, not the current money return, of various occupations are equalized. The suggestion in the text is essentially that we find the appropriate definition of net advantages for the historically evolving economy.

28 In a wider framework there have of course been criticisms of the competitive norm with respect to (i) the ability of individuals to judge their own interests and (ii) the ability of a competitive system to achieve a continuously high level of employment of resources.

References

Auspitz, R. and Lieben, R. (1887): *Theorie des Preises*. Leipsig: Duncker and Humblot.

Cairnes, J. E. (1874): *Some Leading Principles of Political Economy Newly Expounded*. New York: Harper.

Chamberlin, E. H. (1933): *The Theory of Monopolistic Competition*. Cambridge, MA: Harvard University Press.

Clark, J. B. (1899): *The Distribution of Wealth*. New York: Macmillan.

Clarke, W. (1948): "The Basis of Socialism: Industrial," in G. B. Shaw and W. Clarke (eds.), *Fabian Essays in Socialism*, Jubilee edn, London: Allen & Unwin.

Cournot, A. (1927): *Mathematical Principles of the Theory of Wealth*. New York: Macmillan.

Edgeworth, F. Y. (1881): *Mathematical Psychics*. London: Paul.

Edgeworth, F. Y. (1925): *Collected Papers Relating to Political Economy*. London: Macmillan, for the Royal Economic Society.

Engels, F. (1962): "The Conditions of the Working-classes in England," in Marx, K. and Engels, F. *On Britain*, 2nd edn, Moscow: Foreign Language Publishing House.

Fisher, I. (1926): *Mathematical Investigations in the Theory of Value and Prices*. New Haven: Yale University Press.

Hicks, J. R. (1930): "Edgeworth, Marshall, and the Indeterminateness of Wages," *Economic Journal*, 40, 215–31.

James, S. F. and Pierce, I. F. (1951–2): "The Factor Price Equalization Myth," *Review of Economic Studies*, 19, 111–22.

Jevons, W. S. (1871): *Theory of Political Economy*. London: Macmillan.

Knight, F. (1921): *Risk, Uncertainty and Profit*. Boston: Houghton Mifflin.

Leslie, T. E. C. (1879): *Essays in Political and Moral Philosophy*. Dublin: Hodges, Foster and Figgis.

Marshall, A. (1890): *Principles of Economics*. London: Macmillan. Revised: 3rd edn in 1895, 8th edn in 1929.

Marx, K. (1905): *Theorien über den Mehrwert* II. Stuttgart: J. H. W. Diez.

Marx, K. (1906): *Capital*. Reprinted in The Modern Library, New York: Random House.

Marx, K. (1962): "Das Kapital, vol. III," in Marx, K. and Engels, F. *On Britain*, 2nd edn, Moscow: Foreign Language Publishing House.

Moore, H. (1905–6): "Paradoxes of Competition," *Quarterly Journal of Economics*, 20, 209–30.

Pareto, V. (1897): *Cours d'Economie Politique*. Lausanne: Rouge.

Pareto, V. (1927): *Manuel d'Economie Politique*, 2nd edn. Paris: Giard & Briere.

Pigou, A. C. (1912): *Wealth and Welfare*. London: Macmillan.

Samuelson, P. A. (1949): "International Factor-price Equalization once again," *Economic Journal*, 59, 181–97.

Senior, N. W. (1854): *Political Economy*. London: Griffin.

Shaw, G. B. (1948): "The Basis of Socialism: Economic," in G. B. Shaw and W. Clarke (eds), *Fabian Essays in Socialism*, Jubilee edn, London: Allen & Unwin.

Shaw, G. B. and Clarke W. (eds) (1948): *Fabian Essays in Socialism*, Jubilee edn. London: Allen & Unwin.
Sidgwick, H. (1883): *Principles of Political Economy*. London: Macmillan.
Smith, A. (1937): *The Wealth of Nations* (Modern Library edn). New York: Random House.
Walras, L. (1954): *Elements of Pure Economics*. London: Allen & Unwin and Homewood, Ill.: Irwin. Translated by W. Jaffé.
Webb, S. W. (1948): "The Basis of Socialism: Historic," in G. B. Shaw and W. Clarke (eds), *Fabian Essays in Socialism*, Jubilee edn, London: Allen & Unwin.
Webb, S. W. and Webb, B. (1920): *Industrial Democracy*. London: Longmans, Green.

CHAPTER NINE

A Theory of Auctions and Competitive Bidding

PAUL R. MILGROM AND ROBERT J. WEBER

Source: *Econometrica*, 50 (1992), pp. 1089–1122. Reprinted with the permission of the Econometric Society. © The Econometric Society.

A model of competitive bidding is developed in which the winning bidder's payoff may depend upon his personal preferences, the preferences of others, and the intrinsic qualities of the object being sold. In this model, the English (ascending) auction generates higher average prices than does the second-price auction. Also, when bidders are risk-neutral, the second-price auction generates higher average prices than the Dutch and first-price auctions. In all of these auctions, the seller can raise the expected price by adopting a policy of providing expert appraisals of the quality of the objects he sells.

1. Introduction

The design and conduct of auctioning institutions has occupied the attention of many people over thousands of years. One of the earliest reports of an auction was given by the Greek historian Herodotus, who described the sale of women to be wives in Babylonia around the fifth century B.C. During the closing years of the Roman Empire, the auction of plundered booty was common. In China, the personal belongings of deceased Buddhist monks were sold at auction as early as the seventh century A.D.[1]

In the United States in the 1980s, auctions account for an enormous volume of economic activity. Every week, the U.S. Treasury sells billions of dollars of bills and notes using a sealed-bid auction. The Department of the Interior sells mineral rights on federally owned properties at auction.[2] Throughout the public and private sectors, purchasing agents solicit delivery-price offers of products ranging from office supplies to specialized mining equipment; sellers auction antiques and artwork, flowers and live-stock, publishing rights and timber rights, stamps and wine.

The large volume of transactions arranged using auctions leads one to wonder what accounts for the popularity of such common auction forms as the English auction,[3] the Dutch auction,[4] the first-price sealed-bid auction,[5] and the second-price sealed-bid auction.[6] What determines which form will (or should) be used in any particular circumstance?

Equally important, but less thoroughly explored, are questions about the relationship between auction theory and traditional competitive theory. One may ask: Do the prices which arise from the common auction forms resemble competitive prices? Do they approach competitive prices when there are many buyers and sellers? In the case of sales of such things as securities, mineral rights, and timber rights, where the bidders may differ in their knowledge about the intrinsic qualities of the object being sold, do prices aggregate the diverse bits of information available to the many bidders (as they do in some rational expectations market equilibrium models)?

In section 2, we review some important results of the received auction theory, introduce a new general auction model, and summarize the results of our analysis. Section 3 contains a formal statement of our model, and develops the properties of "affiliated" random variables. The various theorems are presented in sections 4–8. In section 9, we offer our views on the current state of auction theory. Following section 9 is a technical appendix dealing with affiliated random variables.

2. An Overview of the Received Theory and New Results[7]

2.1. The independent private values model

Much of the existing literature on auction theory analyzes the *independent private values model*. In that model, a single indivisible object is to be sold to one of several bidders. Each bidder is risk-neutral and knows the value of the object to himself, but does not know the value of the object to the other bidders (this is the *private values* assumption). The values are modeled as being independently drawn from some continuous distribution. Bidders are assumed to behave competitively;[8] therefore, the auction is treated as a noncooperative game among the bidders.[9]

At least seven important conclusions emerge from the model. The first of these is that the Dutch auction and the first-price auction are strategically equivalent. Recall that in a Dutch auction, the auctioneer begins by naming a very high price and then lowers it continuously until some bidder stops the auction and claims the object for that price. An insight due to Vickrey [29] is that the decision faced by a bidder with a particular valuation, is essentially static, i.e. the bidder must choose the price level at which he will claim the object if it has not yet been claimed. The winning bidder will be the one who chooses the highest level, and the price he pays will be equal to that amount. This, of course, is also the way the winner and price are determined in the sealed-bid first-price auction. Thus, the sets of strategies and the mapping from strategies to outcomes are the same for both auction forms. Consequently, the equilibria of the two auction games must coincide.

The second conclusion is that – in the context of the private values model – the second-price sealed-bid auction and the English auction are equivalent, although in a weaker sense than the "strategic equivalence" of the Dutch and first-price auctions. Recall that in an English auction, the auctioneer begins by soliciting bids at a low price level, and he then gradually raises the price until only one willing bidder remains. In this setting, a bidder's strategy must specify, for each of his possible valuations, whether he will be active at any given price level, as a function of the previous activity he has observed during the course of the auction. However, if a bidder knows the value of the object to himself, he has a straightforward dominant strategy, which is to bid actively until the price reaches the value of the object to him. Regardless of the strategies adopted by the other bidders, this simple strategy will be an optimal reply.

Similarly, in the second-price auction, if a bidder knows the value of the object to himself, then his dominant strategy is to submit a sealed bid equal to that value. Thus, in both the English and second-price auctions, there is a unique dominant-strategy equilibrium. In both auctions, at equilibrium, the winner will be the bidder who values the object most highly, and the price he pays will be the value of the object to the bidder who values it second-most highly. In that sense, the two auctions are equivalent. Note that this argument requires that each bidder know the value of the object to himself.[10] If what is being sold is the right to extract minerals from a property, where the amount of recoverable minerals is unknown, or if it is a work of art, which will be enjoyed by the buyer and then eventually resold for some currently undetermined price, then this equivalence result generally does not apply.

A third result is that the outcome (at the dominant-strategy equilibrium) of the English and second-price auctions is Pareto optimal; that is, the winner is the bidder who values the object most highly. This conclusion follows immediately from the argument of the preceding paragraph and, like the first two results, does not depend on the symmetry of the model. In symmetric models the Dutch and first-price auctions also lead to Pareto optimal allocations.

A fourth result is that in the independent private values model, all four auction forms lead to identical expected revenues for the seller (Ortega-Reichert [22], Vickrey [30]). This result remained a puzzle until recently, when an application of the self-selection approach cast it in a new light (Harris and Raviv [8], Myerson [21], Riley and Samuelson [24]). That approach views a bidder's decision problem (when the strategies of the other bidders are fixed) as one of choosing, through his action, a probability p of winning and a corresponding expected payment $e(p)$. (We take $e(p)$ to be the lowest expected payment associated with an action which obtains the object with probability p.) It is important to notice that, because of the independence assumption, the set of $(p, e(p))$ pairs that are available to the bidder depends only on the rules of the auction and the strategies of the others, and not on his private valuation of the object.

Figure 1 displays a typical bidding decision faced by a bidder who values the prize at v. The curve consists of the set of $(p, e(p))$ pairs among which he must choose.[11] Since the bidder's expected utility from a point (p, e) is $v \cdot p - e$, his indifference curves are straight lines with slope v. Let $p^*(\nu)$ denote the optimal choice of p for a bidder with valuation ν. It is clear from the figure that p^* must be nondecreasing.

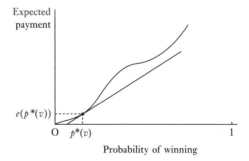

Figure 1

In Figure 1, the tangency condition is $e'(p^*(v)) = v$. Similarly, when the indifference line has multiple points of tangency, a small increase in v causes a jump Δp^* in p^* and a corresponding jump $\Delta e = v \cdot \Delta p^*$ in $e(p^*(v))$. Hence we can conclude quite generally that $e(p^*(v)) = e(p^*(0)) + \int_0^v t \, dp^*(t)$. It then follows that the seller's expected revenue from a bidder depends on the rules of the auction only to the extent that the rules affect either $e(p^*(0))$ or the p^* function. Notice, in particular, that all auctions which always deliver the prize to the highest evaluator have the same p^* function for all bidders. That observation, together with the fact that at the dominant-strategy equilibrium the second-price auction yields a price equal to the second-highest valuation, leads to the fifth result.

Theorem 0: Assume that a particular auction mechanism is given, that the independent private values model applies, and that the bidders adopt strategies which consititute a noncooperative equilibrium. Suppose that at equilibrium the bidder who values the object most highly is certain to receive it, and that any bidder who values the object at its lowest possible level has an expected payment of zero. Then the expected revenue generated for the seller by the mechanism is precisely the expected value of the object to the second-highest evaluator.

At the symmetric equilibria of the English, Dutch, first-price, and second-price auctions, the conditions of the theorem are satisfied. Consequently, the expected selling price is the same for all four mechanisms; this is the so-called "revenue-equivalence" result. It should be noted that Theorem 0 has an attractive economic interpretation. No matter what competitive mechanism is used to establish the selling price of the object, on average the sale will be at the lowest price at which supply (a single unit) equals demand.

The self-selection approach has also been applied to the problem of designing auctions to maximize the seller's expected revenue (Harris and Raviv [8], Myerson [21], Riley and Samuelson [24]). The problem is formulated very generally as a constrained optimal control problem, where the control variables are the pairs $(p_i^*(\cdot), e_i(p_i^*(0)))$. As might be expected, the form of the optimal auction depends on the underlying distribution of bidder valuations. One remarkable conclusion emerging from the analysis is this: For many common sample distributions – including the normal, exponential, and uniform distributions – the four standard auction forms with suitably chosen reserve prices or entry fees are optimal auctions.

The seventh and last result in this list arises in a variation of the model where either the seller or the buyers are risk averse. In that case, the seller will strictly prefer the Dutch or first-price auction to the English or second-price auction (Harris and Raviv [8], Holt [9], Maskin and Riley [11], Matthews [13]).

2.2. Oil, gas, and mineral rights

The private values assumption is most nearly satisfied in auctions for non-durable consumer goods. The satisfaction derived from consuming such goods is reasonably regarded as a personal matter, so it is plausible that a bidder may know the value of the good to himself, and may allow that others could value the good differently.

In contrast, consider the situation in an auction for mineral rights on a tract of land where the value of the rights depends on the unknown amount of recoverable ore, its quality, its ease of recovery, and the prices that will prevail for the processed mineral. To a first approximation, the values of these mineral rights to the various bidders can be regarded as equal, but bidders may have differing estimates of the common value.

Suppose the bidders make (conditionally) independent estimates of this common value V. Other things being equal, the bidder with the largest estimate will make the highest bid. Consequently, even if all bidders make unbiased estimates, the winner will find that he had overestimated (on average) the value of the rights he has won at auction. Petroleum engineers (Capen, Clapp, and Campbell [1]) have claimed that this phenomenon, known as the *winner's curse*, is responsible for the low profits earned by oil companies on offshore tracts in the 1960s.

The model described above, in which risk-neutral bidders make independent estimates of the common value where the estimates are drawn from a single underlying distribution parameterized by V, can be called the *mineral rights model* or the *common value model*. The equilibrium of the first-price auction for this model has been extensively studied (Maskin and Riley [11], Milgrom [15, 16], Milgrom and Weber [20], Ortega-Reichert [22], Reece [23], Rothkopf [25], Wilson [34]). Among the most interesting results for the mineral rights model are those dealing with the relations between information, prices, and bidder profits.

For example, consider the information that is reflected in the price resulting from a mineral rights auction. It is tempting to think that this price cannot convey more information than was available to the winning bidder, since the price is just the amount that he bid. This reasoning, however, is incorrect. Since the winning bidder's estimate is the maximum among all the estimates, the winning bid conveys a bound on all the loser's estimates. When there are many bidders, the price conveys a bound on many estimates, and so can be very informative. Indeed, let $f(x|v)$ be the density of the distribution of a bidder's estimate when $V = v$. A property of many one-parameter sampling distributions is that for $v_1 < v_2, f(x|v_1)/f(x|v_2)$ declines as x increases.[12] If this ratio approaches zero, then the equilibrium price in a first-price auction with many bidders is a consistent estimator of the value V, even if no bidder can estimate V closely from his information alone (Milgrom [15, 16], Wilson [34]). Thus, the price can be surprisingly effective in aggregating private information.

Several results and examples suggest that a bidder's expected profits in a mineral rights auction depend more on the privacy of his information than on its accuracy as information about V. For example, in the first-price auction a bidder whose information is also available to some other bidder must have zero expected profits at equilibrium (Engelbrecht-Wiggans, Milgrom, and Weber [5], Milgrom [15]). Thus, if two bidders have access to the same estimate of V and a third bidder has access only to some less informative but independent estimate, then the two relatively well-informed bidders must have zero expected profits, but the more poorly informed bidder may have positive expected profits. Related results appear in Milgrom [15 and 17] and as Theorem 7 of this paper.

2.3. A general model

Consider the issues that arise in attempting to select an auction to use in selling a painting. If the independent private values model is to be applied, one must make two assumptions:

that each bidder knows his value for the painting, and that the values are statistically independent. The first assumption rules out the possibilities:

  (i)   that the painting may be resold later for an unknown price,
  (ii) that there may be some "prestige" value in owning a painting which is admired by other bidders, and
  (iii) that the authenticity of the painting may be in doubt.

The second assumption rules out the possibility that several bidders may have relevant information concerning the painting's authenticity, or that a buyer, thinking that the painting is particularly fine, may conclude that other bidders also are likely to value it highly. Only if these assumptions are palatable can the theory be used to guide the seller's choice of an auction procedure. Even in this case, however, little guidance is forthcoming: the theory predicts that the four most common auction forms lead to the same expected price.

Unlike the private values theory, the common value theory allows for statistical dependence among bidders' value estimates, but offers no role for differences in individual tastes. Furthermore, the received theory offers no basis for choosing among the first-price, second-price, Dutch, and English auction procedures.

In this paper, we develop a general auction model for risk-neutral bidders which includes as special cases the independent private values model and the common value model, as well as a range of intermediate models which can better represent, for example, the auction of a painting. Despite its generality, the model yields several testable predictions. First, the Dutch and first-price auctions are strategically equivalent in the general model, just as they were in the private values model. Second, when bidders are uncertain about their value estimates, the English and second-price auctions are not equivalent: the English auction generally leads to larger expected prices. One explanation of this inequality is that when bidders are uncertain about their valuations, they can acquire useful information by scrutinizing the bidding behavior of their competitors during the course of an English auction. That extra information weakens the winner's curse and leads to more aggressive bidding in the English auction, which accounts for the higher expected price.

A third prediction of the model is that when the bidders' value estimates are statistically dependent, the second-price auction generates a higher average price than does the first-price auction. Thus, the common auction forms can be ranked by the expected prices they generate. The English auction generates the highest prices followed by the second-price auction and, finally, the Dutch and first-price auctions. This may explain the observation that "an estimated 75 per cent, or even more, of all auctions in the world are conducted on an ascending-bid basis" (Cassady [2, p. 66]).

Suppose that the seller has access to a private source of information. Further, suppose that he can commit himself to any policy of reporting information that he chooses. Among the possible policies are:

  (i)   concealment (never report any information),
  (ii) honesty (always report all information completely),
  (iii) censoring (report only the most favorable information),
  (iv) summarizing (report only a rough summary statistic), and
  (v)   randomizing (add noise to the data before reporting).

The fourth conclusion of our analysis is that for the first-price, second-price, and English auctions policy, (ii) maximizes the expected price: Honesty is the best policy.

The general model and its assumptions are presented in section 3. The analysis of the model is driven by the assumption that the bidders' valuations are *affiliated*. Roughly, this means that a high value of one bidder's estimate makes high values of the others' estimates more likely. This assumption, though restrictive, accords well with the qualitative features of the situations we have described.

Sections 4 through 6 develop our principal results concering the second-price, English, and first-price auction procedures.

In section 7, we modify the general model by introducing reserve prices and entry fees. The introduction of a positive reserve price causes the number of bidders actually submitting bids to be random, but this does not significantly change the analysis of equilibrium strategies nor does it alter the ranking of the three auction forms as revenue generators. However, it does change the analysis of information reporting by the seller, because the number of competitors who are willing to bid at least the reserve price will generally depend on the details of the report: favorable information will attract additional bidders and unfavorable information will discourage them. The seller can offset that effect by adjusting the reserve price (in a manner depending on the particular realization of his information variable) so as to always attract the same set of bidders. When this is done, the information-release results mentioned above continue to hold.

When both a reserve price and an entry fee are used, a bidder will participate in the auction if and only if his expected profit from bidding (given the reserve price) exceeds the entry fee. In particular, he will participate only if his value estimate exceeds some minimum level called the *screening level*. The most tractable case for analysis arises when the "only if" can be replaced by "if and only if," that is, when every bidder whose value estimate exceeds the screening level participates: we call that case the *regular* case. The case of a zero entry fee is always regular.

For each type of auction we study, any particular screening level x^* can be achieved by a continuum of different combinations (r, e) of reserve prices and entry fees. We show that if (r, e) and $(\bar{r}, \bar{e})$ are two such combinations with $e > \bar{e}$, and if the auction corresponding to (r, e) is regular, then the auction corresponding to $(\bar{r}, \bar{e})$ is also regular but generates lower expected revenues than the (r, e) auction. Therefore, so long as regularity is preserved and the screening level is held fixed, it pays to raise entry fees and reduce reserve prices.

In section 8, we consider another variation of the general model, in which bidders are risk-averse. Recall that in the independent private values model with risk aversion, the first-price auction yields a larger expected price than do the second-price and English auctions. In our more general model, no clear qualitative comparison can be made between the first-price and second-price auctions in the presence of risk aversion, and all that can be generally said about reserve prices and entry fees in the first-price auction is that the revenue-maximizing fee is positive (cf. Maskin and Riley [11]). With constant absolute risk aversion, however, both the results that the English auction generates higher average prices than the second-price auction, and that the best information-reporting policy for the seller in either of these two auctions is to reveal fully his information, and retain their validity.

3. The General Symmetric Model

Consider an auction in which n bidders compete for the possession of a single object. Each bidder possesses some information concerning the object up for sale; let $X = (X_1, \cdots, X_n)$ be a vector, the components of which are the real-valued *informational variables*[13] (or *value estimates*, or *signals*) observed by the individual bidders. Let $S = (S_1, \cdots, S_m)$ be a vector of additional real-valued variables which influence the value of the object to the bidders. Some of the components of S might be observed by the seller. For example, in the sale of a work of art, some of the components may represent appraisals obtained by the seller, while other components may correspond to the tastes of art connoisseurs not participating in the auction; these tastes could affect the resale value of the object.

The actual value of the object to bidder i – which may, of course, depend on variables not observed by him at the time of the auction – will be denoted by $V_i = u_i(S, X)$. We make the following assumptions:

Assumption 1: There is a function u on $\mathbb{R}^{m+n}$ such that for all i

$$u_i(S, X) = u(S, X_i \{X_j\}_{j \neq i})$$

Consequently, all of the bidders' valuations depend on S in the same manner, and each bidder's valuation is a symmetric function of the other bidders' signals.

Assumption 2: The function u is nonnegative, and is continuous and nondecreasing in its variables.

Assumption 3: For each i, $E[V_i] < \infty$.
Both the private values model and the common value model involve valuations of this form. In the first case, $m = 0$ and each $V_i = X_i$; in the second case, $m = 1$ and each $V_i = S_1$.

Throughout the next four sections, we assume that the bidders' valuations are in monetary units, and that the bidders are neutral in their attitudes towards risk. Hence, if bidder i receives the object being sold and pays the amount b, his payoff is simply $V_i - b$.

Let $f(s, x)$ denote the joint probability density[14] of the random elements of the model. We make two assumptions about the joint distribution of S and X:

Assumption 4: f is symmetric in its last n arguments.

Assumption 5: The variables $S_1, \cdots, S_m, X_1, \cdots X_n$ are affiliated.

A general definition of affiliation is given in the Appendix. For variables with densities, the following simple definition will suffice.

Let z and z' be points in $\mathbb{R}^{m+n}$. Let $z \vee z'$ denote the component-wise maximum of z and z', and let $z \wedge z'$ denote the component-wise minimum. We say that the variables of the model are *affiliated* if, for all z and z',

$$f(z \vee z')f(z \wedge z') \geqq f(z)f(z') \tag{2}$$

Roughly, this condition means that large values for some of the variables make the other variables more likely to be large than small.

We call inequality (2) the "affiliation inequality" (though it is also known as the "FKG inequality" and the "MTP$_2$ property"), and a function f satisfying (2) is said to be "affiliated." Some consequences of affiliation are discussed by Karlin and Rinott [10] and by Tong [27], and related results are reported by Milgrom [18] and Whitt [32]. For our purposes, the major results are those given by Theorems 1–5 below.

Theorem 1: Let $f: \mathbb{R}^k \to \mathbb{R}$.

(i) If f is strictly positive and twice continuously differentiable, then f is affiliated if and only if for $i \neq j$, $\partial^2 \ln f / \partial z_i \partial z_j \geq 0$.

(ii) If $f(z) = g(z)h(z)$ where g and h are nonnegative and affiliated, then f is affiliated.

A proof of part (i) can be found in Topkis [28, p. 310]. Part (ii) is easily checked.

In the independent private values model, the only random variables are $X_1, \cdots, X_n$, and they are statistically independent. For this case, (2) always holds with equality: Independent variables are always affiliated.

In the mineral rights model, let $g(x_i|s)$ denote the conditional density of any X_i given the common value S and let h be the marginal density of S. Then $f(s, x) = h(s)g(x_i|s) \cdots g(x_n|s)$. Assume that the density g has the monotone likelihood ratio property; that is, assume that $g(x|s)$ satisfies (2).[15] It then follows from Theorem 1 (ii) that f satisfies (2). Consequently, for the case of densities g with the monotone likelihood ratio property, the mineral rights model fits our formulation.

The affiliation assumption also accommodates other forms of the density f. For example, it accommodates a number of variations of the mineral rights model in which the bidders' estimation errors are positively correlated. And, if the inequality in (2) is strict, it formalizes the assumption that in an auction for a painting, a bidder who finds the painting very beautiful will expect others to admire it, too.

In this symmetric bidding environment, we identify competitive behavior with symmetric Nash equilibrium behavior. We will find that, at equilibrium, bidders with higher estimates tend to make higher bids. Consequently, we shall need to understand the properties of the distribution of the highest estimates.

Let $Y_1, \cdots, Y_{n-1}$ denote the largest, ..., smallest estimates from among $X_2, \cdots, X_n$. Then, using (1) and the symmetry assumption, we can rewrite bidder 1's value as follows:

$$V_1 = u(S_1, \ldots, S_m, X_1, Y_1, \ldots, Y_{n-1}) \tag{3}$$

The joint density of $S_1, \ldots, S_m, X_1, Y_1, \ldots, Y_{n-1}$ is

$$(n-1)!f(s_1, \ldots, s_m, x_1, y_1, \ldots, y_{n-1}) 1_{\{y_1 \geqq y_2 \geqq \cdots \geqq y_{n-1}\}} \tag{4}$$

where the last term is an indicator function. Applying Theorem 1 (ii) to (4), we have the following result.

Theorem 2: If f is affiliated and symmetric in $X_2, \ldots, X_n$, then $S_1, \ldots, S_m$, $X_1, Y_1, \ldots, Y_{n-1}$ are affiliated.

The following additional results, which are used repeatedly, are derived in the Appendix.

Theorem 3: If $Z_1, \ldots, Z_k$ are affiliated and $g_1, \ldots, g_k$ are all nondecreasing functions (or all nonincreasing functions), then $g_1(Z_1), \ldots, g_k(Z_k)$ are affiliated.

Theorem 4: If $Z_1, \ldots, Z_k$ are affiliated, then $Z_1, \ldots, Z_{k-1}$ are affiliated.

Theorem 5: Let $Z_1, \ldots, Z_k$ be affiliated and let H be any nondecreasing function. Then the function h defined by

$$h(a_1, b_1; \ldots; a_k, b_k) = E[H(Z_1, \ldots, Z_k)|a_1 \leq Z_1 \leq b_1, \ldots, a_k \leq Z_k \leq b_k]$$

is nondecreasing in all of its arguments. In particular, the functions

$$h_1(z_1, \ldots, z_1) = E[H(Z_1, \ldots, Z_k)|z_1, \ldots, z_l]$$

for $l = 1, \ldots, k$ are all nondecreasing.
In view of Theorems 2 and 5, we can conclude that the function

$$E[V_1|X_1 = x, Y_1 = y_1, \ldots, Y_{n-1} = y_{n-1}]$$

is nondecreasing in x. To simplify later proofs, we add the nondegeneracy assumption that this function is strictly increasing in x. All of our results can be shown to hold without this extra assumption.

4. Second-Price Auctions[16]

In the second-price auction game, a strategy for bidder i is a function mapping his value estimate x_i into a bid $b = b_i(x_i) \geq 0$. Since the auction is symmetric, let us focus our attention on the bidding decision faced by bidder 1.

Suppose that the bidders $j \neq 1$ adopt strategies b_j. Then the highest bid among them will be $W = \max_{j\neq 1} b_j(X_j)$ which, for fixed strategies b_j, is a random variable. Bidder 1 will win the second-price auction if his bid b exceeds W, and W is the price he will pay if he wins. Thus, his decision problem is to choose a bid b to solve

$$\max_b E[(V_1 - W)1_{\{W<b\}}|x_1]$$

If $b_1(x_1)$ solves this problem for every value of x_1, then the strategy b_1 is called a *best reply* to $b_2, \ldots, b_n$. If each b_i in an n-tuple $(b_1, \ldots, b_n)$ is a best reply to the remaining $n-1$ strategies, then the n-tuple is called an *equilibrium point*.

Let us define a function $v: \mathbb{R}^2 \to \mathbb{R}$ by $v(x, y) = E[V_1 | X_1 = x, Y_1 = y]$. In view of (3) and Theorems 2 and 5, v is nondecreasing. Our nondegeneracy assumption ensures that v is strictly increasing in its first argument.

Theorem 6: Let $b^*(x) = v(x, x)$. Then the n-tuple of strategies $(b^*, \ldots, b^*)$ is an equilibrium point of the second-price auction.
Proof: Since b^* is increasing, $W = b^*(Y_1)$. So bidder 1's conditional expected payoff when he bids b is

$$E(V_1 - b^*(Y_1))1_{\{b^*(Y_1) < b\}} | X_1 = x]$$
$$= E[E[(V_1 - v(Y_1, Y_1))1_{\{b^*(Y_1) < b\}} | X_1, Y_1 | X_1 = x]$$
$$= E[(v(X_1, Y_1) - v(Y_1, Y_1))1_{\{b^*(Y_1) < b\}} | X_1 = x]$$
$$= \int_{-\infty}^{b^{*-1}(b)} [v(x, \alpha) - v(\alpha, \alpha)] f_{Y_1}(\alpha | x) d\alpha$$

where $f_{Y_1}(\cdot | x)$ is the conditional density of Y_1 given $X_1 = x$. Since v is increasing in its first argument, the integrand is positive for $\alpha < x$ and negative for $\alpha > x$. Hence, the integral is maximized by choosing b so that $b^{*-1}(b) = x$, i.e., $b = b^*(x)$. This proves that b^* is a best reply for bidder 1.

An important special case arises if we assume that

$$V_1 = V_2 = \cdots = V_n = V$$

We call this the *generalized mineral rights model*. (It differs from the mineral rights model in not requiring the bidders' estimates of V to be conditionally independent.) Suppose that, in this context, we introduce an $(n+1)$st bidder with an estimate X_{n+1} of the common value V. We say that X_{n+1} is a *garbling* of (X_1, Y_1) if the joint density of $(V, X_1, \ldots, X_n, X_{n+1})$ can be written as

$$g(V, X_1, \ldots, X_n) \cdot h(X_{n+1} | X_1, Y_1)$$

For example, if bidder $n+1$ bases his estimate X_{n+1} only on information that was also available to bidder 1, this condition would hold.

Theorem 7: For the generalized mineral rights model, if X_{n+1} is a garbling of (X_1, Y_1), then bidder $n+1$ has no strategy that earns a positive expected payoff when bidders $1, \ldots, n$ use $(b^*, \ldots, b^*)$. Consequently, in this $(n+1)$-bidder second-price auction, the $(n+1)$-tuple $(b^*, \ldots, b^*, b_{n+1})$ where $b_{n+1} \equiv 0$ is an equilibrium point.
Proof: Let $Z = \max(X_1, Y_1)$. If bidder $n+1$ observes X_{n+1} and then makes a winning bid b, then his conditional expected payoff is

$$E[(V - b^*(Z))|X_{n+1}, \{b^*(Z) < b\}]$$
$$= E[E[V - b^*(Z)|X_1, Y_1, X_{n+1}]|X_{n+1}, \{b^*(Z) < b\}]$$
$$= E[v(X_1, Y_1) - v(Z, Z)|X_{n+1}, \{b^*(Z) < b\}]$$

The last equality uses the fact that $E[V|X_1, Y_1, X_{n+1}] = E[V|X_1, Y_1]$, a consequence of the garbling assumption. Since v is nondecreasing, $v(X_1, Y_1) - v(Z, Z) \leq 0$, so the last expectation is nonpositive.

Now consider how the equilibrium is affected when the seller publicly reveals some information X_0 (which is affiliated with all the other random elements of the model). We shall assume the seller's revelations are credible.[17]

Define a function $w: \mathbb{R}^3 \to \mathbb{R}$ by

$$w(x, y; z) = E[V_1|X_1 = x, Y_1 = y, X_0 = z]$$

By Theorems 2 and 5, w is nondecreasing. After X_0 is publicly announced, a new conditional joint density $f(s_1, \ldots, s_m, x_1, \ldots, x_n|x_0)$ applies to the random elements of the model, and it is straightforward to verify that the conditional density satisfies the affiliation inequality. So, carrying out the same analysis as before, there is an equilibrium $(\hat{b}, \ldots, \hat{b})$ given by $\hat{b}(x; x_0) = w(x, x; x_0)$. Note that this time a strategy maps two variables, representing private and public information, into a bid. For any fixed value of X_0, the equilibrium strategy is a function of a single variable and is similar in form to b^*.

Let R_N be the expected selling price when no public information is revealed and let R_I be the expected price when X_0 is made public.

Theorem 8: The expected selling prices are as follows

$$R_N = E[v(Y_1, Y_1)|\{X_1 > Y_1\}]$$
$$R_I = E[w(Y_1, Y_1; X_0)|\{X_1 > Y_1\}]$$

Revealing information publicly raises revenues, that is, $R_I \geq R_N$.
Proof: Recall that $v(Y_1, Y_1)$ is the price paid when bidder 1 wins. Thus, R_N is the expected price paid by bidder 1 when he wins. By symmetry, it is the expected price, regardless of the winner's identity. The same argument applies to R_I.

Next, note the following identities.

$$v(x, y) = E[V_1|X_1 = x, Y_1 = y]$$
$$= E[E[V_1|X_1, Y_1, X_0]|X_1 = x, Y_1 = y]$$
$$= E[w(X_1, Y_1; X_0)|X_1 = x, Y_1 = y]$$

For $x > y$, we apply Theorems 2, 4, and 5 to get:

$$v(y, y) = E[w(X_1, Y_1; X_0)|X_1 = y, Y_1 = y]$$
$$= E[w(Y_1, Y_1; X_0)|X_1 = y, Y_1 = y]$$
$$\leq E[w(Y_1, Y_1; X_0)|X_1 = x, Y_1 = y]$$

So,

$$R_N = E[v(Y_1, Y_1)|\{X_1 > Y_1\}]$$
$$\leq E[E[w(Y_1, Y_1;X_0)|X_1, Y_1]|\{X_1 > Y_1\}]$$
$$= E[w(Y_1, Y_1;X_0)|\{X_1 > Y_1\}] = R_I$$

Theorem 8 indicates that publicly revealing the information X_0 is better, on average, than revealing no information. One might wonder whether it would be better still to censor information sometimes, i.e., to report X_0 only when it exceeds some critical level. Of course, if this policy of the seller were known, rational bidders would correctly interpret the absence of any report as a bad sign.

There are many possible information revelation policies. If one assumes that the bidders know the information policy, then one can also assume without loss of generality that the seller always makes some report, though that report may consist of a blank page. Let Z be a random variable, uniformly distributed on $[0, 1]$ and independent of the other variables of the model. We formulate the seller's report very generally as $X_0' = r(X_0, Z)$, i.e., the seller's report may depend both on his information and the spin of a roulette wheel. We call r the seller's *reporting policy*.

Theorem 9: In the second-price auction, no reporting policy leads to a higher expected price than the policy of always reporting X_0.
Proof: Let r be any reporting policy and let $X_0' = r(X_0, Z)$. The conditional distribution of X_0', given the original variables (S, X), depends only on X_0. We denote the conditional density (if one exists) by $g(X_0'|X_0)$ and the marginal density by $g(X_0')$. For any realization x_0' of X_0', the corresponding conditional joint density[18] of (S, X) is $f(s, x)g(x_0'|x_0)/g(x_0')$, which satisfies the affiliation inequality in (s, x) since f does, by Theorem 1. Therefore, by Theorem 8, revealing X_0 further raises expected revenues. But revealing both X_0 and X_0' leads to the same equilibrium bidding as revealing just X_0, so the result follows.

5. English Auctions

There are many variants of the English auction. In some, the bids are called by the bidders themselves, and the auction ends when no one is willing to raise the bid.[19] In others, the auctioneer calls the bids, and a willing bidder indicates his assent by some slight gesture, usually in a way that preserves his anonymity. Cassady [2] has described yet another variant, used in Japan, in which the price is posted using an electronic display. In that variant, the price is raised continuously, and a bidder who wishes to be active at the current price depresses a button. When he releases the button, he has withdrawn from the auction. These three forms of the English auction correspond to three quite different games. The game model developed in this section corresponds most closely to the Japanese variant. We assume that both the price level and the number of active bidders are continuously displayed. We use the term "English auction" to designate this variant.

In the English auction with only two bidders, each bidder's strategy can be completely described by a single number which specifies how high to compete before ceding the contest to the other bidder. The bidder selecting the higher number wins, and he pays a price equal to the other bidder's number. Thus, with only two bidders, the English and second-price auctions are strategically equivalent. When there are three or more bidders, however, the bidding behavior of those who drop out early in an English auction can convey information to those who keep bidding, and our model of the auction as a game must account for that possibility.

We idealize the auction as follows. Initially, all bidders are active at a price of zero. As the auctioneer raises the price, bidders drop out one by one. No bidder who has dropped out can become active again. After any bidder quits, all remaining active bidders know the price at which he quit.

A strategy for bidder i specifies whether, at any price level p, he will remain active or drop out, as a function of his value estimate, the number of bidders who have quit the bidding, and the levels at which they quit. Let k denote the number of bidders who have quit and let $p_1 \leq \cdots \leq p_k$ denote the levels at which they quit. Then bidder i's strategy can be described by functions $b_{ik}(x_i|p_1, \ldots, p_k)$ which specify the price at which bidder i will quit if, at that point, k other bidders have quit at the prices $p_1, \ldots, p_k$. It is natural to require that $b_{ik}(x_i|p_1, \ldots, p_k)$ be at least p_k.

Now consider the strategy $b^* = (b_0^*, \ldots, b_{n-2}^*)$ defined iteratively as follows.

$$b_0^*(x) = E[V_1|X_1 = x, Y_1 = x, \ldots, Y_{n-1} = x] \tag{5}$$

$$b_k^*(x|p_1, \ldots, p_k) = E[V_1|X_1 = x, Y_1 = x, \ldots, Y_{n-k-1} = x, b_{k-1}^*(Y_{n-k}|p_1, \ldots, p_{k-1}) \tag{6}$$
$$= p_k, \ldots, b_0^*(Y_{n-1}) = p_1]$$

The component strategies reflect a kind of myopic bidding behavior. Suppose, for example, that $k = 0$, i.e., no bidder has quit yet. Suppose, too, that the price has reached the level $b_0^*(y)$ and that bidder 1 has observed $X_1 = x$. If bidders $2, \ldots, n$ were to quit instantly, then bidder 1 could infer from this behavior that $Y_1 = \cdots = Y_{n-1} = y$. In that case, he would estimate his payoff to be

$$E[V_1|X_1 = x, Y_1 = y, \ldots, Y_{n-1} = y] - b_0^*(y)$$

By (5) and Theorem 5, that difference is positive if $x > y$ and negative if $x < y$. Thus, b_0^* calls for bidder 1 to remain active until the price rises to the point where he would be just indifferent between winning and losing at that price. The other strategies b_k^* have similar interpretations, but they assume that bidders infer whatever they can from the quitting prices of those who are no longer active.

Theorem 10: The n-tuple $(b^*, \ldots, b^*)$ is an equilibrium point of the English auction game. *Proof*: It is straightforward to verify from (5) and (6) that each b_k^* is increasing in its first argument. Hence, if bidders $2, \ldots, n$ adopt b^* and bidder 1 wins the auction, the price he will pay is

$$E[V_1|X_1 = y_1, Y_1 = y_1, \ldots, Y_{n-1} = y_{n-1}]$$

where $y_1, \ldots, y_{n-1}$ are the realizations of $Y_1, \ldots, Y_{n-1}$. His conditional estimate of V_1 given $X_1, Y_1, \ldots, Y_{n-1}$ is

$$E[V_1 | X_1 = x, Y_1 = y_1, \ldots, Y_{n-1} = y_{n-1}]$$

so his conditional expected payoff is nonnegative if and only if $x \geq y_1$ Using b^*, bidder 1 will win if and only if $X_1 > Y_1$ (recall that the event $\{X_1 = Y_1\}$ is null). Hence b^* is a best reply for bidder 1.

Theorem 11: The expected price in the English auction is not less than that in the second-price auction.
Proof: This is identical to the proof of Theorem 8, except that $Y_2, \ldots, Y_{n-1}$ play the role of X_0

In effect, the English auction proceeds in two phases. In phase 1, the $n-2$ bidders with the lowest estimates reveal their signals publicly through their bidding behavior. Then, the last two bidders engage in a second-price auction. We know from Theorem 8 that the public information phase raises the expected selling price.

By mimicking the proofs of Theorem 8 and 9, we obtain corresponding results for English auctions. Define $\bar{v}$ and $\bar{w}$ as follows.

$$\bar{v}(x, y_1, \ldots, y_{n-1}) = E[V_1 | X_1 = x, Y_1 = y_1, \ldots, Y_{n-1} = y_{n-1}]$$

$$\bar{w}(x, y_1, \ldots, y_{n-1}; z) = E[V_1 | X_1 = x, Y_1 = y_1, \ldots, Y_{n-1} = y_{n-1}, X_0 = z]$$

Theorem 12: If no information is provided by the seller, the expected price is

$$R_N^E = E[\bar{v}(Y_1, Y_1, Y_2, \ldots, Y_{n-1}) | \{X_1 > Y_1\}]$$

If the seller announces X_0, the expected price is

$$R_I^E = E[\bar{w}(Y_1, Y_1, Y_2, \ldots, Y_{n-1}; X_0) | \{X_1 > Y_1\}]$$

Revealing information publicly raises revenues, that is, $R_I^E \geq R_N^E$.

Theorem 13: In the English auction, no reporting policy leads to a higher expected price than the policy of always reporting X_0.

6. First-Price Auctions

We begin our analysis of first-price auctions by deriving the necessary conditions for an n-tuple $(b^*, \ldots, b^*)$ to be an equilibrium point, when b^* is increasing and differentiable.[20] Suppose bidders $2, \ldots, n$ adopt the strategy b^*. If bidder 1 then observes $X_1 = x$ and bids b, his expected payoff $\Pi(b; x)$ will be given by

$$\Pi(b;x) = E[(V_1 - b)1_{\{b^*(Y_1)<b\}}|X_1 = x]$$
$$= E[E[(V_1 - b)1_{\{b^*(Y_1)<b\}}|X_1, Y_1]|X_1 = x]$$
$$= E[(v(X_1, Y_1) - b)1_{\{b^*(Y_1)<b\}}|X_1 = x]$$
$$= \int_{\underline{x}}^{b^{*-1}(b)} (v(x, \alpha) - b)f_{Y_1}(\alpha|x)d\alpha$$

where $\underline{x}$ is infimum of the support of Y_1. The first-order condition for a maximum of $\Pi(b; x)$ is

$$0 = \Pi_b(b;x)$$
$$= \frac{(v(x, b^{*-1}(b)) - b)f_{Y_1}(b^{*-1}(b)|x)}{b^{*'}(b^{*-1}(b)) - F_{Y_1}(b^{*-1}(b)|x)}$$

where Π_b denotes $\partial\Pi/\partial b$ and F_{Y_1} is the cumulative distribution corresponding to the density f_{Y_1}. If b^* is a best reply for 1, we must have $\Pi_b(b^*(x);x) = 0$. Substituting $b^*(x)$ for b in the first-order condition and rearranging terms leads to a first-order linear differential equation.[21]

$$b^{*'}(x) = (v(x, x) - b^*(x))\frac{f_{Y_1}(x|x)}{F_{Y_1}(x|x)} \tag{7}$$

Condition (7) is just one of the conditions necessary for equilibrium. Another necessary condition is that $(v(x, x) - b^*(x))$ be nonnegative. Otherwise, bidder 1's expected payoff would be negative and he could do better by bidding zero. It is also necessary that $v(\underline{x}, \underline{x}) - b^*(\underline{x})$ be nonpositive. Otherwise, when $X_1 = \underline{x}$, a small increase in the bid from $b^*(\underline{x})$ to $b^*(\underline{x}) + \varepsilon$ would raise 1's expected payoff from zero to some small positive number. These last two restrictions determine the boundary condition: $b^*(\underline{x}) = v(\underline{x}, \underline{x})$.

Theorem 14: The n-tuple $(b^*, \ldots, b^*)$ is an equilibrium of the first-price auction, where:

$$b^*(x) = \int_{\underline{x}}^{x} v(\alpha, \alpha)dL(\alpha|x)$$

and[22]

$$L(\alpha|x) = \exp\left(-\int_{\alpha}^{x} \frac{f_{Y_1}(s|s)}{F_{Y_1}(s|s)}ds\right) \tag{8}$$

Let $t(x) = v(x, x)$. Then b^* can also be written as:

$$b^*(x) = v(x, x) - \int_{\underline{x}}^{x} L(\alpha|x)dt(\alpha)$$

Lemma 1: $F_{Y_1}(x|z)/f_{Y_1}(x|z)$ is decreasing in z.
Proof: By the affiliation inequality, for any $\alpha \le x$ and any $z' \le z$, we have

$$\frac{f_{Y_1}(\alpha|z)}{f_{Y_1}(x|z)} \le \frac{f_{Y_1}(\alpha|z')}{f_{Y_1}(x|z')}$$

Integrating with respect to α over the range $\underline{x} \le \alpha \le x$ yields the desired result.

Proof of Theorem 14: Notice that $L(\cdot|x)$, regarded as a probability distribution on $(\underline{x}, x)$, increases stochastically in x (that is, $L(\alpha|x)$ is decreasing in x). Since $v(\alpha, \alpha)$ is increasing, b^* must be increasing.

Temporarily assume that b^* is continuous in x. Then there is no loss of generality in assuming that b^* is differentiable, since Theorem 3 permits us to rescale the bidders' estimates monotonically.[23] Consider bidder 1's best response problem. It is clear that he need only consider bids in the range of b^*. Therefore, to show that $b^*(z)$ is an optimal bid when $X_1 = z$, it suffices to show that $\Pi_b(b^*(x); z)$ is nonnegative for $x < z$ and non-positive for $x > z$. Now,

$$\Pi_b(b^*(x); z) = \frac{f_{Y_1}(x|z)}{b^{*\prime}(x)}\left[(v(z, x) - b^*(x)) - b^{*\prime}(x) \cdot \frac{F_{Y_1}(x|z)}{f_{Y_1}(x|z)}\right]$$

By (7), the bracketed expression is zero when $x = z$. Therefore, by Lemma 1 and the monotonicity of b^* and v, the bracketed expression (and therefore, $\Pi_b(b^*(x);z)$) has the same sign as $(z - x)$.

It remains to consider the cases where b^* (as defined by (8)) is discontinuous at some point x. That can happen only if for all positive ε, the first of the following expressions is infinite:

$$\int_x^{x+\varepsilon} \frac{f_{Y_1}(s|s)}{F_{Y_1}(s|s)}\,ds \le \int_x^{x+\varepsilon} \frac{f_{Y_1}(s|x+\varepsilon)}{F_{Y_1}(s|x+\varepsilon)}\,ds$$
$$= \ln F_{Y_1}(x+\varepsilon|x+\varepsilon) - \ln F_{Y_1}(x|x+\varepsilon)$$

the inequality follows from Lemma 1. The final difference can be infinite only if

$$F_{Y_1}(x|x+\varepsilon) = 0$$

and that in turn implies that

$$F_{Y_{n-1}}(x|x+\varepsilon) = 0$$

(Otherwise, there would be some point $z = (z_2, \ldots, z_n)$ in the conditional support of $(X_2, \ldots, X_n)$ given $X_1 = x + \varepsilon$, with some $z_i < x$. By symmetry, all of the permutations of z are also in the support and therefore, by affiliation, the component-wise minimum of these permutations is in the support. But that would contradict the earlier conclusion that $F_{Y_1}(x|x+\varepsilon) = 0$.) Thus, if any X_i exceeds x, all must.

It now follows that the bidding game decomposes into two subgames, in one of which it is common knowledge that all estimates exceed x and in the other of which it is common knowledge that none exceed x. Taking the refinement of all such decompositions, we obtain a collection of subgames, in each of which b^* is continuous. The first part of our proof then applies to each subgame separately.

The remaining results in this section, as well as parts of the analyses in Sections 7 and 8, make use of the following simple lemma.

Lemma 2: Let g and h be differentiable functions for which

    (i) $g(\underline{x}) \geq h(\underline{x})$ and
    (ii) $g(x) < h(x)$ implies $g'(x) \geq h'(x)$
Then $g(x) \geq h(x)$ for all $x \geq \underline{x}$.
Proof: If $g(x) < h(x)$ for some $x > \underline{x}$ then, by the mean value theorem, there is some $\hat{x}$ in $(\underline{x}, x)$ such that $g(\hat{x}) < h(\hat{x})$ and $g'(\hat{x}) < h'(\hat{x})$. This contradicts (ii).

Our first application of this lemma is in the proof of the next theorem.

Theorem 15: The expected selling price in the second-price auction is at least as large as in the first-price auction.
Proof: Let $R(x, z)$ denote the expected value received by bidder 1 if his own estimate is z and he bids as if it were x; that is, define

$$R(x, z) = E[V_1 \cdot 1_{\{Y_1 < x\}} | X_1 = z]$$

Let $W^M(x, z)$ denote the conditional expected payment made by bidder 1 in auction mechanism M (in the case at hand, either the first-price or second-price mechanism) if

    (i)   the other bidders follow their equilibrium strategies,
    (ii) bidder 1's estimate is z,
    (iii) he bids as if it were x, and
    (iv) he wins.

For the first-price and second-price mechanisms, we have

$$W^1(x, z) = b^*(x)$$

and

$$W^2(x, z) = E[v(Y_1, Y_1) | Y_1 < x, X_1 = z]$$

In mechanism M, bidder 1's problem at equilibrium when $X_1 = z$ is to choose a bid, or equivalently to choose x, to maximize $R(x, z) - W^M(x, z)F_{Y_1}(x|z)$. The first-order condition must hold at $x = z$:

$$0 = R_1(z, z) - W_1^M(z, z)F_{Y_1}(z|z) - W^M(z, z)f_{Y_1}(z|z) \tag{9}$$

where R_1 and W_1^M denote the relevant partial derivatives. The equilibrium boundary condition is: $W^M(\underline{x}, \underline{x}) = v(\underline{x}, \underline{x})$.

Clearly, $W_2^1(x, z) = 0$. From Theorem 5 it follows that $W_2^2(x, z) \geq 0$. Hence, by (9), if $W^2(z, z) < W^1(z, z)$ for some z, then

$$\frac{dW^2}{dz} = W_1^2 + W_2^2 \geq W_1^1 + W_2^1 = \frac{dW^1}{dz}$$

Therefore, by Lemma 2, $W^2(z, z) \geq W^1(z, z)$ for all $z \geq \underline{x}$. The theorem follows upon noting that the expected prices in the first-price and second-price auctions are

$$E[W^1(X_1, X_1)|\{X_1 > Y_1\}]$$

and

$$E[W^2(X_1, X_1)|\{X_1 > Y_1\}]$$

respectively.

A similar argument is used below to establish that in a first-price auction the seller can raise the expected price by adopting a policy of revealing his information.

Theorem 16: In the first-price auction, a policy of publicly revealing the seller's information cannot lower, and may raise, the expected price.
Proof: Let $b^*(\cdot; s)$ represent the equilibrium bidding strategy in the first-price auction after the seller reveals an informational variable $X_0 = s$. The analogue of equation (7) is:

$$b^{*'}(x; s) = (w(x, x; s) - b^*(x; s)) \frac{f_{Y_1}(x|x, s)}{F_{Y_1}(x|x, s)}$$

By a variant of Lemma 1,

$$\frac{f_{Y_1}(x|x, s)}{F_{Y_1}(x|x, s)}$$

is nondecreasing in s, and by Theorem 5, $w(x, x; s)$ is also nondecreasing in s. The equilibrium boundary condition is $b^*(\underline{x}; s) = w(\underline{x}, \underline{x}; s)$. Hence, applying Lemma 2 to the functions $b^*(\cdot; s)$ for any two different values of s, we can conclude that $b^*(x; s)$ is nondecreasing in s.

Let

$$W^*(x, z) = E[b^*(x; X_0)|Y_1 < x, X_1 = z]$$

By Theorem 5, $W_2^*(x, z) \geq 0$. Note that

$$W^*(\underline{x}, \underline{x}) = E[w(\underline{x}, \underline{x}; X_0) | Y_1 = \underline{x}, X_1 = \underline{x}] = v(\underline{x}, \underline{x})$$

If bidder 1, prior to learning X_0 but after observing $X_1 = z$, were to commit himself to some bidding strategy $b^*(x; \cdot)$, his optimal choice would be $x = z$ (since $b^*(z; x_0)$ is optimal when $X_0 = x_0$). Thus, W^* must satisfy (9). Hence, by Lemma 2, $W^*(z, z) \geq W^1(z, z)$ for all $z \geq \underline{x}$; the details follow just as in the proof of Theorem 15. The expected prices, with and without the release of information, are

$$E[W^*(X_1, X_1) | \{X_1 > Y_1\}]$$

and

$$E[W^1(X_1, X_1) | \{X_1 > Y_1\}]$$

Therefore, releasing information raises the expected price.

If the seller reveals only some of his information, then, conditional on that information, $X_0, X_1, \ldots, X_n$ are still affiliated. Thus, we have the following analogue of Theorems 9 and 13.

Theorem 17: In the first-price auction, no reporting policy leads to a higher expected price than the policy of always reporting X_0.

There is a common thread running through Theorems 8, 11, 12, 15, and 16 that lends some insight into why the three auctions we have studied can be ranked by the expected revenues they generate, and why policies of revealing information raise expected prices. This thread is most easily identified by viewing the auctions as "revelation games" in which each bidder chooses a *report* x instead of a bid $b^*(x)$.

No auction mechanism can determine prices *directly* in terms of the bidders' preferences and information; prices (and the allocation of the object being sold) can depend only on the reports that the bidders make and on the seller's information. However, to the extent that the price in an auction depends directly on variables other than the winning bidder's report, and to the extent that these other variables are (at equilibrium) affiliated with the winner's value estimate, the price is statistically linked to that estimate. The result of this linkage is that the expected price paid by the bidder, as a function of his estimate, increases more steeply in his estimate than it otherwise might. Since a winning bidder with estimate $\underline{x}$ expects to pay $v(\underline{x}, \underline{x})$ in all of the auctions we have analyzed, a steeper payment function yields higher prices (and lower bidder profits).

In the first-price auction, for example, revealing the seller's information links the price to that information, even when the winning bidder's report x is held fixed. In the second-price auction, the price is linked to the estimate of the second-highest bidder, and revealing information links the price to that information as well. In the English auction, the price is linked to the estimates of *all* the non-winning bidders, and to the seller's estimate as well, should he reveal it. The first-price auction, with no linkages to the other bidders' estimates, yields the lowest expected price. The English auction, with linkages to all of their estimates, yields the highest expected price. In all three auctions, revealing information adds a linkage and thus, in all three, it raises the expected price.

7. Reserve Prices and Entry Fees

The developments in sections 4–6 omit any mention of the seller setting a reserve price or charging an entry fee.[24] Such devices are commonly used in auctions and are believed to raise the seller's revenue. Moreover, a great deal of attention has recently been devoted to the problem of setting reserve prices and entry fees optimally (Harris and Raviv [8], Maskin and Riley [11], Matthews [13], Riley and Samuelson [24]).

It is straightforward to adapt the equilibrium characterization theorems (Theorems 6, 10, and 14) to accommodate reserve prices. In the first-price auction, setting a reserve price r above $v(\underline{x}, \underline{x})$ simply alters the boundary condition, and the symmetric equilibrium strategy becomes

$$b^*(x) = r \cdot L(x^*|x) + \int_{x^*}^{x} v(\alpha, \alpha) dL(\alpha|x) \qquad \text{for } x \geq x^*$$

$$b^*(x) < r \qquad \text{for } x < x^*$$

where $x^* = x^*(r)$ is called the *screening level* and is given by

$$x^*(r) = \inf\{x|E[V_1|X_1 = x, Y_1 < x] \geq r\} \qquad (10)$$

It is important to note that when the same reserve price r is used in a first-price, second-price auction, or English auction, the same set of bidders participates. Thus, in the second-price auction with reserve price r,[25] the equilibrium bidding strategy is

$$b^*(x) = v(x, x) \qquad \text{for } x \geq x^*$$

$$b^*(x) < r \qquad \text{for } x < x^*$$

A formal description of equilibrium with a reserve price in an English auction would be lengthy; the equilibrium strategies incorporate the inference that if a bidder does not participate, his valuation must be less than x^*.

With a fixed reserve price, one can again show that the English auction generates higher average prices than the second-price auction, which in turn generates higher average prices than the first-price auction. The introduction of a reserve price does not alter these important conclusions.

More subtle and interesting issues arise when the seller has private information. If he fixes a reserve price and then reveals his information, he will generally affect x^* and hence change the set of bidders who are willing to compete. In our information revelation theorems, we assumed that the reserve price was zero, so that revealing information would not alter the set of competitors.

Given any reserve price $\bar{r}$, and realization z of X_0 let $x^*(\bar{r}|z)$ denote the resulting value of x^*. It is clear from expression (10) that x^* is decreasing in $\bar{r}$ and maps onto the range of

X_1. Hence, there exists a reserve price $r = r(z|\bar{r})$ such that $x^*(r|z) = x^*(\bar{r})$; we call $r(z|\bar{r})$ the reserve price *corresponding to* z, given $\bar{r}$.

Theorem 18: Given any reserve price $\bar{r}$ for the first-price, second-price, or English auction, a policy of announcing X_0 and setting the corresponding reserve price raises expected revenues.
Proof: Let $Y_1^* = \max(Y_1, x^*(\bar{r}))$. Let

$$v^*(x,y) = E[V_1|X_1 = x, Y_1^* = y]$$

and let

$$w^*(x,y,z) = E[V_1|X_1 = x, Y_1^* = y, X_0 = z]$$

By Theorems 2–5, X_0, X_1 and Y_1^* are affiliated and v^* and w^* are nondecreasing, so the arguments used for Theorems 8 and 12 still apply. The argument used in the proof of Theorem 16 generalizes without difficulty.

As with Theorems 8, 12, and 16, Theorem 18 has the corollary that no policy of partially reporting the seller's information leads to a higher expected price than full revelation: Again, "honesty is the best policy."

When both a reserve price r and an entry fee e are given, we more generally define the *screening level* $x^*(r,e)$ to be

$$x^*(r,e) = \inf\{x|E[(V_1 - r)1_{\{Y_1<x\}}|X_1 = x] \geq e\}$$

It is not always true that the set of bidders who will choose to pay the entry fee and participate in an auction consists of all those whose value estimates exceed the screening level. In a first-price auction, an entry fee might discourage participation by some bidder with a valuation x well above $x^*(r,e)$ if he perceives his chance of winning $(F_{Y_1}(x|x))$ as being slight.[26]

If the set of bidders who participate at equilibrium in an auction with reserve price r and entry fee e does consist of those with valuations exceeding $x^*(r,e)$, then we say that the pair (r,e) is *regular* for that auction. The next result shows that among regular pairs with a fixed screening level, it pays to set high entry fees and low reserve prices, rather than the reverse.

Theorem 19: Fix an auction mechanism (first-price, second-price, or English), and suppose that the (reserve price, entry fee) pair (r,e) is regular. Let $(\bar{r}, \bar{e})$ be another pair with the same screening level (i.e., $x^*(r,e) = x^*(\bar{r}, \bar{e})$) and with $\bar{e} < e$. Then $(\bar{r}, \bar{e})$ is regular, but the expected revenue from the $(\bar{r}, \bar{e})$ auction is less than or equal to that from the (r,e) auction.
Proof: Let $P(x,z)$ and $\bar{P}(x,z)$ denote the expected payments made by bidder 1 in the (r,e) auction and the $(\bar{r}, \bar{e})$ auction, respectively, when

   (i)   the other bidders follow their equilibrium strategies,
   (ii)   bidder 1's estimate is z, and
   (iii) he bids as if his estimate were x.

(Notice that P and $\bar{P}$ are *not* conditioned on bidder 1 winning.) Defining R as in the proof of Theorem 15, we have the following equilibrium conditions:

$$P_1(z, z) = R_1(z, z) = \bar{P}_1(z, z)$$

for all $z \geq x^*$ and

$$P(x^*, x^*) = R(x^*, x^*) = \bar{P}(x^*, x^*)$$

If the two auctions are first-price auctions with equilibrium strategies b and $\bar{b}$, then

$$P(x, z) = b(x)F_{Y_1}(x|z) + e$$

and

$$\bar{P}(x, z) = \bar{b}(x)F_{Y_1}(x|z) + \bar{e}$$

Since b and $\bar{b}$ are solutions of the same differential equation, with

$$b(x^*) = r < \bar{r} = \bar{b}(x^*)$$

the functions cannot cross and so $b < \bar{b}$ everywhere. Also,

$$P_2(x, x) - \bar{P}_2(x, x) = [b(x) - \bar{b}(x)]\frac{\partial}{\partial z}|_{z=x} F_{Y_1}(x|z) \geq 0$$

since the partial derivative term is negative (by affiliation). Hence, an application of Lemma 2 yields $P(z, z) \geq \bar{P}(z, z)$ for all $z \geq x^*$.

For the second-price or English auction, the payments made by a bidder when his type is z and he bids as if it were x differ only when he pays the reserve price, i.e., only when $Y_1 < x^*$. Therefore,

$$P_2(x, z) - \bar{P}_2(x, z) = (r - \bar{r})(\frac{\partial}{\partial z})F_{Y_1}(x^*|z) \geq 0$$

Once again, Lemma 2 implies that $P(z, z) \geq \bar{P}(z, z)$.

The expected payoff at equilibrium in the $(\bar{r}, \bar{e})$ auction for a bidder with estimate $z \geq x^*$ is

$$R(z, z) - \bar{P}(z, z) \geq R(z, z) - P(z, z) \geq 0$$

since (r, e) is regular. Hence, such bidders will participate in the $(\bar{r}, \bar{e})$ auction and the seller's expected revenue from each of them is less than it is in the (r, e) auction.

It remains to show that bidders with estimates $z < x^*$ will choose not to participate in the $(\bar{r}, \bar{e})$ auction. In the proofs of Theorems 6, 10, and 14, we argued (implicitly) that the decision problem $\max_x R(x,z) - \bar{P}(x,z)$ is quasiconcave for each of the three auction forms, and that the maximum is attained at $x = z$. Those arguments remain valid in the present context; we shall not repeat them here. Instead, we observe this consequence of quasiconcavity: for $z < x^*$, the optimal choice of x subject to the constraint $x \geq x^*$ is $x = x^*$. The resulting expected payoff to a bidder with estimate z is $R(x^*, z) - \bar{P}(x^*, z)$.

Now,

$$\bar{P}(x^*, z) - P(x^*, z) = \bar{P}(x^*, x^*) - P(x^*, x^*) + (\bar{r} - r)[F_{Y_1}(x^*|z) - F_{Y_1}(x^*|x^*)]$$

But

$$\bar{P}(x^*, x^*) = R(x^*, x^*) = P(x^*, x^*)$$

and, by affiliation, the bracketed term is nonnegative. Therefore $\bar{P}(x^*, z) \geq P(x^*, z)$. Hence, the expected profit of the bidder with estimate z is

$$R(x^*, z) - \bar{P}(x^*, z) \leq R(x^*, z) - P(x^*, z)$$

and this last expression is nonpositive because the (r, e) auction is regular.

8. Risk Aversion

In the model with risk-neutral bidders, we have shown that the English, second-price, and first-price auctions can be ranked by the expected prices they generate. We have also shown that in the English and second-price auctions, the seller benefits by establishing a policy of complete disclosure of his information. In this section, we investigate the robustness of those results when the bidders may be risk averse. For simplicity, we limit attention to the case of zero reserve prices and zero entry fees.

Consider first the independent private values model, in which $V_i = X_i$ and $X_1, \ldots, X_n$ are independent. For this model, the first-and second-price auctions generate identical expected prices. Now let bidder i's payoff be $u(X_i - b)$ when he wins at a price of b, where u is some increasing, concave, differentiable function satisfying $u(0) = 0$. Let b_u^* denote the equilibrium strategy in the first-price auction. Then the analogue of the differential equation (7) is:

$$b_u^{*\prime}(x) = \frac{u(x - b_u^*(x))}{u'(x - b_u^*(x))} \frac{f_{Y_1}(x)}{F_{Y_1}(x)}$$

$$\geq (x - b_u^*(x)) \frac{f_{Y_1}(x)}{F_{Y_1}(x)}$$

(11)

where the inequality follows from the concavity of u. Let b_N^* denote the equilibrium with risk-neutral bidders. From (11) it follows that whenever $b_u^*(x) \leq b_N^*(x), b_u^{*\prime}(x) > b_N^{*\prime}(x)$; the equilibrium boundary condition is:

$$b_N^*(\underline{x}) = b_u^*(\underline{x}) = \underline{x}$$

It then follows from Lemma 2 that, for $x > \underline{x}, b_u^*(x) > b_N^*(x)$: risk aversion raises the expected selling price. It is straightforward to verify that, with $V_i = X_i$, the second-price auction equilibrium strategy is $b^*(x) = x$, independent of risk attitudes. Thus, with independent private values and risk aversion, the first-price auction leads to higher prices than the second-price auction. In conjunction with our earlier result (Theorem 15), this implies that, for models that include both affiliation and risk aversion, the first-and second-price auctions cannot generally be ranked by their expected prices.

To treat the second-price auction when bidders are risk averse and do not know their own valuations, it is useful to generalize the definition of the function v. Let $v(x,y)$ be the unique solution of:

$$E[u(V_1 - v(x,y))|X_1 = x, Y_1 = y] = u(0)$$

The proof of Theorem 6 can be directly generalized to show that $(b^*, \ldots, b^*)$ is an equilibrium point of the second-price auction when $b^*(x) = v(x,x)$.

Similarly, it is useful to generalize the definition of w. Let $w(x,y,z)$ be the unique solution of:

$$E[u(V_1 - w(x,y,z))|X_1 = x, Y_1 = y, X_0 = z] = u(0)$$

In proving that releasing public information raises the expected selling price in Section 4, we used the fact that the relation

$$E[w(X_1, Y_1, X_0)|X_1, Y_1] \geq v(X_1, Y_1)$$

holds with equality when the bidders are risk neutral. Applied to risk-averse bidders, this inequality asserts that resolving uncertainty by releasing information reduces the risk premium demanded by the bidders. If the information being conveyed is perfect information (so that it resolves uncertainty completely), then, clearly, the risk premium is reduced to zero. But for risk-averse bidders, *it is not generally true that partially resolving uncertainty reduces the risk premium.* In fact, the class of utility functions for which any partial resolution of uncertainty tends to reduce the risk premium is a very narrow one.

Let us now rephrase this issue more formally. For a given utility function u and a random pair (V, X), define $R(x)$ by

$$E[u(V - R(x))|X = x] = u(0)$$

and define $\bar{R}$ by

$$E[u(V - R)] = u(0)$$

We shall say that revealing X *raises average willingness to pay* if $E[R(X)] \geq \bar{R}$.

Theorem 20: Let u be an increasing utility function. Then it is true for every random pair (V, X) that revealing X raises average willingness to pay if and only if the coefficient of absolute risk aversion $-u''(\cdot)/u'(\cdot)$ is a nonnegative constant.

Proof: We shall consider a family of random pairs (V_α, X). Let X take values in $\{0, 1\}$ and let $V_\alpha = X(Z + \alpha)$, where Z is some unspecified random variable. Suppose X and Z are independent and $P\{X = 0\} = P\{X = 1\} = \frac{1}{2}$. Finally, suppose $E[u(Z)] = u(0)$, and normalize so that $u(0) = 0$.

Fix u and let $\bar{R}_\alpha$ be the willingness to pay for V_α when there is no information. Let $R_\alpha(x)$ be defined as in the text. Then $R_\alpha(0) = 0$, $R_\alpha(1) = \alpha$, and $E[R_\alpha(X)] = \alpha/2$. If revealing X always increases willingness to pay, then $R_\alpha \leq \alpha/2$. So,

$$0 = E[u(V_\alpha - \bar{R}_\alpha)]$$
$$= \frac{1}{2}E[u(Z + \alpha - \bar{R}_\alpha)] + \frac{1}{2}u(-\bar{R}_\alpha)$$
$$\geq \frac{1}{2}E[u(Z + \frac{\alpha}{2})] + \frac{1}{2}u(-\frac{\alpha}{2})$$

Since this holds with equality at $\alpha = 0$ and since it must hold for all α, positive and negative, the final expression must be maximized when $\alpha = 0$:

$$0 = E[u'(Z)] - u'(0)$$
$$0 \geq E[u''(Z)] + u''(0)$$

(12)

Now, let $g(w) = u'(u^{-1}(w))$ and let $W = u(Z)$. By varying Z, we can obtain any desired random variable W on the range of u. The conclusion reached above can be restated as: $E[W] = 0$ implies $E[g(W)] = u'(0)$. It then follows that

$$g(w) = cw + u'(0)$$

and hence that

$$u'(x) = cu(x) + u'(0)$$

Hence u is linear (and we are done), or

$$u(x) = A + Be^{cx}$$

The inequality condition in (12) rules out $B > 0$; since $u' \geq 0$, it follows that $c \leq 0$. This proves the first assertion of the theorem.

Next fix (V, W) and let $u(x) = -\exp(-ax)$. Then

$$u(0) = E[u(V - \bar{R})]$$
$$= E[E[\exp(a(\bar{R} - R(x)))u(V - R(X))|X]]$$
$$= E[\exp(a(\bar{R} - R(X)))E[u(V - R(X))|X]]$$
$$= E[\exp(a(\bar{R} - R(X)))u(0)]$$
$$\geq u(0)\exp[a(\bar{R} - E[R(X)])]$$

It follows that $\bar{R} - E[R(X)] \leq 0$.

A straightforward corollary of this result is that

$$E[w(X_1, Y_1, X_0)|X_1 = x, Y_1 = y] \geqq v(x, y)$$

This inequality can be used to generalize our various results concerning English and second-price auctions.

Theorem 21: Suppose the bidders are risk averse and have constant absolute risk aversion. Then

   (i)   in the second-price and English auctions, revealing public information raises the expected price,
   (ii) among all possible information reporting policies for the seller in second-price and English auctions, full reporting leads to the highest expected price, and
   (iii) the expected price in the English auction is at least as large as in the second-price auction.

Proof: As in the risk-neutral developments, everything hinges on the initial statement about information release raising the expected price in a second-price auction. We shall prove only this proposition.

Note that w is a nondecreasing function. From this fact, Theorem 5, and the corollary of Theorem 20 observed in the text, we have for all $x > y$ that

$$v(y, y) \leqq E[w(X_1, Y_1, X_0)|X_1 = y, Y_1 = y]$$
$$= E[w(Y_1, Y_1, X_0)|X_1 = y, Y_1 = y]$$
$$\leqq E[w(Y_1, Y_1, X_0)|X_1 = x, Y_1 = y]$$

Hence

$$E[v(Y_1, Y_1)|\{X_1 > Y_1\}] \leqq E[w(Y_1, Y_1, X_0)|\{X_1 > Y_1\}]$$

which is the desired result.

The proof of Theorem 21 suggests that reporting information to the bidders has two effects. First, it reduces each bidder's average profit by diluting his informational advantage. The extent of this dilution is represented by the second inequality in the proof. Second, when bidders have constant absolute risk aversion, reporting information raises the bidders' average willingness to pay. This is represented by the first inequality in the proof.

Generally, partial resolution of uncertainty can either increase or reduce a risk-averse bidder's average willingness to pay. Since only an increase is possible when bidders have constant absolute risk aversion or when the resolution of uncertainty is complete, the cases of reduced average willingness to pay can only arise when the range of possible wealth outcomes from the auction is large (so that the bidders' coefficients of absolute risk aversion may vary substantially over this range) and when the unresolved uncertainty is substantial. For auctions conducted at auction houses, this combination of conditions is unusual. Thus, Theorem 21 may account for the frequent use of English auctions and the reporting of export appraisals by reputable auction houses.

9. Where Now For Auction Theory?

The use of auctions in the conduct of human affairs has ancient roots, and the various forms of auctions in current use account for hundreds of billions of dollars of trading every year. Yet despite the age and importance of auctions, the theory of auctions is still poorly developed.

One obstacle to achieving a satisfactory theory of bidding is the tremendous complexity of some of the environments in which auctions are conducted. For example, in bidding for the development of a weapons system, the intelligent bidder realizes that the contract price will later be subject to profitable renegotiation, when the inevitable changes are made in the specifications of the weapons system. This fact affects bidding behavior in subtle ways, and makes it very difficult to give a meaningful interpretation to bidding data.

Most analyses of competitive bidding situations are based on the assumption that each auction can be treated in isolation. This assumption is sometimes unreasonable. For example, when the U.S. Department of the Interior auctions drilling rights for oil, it may offer about 200 tracts for sale simultaneously. A bidder submitting bids on many tracts may be as concerned about winning too many tracts as about winning too few. Examples suggest that an optimal bidding strategy in this situation may involve placing high bids on a few tracts and low bids on several others of comparable value (Engelbrecht-Wiggans and Weber [6]). Little is understood about these simultaneous auctions, or about the effects of the resale market in drilling rights on the equilibria in the auction games.

Another basic issue is whether the noncooperative game formulation of auctions is a reasonable one. The analysis that we have offered seems reasonable when the bidders do not know each other and do not expect to meet again, but it is less reasonable, for example, as a model of auctions for timber rights on federal land, when the bidders (owners of lumber mills) are members of a trade association and bid repeatedly against each other.

The theory of repeated games suggests that collusive behavior in a single auction can be the result of noncooperative behavior in a repeated bidding situation. That raises the question: which auction forms are most (least) subject to these collusive effects? Issues of collusion also arise in the study of bidding by syndicates of bidders. Why do large oil companies sometimes join with smaller companies in making bids? What effect do these syndicates have on average prices? What forces determine which companies join together into a bidding syndicate?

Another issue that has received relatively little attention in the bidding literature concerns auctions for shares of a divisible object. Recent studies (Harris and Raviv [8], Maskin and Riley [12], Wilson [35]) indicate that such auctions involve a host of new problems that require careful analysis.

Much remains to be done in the theory of auctions. A number of important issues, some of which are described above, simply do not arise in the auctions of a single object that have traditionally been studied and that we have analyzed in this paper (see, for example, the survey by Weber [31]). Nevertheless, the treatment presented here of the role of information in auctions is a first step along the path to understanding auctions which take place in more general environments.

Appendix on affiliation

A general treatment of affiliation requires several new definitions. First, a subset A of $\mathbb{R}^k$ is called *increasing* if its indicator function 1_A is nondecreasing. Second, a subset S of $\mathbb{R}^k$ is a *sublattice* if its indicator function 1_S is affiliated, i.e., if $z \vee z'$ and $z \wedge z'$ are in S whenever z and z' are.

Let $Z = (Z_1, \ldots, Z_k)$ be a random k-vector with probability distribution P. Thus, $P(A) = \text{Prob}(Z \in A)$. We denote the intersection of the sets A and B by AB and the complement of A by $\bar{A}$.

Definition: $Z_1, \ldots, Z_k$ are *associated* if for all increasing sets A and B, $P(AB) \geq P(A)P(B)$.

Remark: It would be equivalent to require $P(\bar{A}\bar{B}) \geq P(\bar{A})P(\bar{B})$ or even $P(\bar{A}B) \leq P(\bar{A})P(B)$.

Definition: $Z_1, \ldots, Z_k$ are *affiliated* if for all increasing sets A and B and every sublattice S, $P(AB|S) \geq P(A|S)P(B|S)$, i.e., if the variables are associated conditional on any sublattice.

With this definition of affiliation, Theorems 3–5 become relatively easy to prove. However, we shall also need to establish the equivalence of this definition and the one in section 3 for variables with densities. We begin by establishing the important properties of associated variables.

Theorem 22: The following statements are equivalent.

(i) $Z_1, \ldots, Z_k$ are associated.
(ii) For every pair of nondecreasing functions g and h,

$$E[g(Z)h(Z)] \geq E[g(Z)] \cdot E[h(Z)]$$

(iii) For every nondecreasing function g and increasing set A,

$$E[g(Z)|A] \geq E[g(Z)] \geq E[g(Z)|\bar{A}]$$

Proof: The inequality in (iii) is equivalent to requiring only (iii'): $E[g(Z)|A] \geq E[g(Z)]$, since

$$E[g(Z)] = P(A)E[g(Z)|A] + P(\bar{A})E[g(Z)|\bar{A}]$$

One can show that (ii) implies (iii') by taking $h = 1_A$. Similarly, to show that (iii') implies (i), take $g = 1_B$. To see that (i) implies (ii), suppose initially that g and h are nonnegative. Then we can approximate g to within $1/n$ by

$$g_n(x) = n^{-1} \sum_{i=1}^{\infty} 1_{A_{ni}(x)}$$

where $A_{ni} = \{x | g(x) > i/n\}$, and h can be similarly approximated using functions h_n and increasing sets B_{nj}. If $Z_1, \ldots, Z_k$ are associated, then

$$E[g_n(Z)h_n(Z)] = n^{-2} \sum_{i=1}^{\infty} \sum_{j=1}^{\infty} P(A_{ni} B_{nj})$$

$$\geq n^{-2} \sum_{i=1}^{\infty} \sum_{j=1}^{\infty} P(A_{ni}) P(B_{nj})$$

$$= E[g_n(Z)] E[h_n(Z)]$$

Letting $n \to \infty$ completes the proof for nonnegative g and h. The extension to general g and h is routine.

The next result is a direct corollary of Theorem 22.

Theorem 23: The following statements are equivalent.

(i) $Z_1, \ldots, Z_k$ are affiliated.
(ii) For every pair of nondecreasing functions g and h and every sublattice S,

$$E[g(Z)h(Z)|S] \geq E[g(Z)|S] \cdot E[h(Z)|S]$$

(iii) For every nondecreasing function g, increasing set A, and sublattice S,

$$E[g(Z)|AS] \geq E[g(Z)|S] \geq E[g(Z)|\bar{A}S]$$

Theorems 3 and 4 follow easily using part (ii) of Theorem 23, and Theorem 5 is a direct consequence of part (iii).

   Finally, we verify that the present definition of affiliation is equivalent to the one given in Section 3.

Theorem 24: Let $Z = (Z_1, \ldots, Z_k)$ have joint probability density f. Then Z is affiliated if and only if f satisfies the affiliation inequality

$$f(z \vee z')f(z \wedge z') \geq f(z)f(z')$$

for μ-almost every $(z, z') \in \mathbb{R}^{2k}$, where μ denotes Lebesgue measure.

Proof: If $k = 1$, both f and Z are trivially affiliated. We proceed by induction to show that if f is affiliated a.e. $[\mu]$, then Z is affiliated. Suppose that the implication holds for $k = m - 1$, and define $Z_{-1} = (Z_2, \ldots, Z_m)$ and $z_{-1} = (z_2, \ldots, z_m)$. In the following arguments, we omit the specification "almost everywhere $[\mu]$."

Let $k = m$, and suppose that f is affiliated. Consider any two points $z_1' > z_1$. Let f_1 denote the marginal density of Z_1, and consider the function

$$\frac{[f(z_1', \cdot) + f(z_1, \cdot)]}{[f_1(z_1) + f_1(z_1')]}$$

which is the conditional density of Z_{-1} given $Z_1 \in \{z_1, z_1'\}$. It can be routinely verified that this function is affiliated.[27] Therefore, by the induction hypothesis, Z_{-1} is affiliated conditional on $Z_1 \in \{z_1, z_1'\}$. Notice that, since f is affiliated, the expression

$$\frac{f(z_1, z_{-1})}{[f(z_1, z_{-1}) + f(z_1', z_{-1})]}$$

is decreasing in z_{-1}. Let g be any increasing function on $\mathbb{R}^k$. Then

$$E[g(Z)|Z_1 = z_1] = \frac{f_1(z_1) + f_1(z_1')}{f_1(z_1)} \cdot E\left[g(Z)\frac{f(z_1, Z_{-1})}{f(z_1, Z_{-1}) + f(z_1', Z_{-1})}\middle| Z_1 \in \{z_1, z_1'\}\right]$$

$$\leq \frac{f_1(z_1) + f_1(z_1')}{f_1(z_1)} \cdot E\left[\frac{f(z_1, Z_{-1})}{f(z_1, Z_{-1}) + f(z_1', Z_{-1})}\middle| Z_1 \in \{z_1, z_1'\}\right] \cdot E\left[g(Z)|Z_1 \in \{z_1, z_1'\}\right]$$

$$= E[g(Z)|Z_1 \in \{z_1, z_1'\}]$$

and it follows that $E[g(Z)|Z_1 = z_1] \leq E[g(Z)|Z_1 = z_1']$, i.e., $E[g(Z)|Z_1 = x]$ is increasing in x.

Now, let h: $\mathbb{R}^k \to \mathbb{R}$ also be increasing. For any non-null sublattice S, the conditional density of Z given S is $f(z) \cdot 1_s(z)/P(S)$, which is affiliated whenever f is. Also, by the induction hypothesis, Z_{-1} is affiliated conditional on Z_1, Hence

$$E[g(\cdot Z)h(Z)|S] = E[E[g(Z)h(Z)|Z_1, S]|S]$$
$$\geq E[E[g(Z)|Z_1, S].E[h(Z)|Z_1, S]|S]$$
$$\geq E[g(Z)|S] \cdot E[h(Z)|S]$$

The second inequality follows from the monotonicity of $E[g(Z)|Z_1 = x, S]$ and $E[h(Z)|Z_1 = x, S]$ in x. Thus we have proved that Z is affiliated if f is.

For the converse, the idea of the proof is to take

$$S = \{z, z', z \vee z', z \wedge z'\}$$

$$A = \{x|x \geq z\}$$

and

$$B = \{x | x \geq z'\}$$

and to apply the definition of affiliation using Bayes' Theorem. This works, but is not rigorous because S is a null event. Instead, we will approximate S, AS, and BS by small but non-null events, and will then pass to the limit.

Let Q^n be the partition of $\mathbb{R}^k$ into k-cubes of the form

$$\frac{i_1}{\frac{2^n \cdot (i_1+1)}{2^n}} \times \cdots \times \frac{i_k}{\frac{2^n \cdot (i_k+1)}{2^n}}$$

Let $Q^n(z)$ denote the unique element of this partition containing the point z. Since $Q^0 \times Q^0$ has only countably many elements, there exists a function $q : Q^0 \times Q^0 \to \mathbb{R}$ such that

(i)   for every $T \in Q^0 \times Q^0, q(T) > 0$, and

(ii) $\sum_{T \in Q^0 \times Q^0} q(T) = 1$

Define a probability measure v on $\mathbb{R}^{2k}$ by

$$v(B) = \sum_{T \in Q^0 \times Q^0} q(T)\mu(BT)$$

(recall that μ denotes Lebesgue measure). Clearly, v is proportional to μ on every $T \in Q^n \times Q^n$ for every $n \geq 0$. Let $E^v[\cdot]$ be the expectation operator corresponding to v.

Let Y and Y' be the projection functions from $\mathbb{R}^{2k}$ to $\mathbb{R}^k$ defined by $Y(z, z') = z$ and $Y'(z, z') = z'$. Y and Y' are random variables when $(\mathbb{R}^{2k}, v)$ is viewed as a probability space. We approximate the vector of densities $(f(z), f(z'), f(z \vee z'), f(z \wedge z'))$ by the function $X^n = (X_1^n, X_2^n, X_3^n, X_4^n)$ defined on $\mathbb{R}^{2k}$ by:

$$X^n(z, z') = E^v[(f(Y), f(Y'), f(Y \vee Y'), f(Y \wedge Y')) | (Y, Y') \in Q^n(z) \times Q^n(z')]$$

X^n is a martingale in $\mathbb{R}^4$, and thus for almost every (z, z'),

$$\lim_{n \to \infty} X^n(z, z') = (f(z), f(z'), f(z \vee z'), f(z \wedge z'))$$

(cf. Chung [3, Theorem 9.4.8]). Also, for almost every (z, z') pair, we have $z_1 \neq z_1', \ldots, z_k \neq z_k'$. For any such pair, for sufficiently large n,

$$X^n(z, z') = 2^{nk}(P(Q^n(z)), P(Q^n(z')), P(Q^n(z \vee z')), P(Q^n(z \wedge z')))$$

Each cube $Q^n(z)$ has a minimal element, so we may define

$$A_n = \{x | x \geq \min Q^n(z)\}$$

$$B_n = \{x | x \geq \min Q''(z')\}$$

and

$$S_n = Q''(z) \cup Q''(z') \cup Q''(z \vee z') \cup Q''(z \wedge z')$$

The sets A_n and B_n are increasing, S_n is a sublattice, and for sufficiently large n the following three identities hold:

$$P(A_n | S_n) = c_n^{-1}(X_1^n + X_4^n)$$
$$P(B_n | S_n) = c_n^{-1}(X_2^n + X_4^n)$$
$$P(A_n B_n | S_n) = c_n^{-1} X_4^n$$

where

$$c_n = X_1^n + X_2^n + X_3^n + X_4^n$$

and each X_j^n is evaluated at z, z'. By the definition of affiliation, we have

$$P(A_n B_n | S_n) \geq P(A_n | S_n) \cdot P(B_n | S_n)$$

or equivalently,

$$c_n^{-1} X_4^n \geq c_n^{-2}(X_1^n + X_4^n)(X_2^n + X_4^n)$$

Letting $n \rightarrow \infty$ yields (for almost every (z, z')):

$$c^{-1} f(z \vee z') \geq c^{-2}[f(z) + f(z \vee z')] \cdot [f(z') + f(z \vee z')]$$

where

$$c = f(z) + f(z') + f(z \vee z') + f(z \wedge z')$$

A rearrangement of terms yields the affiliation inequality.

Notes

1 These and other historical references can be found in Cassady [2].
2 On September 30, 1980, U.S. oil companies paid $2.8 billion for drilling rights on 147 tracts in the Gulf of Mexico. The three most expensive individual tracts brought prices of $165 million, $162 million, and $121 million respectively.
3 The English (ascending, progressive, open, oral) auction is an auction with many variants, some of which are described in section 5. In the variant we study, the auctioneer calls successively higher prices until only one willing bidder remains, and the number of active bidders is publicly known at all times.

4   The Dutch (descending) auction, which has been used to sell flowers for export in Holland, is conducted by an auctioneer who initially calls for a very high price and then continuously lowers the price until some bidder stops the auction and claims the flowers for that price.

5   The first-price auction is a sealed-bid auction in which the buyer making the highest bid claims the object and pays the amount he has bid.

6   The second-price auction is a sealed-bid auction in which the buyer making the highest bid claims the object, but pays only the amount of the second highest bid. This arrangement does not necessarily entail any loss of revenue for the seller, because the buyers in this auction will generally place higher bids than they would in the first-price auction.

7   A more thorough survey of the literature is given by Engelbrecht-Wiggans [4]. A comprehensive bibliography of bidding, including almost 500 titles, has been compiled by Stark and Rothkopf [26].

8   Situations in which bidders collude have received no attention in theoretical studies, despite many allegations of collusion, particularly in bidding for timber rights (Mead [14]).

9   The case in which several identical objects are offered for sale with a limit of one item per bidder has also been analyzed (Ortega-Reichert [22], Vickrey [30]). All of the results discussed below have natural analogues in that more general setting.
Another variation, in which the bidders' private valuations are drawn from a common but unknown distribution, has been treated by Wilson [34].

10   In contrast, the argument concerning the strategic equivalence of the Dutch and first-price auctions does not require any assumptions about the values to the bidders of various outcomes. In particular, it does not require that a bidder know the value of the object to himself.

11   In general, the $(p, e(p))$ curve need not be continuous; there may even be values of p for which no $(p, e(p))$ pair is available. However, there will *always* be a point $(0, e(0))$ on the curve, with $e(0) \leq 0$, for the bidder is free to abstain from participation. The quantity $e(0)$ will be negative only if the seller at times provides subsidies to losing bidders.

12   This property is known to statisticians as the *monotone likelihood ratio property* (Tong [27]). Its usefulness for economic modelling has been elaborated by Milgrom [18].

13   To represent a bidder's information by a single real-valued signal is to make two substantive assumptions. Not only must his signal be a sufficient statistic for all of the information he possesses concerning the value of the object to him, it must also adequately summarize his information concerning the signals received by the other bidders. The derivation of such a statistic from several separate pieces of information is in general a difficult task (see, for example, the discussion in Engelbrecht-Wiggans and Weber [7]). It is in the light of these difficulties that we choose to view each X_i as a "value estimate," which may be correlated with the "estimates" of others but is the only piece of information available to bidder i.

14   This assumption – that the joint distribution of the various signals has an associated density – substantially simplifies the development of our results by making the statement of later assumptions simpler, and by ensuring the existence of equilibrium points in pure strategies. All of the results in this paper, except for the explicit characterizations of equilibrium strategies, continue to hold when this assumption is eliminated. In the general case, equilibrium strategies may involve randomization. These randomized strategies can be obtained directly, or indirectly as the limits of sequences of pure equilibrium strategies of the games studied here, using techniques developed in Engelbrecht-Wiggans, Milgrom, and Weber [5], Milgrom [17], and Milgrom and Weber [19].

15   The density g has the monotone likelihood ratio property if for all $s' > s$ and $x' > x$

$$\frac{g(x|s)}{g(x|s')} \geq \frac{g(x'|s)}{g(x'|s')}$$

This is equivalent to the affiliation inequality:

$$g(x|s)g(x'|s') \geq g(x'|s)g(x|s')$$

16   Our basic analysis of the second-price auction is very similar to that given in Milgrom [17], although the present set-up is a bit different. Theorems 6 and 7 were first proved in that reference.

17   This might be the case if, for example, there were some effective resource available to the buyer if the seller made a false announcement, or if the seller were an institution, like an auction house, which valued its reputation for truthfulness.

18   If $G_{X0}(\cdot|X_0')$ denotes the conditional distribution of X_0 given X_0' then the variables $S_1, \ldots, S_m, X_0, X_1 \ldots, X_n$ always will have a density with respect to the product measure $M^m \times G(\cdot|X_0') \times M^n$, where M is Lebesgue measure, and the density always will have the form $f(s, x)g(x_0|x_0')/f(x_0)$. A density with respect to *any* product measure suffices for our analysis, so the theorem is proved by our argument.

19   A model in which the bidders call the bids has been analyzed by Wilson [33].

20   This derivation of the necessary conditions follows Wilson [34]. The derivation is heuristic: in general, b^* need not be continuous. For example, let $n = 2$ and take X_1 and X_2 to be either independent and uniformly distributed on $[0, 1]$ (with probability $\frac{1}{2}$), or independent and uniform on $[1, 2]$. (Note that X_1 and X_2 are affiliated.) Finally, let $V_i = X_i$. Then b^* jumps from $\frac{1}{2}$ to 1 at $x = 1$.

21   By convention, we take $f_{Y_1}(x|x)/F_{Y_1}(x|x)$ to be zero when x is not in the support of the distribution of Y_1.

22   If the integral is infinite, $L(\alpha|x)$ is taken to be zero.

23   In this proof only, we take special care to argue without assuming that the equilibrium bidding strategies are continuous or differentiable. Subsequent arguments in this paper involve a variety of differentiability assumptions that are made solely for expositional ease.

24   Actually, by permitting only nonnegative bids, we have been making the implicit assumption that there is a reserve price of zero. This reserve price has been "non-binding," in the sense that Assumption 2 (nonnegativity of V_i) ensured that no bidder would wish to abstain from participation in the auction.
      If an auction is conducted with *no* reserve price, other symmetric equilibria may appear. For example, consider a first-price auction in the independent private values setting, when all $V_i = X_i$ are independent and uniformly distributed on $(0, 1)$. For every $k \geq 0$ there is an equilibrium point in which each bidder uses the bidding strategy

$$b(x) = (\frac{n}{(n+1)}) \cdot x - \frac{k}{x^{n-1}}$$

      and each has (ex ante) expected payoff $(1/n(n+1)) + k$. The range of the strategy function is $(0, n/(n+1))$ if $k = 0$, and is $(-\infty, n/(n+1) - k)$ if $k > 0$. This may explain why almost all observed auctions incorporate (at least implicitly) a reserve price.

25   The outcome of this auction is determined as if the seller had bid r. Thus, if only one bidder bids more than r, the price he pays is equal to r. It is of interest to note that, when

$$v(x^*, x^*) = E[V_1|X_1 = x^*, y_1 = x^*] > E[V_1|X_1 = x^*, Y_1 < x^*]$$

      at equilibrium there will be no bids in a neighborhood of r.

26   One such case is the following. There are two variables, X_1 and X_2 so that $Y_1 = X_2$. Assume $V_1 = X_1$. With probability $\frac{1}{2}$, the X_i are drawn independently from a uniform distribution on $[0, 2]$ and, with probability $\frac{1}{2}$, from a uniform distribution on $[1, 2]$. Then $F_{Y_1}(x|x)$ jumps down

from $\frac{1}{2}$ to $\frac{1}{4}$ as x passes up through 1. With a reserve price of zero and an entry fee of 0.32, $x^* = 0.8$ but some bidders with valuations exceeding 1.0 will choose not to bid.

27 The verification amounts to showing that if W_1, W_2, and W_3 are $\{0, 1\}$-valued random variables with a joint probability distribution P satisfying the affiliation inequality, then the joint distribution of W_1 and W_2 also satisfies the inequality. The conclusion follows from the inequalities:

$$(P_{111}P_{000} - P_{101}P_{010})(P_{111}P_{000} - P_{011}P_{100}) \geq 0$$
$$P_{111}P_{001} \geq P_{101}P_{011}$$

and

$$P_{110}P_{000} \geq P_{100}P_{010}$$

References

1 Capen, E. C., Clapp, R. V. and Campbell, W. M. (1971): "Competitive Bidding in High-Risk Situations," *Journal of Petroleum Technology*, 23, 641–53.
2 Cassady, R. Jr. (1967): *Auctions and Auctioneering*. Berkeley: University of California Press.
3 Chung, K. (1974): *A Course in Probability Theory*, 2nd edn. New York: Academic Press.
4 Engelbrecht-Wiggans, R. (1980): "Auctions and Bidding Models: A Survey," *Management Science*, 26, 119–42.
5 Engelbrecht-Wiggans, R., Milgrom, P. R. and Weber, R. J. (1981): "Competitive Bidding and Proprietary Information," CMSEMS discussion paper 465, Northwestern University.
6 Engelbrecht-Wiggans, R. and Weber, R. J. (1979): "An Example of a Multi-Object Auction Game," *Management Science*, 25, 1272–7.
7 ——(1981): Estimates and Information. Unpublished manuscript, Northwestern University.
8 Harris, M. and Raviv A. (1981): "Allocation Mechanisms and the Design of Auctions," *Econometrica*, 49, 1477–99.
9 Holt, C. A., Jr. (1980): "Competitive Bidding for Contracts Under Alternative Auction Procedures," *Journal of Political Economy*, 88, 433–45.
10 Karlin, S. and Rinott, Y. (1980): "Classes of Orderings of Measures and Related Correlation Inequalities. I. Multivariate Totally Positive Distributions," *Journal of Multivariate Analysis*, 10, 467–98.
11 Maskin, E. and Riley, J. (1980): "Auctioning an Indivisible Object," JFK School of Government, discussion paper 87D, Harvard University.
12 ——(1981): "Multi-Unit Auctions, Price Discrimination and Bundling," Economics Department discussion paper 201, U.C.L.A.
13 Matthews, S. (1979): "Risk Aversion and the Efficiency of First-and Second-Price Auctions." CCBA working paper 586, University of Illinois.
14 Mead, W. J. (1967): "Natural Resource Disposal Policy – Oral Auction Versus Sealed Bid," *Natural Resources Planning Journal*, M, 194–224.
15 Milgrom, P. R. (1979): *The Structure of Information in Competitive Bidding*. New York: Garland Publishing Company.
16 ——(1979): "A Convergence Theorem for Competitive Bidding with Differential Information," *Econometrica*, 47, 679–88.
17 —— (1981): "Rational Expectations, Information Acquisition and Competitive Bidding," *Econometrica*, 49, 921–43.
18 ——(1981): "Goods News and Bad News: Representation Theorems and Applications," *Bell Journal of Economics*, 12, 380–91.

19 Milgrom, P. R. and Weber, R. J. (after 1982): "Distributional Strategies for Games with Incomplete Information," *Mathematics of Operations Research*.

20 ——(after 1982): "The Value of Information in a Sealed-Bid Auction," *Journal of Mathematical Economics*.

21 Myerson, R. (1981): "Optimal Auction Design," *Mathematics of Operations Research*, 6, 58–73.

22 Ortega-Reichert, A. (1968): "Models for Competitive Bidding Under Uncertainty," PhD. Thesis, Department of Operations Research technical report 8, Stanford University.

23 Reece, D. K. (1978): "Competitive Bidding for Offshore Petroleum Leases," *Bell Journal of Economics*, 9, 369–84.

24 Riley, J. and Samuelson, W. (1981): "Optimal Auctions," *American Economic Review*, 71, 381–92.

25 Rothkopf, M. (1969): "A Model of Rational Competitive Bidding," *Management Science*, 15, 362–73.

26 Stark, R. M. and Rothkopf, M. H. (1979): "Competitive Bidding: A Comprehensive Bibliography," *Operations Research*, 27, 364–90.

27 Tong, Y. L. (1980): *Probability Inequalities for Multivariate Distributions*. New York: Academic Press.

28 Topkis, D. M. (1978): "Minimizing a Submodular Function on a Lattice," *Mathematics of Operations Research*, 26, 305–21.

29 Vickrey, W. (1961): "Counterspeculation, Auctions, and Competitive Sealed Tenders," *Journal of Finance*, 16, 8–37.

30 ——(1962): "Auctions and Bidding Games," *Recent Advances in Game Theory* (conference proceedings), Princeton University, 15–27.

31 Weber, R. J. (1983): "Multiple-Object Auctions," in R. Englebrecht-Wiggans, M. Shubik and R. M. Stark (eds), *Auctions, Bidding and Contracting: Uses and Theory*, New York: New York University Press.

32 Whitt, W. (1982): "Multivariate Monotone Likelihood Ratio and Uniform Conditional Stochastic Order," *Journal of Applied Probability*, 19 (3), 695–701.

33 Wilson, R. (1982): Comment on: David Hughart, "Informational Asymmetry, Bidding Strategies, and the Marketing of Offshore Petroleum Leases." unpublished notes, Stanford University.

34 ——(1977): "A Bidding Model of Perfect Competition," *Review of Economics Studies*, 4, 511–18.

35 ——(1979): "Auctions of Shares," *Quarterly Journal of Economics*, 93, 675–98.

III C

The Firm's Decision Making Under Certainty: Monopolistically Competitive Markets

CHAPTER TEN

Product Selection, Fixed Costs, and Monopolistic Competition

A. Michael Spence

Source: *Review of Economic Studies*, 43 (1976), pp. 217–35. Reprinted with the permission of Review of Economic Studies Ltd. © Review of Economic Studies Ltd.

1. Introduction

This paper has a simply stated goal. It is to investigate the effects of fixed costs and monopolistic competition on the selection of products and product characteristics in a set of interacting markets. The pursuit of the goal, however, is less easy than the stating of it.

Associated with the production and marketing of many products are fixed costs. These are costs that are incurred sometimes prior to, but always independent of, the volume of output and sales. The marketing fixed costs, though frequently overlooked, are often the more important of the two, quantitatively.

Fixed costs have several implications. They contribute to imperfectly competitive market structures and therefore to non–competitive pricing. But they also restrict the number and variety of products that it is feasible or desirable to supply. Fixed costs, therefore, force an economy to choose from the large set of all conceivable products. The principal criterion for product choice in a market system is profitability. Products that survive are those that are capable of generating revenues sufficient to cover the fixed and variable costs.

No one, I think, would argue that revenues are an accurate measure of the social benefits of a product. For revenues do not capture consumer surplus. On these grounds there is some basis for suspecting that product choice in the market context may not be optimal. There is at least a presumption that there may be a market failure.

The present paper's purpose is to pursue the implications of this type of market failure in the setting of multiple firms and interacting products.

At this stage it is perhaps useful to comment briefly on methodology. The context of the analysis to follow is a comparison of market outcomes with welfare optima. The latter are defined to be points at which the multiple-market sum of consumer and producer surplus is maximized. In using consumer surplus, I shall explicitly assume away income effects. Provided the latter are not large, this will not seriously impair the applicability of the results.[1] Let $P_i(x_1, \ldots, x_n)$ be the inverse demand function for the ith product

$i = 1, \ldots, n$. The gross dollar benefit of the bundle of goods $x = (x_1, \ldots, x_n$ is denoted $u(x)$. Of course, $u_i(x) = P_i(x)$, $i = 1, \ldots, n$: the derivatives of the benefit function are the inverse demand functions.

The analysis is partial equilibrium. It typically deals with a set of products that are linked by significant cross-elasticities of demand; that is to say, it deals with what we normally (albeit somewhat hazily) refer to as an industry.

I have not been primarily interested in the difficult question of the existence of equilibrium, though it is important and is not ignored here. The emphasis is rather on locating the qualitative character of the market failures. I should also add that the location of these failures implies nothing obvious in the way of general policy, at least to me. In particular, the purpose is not to condemn, but to explore in a descriptive fashion, product selection aspects of market performance.[2]

Before proceeding, let me outline the topics with which the paper deals. Section 2 is concerned with showing that if sellers can price discriminate in an appropriate sense, the welfare aspects of the product choice problem are eliminated. This seems to me to establish, in the strongest possible way, that the product choice problem is caused by the incompleteness of prices and profits as signals. It also suggests that price discrimination has some positive virtues that bear investigation, though I shall not disgress on that subject here. Section 3 deals with complementary products and argues that monopolistic competition unambiguously tends to supply too few of them. On the other hand, greater interest attaches to the case of substitute products, and the remainder of the papers deals with them.

Section 4 approaches the problem of substitutes by establishing that there is a class of cases in which monopolistic competition implicitly maximizes some function. But it is not the total surplus that is implicitly maximized. Therefore, by comparing the total surplus function with the one that is implicitly maximized, one can establish the qualitative differences between the market and the optimum.

Section 5 also deals with substitutes, but in a different way. It deals with the case of a benefit function that has a certain amount of separability. The increased analytic tractability allows one to study both biases in product selection and the issue of the number and variety of products. Section 6 concludes with suggestions for further work.

2. Price Discrimination and Product Choice

The aim of this section is to show that if the sellers in a monopolistically competitive industry can price discriminate, then the Nash equilibria in the industry are "local" maxima of the total surplus function. The term "local" has a somewhat special meaning that will be clear shortly.

Let there be n goods in the monopolistically competitive industry indexed by i. Let x_i be the output of the ith good.

It is assumed that each product is produced by one firm whose costs are $c_i(x_i) + F_i$; F_i is a fixed cost and $c_i(x_i)$ are variable costs. The $c_i(x_i)$ are taken to be continuous. The revenues of firm i are denoted by $r^i(x)$, and profits are therefore

$$\pi^i(x) = r^i(x) - c_i(x_i) - F_i \tag{1}$$

We turn now to price discrimination. Let e_i be a vector with a one in the ith place and zeroes elsewhere.

If firm i can price discriminate with respect to each consumer, then it will extract the benefits its good yields. Therefore

$$\pi^i = [u(x) - u(x - x_i e_i)] - c_i(x_i) - F_i \tag{2}$$

That is to say, each firm's profits are exactly equal to its net contribution to consumers' benefits minus the costs that the firm incurs.

The total benefit to consumers of the bundle, x, properly distributed, is $u(x)$. Therefore the net benefits to society are

$$T(x) = u(x) - \Sigma[c_i(x_i) + F_i] \tag{3}$$

This quantity is referred to as the *total surplus*. It is precisely the sum of consumer and producer surpluses in the entire collection of markets, if the price system were being used.

Now if product i is not currently being produced, and then it is added to the set of produced products, the net increase in the total surplus is

$$\Delta T_i = [u(x) - u(x - x_i e_i)] - [c_i(x_i) + F_i] \tag{4}$$

Here we assume that if $x_i = 0$, then fixed costs, F_i are avoidable. But (4) is exactly the expression for the profits of the price discriminating firm, from (2).

We now define a *Nash equilibrium* in the set of markets as a vector $(x_1, \ldots, x_n)$ of quantities such that each firm's quantity is profit maximizing given the quantities of other firms. And we define a *local maximum* of $T(x)$ to be a point, x, such that no single quantity can be adjusted to increase $T(x)$.

Given these two definitions and from the fact that

$$\Delta T_i(x) = \pi^i(x) \tag{5}$$

for each i, we have the following proposition.

Proposition 1: The local optima of T (in terms of produced products and quantities) are in a one-to-one correspondence with the Nash equilibria in the markets. In particular, there exists a global optimum of T and it is sustainable as a Nash equilibrium.

Proof. If product i is currently in production, its output is adjusted to maximize $\pi^i(x)$. But then its contribution to the surplus is maximized. Similarly, if product i is not currently produced, it will be introduced only if for some x_i, $\pi^i(x) \geq 0$. But then its contribution to the total surplus is positive, and the product should be introduced.

Turning to existence, we note that for any given subset of products, there is a maximum in quantities by the continuity of $u(x)$ and $c_i(x_i)$, $i = 1, \ldots, n$.[3] Moreover, there is a finite number of possible subsets of products (2^n to be precise). One of these is the global maximum by enumeration. That maximum is a Nash equilibrium by the previous argument.

In effect, each firm is given a decision variable, x_i, and then, with the ability to price discriminate, acts as if it were maximizing the total surplus

$$T = u(x) - \Sigma(c_i(x_i) + F_i) \tag{6}$$

Since each firm acts as if it were maximizing T, it is not surprising that Nash equilibria exist and correspond to the "local" optima of $T(x)$, where local has this special connotation of decentralized decision making.

It is worth emphasizing that, unlike the monopoly case, price discrimination in this context does *not* imply that consumers receive zero or small net benefits even if the profits of the firms are not distributed to them. On the contrary, if the products are reasonably close substitutes, the contribution of any given product to total surplus may be small. Therefore profits will be small and consumers will benefit. We can be more precise than this. If goods are pairwise substitutes, meaning that $u_{ij}(x) < 0$ for all i and j, then consumers will derive positive benefits. The argument is as follows.

$$u(x) - u(x - x_i e_i) = \int_0^{x_i} u_i(x - x_i e_i + s_i e_i) ds_i$$
$$< \int_0^{x_i} u_i(x - x_i e_i + s_i e_i - \Sigma_{j>i} x_j e_j) ds_i \text{ (from } u_{ij} < 0) \tag{7}$$
$$= u\left(x - \Sigma_{j=i+1}^n x_j e_j\right) - u\left(x - \Sigma_{j=1}^n x_j e_j\right)$$

Therefore, summing over i in (7), we have

$$\Sigma[u(x) - u(x - x_i e_i)] < \Sigma\left[u\left(x - \Sigma_{j=i+1}^n x_j e_j\right) - u\left(x - \Sigma_{j=1}^n x_j e_j\right)\right] \tag{8}$$
$$= u(x)$$

Therefore, the net benefits to consumers,

$$B = u(x) - \Sigma[u(x) - u(x - x_i e_i)] > 0 \tag{9}$$

from (8). Each price discriminating monopolist extracts the marginal surplus contributed by its product. Consumers are indifferent between having and not having any given product, but they are not indifferent between having and not having the entire bundle.

The assumption of perfect price discrimination is not, and is not intended to be, realistic. But the preceding analysis does direct one's attention to several factors. First, price discrimination may be useful if it favourably affects product selection, increases diversity, and helps cover fixed costs. Second, since the product choice problem goes away with price discrimination, we know that the inability of price signals to capture all the information that is presumed to be available to the discriminating firm, is the essence of the potential market failure. Third, since revenues accurately reflect social benefits under price discrimination, there is some reason to believe that revenues without price discrimination will *not* reflect social benefits and may not cover costs for socially valuable products.

It remains to attempt to establish the qualitative directions of biases in product choice in ordinary markets without price discrimination. It perhaps is only fair to warn the reader in advance that perfectly general propositions are hard to come by. Nevertheless, I believe there are a few principal forces at work, that, once identified, are understandable, have intuitive appeal, and have testable implications.

3. Monopolistic Competition and Products that are Complements

Under monopolistic competition there are basically two forces at work in the area of product selection. First, because revenues do not capture the consumer surplus, revenues may not cover costs even when the social value of the product is positive. This is a force tending to eliminate products that should be produced. Second, when a product is introduced, it affects other firm's profits as well as increasing consumer surplus. If the products are substitutes, the effect on other firm's profits is adverse. Since the entering firm does not take these effects into account, it may enter when it is not generating a net social benefit. This is a force tending to generate too many products in the case of substitutes. However, if the products are complements both forces tend toward too few products.

This section, therefore, argues that complementary products are undersupplied in a monopolistically competitive equilibrium. That is to say, there are two few products, and quantities are too low. The intuitive reason is that when a monopolistically competitive firm holds back output and raises price above marginal cost, it reduces the demand for other complementary products. That induces further quantity cut-backs and possibly the exit of products from the market as well. That cycle reinforces itself and leads to an equilibrium where all outputs are below the optimum, and some of the products in the optimal set are not produced at all.

The argument is made rigorous in the following way. Products i and j are complements if, by definition, $u_{ij}(x) > 0$. However, we need a somewhat stronger condition. The profits of the ith firm are

$$\pi^i = x_i u_i - c_i - F_i \tag{10}$$

Given that firm i is in production, profits are maximized when

$$u_i + x_i u_{ii} = c'_i \tag{11}$$

Condition (11) defines the reaction function for the ith firm. By differentiating (11) with respect to x_j, we have

$$\frac{\partial x_i}{\partial x_j} = \frac{u_{ij} + x_i u_{iij}}{c''_i - 2u_{ii} - x_i u_{iii}} \tag{12}$$

The denominator is positive because of the second-order condition for a profit maximum. If the numerator is always positive, the products will be called *strongly complementary*. Products are strongly complementary if an increase in one quantity increases the marginal revenues of other firms.

Proposition 2. If products are strongly complementary, then there is an equilibrium in which all quantities are below the optimal quantities and some of the optimal products are not produced.
Proof (A) For a given set of products, $i = 1, \ldots, n$, the optimum is found by setting price equal to marginal cost:

$$u_i = c_i' \quad i = 1, \ldots, n \tag{13}$$

Moreover, along the surface defined by $u_i = c'$

$$\frac{\partial x_i}{\partial x_j} = \frac{u_{ij}}{c_i'' - u_{ii}} > 0 \tag{14}$$

Therefore, starting at the global optimum, we adjust each product's quantity downward in turn, until the condition

$$u_i + x_i u_{ii} = c_i' \tag{15}$$

is satisfied. When x_i is reduced, $u_j - c_j'$ falls below zero if it started at zero. Similarly, if before x_i is reduced, $u_j + x_j u_{jj} = c_j'$, then afterward $u_j + x_j u_{jj} < c_j'$. Therefore, at every step each quantity has to be reduced.
(B)   Now as x_i is reduced, π_j falls, because

$$\frac{\partial \pi_j}{\partial x_i} = x_j u_{ij} > 0 \tag{16}$$

Thus in the process of reducing quantities, some firms may leave the market. And no firm that is out will want to enter.
(C)   When a firm leaves the market, the profits of those remaining fall further, and further reductions in quantities occur.

Therefore, in the process of moving from the global optimum to a monopolistically competitive equilibrium, quantities are reduced and products removed, but never the reverse.
Monopolistic competition is particularly unsuitable for complementary products, both from the point of view of profits and of total surplus. Indeed, a monopolist might generate a preferred outcome by taking the positive interactions into account. Certainly we would not expect to see a situation in which fountain pens disappear because firms manufacturing ink (but not pens), overprice ink. Horizontal merger will occur.

4. Monopolistic Competition: Maximizing the "Wrong" Function

In discussing price discrimination, we observed that firms implicitly maximize the total surplus function. The mere fact that firms were implicitly maximizing *some* function immediately allowed us to conclude that equilibria exist and correspond to local optima of the function that is maximized.

In general, monopolistic competition yields results grudgingly because the fixed costs can cause equilibria not to exist, or at least to be hard to locate. Thus the notion that there may be some function that is implicitly maximized in the process of entry and exit and the setting of prices recommends itself as a technique for studying the subject of product choice.

It is argued that there is an interesting and reasonably general class of demand structures for which monopolistic competition acts as if it were maximizing some function. We shall determine what this class is, and then, by examining the function that is implicitly maximized, and by comparing it with the total surplus function, identifying biases in product choice under the market system.

We begin with the benefit function $u(x)$. After consumers maximize against a set of prices $(p_1, \ldots, p_n)$, it will be true that

$$u_i(x) = p_i, \quad \text{for } i = 1, \ldots, n \tag{17}$$

Therefore the partial derivatives of the benefit function are the inverse demand functions. The profits of the ith firm (I exclude multi-product firms for the time being) are

$$\pi^i = x_i u_i(x) - c_i(x_i) - F_i \tag{18}$$

As before, F_i are the fixed costs and $c_i(x_i)$ the continuous variable costs. The firm maximizes these with respect to x_i.[4]

The total surplus in the collection of markets is

$$T = u(x) - \Sigma(c_i(x_i) + F_i) \tag{19}$$

It is fairly clear that firms, in maximizing profits (18), do not implicitly maximize T. In fact, one can show that T is implicitly maximized only if $u(x)$ is linear in each variable taken separately.

Suppose, however, that there were another function, $R(x)$, which we shall call the wrong surplus function, which has the property that when firms maximize profits, they implicitly maximize that function. If that were true, then we could compare $T(x)$ and $R(x)$ for differences that suggest biases in product choice.

To proceed, we require some notation. Let Γ_k, $k = 1, \ldots, 2^n$, be the 2^n possible subsets of the integers $(1, \ldots, n)$. Let $H_k(y)$ be a function of a scalar, $k = 1, \ldots, 2^n$, and let $\alpha_1, \ldots, \alpha_n$ be n positive numbers. Let us suppose that $u(x)$ has the following form:

$$u(x) = \Sigma_{k=1}^{2n} H_k \left(\Pi_{i \in \Gamma_k} x_i^{\alpha_i} \right) \qquad (20)$$

If the benefit function has this form, then monopolistic competition implicitly maximizes some function. The argument is relatively straightforward.

We begin with firms' profits. Let $K_i = \{k \mid i \in \Gamma_k\}, i = 1, \ldots, n$. From the previous analysis we know that

$$\pi^i(x) = x_i u_i(x) - c_i(x_i) - F_i = \alpha_i \, \Sigma_{k \in K_i} \, H_k'(y_k) - (c_i(x_i) + F_i) \qquad (21)$$

where

$$y_k = \Pi_{i \in \Gamma_k} x_i^{\alpha_i}$$

Now consider the function,

$$R(x) = \Sigma_{k=1}^{2n} H_k'(y_k) - \Sigma_{i-1}^{n} \frac{(c_i(x_i) + F_i)}{\alpha_i} \qquad (22)$$

We want to assess the contribution of product i, to $R(x)$:

$$R(x) - R(x - x_i e_i) \equiv \Sigma_{k \in K_i} H_k'(y_k) - \frac{(c_i(x_i) + F_i)}{\alpha_i} \qquad (23)$$

$$\equiv \frac{\pi^i(x)}{\alpha_i} \qquad \text{(from (21))}$$

Therefore, when firm i maximizes $\pi^i(x)$ with respect to x_i, it maximizes $R(x)$ with respect to x_i. The preceding is summarized by

Proposition 3. If $u(x)$ has the form (20), then there is a function $R(x)$ given by (22) that is implicitly maximized in the course of monopolistic competition. The Nash equilibria are in one-to-one correspondence with the local maxima of $R(x)$.[5]

Let me digress briefly to comment on the form (20). It contains 2^n arbitrary functions, H_k, and n arbitrary weights, α_i. It therefore provides great flexibility in approximating actual multi-product demand functions. For the analysis to follow, I shall deal with particular cases that illustrate certain fundamental biases in product choice. For example, the quadratic form

$$u(x) = ax - xAx \qquad (24)$$

fits the form (20). More interesting, the generalized quadratic

$$u(x) = \Sigma_i \phi_i(x_i) - \Sigma_{i,j} G_{ij}(x_i x_j) \qquad (25)$$

also fits the general form. Here $G_{ii}(x_i^2) = 0$ for each i. The generalized quadratic gives us considerable flexibility in terms of the shape of the demand function and the pattern of pairwise interactions or substitution effects. It is assumed that the $\phi_i(x_i)$ are concave so that demand is downward sloping, and that the $G_{ij}(x_i x_j)$ are convex, for the same reason.

In what follows, I shall use the generalized quadratic to assess some of the specific, qualitative biases in product choice under monopolistic competition, by comparing $u(x)$ and $R(x)$. To this end, it is useful to write out $R(x)$ for the generalized quadratic case:

$$R(x) = \Sigma_i x_i \phi_i'(x_i) - \Sigma_{i,j} x_i x_j G_{ij}'(x_i x_j) - \Sigma_{i=1}^n (c_i(x_i) + F_i) \tag{26}$$

My approach is to examine various forces affecting product choice by selectively holding various things constant. Since

$$u(x) - u(x - x_i e_i) = \phi_i - 2\Sigma_j G_{ij}(x_i x_j) > x_i \phi_i' - 2\Sigma_j G_{ij}' x_i x_j \tag{27}$$

= the revenues of firm i
the revenues of a firm are below the level of gross benefits that the firm's product delivers. Therefore, certain socially valuable products may not survive in the market because revenues do not cover fixed costs.

In addition to this problem, which afflicts all products, there is the familiar tendency to price above marginal cost. The contribution of the ith product to total surplus is

$$\Delta T_i = \phi_i - 2\Sigma_j G_{ij} - c_i(x_i) - F_i \tag{28}$$

while the profits are

$$\pi_i = x_i \phi_i' - 2\Sigma_j G_{ij}' x_i x_j - c_i - F_i \tag{29}$$

Differentiating, we have

$$\frac{\partial \Delta T_i}{\partial x_i} = \phi_i' - 2\Sigma_j G_{ij}' x_j - c_i'$$
$$> \phi_i' + x_i \phi_i'' - 2\Sigma_j G_{ij}' x_j - 2\Sigma_j G_{ij}'' x_i x_j^2 - c_i' \tag{30}$$
$$= \partial \pi / \partial x_i$$

It follows that the optimal quantity is above the monopolistically competitive one.

More importantly, there are certain biases against particular kinds of products. It is convenient to examine these by means of a special case that isolates the important properties of the demand functions. Suppose that $\phi_i = a_i x_i^{\beta_i}$, $G_{ij} = A_{ij} x_i x_j$, and $c_i(x_i) = c_i x_i$. Let $e_i = 2\Sigma_j A_{ij} x_j - c_i$. It follows that the contribution of the ith product to total surplus is $\Delta T_i = a_i x_i^{\beta_i} - e_i x_i - F_i$, and when this quantity is maximized with respect to x_i, the resulting contribution to the surplus is

$$\Delta T_i = e_i \left(\frac{1}{\beta_i} - 1 \right) \left(\frac{a_i \beta_i}{e_i} \right)^{1/(1-\beta_i)} - F_i \tag{31}$$

On the other hand, profits are $a_i \beta_i x_i^{\beta_i} - e_i x_i - F_i$, and when maximized with respect to x_i, they become

$$\pi^i = e_i \left(\frac{1}{\beta_i} - 1 \right) \left(\frac{a_i \beta_i^2}{e_i} \right)^{1/(1-\beta_i)} - F_i \tag{32}$$

By examining (31) and (32), we note that

$$\beta_i^{1/(1-\beta_i)} (\Delta T_i + F_i) = \left(\pi^i + F_i \right) \tag{33}$$

Now consider two products i and j, for which $\Delta T_i = \Delta T_j = K$. From (5) it follows that

$$\frac{\pi^i + F_i}{\pi^j + F_j} = \frac{\beta_i^{1/(1-\beta_i)}}{\beta_j^{1/(1-\beta_j)}} \left(\frac{K + F_i}{K + F_j} \right) \tag{34}$$

It can be shown that $\beta^{1/(1-\beta)}$ is a function that increases monotonically from zero on the interval $[0, 1]$.[6] Now suppose that $F_i = F_j = F$. If in addition, $\beta_i < \beta_j$, then (34) implies that $\pi_i < \pi_j$.

Proposition 4. If two products contribute equally to total surplus, and have the same fixed costs, then the one with the smaller β will have lower profits.

What is β? It is the parameter that determines the ratio of maximized profits to maximized contribution to the surplus. For it is that ratio that is crucial in determining biases in product selection under the market system.[7] This ratio is not a familiar one in economics. But β_i is related to the more familiar concept of elasticity. If the product were the only one in production ($e_i = 0$), the price elasticity of demand would be

$$\eta_i = \frac{1}{(1 - \beta_i)} \tag{35}$$

With other products, ($e_i \neq 0$), the elasticity has another term. But somewhat roughly, the smaller β_i is, the lower the price elasticity of demand. And hence roughly, the biases are against low elasticity products. But it is preferable to deal directly with the relevant quantity, max $\pi^i /$ max ΔT_i.

Fixed costs also have an impact of their own. To see it, assume that $\beta_i = \beta_j = \beta$ and that $\Delta T_i = \Delta T_j$, but that $F_i > F_j$. It follows from (34) that

$$\pi^i - \pi^j = \left(F_j - F_i \right) \left(1 - \beta^{1/(1-\beta)} \right) < 0 \tag{36}$$

Proposition 5. If two products contribute equally to the total surplus and have the same β, then the one with the larger fixed costs will have smaller profits in the market equilibrium.

This proposition indicates that the market selects against high fixed costs. If it could be shown that high fixed costs tend to go with high quality, then the market would select against quality, even if the elasticities were the same.

We turn now to the terms involving products of quantities, $G_{ij}(x_i x_j)$. The aim is to examine the implications of functions G_{ij} that are convex. The contribution of the *i*th product to total surplus is

$$\Delta T_i = \phi_i - 2\Sigma_j G_{ij} - c_i - F_i \tag{37}$$

while its profits are

$$\pi^i = x_i \phi'_i - 2\Sigma_j G'_{ij} x_i x_j - c_i - F_i \tag{38}$$

We saw above that when $x_i \phi'_i$ is small relative to ϕ_i, then the product *i* is selected against. Similarly, if G_{ij} is convex, then $G'_{ij} x_i x_j$ will be large relative to G_{ij} and the pair of products, *i* and *j*, will be selected against. This means that the market will tend to take one of them even if both contribute positively to total surplus.[8]

The meaning of the convexity of G_{ij} can be seen from examining the inverse demand functions. The *i*th inverse demand function is

$$p_i = \phi'_i - 2\Sigma_j G'_{ij} x_j \tag{39}$$

Therefore, differentiating with respect to x_k, we have

$$\frac{\partial p_i}{\partial x_k} = -2G'_{ik} - 2G''_{ik} x_i x_k \tag{40}$$

Now if G_{ik} were linear, the effect of increasing x_k would be to shift the inverse demand function vertically downward by a constant amount. However, if $G''_{ik} > 0$, the downward shift is larger for larger values of x_i. Hence, when $G''_{ik} > 0$, the effect of an increase in x_k is to shift p_i down and twist it so that it becomes steeper. But, of course, it is steep inverse demand functions that are selected against according to the analysis above. Figure 1 illustrates the twisting effect.

The bias is still that against products whose revenues capture smaller fractions of the contributed surplus. But there are two possible sources of the bias. The product can have a naturally limited set of buyers with highly variegated valuations of the product, or the steepness of the inverse demand function can come from the presence of competitive products, that tend to take away the consumers with the lower valuations of the product. It has been argued that television had this effect on motion picture demand. It removed the mass audience, and caused a shift in the character of films to ones of higher quality and price, and ones that appealed to a more specialized audience.

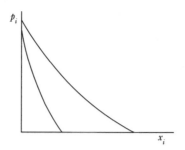

Figure 1

One might suggest that the market is biased against special interest products like odd clothing and shoe sizes. While this may be true, it is necessary to be somewhat careful. The extreme case of a special interest product has a demand like that in Figure 2. But this type of product causes no difficulties: the firm can appropriate the entire surplus. It is rather, extreme variegation in the valuation of the product by consumers that makes survival difficult.

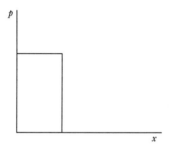

Figure 2

4.1. Multi-product firms

The maximizing the wrong function approach can be applied to multi-product firms. For reasons of space, let me simply sketch the argument and its implications. Let A_f be the set of products that firm f can produce. The surplus is

$$T(x) = \Sigma_f \Sigma_{i \varepsilon A_f} \left[\phi_i(x_i) - \Sigma_j G_{ij}(x_i x_j) - (c_i + F_i) \right] \tag{41}$$

The function that is implicitly maximized is

$$\hat{R}(x) = \Sigma_f \Sigma_{i \varepsilon A_f} \left[\phi_i' x_i - \Sigma_j G_{ij}' x_i x_j - (c_i + F_i) - \Sigma_{j \varepsilon A_f} G_{ij}' x_i x_j \right] \tag{42}$$

The new term is the last one, reflecting the fact that substitution effects among a single firm's products are taken into account (cf. equation (26)).

The multi-product firm takes into account the effect of each of its products on the profits generated by the other products it produces. This is a force tending to limit the number of products. This term indicates that the multi-product firm will tend *not* to introduce products that are close substitutes for each other.

Products that are close substitutes will be produced by separate firms.[9] Firms will spread their products out in the product space, and they are likely to have product lines that compete with other firm's product lines product by product, and not to specialize in groups of products that are close substitutes. Specialization would, however, be the collectively rational strategy for maximizing industry profits.

Given that firms tend not to produce close substitutes, the extra term in $\hat{R}$ is minimized. If the sets of available products for each firm are comparable, then product choice under multi-product firms will be similar to that under monopolistic competition, the implications of which have been examined in detail. However, if the sets $A_f, k = 1, \ldots, F$, are not comparable, so that it is not true that for each $i \varepsilon A_f$ there is a $j \varepsilon A_g$ that is a close substitute, then multi-product firms will reduce the number of products, much as a monopolist would. That is to say, if the feasible sets, A_f force firms to specialize, then the result will be more like the monopoly result. In fact the monopolist case occurs when $F = 1$. In that case, the function that is implicitly maximized is

$$\hat{R} = \Sigma_i x_i \phi_i' - 2\Sigma_{i,j} x_i x_j G_{ij}' - \Sigma_i (c_i + F_i) - F \tag{43}$$

Unless there is a reason for believing that the sets A_f are not comparable, and provided there is no collusion among firms, the multi-product firm market structure will select products in much the same way as monopolistic competition. And one would expect to observe competing product lines. The biases in product selection will be similar to those attributed to monopolistic competition.

5. Monopolistic Competition and Substitutes: The Generalized CES Case

In this section, I should like to discuss the qualitative aspects of product choice and variety for a class of cases in which the equilibria are calculable. The specific form for the benefit function is

$$u(x) = G\left[\int_i \phi_i(x_i) di\right] \tag{44}$$

where G and the ϕ_i are concave functions. It can be thought of as a generalized CES utility function. If $u(x)$ has the form

$$u(x) = \left[\int_i a_i x_i^\beta\right]^\theta \tag{45}$$

then it has the form of a CES function. One could then drop the assumption that all the exponents are the same and write

$$u(x) = \left[\int_i a_i x_i^{\beta_i} \right]^{\theta} \tag{46}$$

And finally, to increase flexibility in approximating demand functions, one could general-ize from $a_i x_i^{\beta_i}$ to an arbitrary function $\phi_i(x_i)$, and from $(\cdot)^{\theta}$ to an arbitrary concave function $G(\cdot)$. That is one way of viewing the form (44). It is a form that has some special properties. These will emerge below. But it may not be entirely without interest as a basis for empirical work.

I should like to accomplish two purposes in using this functional form. The first is to illustrate that the previously identified bias against products for which the firm has difficulty capturing the surplus persists. In this case, the bias is quite closely associated with the elasticity. The second is to discuss the working out of the various forces affecting the number of products, and hence the diversity generated by the market system.

5.1. Biases against products

To get at biases in product selection, one must characterize both the market equilibrium and the optimum. This is done here by means of two algorithms, one for each problem. The algorithms are based on what can be called survival coefficients. These are used in the algorithms to decide in what order to introduce products.

When $u(x)$ has the form (44), the inverse demand functions can be written

$$p_i = u_i = G'(m)\phi_i'(x_i) \tag{47}$$

where

$$m = \int_j \phi_j(x_j)\,dj \tag{48}$$

The quantity m is important. When it increases, $G'(m)$ falls because of the concavity of G. As a result, the inverse demand functions of each firm fall by proportional factors, as can be seen from (47).[10] Thus m can be thought of as an index of congestion in the markets. As it increases, the demand for any particular product is squeezed down.

The profits of the ith firm are

$$\pi^i = G'\phi_i' x_i - (c_i(x_i) + F_i) \tag{49}$$

These are non-negative when $\pi^i \geqq 0$ or

$$G'(m) \geqq \left[\frac{c_i(x_i) + F_i}{x_i \phi_i'(x_i)} \right] \tag{50}$$

Now the firm's ability to survive increases in m or equivalently reductions in $G'(m)$, without incurring negative profits, is determined by how small the quantity $(c_i + F_i)/x_i\phi'_i$ can be made. Let us therefore define the number

$$s_i = \min_{x_i} \left[\frac{c_i(x_i) + F_i}{x_i\phi'_i(x_i)} \right] \tag{51}$$

and refer to it as the *survival coefficient* for product i.

FINDING THE MONOPOLISTICALLY COMPETITIVE EQUILIBRIUM   The interaction among firms takes place through m. Given m, each firm maximizes profits by setting

$$G'\left[\phi'_i + x_i\phi''_i \right] = c'_i(x_i) \tag{52}$$

provided the firm is in business.[11] For any given set of producing firms, the relations (48) and (52) jointly determine the equilibrium levels of the x_i and m. As more products are added, m will rise and the profits of individual firms will fall. If we introduce products in some arbitrary order, we might find that firms introduced early incur negative profits as more products are added, so that they have to be removed.

To avoid this kind of cycling, one uses the survival coefficients, s_i. First, one rank orders products in terms of their survival coefficients, from smallest to largest, so that

$$s_1 \leqq s_2 \leqq \cdots \leqq s_n \tag{53}$$

Then, to find the equilibrium, we introduce products in that order. As products are introduced, firms reset quantities according to (52), m rises and G' falls. At some point, the last firm entering just makes a non-negative profit. If the last firm is n, then $G'(m) = s_n$. But then $G'(m) \geqq s_k$ for all $k > n$, because of the ranking of products by the coefficients s_i. Therefore, no producing firm has negative profits. Similarly, because $G' < s_k$, for $k > n$, no potential entrant could make a profit.[12] And we have an equilibrium. It is depicted in Figure 3.

In short, to find the equilibrium, one introduces products in order of survival capability, until the marginal firm's profits are zero.

THE OPTIMUM   It does not seem necessary here to derive the marginal cost pricing rule for the optimum. The difficult question is which products to introduce, and which to leave out. Formally, the problem is to maximize the total surplus with respect to Γ and x_i:

$$T = G(m) - \int_{i\varepsilon\Gamma} (c_i + F_i) \tag{54}$$

where Γ is the set of products in production. It is convenient to approach this problem obliquely by posing a suboptimization problem. Let us fix m at $\bar{m}$, and minimize the costs of generating the fixed benefits $G(\bar{m})$. Formally, the problem is to minimize

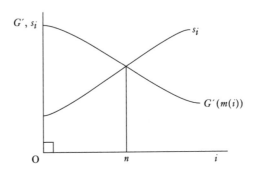

Figure 3

$$c(m) = \int_{i\varepsilon\Gamma} (c_i + F_i) \tag{55}$$

subject to

$$m = \int_{i\varepsilon\Gamma} \phi_i(x_i) \geqq \bar{m} \tag{56}$$

The objective function can be rewritten

$$c = \int_{i\varepsilon\Gamma} \left(\frac{c_i + F_i}{\phi_i} \right) \phi_i \tag{57}$$

This will be minimized subject to the constraint, by selecting products that have the lowest values of $(c_i + F_i)/\phi_i$. Thus we define a new set of coefficients

$$\rho_i = \min_{x_i} \left[\frac{c_i(x_i) + F_i}{\phi_i(x_i)} \right] \tag{58}$$

These coefficients have nothing to do with the particular $\bar{m}$ in the constrained problem (55). To find the optimum, products are rank ordered according to ρ_i from smallest to largest, and introduced in that order.

The cost minimization problem is solved when

$$c_i'(x_i) = \lambda \phi_i'(x_i) \tag{59}$$

and

$$c_n + F_n = \lambda \phi_n \tag{60}$$

where λ is the Lagrange multiplier associated with the constraint (56). However, $(c_n + F_n)/\phi_n = \lambda = c'_n/\phi'_n$. But that is the condition for $(c_n + F_n)/\phi_n$ to be minimized with respect to x_n. Thus $\lambda = \rho_n$. The full surplus maximization problem is now easily solved. The surplus is $G(m) - c(m)$. It is maximized when

$$G'(m) = c'(m) = \lambda = \rho_n \tag{61}$$

Note that since $\lambda = G', G'\phi'_i = \rho_i = c'_i$ from (59) so that the marginal cost pricing rule emerges, as expected. See Figure 4.

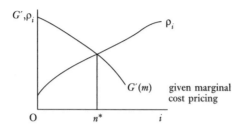

Figure 4

COMPARING THE EQUILIBRIUM AND THE OPTIMUM   The most natural way of contrasting the equilibrium and the optimum is to examine the orderings of the products used in locating the equilibrium and the optimum. If the market system shuffles the optimal ordering, there is a bias in product choice. The qualitative character of the bias is especially easy to see in the case when $\phi_i = a_i x_i^{\beta_i}$. Let us consider this case. We note that $x_i \phi'_i = \beta_i a_i x_i^{\beta_i} = \beta_i \phi_i$. Therefore

$$s_i = \min_{x_i} \left[\frac{c_i + F_i}{x_i \phi'_i} \right] = \min_{x_i} \frac{1}{\beta_i} \left[\frac{c_i + F_i}{\phi_i} \right] = \frac{\rho_i}{\beta_i} \tag{62}$$

Two observations follow immediately.

1   Since $\beta_i < 1, s_i > \rho_i$ for all i, there is a tendency for products to be undervalued by the market.
2   Since $\rho_i/s_i = \beta_i$, those products for which β_i is small tend to be pushed down in the market rank ordering, relative to the optimum, and some of them may be pushed out altogether.

What is the economic interpretation of a small β_i? The inverse demand for product i is

$$p_i = G' a_i \beta_i x_i^{\beta_i - 1} \tag{63}$$

The smaller β_i is, the steeper is the inverse demand function. Thus a small β_i is associated with a steeply sloped inverse demand function or with a product with a low price elasticity of demand. This is the kind of product that fares poorly, other things being equal, under the market system.

For the more general functions, $\phi_i(x_i)$, the same principle holds. The ratio ρ_i/s_i is small for those products for which $x_i\phi_i'/\phi_i$ tends to be small. Such products have steep inverse demand functions, that is to say, small groups of high value users. The ratio $x_i\phi_i'/\phi_i$ can be interpreted in the following way. Revenues for firm i are $G'x_i\phi_i'$. On the other hand. if ϕ_i is small in relation to m, then the contribution of product i to benefits is approximately $G'\phi_i$. Hence the ratio $G/x_i\phi_i'/G'\phi_i = x_i\phi_i'/\phi_i$ is the ratio of revenues to the ith product's incremental contribution to benefits. When revenues are small in relation to incremental benefits, the product has trouble surviving in the market system.

5.2. Numbers and variety of products

The issue relating to the numbers of products under monopolistic competition is whether the entry of new products and the consequent depression of profits of existing firms leads to an excessive number of products or not. That is to say, is the maximum total surplus achieved before or after profits go to zero? Is the profit signal the correct one in determining the number of products?

In analysing the numbers question, it is of interest to compare the market equilibrium not only with the global optimum, but also with two second best optima.

Table 1 indicates the various optima that are of interest. Both prices and the number of products are aspects of both a market equilibrium and an optimum. In constrained problem A, prices are constrained to be monopolistically competitive, and the surplus is maximized with respect to the number of products. In problem B, entry occurs until profits go to zero. The surplus is maximized with respect to the pattern of pricing.

There are conflicting forces at work in respect to the numbers or variety of products. Because of setup costs, revenues may fail to cover the costs of a socially desirable product. As a result, some products may be produced at a loss at an optimum. This is a force tending toward too few products. On the other hand, there are forces tending toward too many products. First, because firms hold back output and keep price above marginal cost, they leave more room for entry than would marginal cost pricing. Second, when a firm enters with a new product, it adds its own consumer and producer surplus to the total surplus, but it also cuts into the profits of the existing firms. If the cross elasticities of demand are high, the dominant effect may be the second one. In this case entry does not increase the size of the pie much; it just divides it into more pieces. Thus in the presence of high cross elasticities of demand, there is a tendency toward too many products.

Table 1

	Prices	Entry
I. Market equilibrium	monopolistically competitive pricing	zero profits
II. Global optimum	optimize price by marginal cost pricing	optimize numbers
III. Constrained problem A	monopolistically competitive pricing	optimize numbers
IV. Constrained problem B	optimize prices	zero profits

In what follows, the outcomes of these conflicting forces are analysed, beginning with simple examples, where the effects are clearest.

The first useful simplification to begin with, is that products are symmetric with respect to both demand and cost though not perfect substitutes. In the model, let us assume that $\phi_i(x) = \phi(x)$, that $c_i(x) = c(x)$ and that $F_i = F$ for all i. Among other things, this permits us to set aside the biases in product choice discussed earlier. Second, it is convenient to begin with the case where $\phi(x) = ax^\beta$. With these two assumptions, the basic quantities of interest are as follows:

$$m = n\phi(x) \tag{64}$$

and

$$T = G(m) - n(c(x) + F) \tag{65}$$

$$\Pi = G'(m)x\phi' - (c + F) \tag{66}$$

Using (64) to solve for $n = m/\phi$, the total surplus can be written:

$$T = G(m) - m(c + F)/\phi \tag{67}$$

It is clear that T is maximized when x minimizes $(c + F)/\phi$, and when

$$G'(m) = (c + F)/\phi \tag{68}$$

On the other hand, profits are maximized with respect to x when

$$G'[\phi' + x\phi''] = c' \tag{69}$$

and then profits are zero when

$$G' = (c + F)/x\phi' \tag{70}$$

From (69) and (70)

$$\frac{c'}{\phi' + x\phi''} = \frac{c + F}{x\phi'} \tag{71}$$

But (71) is the condition that x minimize $(c + F)/x\phi'$. Therefore the quantity x, in the market equilibrium, minimizes $(c + F)/x\phi'$. Finally when $\phi = ax^\beta$, $x\phi' = \beta\phi$, so that the x that minimizes $(c + F)/\phi$ also minimizes $(c + F)/x\phi' = (c + F)/\beta\phi$.

The optimum and the equilibrium are depicted in Figure 5 with x and m on the axes. Each firm produces x^* at both the optimum and the market equilibrium. The optimum is at O, the equilibrium at M. The circular contours around O are iso-total surplus lines.

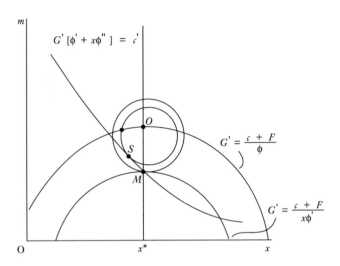

Figure 5

They are vertical through $G' = (c + F)/\phi$, and horizontal through $x = x^*$. The point S is the constrained optimum when monopolistically competitive pricing is taken as given. At S, m is higher and x lower than at M. The point M is the point of tangency between the zero profit constraint and the iso-total surplus line. M is therefore the constrained optimum when the zero profit constraint is adopted. The facts represented in Figure 5 establish the following proposition.

Proposition 6. If $\phi_i(x) = ax^\beta$ for all i and costs are the same, then

(i)   There are more products at the optimum than at the equilibrium.
(ii)   The quantities of each product are the same at O and M.
(iii)   Profits are negative at the optimum.
(iv)   At the optimum constrained by monopolistically competitive pricing, S, there are more products, each selling a smaller quantity than at the market equilibrium. Profits are negative at S.
(v)   The optimum constrained by the zero profit conditions is M, and therefore it is the same as the market equilibrium. M is less satisfactory than S. Given a choice between subsidization to control numbers, and taxing to approximate marginal cost pricing, subsidization is preferable.

We turn now to the case where $\phi(x)$ is an arbitrary concave function. This case is not substantially different from the more special one. It can be established that if $x\phi'/\phi$ is a decreasing function, then the optimal x^* is lower than the market equilibrium quantity, $\bar{x}$. Therefore the configuration of outcomes is as shown in Figure 6.

In this situation, the market equilibrium has too few products relative to both the global optimum O and the optimum constrained to monopolistically competitive pricing, S. The

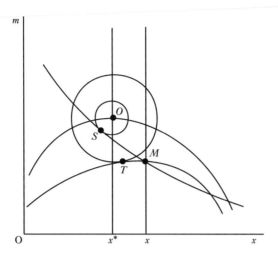

Figure 6

point T is the optimum constrained to non-negative profits for each firm. At T, x is lower than $\bar{x}$, but m is also lower. Therefore, an unambiguous statement about the number of products is not possible.

If $x\phi'/\phi$ is increasing, then the optimal quantity, x, is above the equilibrium quantity, $\bar{x}$. As a result, we get the picture shown in Figure 7. In this case the optimum has a larger quantity, and larger total benefits, $G(m)$, than the market equilibrium. The relative numbers of products is ambiguous. The position of S relative to M is also not determinate. S could be above and to the left of M. Unlike the previous cases, T is preferred to S, so that excise taxes, correctly set, accomplish more than subsidies.

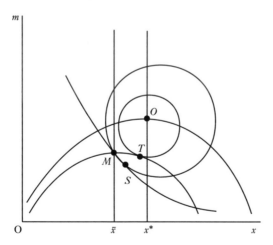

Figure 7

Of these two cases, I find it more plausible that revenues should be a declining fraction of the aggregate benefits generated by a product as price is lowered and quantity increased. If this be accepted, Figure 6 and the conclusions that accompany it represent the normal case. Contrary to most of the literature, the problem in this case is that the output of the monopolistically competitive firms is too high.

6. Concluding Remarks

I should like to conclude first by briefly summarizing the implications of the preceding analysis and then by suggesting areas of application of the models.

Prices do not always permit producers of potentially valuable products to appropriate enough of the social benefits to cover the costs. Several results follow. The market system does not automatically produce the right products. The inability of sellers to appropriate benefits is particularly severe for products with steeply sloped demand curves and these products, which one associates with specialized interests, tend not to be produced. Sellers will look for ways to appropriate more of the benefits by a variety of forms of discrimination. Such efforts may have efficiency costs, but they may also have benefits in increasing the range of choices available.

With fixed costs, there will generally be many market equilibria. I regret not having been able, as yet, to assess the extent of the welfare differences among them.

With multi-product firms that select from sets of products that are comparable, product selection is not likely to differ greatly from that under monopolistic competition. Monopoly, on the other hand, is likely to restrict the range of substitutes supplied, relative to both the optimum and to monopolistic competition.

Given monopolistically competitive pricing, high own price elasticities and high cross-elasticities create an environment in which monopolistic competition is likely to generate too many products. Conversely, low own-price elasticities and low cross-elasticities constitute an environment in which product diversity will be too low.

Given the profitability constraint under a market system, deviations from marginal cost pricing are called for. Monopolistically competitive pricing may not be too far from the second best. In some special instances, it is the second best. In general, the markups of low elasticity products are higher than the optimum at a market equilibrium.

The potential areas of application and extension of these general tendencies are numerous. Spatial competition is a special case of monopolistic competition. One might guess that the range of retail services would be suboptimally low in small communities. It would also be worth investigating whether the higher markups under resale price maintenance tend to generate excessive numbers of retail outlets of various kinds, or whether they compensate for a tendency to have too few.

The models suggest that television programming under pay television will fail to serve special interests. An extension of the models suggests that this particular failing is likely to be even worse under advertiser supported broadcast television. This is discussed in Owen and Spence [4].

Lest fixed costs seem unimportant, it is well to remember that R & D, advertising, and other marketing activities can be counted as fixed costs or at least sources of increasing returns, and they frequently outweigh fixed production costs. Thus, even in consumer non-durables there may be a problem. But there are two influences. High fixed costs tend to reduce product variety, and high cross-elasticities tend to augment it, relative to the optimum. The net effect is an empirical matter.

Formal analysis of entry deals with homogeneous products. Yet the preponderance of consumer goods industries are not homogeneous products. In these, entry is often a matter of finding the right differentiated niche, and deterring entry is a matter of foreclosing such opportunities through careful selection of ranges of products. The subject bears further investigation.

Hopefully the preceding analysis suggests a range of phenomena of potential interest and provides a starting point for the analysis of the qualitative character of the market failures that may arise.

Notes

1 For a discussion of the accuracy of consumer surplus see Willig [8].
2 Edward Chamberlin [2] explicitly raised the product selection problem, and clearly thought of product choice as an integral part of the theory of monopolistic competition. As it evolved, the theory has yielded disappointingly few qualitative insights. Stigler voices this kind of perspective on the theory.
3 I assume here that the set of quantities x for which the surplus is positive, is non-empty, and is contained in a compact subset of R^{nl}.
4 It is well known that quantity and price Nash equilibria are not equivalent. In general, quantity competition yields an outcome closer to the industry contract curve. The reason is that if a firm expects other firms to maintain quantity, then it expects them to cut price in response to price cuts. Thus the anticipated reaction function in the quantity game penalizes the price cutter more. I use quantity here for several reasons. It is analytically tractable. The general results are not sensitive to the assumption. For industries that are not concentrated, the price and quantity equilibria are not very different. And the quantity version captures a part of the tacit coordination to avoid all-out price competition, that I believe characterizes most industries.
5 The form (20) is necessary as well as sufficient for monopolistic competition implicitly to maximize some function (see Spence [6]).
6 To establish this, we take the logarithm of $\beta^{1/(1-\beta)}$, and differentiate with respect to β:

$$\frac{\partial}{\partial\beta}\log\beta^{1/(1-\beta)} = \frac{\partial}{\partial\beta}\left[\frac{1}{1-\beta}\log\beta\right]$$

$$= -\frac{1}{1-\beta^2}\log\beta + \frac{1}{\beta(1-\beta)})$$

$$> 0$$

Moreover, when $\beta = 0, \beta^{1/(1-\beta)} = 0$, and when $\beta = 1, \log(\beta^{1/(1-\beta)}) = -1$, using l'Hôpital's rule. Hence

$$\beta^{1/(1-\beta)} = 1/e$$

when $\beta = 1$.
7 It can be shown that when demand functions are linear, there is no bias in product choice (see Owen and Spence [4]). This is true even if the slopes of the demand functions vary over products. Thus it is not strictly correct to think in terms of slopes or elasticities.

8   In the general case (2), similar biases involving three or more products can be identified in the same way.

9   There are exceptions. General Foods, for example, produces several closely competitive brands of instant coffee. But this, I think, can be explained as an incentive creating device within the firm. The brands are managed by independent managers who compete with each other as well as with other firms. Similar remarks apply to the divisions of the automobile companies, like Chevrolet and Pontiac in General Motors.

10 This important property implies that the ratio of revenues, $G'x_i\phi'_i$ and the product's contribution to aggregate benefits, $G(m) - G(m - \phi_i) \simeq G'\phi_i$, is $x_i\phi'_i/\phi_i$ and is therefore not affected by entry of new firms. The demand for an individual product does not shift from being highly elastic to highly inelastic as a result of the entry of new products.

11 This assumes that the ith firm ignores the effect of changes in x_i on $G'(m)$.

12 Here we use the smallness of the products in relation to the market, specifically by ignoring the effect of change in x_i on $G'(m)$. Without this assumption, difficult linear programming problems arise.

References and Further Reading

1 Chamberlin, E. (1960): *The Theory of Monopolistic Competition*. Cambridge: Harvard University Press.

2 Chamberlin, E. (1953): "The Product as an Economic Variable," *Quarterly Journal of Economics* 67 (1), 1–29.

3 Dixit, A. and Stiglitz, J. E. (1974): "Monopolistic Competition and Optimum Product Diversity," Technical report 153, Institute for Mathematical Studies in the Social Sciences, Stanford University, October.

4 Owen, B. and Spence, A. M. (1975): "Television Programming, Monopolistic Competition and Welfare," Technical report 159, Institute for Mathematical Studies in the Social Sciences, Stanford University, January.

5 Spence, A. M. (1975): "Existence of Equilibrium with Increasing Returns," draft, May.

6 Spence, A. M. (1975): "Monopoly, Quality, and Regulation," Technical report 164, Institute for Mathematical Studies in the Social Sciences, Standford University, April.

7 Stigler, G. (1968): "Monopolistic Competition in Retrospect," in G. Stigler (ed.), *The Organization of Industry*, Homewood, Illinois: Richard D. Irwin.

8 Willig, R. (1973): "Welfare Analysis of Policies Affecting Prices and Products," Research memorandum 153, Center for Research in Economic Growth, Stanford University, September.

III D

The Firm's Decision Making Under Certainty: Oligopoly Markets

CHAPTER ELEVEN

The Role of Potential Competition in Industrial Organization

RICHARD J. GILBERT

Source: *Journal of Economic Perspectives*, 3, 3 (1989), pp. 107–27. Reprinted with the permission of the author and the American Economic Association. © American Economic Association.

Potential competition has been recognized as a mechanism to control the exploitation of market power at least since the work of J. B. Clark (1902), but it was not until 50 years later that economists, most notably Joe Bain and Paolo Sylos-Labini, refocused attention on the idea. With inputs from the theories of imperfect competition, optimal control, and dynamic games, their work evolved into ever more sophisticated models of the reactions of existing competitors to the threat of new competition. Although the most appropriate models of competitive interaction are those which begin with a specific industry, a number of theories have been proposed which attempt to develop more general conclusions. My purpose in this paper is to develop an understanding of the strengths and limitations of these alternative theories by examining the available theoretical, empirical and institutional knowledge.

Rather than attempt the Sisyphean task of recounting every model which relates conditions of entry and market performance, I have partitioned the analysis into four major schools of thought, according to their most central propositions. These are the traditional model of limit pricing, dynamic limit pricing, the theory of contestable markets, and the market efficiency model. Traditional limit pricing models rest on the assumption that firms respond to entry, but are able to earn persistent profits when the structural characteristics of markets make entry difficult. Dynamic limit pricing is similar, but emphasizes that markets can only be temporarily protected from entry. Contestability theory, in its pure form, asserts that potential competition is as effective as actual competition in controlling market performance. The efficient markets hypothesis, broadly interpreted, states that markets are workably competitive and that the market structure reflects differential efficiency, not strategic behavior. While one can construct many other hypotheses about potential competition, these classifications are intended to span a broad range of predictions. This paper attempts to present testable conclusions that follow as consequences from these different schools of thought and to examine these conclusions in light of available data.

A warning is appropriate here. This paper is not an attempt to provide a complete or balanced view of its subject. For example, the theory of contestable markets, developed by Baumol, Panzar and Willig (1982), receives more than an equal share of attention in this paper. This uneven approach is motivated in part by the fact that the specific conclusions of the theory of perfectly contestable markets lend themselves to a critical review, and in part by the excitement and controversy that this theory has stirred in our profession.

1. Hypotheses about Entry

I will consider several alternative hypotheses about the process and consequences of entry. I have intended these hypotheses to conform to prevailing theoretical models, but given the fact that little of the theory of entry prevention has been developed with the intention of providing empirically testable results, I regret that the correspondence between my hypotheses and specific models of entry prevention may be less than exact.

1.1. Hypothesis 1: Markets behave according to the classic limit pricing model

I use the term "classic limit pricing model" to refer generally to the structural theory of market performance developed by Joe Bain and his contemporaries. Bain identified the "conditions of entry" as technological features of markets that affect the exercise of market power. He identified economies of scale, absolute cost advantages, and product differentiation as the primary determinants of "entry barriers," defined to be factors that enable an established firm to maintain price above average cost. While Bain considered these barriers to be partly exogenous, they clearly can be affected by the investments and technology chosen by firms.

The most straightforward application of the classical limit pricing model is to pricing with economies of scale. An established firm (or group of firms) can prevent entry by producing enough so that if a new firm should enter, its additional output would force price to fall below its average cost. A central assumption in the limit pricing model is that entrants expect that established firms will not accommodate entry by reducing their output.[1] (I'll return to this assumption in the discussion of contestability theory.) Following Modigliani's (1958) formulation, the limit output is the smallest pre-entry output for which entry is not profitable. The corresponding limit price is the highest price at which entry is deterred, under the assumption that incumbents would maintain their pre-entry outputs if entry should occur. As Figure 1 illustrates, if an established firm can choose the level of output that it would maintain after entry, the firm can elevate price above its average cost while presenting an entrant (with a similar technology) with no profitable market opportunity. With economies of scale, the limit price exceeds the average cost of production and established firms earn persistent profits.

The limit pricing theory can be applied to other determinants of the conditions of entry, too. As Dixit (1979) has shown, an established firm with a differentiated product can follow a similar strategy to exploit consumer preferences when increasing returns are present in the production technology. With absolute cost advantages, the limit price is the (higher) average cost of an assumed disadvantaged entrant.

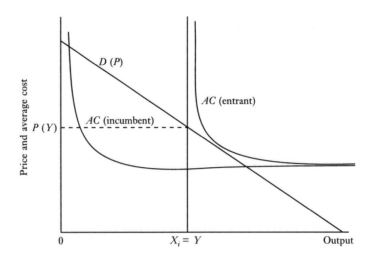

Figure 1   Limit pricing

The particular formulation of the limit pricing model is not important for my purpose. What is important is the essential implication that established firms can exploit structural features of the market to earn persistent above-normal profits. Modest entry barriers could translate into large incumbent profits if entrants expect that entry would trigger aggressive price-cutting behavior (Spence, 1977; Stiglitz, 1987). In the absence of a reputation for aggressive behavior, an established firm wishing to deter entry would need a mechanism to signal potential entrants that it will not act passively in response to an entry attempt. Dixit (1980) shows that sunk costs may offer such a mechanism. To the extent that an established firm has sunk investment expenditures and excess capacity, its marginal cost of production is lower than that of a new firm with the same technology (for which expenditures are not yet sunk). Thus, sunk costs can make operation at capacity profitable for an established firm challenged by new competition, even if competition lowers its marginal revenue. Other possible mechanisms including switching costs (Farrell and Shapiro, 1988; Gelman and Salop, 1983), product differentiation (Dixit, 1979), or pricing practices such as "take or pay" requirements (Aghion and Bolton, 1987).

If equilibrium after entry is unaffected by the behavior of incumbent firms before entry, there is no scope for limit pricing. In this case, entry will be prevented only if the market cannot sustain an additional firm when established firms act without regard to the effects of their behavior on entry. (Bain would say that entry is "blockaded" in this case.) However, if established firms can commit to actions that will make entry less profitable, they may choose to do so, provided the cost of these commitments does not exceed the profits that would be lost if entry occurs. If potential competitors use pre-entry price as a signal of post-entry profitability, incumbent firms may be forced to lower prices to prevent rivals from inferring that their markets are unduly profitable (Salop, 1979; Milgrom and Roberts, 1982).

There are many variants of the limit pricing model, but they all share a few distinguishing features. When limit pricing occurs, dominant firms will earn profits that persist above normal levels. Entry is generally followed by price competition and incumbent firms (approximately) maintain their pre-entry outputs.[2] Potential competition should have a moderating effect on industry profits, but it should not be as effective as actual competition in controlling pricing behavior. Finally, if limit pricing is occurring, we should observe strategic behavior designed to deter entry or to mitigate its consequences.

1.2. Hypothesis 2: Markets follow the dynamic limit pricing model

In the classic limit pricing model, entry is an all or nothing affair. At a price below the limit price, the threat of entry is eliminated; at a price above the limit price, entry occurs instantaneously. In dynamic markets where scale or technical requirements do not restrict entry, however, a reservoir of potential competitors may stand ready to spill into the industry at a rate that depends on expected profits. Knowing this, incumbent firms can trade off the current profitability against the prospect that high profits today will increase the rate at which new competition is attracted to the industry. When an established firm or cartel chooses a high price, competitive fringe producers increase their production and erode the cartel's market share. Geroski (1987) calls this "optimally managed decline."[3] In its simplest guise, it is the "inverted umbrella" story of cartel pricing described by Stigler (1968). More sophisticated versions, which can include nonprice competition, have been developed by Gaskins (1971), Kamien and Schwartz (1971), Friedman (1979), Judd and Peterson (1986), and others.

An internally consistent model of dynamic limit pricing can be difficult to specify. For example, it is not clear why the dominant firm should be a price leader, particularly after its market share has been eroded by entry. In the earlier dynamic limit pricing models, potential competitors were just an exogenously given force, responding to prices chosen by the dominant firm. Judd and Peterson (1986) derive entry from profit-maximizing behavior, but they impose an exogenous internal financing constraint on new competitors.

But despite the limitations of theories of dynamic limit pricing, several distinctive conclusions emerge. Dominant firms will earn supranormal profits, but these profits will gradually erode. The gains from incumbency are transient. Furthermore, pricing behavior should depend not only on interactions between established firms, but also on the threat of potential competition for the industry. Even as dominant firms decline, they are altering their behavior to slow the rate at which they lose market share to new competitors.

1.3. Hypothesis 3: Markets are perfectly contestable

In its pure form, the theory of contestable markets developed by Baumol, Panzar and Willig (1982) is not a description of firm behavior but is rather a statement about the properties of equilibria in a certain kind of market. In a perfectly contestable market, industry prices and outputs are defined as "sustainable" if no new firm (using the same technology as incumbent firms) can choose lower prices (for one or more of the products offered by existing firms) and operate profitably by serving all or part of demand at the new prices. Baumol–Panzar–Willig then define a contestable market as any market which can only be in equilibrium if the market price-quantity vector is sustainable.[4]

The definition, although not related to a particular description of a competitive process, is nonetheless elegant. In a perfectly contestable market equilibrium, total revenue must equal total cost. If revenues exceed costs, a new firm could enter at lower prices and still be profitable. If two or more firms operate in a contestable market, the price for each product that is sold must be equal to marginal cost, since any deviation of price from marginal cost would create opportunities for profitable marginal adjustments in the output(s) of one of the firms. Even if the market is a natural monopoly, if it is also perfectly contestable, price will be sufficient only to cover average cost. In such a situation contestability amounts to a perfect surrogate for price regulation under the constraint that the regulated firm must break even. With two or more firms, a perfectly contestable market replicates the equality of price and marginal cost in a perfectly competitive market.[5]

The concept of a perfectly contestable market does not rely on a description of firm behavior. But when "contestable market" is used in the active voice, it presumes the existence of "hit and run" entrants who are able and willing to enter an industry whenever profit opportunities arise. Such entry makes sense only if the potential entrant has little at risk. According to Baumol and Willig (1986, p. 4), the theory accomplishes this by "stripping away through its assumptions all barriers to entry and exit."

Contestability becomes controversial when it moves from the theory with its assumption of zero entry barriers to situations where entry barriers are modest, but not absent. A key relationship is how quickly prices move in response to entry. Willig (Baumol and Willig, 1986) describes a model that reproduces some of the predictions of perfectly contestable markets with nontrivial barriers to entry, provided prices move slowly in response to entry. On the other hand, Farrell (1986a), Gilbert and Harris (1984), Gilbert (1986) and Stiglitz (1987) present models to show that if prices move quickly, established firms can maintain supra-normal profits even if the sunk costs of entry are small. The key difference is that if prices move quickly in response to entry, then hit and run entry becomes very risky if there are any sunk costs.

Perfect contestability has strong testable implications for market performance. If industry prices are sustainable, established firms will not earn profits that exceed or fall short of normal levels. If barriers to entry or exit are insignificant, profits will be held to negligible levels by the threat of potential entry alone. Incumbency has neither benefits nor costs. Firms will minimize costs subject to the constraint that revenues are sufficient to cover costs; they will not make investments that are inefficient at chosen levels of output, but are intended to deter entrants. If the cost-minimizing industry structure is independent of the number of firms in the industry, then entry or exit of a firm should have no effect on prices. Finally, prices should move slowly relative to the movement of capital into or out of a contestable industry.

1.4. Hypothesis 4: Efficiency differences explain market shares and profit

I will describe this hypothesis as the "Chicago school" of industrial organization, with apologies to those both within and outside the windy city who might be offended by this nomenclature. Without denying the importance of imperfect competition, the Chicago school represents that market evolution reflects differential efficiency. Dominant firms owe their position to superior performance, not to strategic behavior or the history of entry into the industry, and profits are simply the rents that accrue to superior technology (Stigler, 1968, ch. 7; Demsetz, 1973). The Chicago school does not reject the concept of barriers to entry, but believes that they play a relatively minor role (Demsetz, 1982).

The unique perspective of the Chicago school can be illustrated by its definition of "barriers to entry." Stigler proposed that an entry barrier be limited to "a cost of producing (at some or every rate of output) which must be borne by firms seeking to enter an industry but is not borne by firms already in the industry." According to this definition, if both new and old firms have access to the same technology, the extent of scale economies is not a barrier to entry, as it affects equally the costs of both firms. This would be true even if scale economies limited the market to a single firm.

In the classic limit pricing model, remember, scale economies are an entry barrier because the model assumes that incumbents will maintain their outputs and thus constrain the market available to new entrants. If entrants believed they could compete on an equal footing with incumbents (which is implicit in the theory of perfectly contestable markets), scale economies would have no different effect on new entrants than on established firms. They would not be a barrier to entry. Thus, the key difference here is whether established firms can hold on to market share, and can communicate their ability to new entrants.

The Chicago school has not been structured as a formal model of potential competition, but with trepidation I will try to summarize its salient implications. Gains from incumbency should be modest and temporary. Strategic behavior by established firms to affect the conditions of entry should be minimal. Industry structure and profits should reflect cost differences, not accidents of history that determine the order of entry of firms. Market concentration should not, by itself, be a determinant of prices.

In many respects, the Chicago school theory of markets is a weak form of the contestable markets hypothesis. Whereas entry barriers are nonexistent in perfectly contestable markets, they play a minor and temporary role in the Chicago School. With two or more firms contestable markets act as if they are perfectly competitive. In the Chicago School, markets are "workably" competitive.[6]

2. Empirical Evidence on Entry and Market Performance

There is no scarcity of reasonable theories of entry behavior, but theory alone cannot answer the question of which of the many alternative models is the best predictor of entry behavior. We must turn to the empirical evidence which bears on the assumptions and implications of the various hypotheses about entry.

2.1. Experimental studies of entry

Experimental economics provides a way to study alternative hypotheses in settings that are highly structured, if not precisely controlled.[7] Broadly speaking, there are two types of relevant experiments. The first type examines whether a theory performs as expected when the experimental design conforms as closely as possible to both the structural and behavioral assumptions of the theory. This might require imposing specialized rules of the game, such as which competitor moves first and whether firms can commit to prices, which are not always present in actual competitive situations, but such confirming results are a minimal condition for any plausible theory. The second type of experiment does not impose behavioral assumptions other than what might naturally emerge from the structural assumptions of the theory. These experiments can offer practical insights as to the validity of the theory, but only to the extent that the experimental design reflects actual market conditions.

A good example of the first sort of experiment is provided by Harrison (1986), who performed experiments in which the rules of the game were structured to show contestability in its most favorable light. Sellers designated as incumbents were instructed to make public price offers which could not be changed in the subsequent period. Potential competitors faced no costs of entry and demand was simulated by computer, which removed any scope for strategic play by consumers. The institutional design in the Harrison experiment imposed a structure in which the incumbent firm has a first-mover advantage and potential competitors evaluate the profitability of entry with full knowledge of the price that will obtain if entry occurs. It should not be surprising that the outcome of the Harrison game was generally supportive of contestability. In most cases prices converged to average cost, which is also the price predicted by the theory for this market. Convergence to average cost did take some time and at least one case witnessed a successful attempt to maintain a collusive price, although this collusion was subsequently thwarted by introducing an additional seller.

The Harrison experiment was carefully designed to conform to the behavioral assumptions of contestability theory, and the results are supportive of that theory. Thus, the Harrison experiment showed that contestability theory is internally consistent when both the structural and behavioral assumptions of the model are replicated in the experiment.

However, experiments which relax some of the assumptions behind contestability theory, or allow for sunk costs, offer little support for the hypothesis that potential competition can be as effective as actual competition in policing market behavior.

Coursey, Isaac and Smith (1984) ran a series of experiments comparing the outcomes of a monopoly market with the outcome of a duopoly with costless entry and exit. Production exhibited increasing returns to scale, so the efficient market structure called for a single firm. In each iteration of the experimental market, each firm was allowed to post a take-it-or-leave-it price at which deliveries would be made for quantities demanded, subject to the seller's capacity limit. Demand was specified in each experiment, but was not known to the sellers (except as revealed by purchase decisions). The authors reported that as the market was repeated, prices in the duopoly case tended to move closer to average cost than to the monopoly price.[8] They interpreted this result as support for a "weak contestable markets" hypothesis: that prices, quantities, and market efficiency are closer to competitive than to monopoly levels.[9] However, the authors were not clear as to the process by which price moved toward average cost. If the experimental market replicated the predictions of the theory of perfectly contestable markets, a single firm would satisfy demand at a price equal to average cost, and entry would not occur. Coursey, Isaac and Smith did not explain whether price movements reflected the outputs of both firms or the output of a single firm that was pricing to deter entry. This distinction is crucial to the validity of contestability theory.[10]

In a subsequent paper, Coursey, Isaac, Luke and Smith (1984) describe the results of a series of market experiments similar to their earlier study, except for the introduction of sunk costs associated with an entry decision. The experimental design provided for two firms, one established and the other a potential entrant. Entry required the purchase of a permit, which was valid for five periods, and the duopoly game was repeated for a total of twenty periods. When amortized over its useful life, the entry fee would have reduced the level of monopoly profits by 10 percent.[11] As in the earlier paper, the authors conclude with support for a weak contestable markets hypothesis.

However, here it is more apparent that results of these experiments contradict an important prediction of the theory of contestable markets. In every repetition of the experiment, the potential entrant purchased an entry permit at least once (the entrant had four chances to enter, corresponding to the five period duration of the permit and the twenty period duration of the game). Yet entry was clearly inefficient in this experiment. Contestability theory would predict that the incumbent would price at average cost (excluding the entry fee) and there would be no entry. Potential, not actual, entry should police the pricing behavior of the established firm. The authors refer to this outcome as "limit pricing (contestable markets hypothesis)." It did occur, but only at one point in one of the twelve experiments. In four of the twelve cases the incumbent was able to raise price significantly above average cost without triggering an entry decision at a point where entry was feasible. The authors refer to these examples as "unstable pricing," but they are not inconsistent with limit pricing in which the established firm exploits the sunk cost of entry into the market.

These experiments do illustrate the limits of potential entry as a constraint on monopoly pricing. In eleven of the twelve cases, high prices are eroded by actual entry, even though entry is inefficient. In these experiments, attempts to extract monopoly profits are followed by the entry of new competition. But prices are controlled by actual entry, not by the threat of potential entry.[12]

Although economic experiments can sharpen our understanding, only the real world can test the ultimate validity of our models. In what follows, I will draw on industry studies about various aspects of competitive behavior and market performance that bear on the alternative theories of entry described earlier.

2.2. The existence and persistence of industry profits

Joe Bain (1956) made the first systematic attempt to uncover a correlation between measures of market concentration, the conditions of entry, and monopoly profits. Bain identified a positive correlation between profits and both concentration and estimates of the height of barriers to entry, which he categorized as scale economies, absolute cost advantages, and product differentiation. In the absence of substantial barriers to entry, the correlation between profits and market concentration was weak, an observation which lends some support to the contestable market hypothesis.

Bain's studies were highly influential and his correlations have withstood repeated observations, in particular the importance of product differentiation in consumer products industries (Comanor and Wilson, 1967, among others). But Bain's investigations suffered from important deficiencies. The measurement of entry barriers was necessarily subjective and vulnerable to the criticism of circularity: Are barriers high in industries that have persistent profits, or vice versa? Since accounting profits can differ widely from economic profits – for example, in the choice of depreciation schedules and the use of historical asset values – profitability itself is difficult to measure.

Several authors have attempted to estimate the magnitude and persistence of industry profits in other ways. Orr (1974) and Masson and Shaanan (1986) use the relationship between aggregate entry and exit and industry profitability as a means to estimate the importance of barriers to entry. Their estimates of "hurdle profit rates," above which entry becomes significant, can be interpreted as measures of the height of entry barriers in different industries. Mueller (1986; 1977) found that profit levels in a sample of 600 of the largest U.S. manufacturing corporations showed a strong tendency to revert over time to the sample mean, but the process was very slow. Estimated long run profits for the 100 companies with the highest profit levels in 1950 exceeded the sample average by more than 30 percent.

These findings would be consistent with the contestability hypothesis only if the observed profitability figures were accounting artifacts; otherwise these persistent profits should be quickly eliminated. Even if accounting profits are only roughly correlated with economic profits, contestability would predict large changes in market shares in response to even small changes in profitability, and this is not revealed in the data.

Industry studies lend some credence to the classical limit pricing model, since the available data suggests that entry into new industries has been very difficult. In Masson and Shaanan's (1982) sample of 37 U.S. industries over the period 1950–66, new entrants achieved an average market share penetration of only 4.5 percent. Similar studies by Biggadike (1979), Yip (1982) and Hause and Du Reitz (1984) also revealed only modest share gains by new entrants.

Yet the evidence is that new competitors do move into markets and excess profits do not last indefinitely, although the decay rate is quite long. Whatever causes these persistent profits, competitive forces tend to eliminate them over time. Limit pricing is not a perfect tool for blocking new entrants. If structural features of industries are the main cause of limited entry, these barriers are eventually worn down and overcome.

Thus, these interindustry studies are inconsistent with the theory of perfectly contestable markets, but they do not provide much conclusive evidence for any of the other theories of entry behavior. Depending on one's view of how soon is soon enough, the evidence need not contradict either the classic limit pricing model or the model of dynamic limit pricing. The data are not sufficiently detailed to show whether established firms adjust their price (and/or non-price) behavior to moderate the threat of entry, or whether entry simply reflects the development of new managerial and technical skills, which would be consistent with the Chicago school. The dismal performance record of new entrants casts a shadow on the strict view that the evolution of market structure is driven *only* by technological efficiencies with *no* scope for incumbency advantages, but that description of the determinants of market structure probably exaggerates the views of even hard-core Chicagoans.[13]

2.3. Strategic behavior

Strategic behavior to deter entry is an activity that intentionally compromises productive efficiency to protect an established market. To the extent that established firms strategically choose products, locations, outputs, advertising, R&D or other competitive actions that are motivated primarily by their consequences for entry, rather than by efficiency considerations, this behavior contradicts both the perfectly contestable market and the Chicago school hypotheses.[14]

Do established firms actually engage in activities that are designed to protect their markets against entry? An enormous economics literature has examined the theoretical scope for strategic entry deterrence. Corporate strategy, including lessons in entry deterrence, has become a standard component of business school curricula. The business trade press cites product development and marketing strategies that are designed to improve the security of competitive niches, and court cases allege anticompetitive abuses against frustrated entrants. But this combination of anecdotal evidence is not a reliable index of how often strategic entry deterrence is attempted or how often it works.

The empirical literature gives mixed signals on the importance of strategic entry deterrence. Gilbert and Lieberman (1987) found that firms in concentrated chemical product industries could preempt the expansion of rival established firms by investing in new capacity, but it was not possible, from the available data, to discern whether such behavior is intentional or profitable. Moreover, Lieberman (1987) did not find evidence to support preemptive capacity expansion designed to deter new entry. A possible explanation for Lieberman's results is the difficulty of committing to entry-deterring investment. Gilbert (1986) found that the technological characteristics of most industries are such that a single established firm could not commit to a production level that prevented entry, even if it had the desire to do so. For most industries, the fact that some costs are sunk is not sufficient for a single firm to maintain observed levels of output, and this is a necessary condition to deter entry.

Brand proliferation is commonly cited as another instrument to deter entry, as in the models of Schmalensee (1978) and Bonanno (1987). However, Judd (1985) argues that brand proliferation invites the entry of specialized firms, because the incumbent has an incentive to rearrange its product slate to accomodate an entrant. (See Gilbert and Matutes, 1989, for an attempt to reconcile these two opposing views.) A related strategy is spatial preemption. West (1981) examines the pattern of store location by competing supermarkets and concludes that deterrence is a factor in location choice.

Taken together, these studies constitute only fragile evidence that established firms take potential entry into account when developing their competitive policies. Clearly, given the popularity of models of strategic behavior and their central role in the literature on potential competition, more work is needed to confirm or reject this proposition.

2.4. Industry responses to entry

Different theoretical models of potential entry make different assumptions about what new competitors expect to happen if they enter a market. But what responses have actually confronted new entrants in the past?

Yip (1982) surveyed managers in markets that experienced entry over the period 1972–9. Out of 69 instances of entry, Yip selected 36 which he judged to be most successful. These included 21 by direct investment and 15 by acquisition. Managers in the industries that were challenged by these entrants reported that only 29 percent of the entries were viewed as "serious" threats when they occurred. Only 30 percent reported that they responded to entry with price competition, and then only in the case of direct entry, rather than when new management takes over an existing firm.[15] The failure to respond to entry with price competition is not inconsistent with contestability theory or the Chicago school. In a perfectly contestable market, if demand and technological conditions do change, incumbents should not be expected to take entrants seriously because entry would not be viable.

But Yip's data should be interpreted with caution. They are subjective, and the meaning of a "competitive response" is not well-defined. Since they pertain only to the most successful entrants, their success could be a direct consequence of the reluctance of managers of incumbent firms to take the entrants seriously when they first entered the industry. Furthermore, managers might be reluctant to describe their competitive strategies in much detail.

Lieberman (1987) examined how incumbent firms in 39 chemical product industries responded to entry by estimating equations specifying investment rates for established firms and new entrants. He found that entry into the industries characterized by relatively high concentration levels was typically followed by an expansion of capacity by the incumbent firms. Incumbent firms in concentrated industries did not respond positively to expansion by other incumbents, and incumbents in relatively unconcentrated industries did not increase their investment activity in response to new entry.

Lieberman's results are consistent with Caves and Porter's (1977) theory of "mobility deterrence." Incumbent firms (in the relatively concentrated industries in Lieberman's sample) invest to retard the rate of growth of new entrants, but they do not necessarily invest to prevent entry. In an economy with stationary technology and demand, these observations are inconsistent with the contestable market and the Chicago school hypotheses. In an otherwise stationary environment, these models predict that successful entry should coincide with lower output or exit of an incumbent firm. These observations are also inconsistent with common formulations of dynamic limit pricing, in which established firms accommodate entry by reducing their own output in response to production increases by competitive "fringe" firms. Also rejected is the Sylos postulate that established firms will maintain their pre-entry outputs, but an increase in output by established firms is not inconsistent with credible limit pricing, as Bulow, Geanokoplos and Klemperer (1985) explain in discussing Dixit's (1980) limit pricing model.

However, these conclusions from Lieberman's results depend on the assumption of a stationary environment. One might expect entry to coincide with advances in technology or with new information that leads to optimistic expectations of demand growth. In either case, one would expect that both entrants and incumbent firms would react with greater output, so that entrant and incumbent capacity expansion would be positively correlated. However, Lieberman does not find this positive correlation in industries with relatively low concentration levels.

Bresnahan and Reiss (1987) take a different approach to the measurement of incumbent responses to entry. They restrict their set of observations to markets (primarily services in rural areas) that can support no more than a few firms, which allows them to isolate the competitive effects of a discrete entry decision. By examining a cross-section of markets, they are able to estimate a critical market size at which monopoly profits are sufficient to support a single firm. In the same way, they estimate a critical market size that can just support two firms in the same market. Bresnahan and Reiss argue that if firms are equally efficient and if entry does not result in price cutting, then the size of the market that supports two firms should be about twice as large as the size of the market that just supports one firm. However, if entry results in aggressive price competition, then for two firms to survive, the market would have to be more than twice as large as the market that can support a single firm. Their empirical results show a range in the ratio of the critical market size for two firms and for one firm, varying from about two to four. These results suggest that at least in some markets, established firms respond aggressively to entry, which lowers the profit an entrant can expect and should act as a deterrent to potential competitors.[16]

The findings of Bresnahan and Reiss (1987) are consistent with the implications of the classic limit pricing model. Both contestability theory and the Chicago school imply that demand conditions should not adversely affect a second entrant into a market, yet these results suggest otherwise.

2.5. Benefits to incumbency

Much of the preceding discussion was targeted to the question of whether established firms earn persistent, above-normal profits. A related but distinct question is whether these persistent profits result from incumbency, or some other factor. For example, some industries may experience high rates of growth in demand or technological progress that contribute to sustained profits above normal levels. However, if established firms and recent entrants earn similar profits, it would be difficult to conclude that the high profits are a result of incumbency.

Urban, Carter, Gaskin and Mucha (1984) examined 129 frequently purchased consumer brands in 12 U.S. markets. They found that market shares were a decreasing function of the order of the entry of the brand. Early entrants enjoyed larger market shares, all else equal. Large market shares need not imply higher profitability, but the study does suggest that the history of entry into an industry produces some asymmetry in the condition of firms.

Contestability theory predicts that no rents are derived from incumbency. An incumbent firm can protect a natural monopoly, but it cannot earn rents as a result. In addition, the sequence of entry into a market should not, by itself, account for differences in profits or market shares, as all firms are presumed to have access to the same technology.

However, the empirical evidence from Urban, Carter, Gaskin and Mucha is not inconsistent with the weaker hypothesis of the Chicago school, if it happens that earlier entrants tend to be better able to satisfy consumer demands and therefore have higher market shares.

2.6. Entry in deregulated markets

Alfred Kahn once characterized the airlines as "marginal costs on wings." Indeed, sunk costs are small relative to total expenditures in the airline industry. The capital costs of entry into the industry are relatively low and the main component of fixed plant, the aircraft, is extraordinarily mobile and can be put to use in alternative markets in response to changing market conditions. Thus, many expected that the deregulated U.S. airline industry would become the classic example of the effectiveness of the contestability thesis, with industry performance determined more by the threat of entry than by actual competitive circumstances.

This sanguine view was expressed by Bailey and Panzar (1981) shortly after the passage of the Airline Deregulation Act of 1978. Although their findings were qualified by the limited evidence that became available between deregulation and the date of their study, they concluded that potential competition from the major trunk carriers was sufficient to police monopoly pricing behavior in long-haul local markets (greater than 400 miles), but not in local markets of shorter distances where specialized equipment requirements make them less vulnerable to entry. They also concluded that equipment availability limited the effectiveness of potential competition in controlling pricing by trunk carriers.

Subsequent studies of competitive conditions in the U.S. airline industry have generally praised the results of deregulation, but find little support for contestability theory in airline pricing behavior. Airline route prices are sensitive to actual market concentration levels and prices have responded rapidly to entry and exit. There is widespread price discrimination for apparently similar services. The industry has evolved into a network of major hubs where a few airlines account for a major share of enplanements at each airport and entry of new competitors into these hubs has proved difficult (Maldutis, 1987).

Call and Keeler (1985) estimated a model of how fares were determined in major city-pair markets, including as explanatory variables the level of concentration in the market, the estimated elasticity of demand, and the entry of new carriers. They concluded that fares tend to be high in markets where concentration is high and estimated demand elasticity is low, and that incumbent carriers price aggressively in response to entry. Similarly, Bailey, Graham and Kaplan (1984) found that fare levels were positively correlated with the degree of market concentration and that average fares in markets served by newly certified carriers were 20 percent lower than in similar markets that did not experience entry of new carriers.

Call and Keeler used these observations and the behavior of restricted and unrestricted fares to evaluate the predictive power of several alternative models of oligopoly behavior, including contestability theory, dynamic limit pricing, and a variant of classical limit pricing emphasizing differentiated products.[17] The authors reject the hypothesis that airline markets were contestable over the period they studied.[18] They found support for pricing behavior reflective of dynamic limit pricing, concluding (p. 243) that "the evidence strongly supports the hypothesis that unrestricted fares have fallen on high-density routes, and that the fall has not been immediate, but gradual, occurring with the entry of new and existing firms on to new routes." However, this finding is only partial support for dynamic limit pricing, because it shows only that entry took time and not that established firms adjusted their pricing to retard entry. Call and Keeler also found support for a variant of classical limit pricing exploiting product differentiation barriers to entry.

Using data collected over a longer post-deregulation time period, Morrison and Winston (1987) also conclude that airline pricing does not support the contestability hypothesis. Rather than looking at the effects of entry as in Call and Keeler (1985), Morrison and Winston focus on the role of potential competitors, which they define as carriers that serve at least one of the two airports in a particular city-pair route but do not serve that route. These carriers should have relatively small sunk costs of entry and exit. They found that the existence of potential competitors did act to control prices, but the effect was not as large as the control influenced by actual competitors, and prices tended to be above competitive levels. Their findings offer strong support for the classic model of limit pricing. Potential competition matters, but established firms are able to exploit barriers to entry and maintain prices above competitive levels.[19]

These studies and the observations in Kahn (1988) provide generous evidence that incumbent airline carriers typically responded to the entry of aggressive carriers by selectively cutting prices on those routes which were challenged, and typically the competition took the particular form of lower prices for restricted travel. The industry went through periods of price-cutting that, in Kahn's opinion, were not sustainable. Industry profitability experienced wide swings, a result that is inconsistent with free entry and exit.

The industry has experienced a massive restructuring since deregulation in 1978. Entry occurred on a large scale, followed by bankruptcies and mergers. Low cost carriers forced reorganization by the major carriers. The structure of airline service changed to a "hub and spoke" travel network. These changes make it more difficult to reach conclusions about the role of potential entry, but we know enough to suggest serious defects in contestability theory as it might apply to the airlines. For example, Call and Keeler found that entry into new markets by trunk airlines depressed prices in much the same way as entry by non-trunks, despite the fact that the trunks should have cost structures that are similar to the costs of established firms. Deregulation has brought an increasing awareness of the importance of sunk costs and other factors that limit the effectiveness of potential entry in the industry. These include ground support facilities (both cost and availability) and marketing innovations such as the frequent flyer program which increase brand loyalty. There are also indications that control of computerized reservation systems is a factor in the ability of an airline to achieve success in new markets (U.S. Department of Transportation, 1988).

The present hub and spoke organization of the airline market is consistent with the conclusion that potential competition is only partially effective in this industry, and thus not consistent with the theory of contestable markets. Market concentration at airport hubs is typically high, and the dominant firms at these hubs appear to enjoy market power that is not controlled by potential competition (Borenstein, 1988; 1989). It also casts doubt on the model of dynamic limit pricing, where a steady flow of entry slowly but surely erodes the market power of established firms. With the evidence that was available in 1985, Call and Keeler concluded that entry would eventually undermine any substantial exercise of market power in the airline industry. Later findings do not support this conclusion. The long-run behavior of the industry may be more indicative of the limit pricing model, where scale and product differentiation barriers to entry translate into persistent advantages for incumbent firms.

3. A Summing Up

Potential competition is important as a mechanism to control market power, as was observed by Clark, Bain, Sylos-Labini and others. But these scholars considered potential competition to be an imperfect control. With the theory of perfectly contestable markets, potential competitors were elevated to a status comparable to that of actual competitors. In the theory of contestability, potential competition is an almost perfect control on monopoly power, the qualification being that price will equal average cost with potential competition, whereas price will equal marginal cost with actual competition in contestable markets. The observations presented here suggest that potential competition is important, but not as powerful as the theory of contestable markets implies.

With the diverse observations available and the rather loose connection between theoretical models and testable hypotheses, one can search for and find some support to bolster almost any theory of behavior with potential competition. This should be expected, since the circumstances of each industry are unique and models that explain competitor behavior in one industry may be inappropriate to describe behavior in another. Yet, one function of economics is to make testable generalizations about economic behavior, and in this role we have a responsibility to draw conclusions that apply as accurate generalizations, if not in every individual situation.

My strongest conclusions focus on the general validity of the model of perfectly contestable markets. There is only weak evidence consistent with this theory, and the amount of inconsistent evidence is substantial. In fairness to the proponents of the contestable markets theory, it was developed under the assumption that entry and exit are free, and tests of the theory should recognize this condition. Adherents of contestability theory can argue that many of the observations discussed in this paper are irrelevant to the theory because no one expects industries with substantial entry costs to be contestable. But a theory that applies only when entry and exit costs are strictly zero is of little practical value. The central question is whether contestability theory makes useful predictions about markets that are close to being perfectly contestable.

The experimental evidence provides some support for contestability theory, but the support depends on careful specification of strategies for the market participants. When strategies are not so tightly constrained, the experiments show only that competition is effective in controlling monopoly prices when entry barriers are small, a conclusion that follows from any of the models considered here. The specific conclusion of contestability theory – that potential competition is as good as actual competition – is not clearly supported by the outcomes of market experiments.

Airline markets were expected to have relatively low entry and exit costs, and with their availability of data, they have been a popular testing ground for the theory of contestable markets. Here again, most of the studies cast doubts on the theory. Although sunk costs may be relatively low for airlines, the validity of contestability theory also depends on the assumption that prices move slowly relative to capital. The speed with which airline competitors can respond to pricing initiatives, along with other factors that limit entry at airports and encourage brand recognition, have undermined the recent effectiveness of potential entry in this industry. These observations do not invalidate the theory of contestable markets, but they do suggest that different examples are needed to illustrate how the theory is relevant to actual markets.

The evidence is much less conclusive among the other competing theories of potential entry, which probably results from the large variation in the conditions of entry across industries. A host of studies find that some industries change in ways that are consistent with the dynamic limit pricing model. Profits are eroded over time as new entry occurs, but the success rate of new entrants is low and above-normal profits persist for a long time. These observations could also be construed as consistent with the classic limit pricing model. The Chicago school cannot be dismissed either, because evidence that established firms act strategically to discourage entry is more anecdotal than actual.

It should be all too clear that despite a large body of data, the need for further empirical work in this area is abundant. But what is needed is rather different from the focus of most of the empirical work to date. Most existing studies have concentrated on the magnitude of entry and exit and the persistence of profits. Instead, what is needed is a better understanding of competitive behavior in the presence of potential competition. Economists need to learn more about the extent to which price and non-price behavior of established firms is conditioned on the threat of potential entry. Do new entrants respond to past episodes of entry and to the present strategies of established firms? Are potential entrants affected by the behavior of established firms as assumed in the classic limit pricing model? Both contestability theory and the Chicago school implicitly assume that present prices are good indicators of post-entry profitability. When are these assumptions valid?

Progress has been made on these fronts, with recent advances coming from the study of specific industries, such as airlines, where the responses to competitive strategies can be examined in microscopic detail. Continued research that integrates theoretical models of competitive strategy with industry-level observations should be a productive tool in understanding the real potential of potential competition.

Notes

1 A particular example of the non-accommodation assumption is the "Sylos postulate" that established firms will maintain their pre-entry outputs, named after the work of Sylos-Labini (1962, originally published in Italian in 1958). Game theorists will recognize this assumption as Nash–Cournot behavior on the part of entrants, with the incumbent acting as a Stackelberg leader.

2 Although limit pricing is consistent with a range of incumbent responses to entry, we should not observe that established firms consistently reduce output to accommodate new entry.

3 For example, as formulated by Gaskins (1971), a dominant firm chooses a price path (p_t) to maximize

$$\prod (t_0) = \int_{t_0}^{T} (p_t - c)[D(p_t) - x_t]dt$$

where $D(p_t)$ is total demand at price p_t, x_t is the total supply from competing firms, and c is the dominant firm's average cost of production (taken to be constant). It is assumed that the rate of change of x_t is an increasing function of the price set by the dominant firm.

4 Much criticism of contestability theory has focused on the extent to which sustainability is a feasible and necessary condition of market equilibria. It is not difficult to construct examples of markets in which sustainable price-quantity pairs do not exist. Some familiar models of imperfect competition, such as the Nash–Cournot model, generate equilibria that do not satisfy the conditions of sustainability.

5 A perfectly contestable market does not assure that the selection of products that are offered for sale will maximize total economic surplus subject to the break-even constraint. With economies of scale, there is a particular set of products that results in the largest economic surplus. Perfectly contestable market equilibria may exist with more than one set of products. Taking prices as given, an entrant firm may not be able to introduce the most efficient set of products without making losses. This would not be the case if firms were able to price discriminate, but contestability theory as formulated by Baumol, Panzar, and Willig (1982), assumes that firms are restricted to linear prices.

6 In principle, contestability could be generalized to make it more similar to the predictions of the Chicago school. Suppose firms had access to different technologies. Then the contestability

result might imply that established firms are winners of a second price auction, in which the market price is determined by the next most efficient firm. Although a model with these properties has been described by Grossman (1981), there has been little attempt to apply this theory to actual markets.

7   The following discussion parallels that in Schwartz (1986).

8   In these experiments, when a single firm supplies the entire market, average cost is equal to marginal cost because the firm is capacity constrained. Therefore the competitive price and the efficient price subject to nonnegative profits are the same.

9   Harrison and McKee (1985) conducted market experiments with a design similar to that in Coursey, Isaac and Smith (1984) (no sunk costs, symmetric price offers). They also found that prices were closer to competitive than to monopoly levels, but they concluded that a system of regulation through franchise bidding was superior to market competition in limiting profits.

10 In Table 1, Coursey, Isaac and Smith (1984, p. 67) state the supply side of the contestable markets hypothesis as "supply unrestricted at the competitive price by at least one firm." But the prediction of the theory for their experimental design is supply at a price equal to average cost by only one firm.

11 The experimental design is complicated by the fact that the incumbent pre-commits to an entry permit that lasts from period 1–10, but thereafter is on an equal footing with the entrant.

12 Comparing their results to an earlier set of experiments with no sunk costs, Coursey, Isaac, Luke and Smith (1984, p. 82) conclude that "the effect of an entry cost is to weaken support for the strong form of the contestable markets hypothesis," in that prices converge to average cost in fewer cases. But once entry occurs, sunk costs should be irrelevant (except, perhaps for any role they might play in the formation of reputations).

13 For example, Demsetz (1982) attributes informational and reputational advantages of early entrants as part of the costs of doing business and not barriers to entry. But Farrell (1986b) argues that such factors can work decidedly against new entrants.

14 Of course, the line between deterring entry and efficiency is not always clear. It is possible that entry prevention results in outcomes that are more efficient than when entry is accommodated by established firms, and actions that are economically efficient may have incidental deterrence effects (von Weizsacker, 1980, Demsetz, 1982).

15 None of the alternative theories presented here predict the consequences for industry performance of a change in management, in the absence of a change in industry concentration. Given the prevalence of entry by acquisition of existing assets, this is an important deficiency.

16 Some of the Bresnahan and Reiss findings are counterintuitive. For example, the ratio was highest for veterinarians and lowest for auto dealers, while casual observations on the extent of rivalry might suggest the opposite. A difficulty with their approach is that their market measures are static, whereas entry should depend on the present value of profit streams that can be earned in a market. Bresnahan and Reiss measure only current market size, not present value profits, and the relationship between the two can be tenuous.

17 The variant on limit pricing was the "fat cat" model in Fudenberg and Tirole (1984). Models with similar consequences include Farrell and Shapiro (1988) and Gelman and Salop (1983).

18 The correlation between prices and concentration is not, by itself, a rejection of contestability theory. For example, some markets could be natural monopolies while others are natural oligopolies, and the (perfectly contestable) price could be higher in the first instance. Also, shifts in demand or technology can change a market from a natural monopoly to a natural duopoly, with a lower (perfectly contestable) price. Then entry would correlate with lower prices, even if the market is contestable. (I am grateful to John Panzar for this observation.) However, Call and Keeler's observed significance of demand elasticity is not consistent with contestability theory, and the observations on entry and exit suggest that the price movements

reflect competition and not technology. Moreover, Caves, Christensen and Tretheway (1984)
find constant returns to scale for trunk and local carriers.

19   Peteraf (1988) also suggests that potential competition has not affected pricing behavior in the
way expected by contestability theory. Specifically, potential competition was not observed to
be more effective in situations where the sunk costs associated with entry are less.

References and Further Reading

Aghion, P. and Bolton, P. (1987): "Entry Prevention through Contracts with Customers," *American
Economic Review*, 77, 308–402.

Bailey, E. and Panzar, J. (1981): "The Contestability of Airline Markets During the Transition to
Deregulation," *Law and Contemporary Problems*, 44, 125–45.

Bailey, E., Graham, D. and Kaplan, D. (1984): *Deregulating the Airlines: An Economic Analysis*.
Cambridge: MIT Press.

Bain, J. (1956): *Barriers to New Competition*. Cambridge: University Press.

Baumol, W. and Willig, R. (1986): "Contestability: Developments Since the Book," in D. J. Morris,
P. J. Sinclair, M. D. Slater and J. S. Vickers (eds), *Strategic Behavior and Industrial Competition*,
Oxford: Clarendon Press.

Baumol, W., Panzar, J. and Willig, R. (1982): *Contestable Markets and the Theory of Industry
Structure*. New York: Harcourt, Brace, Jovanovich.

——— (1986): "On the Theory of Perfectly-Contestable Markets," in J. E. Stiglitz and F. Mathewson
(eds), *New Developments in the Analysis of Market Structure*, Cambridge: MIT Press.

Biggadike, E. (1979): *Corporate Diversification: Entry, Strategy and Performance*. Boston: Division of
Research, Graduate School of Business Administration, Harvard University.

Bonanno, G. (1987): "Location Choice, Product Proliferation and Entry Deterrence," *The Review of
Economic Studies*, 54, 37–45.

Borenstein, S. (1988): "Hubs and High Fares: Airport Dominance and Market Power in the U.S.
Airline Industry," Institute of Public Policy Studies discussion paper 278, University of Michigan.

——— (1989): "The Competitive Advantage of a Dominant Airline," Institute of Public Policy
Studies discussion paper 280, University of Michigan.

Bresnahan, T. and Reiss, P. (1987): "What Kinds of Markets Have Too Few Firms?," working
paper, Stanford University.

Bulow, J., Geanakoplos, J. and Klemperer, P. (1985): "Holding Idle Capacity to Deter Entry,"
Economic Journal, 95, March, 178–82.

Call, G. and Keeler, T. (1985): "Airline Deregulation, Fares, and Market Behavior: Some Empirical
Evidence," in A. Daugherty (ed.), *Analytical Studies in Transport Economics*, Cambridge: Cambridge University Press.

Caves, D., Christensen, L. and Tretheway, M. (1984): "Economies of Density versus Economies of
Scale: Why Trunk and Local Service Airline Costs Differ," *Rand Journal of Economics*, 15,
Winter, 471–89.

Caves, R. and Porter, M. (1977): "From Entry Barriers to Mobility Barriers: Conjectural Decisions
and Contrived Deterrence to New Competition," *Quarterly Journal of Economics*, 97, May,
247–61.

Clark, J. B. (1902): *The Control of Trusts*. New York: Macmillan.

Comanor, W. S. and Wilson, T. (1967): "Advertising, Market Structure and Performance," *Review
of Economic Studies*, 49, November 423–40.

Coursey, D., Isaac, R. M. and Smith, V. L. (1984): "Natural Monopoly and Contested Markets:
Some Experimental Results," *Journal of Law and Economics*, 27, April, 91–113.

Coursey, D., Isaac, R.M., Luke, M. and Smith, V. L. (1984): "Market Contestability in the Presence
of Sunk (Entry) Costs," *Rand Journal of Economics*, 15, Spring, 69–84.

Demsetz, H. (1973): "Industry Structure, Market Rivalry and Public Policy," *Journal of Law and Economics*, 16, 1–9.

Desmsetz, H. (1982): "Barriers to Entry," *American Economic Review*, 72, March, 47–57.

Dixit, A. (1979): "A Model of Duopoly Suggesting a Theory of Entry Barriers," *Bell Journal of Economics*, 10, Spring 20–32.

Dixit, A. (1980): "The Role of Investment in Entry Deterrence," *Economic Journal*, 90, March, 95–106.

Farrell, J. (1986a): "How Effective is Potential Competition?" *Economic Letters*, 20, 67–70.

—— (1986b): "Moral Hazard as an Entry Barrier," *Rand Journal of Economics*, 17, 440–9.

—— and Shapiro, C. (1988): "Dynamic Competition with Switching Costs," *Rand Journal of Economics*, 19, 123–37.

Friedman, J. (1979): "On Entry Preventing Behavior and Limit Price Models of Entry," in S. Brams, A. Schotter and G. Schwodiauer (eds), *Applied Game Theory*, Vienna: Springer.

Fudenberg, D. and Tirole, J. (1984): "The Fat-Cat Effect, the Puppy-Dog Ploy, and the Lean and Hungry Look," *American Economic Review: Papers and Proceedings*, 74, May, 361–6.

Gaskins, D. W. Jr. (1971): "Dynamic Limit Pricing: Optimal Pricing Under Threat of Entry," *Journal of Economic Theory*, 2, September, 306–22.

Gelman, J. R. and Salop, S. (1983): "Capacity Limitation and Coupon Competition," *Bell Journal of Economics*, 14, Autumn, 315–25.

Geroski, P. (1987): "Do Dominant Firms Decline?" in D. Hay and J. Vickers (eds), *The Economics of Market Dominance*, Oxford: Basil Blackwell.

—— Gilbert, R. J. and Jacquemin, A. (*nd*): "Barriers to Entry and Strategic Competition," in H. Sonnenschein and J. Lesourne (eds), *Fundamentals of Pure and Applied Economics: Encyclopedia of Economics*, Harwood Academic Publishers.

Gilbert, R. J. (1986): "Preemptive Competition," in J. E. Stiglitz and F. Mathewson (eds), *New Developments in the Analysis of Market Structure*, Cambridge: MIT Press. 90–125.

—— and Harris, R. G. (1984): "Competition with Lumpy Investment," *Rand Journal of Economics*, 15, September, 197–212.

—— and Lieberman, M. (1987): "Investment and Coordination in Oligopolistic Industries," *Rand Journal of Economics*, 18, 17–33.

—— and Matutes, C. (1989): "Product Line Rivalry with Brand Differentiation," working paper, University of California.

Grossman, S. J. (1981): "Nash Equilibrium and the Industrial Organization of Markets with Large Fixed Costs," *Econometrica* 49, September, 1149–72.

Harrison, G. W. (1986): "Experimental Evaluation of the Contestable Markets Hypothesis," in E. Bailey (ed.), *Public Regulation*, Cambridge: MIT Press.

—— and McKee, M. (1985): "Monopoly Behavior, Decentralized Regulation, and Contestable Markets: An Experimental Evaluation," *Rand Journal of Economics*, 16, Spring, 51–69.

Hause, J. C. and du Reitz, G. (1984): "Entry, Industry Growth and the Microdynamics of Industry Supply," *Journal of Political Economy*, 92, August, 733–57.

Judd, K. L. (1985): "Credible Spatial Preemption," *Rand Journal of Economics*, 16, Summer, 153–66.

—— and Peterson, B. (1986): "Dynamic Limit Pricing and Optimal Finance," *Journal of Economic Theory*, 39, 368–99.

Kahn, A. E. (1988): "Surprises of Airline Deregulation," *American Economic Review: Papers and Proceedings*, 78, 316–22.

Kamien, M. I. and Schwartz, N. L. (1971): "Limit Pricing and Uncertain Entry," *Econometrica*, 39, May, 441–54.

Lieberman, M. (1987): "Post-Entry Investment and Market Structure in the Chemical Processing Industries," *Rand Journal of Economics*, 18, 533–49.

Maldutis, J. (1987): "Airline Competition at the Fifty Largest U.S. Airports," Salomon Brothers, Inc., August.

Masson, R. and Shaanan, J. (1982): "Stochastic Dynamic Limit Pricing: An Empirical Test," *Review of Economics and Statistics*, 64, August, 413–23.

—— and —— (1986): "Excess Capacity and Limit Pricing: An Empirical Test," *Economica*, 53, 365–78.

Milgrom, P. and Roberts, J. (1982): "Limit Pricing and Entry Under Incomplete Information: An Equilibrium Analysis," *Econometrica*, 50, March, 443–59.

Modigliani, F. (1958): "New Developments on the Oligopoly Front," *Journal of Political Economy*, 66, June, 215–32.

Morrison, S. and Winston, C. (1987): "Empirical Implications and Tests of the Contestability Hypothesis," *Journal of Law and Economics*, 30, 53–66.

Mueller, D. C. (1977): "The Persistence of Profits above the Norm," *Economica*, 44, November, 369–80.

—— (1986): *Profits in the Long Run*, Cambridge: Cambridge University Press.

Omori, T. and Yarrow, G. (1982): "Product Diversification, Entry Prevention and Limit Pricing," *Bell Journal of Economics*, 13, Spring, 242–8.

Orr, D. (1974): "An Index of Entry Barriers and Its Application to the Market Structure Performance Relationship," *Journal of Industrial Economics*, 23, September, 39–49.

Pakes, A. (1987): "Mueller's 'Profits in the Long Run'," *Rand Journal of Economics*, 18, 319–32.

Peteraf, M. (1988): "Contestability in Monopoly Airline Markets," Northwestern University discussion paper 10.

Salop, S. (1979): "Strategic Entry Deterrence," *American Economic Review*, 69, May, 335–8.

Schmalensee, R. (1978): "Entry Deterrence in the Ready-to-Eat Breakfast Cereal Industry," *Bell Journal of Economics*, 9, Autumn, 305–27.

Schwartz, M. (1986): "The Nature and Scope of Contestability Theory," in D. J. Morris, P. J. Sinclair, M. D. Slater and J. S. Vickers (eds), *Strategic Behavior and Industrial Competition*, Oxford: Oxford University Press.

Spence, A. M. (1977): "Entry, Capacity, Investment and Oligopolistic Pricing," *Bell Journal of Economics*, 8, Autumn, 534–44.

Stigler, G. J. (1968): *The Organization of Industry*. Homewood, Illinois: Richard D. Irwin.

Stiglitz, J. E. (1981): "Potential Competition May Reduce Welfare," *American Economic Review*, 71, May, 184–9.

—— (1987): "Technological Change, Sunk Costs and Competition," *Brookings Papers on Economic Activity*, 3, 883–937.

Sylos-Labini, P. (1962): *Oligopoly and Technical Progress*. Cambridge: Harvard University Press.

Urban, G., Carter, T., Gaskin, S. and Mucha, Z. (1984): "Market Share Reward to Pioneering Brands," *Management Science*, 32, 645–59.

U.S. Department of Transportation, (1988): *Study of Airline Computer Reservation Systems*, May.

von, Weizsacker, C. C. (1980): "A Welfare Analysis of Barriers to Entry," *Bell Journal of Economics*, 11, Autumn, 399–420.

West, D. S. (1981): "Testing for Market Preemption Using Sequential Location Data," *Bell Journal of Economics*, 12, Spring, 129–43.

Weitzman, M. L. (1983): "Contestable Markets: An Uprising in the Theory of Industry Structure: Comment," *American Economic Review*, 73, June, 486–7.

Yip, G. S. (1982): *Barriers to Entry: A Corporate Strategy Perspective*. Lexington: Ballinger.

CHAPTER TWELVE

The Evolution of U.S. Airline Competition

SEVERIN BORENSTEIN

Source: *Journal of Economic Perspectives*, 6, 2 (1991), pp. 45–73.
Reprinted with the permission of the author and the American
Economic Association. © American Economic Association.

Studies by academic economists were a significant force in the movement towards deregulation of the domestic airline industry in the early 1970s (Levine, 1965; Jordan, 1970; Keeler, 1972; Douglas and Miller, 1974). During the critical 1977–8 period in which deregulation was imposed first *de facto* by the Civil Aeronautics Board (CAB) and then *de jure* by Congress, the chairman and vice-chairman of the CAB were economists. For the 14 years since deregulation, economists have continued intensive study of the industry, in part because of the unusual availability of reliable firm-and transaction-level data and in part because of the rare opportunity to observe an industry as it evolves from strict economic regulation to fairly unimpeded competition and strategic behavior.

The simplest prediction of economists about airline deregulation, and one of the few on which nearly all economists agreed, was that deregulation would improve consumer welfare in comparison to continued price and entry regulation. Fourteen years later, nearly all economists still agree on this, though the degree of enthusiasm for the deregulation outcome varies considerably. There was substantial disagreement among economists about the market structure that would result. Because studies of scale economies in the airline industry had concluded that none existed beyond the scale of the smaller major airlines of the 1970s (Caves, 1962; Eads et al., 1969), many economists argued that deregulation would result in more than the 11 major airlines that existed at the time of deregulation. Others predicted that only a few, or possibly only one, airline would survive at a large scale. Two noted University of Chicago economists, Sam Peltzman and Lester Telser, made a bet in 1979 on whether the 4-firm concentration ratio would be above or below 90 percent by 1985. Peltzman bet that it would be below 90 percent and, as he put it, "won the bet, but lost the war." Nationwide, concentration decreased during the first few years following deregulation, but has turned upward since then.

Though comparisons of the airline industry under regulation and deregulation continue, this is not my primary focus here.[1] As the time since deregulation grows, such comparisons to the "straw man" of regulation are increasingly speculative and decreasingly relevant to the issues at hand. Regulation under the CAB was far from ideal; if it were reimposed today, it would probably be more efficient than the pre-1978 regulation.

Deregulation has also entailed missteps that would not be repeated were the process to be replayed. Therefore, an estimate of the net welfare gain (or loss) resulting from deregulation gives little guidance about the relevant choices that will face policy makers in the future.

For the most part, the lessons that have been learned from the deregulated domestic airline industry are not about government regulation or the process of deregulation, but about the tactics, strategies, and results of competition in a dynamic, complex, and innovative service industry. These lessons are more likely to inform economists about the market process in, for instance, the hotel or fast-food industries than in electric power distribution or other traditional areas of regulation.

The next section reviews the evolution of the domestic airline industry since the late 1970s, when it was abruptly freed from most regulatory constraints on pricing, entry and exit. (International air travel is considered here only as it relates to competition in the domestic industry. This is due both to space limitations and because international air travel remains heavily and idiosyncratically regulated.[2]) The following sections will examine the competitive issues that have arisen since deregulation; the conclusions, and in some cases consensus, that economists have reached on these issues; and the public policy options in dealing with the airline industry in light of these issues.

1. A Brief History of the Deregulated Airline Industry

In the early 1970s, just a few years prior to deregulation, government intervention in the airline industry reached its apex. The CAB had prevented entry of new start-up airlines for many years, but in the early 1970s it also imposed a "route moratorium," ceasing to assign new authority for existing airlines to serve new city-pairs and preventing many airlines from abandoning routes that they no longer wished to serve. At the same time, the CAB decided that the discounts with which it had experimented in the 1960s – such as student fares and discounts for a spouse accompanying a full-fare passenger – conflicted with its mandate for fair and equitable prices, so it greatly reduced the scope for such fares.

By 1976, however, the CAB began to move towards deregulation by again permitting discriminatory fare discounts. In the following two years, the Board permitted free entry of any certified carrier on a few selected routes, breaking with its history of choosing which airlines would compete in each market. It also relaxed the restrictions on chartered service to the extent that charters became close substitutes for regular scheduled flights. Just as some of the major airlines had begun to sue the CAB for violating its congressional mandate by allowing too much competition, Congress passed the Airline Deregulation Act of 1978. The Act set out a time schedule for relaxation of price and entry regulation and permitted the CAB to accelerate that schedule as it deemed appropriate.

New entry boomed and prices fell substantially on most routes, especially long-distance routes. On the shorter routes, which had been cross-subsidized under regulation, real prices did not fall as much and even increased in some cases. Airline profits were at record levels in 1978, but the 1979 oil price shock dampened these gains. As the deep recession of the early 1980s set in, the profits turned to large losses. Entry of new airlines slowed markedly and came to a nearly complete halt by 1983. In the next few years, many of the new entrants and the pre-deregulation smaller carriers either merged with a major carrier or declared bankruptcy and ceased operations. Table 1 presents the evolution of three different measures of nationwide concentration in the industry. By all three measures, concentration increased between 1982 and 1990, and is now higher than it was in 1977. Figure 1 tracks the lineage of the major carriers that operated in 1991.

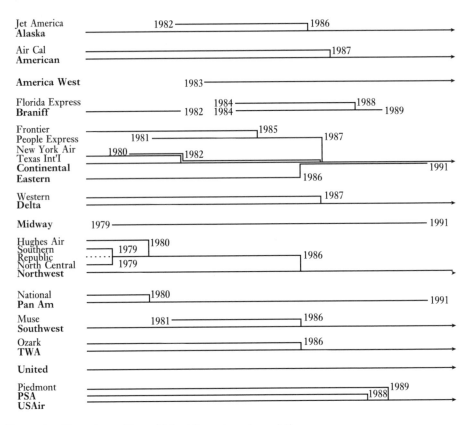

Figure 1   Chronology of large U.S. airlines since deregulation
Source: Kaplan (1986) and *Wall Street Journal,* various issues

Table 1   Measures of domestic airline industry concentration since deregulation

	1977	*1982*	*1987*	*1990*
4-firm concentration ratio	56.2%	54.2%	64.8%	61.5%
8-firm concentration ratio	81.1%	80.4%	86.5%	90.5%
Herfindahl index	0.106	0.093	0.123	0.121

The 4- and 8-firm concentration ratios are the sums of the market shares of the 4 and 8 largest firms, respectively. The Herfindahl index, the sum of the squared market shares of all firms, ranges between 0 and 1.
Source: U.S.D.O.T. Air Carrier Traffic Statistics, Revenue Passenger-Miles.

Measures of national concentration are convenient reference points, but the increase in concentration is less apparent at the city-pair route level, where competitors' products are effective substitutes for one another. Table 2 shows that looking at all traffic, route level concentration decreased substantially between 1984 and 1987, and showed a slight drop between 1987 and 1990. If we examine direct trips, however – those in which the passenger does not change planes – concentration has steadily increased from 1984 to 1990.

This outcome reflects the growth of hub-and-spoke operations. All major airlines now have one or more hubs at which many of their long-distance passengers change planes. This approach has allowed carriers to fill a higher proportion of the seats on their planes and to increase flight frequency of nonstop routes between their hubs and other airports. Since most hub airports can accommodate large-scale operations of only one airline, both logistically and economically, competition has tended to decrease on direct routes to and from the hubs. Yet, because a hub allows an airline to serve a large number of routes with a change of plane at the hub, longer routes and ones on which most passengers change planes are now served by many airlines, each channeling passengers through its particular hub airport. This explains the decline in concentration on longer routes and increase on shorter routes – usually served without a change of plane – when all trips are examined.

One drawback to hub-and-spoke operations is that a larger proportion of passengers change planes, especially on longer trips, instead of flying nonstop from their origin to their destination. The share of trips over 1500 miles that involve a flight change rose from 42 percent in 1978 to 52 percent in 1990. On trips between 500 and 1500 miles, it increased from 33 percent in 1978 to 38 percent in 1990. Gordon (1992) finds that nonstop service has increased on most of the top 500 routes since deregulation, but even on these higher density routes, the increase in nonstop flights has not kept pace with the increase in traffic. Furthermore, the loss of nonstop service is more likely to be evident on smaller routes.

Table 2 Average city-pair Herfindahl indexes

	Market distance in miles					
Year	0–200	201–500	501–1000	1001–1500	1500 +	ALL
All trips						
1984	0.600	0.588	0.537	0.479	0.415	0.531
1987	0.689	0.616	0.498	0.444	0.363	0.512
1990	0.618	0.614	0.518	0.424	0.357	0.506
Direct trips only						
1984	0.601	0.598	0.601	0.581	0.536	0.590
1987	0.691	0.648	0.612	0.587	0.532	0.620
1990	0.612	0.641	0.672	0.625	0.536	0.632

Excludes interline tickets and markets with less than 10 passengers per day. The numbers shown are unweighted averages across routes. The sign and approximate magnitudes of these changes are the same if routes are weighted by either passengers or passenger-miles. All data are for the second quarter of the given year.
Source: U.S.D.O.T. Databank 1A.

Still, by allowing each airline to serve more city-pairs with change-of-plane service, hub systems have decreased the proportion of passengers who need to change airlines as well as planes during their trip. Carlton, Landes, and Posner (1980) and many passenger surveys have concluded that changing airlines imposes substantial additional costs on passengers, due to increased probability of missed connections and lost baggage. The proportion of trips that included a change of airline fell from 11.2 percent in 1978 to 6.9 percent in 1981, 4.0 percent in 1984, and 1.2 percent in 1987 and 1990. While the more recent changes are due in substantial part to mergers among major carriers, the earlier and more significant declines are explained largely by formation of hub-and-spoke systems.

Furthermore, for most travel between non-hub airports, the choice of departure times has been enhanced substantially by hub-and-spoke operations. A thinly traveled route that had one or two nonstops a day under regulation is likely now to have 10 or more possible change-of-plane routings through different hubs spread throughout the day. Finally, hub-and-spoke operations have contributed to the increased use of satellite airports such as Oakland, Burbank, or Orange County in California. Many people would rather fly to these airports with a change of plane than to San Francisco or Los Angeles airports nonstop.

Concerns about the possible anticompetitive effects of hub-and-spoke systems have been fueled by mergers and bankruptcies among some of the larger airlines in the last few years. Eight mergers among major airlines were approved in 1986 and 1987. Two of these mergers, Northwest-Republic and TWA-Ozark, involved airlines that shared the same primary hub. The Department of Transportation (DOT) approved these two combinations over the objections of participants from the Department of Justice.

The industry shakeout intensified following the August 1990 Iraqi invasion of Kuwait that increased jet fuel prices, for a brief period by more than 100 percent. Since then, America West, TWA and Continental have filed for Chapter 11 bankruptcy protection, but continued to operate. Midway, Pan Am, and Eastern have been liquidated, but only after hundreds of millions of shareholders' and creditors' dollars had been spent trying to revive these companies.

Despite the spate of airline mergers and failures, or some have argued because of them, domestic airline prices have not increased relative to costs since most new entry ended in the early 1980s. From the second quarter of 1984 to the second quarter of 1990, before the events in the Persian Gulf, prices increased 4 percent less than DOT's index of airline costs. Many managers in the industry have claimed that cash flow requirements of airlines near bankruptcy or operating under bankruptcy court protection have led to cut-throat pricing. The industry average comparison, however, hides an important dichotomy: prices on short-haul routes, under 500 miles, increased 5 percent more than the cost index between 1984 and 1990, while prices on longer routes increased 10 percent less than cost. Nearly all of these changes occurred between 1984 and 1987; from 1987 to 1990 prices moved closely in line with the DOT cost index.

Many analysts have pointed to airport capacity shortages as the most critical factor affecting competition and efficiency in the domestic airline industry. Though a few airports suffered significant congestion before deregulation, the problem has worsened dramatically since 1978. In part, the increase in airport congestion is a cost of the success of airline deregulation. From 1977 to 1990, domestic air travel increased by 120 percent.[3] During this time, no new airports were built, while expansion of existing airports was greatly hampered by environmental concerns and local zoning and noise restrictions. The formation of hubs also increased the strain on many airports. A hub operates by scheduling many incoming flights at virtually the same time and then many departures 30 to 60 minutes later, thereby increasing airport capacity demands for a given number of flights.

One approach to allocating scarce airport capacity would be to impose congestion-based landing fees, which would increase at times of peak demand. Historically, landing fees have been kept quite low; for example, from $25 for a small private plane (known as general aviation) to $800 for a jumbo jet at Boston's Logan airport. To date, political resistance to peak-load pricing of runway use, particularly from general aviation operators, has successfully prevented its implementation, but recent moves by the FAA indicate that this may soon change. Congestion-based landing fees would also imply that fees would cease to be a linear function of weight, as is common now, raising the cost to smaller commercial planes and general aviation and lowering the cost to large planes. This would reduce use of congested airports by aircraft carrying few passengers. An attempt to implement such a plan in Massachusetts in 1987, however, was successfully challenged in the courts for being "discriminatory."

At a few U.S. airports, permission to have a plane takeoff or land at a given time of the day has been converted into a transferable property right. Such landing slots at Washington National airport and O'Hare in Chicago have recently sold for $.5 to $1.2 million, with the higher prices going for peak time slots. Unfortunately, congestion delays appear to be just as high at "slot-controlled" airports as at similar-size airports without slots, though changing the number of slots permitted would surely affect this result. The issue of airport congestion is likely to become more important in the future.

Innovation has also occurred in the technology and strategy of selling air travel. Computer reservation systems (CRSs) used by travel agents have become a central and critical part of airline ticketing. Travel agents now write more than 80 percent of all tickets, up from about 50 percent before deregulation. There are four CRS systems currently in use, but Sabre (owned by American) and Apollo (owned principally by United, but also by USAir and some foreign airlines) have more than 75 percent of the business. Worldspan (Delta, TWA, and Northwest) is still a distant third in volume. System One (Continental) is considered the poorest sister of the industry and may cease operations soon. Most tickets written by travel agents are booked through one of these systems.

The airlines, led principally by American, have also successfully explored marketing strategies to increase customer loyalty. Frequent flyer programs (FFPs) and travel agent commission override programs (TACOs) were introduced shortly after deregulation. Most travelers are aware of frequent flyer programs, which give free travel or other bonuses to passengers who have flown some preset amount with a firm. TACOs have been called "frequent booker" programs for travel agents. In a typical TACO agreement, airline X promises a travel agency a 15 percent commission rate, instead of the usual 10 percent, if that agency books more than 80 percent of its tickets on airline X. In a 1990 study by the General Accounting Office, more than half of all agents reported receiving commission overrides.

The biggest surprise from the first 13 years of deregulation has been the pervasive importance of hub-and-spoke operations in the logistic and competitive development of the domestic airline industry. Hubbing has enhanced the efficiency of airline operations, increased the effectiveness of marketing devices such as frequent flyer programs, changed the scale at which an airline must operate to be competitive, and exacerbated problems of congestion at major airports. For this reason, much of the economic research on the industry since deregulation has investigated issues related to the hubs and airline networks in a deregulated industry. The result has been a few well-established facts, and a growing number of questions that remain to be answered.

Nearly all of the research on airline competition addresses one or both of the two critical questions that underlie most work in applied industrial organization: "What equilibrium will evolve in the industry and what will be the speed and path of transition to that equilibrium?" and "What type or degree of government intervention will maximize social welfare?" The next two sections focus on the first question, though the observations have immediate consequences for the second. The topics divide roughly into what might be called "structure" and "strategic" issues; the former covers questions of the effect of market structure on market power – the influence of potential competition, airline net-works, and mergers—while the latter includes the complexities in airline competition that result from the sophisticated marketing strategies that have developed – frequent flyer plans, TACOs, price discrimination, and computer reservation systems.

2. Structure Issues in Airline Competition

Many of the pre-deregulation predictions about competition in the airline industry relied on simple textbooks models. The application of contestability theory to the airline industry generally assumed an industry of independent city-pair markets, failing to take account of the importance of airline networks and hub operations. Likewise, the strategic advantages to an airline of dominating service at an airport were not foreseen by many. The textbook theories generally concluded that actual or potential competition would drive all prices to the marginal costs of the most efficient firms, with less efficient airlines reorganizing or exiting the industry. The actual outcome has been quite a bit different.

2.1. The disappointing evidence on contestability and potential competition

For many economists and policy makers, advocacy of airline deregulation was simply a rejection of the incredibly inefficient regulation of the previous 50 years. For others, however, a cornerstone of support for airline deregulation was contestability theory, reliance on the disciplining effect of potential competition. It was argued that an airline can enter a new market quickly and with low sunk costs, particularly if the entrant already serves one or both of the endpoints of the route (Bailey and Panzar, 1981). The importance of a potential entrant serving both ends of a route before entering has been demonstrated by Berry (1990a) and Morrison and Winston (1990). Berry, for example, finds that in a sample of 281 new markets entries that occurred between the first and third quarters of 1980, the new competitor already served both endpoints in 245 cases and at least one endpoint in 277 cases.

Unfortunately, potential competition appears to be no substitute for actual competition. While contestability theory in its pure form suggests that the number of actual competitors should have no effect on prices, many studies have found that the number of airlines actually competing on a route has a significant effect on the price level (Bailey, Graham, and Kaplan, 1985; Call and Keeler, 1985; Morrison and Winston, 1987; Borenstein, 1989; Hurdle et al., 1989). In 1990, prices on routes with two active competitors averaged about 8 percent lower than on monopoly routes. A third active competitor was associated with another 8 percent price drop. Nor can these effects be attributed to cost savings from higher traffic volume on more competitive routes; volume per airline is smaller on average on routes with more competitors.

Studies that attempt to explain cross-sectional variation in average prices find that a potential competitor in a market has from one-tenth to one-third the competitive impact of an actual competitor (Morrison and Winston, 1987; Borenstein, 1989; Brueckner, Dyer, and Spiller, 1990). In retrospect, the result is not very surprising. If sunk costs are non-trivial, albeit small, and an incumbent can respond in price and quantity as quickly as a new competitor can enter, then the incumbent has little incentive to respond in advance of actual entry (Stiglitz, 1987). Advertising and the short-run losses associated with inauguration of service on a new route seem to be sufficient sunk costs to inhibit contestability in the airline industry.

Even the small estimates of potential competition effects that have been made may be too high. The measure of potential competition – the number of airlines serving one or both endpoints, but not the route itself – is almost certainly endogenous. A low price in a market will encourage well-positioned potential competitors to stay out of the market, thus increasing the number of potential competitors observed. This effect is likely to bias the analysis towards a larger estimated impact of potential competition. Reiss and Spiller (1989) make an ambitious attempt to model this problem explicitly.

A related approach to comparing the effects of actual and potential competition is to observe when entry and exit occur; that is, the result of a potential competitor becoming an actual competitor and *vice versa*. Joskow, Werden, and Johnson (1990) find that after controlling for cost factors, routes with unusually low prices are subject to more exit than others, and that exit of a competitor leads to a 10 percent average price increase for the incumbents that remain. Routes with abnormally high prices, however, are no more likely to experience new entry than are other routes. Still, they estimate that new entry on average drives down prices by about 9 percent. Morrison and Winston (1990) find that routes with lower-than-average prices, controlling for distance, are actually more likely to be entered than other routes and that routes with higher-than-average prices are more likely to experience exit of a competitor. These studies lend little support to a belief that potential competition disciplines airline markets. They do, however, strongly indicate that prices and entry are jointly determined by some process that is not well understood.

Whinston and Collins (1990) use a stock market event study to analyze the effect of entry. They look at a series of announcements by People Express during 1984–5 about specific routes that it planned to enter in the ensuing weeks. They find that the average combined equity value loss to the incumbents in these markets reflect a pretax loss in future profits of 25 percent to 43 percent of the annual revenues earned on these routes. Such a finding indicates that substantial rents were being earned prior to new entry, again reinforcing the conclusion that potential competition cannot substitute for actual competition in airline markets.

2.2. *Airport concentration and market power*

The value of hub-and-spoke networks for the cost savings they offered was recognized before deregulation, but few saw that hubs would also be valued for the market power that they permit. For people whose origin or destination is the hub city, there is often very little competition. The hub-and-spoke networks have evolved to the point that one airline will generally fly to another airline's hub only from its own hub. United, for instance, offers nonstop service to Atlanta – Delta's major hub – only from Denver, Chicago-O'Hare, and Washington-Dulles, three of United's four largest hubs.

Table 3 lists the 30 largest U.S. airports in declining order of what might be called "hubness" – the percentage of passengers using the airport who are traveling through,

Table 3   Hubbing and airport concentration at the 30 largest U.S. airports

Airport	Percent changing planes	Airport Herfindahl	Airport fare premium	Rank by size
Charlotte	75.7%	0.579	18.8%	20
Atlanta	69.0%	0.347	17.2%	3
Memphis	67.7%	0.355	27.4%	29
Dallas/Ft. Worth	65.8%	0.386	20.5%	2
Pittsburgh	62.1%	0.529	15.9%	16
Salt Lake City	61.3%	0.430	19.1%	28
St. Louis	56.2%	0.354	−4.0%	13
Chicago – O'Hare	55.7%	0.270	14.8%	1
Denver	54.1%	0.272	15.3%	7
Minneapolis	51.0%	0.418	31.5%	15
Houston – Intercontinental	49.5%	0.423	15.6%	19
New York – Kennedy	47.3%	0.202	2.9%	6
Detroit	43.6%	0.296	−0.7%	11
Baltimore	40.5%	0.299	9.1%	26
Phoenix	33.1%	0.205	−28.4%	9
Miami	31.0%	0.171	−14.3%	14
Seattle	27.3%	0.145	8.7%	24
San Francisco	25.3%	0.145	−1.5%	5
Los Angeles	25.2%	0.110	−5.3%	4
Philadelphia	24.9%	0.217	11.2%	22
Honolulu	22.4%	0.199	−20.8%	17
Newark	19.6%	0.292	11.5%	12
Las Vegas	18.9%	0.177	−27.8%	23
Houston – Hobby	17.5%	0.481	−23.4%	30
Orlando	16.8%	0.180	−15.6%	21
Boston	13.8%	0.120	9.0%	10
Washington D.C. – National	11.1%	0.125	10.7%	18
Tampa	11.0%	0.181	−12.4%	27
San Diego	6.6%	0.138	−18.1%	25
New York – La Guardia	6.2%	0.118	9.5%	8

Source: U.S.D.O.T. Databank IA, second quarter, 1990.

rather than to or from, the city. Not surprisingly, the hubs tend to be located towards the center of the country. Table 3 also demonstrates that the markets for travel to and from hub airports tend to be more concentrated than at nonhub airports. The third column shows the Herfindahl index of to/from traffic, known as local traffic, at the airport. The correlation between the percentage of passengers changing planes at the airport and the local traffic Herfindahl is 0.74 in this list.

It has been clearly and frequently demonstrated that average prices for local traffic at concentrated airports are significantly higher than prices on other routes (Borenstein, 1989; GAO, 1990a; DOT, 1990; Berry, 1990b; Abramowitz and Brown, 1990; Evans and Kessides, 1992 or later). This is illustrated by the fourth column of Table 3, which presents the average ratio of fares on local routes at these airports compared to national average fares on routes of the same distance. The correlation between this "airport fare premium" and airport concentration is 0.44 in this table. Econometric studies have found this effect while controlling for traffic volume, business/tourist mix, the number of plane changes a passenger must make, heterogeneous costs of airlines, concentration and market share on specific routes, airport-specific congestion, and many other factors. The effect, however, does not carry over to itineraries in which the passenger just changes planes at concentrated airports; "through" passengers using these airports pay prices about equal to the national average.

One of the leading explanations for this result is the market power and customer loyalty advantage that a locally dominant airline can achieve through use of frequent flyer plans and travel agent commission override programs (TACOs). One piece of evidence for this theory is that the dominant carrier at a concentrated airport charges higher average prices on routes to and from the airport than other airlines serving the same routes (Borenstein, 1989; Evans and Kessides, 1992 or later). Borenstein (1991) also demonstrates that, controlling for price and service quality, the dominant airline at an airport attracts a disproportionate share of passengers who originate their trips at the airport, with the advantage being especially great on business-oriented routes. As explained below, one would expect that frequent flyer programs give a dominant airline a greater advantage in attracting business travelers than others. Other studies have included airport-level entry barriers as an explanation for the higher prices at dominated hubs. Abramowitz and Brown (1990) control explicitly for the effect of majority-in-interest (MII) clauses in gate lease contracts, which allow a dominant airline to block construction of new airport facilities. The effect of MII's is statistically significant, but small, increasing prices by less than 2 percent.

Thus, hub-and-spoke networks are not just a source of increased production efficiency; they are also associated with airport concentration and dominance of a hub airport by one or, occasionally, two airlines. This airport dominance ensures a degree of protection from competition and control over price that was not foreseen prior to deregulation and has significantly altered airlines' strategies in the deregulated industry.

2.3. Horizontal mergers

For better or worse, the Reagan administration's *laissez-faire* views of mergers provided an experiment in industry restructuring, especially in the airline industry. In particular, two mergers between hub-sharing carriers in October 1986 were an excellent opportunity to observe the effect of increased airport dominance.

The merger between Northwest and Republic caused prices at Minneapolis, the primary hub they shared, to increase substantially faster than the national average immediately before and after the merger. The largest price increase occurred on routes where the two merging airlines had been the only competitors, increasing 23 percent faster than the national average. Overall, the average Minneapolis/St. Paul passenger's ticket price went up 11 percent faster than the national average between the year before the merger and the year after (Borenstein, 1990; see also Werden, Joskow, and Johnson, 1991).

The effect of the TWA-Ozark merger on prices at St. Louis is more mixed. When all tickets to and from St. Louis are considered, price went up 8 percent faster than the national average (GAO, 1988; Borenstein, 1990). The increase, however, is driven by a few high-volume routes on which prices increased dramatically following the merger. These were routes on which TWA and Ozark competed prior to the merger along with at least one other airline. Increases on routes with just TWA and Ozark were not faster than the national average. Finally, as Table 3 indicates, St. Louis remains a remarkably low cost city to fly to or from given that it is a concentrated hub airport dominated by TWA.

Such hub mergers appear to decrease service on routes where the merging airlines had competed. This may reflect the elimination of "redundant" service or it could be indicative of reduced competition. The interpretations are not mutually exclusive. Overall, the number of flights offered by the dominant airlines fell 7 percent at Minneapolis following the merger and 11 percent at St. Louis (Borenstein, 1990). Both mergers led to an increase in the total number of cities served from the hubs and to a large increase in the number of connections passengers could make without changing airlines (Huston and Butler, 1988).

The overall welfare effects of these and other mergers require a balancing of the increased market power that may result with the possibility of improved service and efficiency. Brueckner, Dyer, and Spiller (1990) estimate that increased traffic for a dominant airline at a hub will significantly lower the prices it charges to consumers changing planes at the hub on their way to another location. Thus, the merger of two airlines' operating hubs at the same airport would be expected to increase the volume of the traffic carried by the surviving carrier on the spokes of the network and thus decrease costs and prices to through passengers. In fact, prices for passengers traveling through Minneapolis on Northwest-Republic fell by 1.5 percent relative to industry average prices between the second quarters of 1986 and 1987, while passengers traveling through St. Louis on TWA-Ozark saw their prices increase by 0.5 percent relative to industry average during this period.

Morrison and Winston (1989) attempt to compare the costs of market power and the benefits of improved efficiency for six mergers among jet carriers that took place between 1985 and 1988. Besides the two mentioned above, these included Delta-Western, American-Air California, USAir-Piedmont, and USAir-Pacific Southwest Airlines. They find that the six mergers in total had a small positive effect on consumers. This result, however, depends on a large positive estimate of the change in the value of frequent flyer bonuses, an estimate that is probably too optimistic.

Morrison and Winston estimated that frequent flyer miles were valued by consumers at an average of 2.7 per mile earned in 1983, about 20 percent of the average fair paid per mile at that time, implying that the minimum 20,000 miles necessary for a free domestic ticket would produce a bonus worth $540. The estimate seems high, considering that supersaver fares for the longest transcontinental trips were under $400 at the time. More importantly, most frequent flyer mileage is never cashed in for free travel, because the consumer either never earns enough mileage for a bonus, never uses the bonus once it is earned, or uses it only for a first-class upgrade, which is likely to be a less valued use. In fact, only 5 to 8 percent of passenger miles are "non-revenue," which includes both frequent-flyer bonus tickets and employee travel. If frequent flyer program bonus trips are valued as much as paid-for trips, then the value enhancement of FFPs would be in the 3 to 7 percent range, after deducting the 1 to 2 percent of passenger miles comprised by employee travel. The actual value enhancement is probably much lower than 3 to 7 percent, since many FFP trips would not have been taken had the traveler had to pay actual fares. On the other hand, to the extent that FFP mileage is used for upgrades and other perks, the actual figure could be somewhat higher. If one assumes that FFPs enhance average ticket value by 6 percent instead of 20 percent, or about 0.8 cents per mile, the overall impact of the mergers they analyze falls from a $67 million annual increase in consumer welfare to about a $200 million loss (Morrison and Winston, 1989, Table 7).[4]

In reality, the short-run welfare effect of the mergers between direct competitors was probably significantly negative. Whatever production efficiency that the mergers may have permitted does not seem to have been reflected in prices, but the increased market power was often evident. The long-run effect is much more difficult to estimate, because many of the firms – Ozark being the most notable – would probably have failed within a few years absent these mergers. Morrison and Winston (1989) point out that since mergers are extremely unlikely to be "unscrambled" once they have occurred, the appropriate long-run comparison is not to that market structure before the merger, but to the alternative possible market structures and mergers – with the potential for greater efficiency and competition increases – that are foreclosed by the merger.

2.4. Vertical mergers with commuter airlines

As the much-publicized horizontal airline mergers were taking place in the mid-1980s, less-publicized vertical network mergers and joint marketing agreements were forming between major airlines and commuter carriers who serve short routes that transport passengers to larger airports. In the early part of deregulation, many commuters agreed to operate in coordination with, and under the name of, a major jet airline. These "codesharing" agreements meant that the commuter airline's flights would be timed to connect with the major airline and would be listed on computer reservation systems under the airline code of the major. In the later 1980s, these agreements were often replaced by vertical integration.

Such agreements and mergers permit greater coordination of flight schedules, baggage handling, marketing, and frequent flyer programs, which may increase the consumer's value of the joint product and may lower actual production costs. In addition, however, they can raise the costs of entry for a new airline at airports where the major and the commuter airline connect. These agreements and mergers do not lead to strict exclusivity – it is possible to connect from a United-affiliated or -owned commuter airline to an American flight – but realistically, a commuter airline cannot coordinate its schedule, airport location, and marketing with many different major airlines. If a new major carrier can compete with the commuter-affiliated major at an airport only by having its own coordinated commuter carrier, there is an associated increase in the sunk cost of starting service at the airport. The theoretical debate over whether efficiency-enhancing vertical coordination might also be used anticompetitively is far from settled.

Consumers occasionally complain that codesharing agreements are an attempt to mislead consumers about who is operating their flights. Most of these complaints are about flying on a propeller plane, however, not about the ownership or operation of the flight. Since both ownership and equipment information are available when the ticket is purchased, and since an airline will have incentive to make sure that an affiliated commuter does not harm the airline's good name, government intervention here does not seem wise.

2.5. Cost heterogeneity among airlines

The absence of substantial economies of scale was one of the leading arguments for deregulation of the airline industry. The inference drawn by many economists was that all airlines would attain approximately the same costs of production. Yet the studies on which this conclusion was based were not very sophisticated. Essentially, they regressed the total costs of an airline on a measure of output and the costs of inputs, with little focus on the actual production process. Caves, Christensen, and Tretheway (1984) improved upon the earlier studies by distinguishing economies of density – additional passengers on a given set of routes – from economies of scope – a proportional expansion of the size of the network as output expands. Using data from 1970 to 1981, they found substantial density economies, but did not find that increases in the scope of operations lowers an airline's unit costs.

One of the most remarkable results of the various cost studies has received little attention: the significant variation in unit production costs across firms. After controlling for input prices and output characteristics, the carrier-fixed effects in the study by Caves, Christensen, and Tretheway (1984) exhibit a substantial spread, with the least efficient major airline estimated to have 40 percent higher unit costs than the most efficient ones. Since none of these studies corrects for the endogeneity of wages – wages tend to decline when an exogenous cost increase causes the firm's profits to decline – these spreads might well be understated.[5]

Table 4 presents the cost per passenger-mile and per seat-mile for the 12 largest U.S. carriers during 1990. The cost heterogeneity appears to be as significant as ever, with the highest cost airline, USAir, exhibiting unit costs about 64 percent above Southwest's. Caves, Christensen, and Tretheway identify average flight length as the most significant cause of costs heterogeneity, but Southwest actually has a shorter average flight length than USAir, implying that Southwest should exhibit higher costs. America West, which operates a more traditional hub-and-spoke system than Southwest and makes greater use of travel agents and computer reservation system ticketing also has much lower costs than the other major airlines while flying shorter average trips than most of the others.

What is the source of these cost differences? One answer seems to be managerial ability. The managers of Southwest and American, which has the lowest costs among the large major airlines, are recognized in the industry for being smart and sophisticated. USAir has a reputation for poor management that dates back to the days of regulation.

Table 4 Costs of major U.S. airlines, 1990

Airline	Average cost per passenger-mile	Average cost per seat-mile	Average flight distance
Southwest	0.111	0.067	376
America West	0.122	0.075	544
Eastern	0.128	0.078	606
Midway	0.144	0.084	636
American	0.144	0.088	776
United	0.145	0.093	809
Continental	0.150	0.087	743
Northwest	0.150	0.094	665
TWA	0.151	0.089	719
Delta	0.155	0.090	626
Pan Am	0.168	0.101	693
USAir	0.189	0.112	463

Source: U.S.D.O.T. Air Carrier Traffic and Financial Statistics.

Still, that just leads to the question of how the inefficient managers hold on to their jobs. Levine (1987) and others have argued that the separation between ownership and control explains the persistence of bad management at some U.S. airlines. The canonical case in the industry is Pan Am, which lost money in all but one year between 1980 and its 1991 demise – a net loss of more than $2 billion – but survived by selling off assets on which huge capital gains were realized, such as land that the company owned in Tokyo. To survive, inefficient firms must retain substantial market power. USAir is a good example. It has two significant dominated hubs, Pittsburgh and Charlotte, where it has over 80 percent of the enplanements. Eastern, which had high costs prior to its bankruptcy declaration and associated wage concessions, exemplifies the alternate outcome. Before its demise, Eastern's most significant airport position was at Atlanta, where it had to coexist with Delta, a much more efficient and sophisticated airline.

These answers, however, are *ad hoc* and the evidence is largely anecdotal. The heterogeneity of management ability and entrenchment in the airline industry, along with the detailed public data on company operations and finances, may offer an unusual opportunity to look more systematically at the internal dynamics of large corporations. These heterogeneities appear to play as large a role in the competitive evolution of the industry as the differences in market shares and concentration across firms and markets.

3. Strategic Developments in Airline Competition

Under government regulation, airline managers had few marketing decisions to make beyond reviewing the latest brand-image advertisements. Not only did the CAB tell each airline which products it could sell, it also dictated the ways in which they could be sold and the prices that could be charged. When these constraints were lifted, the marketing of air travel quickly became a dynamic and central part of the airline business. The airlines that innovated most quickly gained in market share and profitability.

3.1. Loyalty-inducing marketing devices

The first frequent flyer program was introduced in 1981 by American Airlines, but it took until 1986 for all of the major airlines to start one. In some ways, frequent flyer programs (FFPs) are just quantity discounts: "Buy four trips, get the fifth one free." Supporters of this view have pointed out that quantity discounts are present in many industries and that they are particularly appropriate if marginal cost is below average cost, because they allow total costs to be covered while decreasing the inefficiency that results when the marginal price is above marginal cost.[6] However, FFPs also create strategic advantages for an airline with a large market share and reduce the threat of potential competition.

Strategic advantages may result both from the way frequent flyer mileage is accumulated and the way that bonuses are paid out. Because the marginal value of the reward increases as the customer builds up miles or points on a single airline, FFPs encourage travelers to choose the airline that they are most likely to fly on in the future. Thus, the airline with the most service from the traveler's home airport is particularly attractive, because it serves many markets that the consumer may need to travel in the future. Furthermore, the most common bonus – a free flight anywhere in the U.S. – will be more valuable on an airline that offers substantial service from the consumer's home airport than on an airline with little service there.

Frequent flyer programs are targeted primarily at business travelers, taking advantage of the principal-agent problem resulting when the traveler, monitored imperfectly by his employer, does not make the efficient tradeoff between lower prices, or reduced travel time, and extra FFP bonuses (Levine, 1987). In essence, the frequent flyer bonus is a kickback to the purchasing agent, in this case the employee. In a survey of travel agents conducted by the General Accounting Office (1990b), more than half said that their business customers select flights to match their frequent flyer program "always or almost always."

Bonuses earned on business travel are also untaxed fringe benefits which may jointly benefit the employer and employee while harming the government and other taxpayers. Defenders of frequent flyer programs argue that even if the employer finds it costly to monitor frequent flyer miles and bonuses directly, it can still calculate an expected value of the bonuses earned by certain types of employees, and count that toward the employees' compensation. Though this will transfer some of the agent's gains to the principal, it does nothing on the margin to lessen inefficient (and cost-increasing) schedule choices of the employee. Nor does it address the advantage that the dominant airline in an area gains through such bonuses.

What frequent flyer programs are to business travelers, travel agent commission overrides (TACOs) are to travel agents. Most travel agents earn increased commission rates from at least one airline in return for steering passengers to those airlines. No work has explicitly modeled the effect of TACOs on competition among airlines, but there is widespread belief within the industry that TACOs are most effectively used by the dominant airline in an area (Levine, 1987; Borenstein, 1991). Just as with FFPs, the rewards for increased bookings on an airline are designed to encourage the agent to concentrate bookings on a single carrier. The anecdotal evidence that exists supports the notion that travel agents will be most affected by the TACO program of the dominant airline in the area (DOT, 1988). This is due in part to the correlation between use of a carrier's computer reservation system and receipt of commission overrides from that airline, as discussed below.

Of course, salespeople of many goods and services receive different commissions on various brands and are thus biased toward the high-commission sale. Are commission overrides for travel agents any different? Probably. Most travelers are not aware of TACOs and do not realize that the agent has a reason to prefer one airline over another, so are less likely to be wary of the agent's advice. Agents hold themselves out as unbiased conveyors of travel information. Moreover, even if customers were aware, it is extremely difficult for any customer to monitor travel agent performance, due to the complexity and constant flux of prices and seat availability in a market.

Increases in brand loyalty or switching costs, such as from FFPs or TACOs, may also facilitate market division and tacit collusion (Banerjee and Summers, 1987). These programs lower the cross-elasticity of demand between products, reducing the incentive for competitive price cutting. This effect may be less important than the dominant firm advantage that the devices permit, because airlines use these strategies most aggressively in areas where they have large market shares, but the two uses are not mutually exclusive. In either case, it is clear that the airlines view these aspects of retailing their product as much more than simple price cuts or commission payments.

3.2. Information and distribution channels

At the time of deregulation, many industry analysts forecast a streamlined distribution system, possibly with most ticketing done through machines similar to automatic teller machines, so that the travel agent industry would shrink or even disappear. Instead, travel agents are now more central to the distribution of air travel services than ever before, thanks to the complexity of airline fare structures and the frequency of price changes. With the current computer reservation systems (CRSs), the agent can look up the schedules, fares, and seat availability on all airlines simultaneously, then reserve a ticket and seat assignment, enter the traveler's frequent flyer number, and even print out boarding passes.

The earliest entrants in the computer reservation service industry, American's Sabre and United's Apollo systems, signed up many travel agents before competing CRSs became widely available. Later entrants have never attained significant penetration in more than a few locations, areas in which the airline owning the CRS has a large share of the flights and traffic. In recent years, Sabre and Apollo have been accused of attempting to lock travel agents into exclusive use of their systems through various contract requirements: damages charged to agents who choose to switch systems may have been out of proportion to actual costs; access to an airline's TACO program may have been illegally tied to use of its CRS; and minimum use clauses may be the reason that nearly all travel agents use only one airline's CRS for all bookings. These complaints continue, but so far have not been confirmed in court.

The earliest complaints registered against the CRSs were by airlines that did not own a system of their own, in reaction to the biased presentation of flight information. Prior to a

1984 CAB rule outlawing the practice, airlines would systematically list their own flights more prominently than those of their competitors, a practice known as "screen bias." A recurrent and naive view of computer reservation systems is that they are equivalent to advertising for an airline, and that every airline could start a reservation system and engage in such promotion. In reality, the sunk costs for starting a computer reservation system are substantial, because complex industry-specific software must be developed, tested, and marketed. The learning effects also appear to be significant; Sabre and Apollo systems continue to exhibit more sophistication and capabilities, as well as much larger market shares, than the other CRSs. Economies of scale are quite substantial, because the software production and updating expenses are unrelated to the number of users on the system. The 1984 CAB rule forbidding "screen bias" was implicitly based on the decision that CRSs are essential facilities for selling air transport, and so should be available on a comparable basis to all airlines. Because the software that runs a computer reservation system is so complex, some screen bias almost surely remains, though it is certainly less obvious or important than before 1984.

Computer reservation systems have also become a critical tool in the administration of travel agent commission overrides. Although the 1984 rule explicitly forbids tying of TACOs to use of a carrier's CRS, such practices almost certainly continue (DOT, 1988). Ownership of the CRS used by an agent makes it easier for an airline to implement a TACO program, because most programs are based on the *share* of the agent's bookings that go to an airline, requiring reliable information on all of the agents' sales.

The bias in travel agent booking associated with the CRS it uses, called the "halo effect," was studied in 1988 by the DOT. They found that the airline owning a travel agent's CRS receives a disproportionate share of the bookings from the agent, even after a rough control for commission overrides. The strong results they get, however, could reflect factors other than CRS influence and are certainly subject to endogeneity bias. In a city with a dominant airline that owns a reservation system most of the agents in that city are likely to adopt that CRS for its superior information on the airline's flights and a greater share of agents are likely to be on the dominant airline's TACO program. Furthermore, the dominance will likely inspire greater customer loyalty through frequent flyer programs, which is not controlled for at all.

The ownership of a computer reservation system may also be a deterrent to new entry and price competition, both because of the halo effect, and also because airline B must pay a booking fee to airline A for every airline B ticket booked through airline A's CRS. Under the 1984 CAB rules, a CRS must charge the same booking fees to all airlines, but such a non-discrimination rule cannot affect the internal price or cost paid by the airline-owner for booking its own tickets. In Dallas, for instance, where more than 90 percent of the travel agent bookings go through American's Sabre system, high booking fees on Sabre could discourage entry into all Dallas routes. The DOT study found that booking fees are well above marginal or average cost.

The high-speed transmission of complex information through computer reservation systems has also raised concerns about collusion among the airlines. It appears to be common practice for an airline to announce, through the CRSs, that its price on a certain route will increase by some amount beginning on a certain date in the future. The carrier then waits to see if others will match. If they do, the price increase is implemented. If they do not, the airline suggesting the increase will either withdraw it or push back the implementation date. Other airlines might counteroffer with a smaller increase, effective a day after the first increase. Then the first airline many proceed with a smaller increase, or counteroffer again. All of this occurs without the airlines changing any prices on actual sales, because the negotiation goes on with effective dates two or three weeks hence.

Each airline's fare on the computer reservation system for each route has a descriptive code, usually a string of 5 or more letters and numbers, that may contain further information about what the airline is suggesting or at which competitor a price change might be targeted (Nomani, 1990). In one incident reported in the *Wall Street Journal*, Continental introduced a new fare on a certain route with a fare code that included "HP," the two-letter designation for America West, which Continental appeared to be attacking with the discount. The code may have included "HP" to inform other airlines that Continental was targeting the fare cut at America West and was not interested in starting a widespread fare war.

If such signaling and possible attempts at collusive price fixing exist, they give a basis for concern over the increased national concentration figures, even if route concentration has been fairly stable. The language of signaling is easier to develop and communicate if there are many opportunities for a small number of firms to interact, than if there are many firms. The impact of multimarket contact on tacit or explicit collusion and thus prices has been examined in many industries, but only Evans and Kessides (1991) has focused on domestic airlines. They find that multimarket contact has a significant effect on prices, increasing average round-trip ticket prices by more than $20. The Department of Justice has announced an investigation of airline price signaling. There is sure to be more work done in this area.

3.3. Price discrimination and dispersion

In the early days of deregulation, some economists called the prevalence of discount fares a sign that the new competitive equilibrium had not yet been reached. As time went by, however, and more airlines adopted complex fare structures, explanations shifted. Unlike the pre-deregulation discounts, availability of today's low fares is limited to a given number on a flight, with that number differing across flights in response to differences in demand. In this way, discounts may reflect peak-load pricing (Salop, 1978; Gale and Holmes, 1990). The restrictions on discounts have also been refined, however, so as to approach the discriminating firm's ideal: imposing prohibitive discount-qualification costs on members of the less-elastic demand group (for example, business travelers are almost never willing to stay over a Saturday night), while retaining relatively easy availability to the group with more elastic demand.

Frank (1983) suggested that the fare differentials were cost-based, because the travelers paying higher prices were those who demanded more frequent service and were thus responsible for higher fixed costs. In models of price discrimination under imperfect competition, Borenstein (1985) and Holmes (1989) have made this argument more rigorous, while clarifying that such pricing is still discriminatory in the traditional sense of differential mark-ups above marginal cost. Even though airline prices are discriminatory, there is no clear reason to believe they are less efficient than a single price set by firms with the same market power. While price discrimination necessarily results in exchange inefficiency – any given quantity produced is not allocated to the users who value it most highly – it also may increase total output compared with firms that face the same demand functions and each charge a single price.

The pattern of price discrimination in the airline industry is in itself interesting and surprising. After controlling for peak-load pricing effects, Borenstein and Rose (1991) find that discrimination is greater on more competitive routes. The theoretical works by Borenstein and Holmes predict this pattern if discrimination is based more on variations in customer willingness to switch flights – scheduling flexibility and brand loyalty – than on variations in customer reservation prices for the trip. Borenstein and Rose also find that airlines owning CRSs have significantly more price dispersion on a route, supporting the industry wisdom that effective market segmentation requires the sort of management and computer sophistication that varies widely among the airlines.

4. Bankruptcies, Bailouts, and Public Policy

The crisis in the airline industry that began in the last half of 1990 raised numerous public policy issues. Unsecured debt markets were closed to the weaker airlines, many of which requested financial assistance from the federal government. Did this represent a failure of capital markets, or simply a market signal that these companies should not be extended loans because they are unlikely to be able to repay them? In late 1990, the government considered several short-run fixes, including short-term loans, tapping the Strategic Petroleum Reserve specifically to lower jet fuel prices, and permitting airlines to delay remitting some of the 10 percent ticket tax to the government, thereby making interest-free loans to the airlines.

None of these steps was taken. The main reasons seemed to be that the industry was not yet so close to anticompetitive levels of concentration that the impending bankruptcies would be pivotal and, in addition, that a bailout appeared likely to spend taxpayer's money without a real hope of benefits. Bankruptcy courts handling the Eastern and Pan Am cases took a very different view, willingly spending the remaining funds of these firms to give the companies every possible chance to survive. Effectively, these courts were taxing the holders of the firms' debt. Their motivation seemed to be the preservation of competitors in the marketplace, not protection of creditors' wealth.

The bankruptcy proceedings have highlighted the fact that large corporate failures in the U.S. always involve some government intervention. The default regulator of the industry is the bankruptcy court judge. The fact that government will be involved does not mean, of course, that earlier intervention by some other government body will necessarily lead to better outcomes, but it does imply that a simple hands-off approach to the disruption and increasing concentration in the airline industry is not realistic.

The policies that have been suggested to respond to declining competition in the domestic airline industry range from more deregulation to complete reregulation. Here is a brief summary and critique of the most probable actions, ordered from least to most interventionist.

4.1. Foreign ownership and foreign competition

Currently, foreign interests can hold no more than a 49 percent voting share in a U.S. airline (increased from 25 percent in 1991) and cannot otherwise control the company.

Advocates of permitting greater foreign ownership argue that it would provide a quick infusion of capital to the distressed airlines.

Opposition to this proposal has rested on national defense arguments, such as the questionable view that the aircraft of foreign-controlled airlines might be unavailable for government use in times of war or other disaster. The obvious response is to require that all aircraft serving U.S. routes are subject to confiscation during national emergencies. The real weakness of this plan is that no queue of foreign investors is waiting to sink money into the crippled U.S. airlines; they are more interested in buying part of American or United than Continental or TWA. Again, the capital markets might be telling us something about these airlines.

The corollary to foreign investment is competition from foreign airlines on domestic U.S. routes. Among economists and policy makers, this idea is seen as one whose time has come, but it will still be a long time in the implementation. The main sticking point is that the European Community and most Asian countries are not yet ready to allow U.S. airlines to fly domestic and international routes within and between their countries. U.S. negotiators are understandably hesitant to drop barriers to foreign airlines in the U.S. without gaining access to foreign markets. In fact, most foreign carriers are much less efficient than U.S. airlines, due to years of government ownership and protection, and they have comparatively little sophistication in modern airline marketing strategies. Without subsidies from their home governments, they would not be likely to offer much competition to U.S. airlines. As with foreign ownership, foreign competition is probably a good idea, but not one likely to have a dramatic effect on the domestic airline industry.

4.2. Airport expansion, peak-load pricing, and privatization

Some critics believe that the only remaining problem in the U.S. domestic airline industry is that the government is still in the airport business. They argue that if airports were privatized, the operators would charge efficient peak/off-peak prices and would respond to market incentives for expansion. This argument ignores the fact that airports are natural monopolies, which would lead to restricted output in the absence of regulation, and that airports create large externalities, which would lead to *de facto* regulation even without an explicit regulatory body. Furthermore, without competition from other airports, an operator's profits would probably be maximized by permitting dominance of the airport by a single carrier and then extracting the carrier's rents with high facility fees.

Still, there is no doubt that current airport management fails to implement many of the market-based incentives, most notably peak-load pricing of runway and facility use, that would lessen the inefficiencies that permeate the system (Morrison, 1987). A switch to peak-load pricing – including a recognition that a general aviation plane landing or taking off creates about as much congestion as a commercial jet – would significantly improve allocation of limited airport capacity.

Rational funding of airport expansion would also greatly improve airport congestion. In a program that seems to be based more on politics than economics, the DOT currently distributes most funds for airport improvements through a program that is strongly biased towards thousands of small general aviation and commercial "reliever" airports. These airports are not operating at capacity and are not used by jet aircraft. Shifting funds towards improvements that have the highest shadow value would substantially lessen airport congestion without increased funding.

Funding is not the only constraint on airport expansion, however, Neighborhood opposition to increased air traffic is often quite strong and the incumbent dominant airlines at many airports are powerful opponents to facility expansion. Improved airport management and expansion planning would increase competition, but the impact may be disappointingly small. Even with higher capacity and peak-load pricing, airport access problems may remain. While additional capacity at an airport could facilitate new entry, the monopoly rents earned by a dominant incumbent would probably give it the incentive to outbid potential new entrants for rights to the additional capacity. Anecdotes about control of gates for the purpose of excluding competitors are commonplace. At the four slot-controlled airports, minimum-use rules have been imposed to keep the owner of a slot from holding it for exclusionary purposes.

4.3. Limiting loyalty-inducing devices for flyers and travel agents

Since frequent flyer programs and travel agent commission overrides are widely thought to give a competitive advantage to the dominant airline in an area, their elimination or curtailment has been suggested. Discussion continues at DOT and in Congress about the possibility of banning frequent flyer programs or taxing them as fringe benefits. The latter approach poses practical difficulties, since the IRS would have to distinguish between awards earned from personal travel and those earned from business travel. An alternative approach would be to require that airlines allow sale and transfer of frequent flyer miles, and thus lessen the lock-in effect of these programs. The airlines have made it clear that they would respond to such a rule by cancelling their frequent flyer programs. FFPs do seem to present a barrier to entry in areas where one airline is dominant. There are clear inefficiencies from the principal-agent problem that they create, without which they would probably be abandoned by the airlines. No good data have been found on FFPs, however, so reliable estimates of the magnitudes of these effects are still lacking.

The principle argument against eliminating frequent flyer programs seems to be the generic concern that limits on the forms in which companies can do business should be enacted only in extreme situations, because the results of such rules can be unpredictable. For example, some have argued that sustainable prices may not exist for hub operations, and that the loyalty induced by frequent flyer programs could allow an airline to maintain efficient economies of density at their hubs. However, such an effect would be empirically indistinguishable from barriers to entry that enhance market power and lead to supra-competitive prices.

A minimalist proposal to address the principal-agent problem induced by travel agent commission overrides would require that agents disclose the average commission rates that they receive from each airline. If this information were posted at the travel agency and enclosed with each ticket sold, customers would be made aware that the agent receives different commission rates from different airlines and would know the direction in which the agent is likely to be biased. A more significant step would be to require that airlines pay equal commission rates to all agents. This, however, intervenes in the retailing process to a much greater extent than in other industries and possibly to a greater extent than is justified by the principal-agent problem.

Opponents of policy actions on TACOs make the arguments that the travel agent industry is very competitive and that differential commission rates are common in many industries. However, given that airlines think TACOs have an effect on the agents' airline choice and travel agents report in surveys that they do (*Travel Weekly*, 1988), the commission disclosure proposal seems a minimally invasive way to alert consumers to the bias.

4.4. *Divestiture or new restrictions on computer reservation systems*

The most frequent suggestion to correct biased treatment of carriers in listing flights and updating information on computer reservation systems is to require that airlines sell off their systems. The proposal would also eliminate differential booking fees that effectively result when one carrier owns the CRS that is charging above-cost fees. To the extent that owner-airlines use their CRSs to coordinate or enforce TACOs, divestiture will weaken the impact of commission overrides. Levine (1987) and others who are very familiar with CRSs argue that no realistic amount of rule making and enforcement will remove these advantages without divestiture.

The problem with divestiture is that it would be a very costly form of intervention. Separated from one another, the computer reservation systems and the airlines would each be worth quite a bit less, because both the "bias" advantages for the airlines and any economies of jointly operating and making innovations in these two related businesses would disappear. The litigation that would precede and follow such a move would be lengthy. The net benefits of divestiture could well be positive, but the variance of most guesses about the benefits is large both relative to the expected benefit and in actual dollar terms. CRS divestiture would not reduce concerns about tacit collusion through CRS pre-announcement of price changes.

5. Conclusion

The airline industry was deregulated not because economists or politicians knew what the deregulated equilibrium would look like, but because they believed that the deregulated outcome would be better than regulation. Airline executives also did not know what the new equilibrium would be. The managements of Delta and American vigorously opposed deregulation, but they have reaped the greatest benefits from it. The industry has gone through a wave of new entry and mass exit, while the survivors have reorganized to focus on hub and spoke operations. Movement towards equilibrium has been slow in part because the structure of the new equilibrium has not been clear; the players were guessing about the outcome as much as the observers, and were probably not much better informed.

The long-run equilibrium in the airline industry is still not clear. Eventually, the number of major airlines might be reduced to just a few, reinforcing calls for renewed price regulation. If so, that may be the inevitable result of network economies that may make competition unworkable. More likely, however, it would result from marketing devices that give strategic advantages to larger firms and incumbents operating hub and spoke systems.

The current task for policy makers is to make sure that efficient production and competition, not anticompetitive marketing devices, determine the winners and losers in the airline industry as it moves towards a new equilibrium. At the least, this requires opening markets to foreign competition, improving access to and pricing of airport ground facilities, requiring that travel agents disclose their commission rates, and monitoring CRSs closely for biased and strategic uses. Of course, any future mergers among major airlines must also be examined with great skepticism. As the number of competitors has continued to decline in the last year, the arguments have been bolstered for more aggressive actions: banning frequent flyer programs, requiring airlines to pay flat and equal commission rates to all agents, and forcing divestiture of the CRSs. These moves would imply a heavier hand of government intervention, but still much less than the price and entry regulation that may otherwise result.

Notes

1 See Bailey, Graham, and Kaplan (1985), and Morrison and Winston (1986) for the most complete analyses of the effects of deregulation during the first half decade. Dempsey (1990) compares the trend in average prices since 1978 to the pre-deregulation trend, adjusting only for fuel price changes, and finds that prices are higher than they would have been under deregulation. The significant weakness in this comparison is that real fuel prices fell during the period Dempsey analyzes, while most other airline input prices, for which Dempsey does not control, were constant or increased in real terms. The Morrison and Winston study does a much more complete comparison and finds substantial price decrease relative to regulation.

2 Those interested in whether the single European market scheduled to go into effect at the end of 1992 might offer some hope for increased international airline competition should consult the cautious view of McGowan and Seabright (1989) and Borenstein (1992).

3 Growth in travel was even greater in the 13 years prior to 1977, but this was probably due to improvements in speed and comfort of travel with the introduction of jet aircraft. Since deregulation, there have been very few technological improvements in air transport quality.

4 Furthermore, Morrison and Winston assume that the value of a FFP bonus ticket increase linearly with an increase in the number of cities that the airline serves, implying that a merger in which the surviving carrier serves 50 percent more cities than either merging carrier did would increase the value of all FFP on the carrier tickets by 50 percent. Given that one always has the option of paying for a ticket to fly where one wants, the size and unbounded nature of the value increase does not seem credible.

5 Greenwald, Salinger, and Stiglitz (1991) argue that the cost disparities may be self-enforcing. In a theoretical model and empirical application to the airline industry, they find that firms in financial distress may be less able to invest in productivity-enhancing improvements, thus increasing their cost disadvantage.

6 This argument is frequently made in support of declining block pricing schedules for public utilities.

References

Abramowitz, A. D. and Brown, S. M. (1990): *The Effects of Hub Dominance and Barriers to Entry on Airline Competition and Fares*, mimeo, U.S. General Accounting Office, Washington DC, October.

Bailey, E. E. and Panzar, J. C. (1991): "The Contestability of Airline Markets During the Transition to Deregulation," *Law and Contemporary Problems*, 44: 1 Winter, 125–45.

——Graham, D. R. and Kaplan, D. P. (1985): *Deregulating the Airlines*, Cambridge: MIT Press.

Banerjee, A. and Summers, L. (1987): "On Frequent-Flyer Programs and Other Loyalty-Inducing Economics Arrangements," Harvard Institute of Economic Research discussion paper 1337, September.

Berry, S. T. (1990a): "Estimating a Model of Entry in the Airline Industry," Yale University working paper.

——(1990b): "Airport Presence as Product Differentiation," *American Economic Review*, 80, May, 394–9.

Borenstein, S. (1985): "Price Discrimination in Free-Entry Markets," *Rand Journal of Economics*, 16, Autumn, 380–97.

—— (1989): "Hubs and High Fares: Airport Dominance and Market Power in the U.S. Airline Industry," *Rand Journal of Economics*, 20, Autumn, 344–65.

——(1990): "Airline Mergers, Airport Dominance, and Market Power," *American Economic Review*, 80, May, 400–04.

——(1991): "The Dominant-Firm Advantage in Multi-Product Industries: Evidence from the U.S. Airlines," *Quarterly Journal of Economics*, 106, November, 1237–66.

——(1992): "Prospects for Competitive European Air Travel," in W. J. Adams (ed.), *Europe After 1992*, Ann Arbor: The University of Michigan Press.

——and Rose, N. L. (1991): "Competition and Price Dispersion in the U.S. Airline Industry," National Bureau of Economic Research working paper 3785, July.

Brueckner, J. K., Dyer, N. J. and Spiller, P. T. (1990): "Fare Determination in Airline Hub-and-Spoke Networks," University of Illinois working paper, June.

Call, G. D. and Keeler, T. E. (1985): "Airline Deregulation, Fares and Market Behavior: Some Empirical Evidence," in A. H. Daugherty (ed.), *Analytic Studies in Transport Economics*, Cambridge: Cambridge University Press, 221–47.

Carlton, D. W., Landes, W. M. and Posner, R. A. (1980): "Benefits and Costs of Airline Mergers: A Case Study," *Bell Journal of Economics and Management Science*, 11, Spring, 65–83.

Caves, D. W. (1962): *Air Transport and Its Regulators: An Industry Study*. Cambridge: Harvard University Press.

——Christensen, L. R. and Tretheway, M. W. (1984): "Economies of Density Versus Economies of Scale: Why Trunk and Local Service Airline Costs Differ," *Rand Journal of Economics*, 15, Winter, 471–89.

Dempsey, P. S. (1990): *Flying Blind: The Failure of Airline Deregulation*. Washington, DC: Economic Policy Institute.

Douglas, G. W. and Miller J. C. III, (1974): *Economic Regulation of Domestic Air Transport: Theory and Policy*. Washington DC: Brookings Institution.

Eads, G., Nerlove, M. and Raduchel, W. (1969): "A Long-Run Cost Function for the Local Service Airline Industry," *Review of Economics and Statistics*, 51(3): August, 258–70.

Evans, W. N. and Kessides, I. N. (1991): "Living by the 'Golden Rule': Multi-market Contact in the U.S. Airline Industry," University of Maryland working paper, January.

——"Localized Market Power in the U.S. Airline Industry," *Review of Economics and Statistics*.

Frank, R. (1983): "When Are Price Differentials Discriminatory?" *Journal of Policy Analysis and Management*, 2(2), Winter, 238–55.

Gale, I. and Holmes, T. J. (1990): "Advance-Purchase Discounts and Monopoly Allocation of Capacity," SSRI working paper 9005.

Gordon, R. J. (1992): "Productivity in the Transportation Sector," in Z. Griliches, E. R. Berndt, T. F. Bresnahan and M. E. Manser (eds), *Measurement Output in the Services Sector*, University of Chicago Press for NBER.

Greenwald, B. C., Salinger, M. A. and Stiglitz, J. E. (1991): *Imperfect Capital Markets and Productivity Growth*, mimeo, Stanford University, March. Paper presented at NBER Conference in Vail, Colorado, April.

Holmes, T. J. (1989): "The Effects of Third-Degree Price Discrimination in Oligopoly," *American Economic Review*, 79, March, 244–50.

Hurdle, G. J., Johnson, R. L., Joskow, A. S., Werden, G. J. and Williams, M. A. (1989): "Concentration, Potential Entry, and Performance in the Airline Industry," *Journal of Industrial Economics*, 38, December, 119–39.

Huston, J. H. and Butler, R. V. (1988): "The Effects of Fortress Hubs on Airline Fares and Service: The Early Returns," *Logistics and Transportation Review*, 24, September, 203–15.

Jordan, W. A. (1970): *Airline Regulation in America: Effects and Imperfections*. Baltimore: The Johns Hopkins University Press.

Joskow, A. S., Werden, G. J. and Johnson, R. L. (1990): "Entry, Exit and Performance in Airline Markets," Department of Justice discussion paper EAG90–10, December.

Kaplan, D. P. (1986): "The Changing Airline Industry," in L. W. Weiss and M. W. Klass, (eds), *Regulatory Reform: What Actually Happened*, Boston: Little, Brown and Company, 40–77.

Keeler, T. E. (1972): "Airline Regulation and Market Performance," *Bell Journal of Economics and Management Science*, 3, Autumn, 399–424.

Levine, M. E. (1965): "Is Regulation Necessary? California Air Transportation and National Regulatory Policy," *Yale Law Journal*, 74, July, 1416–47.

——(1987): "Airline Competition in Deregulated Markets: Theory, Firm Strategy, and Public Policy," *Yale Journal on Regulation*, 4, Spring, 393–494.

McGowan, F. and Seabright, P. (1989): "Deregulating European Airlines," *Economic Policy*, 4, October, 283–344.

Morrison, S. A. (1987): "The Efficiency and Equity of Runway Pricing," *Journal of Public Economics*, 34, October 45–60.

——and Clifford Winston, (1986): *The Economic Effects of Airline Deregulation*. Washington DC: Brookings Institution.

——(1987): "Empirical Implications and Tests of the Contestability Hypothesis," *Journal of Law and Economics*, 30, April, 53–66.

——(1989): "Enhancing the Performance of the Deregulated Air Transportation System," *Brookings Papers on Economic Activity: Microeconomics*, 61–112.

——(1990): "The Dynamics of Airline Pricing and Competition," *American Economic Review*, 80, May, 389–93.

Nomani, A. Q. (1990): "Airlines May Be Using a Price-Data Network to Lessen Competition," *Wall Street Journal*, June 28, 122, A1, A6.

Reiss, P. C. and Spiller, P. T. (1989): "Competition and Entry in Small Airline Markets," *Journal of Law and Economics*, 32, October, S179–202.

Salop, S. C. (1978): "Alternative Reservation Contracts," Civil Aeronautics Board memo.

Stiglitz, J. E. (1987): "Technological Change, Sunk Costs, and Competition," *Brookings Papers on Economic Activity: Microeconomics*, 3, 883–937.

Travel Weekly (1988): "The 1988 Louis Harris Survey," XLVII, June 29, 9–142.

U.S. General Accounting Office (1988): *Airline Competition: Fare and Service Changes at St. Louis Since the TWA-Ozark Merger*, September.

——(1990a) *Airline Competition: Higher Fares and Reduced Competition at Concentrated Airports* July.

——(1990b): *Airline Competition: Industry Operating and Marketing Practices Limit Market Entry*, August.

U.S. Department of Transportation (1988): *Study of Airline Computer Reservation Systems*, Washington, DC: U.S. Government Printing Office.

—— (1990): *Secretary's Task Force on Competition in the U.S. Domestic Airline Industry*, Washington, DC: U.S. Government Printing Office.

Werden, G. J., Joskow, A. S. and Johnson, R. L. (1991): "The Effects of Mergers of Price and Output: Two Case Studies from the Airline Industry," *Managerial and Decision Economics*, 12, October, 341–52.

Whinston, M. D. and Collins, S. C. (1990): "Entry and Competitive Structure in Deregulated Airline Markets: An Event Study Analysis of People Express," Harvard University working paper, August.

CHAPTER THIRTEEN

An Introduction to
Applicable Game Theory

Robert S. Gibbons

Source: *Journal of Economic Perspectives*, 11 (1) (1997), pp. 127–49.
Reprinted with the permission of the author and the American
Economic Association. © American Economic Association.

Game theory is rampant in economics. Having long ago invaded industrial organization, game-theoretic modeling is now commonplace in international, labor, macro and public finance, and it is gathering steam in development and economic history. Nor is economics alone: accounting, finance, law, marketing, political science and sociology are beginning similar experiences. Many modelers use game theory because it allows them to think like an economist when price theory does not apply. That is, game-theoretic models allow economists to study the implications of rationality, self-interest and equilibrium, both in market interactions that are modeled as games (such as where small numbers, hidden information, hidden actions or incomplete contracts are present) and in nonmarket inter-actions (such as between a regulator and a firm, a boss and a worker, and so on).

Many applied economists seem to appreciate that game theory can complement price theory in this way, but nonetheless find game theory more an entry barrier than a useful tool. This paper is addressed to such readers. I try to give clear definitions and intuitive examples of the basic kinds of games and the basic solution concepts. Perhaps more importantly, I try to distill the welter of solution concepts and other jargon into a few basic principles that permeate the literature. Thus, I envision this paper as a tutorial for economists who have brushed up against game theory but have not (yet) read a book on the subject.

The theory is presented in four sections, corresponding to whether the game in question is static or dynamic and to whether it has complete or incomplete information. ("Complete information" means that there is no private information: the timing, feasible moves and payoffs of the game are all common knowledge.) We begin with static games with complete information; for these games, we focus on Nash equilibrium as the solution concept. We turn next to dynamic games with complete information, for which we use backward induction as the solution concept. We discuss dynamic games with complete information that have multiple Nash equilibria, and we show how backward induction selects a Nash equilibrium that does not rely on noncredible threats. We then return to the context of static games and introduce private information; for these games we extend the concept of Nash equilibrium to allow for private information and call the resulting solution concept Bayesian Nash equilibrium. Finally, we consider signaling games (the simplest dynamic games with private information) and blend the ideas of backward induction and Bayesian Nash equilibrium to define perfect Bayesian equilibrium.

This outline may seem to suggest that game theory invokes a brand new equilibrium concept for each new class of games, but one theme of this paper is that these equilibrium concepts are very closely linked. As we consider progressively richer games, we progressively strengthen the equilibrium concept to rule out implausible equilibria in the richer games that would survive if we applied equilibrium concepts suitable for simpler games. In each case, the stronger equilibrium concept differs from the weaker concept only for the richer games, not for the simpler games.

Space constraints prevent me from presenting anything other than the basic theory, I omit several natural extensions of the theory; I only hint at the terrific breadth of applications in economics; I say nothing about the growing body of field and experimental evidence; and I do not discuss recent applications outside economics, including fascinating efforts to integrate game theory with behavioral and social-structural elements from other social sciences. To conclude the paper, therefore, I offer a brief guide to further reading.[1]

1. Static Games with Complete Information

We begin with two-player, simultaneous-move games. (Everything we do for two-player games extends easily to three or more players; we consider sequential-move games below.) The timing of such a game is as follows:

1 Player 1 chooses an action a_1 from a set of feasible actions A_1. Simultaneously, player 2 chooses an action a_2 from a set of feasible actions A_2.
2 After the players choose their actions, they receive payoffs: $u_1(a_1, a_2)$ to player 1 and $u_2(a_1, a_2)$ to player 2.

A classic example of a static game with complete information is Cournot's (1838) duopoly model. Other examples include Hotelling's (1929) model of candidates' platform choices in an election, Farber's (1980) model of final-offer arbitration and Grossman and Hart's (1980) model of takeover bids.

1.1. Rational play

Rather than ask how one *should* play a given game, we first ask how one *should not* play the game. Consider the game in Figure 1. Player 1 has two actions, {Up, Down}; player 2 has three, {Left, Middle, Right}. For player 2, playing Right is dominated by playing Middle: if player 1 chooses Up, then Right yields 1 for player 2, whereas Middle yields 2; if 1

		Player 2		
		Left	Middle	Right
Player 1	Up	1, 0	1, 2	0, 1
	Down	0, 3	0, 1	2, 0

Figure 1 An example of iterated elimination of dominated strategies

chooses Down, then Right yields 0 for 2, whereas Middle yields 1. Thus, a rational player 2 will not play Right.[2]

Now take the argument a step further. If player 1 knows that player 2 is rational, then player 1 can eliminate Right from player 2's action space. That is, if player 1 knows that player 2 is rational, then player 1 can play the game *as if* player 2's only moves were Left and Middle. But in this case, Down is dominated by Up for player 1: if 2 plays Left, then Up is better for 1, and likewise if 2 plays Middle. Thus, if player 1 is rational (and player 1 knows that player 2 is rational, so that player 2's only moves are Left and Middle), then player 1 will not play Down.

Finally, take the argument one last step. If player 2 knows that player 1 is rational, *and* player 2 knows that player 1 knows that player 2 is rational, then player 2 can eliminate Down from player 1's action space, leaving Up as player 1's only move. But in this case, Left is dominated by Middle for player 2, leaving (Up, Middle) as the solution to the game.

This argument shows that some games can be solved by (repeatedly) asking how one should not play the game. This process is called *iterated elimination of dominated strategies*. Although it is based on the appealing idea that rational players do not play dominated strategies, the process has two drawbacks. First, each step requires a further assumption about what the players know about each other's rationality. Second, the process often produces a very imprecise prediction about the play of the game. Consider the game in Figure 2, for example. In this game there are no dominated strategies to be eliminated. Since all the strategies in the game survive iterated elimination of dominated strategies, the process produces no prediction whatsoever about the play of the game. Thus, asking how one should not play a game sometimes is no help in determining how one should play.

	L	C	R
T	0, 4	4, 0	5, 3
M	4, 0	0, 4	5, 3
B	3, 5	3, 5	6, 6

Figure 2 A game without dominated strategies to be eliminated

We turn next to Nash equilibrium – a solution concept that produces much tighter predictions in a very broad class of games. We will see that each of the two games above has a unique Nash equilibrium. In any game, the players' strategies in a Nash equilibrium always survive iterated elimination of dominated strategies; in particular, we will see that (Up, Middle) is the unique Nash equilibrium of the game in Figure 1.

1.2. Nash equilibrium

We have just seen that asking how one should not play a given game can shed some light on how one should play. To introduce Nash equilibrium, we take a similarly indirect approach: instead of asking what the solution of a given game is (that is, what all the players should do), we ask what outcomes cannot be the solution. After eliminating some outcomes, we are left with one or more possible solutions. We then discuss which of these possible solutions, if any, deserves further attention. We also consider the possibility that the game has no compelling solution.

Suppose game theory offers a unique prediction about the play of a particular game. For this predicted solution to be correct, it is necessary that each player be willing to choose the strategy that the theory predicts that individual will play. Thus, each player's predicted strategy must be that player's best response to the predicted strategies of the other players. Such a collection of predicted strategies could be called "strategically stable" or "self-enforcing," because no single player wants to deviate from his or her predicted strategy. We will call such a collection of strategies a *Nash equilibrium*.[3]

To relate this definition to the motivation above, suppose game theory offers the actions (a_1^*, a_2^*) as a solution. Saying that (a_1^*, a_2^*) is *not* a Nash equilibrium is equivalent to saying that either a_1^* is not a best response for player 1 to a_2^*, or a_2^* is not a best response for player 2 to a_1^*, or both. Thus, if the theory offers the strategies (a_1^*, a_2^*) as the solution, but these strategies are not a Nash equilibrium, then at least one player will have an incentive to deviate from the theory's prediction, so the prediction seems unlikely to be true.

To see the definition of Nash equilibrium at work, consider the games in Figures 1 and 2. For five of the six strategy pairs in Figure 1, at least one player would want to deviate if that strategy pair were proposed as the solution to the game. Only (Up, Middle) satisfies the mutual-best-response criterion of Nash equilibrium. Likewise, of the nine strategy pairs in Figure 2, only (B, R) is "strategically stable" or "self-enforcing." In Figure 2, it happens that the unique Nash equilibrium is efficient: it yields the highest payoffs in the game for both players. In many games, however, the unique Nash equilibrium is not efficient – consider the Prisoners' Dilemma in Figure 3.[4]

Some games have multiple Nash equilibria, such as the Dating Game (or Battle of the Sexes, in antiquated terminology) shown below in Figure 4. The story behind this game is that Chris and Pat will be having dinner together but are currently on their separate ways home from work. Pat is supposed to buy the wine and Chris the main course, but Pat could buy red or white wine and Chris steak or chicken. Both Chris and Pat prefer red wine with steak and white with chicken, but Chris prefers the former combination to

		Player 2	
		L_2	R_2
Player 1	L_1	1, 1	5, 0
	R_1	0, 5	4, 4

Figure 3   The prisoners' dilemma

		Pat	
		Red	White
Chris	Steak	2, 1	0, 0
	Chicken	0, 0	1, 2

Figure 4   The dating game

the latter and Pat the reverse; that is, the players prefer to coordinate but disagree about how to do so.[5] In this game, red wine and steak is a Nash equilibrium, as is white wine and chicken, but there is no obvious way to decide between these equilibria. When several Nash equilibria are equally compelling, as in the Dating Game, Nash equilibrium loses much of its appeal as a prediction of play. In such settings, which (if any) Nash equilibrium emerges as a convention may depend on accidents of history (Young, 1996).

Other games, such as Matching Pennies in Figure 5, do not have a pair of strategies satisfying the mutual-best-response definition of Nash equilibrium given above. The distinguishing feature of Matching Pennies is that each player would like to outguess the other. Versions of this game also arise in poker, auditing and other settings. In poker, for example, the analogous question is how often to bluff: if player i is known never to bluff, then i's opponents will fold whenever i bids aggressively, thereby making it worthwhile for i to bluff on occasion; on the other hand, bluffing too often is also a losing strategy. Similarly, in auditing, if a subordinate worked diligently, then the boss prefers not to incur the cost of auditing the subordinate, but if the boss is not going to audit, then the subordinate prefers to shirk, and so on.

		Player 2	
		Heads	Tails
Player 1	Heads	−1, 1	1, −1
	Tails	1, −1	−1, 1

Figure 5   Matching pennies

In any game in which each player would like to outguess the other, there is no pair of strategies satisfying the definition of Nash equilibrium given above. Instead, the solution to such a game necessarily involves uncertainty about what the players will do. To model this uncertainty, we will refer to the actions in a player's action space (A_i) as *pure strategies*, and we will define a *mixed strategy* to be a probability distribution over some or all of the player's pure strategies. A mixed strategy for player i is sometimes described as player i rolling dice to pick a pure strategy, but later in the paper we will offer a much more plausible interpretation based on player j's uncertainty about the strategy player i will choose. Regardless of how one interprets mixed strategies, once the mutual-best-response definition of Nash equilibrium is extended to allow mixed as well as pure strategies, then any game with a finite number of players, each of whom has a finite number of pure strategies, has a Nash equilibrium (possibly involving mixed strategies). See Nash's (1950) classic paper for the proof, based on a fixed-point theorem.

2. Dynamic Games with Complete Information

We turn next to dynamic games, beginning with two-player, sequential-move games. The timing of such a game is as follows:

1 Player 1 chooses an action a_1 from a set of feasible actions A_1.
2 Player 2 observes 1's choice and then chooses an action a_2 from a set of feasible actions A_2.
3 After the players choose their actions, they receive payoffs: $u_1(a_1, a_2)$ to player 1 and $u_2(a_1, a_2)$ to player 2.

A classic example of a dynamic game with complete information is von Stackelberg's (1934) sequential-move version of Cournot duopoly. Other examples include Leontief's (1946) monopoly-union model and Rubinstein's (1982) bargaining model (although the latter may not end after only two moves).

The new solution concept in this section is backward induction. We will see that in many dynamic games there are many Nash equilibria, some of which depend on non-credible threats – defined as threats that the threatener would not want to carry out, but will not have to carry out if the threat is believed. Backward induction identifies a Nash equilibrium that does not rely on such threats.

2.1. Backward induction

Consider the Trust Game in Figure 6, in which player 1 first chooses either to trust or not trust player 2. For simplicity, suppose that if player 1 chooses not trust then the game ends – 1 terminates the relationship. If player 1 chooses to trust 2, however, then the game continues, and 2 chooses either to honor or to betray 1's trust. If player 1 chooses to end the relationship, then both players' payoffs are 0. If 1 chooses to trust 2, then both players' payoffs are 1 if 2 honors 1's trust, but player 1 receives -1 and player 2 receives 2 if player 2 betrays 1's trust. All of this is captured by the game tree on the left-hand side of Figure 6. The game begins with a decision node for player 1 and reaches a decision node for player 2 if 1 chooses Trust. At the end of each branch of the tree, player 1's payoff appears above player 2's. The bold branches in the tree will be explained momentarily.

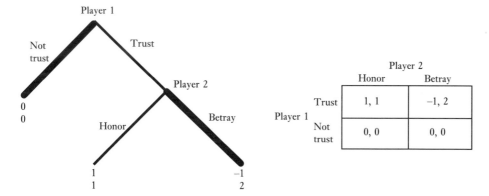

Figure 6   The trust game

We solve the Trust Game by working backward through the game tree. If player 2 gets to move (that is, if player 1 chooses Trust) then 2 can receive a payoff of 1 by choosing to honor 1's trust or a payoff of 2 by choosing to betray 1's trust. Since 2 exceeds 1, player 2 will betray 1's trust. Knowing this, player 1's initial choice amounts to ending the relationship (and so receiving a payoff of 0) or trusting player 2 (and so receiving a payoff of −1, after player 2 betrays 1's trust). Since 0 exceeds −1, player 1 should Not trust. These arguments are summarized by the bold lines in the game tree.

Thus far, it may appear that simultaneous-move games must be represented in matrix (or "normal") form, as in the previous section, while sequential-move games must be represented using game trees. Similarly, it may appear that we use two different methods to solve these two kinds of games: Nash equilibrium in simultaneous-move games and backward induction in sequential-move games. *These perceptions are not correct.* Either kind of game can be represented in either normal form or a game tree, but for some games it is more convenient to use one than the other. The Trust Game, for example, is represented in normal form on the right-hand side of Figure 6, and using this representation one can verify that the Nash equilibrium is (Not trust, Betray), just as we found by working backward through the game tree.

The reassurances just offered obscure one subtle point: in some games, there are several Nash equilibria, some of which rely on noncredible threats or promises. Fortunately, the backward-induction solution to a game is always a Nash equilibrium that does not rely on noncredible threats or promises. As an illustration of a Nash equilibrium that relies on a noncredible threat (but does not satisfy backward induction), consider the game tree and associated normal form in Figure 7. Working backward through this game tree shows that the backward-induction solution is for player 2 to play R' if given the move and for player 1 to play R. But the normal form reveals that there are two Nash equilibria: (R, R') and (L, L'). The second Nash equilibrium exists because player 1's best response to L' by 2 is to end the game by choosing L. But (L, L') relies on the noncredible threat by player 2 to play L' rather than R' if given the move. If player 1 believes 2's threat, then 2 is off the hook because 1 will play L, but 2 would never want to carry out this threat if given the opportunity.

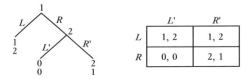

Figure 7   A game that relies on a noncredible threat

Backward induction can be applied in any finite-horizon game of complete information in which the players move one at a time and all previous moves are common knowledge before the next move is chosen. The method is simple: go to the end of the game and work backward, one move at a time. In dynamic games with simultaneous moves or an infinite horizon, however, we cannot apply this method directly. We turn next to subgame-perfect Nash equilibrium, which extends the spirit of backward induction to such games.

2.2. Subgame-perfect Nash equilibrium

Subgame-perfect Nash equilibrium is a *refinement* of Nash equilibrium; that is, to be subgame-perfect, the players' strategies must first be a Nash equilibrium and must then fulfill an additional requirement. The point of this additional requirement is, as with backward induction, to rule out Nash equilibria that rely on non-credible threats.

To provide an informal definition of subgame-perfect Nash equilibrium, we return to the motivation for Nash equilibrium – namely, that a unique solution to a game-theoretic problem must satisfy Nash's mutual-best-response requirement. In many dynamic games, the same argument can also be applied to certain pieces of the game, called subgames. A subgame is the piece of an original game that remains to be played beginning at any point at which the complete history of the play of the game thus far is common knowledge. In the one-shot Trust Game, for example, the history of play is common knowledge after player 1 moves. The piece of the game that then remains is very simple – just one move by player 2.

As a second example of a subgame (and, eventually, of subgame-perfect Nash equilibrium), consider Lazear and Rosen's (1981) model of a tournament. First, the principal chooses two wages – W_H for the winner, W_L for the loser. Second, the two workers observe these wages and then simultaneously choose effort levels. Finally, each worker's output (which equals the worker's effort plus noise) is observed, and the worker with the higher output earns W_H. In this game, the history of play is common knowledge after the principal chooses the wages. The piece of the game that then remains is the effort-choice game between the workers.

Because the workers' effort-choice game has simultaneous moves, we cannot go to the end of the game and work backward *one move at a time*, as with backward induction. (If we go to the end of the game, which worker's move should we analyze first?) Instead, we analyze both workers' moves together. That is, we analyze the entire subgame that remains after the principal sets the wages by solving for the Nash equilibrium in the workers' effort-choice game given arbitrary wages chosen by the principal. Given the workers' equilibrium response to these arbitrary wages, we can then work backward, solving the principal's problem: choose wages that maximize expected profit given the workers' equilibrium response. This process yields the subgame-perfect Nash equilibrium of the tournament game.

There typically are other Nash equilibria of the tournament game that are not subgame-perfect. For example, the principal might pay very high wages because the workers both threaten to shirk if she pays anything less. Solving for the workers' equilibrium response to an arbitrary pair of wages reveals that this threat is not credible. This solution process illustrates Selten's (1965) definition of a subgame-perfect Nash equilibrium: a Nash equilibrium (of the game as whole) is subgame-perfect if the players' strategies constitute a Nash equilibrium in every subgame.[6]

2.3. Repeated games

When people interact over time, threats and promises concerning future behavior may influence current behavior. Repeated games capture this fact of life, and hence have been applied more broadly than any other game-theoretic model (by my armchair count) – not only in virtually every field of economics but also in finance, law, marketing, political science and sociology.

In this section, we analyze the infinitely repeated Trust Game, borrowed from Kreps's (1990a) analysis of corporate culture. All previous outcomes are known before the next period's Trust Game is played. Both players share the interest rate r per period.[7] Consider the following "trigger" strategies:

> *Player 1* In the first period, play Trust. Thereafter, if all moves in all previous periods have been Trust and Honor, play Trust; otherwise, play Not trust.
> *Player 2* If given the move this period, play Honor if all moves in all previous periods have been Trust and Honor; otherwise, play Betray.

Recall that in the one-shot version of the Trust Game, backward induction yields (Not trust, Betray), with payoffs of (0, 0). Given the trigger strategies stated above for the repeated game, this backward-induction outcome of the stage game will be the "punishment" outcome if cooperation collapses in the repeated game. Under these trigger strategies, the payoffs from "cooperation" are (1, 1), but cooperation creates an incentive for "defection," at least for player 2: if player 1 chooses Trust, player 2's one-period payoff would be maximized by choosing to betray, producing payoffs of $(-1, 2)$. Thus, player 2 will cooperate if the present value of the payoffs from cooperation (1 in each period) exceeds the present value of the payoffs from detection followed by punishment (2 immediately, but 0 thereafter). The former present value exceeds the latter if the interest rate is sufficiently small (here, $r \leq 1$).[8]

What about player 1? Suppose player 2 is playing his strategy given above. Because player 1 moves first, she has no chance to defect, in the sense of cheating while player 2 attempts to cooperate. The only possible deviation for player 1 is to play Not trust, in which case player 2 does not get the move that period. But 2's strategy then specifies that any future Trusts will be met with Betrayal. Thus, by playing Not trust, player 1 gets 0 this period and 0 thereafter (because playing Not trust forever after is 1's best response to 2's anticipated betrayal of trust). So if player 2 is playing his strategy given above, then it is optimal for player 1 to play hers. Thus, if the interest rate is sufficiently small, then the trigger strategies stated above are a Nash equilibrium of the repeated game.[9]

The general point is that cooperation is prone to defection – otherwise we should call it something else, such as a happy alignment of the players' self-interests. But in some circumstances, defection can be met with punishment, in which case a potential defector must weigh the present value of continued cooperation against the short-term gain from defection followed by the long-term loss from punishment. If the players are sufficiently patient (that is, the interest rate is sufficiently small), then cooperation can occur in an equilibrium of the repeated game when it cannot in the one-shot game.

3. Static Games with Incomplete Information

We turn next to games with *incomplete information*, also called *Bayesian games*. In a game of complete information, the players' payoff functions are common knowledge, whereas in a game of incomplete information at least one player is uncertain about another player's payoff function. One common example of a static game of incomplete information is a sealed-bid auction: each bidder knows his or her own valuation for the good being sold, but does not know any other bidder's valuation; bids are submitted in sealed envelopes, so the players' moves are effectively simultaneous. Most economically interesting Bayesian games are dynamic, however, because the existence of private information leads naturally to attempts by informed parties to communicate (or mislead) and to attempts by uninformed parties to learn and respond.

We first use the idea of incomplete information to provide a new interpretation for mixed-strategy Nash equilibria in games with *complete* information – an interpretation of player i's mixed strategy in terms of player j's uncertainty about i's action, rather than in terms of actual randomization on i's part. Using this simple model as a template, we then define a static Bayesian game and a Bayesian Nash equilibrium. Reassuringly, we will see that a Bayesian Nash equilibrium is simply a Nash equilibrium in a Bayesian game: the players' strategies must be best responses to each other.

3.1. Mixed strategies reinterpreted

Recall that in the Dating Game discussed earlier, there are two pure-strategy Nash equilibria: (Steak, Red wine) and (Chicken, White wine). There is also a mixed-strategy Nash equilibrium, in which Chris chooses steak with probability $\frac{2}{3}$ and chicken with probability $\frac{1}{3}$, and Pat chooses white wine with probability $\frac{2}{3}$ and red wine with probability $\frac{1}{3}$. To verify that these mixed strategies constitute a Nash equilibrium, check that given Pat's strategy, Chris is indifferent between the pure strategies of steak and chicken and so also indifferent among all probability distributions over these pure strategies. Thus, the mixed strategy specified for Chris is one of a continuum of best responses to Pat's strategy. The same is true for Pat, so the two mixed strategies are a Nash equilibrium.

Now suppose that, although they have known each other for quite some time, Chris and Pat are not quite sure of each other's payoffs, as shown in Figure 8. Chris's payoff from steak with red wine is now $2 + t_c$, where t_c is privately known by Chris; Pat's payoff from chicken with white wine is now $2 + t_p$, where t_p is privately known by Pat; and t_c and t_p are independent draws from a uniform distribution on $[0, x]$. The choice of a uniform distribution is only for convenience, but we do have in mind that the values of t_c and t_p only slightly perturb the payoffs in the original game, so think of x as small. All the other payoffs are the same as in the original complete-information game.

We will construct a pure-strategy Bayesian Nash equilibrium of this incomplete-information version of the Dating Game in which Chris chooses steak if t_c exceeds a

		Pat	
		Red	White
Chris	Steak	$2 + t_c$, 1	0, 0
	Chicken	0, 0	1, $2 + t_p$

Figure 8 The dating game with incomplete information

critical value, c, and chooses chicken otherwise, and Pat chooses white wine if t_p exceeds a critical value, p, and chooses red wine otherwise. In such an equilibrium, Chris chooses steak with probability $(x - c)/x$, and Pat chooses white wine with probability $(x - p)/x$. (For example, if the critical value c is nearly x, then the probability that t_c will exceed c is almost zero.) We will show that as the incomplete information disappears – that is, as x approaches zero – the players' behavior in this pure-strategy Bayesian Nash equilibrium of the incomplete-information game approaches their behavior in the mixed-strategy Nash equilibrium in the original complete-information game. That is, both $(x - c)/x$ and $(x - p)/x$ approach $\frac{2}{3}$ as x approaches zero.

Suppose that Pat will play the strategy described above for the incomplete-information game. Chris can then compute that Pat chooses white wine with probability $(x - p)/x$ and red with probability p/x, so Chris's expected payoffs from choosing steak and from choosing chicken are $p(2 + t_c)/x$ and $(x - p)/x$, respectively. Thus, Chris's best response to Pat's strategy has the form described above: choosing steak has the higher expected payoff if and only if

$$t_c \geq (x - 3p)/p \equiv c$$

Similarly, given Chris's strategy, Pat can compute that Chris chooses steak with probability $(x - c)/x$ and chicken with probability c/x, so Pat's expected payoffs from choosing white wine and from choosing red wine are $c(2 + t_p)/x$ and $(x - c)/x$, respectively. Thus, choosing white wine has the higher expected payoff if and only if

$$t_p \geq (x - 3c)/c \equiv p$$

We have now shown that Chris's strategy (namely, steak if and only if $t_c \geq c$) and Pat's strategy (namely, white wine if and only if $t_p \geq p$) are best responses to each other if and only if $(x - 3p)/p = c$ and $(x - 3c)/c = p$. Solving these two equations for p and c shows that the probability that Chris chooses steak, namely, $(x - c)/x$, and the probability that Pat chooses white wine, namely, $(x - p)/x$, are equal. This probability approaches $\frac{2}{3}$ as x approaches zero (by application of l'Hôpital's rule). Thus, as the incomplete information disappears, the players' behavior in this pure-strategy Bayesian Nash equilibrium of the incomplete-information game approaches their behavior in the mixed-strategy Nash equilibrium in the original game of complete information.

Harsanyi (1973) showed that this result is quite general: a mixed-strategy Nash equilibrium in a game of complete information can (almost always) be interpreted as a pure-strategy Bayesian Nash equilibrium in a closely related game with a little bit of incomplete information. Put more evocatively, the crucial feature of a mixed-strategy Nash equilibrium is not that player j chooses a strategy randomly, but rather that player i is uncertain about player j's choice; this uncertainty can arise either because of randomization or (more plausibly) because of a little incomplete information.

3.2. Static Bayesian games and Bayesian Nash equilibrium

Recall from the first section that in a two-player, simultaneous-move game of complete information, first the players simultaneously choose actions (player i chooses a_i from the feasible set A_i) and then payoffs $u_i(a_i, a_j)$ are received. To describe a two-player, simultaneous-move game of incomplete information, the first step is to represent the idea that each player knows his or her own payoff function but may be uncertain about the other player's payoff function. Let player i's possible payoff functions be represented by $u_i(a_i, a_j; t_i)$, where t_i is called player i's *type* and belongs to a set of possible types (or *type space*) T_i. Each type t_i corresponds to a different payoff function that player i might have. In an auction, for example, a player's payoff depends not only on all the players' bids (that is, the players' actions a_i and a_j) but also on the player's own valuation for the good being auctioned (that is, the player's type t_i).

Given this definition of a player's type, saying that player i knows his or her own payoff function is equivalent to saying that player i knows his or her type. Likewise, saying that player i may be uncertain about player j's payoff function is equivalent to saying that player i may be uncertain about player j's type t_j. (In an auction, player i may be uncertain about player j's valuation for the good.) We use the probability distribution $p(t_j|t_i)$ to denote player i's belief about player j's type, t_j, given player i's knowledge of her own type, t_i. For notational simplicity we assume (as in most of the literature) that the players' types are independent, in which case $p(t_j|t_i)$ does not depend on t_i, so we can write player i's belief as $p(t_j)$.[10]

Joining these new concepts of types and beliefs with the familiar elements of a static game of complete information yields a *static Bayesian game*, as first defined by Harsanyi (1967, 1968a, b). The timing of a two-player static Bayesian game is as follows:

1 Nature draws a type vector $t = (t_1, t_2)$, where t_i is independently drawn from the probability distribution $p(t_i)$ over player i's set of possible types T_i.
2 Nature reveals t_i to player i but not to player j.
3 The players simultaneously choose actions, player i choosing a_i from the feasible set A_i.
4 Payoffs $u_i(a_i, a_j; t_i)$, are received by each player.[11]

It may be helpful to check that the Dating Game with incomplete information described above is a simple example of this abstract definition of a static Bayesian game.

We now need to define an equilibrium concept for static Bayesian games. To do so, we must first define the players' strategy spaces in such a game, after which we will define a Bayesian Nash equilibrium to be a pair of strategies such that each player's strategy is a best response to the other player's strategy. That is, given the appropriate definition of a strategy in a static Bayesian game, the appropriate definition of equilibrium (now called *Bayesian Nash equilibrium*) is just the familiar definition from Nash.[12]

A strategy in a static Bayesian game is an action rule, not just an action. More formally, a (pure) strategy for player i specifies a feasible action (a_i) for *each* of player i's possible types (t_i). In the Dating Game with incomplete information, for example, Chris's strategy was a rule specifying Chris's action for each possible value of t_c: steak if t_c exceeds a critical value, c, and chicken otherwise. Similarly, in an auction, a bidder's strategy is a rule specifying the player's bid for each possible valuation the bidder might have for the good.

In a static Bayesian game, player 1's strategy is a best response to player 2's if, for each of player 1's types, the action specified by 1's action rule for that type maximizes 1's expected payoff, given 1's belief about 2's type and given 2's action rule. In the Bayesian

Nash equilibrium we constructed in the Dating Game, for example, there was no incentive for Chris to change even one action by one type, given Chris's belief about Pat's type and given Pat's action rule (namely, choose white wine if t_p exceeds a critical value, p, and choose red wine otherwise). Likewise, in a Bayesian Nash equilibrium of a two-bidder auction, bidder 1 has no incentive to change even one bid by one valuation-type, given bidder 1's belief about bidder 2's type and given bidder 2's bidding rule.[13]

4. Dynamic Games with Incomplete Information

As noted earlier, the existence of private information leads naturally to attempts by informed parties to communicate (or to mislead) and to attempts by uninformed parties to learn and respond. The simplest model of such attempts is a signaling game: there are two players – one with private information, the other without; and there are two stages in the game – a signal sent by the informed party, followed by a response taken by the uninformed party. In Spence's (1973) classic model, for example, the informed party is a worker with private information about his or her productive ability, the uninformed party is a potential employer (or a market of same), the signal is education, and the response is a wage offer.

Richer dynamic Bayesian games allow for reputations to be developed, maintained or milked. In the first such analysis, Kreps, Milgrom, Roberts and Wilson (1982) showed that a finitely repeated prisoners' dilemma that begins with a little bit of (the right kind of) private information can have equilibrium cooperation in all but the last few periods. In contrast, a backward-induction argument shows that equilibrium cooperation cannot occur in any round of a finitely repeated prisoner's dilemma under complete information, because knowing that cooperation will break down in the last round causes it to break down in the next-to-last round, and so on back to the first round. Signaling games, reputation games and other dynamic Bayesian games (like bargaining games) have been very widely applied in many fields of economics and in accounting, finance, law, marketing and political science. For example, see Benabou and Laroque (1992) on insiders and gurus in financial markets, Cramton and Tracy (1992) on strikes and Rogoff (1989) on monetary policy.

4.1. Perfect Bayesian equilibrium

To analyze dynamic Bayesian games, we introduce a fourth equilibrium concept: perfect Bayesian equilibrium. The crucial new feature of perfect Bayesian equilibrium is due to Kreps and Wilson (1982): beliefs are elevated to the level of importance of strategies in the definition of equilibrium. That is, the definition of equilibrium no longer consists of just a strategy for each player but now also includes a belief for each player whenever the player has the move but is uncertain about the history of prior play.[14] The advantage of making the players' beliefs an explicit part of the equilibrium is that, just as we previously insisted that the players choose credible (that is, subgame-perfect) strategies, we can now also insist that they hold reasonable beliefs.

To illustrate why the players' beliefs are as important as their strategies, consider the example in Figure 9. (This example shows that perfect Bayesian equilibrium refines

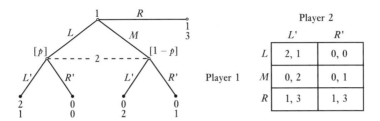

Figure 9 Why players' beliefs are as important as their strategies

subgame-perfect Nash equilibrium; we return to dynamic Bayesian games in the next subsection.) First, player 1 chooses among three actions: L, M and R. If player 1 chooses R then the game ends without a move by player 2. If player 1 chooses either L or M then player 2 learns that R was not chosen (but not which of L or M was chosen) and then chooses between two actions, L' and R', after which the game ends. (The dashed line connecting player 2's two decision nodes in the game tree on the left of Figure 9 indicates that if player 2 gets the move, player 2 does not know which node has been reached – that is, whether player 1 has chosen L or M. The probabilities p and $1 - p$ attached to player 2's decision nodes will be explained below.) Payoffs are given in the game tree.

The normal-form representation of this game on the right-hand side of Figure 9 reveals that there are two pure-strategy Nash equilibria: (L, L') and (R, R'). We first ask whether these Nash equilibria are subgame-perfect. Because a subgame is defined to begin when the history of prior play is common knowledge, there are no subgames in the game tree above. (After player 1's decision node at the beginning of the game, there is no point at which the complete history of play is common knowledge: the only other nodes are player 2's, and if these nodes are reached, then player 2 does not know whether the previous play was L or M.) If a game has no subgames, then the requirement of subgame-perfection – namely, that the players' strategies constitute a Nash equilibrium on every subgame – is trivially satisfied. Thus, in any game that has no subgames the definition of subgame-perfect Nash equilibrium is equivalent to the definition of Nash equilibrium, so in this example both (L, L') and (R, R') are subgame-perfect Nash equilibria. Nonetheless, (R, R') clearly depends on a noncredible threat: if player 2 gets the move, then playing L' dominates playing R', so player 1 should not be induced to play R by 2's threat to play R' if given the move.

One way to strengthen the equilibrium concept so as to rule out the sub-game-perfect Nash equilibrium (R, R') is to impose two requirements.

Requirement 1: Whenever a player has the move and is uncertain about the history of prior play, the player must have a *belief* over the set of feasible histories of play.

Requirement 2: Given their beliefs, the players' strategies must be *sequentially rational*. That is, whenever a player has the move, the player's action (and the player's strategy from then on) must be optimal given the player's belief at that point (and the other players' strategies from then on).

In the example above, Requirement 1 implies that if player 2 gets the move, then player 2 must have a belief about whether player 1 has played L or M. This belief is represented by the probabilities p and $1 - p$ attached to the relevant nodes in the game tree. Given player 2's belief, the expected payoff from playing R' is

$$p \cdot 0 + (1 - p) \cdot 1 = 1 - p$$

while the expected payoff from playing L' is

$$p \cdot 1 + (1 - p) \cdot 2 = 2 - p$$

Since $2 - p > 1 - p$ for any value of p, Requirement 2 prevents player 2 from choosing R'. Thus, simply requiring that each player have a belief and act optimally given this belief suffices to eliminate the implausible equilibrium (R, R') in this example.

What about the other subgame-perfect Nash equilibrium, (L, L')? Requirement 1 dictates that player 2 have a belief but does not specify what it should be. In the spirit of rational expectations, however, player 2's belief in this equilibrium should be $p = 1$. We state this idea a bit more formally as:

Requirement 3: Where possible, beliefs should be determined by Bayes' rule from the players' equilibrium strategies.

We give other examples of Requirement 3 below.

In simple economic applications, including the signaling games discussed below, Requirements 1 through 3 constitute the definition of *perfect Bayesian equilibrium*. In richer applications, more requirements need to be imposed to eliminate implausible equilibria.[15]

4.2. Signaling games

We now return to dynamic Bayesian games, where we will apply perfect Bayesian equilibrium. For simplicity, we restrict attention to (finite) signaling games, which have the following timing:

1 Nature draws a type t_i for the Sender from a set of feasible types $T = \{t_1, \ldots, t_I\}$ according to a probability distribution $p(t_i)$.
2 The Sender observes t_i and then chooses a message m_j from a set of feasible messages $M = \{m_1, \ldots, m_J\}$.
3 The Receiver observes m_j (but not t_i) and then chooses an action a_k from a set of feasible actions $A = \{a_1, \ldots, a_K\}$.
4 Payoffs are given by $U_S(t_i, m_j, a_k)$ and $U_R(t_i, m_j, a_k)$.

In Cho and Kreps's (1987) "Beer and Quiche" signaling game, shown in Figure 10, the type, message and action spaces (T, M and A, respectively) all have only two elements. While most game trees start at the top, a signaling game starts in the middle, with a move

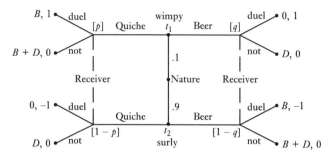

Figure 10   The beer and quiche signaling game

by Nature that determines the Sender's type: here $t_1 =$ "wimpy" (with probability .1) or $t_2 =$ "surly" (with probability .9).[16] Both Sender types then have the same choice of messages – Quiche or Beer (as alternative breakfasts). The Receiver observes the message but not the type. (As above, the dashed line connecting two of the Receiver's two decision nodes indicates that the Receiver knows that one of the nodes in this "information set" was reached, but does not know which node – that is, the Receiver observes the Sender's breakfast but not his type.) Finally, following each message, the Receiver chooses between two actions – to duel or not to duel with the Sender.

The qualitative features of the payoffs are that the wimpy type would prefer to have quiche for breakfast, the surly type would prefer to have beer, both types would prefer not to duel with the Receiver, and the Receiver would prefer to duel with the wimpy type but not to duel with the surly type. Specifically, the preferred breakfast is worth $B > 0$ for both sender types, avoiding a duel is worth $D > 0$ for both Sender types, and the payoff from a duel with the wimpy (respectively, surly) type is 1 (respectively, -1) for the Receiver; all other payoffs were zero.

The point of a signaling game is that the Sender's message may convey information to the Receiver. We call the Sender's strategy *separating* if each type sends a different message. In Beer and Quiche, for example, the strategy [Quiche if wimpy, Beer if surly] is a separating strategy for the Sender. At the other extreme, the Sender's strategy is called *pooling* if each type sends the same message. In a model with more than two types there are also *partially* pooling (or *semiseparating*) strategies in which all the types in a given set of types send the same message, but different sets of types send different messages. Perfect Bayesian equilibria involving such strategies for the Sender are also called separating, pooling, and so on.

If $B > D$, then the Sender's strategy [Quiche if wimpy, Beer if surly] and the Receiver's strategy [duel after Quiche, no duel after Beer], together with the beliefs $p = 1$ and $q = 0$ satisfy Requirements 1 through 3 and so are a perfect Bayesian equilibrium of the Beer and Quiche signaling game. Put more evocatively, when $B > D$, having the preferred breakfast is more important than avoiding a duel, so each Sender type chooses its preferred breakfast, thereby signaling its type; signaling this information works against the wimpy type (because it induces the Receiver to duel), but this consideration is outweighed by the importance of getting the preferred breakfast.

We can also ask whether Beer and Quiche has other perfect Bayesian equilibria. The three other pure strategies the Sender could play are [Quiche if wimpy, Quiche if surly], [Beer if wimpy, Quiche if surly] and [Beer if wimpy, Beer if surly]. When $B > D$, the lowest payoff the wimpy Sender-type could receive from playing Quiche (B) exceeds the highest available from playing Beer (D), so the wimpy type will not play Beer, leaving [Quiche if wimpy, Quiche if surly] as the only other strategy the Sender might play. Analogously, the lowest payoff the surly Sender-type could receive from playing Beer (B) exceeds the highest available from playing Quiche (D), so the surly type will not play Quiche. Thus, the separating perfect Bayesian equilibrium derived above is the unique perfect Bayesian equilibrium of the Beer and Quiche signaling game when $B > D$.

What about when $B < D$? Now there is no separating perfect Bayesian equilibrium.[17] But there are two pooling perfect Bayesian equilibria. It is straightforward to show that when $B < D$, the Sender's strategy [Beer if wimpy, Beer if surly] and the Receiver's strategy [duel after Quiche, no duel after Beer], together with the beliefs $p = 1$ and $q = \cdot 1$ satisfy Requirements 1 through 3. (In fact, any $p \geq .5$ would work as well.) This pooling equilibrium makes sense (just as the separating equilibrium above made sense when $B \geq D$): the surly type gets its preferred breakfast and avoids a duel; because $B < D$, the wimpy type now prefers to hide behind the high prior probability of the surly type (.9, which dissuades the Receiver from dueling without further information) rather than have its preferred breakfast.

There is also another pooling equilibrium: when $B < D$, the Sender's strategy [Quiche if wimpy, Quiche if surly] and the Receiver's strategy [no duel after Quiche, duel after Beer], together with the beliefs $p = .1$ and $q = 1$ satisfy Requirements 1 through 3. (In fact, any $q \geq .5$ would work as well.) Cho and Kreps argue that the Receiver's belief in this equilibrium is counterintuitive. Their "Intuitive Criterion" refines perfect Bayesian equilibrium by putting additional restrictions on beliefs (beyond Requirement 3) that rule out this pooling equilibrium (but not the previous pooling equilibrium, in which both types choose Beer).

Further Reading

I hope this paper has clearly defined the four major classes of games and their solution concepts, as well as sketched the motivation for and connections among these concepts. This may be enough to allow some applied economists to grapple with game-theoretic work in their own research areas, but I hope to have interested at least a few readers in more than this introduction.

An economist seeking further reading on game theory has the luxury of a great deal of choice – at least eight new books, as well as at least two earlier texts, one now in its second edition. (I apologize for excluding several other books written either for or by non-economists, as well as any books by and for economists that have escaped my attention.) These ten books are Binmore (1992), Dixit and Nalebuff (1991), Friedman (1990), Fudenberg and Tirole (1991b), Gibbons (1992), Kreps (1990b), McMillan (1992), Myerson (1991), Osborne and Rubinstein (1994) and Rasmussen (1989). These books are all excellent, but I think it fair to say that different readers will find different books appropriate, depending on the reader's background and goals. At the risk of offending my fellow authors, let me hazard some characterizations and suggestions.

Roughly speaking, some books emphasize theory, others economic applications, and still others "the real world." Given a book's emphasis, there is then a question regarding its level. I see Binmore, Friedman, Fudenberg–Tirole, Kreps, Myerson and Osborne–Rubinstein as books that emphasize theory. If I were trying to transform a bright undergraduate into a game theorist (as distinct from an applied modeler), I would start with either or both of Binmore and Kreps, and then proceed to any or all of Friedman, Fudenberg–Tirole, Myerson and Osborne–Rubinstein. In contrast, I see Gibbons and Rasmussen (and, to some extent, McMillan) as books that emphasize economic applications. Each is accessible to a bright undergraduate, but could also provide the initial doctoral training for an applied modeler and perhaps the full doctoral training for an applied economist wishing to consume (rather than construct) applied models. The next step for those who wish to construct such models might be to sample from Fudenberg–Tirole, as the most applications oriented of the advanced theory books. Finally, I see Dixit–Nalebuff and McMillan as books that emphasize the real world (McMillan being more closely tied to applications from the economics literature). These are the texts to use to teach an undergraduate (or an MBA) to think strategically, although for this purpose one should also read the collected works of Thomas Schelling. These books would also be useful additions to the training of an applied modeler, in the hope that the student would learn to keep his or her eye on the empirical ball.

All of this further reading is for economists seeking a deeper treatment of the theory. I wish I could offer analogous recommendations for those seeking further reading on the many ways game theory has been used to build new theoretical models, both inside and outside economics; this will have to await a future survey. More importantly, I eagerly await the first thorough assessment of how game-theoretic models in economics have fared when confronted with field data of the kind commonly used to assess price-theoretic models. For an important step in a related direction, see Roth and Kagel's (1995) excellent *Handbook of Experimental Economics*, which describes laboratory evidence pertaining to many game-theoretic models.

Notes

1 Full disclosure requires me to reveal that I wrote one of the books mentioned in this guide to further reading, so readers should discount my objectivity accordingly. By the gracious consent of the publisher, much of the material presented here is drawn from that book.

2 More generally, action a_1' is *dominated* by action a_1'' for player 1 if, for each action player 2 might choose, 1's payoff is higher from playing a_1'' than from playing a_1'. That is, $u_1(a_1', a_2) < u_1(a_1'', a_2)$ for each action a_2 in 2's action set, A_2. A rational player will not play a dominated action.

3 Formally, in the two-player, simultaneous-move game described above, the actions (a_1^*, a_2^*) are a Nash equilibrium if a_1^* is a best response for player 1 to a_2^*, and a_2^* is a best response for player 2 to a_1^*. That is, a_1^* must satisfy $u_1(a_1^*, a_2^*) \geq u_1(a_1, a_2^*)$ for every a_1 in A_1, and a_2^* must satisfy $u_2(a_1^*, a_2^*) \geq u_2(a_1^*, a_2)$ for every a_2 in A_2.

4 Another well-known example in which the unique Nash Equilibrium is not efficient is the Cournot duopoly model.

5   I owe the nonsexist, nonheterosexist player names to Matt Rabin. Allison Beezer noted, however, that no amount of Rabin's relabeling could overcome the game's original name, so she suggested the Dating Game. Larry Samuelson suggested the updated choices available to the players.

There are of course many applications of this game, including political groups attempting to establish a constitution, firms attempting to establish an industry standard, and colleagues deciding which days to work at home.

6   Any finite game has a subgame-perfect Nash equilibrium, possibly involving mixed strategies, because each subgame is itself a finite game and hence has a Nash equilibrium.

7   The interest rate r can be interpreted as reflecting both the rate of time preference and the probability that the current period will be the last, so that the "infinitely repeated" game ends at a random date.

8   If player 1 is playing her strategy given above, then it is a best response for player 2 to play his strategy if

$$\left\{ 1 + \left(\frac{1}{r} \right) \right\} 1 \geq 2 + \left(\frac{1}{r} \right) \cdot 0$$

or $r \leq 1$. More generally, if a player's payoffs (per period) are C from cooperation, D from defection and P from punishment, then the player has an incentive to cooperate if

$$\left\{ 1 + \left(\frac{1}{r} \right) \right\} C \geq D + \left(\frac{1}{r} \right) P$$

or

$$r \leq \frac{(C - P)}{(D - C)}$$

9   In fact, this Nash equilibrium of the repeated game is subgame-perfect.

10 As an example of correlated types, imagine that two firms are racing to develop a new technology. Each firm's chance of success depends in part on how difficult the technology is to develop, which is not known. Each firm knows only whether it has succeeded, not whether the other has. If firm 1 has succeeded, however, then it is more likely that the technology is easy to develop and so also more likely that firm 2 has succeeded. Thus, firm 1's belief about firm 2's type depends on firm 1's knowledge of its own type.

11 There are games in which one player has private information not only about his or her own payoff function but also about another player's payoff function. As an example, consider an asymmetric-information Cournot model in which costs are common knowledge, but one firm knows the level of demand and the other does not. Since the level of demand affects both players' payoff functions, the informed firm's type enters the uninformed firm's payoff function. To allow for such information structures, the payoff functions in a Bayesian game can be written as $u_i(a_i, a_j; t_i, t_j)$.

12 Given the close connection between Nash equilibrium and Bayesian Nash equilibrium, it should not be surprising that a Bayesian Nash equilibrium exists in any finite Bayesian game.

13 It may seem strange to define equilibrium in terms of action rules. In an auction, for example, why can't a bidder simply consider what bid to make given her actual valuation? Why does it matter what bids she would have made given other valuations? To see through this puzzle, note that for bidder 1 to compute an optimal bid, bidder 1 needs a conjecture about bidder 2's entire bidding rule. And to determine whether even one bid from this rule is optimal, bidder 2 would need a conjecture about bidder 1's entire bidding rule. Akin to a rational expectations equilibrium, these conjectured bidding rules must be correct in a Bayesian Nash equilibrium.

14 Kreps and Wilson (1982) formalize this perspective on equilibrium by defining *sequential equilibrium*, an equilibrium concept that is equivalent to perfect Bayesian equilibrium in many economic applications but in some cases is slightly stronger. Sequential equilibrium is more complicated to define and to apply than perfect Bayesian equilibrium, so most authors now use the latter. Kreps and Wilson show that any finite game (with or without private information) has a sequential equilibrium, so the same can be said for perfect Bayesian equilibrium.

15 To give a sense of the issues not addressed by Requirements 1 through 3, suppose players 2 and 3 have observed the same events, and then both observe a deviation from the equilibrium by player 1. Should players 2 and 3 hold the same belief about earlier unobserved moves by player 1? Fudenberg and Tirole (1991a) give a formal definition of perfect Bayesian equilibrium for a broad class of dynamic Bayesian games and provide conditions under which their perfect Bayesian equilibrium is equivalent to Kreps and Wilson's (1982) sequential equilibrium.

16 Readers over the age of 35 may recognize that the labels in this game were inspired by *Real Men Don't Eat Quiche*, a highly visible book when this example was conceived.

17 To see why, work out what the Receiver would do if, say, the wimpy Sender-type chose Quiche and the surly choose Beer, and then work out whether these Sender-types would in fact make these choices, given the response just calculated for the Receiver.

References

Benabou, R. and Laroque, G. (1992): "Using Privileged Information to Manipulate Markets: Insiders, Gurus, and Credibility," *Quarterly Journal of Economics*, 107, August, 921–58.

Binmore, K. (1992): *Fun and Games: A Text on Game Theory*. Lexington, Mass: D. C. Heath & Co.

Cho, I. K., and Kreps, D. (1987): "Signaling Games and Stable Equilibria," *Quarterly Journal of Economics*, 102, May, 179–222.

Cournot, A. (1838): *Recherches sur les Principes Mathématiques de la Théorie des Richesses*. English edition, Bacon, N. (ed.) *Researches into the Mathematical Principles of the Theory of Wealth*. New York: Macmillan, 1897.

Cramton, P. and Tracy, J. (1992): "Strikes and Holdouts in Wage Bargaining: Theory and Data," *American Economic Review*, 82, March, 100–21.

Dixit, A. and Nalebuff, B. (1991): *Thinking Strategically: The Competitive Edge in Business, Politics, and Everyday Life*. New York: Norton.

Farber, H. (1980): "An Analysis of Final-Offer Arbitration," *Journal of Conflict Resolution*, 35, December, 683–705.

Friedman, J. (1990): *Game Theory with Applications to Economics*, 2nd edn. Oxford: Oxford University Press.

Fudenberg, D. and Tirole, J. (1991a): "Perfect Bayesian Equilibrium and Sequential Equilibrium," *Journal of Economic Theory*, 53, April, 236–60.

—— and —— (1991b): *Game Theory*. Cambridge, Mass: Massachusetts Institute of Technology Press.

Gibbons, R. (1992): *Game Theory for Applied Economists*. Princeton, NJ: Princeton University Press.

Grossman, S. and Hart, O. (1980): "Takeover Bids, the Free-Rider Problem, and the Theory of the Corporation," *Bell Journal of Economics*, 11, Spring, 42–64.

Harsanyi, J. (1967): "Games with Incomplete Information Played by 'Bayesian Players': I. The Basic Model," *Management Science*, 14, November, 159–82.

——(1968a): "Games with Incomplete Information Played by 'Bayesian Players': II. Bayesian Equilibrium Points," *Management Science*, 14, January, 320–34.

——(1968b): "Games with Incomplete Information Played by 'Bayesian Players': III. The Basic Probability Distribution of the Game," *Management Science*, 14, March, 486–502.

—— (1973): "Games with Randomly Disturbed Payoffs: A New Rationale for Mixed Strategy Equilibrium Points," *International Journal of Game Theory*, 2 (1), 1–23.

Hotelling, H. (1929): "Stability in Competition," *Economic Journal*, 39, March, 41–57.

Kreps, D. (1990a): "Corporate Culture and Economic Theory," in J. Alt and K. Shepsle (eds), *Perspectives on Positive Political Economy*, Cambridge: Cambridge University Press, 90–143.

—— (1990b): *Game Theory and Economic Modeling*. Oxford: Oxford University Press.

—— and Wilson, R. (1982): "Sequential Equilibrium," *Econometrica*, 50, July, 863–94.

——, Milgrom, P., Roberts, J. and Wilson, R. (1982): "Rational Cooperation in the Finitely Repeated Prisoners' Dilemma," *Journal of Economic Theory*, 27, August, 245–52.

Lazear, E. and Rosen, S. (1981): "Rank-Order Tournaments as Optimum Labor Contracts," *Journal of Political Economy*, 89, October, 841–64.

Leontief, W. (1946): "The Pure Theory of the Guaranteed Annual Wage Contract," *Journal of Political Economy*, 54, February, 76–9.

McMillan, J. (1992): *Games, Strategies, and Managers*, Oxford: Oxford University Press.

Myerson, R. (1991): *Games Theory: Analysis of Conflict*. Cambridge, Mass: Harvard University Press.

Nash, J. (1950): "Equilibrium Points in *n*-Person Games," *Proceedings of the National Academy of Sciences*, 36, 48–9.

Osborne, M. and Rubinstein, A. (1994): *A Course in Game Theory*. Cambridge, Mass: Massachusetts Institute of Technology Press.

Rasmussen, E. (1989): *Games and Information: An Introduction to Game Theory*, New York: Basil Blackwell.

Rogoff, K. (1989): "Reputation, Coordination, and Monetary Policy," in R. Barro (ed.), *Modern Business Cycle Theory*, Cambridge, Mass: Harvard University Press, 236–64.

Roth, A. and Kagel, J. (1995): *Handbook of Experimental Economics*. Princeton, NJ: Princeton University Press.

Rubinstein, A. (1982): "Perfect Equilibrium in a Bargaining Model," *Econometrica*, 50, January, 97–109.

Selten, R. (1965): "Spieltheoretische Behandlung eines Oligopolmodells mit Nachfragetragheit," *Zeitschrift für Gesamle Staatswissenschaft*, 121, 301–24.

Spence, A. M. (1973): "Job Market Signaling," *Quarterly Journal of Economics*, 87, August, 355–74.

von Stackelberg, H. (1934): *Marktform und Gleichgewicht*. Vienna: Julius Springer.

Young, H. P. (1996): "The Economics of Convention," *Journal of Economic Perspectives*, 10, Spring, 105–22.

III E

The Firm's Decision Making Under Uncertainty

CHAPTER FOURTEEN

The Economics of Moral Hazard: Comment

MARK V. PAULY

Source: *American Economic Review*, 58 (1968), pp. 531–37. Reprinted with the permission of the author and the American Economic Association. © American Economic Association.

When uncertainty is present in economic activity, insurance is commonly found. Indeed, Kenneth Arrow [1] has identified a kind of market failure with the absence of markets to provide insurance against some uncertain events. Arrow stated that "the welfare case for insurance of all sorts is overwhelming. It follows that the government should undertake insurance where the market, for whatever reason, has failed to emerge" [1, pp. 945, 961]. This paper will show, however, that even if all individuals are risk–averters, insurance against some types of uncertain events may be nonoptimal. Hence, the fact that certain kinds of insurance have failed to emerge in the private market may be no indication of nonoptimality, and compulsory government insurance against some uncertain events may lead to inefficiency. It will also be shown that the problem of "moral hazard" in insurance has, in fact, little to do with morality, but can be analyzed with orthodox economic tools.

The particular type of insurance for which the argument will be presented is that of insurance against medical care expenses, for it was in a discussion of medical expense insurance that Arrow framed the propositions cited above. However, the analysis is applicable as well to other types of insurance, such as automobile collision insurance.

1. The Welfare Implications of Insurance

It is assumed that all individuals are expected utility maximizers and are risk–averters, and that the incidence of illness is a random event. This excludes preventive medicine from consideration, and it also ignores the effect that medical insurance might have on the purchase of preventive care. Bernoulli's theorem, as cited by Arrow [1, pp. 959–61], states that such individuals will prefer insurance with a premium m which indemnifies against all costs of medical care to facing without insurance a probability distribution of such expenditures with mean m.

There is a social gain obtained by purchase of this insurance (as long as the insurer suffers no social loss) since pooling of risks reduces the total risk, and therefore the risk per insured, because of the Law of Large Numbers. Of course, the existence of transactions costs means that the policy is not really offered at the actuarially fair premium m.

However, since the individual preferred actuarially fair insurance to self-insurance, he will prefer some insurance with an actuarially unfair premium to self-insurance, so long as the premium is not too "unfair." His preference in this regard will depend on the intensity of his risk aversion and the strength of the Law of Large Numbers in reducing risk.

As indicated above, Arrow concluded from this analysis that the absence of commercial insurance against some uncertain medical-care expenses provides a case for government intervention to provide such insurance. Dennis Lees and R. D. Rice [6] answered that this insurance was not offered because of selling and transactions costs. Arrow [2] replied, in effect, that such costs were dead-weight losses anyway, and indeed would be eliminated by compulsory social insurance. It seems clear, however, that there is another and better way to explain why some insurances are not offered commercially. It is to show that some, perhaps many, medical care expenses are not "insurable" in the standard sense.

In order for the welfare proposition given above to be valid, the costs of medical care must be random variables. But if such expenses are not completely random, the proposition no longer holds. The quantity of medical care an individual will demand depends on his income and tastes, how ill he is, and the price charged for it. The effect of an insurance which indemnifies against all medical care expenses is to reduce the price charged to the individual at the point of service from the market price to zero. Even if the incidence of illness is a random event, whether the presence of insurance will alter the randomness of medical *expenses* depends on the elasticity of demand for medical care. Only if this demand is perfectly inelastic with respect to price in the range from the market price to zero is an expense "insurable" in the strict sense envisioned by Arrow's welfare proposition.

Suppose, for example, that an individual faces the probability $p_1 = \frac{1}{2}$ that he will not be sick at all during a given time period (event I_1) and so will demand no medical care, probability $p_2 = \frac{1}{4}$ that he will contract sickness I_2, and probability $p_3 = \frac{1}{4}$ that he will contract "more serious" sickness I_3. The position of his demand curve for medical care depends on which illness, if any, he contracts. In Figure 1, it is assumed that his demand curves D_2' and D_3' are perfectly inelastic, and that his demand curve for the "no illness"

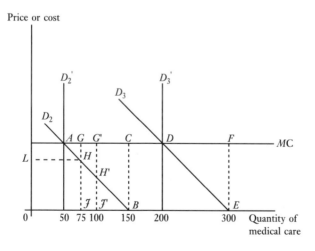

Figure 1

case is identical with the y-axis. Without insurance, the individual faces the probability p_1 that he will incur no medical expenses, the probability p_2 that he will need 50 units of medical care (which is assumed to be priced at marginal cost), and the probability p_3 that he will need 200 units of medical care at a cost of 200 MC. The mean of this probability distribution (or the expected values of the individual's medical care expenses) equals

$$(\frac{1}{2} \times 0 + \frac{1}{4} \times 50\ MC + \frac{1}{4} \times 200\ MC)$$

or 62.5 MC. Hence, an actuarially fair insurance which indemnifies the individual against all costs of medical care could be offered at a premium P of 62.5 MC. Arrow's welfare proposition indicates that the individual would prefer paying a premium of 62.5 MC to risking the probability distribution with the mean $m = 62.5\ MC$.

Suppose, however, that the individual's demand curves are not all perfectly inelastic, but are as D_2 and D_3. Then the individual has to choose between facing, without insurance, the probability distribution

$$(\frac{1}{2} \times 0 + \frac{1}{4} \times 50\ MC + \frac{1}{4} \times 200\ MC)$$

with a mean m of 62.5 MC, and paying a premium of

$$P = (\frac{1}{2} \times 0 + \frac{1}{4} \times 150\ MC + \frac{1}{4} \times 300\ MC) = 112.5\ MC$$

in order to obtain insurance. In such a case, he may well prefer the risk to the insurance.

The presence of elasticity in the demand curves implies therefore that the individual will alter his desired expenditures for medical care because of the fact of insurance. The individual who has insurance which covers all costs demands medical care as though it had a *zero* price, but when he purchases insurance, he must take account of the *positive* cost of that care, as "translated" to him through the actuarially necessary premium. Hence, he may well not wish to purchase such insurance at the premium his behavior as a purchaser of insurance and as a demander of medical care under insurance makes necessary.[1]

The presence of a "prisoners' dilemma" motivation makes this inconsistency inevitable.[2] Each individual may well recognize that "excess" use of medical care makes the premium he must pay rise. No individual will be motivated to restrain his own use, however, since the incremental benefit to him for excess use is great, while the additional cost of his use is largely spread over other insurance holders, and so he bears only a tiny fraction of the cost of his use. It would be better for all insurance beneficiaries to restrain their use, but such a result is not forthcoming because the strategy of "restrain use" is dominated by that of "use excess care."

If the demand for medical care is of greater than zero elasticity, the existence of this "inconsistency" implies that inefficiency may well be created if individuals are forced, by taxation, to "purchase" insurance which indemnifies against some kinds of medical care expense. For an efficient solution, at least some price-rationing at the point of service may be necessary.

Suppose there are no significant income effects on the individual's demand for medical care resulting from his payment of a lump-sum premium for insurance. In Figure 1, the inefficiency loss due to behavior under insurance, if that insurance were compulsory, would then be roughly measured by triangles ABC and DEF. These areas represent the excess that individuals do pay over what they would be willing to pay for the quantity of medical care demanded under insurance. Against this loss must be offset the utility gain from having these uncertain expenses insured, but the net change in utility from a compulsory purchase of this "insurance" could well be negative.

Moreover, if individual demands for medical care differ, it is possible that the loss due to "excess" use under insurance may exceed the welfare gain from insurance for one individual but fall short of it for another individual. It follows that it may not be optimal policy to provide compulsory insurance against particular events for all individuals. Some events may be "insurable" for some persons but not for others. It also follows that some events, though uncertain, may not be insurable for anyone. If persons differ

(a)   in the strength of their risk aversion or
(b)   in the extent to which insurances of various types alter the quantity of medical care they demand

an optimal state will be one in which various types of policies are purchased by various groups of people. There may be some persons who will purchase no insurance against some uncertain events.

Insurance is more likely to be provided against those events

(a)   for which the quantity demanded at a zero price does not greatly exceed that demanded at a positive price,
(b)   for which the extent of randomness is greater, so that risk-spreading reduces the risk significantly, and
(c)   against which individuals have a greater risk-aversion.

There is uncertainty attached to "catastrophic" illness, but it appears that the elasticity of demand for treatment against such illness is not very great (in the sense that there is one and only one appropriate treatment). Furthermore, the "randomness" attached to such illnesses is relatively great, in the sense that they are unpredictable for any individual, and people's aversion to such risk is relatively great. Hence, one would expect to find, and does find, insurance offered against such events. Similar statement might be made with respect to ordinary hospitalization insurance.

There is also some uncertainty attached to visits to a physician's office, but the extent of randomness and risk-aversion is probably relatively low for most persons. The increase in use in response to a zero price would be relatively great. One would not expect to find, and does not in general find, "insurance" against such events. Similar analysis applies to insurance against the cost of dental care, eyeglasses, or drugs.

2. Moral Hazard

It has been recognized in the insurance literature that medical insurance, by lowering the marginal cost of care to the individual, may increase usage; this characteristic has been termed "moral hazard." Moral hazard is defined as "the intangible loss-producing propensities of the individual assured" [4, p. 463] or as that which "comprehends all of the nonphysical hazards of risk" [5, p. 42]. Insurance writers have tended very strongly to look upon this phenomenon (of demanding more at a zero price than at a positive one) as a moral or ethical problem, using emotive words such as "malingering" and "hypochon-dria," lumping it together with outright fraud in the collection of benefits, and providing value-tinged definitions as "moral hazard reflects the hazard that arises from the failure of individuals who are or have been affected by insurance to uphold the accepted moral qualities" [5, p. 327], or "moral hazard is every deviation from correct human behavior that may pose a problem for an insurer" [3, p. 22]. It is surprising that very little economic analysis seems to have been applied here.[3]

The above analysis shows, however, that the response of seeking more medical care with insurance than in its absence is a result not of moral perfidy, but of rational economic behavior. Since the cost of the individual's excess usage is spread over all other purchasers of that insurance, the individual is not prompted to restrain his usage of care.

3. Deductibles and Coinsurance

The only type of insurance so far considered has been an insurance which provides full coverage of the cost of medical care. However, various devices are written into insurance, in part to reduce the moral hazard, of which the most important are deductibles and coinsurance.[4] The individual may well prefer no insurance to full coverage of all expenses, but may at the same time prefer an insurance with these devices to no insurance.[5]

3.1. Deductibles

Suppose the insurance contains a deductible. The individual will compare the position he would attain if he covered the deductible and received additional care free with the position he would attain if he paid the market price for all the medical care he consumed but did not cover the deductible. If income effects are absent in Figure 1, the individual will cover a deductible and consume 150 units of medical care when event I_2 occurs as long as the "excess" amount he pays as a deductible (e.g., area AGH for a deductible of 75 MC) is less than the consumer's surplus he gets from the "free" units of care this coverage allows him to consume (e.g., area HJB). If the deductible exceeds 100 MC (at which point area $AG'H'$ equals area $H'J'B$), the individual will not cover the deductible and will purchase 50 units. Hence, the deductible either

  (a)   has no effect on an individual's usage, or

(b) induces him to consume that amount of care he would have purchased if he had no insurance.

If there are income effects on individual demands, because the deductible makes the individual poorer his usage will be restrained somewhat even if he covers the deductible.

3.2. Coinsurance

Coinsurance is a scheme in which the individual is, in effect, charged a positive price for medical care, but a price less than the market price. The higher the fraction paid by the individual, the more his usage will be curtailed. In Figure 1, if he had to pay OL of each unit's cost, he would reduce his usage if event I_2 occurred from 150 units to 75 units. The smaller the price elasticity of demand for medical care, the less will be the effect of coinsurance on usage.

It is possible for the restraining effect of coinsurance to reduce moral hazard enough to make insurance attractive to an individual who would have preferred no insurance to full-coverage insurance. Indeed, there is an optimal extent of coinsurance for each individual. The optimal extent of coinsurance is the coverage of that percentage of the cost of each unit of medical care at which the utility gain to the individual from having an additional small fraction of the cost of each unit of care covered by insurance equals the utility loss to him upon having to pay for the "excess" units of care whose consumption the additional coverage encourages. If the marginal gain from the coverage of additional fractions of cost always exceeds the marginal inefficiency loss, he will purchase full coverage insurance; if the marginal loss exceeds the marginal gain for all extends of coinsurance, the individual will purchase no insurance. If individual demands differ, the optimal extent of coinsurance will differ for different individuals.

4. Conclusion

It is possible to conclude that even if all individuals are risk-averters, some uncertain medical care expenses will not and should not be insured in an optimal situation. No single insurance policy is "best" or "most efficient" for a whole population of diverse tastes. Which expenses are insurable is not an objective fact, but depends on the tastes and behavior of the persons involved.

Notes

1 This is exactly the same sort of "inconsistency" that Buchanan has noted in connection with the British National Health Service. Individuals demand medical care as though it were free but in voting decisions consider the positive cost of such care. Hence, they vote, through their representatives in the political process, to provide facilities for less medical care than they demand in the market. See [4].
2 For a discussion of the prisoners' dilemma problem, see [7].

3   In his original article, Arrow mentions moral hazard as a "practical limitation" on the use of insurance which does not "alter the case for creation of a much wider class of insurance policies than now exist" [1, p. 961]. However, Arrow appears to consider moral hazard as an imperfection, a defect in physician control, rather than as a simple response to price reduction. He does not consider the direct relationship which exists between the existence of moral hazard and the validity of the welfare proposition. More importantly, in the controversy that followed [2] [6], moral hazard seems to have been completely overlooked as an explanation of why certain types of expenses are not insured commercially.

4   A deductible is the exclusion of a certain amount of expense from coverage; coinsurance requires the individual to pay some fraction of each dollar of cost.

5   Arrow [1, pp. 969–73] gives some other arguments to explain why the individual will prefer insurance with deductibles or coinsurance to insurance without such devices.

References and Further Reading

1 Arrow, K. J. (1963): "Uncertainty and the Welfare Economics of Medical-Care," *American Economic Review*, 53, December, 941–73.

2 ——(1965): "Reply," *American Economic Review*, 55, March, 154–8.

3 Buchanan, J. M. (1965): *The Inconsistencies of the National Health Service*, Occasional paper 7, London: Institute of Economic Affairs.

4 Dickerson, O. D. (1963): *Health Insurance*, revised edn Homewood, Ill.: Irwin.

5 Faulkner, E. J. (1960): *Health Insurance*. New York: McGraw-Hill.

6 Lees, D. S. and Rice, R. G. (1965): "Uncertainty and the Welfare Economics of Medical Care: Comment," *American Economic Review*, 55, March, 140–54.

7 Luce, R. D. and Raiffa, H. (1957): *Games and Decisions*. New York: Wiley.

8 Michelbacher, G. F. (1957): *Multiple-line Insurance*. New York: McGraw-Hill.

CHAPTER FIFTEEN

Job Market Signaling

A. Michael Spence

Source: *Quarterly Journal of Economics*, 87 (1973), pp. 355–74.

1. Introduction

The term "market signaling" is not exactly a part of the well-defined, technical vocabulary of the economist. As a part of the preamble, therefore, I feel I owe the reader a word of explanation about the title. I find it difficult, however, to give a coherent and comprehensive explanation of the meaning of the term abstracted from the contents of the essay. In fact, it is part of my purpose to outline a model in which signaling is implicitly defined and to explain why one can, and perhaps should, be interested in it. One might accurately characterize my problem as a signaling one, and that of the reader, who is faced with an investment decision under uncertainty, as that of interpreting signals.

How the reader interprets my report of the content of this essay will depend upon his expectation concerning my stay in the market. If one believes I will be in the essay market repeatedly, then both the reader and I will contemplate the possibility that I might invest in my future ability to communicate by accurately reporting the content of this essay now. On the other hand, if I am to be in the market only once, or relatively infrequently, then the above-mentioned possibility deserves a low probability. This essay is about markets in which signaling takes place and in which the primary signalers are relatively numerous and in the market sufficiently infrequently that they are not expected to (and therefore do not) invest in acquiring signaling reputations.

I shall argue that the paradigm case of the market with this type of informational structure is the job market and will therefore focus upon it. By the end I hope it will be clear (although space limitations will not permit an extended argument) that a considerable variety of market and quasi-market phenomena like admissions procedures, promotion in organizations, loans and consumer credit, can be usefully viewed through the conceptual lens applied to the job market.

If the incentives for veracity in reporting anything by means of a conventional signaling code are weak, then one must look for other means by which information transfers take place. My aim is to outline a conceptual apparatus within which the signaling power of education, job experience, race, sex, and a host of other observable, personal characteristics can be determined. The question, put crudely, is what in the interactive structure of a market accounts for the informational content, if any, of these potential signals. I have placed primary emphasis upon

  (i)   the definition and properties of signaling equilibria,
  (ii) the interaction of potential signals, and
  (iii) the allocative efficiency of the market.

2. Hiring as Investment under Uncertainty

In most job markets the employer is not sure of the productive capabilities of an individual at the time he hires him.[1] Nor will this information necessarily become available to the employer immediately after hiring. The job may take time to learn. Often specific training is required. And there may be a contract period within which no recontracting is allowed. The fact that it takes time to learn an individual's productive capabilities means that hiring is an investment decision. The fact that these capabilities are not known beforehand makes the decision one under uncertainty.

To hire someone, then, is frequently to purchase a lottery.[2] In what follows, I shall assume the employer pays the certain monetary equivalent of the lottery to the individual as wage.[3] If he is risk-neutral, the wage is taken to be the individual's marginal contribution to the hiring organization.

Primary interest attaches to how the employer perceives the lottery, for it is these perceptions that determine the wages he offers to pay. We have stipulated that the employer cannot directly observe the marginal product prior to hiring. What he does observe is a plethora of personal data in the form of observable characteristics and attributes of the individual, and it is these that must ultimately determine his assessment of the lottery he is buying. (The image that the individual presents includes education, previous work, race, sex, criminal and service records, and a host of other data.) This essay is about the endogenous market process whereby the employer requires (and the individual transmits) information about the potential employee, which ultimately determines the implicit lottery involved in hiring, the offered wages, and in the end the allocation of jobs to people and people to jobs in the market.

At this point, it is useful to introduce a distinction, the import of which will be clear shortly. Of those observable, personal attributes that collectively constitute the image the job applicant presents, some are immutably fixed, while others are alterable. For example, education is something that the individual can invest in at some cost in terms of time and money. On the other hand, race and sex are not generally thought to be alterable. I shall refer to observable, unalterable attributes as *indices*, reserving the term *signals* for those observable characteristics attached to the individual that are subject to manipulation by him.[4] Some attributes, like age, do change, but not at the discretion of the individual. In my terms, these are indices.

Sometime after hiring an individual, the employer will learn the individual's productive capabilities. On the basis of previous experience in the market, the employer will have conditional probability assessments over productive capacity given various combinations of signals and indices. At any point of time when confronted with an individual applicant with certain observable attributes, the employer's subjective assessment of the lottery with which he is confronted is defined by these conditional probability distributions over productivity given the new data.

From one point of view, then, signals and indices are to be regarded as parameters in shifting conditional probability distributions that define an employer's beliefs.[5]

3. Applicant Signaling

For simplicity I shall speak as if the employer were risk-neutral. For each set of signals and indices that the employer confronts, he will have an expected marginal product for an individual who has these observable attributes. This is taken to be the offered wage to applicants with those characteristics. Potential employees therefore confront an offered wage schedule whose arguments are signals and indices.

There is not much that the applicant can do about indices. Signals, on the other hand, are alterable and therefore potentially subject to manipulation by the job applicant. Of course, there may be costs of making these adjustments. Education, for example, is costly. We refer to these costs as *signaling costs*. Notice that the individual, in acquiring an education, need not think of himself as signaling. He will invest in education if there is sufficient return as defined by the offered wage schedule.[6] Individuals, then, are assumed to select signals (for the most part, I shall talk in terms of education) so as to maximize the difference between offered wages and signaling costs. Signaling costs play a key role in this type of signaling situation, for they functionally replace the less direct costs and benefits associated with a reputation for signaling reliability acquired by those who are more prominent in their markets than job seekers are in theirs.

3.1. A critical assumption

It is not difficult to see that a signal will not effectively distinguish one applicant from another, unless the costs of signaling are negatively correlated with productive capability. For if this condition fails to hold, given the offered wage schedule, everyone will invest in the signal in exactly the same way, so that they cannot be distinguished on the basis of the signal. In what follows, we shall make the assumption that signaling costs are negatively correlated with productivity. It is, however, most appropriately viewed as a *prerequisite* for an observable, alterable characteristic to be a persistently informative signal in the market. This means, among other things, that a characteristic may be a signal with respect to some types of jobs but not with respect to others.[7]

Signaling costs are to be interpreted broadly to include psychic and other costs, as well as the direct monetary ones. One element of cost, for example, is time.

4. Information Feedback and the Definition of Equilibrium

At this point it is perhaps clear that there is informational feedback to the employer over time. As new market information comes in to the employer through hiring and subsequent observation of productive capabilities as they relate to signals, the employer's conditional probabilitic beliefs are adjusted, and a new round starts. The wage schedule facing the new entrants in the market generally differs from that facing the previous group. The elements in the feedback loop are shown in Figure 1.

It is desirable to find a way to study this feedback loop in the market over time. To avoid studying a system in a continual state of flux, it is useful to look for nontransitory configuration of the feedback system. The system will be stationary if the employer starts

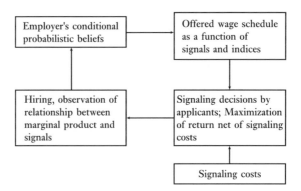

Figure 1   Information feedback in the job market

out with conditional probabilistic beliefs that after one round are not disconfirmed by the incoming data they generated. We shall refer to such beliefs as self-confirming. The sense in which they are self-confirming is defined by the feedback loop in Figure 1.

4.1. A signaling equilibrium

As successive waves of new applicants come into the market, we can imagine repeated cycles around the loop. Employers' conditional probabilistic beliefs are modified, offered wage schedules are adjusted, applicant behavior with respect to signal choice changes, and after hiring, new data become available to the employer. Each cycle, then, generates the next one. In thinking about it, one can interrupt the cycle at any point. An equilibrium is a set of components in the cycle that regenerate themselves. Thus, we can think of employer beliefs being self-confirming, or offered wage schedules regenerating themselves, or applicant behavior reproducing itself on the next round.[8]

I find it most useful to think in terms of the self-confirming aspect of the employer beliefs because of the continuity provided by the employer's persistent presence in the market.[9] Thus, in these terms an equilibrium can be thought of as a set of employer beliefs that generate offered wage schedules, applicant signaling decisions, hiring, and ultimately new market data over time that are consistent with the initial beliefs.

A further word about the definition of equilibrium is in order. Given an offered wage schedule, one can think of the market as generating, via individual optimizing decisions, an empirical distribution of productive capabilities given observable attributes or signals (and indices). On the other hand, the employer has subjectively held conditional probabilistic beliefs with respect to productivity, given signals. In an equilibrium the subjective distribution and the one implicit in the market mechanism are identical, *over the range of signals that the employer actually observes.*[10] Any other subjective beliefs will eventually be disconfirmed in the market because of the employer's persistent presence there.

Indices continue to be relevant. But since they are not a matter of individual choice, they do not figure prominently in the feedback system just described. I shall return to them later.

5. Properties of Informational Equilibria: An Example

I propose to discuss the existence and properties of market signaling equilibria via a specific numerical example.[11] For the time being, indices play no part. The properties of signaling equilibria that we shall encounter in the example are general (Spence, 1974).

Let us suppose that there are just two productively distinct groups in a population facing one employer. Individuals in Group I have a productivity of 1, while those in Group II have a productivity of 2.[12] Group I is a proportion q_1 of the population; Group II is a proportion of $1 - q_1$. There is, in addition, a potential signal, say education, which is available at a cost. We shall assume that education is measured by an index y of level and achievement and is subject to individual choice. Education costs are both monetary and psychic. It is assumed that the cost to a member of Group I of y units of education is y, while the cost to a member of Group II is $y/2$.

We summarize the underlying data of our numerical example in Table 1.

Table 1 Data of the model

Group	Marginal product	Proportion of population	Cost of education level y
I	1	q_1	y
II	2	$1 - q_1$	$y/2$

To find an equilibrium in the market, we guess at a set of self-confirming conditional probabilistic beliefs for the employer and then determine whether they are in fact confirmed by the feedback mechanisms described above. Suppose that the employer believes that there is some level of education, say y^* such that if $y < y^*$, then productivity is one with probability one, and that if $y \geq y^*$, then productivity will be two with probability one. If these are his conditional beliefs, then his offered wage schedule, $W(y)$, will be as shown in Figure 2.

Given the offered wage schedule, members of each group will select optimal levels for education. Consider the person who will set $y < y^*$. If he does this, we know he will set $y = 0$ because education is costly, and until he reaches y^*, there are no benefits to increasing y, given the employer's hypothesized beliefs. Similarly, any individual who sets $y \geq y^*$ will in fact set $y = y^*$, since further increases would merely incur costs with no corresponding benefits. Everyone will therefore either set $y = 0$ or set $y = y^*$. Given the employer's initial beliefs and the fact just deduced, if the employer's beliefs are to be confirmed, then members of Group I must set $y = 0$, while members of Group II set $y = y^*$. Diagrams of the options facing the two groups are shown in Figure 3.

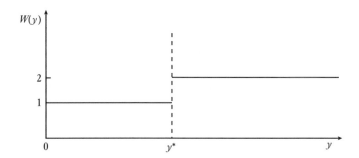

Figure 2   Offered wages as a function of level of economics

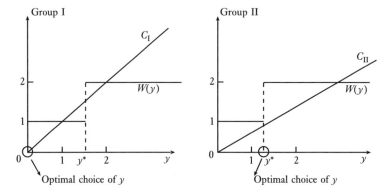

Figure 3   Optimizing choice of education for both groups

   Superimposed upon the wage schedule are the cost schedules for the two groups. Each group selects y to maximize the difference between the offered wages and the costs of education. Given the level of y^* in the diagram, it is easy to see that Group I selects $y = 0$, and Group II sets $y = y^*$. Thus, in this case the employer's beliefs are confirmed, and we have a signaling equilibrium. We can state the conditions on behavior by the two groups, in order that the employer's beliefs be confirmed, in algebraic terms. Group I sets $y = 0$ if

$$1 > 2 - y^*$$

Group II will set $y = y^*$ as required, provided that

$$2 - \frac{y^*}{2} > 1$$

Putting these two conditions together, we find that the employer's initial beliefs are confirmed by market experience, provided that the parameter y^* satisfies the inequality,

$$1 < y^* < 2$$

It is worth pausing at this point to remark upon some striking features of this type of equilibrium. One is that within the class of employer expectations used above, there is an infinite number of possible equilibrium values for y^*. This means that there is an infinite number of equilibria. In any one of the equilibria the employer is able to make perfect point predictions concerning the productivity of any individual, having observed his level of education. The reader will realize that this property is special and depends, at least in part, upon the assumption that education costs are perfectly negatively correlated with productivity. However, even in this case, there are equilibria in which the employer is uncertain, as we shall shortly see.

The equilibria are not equivalent from the point of view of welfare. Increases in the level of y^* hurt Group II, while, at the same time, members of Group I are unaffected. Group I is worse off than it was with no signaling at all. For if no signaling takes place, each person is paid his unconditional expected marginal product, which is just

$$q_1 + 2(1 - q_1) = 2 - q_1$$

Group II may also be worse off than it was with no signaling. Assume that the proportion of people in Group I is 0.5. Since $y^* > 1$ and the net return to the member of Group II is $2 - y^*/2$, in equilibrium his net return must be below 1.5, the no–signaling wage. Thus, everyone would prefer a situation in which there is no signaling.

No one is acting irrationally as an individual. Coalitions might profitably form and upset the signaling equilibrium.[13] The initial proportions of people in the two groups q_1 and $1 - q_1$ have no effect upon the equilibrium. This conclusion depends upon this assumption that the marginal product of a person in a given group does not change with numbers hired.

Given the signaling equilibrium, the education level y^*, which defines the equilibrium, is an entrance requirement or prerequisite for the high-salary job – or so it would appear from the outside. From the point of view of the individual, it is a prerequisite that has its source in a signaling game. Looked at from the outside, education might appear to be productive. It is productive for the individual, but, in this example, it does not increase his real marginal product at all.[14]

A sophisticated objection to the assertion that private and social returns differ might be that, in the context of our example, the social return is not really zero. We have an information problem in the society and the problem of allocating the right people to the right jobs. Education, in its capacity as a signal in the model, is helping us to do this properly. The objection is well founded. To decide how efficient or inefficient this system is, one must consider the realistic alternatives to market sorting procedures in the society.[15] But notice that even within the confines of the market model, there are more or less efficient ways of getting the sorting accomplished. Increases in y^* improve the quality of the sorting not one bit. They simply use up real or psychic resources. This is just another way of saying that there are Pareto inferior signaling equilibria in the market.

It is not always the case that all groups lose due to the existence of signaling. For example, if, in the signaling equilibrium, $y^* < 2q_1$, then Group II would be better off when education is functioning effectively as a signal than it would be other- wise. Thus, in our example if $q_1 > \frac{1}{2}$ so that Group II is a minority, then there exists a signaling equilibrium in which the members of Group II improve their position over the no-signaling case. Recall that the wage in the no-signaling case was a uniform $2 - q_1$ over all groups.

We may generalize this bit of analysis slightly. Suppose that the signaling cost schedule for Group I was given by $a_1 y$ and that for Group II by $a_2 y$.[16] Then with a small amount of calculation, we can show that there is a signaling equilibrium in which Group II is better off than with no signaling,[17] provided that

$$q_1 > \frac{a_2}{a_1}$$

How small a "minority" Group II has to be to have the possibility of benefiting from signaling depends upon the ratio of the marginal signaling costs of the two groups.[18]

Before leaving our education signaling model, it is worth noting that there are other equilibria in the system with quite different properties. Suppose that the employer's expectations are of the following form:

If $y < y^*$:   Group I with probability q_1,
              Group II with probability $1 - q_1$;
if $y \geq y^*$:   Group II with probability 1.

As before, the only levels of y that could conceivably be selected are $y = 0$ and $y = y^*$. The wage for $y = 0$ is $2 - q_1$, while the wage for $y = y^*$ is simply 2. From Figure 4 it is easy to see that both groups rationally set $y = 0$, provided that $y^* > 2q_1$. If they both do this, then the employer's beliefs are confirmed, and we have an equilibrium.

It should be noted that the employer's beliefs about the relationship between productivity and education for $y \geq y^*$ are confirmed in a somewhat degenerate, but perfectly acceptable, sense. There are no data relating to these levels of education and hence, by logic, no disconfirming data. This is an example of a phenomenon of much wider potential importance. The employer's beliefs may drive certain groups from the market and into another labor market. We cannot capture this situation in a simple one-employer,

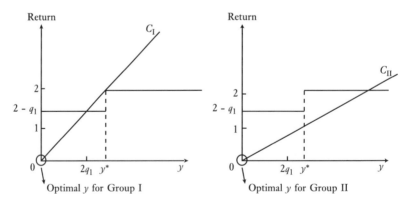

Figure 4   Optimal signaling decisions for the two groups

one-market model. But when it happens, there is no experience forthcoming to the employer to cause him to alter his beliefs.[19]

Education conveys no information in this type of equilibrium. In fact, we have reproduced the wages and information state of the employer in the no-signaling model, as a signaling equilibrium.

Just as there exists a signaling equilibrium in which everyone sets $y = 0$, there is also an equilibrium in which everyone sets $y = y^*$ for some positive y^*. The requisite employer beliefs are as follows:

If $y < y^*$: Group I with probability 1;
if $y \geq y^*$: Group I with probability q_1,
Group II with probability $1 - q_1$.

Following our familiar mode of analysis, one finds that these beliefs are self-confirming in the market, provided that

$$y^* < 1 - q_1$$

Again, the education level conveys no useful information, but in this instance individuals are rationally investing in education. If they as individuals did not invest, they would incur lower wages, and the loss would exceed the gain from not making the educational investment. The implication of this version of the signaling equilibrium is that there can be stable prerequisites for jobs that convey no information by virtue of their existence and hence serve no function.

It is interesting to note that this last possibility does not depend upon costs being correlated with productivity at all. Suppose that the signaling costs *for both groups* were given by the one schedule y. And suppose further that employer beliefs were as described above. Then everyone will rationally select $y = y^*$, provided that

$$y^* < 1 - q_1$$

The outcome is the same. But the interesting thing is that, because of the absence of any correlation between educational costs and productivity, education could *never* be an effective signal, in the sense of conveying useful information, in an equilibrium in this market.

We have dwelt enough upon the specifics of this model to have observed some of the effects the signaling game may have upon the allocational functioning of the market. The numerical example is not important. The potential effects and patterns of signaling are.

An alterable characteristic like education, which is a potential signal, becomes an actual signal if the signaling costs are negatively correlated with the individual's unknown productivity. Actually, the negative correlation is a necessary but not sufficient condition for signaling to take place. To see this in the context of our model, assume that the only values y can have are one and three. That is to say, one can only get units of education in lumps. If this is true, then there is no feasible value of y^* that will make it worthwhile for Group II to acquire an education. Three units is too much, and one unit will not distinguish Group II from Group I. Therefore, effective signaling depends not only upon the negative correlation of costs and productivities, but also upon there being a "sufficient" number of signals within the appropriate cost range.[20]

An equilibrium is defined in the context of a feedback loop, in which employer expectations lead to offered wages to various levels of education, which in turn lead to investment in education by individuals. After hiring, the discovery of the actual relationships between education and productivity in the sample leads to revised expectations or beliefs. Here the cycle starts again. An equilibrium is best thought of as a set of beliefs that are confirmed or at least not contradicted by the new data at the end of the loop just described. Such beliefs will tend to persist over time as new entrants into the market flow through.

Multiple equilibria are a distinct possibility. Some may be Pareto inferior to others. Private and social returns to education diverge. Sometimes everyone loses as a result of the existence of signaling. In other situations some gain, while others lose. Systematic overinvestment in education is a distinct possibility because of the element of arbitrariness in the equilibrium configuration of the market. In the context of atomistic behavior (which we have assumed thus far) everyone is reacting rationally to the market situation. Information is passed to the employer through the educational signal. In some of our examples it was perfect information. In other cases this is not so. There will be random variation in signaling costs that prevent the employer from distinguishing perfectly among individuals of varying productive capabilities.

In our examples, education was measured by a scalar quantity. With no basic adjustment in the conceptual apparatus, we can think of education as a multidimensional quantity: years of education, institution attended, grades, recommendations and so on. Similarly, it is not necessary to think in terms of two groups of people. There may be many groups, or even a continuum of people: some suited to certain kinds of work, others suited to other kinds. Nor need education be strictly unproductive. However, if it is too productive relative to the costs, everyone will invest heavily in education, and education may cease to have a signaling function.

6. The Informational Impact of Indices

In the educational signaling model we avoided considering any observable characteristics other than education. In that model education was a signal. Here we consider what role, if any, is played by indices. For concreteness I shall use sex as the example. But just as education can stand for any set of observable, alterable characteristics in the first model, sex can stand for observable, unalterable ones here. The reader may wish to think in terms of race, nationality, size, or in terms of criminal or police records and service records. The latter is potentially public information about a person's history and is, of course, unalterable when viewed retrospectively from the present.[21]

Let us assume that there are two groups, men and women. I shall refer to these groups as M and W. Within each group the distribution of productive capabilities and the incidence of signaling costs are the same. Thus, within M the proportion of people with productivity one and signaling (education) costs of y is q_1. The remainder have productivity two and signaling costs $y/2$. The same is true for group W. Here m is the proportion of men in the overall population of job applicants.

Table 2 Data of the Model [Table IV]

Race	Productivity	Education costs	Proportion within group	Proportion of total population
W	1	y	q_1	$q_1(1-m)$
W	2	$y/2$	$1-q_1$	$(1-q_1)(1-m)$
M	1	y	q_1	$q_1 m$
M	2	$y/2$	$1-q_1$	$(1-q_1)m$

Given the assumptions the central question is, "how could sex have an informational impact on the market?" The next few paragraphs are devoted to arguing that indices do have a potential impact and to explaining why this is true. We begin by noting that, under the assumptions, the conditional probability that a person drawn at random from the population has a productivity of two, given that he is a man (or she is a woman), is the same as the unconditional probability that his productivity is two. Sex and productivity are uncorrelated in the population. Therefore, *by itself*, sex could never tell the employer anything about productivity.

We are forced to the conclusion that if sex is to have any informational impact, it must be through its interaction with the educational signaling mechanism. But here again we run up against an initially puzzling symmetry. Under the assumptions, men and women of equal productivity have the same signaling (education) costs. It is a general maxim in economics that people with the same preferences and opportunity sets will make similar decisions and end up in similar situations. We may assume that people maximize their income net of signaling costs so that their preferences are the same. And since signaling costs are the same, it would appear that their opportunity sets are the same. Hence, again we appear to be driven to the conclusion that sex can have no informational impact. But the conclusion is wrong, for an interesting reason.

The opportunity sets of men and women of comparable productivity are *not* necessarily the same. To see this, let us step back to the simple educational signaling model. There are externalities in that model. One person's signaling strategy or decision affects the market data obtained by the employer, which in turn affect the employer's conditional probabilities. These determine the offered wages to various levels of education and hence of rates of return on education for the next group in the job market. The same mechanism applies here, with a notable modification. If employers' distributions are conditional on sex as well as education, then the external impacts of a man's signaling decision are felt only by other men. The same holds for women.

If at some point in time men and women are not investing in education in the same ways, then the returns to education for men and women will be different in the next round. In short, their opportunity sets differ. In what follows, we demonstrate rigorously that this sort of situation can persist in an equilibrium. The important point, however, is that there are externalities implicit in the fact that an individual is treated as the average member of the group of people who look the same and that, as a result, and in spite of an apparent sameness the opportunity sets facing two or more groups that are visibly distinguishable may in fact be different.

The employer now has two potential signals to consider: education and sex. At the start he does not know whether either education or sex will be correlated with productivity. Uninformative potential signals or indices are discarded in the course of reaching an equilibrium. As before we must guess at an equilibrium form for the employer's expectations and then verify that these beliefs can be self-confirming via the market informational feedback mechanisms. We will try beliefs on the following form.

If W and $y < y_W^*$, productivity $= 1$ with probability 1.
If W and $y \geq y_W^*$, productivity $= 2$ with probability 1.
If M and $y < y_M^*$, productivity $= 1$ with probability 1.
If M and $y \geq y_M^*$, productivity $= 2$ with probability 1.

These lead to offered wage schedules $W_W(y)$ and $W_M(y)$ as shown in Figure 5.

Because groups W and M are distinguishable to the employer, their offered wages are not connected at the level of employer expectations. Applying the reasoning used in the straightforward educational signaling model, we find that the required equilibrium conditions on y_W^* and y_M^* are

$$1 < y_W^* < 2$$

and

$$1 < y_M^* < 2$$

No logical condition requires that y_W^* equals y_M^* in an equilibrium.

Essentially we simply have the educational signaling model iterated twice. Because sex is observable, the employer can make his conditional probability assessments depend upon sex as well as education. This has the effect of making signaling interdependencies between two groups, W and M, nonexistent. They settle into signaling equilibrium configurations in the market independently of each other. But in the first model there was not one equilibrium, there were many. Therefore, there is at least the logical possibility that men and women will settle into *different* stable signaling equilibria in the market and stay there.

As we noted earlier, the signaling equilibria are not equivalent from the point of view of social welfare. The higher that y_W^* (or y_M^*) is, the worse off is the relevant group or, more accurately, the high-productivity portion of the group. One example of an asymmetrical equilibrium would be given by $y_M^* = 1.1$ and $y_W^* = 1.9$ (Figure 6). In this case high-productivity women have to spend more on education and have less left over to consume in order to convince the employer that they are in the high-productivity group.

Notice that the proportions of high- and low-productivity people in each group do not affect the signaling equilibrium in the market. Hence, our initial assumption that the groups were identical with respect to the distribution of productive characteristics and the incidence of signaling costs was superfluous. More accurately, it was superfluous with respect to this type of equilibrium. As we saw in the educational signaling model, there are other types of equilibrium in which the proportions matter.

Since from an equilibrium point of view men and women really are independent, they might settle into different types of equilibrium. Thus, we might have men signaling

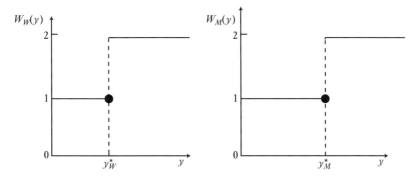

Figure 5   Offered wages to W and M

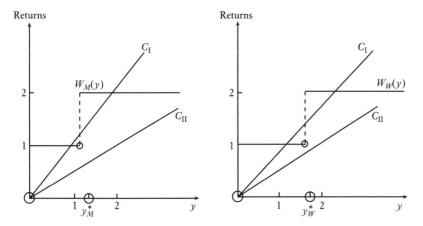

Figure 6   Market equilibrium with sex as an index

$y = y_M^* = 1.1$ if they are also in the higher productivity group, while other men set $y = 0$. On the other hand, we may find that all women set $y = 0$. In this case all women would be paid $2 - q_1$, and the upper signaling cutoff point y_M^* would have to be greater than $2q_1$. Notice that all women, including lower productivity women, would be paid more than low-productivity men in this situation.[22] High-productivity women would, of course, be hurt in terms of wages received. It is conceivable, however, that returns net of signaling would be higher for women with productivity of two. In other words, it is possible that

$$2 - q_1 > w - y_M^*/2$$

This will occur when

$$2q_1 < y_M^*$$

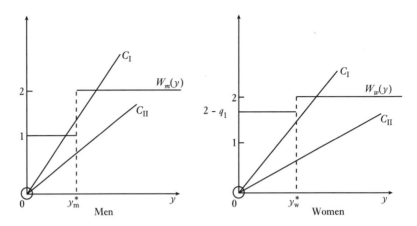

Figure 7   Another equilibrium configuration in the market

Looking at this situation from outside, one might conclude that women receive lower wages than some men because of a lack of education, which keeps their productivity down. One might then go looking outside the job market for the explanation for the lack of education. In this model the analysis just suggested would be wrong. The source of the signaling and wage differentials is in the informational structure of the market itself.[23]

Because of the independence of the two groups, M and W, at the level of signaling, we can generate many different possible equilibrium configurations by taking any of the educational signaling equilibria in our first model and assigning it to W and then taking any education equilibrium and assigning it to M. However, an exhaustive listing of the possibilities seems pointless at this stage.

We have here the possibility of arbitrary differences in the equilibrium signaling config-urations of two or more distinct groups. Some of them may be at a disadvantage relative to the others. Subsets of one may be at a disadvantage to comparable subsets of the others. Since the mechanism that generates the equilibrium is a feedback loop, we might, following Myrdal and others, wish to refer to the situation of the disadvantaged group as a vicious cycle, albeit it an informationally based one. I prefer to refer to the situation of the disadvantaged group as a lower level equilibrium trap, which conveys the notion of a situation that, once achieved, persists for reasons endogenous to the model. The multiple equilibria of the education model translate into arbitrary differences in the equilibrium configuration and status of two groups, as defined as observable, unalterable characteristics.

7. Conclusions

We have looked at the characteristics of a basic equilibrium signaling model and at one possible type of interaction of signals and indices. There remains a host of questions, which can be posed and partially answered within the conceptual framework outlined here. Among them are the following:

1   What is the effect of cooperative behavior on the signaling game?
2   What is the informational impact of randomness in signaling costs?
3   What is the effect of signaling costs that differ systematically with indices?
4   How general are the properties of the examples considered here?
5   In a multiple-market setting, does the indeterminateness of the equilibrium remain?
6   Do signaling equilibria exist in general?
7   What kinds of discriminatory mechanisms are implicit in, or interact with, the informational structure of the market, and what policies are effective or ineffective in dealing with them?

I would argue further that a range of phenomena from selective admissions procedures through promotion, loans and consumer credit, and signaling status via conspicuous consumption lends itself to analysis with the same basic conceptual apparatus. Moreover, it may be as important to explain the absence of effective signaling as its presence, and here the prerequisites for effective signaling are of some use.

On the other hand, it is well to remember that the property of relative infrequency of appearance by signalers in the market, which defines the class signaling phenomena under scrutiny here, is not characteristic of many markets, like those for consumer durables, and that, as a result, the informational structures of these latter are likely to be quite different.

Notes

1   There are, of course, other informational gaps in the job market. Just as employers have less than perfect information about applicants, so also will applicants be imperfectly informed about the qualities of jobs and work environments. And in a different vein neither potential employees nor employers know all of the people in the market. The resulting activities are job search and recruiting. For the purpose of this essay I concentrate upon employer uncertainty and the signaling game that results.

2   The term "lottery" is used in the technical sense, imparted to it by decision theory.

3   The certain monetary equivalent of a lottery is the amount the individual would take, with certainty, in lieu of the lottery. It is generally thought to be less than the actuarial value of the lottery.

4   The terminological distinction is borrowed from Robert Jervis (1970). My use of the terms follows that of Jervis sufficiently closely to warrant their transplantation.

5   The shifting of the distributions occurs when new market data are received and conditional probabilities are revised or updated. Hiring in the market is to be regarded as sampling, and revising conditional probabilities as passing from prior to posterior. The whole process is a learning one.

6   There may be other returns to education. It may be a consumption good or serve as a signal of things other than work potential (status for example). These returns should be added to the offered wage schedule.

7   The reason is that signaling costs can be negatively correlated with one type of productive capability but not with another.

8   In pursuing the properties of signaling equilibria, we select as the object for regeneration whatever is analytically convenient, but usually employer beliefs or offered wage schedules.

9   The mathematically oriented will realize that what is at issue here is a fixed point property. A mapping from the space of conditional distributions over productivity given signals into itself is

defined by the market response mechanism. An equilibrium can be thought of as a fixed point of this mapping. A mathematical treatment of this subject is contained in Spence (1974).

10   In a multi-market model one faces the possibility that certain types of potential applicants will rationally select themselves out of certain job markets, and hence certain signal configurations may never appear in these markets. When this happens, the beliefs of the employers in the relevant market are not disconfirmed in a degenerate way. No data are forthcoming. This raises the possibility of persistent informationally based discrimination against certain groups. The subject is pursued in detail in Spence (1974).

11   Obviously, an example does not prove generality. On the other hand, if the reader will take reasonable generality on faith, the example does illustrate some essential properties of signaling equilibria.

12   For productivity the reader may read "what the individual is worth to the employer." There is no need to rely on marginal productivity here.

13   Coalitions to change the patterns of signaling are discussed in Spence (1974).

14   I am ignoring external benefits to education here. The assertion is simply that in the example education does not contribute to productivity. One might still claim that the social product is not zero. The signal cost function does, in principle, capture education as a consumption good, an efect that smily reduces the cost of education.

15   This question is pursued in Spence (1974).

16   It is assumed that $a_2 < a_1$.

17   Notice that the statement is that there exists a signaling equilibrium in which Group II is better off. It turns out that there always exists a signaling equilibrium in which Group II is worse off as well.

18   The calculation is straightforward. Given these signaling costs groups will make the requisite choice to confirm the employer's beliefs provided that

$$1 > 2 - a_1 y^*$$

and

$$2 - a_2 y^* > 1$$

These translate easily into the following condition on y^*:

$$\frac{1}{a_2} < y^* < \frac{1}{a_1}$$

Now, if Group II is to be better off for some signaling equilibrium, then

$$2 - \frac{a_2}{a_1} > 2 - q_1$$

or

$$q_1 > \frac{a_2}{a_1}$$

This is what we set out to show.

19   This is discussed in detail in Spence (1974).

20   Spence (1974) argues that many potential signals in credit and loan markets effectively become indices because the "signaling" costs swamp the gains, so that characteristics that could be manipulated in fact are not. House ownership is an example of a potential signal that, in the context of the loan market, fails on this criterion and hence becomes an index.

21   It is, or ought to be, the subject of policy decisions as well.

22   I have not assumed that employers are prejudiced. If they are, this differential could be wiped out. Perhaps more interestingly laws prohibiting wage discrimination, if enforced, would also wipe it out.
23   Differential signaling costs over groups are an important possibility pursued in Spence (1974).

References

Jervis, R. (1970): *The Logic of Images in International Relations*. Princeton, NJ: Princeton University Press.
Spence, A. M. (1974): *Market Signaling: Information Transfer in Hiring and Related Screening Processes*. Cambridge, Mass.: Harvard University Press.

CHAPTER SIXTEEN

The Economic Theory of Agency: The Principal's Problem

Stephen A. Ross

Source: *American Economic Review, Papers and Proceedings*, 63 (1973), pp. 134–9. Reprinted with the permission of the author and the American Economic Association. © American Economic Association.

The relationship of agency is one of the oldest and commonest codified modes of social interaction. We will say that an agency relationship has arisen between two (or more) parties when one, designated as the agent, acts for, on behalf of, or as representative for the other, designated the principal, in a particular domain of decision problems. Examples of agency are universal. Essentially all contractural arrangements, as between employer and employee or the state and the governed, for example, contain important elements of agency. In addition, without explicitly studying the agency relationship, much of the economic literature on problems of moral hazard (K. J. Arrow, 1971) is concerned with problems raised by agency. In a general equilibrium context the study of information flows (J. Marschak and R. Radner, 1972) or of financial intermediaries in monetary models is also an example of agency theory.

The canonical agency problem can be posed as follows. Assume that both the agent and the principal possess state independent von Neumann–Morgenstern utility functions, $G(\cdot)$ and $U(\cdot)$ respectively, and that they act so as to maximize their expected utility. The problems of agency are really most interesting when seen as involving choice under uncertainty and this is the view we will adopt. The agent may choose an act, $a \varepsilon A$, a feasible action space, and the random payoff from this act, $\omega(a, \theta)$, will depend on the random state of nature θ ($\varepsilon \Omega$ the state space set), unknown to the agent when a is chosen. By assumption the agent and the principal have agreed upon a fee schedule f to be paid to the agent for his services. The fee, f, is generally a function of both the state of the world, θ, and the action, a, but we will assume that the action can influence the parties and, hence, the fee only through its impact on the payoff. This permits us to write,

$$f = f(\omega(a, \theta); \theta) \tag{1}$$

Two points deserve mention. Obviously the choice of a fee schedule is the outcome of a bargaining problem or, in large games, of a market process. Much of what we have to say is relevant for this view but we will not treat the bargaining problem explicitly. Second, while it is possible to conceive of the fee as being directly functionally dependent on the act, the theory loses much of its interest, since without further conditions, such a fee can always be chosen as a Dirac δ-function forcing a particular act (S. Ross, 1972 or later). In some sense, then, we are assuming that only the payoff is operational and we will take this point up below. Now, the agent will choose an act, a, so as to

$$\max_{a} \underset{\theta}{E}\, G[f(\omega(a,\theta);\theta)] \tag{2}$$

where the agent takes the expectation over his subjectively held probability distribution. The solution to the agent's problem involves the choice of an optimal act, a°, conditional on the particular fee schedule, i.e., $a^{\circ}= a(\langle f \rangle)$, where $a(\cdot)$ is a mapping from the space of fee schedules into A.

If the principal has complete information about the fee to act mapping, $a(\langle f \rangle)$, he will now choose a fee so as to

$$\max_{\langle f \rangle} \underset{\theta}{E}\, \{U[\omega(a(\langle f \rangle),\theta),\theta) - f(\omega(a(\langle f \rangle),\theta);\theta)]\} \tag{3}$$

where the expectation is taken over the principal's subjective probability distribution over states of nature. If the principal is not fully informed about $a(\cdot)$, then $a(\cdot)$ will be a random function from his point of view. Formally, at least, by appropriately augmenting the state space the criterion (3) could still be made to apply. In general some side constraints on $\langle f \rangle$ would also have to be imposed to insure that the problem possesses a solution (Ross, 1972 or later). A market-imposed minimum expected fee or expected utility of fee by the agent would be one economically sensible constraint:

$$\underset{\theta}{E}\, \{G[f(\omega(a,\theta);\theta)]\} \geq k \tag{4}$$

Since utility functions are assumed to be independent of states, θ, one of the important reasons for a fee to depend directly on θ would be if individual subjective probability distributions differed. In what follows we will assume that both the agent and the principal share the same subjective beliefs about the occurrence of θ and write the fee as a function of the payoff only,

$$f = f(\omega(a,\theta)) \tag{5}$$

Notice that this interpretation would not in general be permissible if the principal lacked perfect knowledge of $a(\cdot)$. More importantly, though, surely aside from simple comparative advantage, for some questions the *raison d'être* for an agency relationship is that the agent (or the principal) may possess different (better or finer) information about the states of the world than the principal (agent). If we abstract from this possibility we will have to show that we are not throwing out the baby with the bath water.

Under this assumption the problem is considerably simplified but much of interest does remain. Suppose, first, that we are simply interested in the properties of Pareto-efficient arrangements that the agent and the principal will strike. Notice that the optimal fee schedule as seen by the principal is found by solving (3) and is dependent on the desire to motivate the agent. In general, then, we would expect such an arrangement to be Pareto-inefficient, but we will return to this point below. The family of Pareto-efficient fee schedules can be characterized by assuming that the principal and the agent cooperate to choose a schedule that maximizes a weighted sum of utilities

$$\max_{\langle f \rangle} E\{U[\omega - f] + \lambda G[f]\} \tag{6}$$

where λ is a relative weighting factor (and where strategies have been randomized to insure convexity). K. Borch (1962) recognized that the solution to (6) is obtained by maximizing the function internal to the expectation which requires setting.

$$U'[\omega - f] = \lambda G'[f] \tag{P.E.}$$

when U and G are monotone and concave. (See H. Raiffa, 1968 for a good exposition.) The P.E. condition defines the fee schedule, $f(\cdot)$, as a function of the payoff ω (and the weight, λ). (See R. Wilson (1968) or Ross (1972 or later) for a fuller discussion of this derivation and the functional aspect of the fee schedule.)

An alternative approach to finding optimal fee schedules was first proposed by Wilson in the theory of syndicates and studied by Wilson (1968, 1969) and Ross (1972 or later). This is the similarity condition that solves for the fee schedule by setting.

$$U[\omega - f] = aG[f] + b \tag{S}$$

for constants $a > 0, b$. If $\langle f \rangle$ satisfies S then, given the fee schedule, it should be clear that the agent and the principal have identical attitudes towards risky payoffs and, consequently, the agent will always choose the act that the principal most desires. Ross was able to completely characterize the class of utility functions that satisfied both P.E. and S (for a range of λ) and show that in such situations the fee schedule is (affine) linear, L, in the payoff. (The class is simply that of pairs $\langle U, G \rangle$ with linear risk tolerance,

$$-\frac{U'}{U''} = c\omega + d \quad \text{and} \quad -\frac{G'}{G''} = c\omega + e$$

where c, d and e are constants.) In fact, it can be shown that any two of S, P.E., or L imply the third.

A question of interest that naturally arises is that of the relation that S and P.E. bear to the exact solution to the principal's problem. (A comparable "agent's problem" can also be posed but we will not be concerned with that here. Some observations on such a problem are contained in Ross (1972 or later). The solution to the principal's problem (3) subject to the constraint (4) and to the constraint imposed by the condition that the agent chooses the optimal act from his problem (2) can, under some circumstances, be posed as a classical variational problem. To do so we will assume that the payoff function is (twice) differentiable and that the agent chooses an optimal act, given a fee schedule, by the first order condition

$$\underset{\theta}{E}\left\{G'[f(\omega)]f'(\omega)\omega_a\right\}=0 \tag{7}$$

where a subscript indicates partial differentiation. The principal's problem is now to

$$\max_{\langle f\rangle}\underset{\theta}{E}\left\{H\right\}\equiv\max_{\langle f\rangle}\underset{\theta}{E}\left\{U[\omega-f]+\Psi G'f'\omega_a+\lambda G\right\} \tag{8}$$

where Ψ and λ are Lagrange multipliers associated with the constraints (7) and (4) respectively. Changing variables to $V(\theta)\equiv f(\omega(a,\theta))$ where we have suppressed the impact of a on V and assuming, without loss of generality, that θ is uniformly distributed on [0, 1] permits us to solve (8) by the Euler–Lagrange equation. Thus, at an optimum

$$\frac{\mathrm{d}}{\mathrm{d}\theta}\left\{\frac{\partial H}{\partial V'}\right\}-\frac{\partial H}{\partial V}=U'+\Psi G'\frac{\mathrm{d}}{\mathrm{d}\theta}\left[\frac{\omega_a}{\omega_\theta}\right]-\lambda G' \tag{9}$$
$$=0$$

or the marginal rate of substitution,

$$\frac{U'}{G'}=\lambda-\Psi\frac{\mathrm{d}}{\mathrm{d}\theta}\left[\frac{\omega_a}{\omega_\theta}\right] \tag{10}$$

This is an intuitively appealing result; the marginal rate of substitution is set equal to a constant as in the P.E. condition plus an additional term which captures the constraint (7) imposed on the principal by the need to motivate the agent. To determine the optimal act, a, we differentiate (8) with respect to a which yields

$$\underset{\theta}{E}\left\{U'[1-f']\omega_a+\Psi G''(f'\omega_a)^2+\Psi G'f''(\omega_a)^2+\Psi G'f'\omega_{aa}\right\}=0 \tag{11}$$

where we have made use of (7). Substituting the boundary conditions permits us to solve for the multipliers Ψ and λ.

Like S or P.E. (10) defines the fee schedule as a function of ω. (Notice that we are tacitly assuming that, at least for the optimal act, the payoff is (a.e. locally) state invertible. This allows the fee to take the form of (5).) It follows that (10) will coincide with P.E. if and only if Ψ is zero, or if $\Psi\neq 0$, we must have

$$\frac{\mathrm{d}}{\mathrm{d}\theta}\left[\frac{\omega_a}{\omega_\theta}\right]=b(a) \tag{12}$$

a function of a alone.

In particular, using these conditions we can ask what class of (pairs of) utility functions $\langle U,G\rangle$ has the property that, for any payoff structure, $\omega(a,\theta)$, the solution to the principal's problem is Pareto-efficient. Conversely, we can ask what class of payoff structures has the property that the principal's problem yields a Pareto-efficient solution for any pair of utility functions $\langle U,G\rangle$.

A little reflection reveals that the only pairs of $\langle U, G \rangle$ that could possibly belong to the first class must be those which satisfy S and P.E. for a range of schedules (indexed by the λ weight in P.E.). Clearly if (10) is to be equivalent to P.E. for all payoff functions, $w(a, \theta)$, then Ψ must be zero and the motivational constraint (7) must not be binding. For this to be the case, for an interval of values of k (in (4)), the satisfaction of P.E. must imply that the agent chooses the principal's most desired act by (7). For any fee schedule, $\langle f \rangle$, the principal wants the act to be chosen to maximize $\underset{\theta}{E} \{ U[w - f] \}$ which implies that

$$\underset{\theta}{E} \{ U'(1 - f')w_a \} = 0 \tag{13}$$

If (13) is to be equivalent to the motivational constraint (7) for all possible payoff structures, then we must have

$$U'(1 - f') = G'f' \tag{14}$$

which, with P.E. (or (10) with $\Psi = 0$) yields a linear fee schedule in the payoff. But, as shown in Ross (1972 or later), linearity of the fee schedule and P.E. imply the satisfaction of S and the $\langle U, G \rangle$ pair must belong to the linear risk-tolerance class of utility functions described above.

Since the linear risk-tolerance class, while important, is very limited, we turn now to the converse question of what payoff structures permit a Pareto-efficient solution for all $\langle U, G \rangle$ pairs. If $\Psi = 0$ we must, as before, have that the motivational constraint is not binding for all $\langle U, G \rangle$ or (13) must always imply (7). The implication will always hold if there exists an a^* such that for all a there is some choice of the state domain, I, for which

$$w(a^*, \theta) \geq w(a, \theta) \quad \theta \varepsilon I \tag{15}$$

Conversely, from P.E., we must have that for all $G(\cdot)$

$$\underset{\theta}{E} \{ G'[f](1 - f')w_a \} = 0 \tag{16}$$

implies (7) where f is determined by P.E. Since $\langle U, G \rangle$ can always be chosen so as to attain any desired weightings of w_a in (7) and (16) the special case of (15) is the only one for which motivation is irrelevant. Given (15) all individuals have a uniquely optimal act irrespective of their attitudes towards risk.

If $\Psi \neq 0$, then to assure Pareto efficiency we must satisfy (12). This is a partial differential equation and its solution is given by

$$w(a, \theta) = H[\theta B(a) - C(a)] \tag{17}$$

where $H(\cdot)$, $B(\cdot)$ and $C(\cdot)$ are arbitrary functions. (The detailed computations are carried out in an appendix.) This is a rich and interesting class of payoff functions. In particular, (17) is a generalization of the class of functions of the form $l(\theta - a)$, where the object is to pick an act, a, so as to best guess the state θ. It therefore includes, for example, traditional estimation problems, problems with a quadratic payoff function, and all problems with payoff functions of the form $|\theta - a|\xi h(a)$, and many asymmetric ones as well. It is not, however, difficult to find plausible payoff functions which do not take the form of (17). (The class of the form (15) will generate such functions.)

We may conclude, then, that the class of payoff structures that simultaneously solve the principal's problem and lead to Pareto efficiency for all $\langle U, G \rangle$ pairs is quite important and quite likely to arise in practice.

In general, though, it is clear that the solution to the principal's problem will not be Pareto-efficient. This is, however, a somewhat naive view to take. Pareto efficiency as defined above assumes that perfect information is held by the participants. In fact, the optimal solution to the principal's problem implied that the fee-to-act mapping induced by the agent was completely known to the principal. In such a case it might be thought that the principal could simply tell the agent to perform a particular act. The difficulty arises in monitoring the act that the agent chooses. Michael Spence and Richard Zeckhauser (1971) have examined this problem in detail in the case of insurance. In addition, if agents are numerous the fee may be the only communication mechanism. While it might in principle be feasible to monitor the agent's actions, it would not be economically viable to do so.

The format of this paper has been such as to allow us to only touch on what is surely the most challenging aspect of agency theory; embedding it in a general equilibrium market context. Much is to be learned from such attempts. One would naturally expect a market to arise in the services of agents. Furthermore, in some sense, such a market serves as a surrogate for a market in the information possessed by agents. To the extent to which this occurs, the study of agency in market contexts should shed some light on the economics of information. To mention one more path of interest – in a world of true uncertainty where adequate contingent markets do not exist, the manager of the firm is essentially an agent of the shareholders. It can, therefore, be expected that an understanding of the agency relationship will aid our understanding of this difficult question.

The results obtained here provide some of the micro foundations for such studies. We have shown that, for an interesting class of utility functions and for a very broad and relevant class of payoff structures, the need to motivate agents does not conflict with the attainment of Pareto efficiency. At the least, a callous observer might view these results as providing some solace to those engaged in econometric activity.

Appendix

This appendix solves the partial differential equation (12) in the text.
Integrating (12) over θ yields

$$\frac{\partial \omega}{\partial a} + [b(a)\theta + c(a)]\frac{\partial \omega}{\partial \theta} = 0$$

Along a locus of constant ω,

$$\frac{d\theta}{da} = -\frac{\partial \omega / \partial a}{\partial \omega / \partial \theta} = b(a)\theta + c(a)$$

is a first-order Bernoulli equation that integrates to

$$\theta = e^{\int^{b(a)} \left[\int e^{-\int^{b(a)} } c(a)+k \right]}$$

where k is a constant of integration. It follows that

$$\omega(a, \theta) = H[\theta B(a) - C(a)]$$

where

$$B(a) \equiv e^{-\int^{b(a)}}$$

and

$$C(a) \equiv \int e^{-\int b(a)} c(a) + k$$

and $H(\cdot)$ is an arbitrary function.

References

Arrow, K. J. (1971): *Essays in the Theory of Risk-Bearing*. Chicago: Markham.

Borch, K. (1962): "Equilibrium in a Reinsurance Market," *Econometrica*, 30, July, 424–44.

Marschak J. and Radner, R. (1972): *The Economic Theory of Teams*. New Haven: Yale University Press.

Raiffa, H. (1968): *Decision Analysis; Introductory Lectures on Choices Under Uncertainty*. Reading, MA.: Addison-Wesley.

Ross, S. (1972 or later) "On the Economic Theory of Agency: The Principle of Similarity," *Proceedings of the NBER-NSF Conference on Decision Making and Uncertainty*.

Spence, M. and Zeckhauser, R. (1971): "Insurance, Information and Individual Action," *American Economical Review Proceedings*, 61, May, 380–7.

Wilson, R. (1968): "On the Theory of Syndicates," *Econometrica*, 36 January, 119–32.

——(1969) "The Structure of Incentives for Decentralization Under Uncertainty," *La Décision*, Editions du Centre National de la Recherche Scientifique, Paris.

CHAPTER SEVENTEEN

Choice Under Uncertainty: Problems Solved and Unsolved

MARK J. MACHINA

Source: *Journal of Economic Perspectives*, 1, 1 (1987), pp. 121–54.
Reprinted (with minor changes and an additional final section) with
the permission of the author and the American Economic Association.
© American Economic Association.

1. Introduction

Twenty years ago, the theory of choice under uncertainty could be considered one of the "success stories" of economic analysis: it rested on solid axiomatic foundations (von Neumann and Morgenstern, 1947; Marschak, 1950; Savage 1954), it had seen important breakthroughs in the analytics of risk, risk aversion, and their applications to economic issues,[1] and it stood ready to provide the theoretical underpinnings for the newly emerging "information revolution" in economics (Akerlof, 1970; Spence and Zeckhauser, 1971; Stiglitz, 1975, 1985). Today, choice under uncertainty is a field in flux: the standard theory, and implicitly, its public policy implications, are being challenged on several grounds from both within and outside economics. The nature of these challenges, and of economists' responses to them, is the topic of this paper.

The following section provides a brief but self-contained description of the economist's canonical model of individual choice under uncertainty, the *expected utility* model of preferences over lotteries. I shall describe this model from two different perspectives. The first perspective is the most familiar, and has traditionally been the most useful for addressing standard economic questions. However the second, more modern perspective will be the most useful for illustrating some of the problems that have beset this model, as well as some of the proposed responses.

Each of sections 3–6 is devoted to one of these problems. All are important; some are more completely "solved" than others. In each case I shall begin with a specific example or description of the phenomenon in question. I shall then review the empirical evidence regarding the uniformity and extent of the phenomenon. I conclude each section with thoughts on how these empirical findings have changed, or in my view ought to change, the way economists construct their *descriptive* ("positive") models of individual decision making and/or the operation of markets. Table 3, which follows section 6, provides a summary of these findings, their major sources, and significant responses to them.

The final section of the paper treats a much more difficult issue: namely, how private sector decision analysts, government agencies and environmental policy makers should adjust their *prescriptive* ("normative") decision practices in light of these empirical findings. Here my thoughts are – of necessity – much more speculative, and the disclaimer that "my opinions are my own" has more than the usual significance.

2. The Expected Utility Model

2.1. The classical perspective: Cardinal utility and attitudes toward risk

In light of current trends toward generalizing this model, it is useful to note that the expected utility hypothesis was *itself* first proposed as an alternative to an earlier, more restrictive theory of risk bearing. During the development of modern probability theory in the 17th century, mathematicians such as Blaise Pascal and Pierre de Fermat assumed that the attractiveness of a gamble offering the payoffs $(x_1, \cdots, x_n)$ with probabilities $(p_1, \cdots, p_n)$ was given by its *expected value* $\bar{x}$, i.e., the weighted average of the payoffs where each payoff is multiplied by its associated probability, so that

$$\bar{x} = x_1 \cdot p_1 + \cdots + x_n \cdot p_n$$

The fact that individuals consider more than just expected value, however, was dramatically illustrated by an example posed by Nicholas Bernoulli in 1728 and now known as the *St. Petersburg Paradox:*

> "Suppose someone offers to toss a fair coin repeatedly until it comes up heads, and to pay you $1 if this happens on the first toss, $2 if it takes two tosses to land a head, $4 if it takes three tosses, $8 if it takes four tosses, etc. What is the largest sure payment you would forgo in order to undertake a *single* play of this game?"

Since this gamble offers a $\frac{1}{2}$ chance of winning $1, a $\frac{1}{4}$ chance of winning $2, etc., its expected value is

$$\left(\frac{1}{2}\right) \cdot \$1 + \left(\frac{1}{4}\right) \cdot \$2 + \left(\frac{1}{8}\right) \cdot \$4 + \cdots = \$\frac{1}{2} + \$\frac{1}{2} + \$\frac{1}{2} + \cdots = \$\infty$$

so it should be preferred to *any* finite sure gain. However, it is clear that few individuals would forgo more than a moderate amount for a one-shot play. Although the unlimited financial backing needed to actually make this offer is somewhat unrealistic, it is not essential for making the point: agreeing to limit the game to at most one million tosses will still lead to a striking discrepancy between a typical individual's valuation of the modified gamble and its expected value of $500,000.

The resolution of this paradox was proposed independently by Gabriel Cramer and Nicholas's cousin Daniel Bernoulli.[2] Arguing that a gain of $2,000 was not necessarily "worth" twice as much as a gain of $1,000, they hypothesized that individuals possess what is now termed a *von Neumann–Morgenstern utility of wealth function* $U(\cdot)$, and rather than evaluating gambles on the basis of their expected value

$$\bar{x} = x_1 \cdot p_1 + \cdots + x_n \cdot p_n$$

evaluate them on the basis of their expected *utility*

$$\bar{u} = U(x_1) \cdot p_1 + \cdots + U(x_n) \cdot p_n$$

which is calculated by weighting the *utility* of each possible outcome by its associated probability, and can therefore incorporate the fact that successive increments to wealth may yield successively diminishing increments to utility. Thus if utility took the logarithmic form $U(x) = \ln(x)$ (which exhibits this property of diminishing increments) and the individual's wealth at the start of the game were (say) $50,000, the sure gain that would yield just as much utility as taking this gamble, i.e., the individual's *certainty equivalent* of the gamble, would be about $9, even though the gamble has an infinite expected value.[3]

Although it shares the name "utility," this function $U(\cdot)$ is quite distinct from the ordinal utility function of standard consumer theory. While the latter can be subjected to any monotonic transformation, a von Neumann–Morgenstern utility function is *cardinal* in that it can only be subjected to transformations that change the intercept and/or scale of the vertical axis, but do not affect the "shape" of the function. Our ability to choose the intercept and scale is often used to *normalize* the utility function, for example to set $U(0) = 0$ and $U(M) = 1$ for some fixed value M.

To see how this shape determines risk attitudes, consider Figures 1a and 1b. The monotonicity of the curves in each figure reflects the property of (first order) stochastic dominance preference, where one lottery is said to *stochastically dominate* another if it can be obtained from it by shifting probability from lower to higher outcome levels.[4] Stochastic dominance preference is thus the probabilistic extension of the attitude that "more is better."

Consider a gamble offering a $\frac{2}{3}$ chance of a wealth level of x' and a $\frac{1}{3}$ chance of a wealth level of x''. The amount

$$\bar{x} = \left(\frac{2}{3}\right) \cdot x' + \left(\frac{1}{3}\right) \cdot x''$$

in the figures gives the expected value of this gamble, and

$$\bar{u}_a = \left(\frac{2}{3}\right) \cdot U_a(x') + \left(\frac{1}{3}\right) \cdot U_a(x'')$$

and

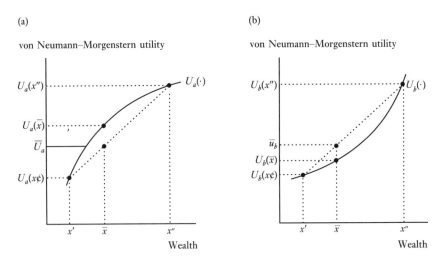

Figure 1   (a) Concave utility function of a risk averter; (b) Convex utility function of a risk lover

$$\bar{u}_b = \left(\frac{2}{3}\right) \cdot U_b(x') + \left(\frac{1}{3}\right) \cdot U_b(x'')$$

give its expected *utility* for the utility functions $U_a(\cdot)$ and $U_b(\cdot)$. For the concave (i.e., bowed upward) utility function $U_a(\cdot)$ we have $U_a(\bar{x}) > \bar{u}_a$, which implies that this individual would prefer a sure gain of $\bar{x}$ (which yields utility $U_a(\bar{x})$) over the gamble. Since someone with a concave utility function will in fact *always* rather receive the expected value of a gamble over the gamble itself, concave utility functions are termed *risk averse*. For the convex (bowed downward) utility function $U_b(\cdot)$ we have $\bar{u}_b > U_b(\bar{x})$, and since this preference for bearing the risk rather than receiving the expected value extends to all gambles, $U_b(\cdot)$ is termed *risk loving*. In their famous article, Friedman and Savage (1948) showed how a utility function that was concave at low wealth levels and convex at high wealth levels could explain the behavior of individuals who *incur* risk by purchasing lottery tickets as well as *avoid* risk by purchasing insurance.[5] Algebraically, Arrow (1963, 1974), Pratt (1964), and others have shown that the *degree* of concavity of a utility function, as measured by the curvature index $-U''(x)/U'(x)$, can lead to predictions of how risk attitudes, and hence behavior, will vary with wealth or across individuals in a variety of situations.[6]

Since a knowledge of $U(\cdot)$ would allow us to predict preferences (and hence behavior) in any risky situation, experimenters and applied decision analysts are frequently interested in eliciting or *recovering* their subjects' (or clients') von Neumann–Morgenstern utility functions. One means of doing this is termed the *fractile method*. This approach begins by adopting the normalization $U(0) = 0$ and $U(M) = 1$ for some positive amount M and fixing a "mixture probability" $\bar{p}$, say $\bar{p} = \frac{1}{2}$. The next step involves obtaining the individual's certainty equivalent ξ_1 of a gamble yielding a $\frac{1}{2}$ chance of M and a $\frac{1}{2}$ chance of 0, which will have the property that $U(\xi_1) = \frac{1}{2}$.[7] Finding the certainty equivalent of a gamble yielding a $\frac{1}{2}$ chance of ξ_1 and a $\frac{1}{2}$ chance of 0 yields the value ξ_2 satisfying $U(\xi_2) = \frac{1}{4}$, and finding the certainty equivalent of a gamble yielding a $\frac{1}{2}$ chance of M and a $\frac{1}{2}$ chance of ξ_1 yields the value ξ_3 satisfying $U(\xi_3) = \frac{3}{4}.$[8] By repeating this procedure ($\frac{1}{8}, \frac{3}{8}, \frac{5}{8}, \frac{7}{8}, \frac{1}{16}, \frac{3}{16}$, etc.) the utility function can (in the limit) be completely assessed.

To see how the expected utility model can be applied to risk policy, consider a disastrous event which is expected to occur with probability p and involve a loss of L (lost dollars or lost lives). In many cases there will be some scope for influencing the levels of either p and/or L, often at the expense of the other. For example, building two small separate nuclear power plants instead of a single large may raise the probability that there is *some* nuclear accident, but presumably lowers the magnitude of the loss (however measured) should one occur. Within a given reactor, we can move along this probability-loss tradeoff by shifting resources (material or human) between the reactor's early sensing system, which determines p, and its containment system, which determines L (we return to this example in section 7 below).

The key tool used in evaluating whether such adjustments should be undertaken is the individual's (or society's) *marginal rate of substitution (MRS)*, which specifies the rate at which they would just be willing to trade off small changes in p against small changes in L. If a potential adjustment involves better terms than this minimum acceptable rate it will be preferred, if it involves worse terms it will be rejected. Since expected utility in this situation is given by

$$\bar{u} = (1-p) \cdot U(W) + p \cdot U(W-L)$$

where W is initial wealth or initial lives, this willingness to trade off changes in p against changes in L is given by the formula

$$MRS(p, L) = \frac{\partial p}{\partial L}\Big|_{\bar{u}\text{constant}} = -\frac{\frac{\partial \bar{u}}{\partial L}}{\frac{\partial \bar{u}}{\partial P}} = \frac{-p \cdot U'(W-L)}{[U(W) - U(W-L)]}$$

Although the specific value of this marginal rate of substitution depends upon the specific utility function $U(\cdot)$, this formula offers some general guidance independent of the particular utility function: given the value of L, the local tradeoff rate from any existing situation (p, L) is exactly proportional to its value of p.

Our discussion so far has paralleled the economic literature of the 1960s and 1970s by emphasizing the *flexibility* of the expected utility model, compared to the Pascal–Fermat expected value approach. However, starting in the 1980s, the need to analyze and respond to growing empirical challenges has led economists to examine the *behavioral restrictions* implied by the expected utility hypothesis. It is to these restrictions that we now turn.

2.2. A modern perspective: Linearity in the probabilities as a testable hypothesis

As a theory of individual behavior, the expected utility model shares many of the underlying assumptions of standard economic consumer theory. In each case we assume that the objects of choice, either commodity bundles or lotteries, can be unambiguously and objectively described, and that situations which ultimately imply the same set of avail-abilities (e.g., the same budget set) will lead to the same choice. In each case we also assume that the individual is able to perform the mathematical operations necessary to actually determine the set of availabilities, e.g., to add up the quantities in different sized containers or calculate the probabilities of compound or conditional events. Finally, in each case we assume that preferences are *transitive*, so that if an individual prefers one object (either a commodity bundle or a risky prospect) to a second, and prefers this second object to a third, then he or she will prefer the first object to the third. We shall examine the validity of these assumptions for choice under uncertainty in sections 4–6.

However the strongest and most specific implication of the expected utility hypothesis stems from the form of the expected utility maximand or *preference function*

$$U(x_1) \cdot p_1 + \cdots + U(x_n) \cdot p_n$$

Although this preference function generalizes the expected value form

$$x_1 \cdot p_1 + \cdots + x_n \cdot p_n$$

by dropping the property of linearity in the *payoff levels* (the x_i), it retains the other key property of this form, namely *linearity in the probabilities*.

Graphically, we may illustrate the property of linearity in the probabilities by consider-ing the set of all lotteries or prospects over some set of fixed outcome levels $x_1 < x_2 < x_3$, which can be represented by the set of all probability triples[9] of the form $\mathbf{P} = (p_1, p_2, p_3)$ where $p_i = \text{prob}\ (x_i)$ and

$$p_1 + p_2 + p_3 = 1$$

Making the substitution $p_2 = 1 - p_1 - p_3$, we can represent this set of lotteries by the points in the unit triangle in the (p_1, p_3) plane, as in Figure 2.[10] Since upward movements in the triangle increase p_3 at the expense of p_2 (i.e., shift probability from the outcome x_2 up to x_3) and leftward movements reduce p_1 to the benefit of p_2 (i.e., shift probability from x_1 up to x_2), these movements (and more generally, all northwest movements) lead to stochastically dominating lotteries and thus are always preferred. For purposes of illustrating many of the following discussions it will be useful to plot the individual's *indifference curves* in this diagram, i.e., loci of points having the same expected utility.[11] Since each such curve will consist of the set of all (p_1, p_3) points that solve the equation

$$\bar{u} = U(x_1) \cdot p_1 + U(x_2) \cdot (1 - p_1 - p_3) + U(x_3) \cdot p_3 = k$$

for some constant k, and since the probabilities p_1 and p_3 enter linearly (i.e., as multi-plicative coefficients) into this equation, the indifference curves will consist of parallel straight lines, with more preferred indifference curves lying to the northwest. This means that in order to know an expected utility maximizer's preferences over the entire triangle, it suffices to know the slope of a single indifference curve through a single point (i.e., lottery) in the diagram.

To see how this diagram can be used to illustrate attitudes toward risk, consider Figures 3a and 3b. The dashed lines in the figures are not indifference curves, but rather *iso-expected value lines*, i.e., loci of points having the same expected value, and hence given by the solutions to equations of the form

$$\bar{x} = x_1 \cdot p_1 + x_2 \cdot (1 - p_1 - p_3) + x_3 \cdot p_3 = k$$

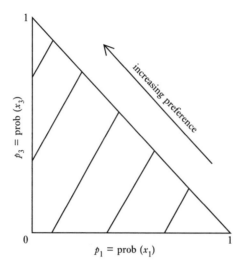

Figure 2   Expected utility indifference curves in the triangle diagram

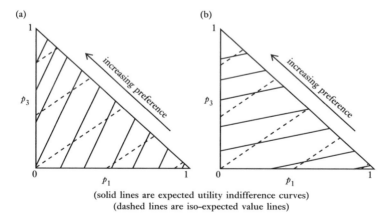

(solid lines are expected utility indifference curves)
(dashed lines are iso–expected value lines)

Figure 3   (a) Relatively steep indifference curves of a risk averter; (b) Relatively flat indifference curves of a risk lover

for some constant k. Since northeast movements along these lines do not change the expected value of the prospect but do increase the probabilities of the extreme outcomes x_1 and x_3 at the expense of the middle outcome x_2, they are simple examples of *mean preserving spreads* or "pure increases in risk" (Rothschild and Stiglitz, 1970, 1971). When the utility function $U(\cdot)$ is concave (i.e., risk averse), its indifference curves can be shown to be steeper than the iso-expected value lines (as in Figure 3a),[12] and such increases in risk will lead to less preferred indifference curves. When $U(\cdot)$ is convex (risk loving), its indifference curves will be flatter than the iso-expected value lines (as in Figure 3b), and these increases in risk will lead to more preferred indifference curves. Finally, if we compare two different utility functions, the one that is more risk averse (in the above Arrow–Pratt sense) will possess the steeper indifference curves.[13]

Behaviorally, we can view the property of linearity in the probabilities as a restriction on the individual's preferences over *probability mixtures* of lotteries. If

$$\mathbf{P}^* = (p_1^*, \ldots, p_n^*)$$

and

$$\mathbf{P} = (p_1, \ldots, p_n)$$

are two lotteries over a common outcome set $\{x_1, \ldots, x_n\}$, the $\alpha:(1-\alpha)$ probability mixture of $\mathbf{P}^*$ and $\mathbf{P}$ is the lottery

$$\alpha \cdot \mathbf{P}^* + (1-\alpha) \cdot \mathbf{P} = (\alpha \cdot p_1^* + (1-\alpha) \cdot p_1, \ldots, \alpha \cdot p_n^* + (1-\alpha) \cdot p_n)$$

This may be thought of as the prospect that yields the same ultimate probabilities over $\{x_1, \ldots, x_n\}$ as the two-stage lottery offering an $\alpha:(1-\alpha)$ chance of winning $\mathbf{P}^*$ or $\mathbf{P}$ respectively. It can be shown that expected utility maximizers all exhibit the following property, known as the *Independence Axiom* (Marschak, 1950; Samuelson, 1952).

> If the lottery $\mathbf{P}^*$ is preferred (respectively, indifferent) to the lottery $\mathbf{P}$, then the mixture $\alpha \cdot \mathbf{P}^* + (1-\alpha) \cdot \mathbf{P}^{**}$ will be preferred (respectively, indifferent) to the mixture $\alpha \cdot \mathbf{P} + (1-\alpha) \cdot \mathbf{P}^{**}$ for all $\alpha > 0$ and $\mathbf{P}^{**}$

This property, which is in fact *equivalent* to linearity in the probabilities, can be interpreted as follows:

> In terms of the ultimate probabilities over the outcomes $\{x_1, \cdots, x_n\}$, choosing between the mixtures $\alpha \cdot \mathbf{P}^* + (1-\alpha) \cdot \mathbf{P}^{**}$ and $\alpha \cdot \mathbf{P} + (1-\alpha) \cdot \mathbf{P}^{**}$ is the same as being offered a coin with a probability $1-\alpha$ of landing tails, in which case you will obtain the lottery $\mathbf{P}^{**}$, and being asked *before the flip* whether you would rather obtain $\mathbf{P}^*$ or obtain $\mathbf{P}$ in the event of a head. Now either the coin will land tails, in which case your choice won't have mattered, or else it will land heads, in which case your are "in effect" back to a choice between $\mathbf{P}^*$ or $\mathbf{P}$, and it is only "rational" to make the same choice as you would before.

Although this is a *prescriptive* argument, it has played a key role in economists' adoption of expected utility as a *descriptive* theory of choice under uncertainty. As the evidence against the model mounts, this has led to a growing tension between those who view economic analysis as the description and prediction of what they consider to be *rational* behavior and those who view it as the description and prediction of *observed* behavior. We turn now to this evidence.

3. Violations of Linearity in the Probabilities

3.1. The Allais paradox and "fanning out"

One of the earliest and best known examples of systematic violation of linearity in the probabilities (or equivalently, of the independence axiom) is the well known *Allais Paradox* (1952, 1953, 1979a). This problem involves obtaining the individual's preferred option from each of the following two pairs of gambles (readers who have never seen this problem may want to note down their own choices before proceeding):

$$a_1: \{1.00 \text{ chance of } \$1,000,000 \qquad \text{versus} \qquad a_2: \begin{cases} .10 \text{ chance of } \$5,000,000 \\ .89 \text{ chance of } \$1,000,000 \\ .01 \text{ chance of } \$0 \end{cases}$$

and

$$a_3: \begin{cases} .10 \text{ chance of } \$5,000,000 \\ .90 \text{ chance of } \$0 \end{cases} \qquad \text{versus} \qquad a_4: \begin{cases} .11 \text{ chance of } \$1,000,000 \\ .89 \text{ chance of } \$0 \end{cases}$$

Defining $\{x_1, x_2, x_3\} = \{0; \$1,000,000; \$5,000,000\}$, these four gambles are seen to form a parallelogram in the (p_1, p_3) triangle, as in Figures 4a and 4b. Under the expected utility hypothesis, therefore, a preference for a_1 in the first pair would indicate that the individual's indifference curves were relatively steep (as in Figure 4a), which would imply a preference for a_4 in the second pair. In the alternative case of relatively flat indifference curves, the gambles a_2 and a_3 would be preferred.[14] However, researchers such as Allais (1953), Morrison (1967), Raiffa (1968), Slovic and Tversky (1974) and many others have found that the most common choice has been for a_1 in the first pair and a_3 in the second, which implies that indifference curves are not parallel but rather *fan out*, as in Figure 4b.

One of the criticisms of this evidence has been that individuals whose choices violated the independence axiom would "correct" themselves once the nature of their violations were revealed by an application of the above coin flip argument.[15] Thus, while even Leonard Savage chose a_1 and a_3 when first presented with this problem, he concluded upon reflection that these preferences were in error.[16] Although his own reaction was undoubtedly sincere, the prediction that individuals would *invariably* react in such a manner has not been sustained in direct empirical testing. In experiments where subjects

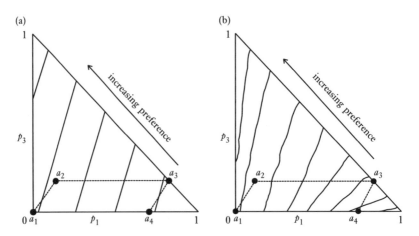

Figure 4 (a) Expected utility indifference curves and the Allais paradox; (b) Indifference curves that "fan out" and the Allais paradox

were asked to respond to Allais-type problems and then presented with written arguments both for *and against* the expected utility position, neither MacCrimmon (1968), Moskowitz (1974) nor Slovic and Tversky (1974) found predominant net swings toward the expected utility choices.[17]

3.2. Additional evidence of fanning out

Although the Allais Paradox was originally dismissed as an isolated example, it is now known to be a special case of a general empirical pattern termed the *common consequence effect*. This effect involves pairs of probability mixtures of the form:

$$
b_1: \begin{cases} \alpha \text{ chance of } c \\ 1 - \alpha \text{ chance of } \mathbf{P}^{**} \end{cases} \quad \text{versus} \quad b_2: \begin{cases} \alpha \text{ chance of } \mathbf{P} \\ 1 - \alpha \text{ chance of } \mathbf{P}^{**} \end{cases}
$$

and

$$
b_3: \begin{cases} \alpha \text{ chance of } c \\ 1 - \alpha \text{ chance of } \mathbf{P}^{*} \end{cases} \quad \text{versus} \quad b_4: \begin{cases} \alpha \text{ chance of } \mathbf{P} \\ 1 - \alpha \text{ chance of } \mathbf{P}^{*} \end{cases}
$$

where $\mathbf{P}$ involves outcomes both greater and less than c, and $\mathbf{P}^{**}$ stochastically dominates $\mathbf{P}^{*}$.[18] Although the independence axiom clearly implies choices of either b_1 and b_3 (if x is preferred to $\mathbf{P}$) or else b_2 and b_4 (if $\mathbf{P}$ is preferred to x), researchers have again found a tendency for subjects to choose b_1 in the first pair and b_4 in the second (MacCrimmon, 1968; MacCrimmon and Larsson, 1979; Kahneman and Tversky, 1979; Chew and Waller, 1986). When the distributions $\mathbf{P}, \mathbf{P}^{*}$ and $\mathbf{P}^{**}$ are each over a common outcome set

$\{x_1, x_2, x_3\}$ which includes x, the prospects b_1, b_2, b_3 and b_4 will again form a parallelogram in the (p_1, p_3) triangle, and a choice of b_1 and b_4 again implies indifference curves which fan out as in Figure 4b.

The intuition behind this phenomenon can be described in terms of the above "coin-flip" scenario. According to the independence axiom, preferences over what would occur in the event of a head should not depend upon what would occur in the event of a tail. In fact, however, they *may well* depend upon what would otherwise happen.[19] The common consequence effect states that the *better off* individuals would be in the event of a tail (in the sense of stochastic dominance), the *more risk averse* they become over what they would receive in the event of a head. Intuitively, if the distribution $\mathbf{P}^{**}$ in the pair $\{b_1, b_2\}$ involves very high outcomes, I may prefer not to bear further risk in the unlucky event that I don't receive it, and prefer the sure outcome x over the distribution $\mathbf{P}$ in this event (i.e., choose b_1 over b_2). But if $\mathbf{P}^*$ in $\{b_3, b_4\}$ involves very low outcomes, I may be more willing to bear risk in the (lucky) event that I don't receive it, and prefer the lottery $\mathbf{P}$ to the outcome x in this case (i.e., choose b_4 over b_3). Note that it is not my *beliefs* regarding the probabilities or conditional probabilities that are affected here, merely my willingness to bear them.[20]

A second class of systematic violations, stemming from another early example of Allais (1953), is known as the *common ratio effect*. This phenomenon involves pairs of prospects of the form:

$$c_1 : \begin{cases} p & \text{chance of } \$X \\ 1-p & \text{chance of } \$0 \end{cases} \quad \text{versus} \quad c_2 : \begin{cases} q & \text{chance of } \$Y \\ 1-q & \text{chance of } \$0 \end{cases}$$

and

$$c_3 : \begin{cases} \alpha \cdot p & \text{chance of } \$X \\ 1-\alpha \cdot p & \text{chance of } \$0 \end{cases} \quad \text{versus} \quad c_4 : \begin{cases} \alpha \cdot q & \text{chance of } \$Y \\ 1-\alpha \cdot q & \text{chance of } \$0 \end{cases}$$

where $p > q$, $0 < X < Y$, and $0 < \alpha < 1$, and includes the "certainty effect" of Kahneman and Tversky (1979) and the ingenious "Bergen Paradox" of Hagen (1979) as special cases.[21] Setting $\{x_1, x_2, x_3\} = \{0, X, Y\}$ and plotting these prospects in the (p_1, p_3) triangle, the line segments $\overline{c_1 c_2}$ and $\overline{c_3 c_4}$ are seen to be parallel (as in Figure 5a), so that the expected utility model again predicts choices of c_1 and c_3 (if the individual's indifference curves are steep) or else c_2 and c_4 (if they are flat). However, experimental studies have found a systematic tendency for choices to depart from these predictions in the direction of preferring c_1 and c_4 (Tversky, 1975; MacCrimmon and Larsson, 1979. Chew and Waller, 1986)., which again suggests that indifference curves fan out, as in the figure. In a variation on this approach, Kahneman and Tversky (1979) replaced the gains of $\$X$ and $\$Y$ in the above gambles with losses of these magnitudes, and found a tendency to depart from expected utility in the direction of c_2 and c_3. Defining $\{x_1, x_2, x_3\}$ as $\{-Y, -X, 0\}$ (to maintain the ordering $x_1 < x_2 < x_3$) and plotting these gambles in Figure 5b, a choice of c_2 and c_3 is again seen to imply that indifference curves fan out. Finally, Battalio, Kagel and MacDonald (1985) found that laboratory rats choosing among

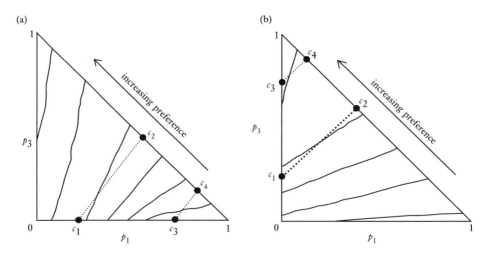

Figure 5   (a) Indifference curves that fan out and the common ratio effect; (b) Indifference curves that fan out and the common ratio effect with negative payoffs

gambles which involved substantial variations in their actual daily food intake also exhibited this pattern of choices.

A third class of evidence stems from the elicitation method described in the previous section. In particular, note that there is no reason why the mixture probability $\bar{p}$ *must* be $\frac{1}{2}$, as in our earlier example. Picking any other value, say $\bar{p}^* = \frac{1}{4}$, and obtaining the individual's certainty equivalent ξ_1^* of the gamble offering a $\frac{1}{4}$ chance of M and a $\frac{3}{4}$ chance of 0 will lead to the property that $U(\xi_1^*) = \frac{1}{4}$, and just as in the previous case of $\bar{p} = \frac{1}{2}$, the procedure using $\bar{p}^* = \frac{1}{4}$ (or any other fixed value) can also be continued to (in the limit) completely recover $U(\cdot)$.

Although this procedure should recover the same (normalized) utility function for any value of the mixture probability $\bar{p}$, researchers such as Karmarkar (1974, 1978) and McCord and de Neufville (1983, 1984) have found a tendency for higher values of $\bar{p}$ to lead to the "recovery" of higher valued utility functions, as in Figure 6a. By illustrating the gambles used to obtain the certainty equivalents ξ_1, ξ_2 and ξ_3 for the mixture probability $\bar{p} = \frac{1}{2}$, ξ_1^* for $\bar{p}^* = \frac{1}{4}$, and ξ_1^{**} for $\bar{p}^{**} = \frac{3}{4}$, Figure 6b shows that, as with the common consequence and common ratio effects, this *utility evaluation effect* is precisely what would be expected from an individual whose indifference curves departed from expected utility by fanning out.[22]

3.3. Non-expected utility models of preferences

The systematic nature of these departures from linearity in the probabilities have led several researchers to generalize the expected utility model by positing *nonlinear* functional forms for the individual preference function $V(x_1, p_1; \ldots; x_n, p_n)$. Some examples of such forms and researchers who have studied them are given in Table 1.

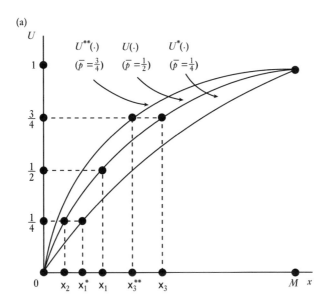

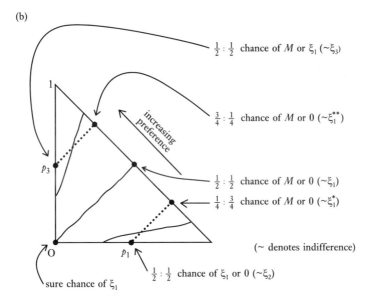

Figure 6 (a) "Recovered" utility functions for mixture probabilities $\frac{1}{4}$, $\frac{1}{2}$ and $\frac{3}{4}$; (b) Fanning out indifference curves which generate the responses of Fig. 6a

Table 1   Examples of non-expected utility preference functions

Name	$V(x_1p_1; \ldots; x_np_n)$	*References*
"Subjective expected utility"/[a] Prospect theory	$\sum_{i=1}^n v(x_i) \cdot \pi(p_i)$	Edwards (1955, 1962) Kahneman and Tversky (1979)
Subjectively weighted utility	$\dfrac{\sum_{i=1}^n v(x_i) \cdot \pi(p_i)}{\sum_{i=1}^n \pi(p_i)}$	Karmarkar (1978, 1979)
Moments of utility	$f\left(\sum_{i=1}^n v(x_i) \cdot p_i, \sum_{i=1}^n v(x_i)^2 \cdot p_i, \ldots\right)$	Múnera and de Neufville (1983), Hagen (1979)
Weighted utility	$\dfrac{\sum_{i=1}^n v(x_i) \cdot p_i}{\sum_{i=1}^n \tau(x_i) \cdot p_i}$	Chew (1983) Fishburn (1983)
Rank-dependent[b]	$\sum_{i=1}^n v(x_i) \cdot \left[G\left(\sum_{j=1}^i p_j\right) - G\left(\sum_{j=1}^{i-1} p_j\right)\right]$	Quiggin (1982) Yaari (1987), Allais (1988)
Quadratic in the probabilities	$\sum_{i=1}^n \sum_{j=1}^n \tau(x_i, x_j) \cdot p_i \cdot p_j$	Chew, Epstein and Segal (1991)
Optimism–Pessimism	$\sum_{i=1}^n v(x_i) \cdot g(p_i, x_1, \ldots, x_n)$	Hey (1984)
Ordinal independence	$\sum_{i=1}^n h\left(x_i, \sum_{j=1}^i p_j\right) \cdot \left[G\left(\sum_{j=1}^i p_j\right) - G\left(\sum_{j=1}^{i-1} p_j\right)\right]$	Segal (1984) Green and Jullien (1988)

[a] The term "subjective expected utility" as used to describe the preference function $v(x_i) \cdot (p_i)$ the 1950s and 1960s, should not be confused with the "expected utility under subjective uncertainty" approach of Savage (1954), which posits neither a nonlinear weighting function ($\cdot$) nor objective probabilities p_i, but rather, derives the individual's subjective probabilities over events from their preferences over bets on these events.
[b] The "Rank-dependent and "Ordinal independence" forms assume the outcomes are labeled so that $x_1 \leq \cdots \leq x_n$.

Many (though not all) of these forms are flexible enough to exhibit the properties of stochastic dominance preference, risk aversion/risk preference and fanning out, and the Chew–MacCrimmon–Fishburn and Quiggin forms have proven to be particularly useful, both theoretically and empirically. Additional analyses of the above forms can be found in Chew, Karni and Safra (1987), Fishburn (1982, 1984a, 1984b), Röell (1987), Segal (1984, 1987) and Yaari (1987). For general surveys of these models, see Machina (1983a), Sugden (1986) and Weber and Camerer (1987).

Although such forms allow for the modeling of preferences that are more general than those allowed by the expected utility hypothesis, each requires a different set of conditions on its component functions $v(\cdot)$, $\pi(\cdot)$, $\tau(\cdot)$ or $g(\cdot)$ for the properties of stochastic dominance preference, risk aversion/risk preference, comparative risk aversion, etc. In particular, the standard expected utility results that link properties of the function $U(\cdot)$ to such aspects of behavior will generally *not* extend to the corresponding properties of any function $v(\cdot)$ in the above forms. Does this imply that the study of non-expected utility preferences requires us to abandon the vast body of theoretical results and intuition we have developed within the expected utility framework?

Fortunately, the answer is no. An alternative approach to the analysis of non-expected utility preferences proceeds not by proposing a *specific* nonlinear function, but rather by considering nonlinear functions *in general*, and using calculus to extend results from expected utility theory in the same manner in which it is typically used to extend results involving linear functions.[23]

Specifically, consider the set of all probability distributions $\mathbf{P} = (p_1, \ldots, p_n)$ over a fixed outcome set $\{x_1, \ldots, x_n\}$, so that the expected utility preference function can be written as

$$V(\mathbf{P}) = V(p_1, \ldots, p_n) = U(x_1) \cdot p_1 + \ldots + U(x_n) \cdot p_n$$

and think of $U(x_i)$ not as a "utility level" but rather as the *coefficient* of $p_i = \text{prob}(x_i)$ in this linear function. If we plot these coefficients against x_i as in Figure 7, the expected utility results of the previous section can be stated as:

- *Stochastic Dominance Preference*: $V(\cdot)$ will exhibit global stochastic dominance preference if and only if the coefficients $\{U(x_i)\}$ are increasing in x_i, as in Figure 7.
- *Risk Aversion*: $V(\cdot)$ will exhibit global risk aversion if and only if the coefficients $\{U(x_i)\}$ are concave in x_i,[24] as in Figure 7.
- *Comparative Risk Aversion*: The expected utility preference function

$$V^*(\mathbf{P}) = U^*(x_1) \cdot p_1 + \cdots + U^*(x_n) \cdot p_n$$

will be at least as risk averse as $V(\cdot)$ if and only if the coefficients $\{U^*(x_i)\}$ are at least as concave in x_i as $\{U(x_i)\}$.[25]

Now consider the case where the individual's preference function $V(\mathbf{P}) = V(p_1, \cdots, p_n)$ is not linear (i.e., not expected utility) but at least differentiable, and consider its *probability derivatives*

$$U(x_i; \mathbf{P}) = \frac{\partial V(\mathbf{P})}{\partial p_i} = \frac{\partial V(\mathbf{P})}{\partial \text{prob}(x_i)}$$

Start at any probability distribution $\mathbf{P}_0$ and plot these $U(x_i; \mathbf{P}_0)$ values against x_i. If they are increasing in x_i, it is clear that any *infinitesimal* stochastically dominating shift from $\mathbf{P}_0$, such as a decrease in some p_i and matching increase in p_{i+1}, will be preferred. If they are concave in x_i, any *infinitesimal* mean preserving spread, such as a drop in p_i and (mean preserving) rise in p_{i-1} and p_{i+1}, will make the individual worse off. In light of this correspondence between the *probability coefficients* $\{U(x_i)\}$ of the expected utility preference function $V(\cdot)$ and the *probability derivatives* $\{U(x_i; \mathbf{P}_0)\}$ of the non-expected utility preference function $V(\cdot)$, we refer to $\{U(x_i; \mathbf{P}_0)\}$ as the individual's *local utility indices* at $\mathbf{P}_0$.

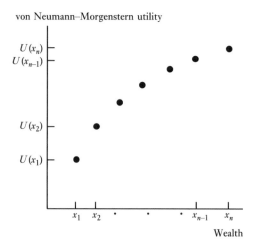

Figure 7 von Neumann-Morgenstern utilities as coefficients of the expected utility preference function $V_{p1}\ldots,P_n = U(x_1)p_1 + \cdots + U(x_n)p_n$

Of course, the above results only hold exactly for infinitesimal shifts from the distribution $\mathbf{P}_0$. However, we can exploit another result from standard calculus to show how "expected utility" results may be applied to the exact *global* analysis of non-expected utility preferences. Recall that in many cases, a differentiable function will exhibit a specific global property if and only if that property is exhibited by its *linear approximations* at each point. For example, a differentiable function will be globally nondecreasing if and only if its linear approximation at each point is nondecreasing. In fact, most of the fundamental properties of risk attitudes and their expected utility characterizations are precisely of this type. In particular, it can be shown that:

- *Stochastic Dominance Preference*: A non-expected utility preference function $V(\cdot)$ will exhibit *global* stochastic dominance preference if and only if its local utility indices $\{U(x_i; \mathbf{P})\}$ are increasing in x_i at each distribution $\mathbf{P}$.
- *Risk Aversion*: $V(\cdot)$ will exhibit global risk aversion if and only if its local utility indices $\{U(x_i; \mathbf{P})\}$ are concave in x_i at each distribution $\mathbf{P}$.
- *Comparative Risk Aversion*: The preference function $V^*(\cdot)$ will be globally at least as risk averse[26] as $V(\cdot)$ if and only if its local utility indices $\{U^*(x_i; \mathbf{P})\}$ are at least as concave in x_i as $\{U(x_i; \mathbf{P})\}$ at each $\mathbf{P}$.

Figures 8a and 8b give a graphical illustration of this approach for the outcome set $\{x_1, x_2, x_3\}$. Here the solid curves denote the indifference curves of the non-expected utility preference function $V(\mathbf{P})$. The parallel lines near the lottery $\mathbf{P}_0$ denote the tangent "expected utility" indifference curves that correspond to the local utility indices $\{U(x_i; \mathbf{P}_0)\}$ at $\mathbf{P}_0$. As always with differentiable functions, an infinitesimal change in the probabilities at $\mathbf{P}_0$ will be preferred if and only if it would be preferred by this tangent linear (i.e., expected utility) approximation. Figure 8b illustrates the above "risk aversion"

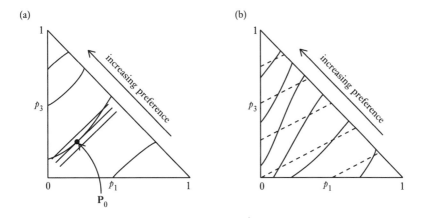

(a)   (b)

(solid lines are local expected utility approximation   (dashed lines are iso-expected value lines)
to non-expected utility indifference curves at P_0)

Figure 8 (a) Tangent "expected utility" approximation to non-expected utility indifference curves; (b) Risk aversion of every local expected utility approximation is equivalent to global risk of aversion

result. It is clear that these indifference curves will be globally risk averse (averse to mean preserving spreads) if and only if they are everywhere steeper than the dashed iso-expected value lines. However, this is equivalent to all of their *tangents* being steeper than these lines, which is in turn equivalent to all of their *local expected utility approximations* being steeper, or in other words, to the local utility indices $\{U(x_i; \mathbf{P})\}$ being concave in x_i at each distribution $\mathbf{P}$.

My fellow researchers and I have shown how this and similar techniques can be applied to further extend the results of expected utility theory to the case of non-expected utility preferences, to characterize and explore the implications of preferences that "fan out," and to conduct new and more general analyses of economic behavior under uncertainty. (Allen, 1987; Chew, 1983; Chew, Karni and Safra, 1987; Dekel, 1986; Epstein, 1985; Fishburn, 1984a; Karni and Safra, 1987, Machina, 1982, 1983b, 1984; Machina and Neilson, 1987. However, while I feel that they constitute a useful and promising response to the phenomenon of nonlinearities in the probabilities, these models do *not* provide solutions to the more problematic empirical phenomena of sections 4 through 6 below.

3.4. Safety-based models

Besides the class of models just discussed, another class of alternative models that has been applied to various types of real-world decisions are the so-called "safety-based" models, which place a special emphasis on the probability that wealth might take a very low value. Examples of such criteria and some researchers who have proposed them include:[27]

- "*Safety Principle*": Choose the option that maximizes the probability that wealth will be at least $\hat{x}$, for some prespecified value $\hat{x}$ (Cramér, 1930; Roy, 1952).

- "*Strict Safety-First Principle*": Choose the option that maximizes expected utility (or expected value) subject to the constraint it guarantee at least a $\hat{p}$ chance that wealth is at least $\hat{x}$, for some prespecified probability $\hat{p}$ and value $\hat{x}$ (Shackle, 1949; Telser, 1955)).
- "*Safety-Fixed Principle*": Choose the option that maximizes the minimum wealth level that can be guaranteed to occur with probability $\hat{p}$, for some prespecified value of $\hat{p}$ (Kataoka, 1963).

For further discussions of these models, including applications to agricultural, development, and business pricing decisions, the reader is referred to Day, Aigner and Smith (1971) as well as the collection of papers in Roumasset, Boussard and Singh (1979). Note that the Safety Principle and the Safety-Fixed Principle are "dual" in the sense that the former says to maximize the probability that you can count on a prespecified wealth level $\hat{x}$, whereas the second says to maximize the wealth level that you can count on with a prespecified probability $\hat{p}$.

Although the Safety Principle is actually a special case of the expected utility model, where the von Neumann–Morgenstern utility function $U(x)$ takes on the values 0:1 for x less: greater than $\hat{x}$, neither the Strict Safety-First nor the Safety-Fixed Principles are consistent with the expected utility hypothesis.[28] Accordingly, these latter two models might seem useful candidates for more general decision models under uncertainty. However, there are two reasons why (at least in the present author's view) they do not constitute useful alternatives to the expected utility model.

The first is that neither the Strict Safety-First and Safety-Fixed principles especially imply the types of departures from linearity in the probabilities that researchers have observed (namely, indifference curves that fan out). Nor are they capable of accommodating the other types of evidence we shall discuss in sections 4 through 6 below.

The second and more serious problem is that all three of these safety-based models exhibit an extreme sensitivity to very slight changes in the probabilities and/or payoffs near their respective cutoff levels, to the point where they propose almost nonsensical behavior. To see this, say that the cutoff wealth $\hat{x}$ is $100, the cutoff probability $\hat{p}$ is .95, and consider the risky projects A and B, with payoffs and probabilities given as in Table 2.

Table 2 Outcomes and probabilities for two competing risky projects

	0.949	0.001	0.05
Project A	$290.00	$99.99	$95.00
Project B	$200.00	$101.01	$5.00

Neither of these projects stochastically dominates the other in the sense of section 2. However, there is a .999 chance that Project A will yield *90 dollars more* than Project B (if either of the outer columns occur), and a .001 chance that it will yield *two cents less* than Project B (if the middle column occurs). Now a probability of .001 is very small, and even if this middle event did occur, the stakes would only be two cents, so it would seem that Project A ought to be clearly preferred.

However, each of the above three principles would instruct us to choose *Project B*:

- *Safety Principle*: Project B is preferred since it gives a .95 chance that wealth will be above the cutoff level $\hat{x} = 100$, whereas Project A only gives a .949 chance that wealth will be above this cutoff level.
- *Strict Safety-First Principle*: Project B is preferred since Project A fails to meet the requirement of a $\hat{p} = .95$ chance that wealth will be above the cutoff level $\hat{x} = 100$.
- *Safety-Fixed Principle*: Project B is preferred since it guarantees a $\hat{p} = .95$ chance of at least $101.01, whereas Project A can only guarantee a .95 chance of at least $99.99.

Of course, a proponent of these models might respond that in such circumstances we would want to neglect the .001 probability event or the 2¢ payoff difference in making our choice. However, this is precisely the problem with safety-based models – whereas it is *automatically the case* that extremely small probabilities and/or payoff differences have extremely small effects on the continuous preference functions of Table 1, such small probabilities or payoff differences could be the *sole determining factor* in a safety-based model. Those who advocate adherence to a safety-based model "except when it needs to be adjusted" for such cases should ask themselves whether they aren't in fact revealing preferences more along the line of one of the preference functions of Table 1, which are capable of exhibiting the same type of attention to the probability that wealth might take a low value, without implying the type of rigid discontinuities about a single $\hat{p}$ or $\hat{x}$ level.

4. The Preference Reversal Phenomenon

4.1. The evidence

The finding now known as the *preference reversal phenomenon* was first reported by psychologists Lichtenstein and Slovic (1971). In this study, subjects were first presented with a number of pairs of bets and asked to choose one bet out of each pair. Each of these pairs took the following form:

$$P\text{-bet} : \begin{cases} p & \text{chance of } \$X \\ 1-p & \text{chance of } \$ x \end{cases} \quad \text{versus} \quad \$\text{-bet} : \begin{cases} q & \text{chance of } \$Y \\ 1-q & \text{chance of } \$y \end{cases}$$

where X and Y are respectively greater than x and y, p is greater than q, and Y is greater than X (the names "P-bet" and "$-bet" come from the greater probability of winning in the first bet and greater possible gain in the second). In some cases, x and y took on small negative values. The subjects were next asked to "value" (state certainty equivalents for) each of these bets. The different valuation methods used consisted of

(a) asking subjects to state their minimum selling price for each bet if they were to own it,
(b) asking them to state their maximum bid price for each bet if they were to buy it, and

(c)   the elicitation procedure of Becker, DeGroot and Marschak (1964), where it is in a
       subject's best interest to reveal his or her true certainty equivalent.[29]

In the latter case, real money was in fact used.

The expected utility model, as well as each of the *non*-expected utility models of the
previous section, clearly implies that the bet that is actually chosen out of each pair will
also be the one that is assigned the higher certainty equivalent.[30] However, Lichtenstein
and Slovic (1971) found a systematic tendency to violate this prediction in the direction of
choosing the *P-bet* in a direct choice but assigning a higher value to the *$-bet*. In one
experiment, for example, 127 out of 173 subjects assigned a higher sell price to the $-bet in
every pair in which the P-bet was chosen. Similar findings were obtained by Lindman
(1971), and in an interesting variation on the usual experimental setting, by Lichtenstein
and Slovic (1973) in a Las Vegas casino where customers actually staked (and hence
sometimes lost) their own money. In another real money experiment, Mowen and Gentry
(1980) found that groups who were allowed to discuss their (joint) decisions were, if
anything, more likely than individuals to exhibit the phenomenon.

Although the above studies involved deliberate variations in experimental design
in order to check for the robustness of this phenomenon, they were nevertheless received
skeptically by economists, who perhaps not unnaturally felt they had more at stake than
psychologists in this type of finding. In an admitted attempt to "discredit" this work,
economists Grether and Plott (1979) designed a pair of experiments which, by correcting
for issues of incentives, income effects,[31] strategic considerations, ability to indicate
indifference, and others, would presumably not generate this phenomenon. They
nonetheless found it in both experiments. Further design modifications by Pommerehne,
Schneider and Zweifel (1982) and Reilly (1982) yielded the same results. Finally,
the phenomenon has been found to persist (although in mitigated form) even
when subjects are allowed to engage in experimental market transactions involving
the gambles (Knez and Smith (1987)), or when the experimenter is able to act as
an arbitrageur and make money from such reversals (Berg, Dickhaut and O'Brien
(1983)).

4.2. Two interpretations of this phenomenon

How you interpret these findings depends on whether you adopt the worldview of an
economist or a psychologist. An economist would reason as follows: Each individual
possesses a unique underlying *preference ordering* over objects (in this case lotteries), and
information about this preference ordering can be gleaned from either direct choice
questions or (properly designed) valuation questions.[32] Someone exhibiting the preference
reversal phenomenon is therefore telling us that they

(a)   are indifferent between the P-bet and some sure amount ξ_p,
(b)   strictly prefer the P-bet to the $-bet, and
(c)   are indifferent between the $-bet and an amount $\xi_\$$ *greater than* ξ_p.

Assuming that they in fact prefer $\xi_\$$ to the lesser amount ξ_p, this implies that their
preferences over these four objects are cyclic or *intransitive*.

Psychologists on the other hand would deny the premise of an common underlying mechanism generating both choice and valuation behavior. Rather, they view choice and valuation (even different forms of valuation) as distinct processes, subject to possibly different influences. In other words, individuals exhibit what are termed *response-mode effects*. Excellent discussions and empirical examinations of this phenomenon and its implications for the elicitation of both probabilistic beliefs and utility functions can be found in Hogarth (1975, 1980), Hershey, Kunreuther and Schoemaker (1982), Slovic, Fischhoff and Lichtenstein (1982), Hershey and Schoemaker (1985) and MacCrimmon and Wehrung (1986). In reporting how the response-mode study of Slovic and Lichtenstein (1968) actually led them to *predict* the preference reversal phenomenon, I can do no better than quote the authors themselves (Slovic and Lichtenstein, 1983, p. 597):

> The impetus for this study [Lichtenstein and Slovic (1971)] was our observation in our earlier 1968 article that choices among pairs of gambles appeared to be influenced primarily by probabilities of winning and losing, whereas buying and selling prices were primarily determined by the dollar amounts that could be won or lost.... In our 1971 article, we argued that, if the information in a gamble is processed differently when making choices and setting prices, it should be possible to construct pairs of gambles such that people would choose one member of the pair but set a higher price on the other.

4.3. Implications of the economic worldview

The issue of intransitivity is new neither to economics nor to choice under uncertainty. May (1954), for example, observed intransitivities in pairwise rankings of three alternative marriage partners, where each candidate was rated highly in two of three attributes (intelligence, looks, wealth) and low in the third. In an uncertain context, Blyth (1972) has adapted this approach to construct a set of random variables $(\tilde{x}, \tilde{y}, \tilde{z})$ such that

$$\text{prob}(\tilde{x} > \tilde{y}) = \text{prob}(\tilde{y} > \tilde{z}) = \text{prob}(\tilde{z} > \tilde{x}) = \frac{2}{3}$$

so that individuals making pairwise choices on the basis of these probabilities would also be intransitive. In addition to the preference reversal phenomenon, Edwards (1954a)[33] and Tversky (1969) have also observed intransitivities in preferences over risky prospects. On the other hand, researchers have also shown that many aspects of economic theory, in particular the existence of demand functions and of general equilibrium, are surprisingly robust to the phenomenon of intransitivity (e.g., Sonnenschein (1971), Shafer (1974, 1976), Mas-Colell (1974), Epstein (1987) and Kim and Richter (1986)).

In any event, economists have begun to develop and analyze models of nontransitive preferences over lotteries. The leading example of this is the "regret theory" model developed independently by Bell (1982, 1983) (see also Bell and Raiffa (1980)), Fishburn (1981, 1982, 1984a, 1984b) and Loomes and Sugden (1982, 1983a, 1983b)). In this model of pairwise choice the von Neumann–Morgenstern utility function $U(x)$ is replaced by a *regret/rejoice function* $r(x,y)$ that represents the level of satisfaction (or if negative, dissatisfaction) the individual would experience if he or she were to receive the outcome

x when the alternative choice would have yielded the outcome y (this function is assumed to satisfy $r(x,y) = -r(y,x)$ for all values of x and y). In choosing between statistically independent gambles $\mathbf{P} = (p_1, \ldots, p_n)$ and $\mathbf{P}^* = (p_1^*, \ldots, p_n^*)$ over a common outcome set $\{x_1, \ldots, x_n\}$, the individual will choose $\mathbf{P}^*$ if the expected value of the function $r(x,y)$ is positive, and $\mathbf{P}$ if it is negative.[34]

It is interesting to note that when the regret/rejoice function takes the special form

$$r(x,y) = U(x) - U(y)$$

this model reduces to the expected utility model.[35] But in general such an individual will not be an expected utility maximizer, nor will he or she have transitive preferences.

However, this intransitivity does not prevent us from illustrating such preferences graphically. To see this, consider the case when the individual is facing alternative independent lotteries over a common outcome set $\{x_1, x_2, x_3\}$, so that we may again use the triangle diagram to illustrate their "indifference curves," which will appear as in Figure 9. In such a case it is important to understand what is and is not still true of these indifference curves. The curve through $\mathbf{P}$ will still correspond to the points (i.e., lotteries) that are indifferent to $\mathbf{P}$, and it will still divide the points that are strictly preferred to $\mathbf{P}$ (the points in the direction of the arrow) from the ones to which $\mathbf{P}$ is strictly preferred. Furthermore, if (as in the figure) $\mathbf{P}^*$ lies above the indifference curve through $\mathbf{P}$, then $\mathbf{P}$ will lie below the indifference curve through $\mathbf{P}^*$ (i.e., the individual's ranking of $\mathbf{P}$ and $\mathbf{P}^*$ will be unambiguous). However unlike indifference curves for transitive preferences, these curves will cross,[36] and preferences over the lotteries $\mathbf{P}$, $\mathbf{P}^*$, and $\mathbf{P}^{**}$ are seen to form an intransitive cycle. But in regions where the indifference curves do *not* cross (such as near the origin) the individual will be indistinguishable from someone with transitive (albeit non-expected utility) preferences.

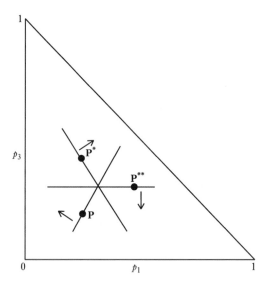

Figure 9   "Indifference curves" for the expected regret model

Bell, Raiffa, Loomes and Sugden, and Fishburn have shown how specific assumptions on the form of the regret/rejoice function will generate the common consequence effect, the common ratio effect, the preference reversal phenomenon and other observed properties of choice over lotteries.[37] The theoretical and empirical prospects for this approach seem quite impressive.

4.4. Implications of the psychological worldview

On the other hand, how should economists respond if it turns out that the psychologists are right, and the preference reversal phenomenon really *is* generated by some form of response-mode effect (or effects)? In that case, the first thing to do would be to try to determine if there were analogues of such effects in real world economic situations.[38] Will individuals behave differently when determining their valuation of an object (e.g., a reservation bid on a used car) than when reacting to a fixed and nonnegotiable price for the same object? Since a proper test of this would require correcting for any possible strategic and/or information-theoretic (e.g., signaling) issues, it would not be a simple undertaking. However, in light of the experimental evidence, I feel it is crucial that we attempt it.

Say we found that response-mode effects did not occur outside of the laboratory. In that case we could rest more easily, although we could not forget about such issues completely: experimenters testing *other* economic theories and models (e.g., auctions) would have to be forever mindful of the possible influence of the particular response mode used in their experimental design.

On the other hand, what if we *did* find response-mode effects out in the field? In such a case we would want to determine, perhaps by going back to the laboratory, whether the rest of economic theory remained valid *provided the response mode is held constant*. If this were true, then with further evidence on exactly *how* the response mode mattered, we could presumably incorporate it as a new independent variable into existing theories. Since response modes tend to be constant *within* specific economic models, e.g., quantity responses to fixed prices in competitive markets, valuation announcements (truthful or otherwise) in auctions, etc., we should expect most of the testable implications of this approach to appear as *cross-institutional predictions*, such as systematic violations of the various equivalency results involving prices versus quantities or second price sealed bid versus oral English auctions. I feel that the new results and implications for our theories of institutions and mechanisms would be exciting indeed.[39]

5. Framing Effects

5.1. Evidence

In addition to response-mode effects, psychologists have uncovered an even more disturbing phenomenon, namely that alternative means of representing or "framing" probabilistically equivalent choice problems can lead to systematic differences in choice. An early example of this phenomenon is reported by Slovic (1969a), who found (for example) that offering a gain or loss contingent on the joint occurrence of four independent events with probability p elicited different responses than offering it on the occurrence of a single event with probability p^4 (all probabilities were stated explicitly). In comparison with the single-event case, making a gain contingent on the joint occurrence of events was found to make it more attractive, and making a loss contingent on the joint occurrence of events made it more unattractive.[40]

In another study, Payne and Braunstein (1971) used pairs of gambles of the type illustrated in Figure 10. Each of the gambles in the figure, known as a *duplex gamble*, involves spinning the pointers on both its "gain wheel" (on the left) and its "loss wheel" (on the right), with the individual receiving the sum of the resulting amounts. Thus an individual choosing Gamble A would win $.40 with probability .3 (i.e., if the pointer in the gain wheel landed up and the pointer in the loss wheel landed down), would lose $.40 with probability .2 (if the pointers landed in the reverse positions), and would break even with probability .5 (if the pointers landed either both up or both down). An examination of Gamble B reveals that it has an identical implied distribution, so that subjects should be indifferent between the two gambles regardless of their risk preferences. However, Payne and Braunstein found that individuals in fact chose between such pairs (and indicated nontrivial strengths of preference) in manners which were systematically affected by the attributes of the component wheels. When the probability of winning in the gain wheel was greater than the probability of losing in the loss wheel for each gamble (as in the figure), subjects tended to choose the gamble whose gain wheel yielded the greater probability of a gain (Gamble A). In cases where the probabilities of losing in the loss wheels were greater than the probabilities of winning in the gain wheels, subjects tended toward the gamble with the lower probability of losing in the loss wheel.

Finally, although the gambles in Figure 10 possess identical implied distributions, continuity suggests that worsening of the terms of the preferred gamble could result in

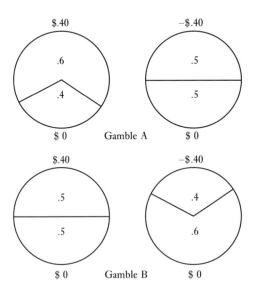

Figure 10   Duplex gambles with identical underlying distributions

a pair of nonequivalent duplex gambles in which the individual will actually choose the one with the *stochastically dominated* implied distribution. In an experiment where subjects were allowed to construct their own duplex gambles by choosing one from a pair of prospects involving gains and one from a pair of prospects involving losses, stochastically dominated combinations were indeed chosen (Tversky and Kahneman (1981) and Kahneman and Tversky (1984)).[41]

A second class of framing effects exploits the phenomenon of a *reference point*. Theoretically, the variable that enters an individual's von Neumann–Morgenstern utility function should be total (i.e., final) wealth, and gambles phrased in terms of gains and losses should be combined with current wealth and re-expressed as distributions over final wealth levels before being evaluated. However, economists since Markowitz (1952) have observed that risk attitudes over gains and losses are more stable than can be explained by a fixed utility function over final wealth, and have suggested that the utility function might be best defined in terms of *changes* from the "reference point" of current wealth. The stability of risk attitudes in the face of wealth variations has also been observed in several experimental studies.[42]

Markowitz (p. 155) also suggested that certain circumstances may cause the individual's reference point to temporarily deviate from current wealth. If these circumstances include the manner in which a given problem is verbally described, then differing risk attitudes over gains and losses can lead to different choices depending upon the exact description. A simple example of this, from Kahneman and Tversky (1979), involves the following two questions:

> "In addition to whatever you own, you have been given 1,000 (Israeli pounds). You are now asked to choose between a $\frac{1}{2} \cdot \frac{1}{2}$ chance of a gain of 1,000 or 0 or a sure chance of a gain of 500."

and

> "In addition to whatever you own, you have been given 2,000. You are now asked to choose between a $\frac{1}{2} \cdot \frac{1}{2}$ chance of a loss of 1,000 or 0 or a sure loss of 500."

These two problems involve identical distributions over final wealth. However, when put to two different groups of subjects, 84% chose the sure gain in the first problem but 69% chose the $\frac{1}{2} \cdot \frac{1}{2}$ gamble in the second. A nonmonetary version of this type of example, from Tversky and Kahneman (1981), posits the following scenario:

> "Imagine that the U.S. is preparing for the outbreak of an unusual Asian disease, which is expected to kill 600 people. Two alternative programs to combat the disease have been proposed. Assume that the exact scientific estimate of the consequences of the programs are as follows:
>
> If Program *A* is adopted, 200 people will be saved.
> If Program *B* is adopted, there is $\frac{1}{3}$ probability that 600 people will be saved, and $\frac{2}{3}$ probability that no people will be saved."

72% of the subjects who were presented with this form of the question chose program *A*. A second group was given the same initial information, but the descriptions of the programs were changed to read:

"If Program C is adopted 400 people will die.
If Program D is adopted there is $\frac{1}{3}$ probability that nobody will die, and $\frac{2}{3}$ probability that 600 people will die."

Although this statement once again implies choices identical to the former one, 78% of the respondents chose Program D.

In other studies, Schoemaker and Kunreuther (1979), Hershey and Schoemaker (1980a), Kahneman and Tversky (1982, 1984), Hershey, Kunreuther and Schoemaker (1982), McNeil, Pauker, Sox and Tversky (1982) and Slovic, Fischhoff and Lichtenstein (1982) have found that subjects' choices in otherwise identical problems will depend upon whether they are phrased as decisions whether or not to gamble or whether or not to insure, whether the statistical information for different therapies is presented in terms of cumulative survival probabilities over time or cumulative mortality probabilities over time, etc. (see also the additional references in Tversky and Kahneman (1981) as well as the examples of this phenomenon in nonstochastic situations given in Thaler (1980, 1985)).

In a final class of examples, not based on reference point effects, Moskowitz (1974) and Keller (1985) found that the proportion of subjects choosing in conformity with or in violation of the independence axiom in examples like the Allais Paradox was significantly affected by whether the problems were described in the standard matrix form (e.g., Raiffa (1968, p.7)), decision tree form, or as minimally structured written statements. Interestingly enough, the form that was judged the "clearest representation" by the majority of Moskowitz's subjects (the tree form) led to the lowest degree of consistency with the independence axiom, the highest proportion of Allais-type (i.e., fanning out) choices, and the highest persistency rate of these choices (Moskowitz 1974, pp. 234, 237–8).

5.2. Two issues regarding framing

The replicability and pervasiveness of the above group of examples is indisputable. Their implications for economic modeling involve (at least) two issues. The first is whether these experimental observations possess any analog outside of the laboratory. Since real world decision problems do not present themselves as neatly packaged as the ones on experimental questionnaires, monitoring such effects would not be as straightforward. However this does not mean that they do not exist, nor that they cannot be objectively observed or quantitatively measured. The real world example that comes most quickly to mind, and is presumably of no small importance to the involved parties, is whether gasoline price differentials should be represented as "cash discounts" or "credit surcharges." Similarly, Russo, Krieser and Miyashita (1975) and Russo (1977) found that the practice, and even method, of displaying unit price information in supermarkets (information which consumers could calculate for themselves) affected both the level and distribution of consumer expenditures. The empirical marketing literature is no doubt replete with findings that we could legitimately interpret as real world framing effects.

The second, more difficult issue is that of the independent observability of the particular frame that an individual will adopt in a given problem. In the duplex gamble and the /matrix/ decision tree/written statement / examples of the previous section, the different frames seem unambiguously determined by the form of presentation. However, in instances where framing involves the choice of a reference point, which presumably include the majority of real world cases, this point might not be objectively determined by the form of presentation, and might be chosen differently, and what is worse, *unobservably*, by each individual.[43] In a particularly thorough and insightful study, Fischhoff (1983) presented subjects with a written decision problem which allowed for different choices of a reference point, and explored different ways of predicting which frame individuals would adopt, in order to be able to predict their actual choices. While the majority choice of subjects was consistent with what would appear to be the most appropriate frame, Fischhoff noted "the absence of any relation within those studies between [separately elicited] frame preference and option preference." Indeed to the extent that frame preferences varied across his experiments, they did so *inversely* to the incidence of the predicted choice.[44] If such problems can occur in predicting responses to specific written questions in the laboratory, imagine how they could plague the modeling of real world choice behavior.

5.3. *Framing effects and economic analysis: Have we already solved this problem?*

How should we then respond if it turns out that framing actually is a real world phenomenon of economic relevance, and in particular, if individuals' frames cannot always be observed? I would argue that the means of responding to this issue can already be found in the "tool box" of existing economic analysis.

Consider first the case where the frame of a particular economic decision problem, even though it should not matter from the point of view of standard theory, can at least be independently and objectively observed. I believe that economists have in fact already solved such a problem in their treatment of the phenomenon of "uninformative advertising." Although it is hard to give a formal definition of this term, it is widely felt that economic theory is hard put to explain a large portion of current advertising in terms of traditional informational considerations.[45] However this has hardly led economists to abandon classical consumer theory. Rather, models of uninformative advertising proceed by quantifying this variable (e.g., air time) and treating it as an additional independent variable in the utility and/or demand function. Standard results like the Slutsky equation need not be abandoned, but rather simply reinterpreted as properties of demand functions *holding this new variable constant*. The degree of advertising itself is determined as a maximizing variable on the part of the firm (given some cost curve) and subject to standard comparative statics analysis.

In the case when decision frames can be observed, framing effects can presumably be modeled in an analogous manner. To do so, we would begin by adopting a method of quantifying, or at least categorizing, frames. The second step, some of which has of course already been done, would be to study both the effect of this new independent variable holding the standard economic variables constant, and conversely, to retest our standard economic theories in conditions where we carefully held the frame fixed. With any luck we would find that, holding the frame constant, the Slutsky equation still held.

The next step in any given modeling situation would be to ask "who determines the frame?" If (as with advertising) it is the firm, then the effect of the frame upon consumer demand, and hence upon firm profits, can be incorporated into the firm's maximization problem, and the choice of the frame as well as the other relevant variables (e.g., prices and quantities) can be simultaneously determined and subjected to comparative static analysis just as in the case of uninformative advertising.

A seemingly more difficult case is when the individual chooses the frame (for example, a reference point) and this choice cannot be observed. Although we should not forget the findings of Fischhoff (1983), assume that this choice is at least systematic in the sense that the consumer will jointly choose the frame and make the subsequent decision in a manner that maximizes a "utility function" which depends both on the decision *and* the choice of frame. In other words, individuals make their choices as part of a *joint maximization problem*, the other component of which (the choice of frame or reference point) cannot be observed.

Such models are hardly new to economic analysis. Indeed, *most* economic models presuppose that the agent is simultaneously maximizing with respect to variables other than the ones being studied. When assumptions are made on the individual's joint preferences over the unobserved and observed variables, the well known *theory of induced preferences* can be used to derive testable implications on choice behavior over the observables.[46] With a little more knowledge on exactly how frames are chosen, such an approach could presumably be applied here as well.

The above remarks should *not* be taken as implying that we have already solved the problems of framing in economic analysis or that there is no need to adapt, and if necessary abandon, our standard models in light of this phenomenon. Rather, they reflect the view that when the psychologists are able to present enough systematic evidence on how these effects operate, economists will be able to respond appropriately.

6. Other Issues: Is Probability Theory Relevant?

6.1. The manipulation of subjective probabilities

The evidence discussed so far has primarily consisted of cases where subjects have been presented with explicit (i.e., "objective") probabilities as part of their decision problems, and the models that have addressed these phenomena possess the corresponding property of being defined over objective probability distributions. However, there is extensive evidence that when individuals have to estimate or revise probabilities for themselves they will make systematic mistakes in doing so.

The psychological literature on the processing of probabilistic information is way too large even to summarize here. However, it is worth noting that experimenters have uncovered several "heuristics" used by subjects which can lead to predictable errors in the formation and manipulation of subjective probabilities. Kahneman and Tversky (1973), Bar-Hillel (1974) and Grether (1980), for example, have found that probability updating systematically departs from Bayes' Law in the direction of underweighting prior information and overweighting the "representativeness" of the current sample. In a related phenomenon termed the "law of small numbers," Tversky and Kahneman (1971) found that individuals overestimated the probability of drawing a perfectly representative sample out of a heterogeneous population. Finally, Bar-Hillel (1973), Tversky and Kahneman (1983) and others have found systematic biases in the formation of the probabilities of conjunctions of both independent and nonindependent events. For surveys, discussions and examples of the psychological literature on the formation and handling of probabilities, see Edwards, Lindman and Savage (1963), Edwards (1971), Slovic and Lichtenstein (1971), Tversky and Kahneman (1974), Grether (1978), as well as the collections in *Acta Psychologica* (Vanschie and Vandespligt, 1970), in Kahneman, Slovic and Tversky (1982), and in Arkes and Hammond (1986). For examples of how economists have responded to some of these issues, see Arrow (1982), Viscusi (1985a, 1985b) and the references cited there.

6.2. The existence of subjective probabilities

The evidence referred to above indicates that when individuals are asked to formulate probabilities they don't do it correctly. However, these findings may be rendered moot by evidence which suggests that when individuals making decisions under uncertainty are *not* explicitly asked to form subjective probabilities they might not do it *at all*.

In one of a class of examples due to Ellsberg (1961), subjects were presented with a pair of urns, the first containing 50 red balls and 50 black balls and the second also containing 100 red and black balls but in an unknown proportion. When faced with the choice of staking a prize on:

R_1 = drawing a red ball from the first urn;
R_2 = drawing a red ball from the second urn;
B_1 = drawing a black ball from the first urn; or
B_2 = drawing a black ball from the second urn

a majority of subjects strictly preferred R_1 over R_2 *and* strictly preferred B_1 over B_2. It is clear that there can exist *no* subjective probabilities $p : (1 - p)$ of drawing a red:black ball from the second urn – even the probabilities $\frac{1}{2}:\frac{1}{2}$ – that can simultaneously generate *both* of these strict preferences. Similar behavior in this and related problems has been observed by Raiffa (1961), Becker and Brownson (1964), MacCrimmon (1965), Slovic and Tversky (1974) and MacCrimmon and Larsson (1979).[47]

6.3. Life (and economic analysis) without probability theory

One response to this type of phenomenon as been to suppose that individuals "slant" whatever subjective probabilities they might otherwise form in a manner which reflects the amount of confidence/ambiguity associated with them (Fellner (1961, 1963), Brewer and Fellner (1965), Becker and Brownson (1964), Einhorn and Hogarth (1986), Fishburn (1986, 1988) and Hogarth and Kunreuther (1985, 1989)). In the case of complete ignorance regarding probabilities, Arrow and Hurwicz (1972), Maskin (1979) and others have presented axioms which imply principles such as ranking options solely on the basis of their best and/or worst possible outcomes (e.g., maximin, maximax), the unweighted average of their outcomes ("principle of insufficient reason") or similar criteria.[48] Finally generalizations of expected utility theory which drop the standard additivity and/or compounding laws of probability theory have been developed by Schmeidler (1989) and Segal (1987).

Table 3 Typology of violations of the expected utility hypothesis and alternative models[a]

Violation	Description	Empirical references	Models consistent with the phenomenon
Allais paradox, Common consequence effect, Common ratio effect, Utility evaluation effect	Indifference curves over lotteries are not linear in the probabilities, but rather "fan out"	Allais (1953, 1979a), Karmarkar (1974), MacCrimmon and Larsson (1979), Kahneman and Tversky (1979)	Edwards (1955, 1962), Kahneman and Tversky (1979), Machina (1982), Quiggin (1982), Chew (1983), Fishburn (1983)
Preference reversal phenomenon	"P-Bet" preferred to "$-bet" in direct choice, but assigned a lower certainty equivalent	Lichtenstein and Slovic (1971, 1973), Lindman (1971), Reilly (1982), Grether and Plott (1979)	Bell (1982, 1983), Fishburn (1981, 1982), Loomes and Sugden (1982, 1983b)
Reference point effects	Preferences over gambles with identical final distributions affected by status quo or "reference point"	Markowitz (1952), Schoemaker and Kunreuther (1979), Kahneman and Tversky (1979)	Markowitz (1952), Kahneman and Tversky (1979)
Other framing effects	Preferences over gambles with identical distributions are affected by the manner of presentation	Slovic (1969a), Moskowitz (1974), Payne and Braunstein (1971), Kahneman and Tversky (1984)	Kahneman and Tversky (1984) (consistent with some, but not all, of these effects)
Incorrect manipulation of Probabilities	Systematic errors in the use of Bayes' Law, probabilities of compound events, etc.	Bar-Hillel (1973, 1974), Kahneman and Tversky (1973), Grether (1980)	Viscusi (1985a, 1989), Segal (1987, 1990)
Non-Existence of subjective probabilities	Choices inconsistent with the existence of well-defined subjective probabilities	Ellsberg (1961), Raiffa (1961), Slovic and Tversky (1974), MacCrimmon and Larsson (1979)	Schmeidler (1989), Gilboa (1987), Hazen (1987)

[a] See the text for additional details and references on observed violations and alternative models.

Although the above models may well capture aspects of actual decision processes, the *analytically* most useful approach to choice in the presence of uncertainty but the absence of probabilities is the so-called *state-preference* model of Arrow (1953/1964), Debreu (1959) and Hirshleifer (1965, 1966).[49] In this model uncertainty is represented by a set of mutually exclusive and exhaustive *states of nature* $S = \{s_t\}$. This partition of all possible unfoldings of the future could be either coarse, such as the pair of states {it rains here tomorrow, it doesn't rain here tomorrow} or else very fine, so that the definition of an individual state might read "it rains here tomorrow *and* the temperature at Gibraltar is 75° at noon *and* the price of gold in London is below \$700.00/ounce." Note that it is neither feasible nor desirable to capture *all conceivable* sources of uncertainty when specifying the set of states for a given problem: it is not feasible since no matter how finely the states are defined there will always be some other random criterion on which to further divide them, and not desirable since such criteria may affect neither individuals' preferences nor their opportunities. Rather, the key requirements are that the states be mutually exclusive and exhaustive so that exactly one will be realized, and that the extent to which the individual is able to influence their probabilities (if at all) be *explicitly* specified.

Given a fixed (and say finite) set of states, the objects of choice in this framework consist of alternative *state-payoff bundles*, each of which specifies the outcome the individual will receive in every possible state. When the outcomes are monetary payoffs, for example, state-payoff bundles take the form $(c_1, \ldots, c_n)$, where c_i denotes the payoff the individual will receive should state i occur. In the case of exactly two states of nature we can represent this set by the points in the (c_1, c_2) plane. Since bundles of the form (c, c) represent prospects that yield the same payoff in each state of nature, the 45° line in this plane is known as the *certainty line*.

Now if the individual happens to assign some set of probabilities $\{p_i\}$ to the states $\{s_i\}$, each bundle $(c_1, \ldots, c_n)$ will imply a specific probability distribution over the payoffs, and we could infer their preferences (i.e., indifference curves) over state-payoff bundles.[50] However, since these bundles are defined directly over the respective states and *without reference* to any probabilities, it is possible to speak of preferences over such bundles without making any assumptions regarding the coherency, or even existence, of probabilistic beliefs. Researchers such as the ones listed above as well as Yaari (1969), Diamond and Yaari (1972) and Mishan (1976) have used this indifference curve-based approach to derive results from individual demand behavior through general equilibrium in a context which requires neither the expected utility hypothesis nor the existence or commonality of subjective probabilities. In other words, life without probability theory does not imply life without economic analysis.[51]

7. Implications for Private, Public and Environmental Decision Making

Twenty years ago, a decision analyst advising an individual, private firm, or government agency in a business, social, or environmental choice under uncertainty might proceed through something like the following stylized procedure:

Step 1: Collect as much information as possible about the decision and construct an explicit list of the currently or potentially available options.

Step 2: Assess the decision maker's (or alternatively, "expert's") subjective probability distributions over consequences implied by each option.

Step 3: Evaluate the decision maker's (or "society's") preferences over the alternative consequences, as well as their attitudes toward risk (in other words, their von Neumann-Morgenstern utility function).

Step 4: Determine the option that would yield the highest (individual or social) expected utility.[52]

Of course, the consequences might involve several dimensions (requiring the assessment of a multivariate utility function) (Keeny and Raiffa, 1976), or the experts might disagree on the probabilities (requiring some form of consensus, aggregation, or pooling of beliefs) (Grofman and Owen, 1986), but researchers working on these aspects remained confident of the validity of this overall, expected utility-based, approach.

Should the developments surveyed in this paper change the way private decision analysts or public decision makers go about their jobs, or how environmental decision policy should be conducted? Do they imply new or different business or governmental responsibilities in keeping customers or citizens informed of any voluntary (or involuntary) risks they may be facing? The following is a discussion of some issues that these new developments raise.

7.1. Implications for private sector decision analysis

How should private sector decision analysts adapt their procedures in light of these new empirical findings and theoretical models? It is hard to see how Step 1 (formulating the options) could, or should, change. However, the types of systematic biases in the formulation and manipulation of subjective probabilities presented in section 6 should cause the analyst to be especially careful in obtaining mutually consistent estimates of the underlying event likelihoods used in constructing the probability distributions over consequences implied by each option in Step 2. Note that this step has nothing to do with the client's attitudes toward *bearing* such risks (namely whether they are, or should be, expected utility maximizing). Rather, it consists of applying probability theory to establish the internal consistency and (once established) the logical implications of the client's or expert's probabilistic beliefs. If the client assigns probability .3 to some event A occurring, probability .2 to some mutually exclusive event B occurring, and a probability .6 that neither will occur, then at least one of these numbers will have to change before the pieces will fit. This is no different from asking a client for the length, the width and the area of his or her living room before advising them on a choice of carpet: if the numbers don't multiply out correctly then something is wrong, and the advising process should stop short until they do. While practitioners in the field have been aware of such inconsistencies (and how to iron them out) for some time now, the type of systematic and specific biases that psychologists have been uncovering now give decision analysts the opportunity, and I feel much more of an obligation, to explicitly search for and eliminate what might otherwise remain hidden biases and inconsistencies in clients' probabilistic beliefs.

Although I feel they are important, the suggestions of the previous paragraph represent more of a technical improvement rather than a basic change in how Step 2 is carried out. On the other hand, I would argue that the developments reviewed in this paper *do* imply a fundamental change in the way modern decision analysts should proceed with Steps 3 and 4 (explicating clients' risk preferences and determining their optimal action). The classical approach would be to essentially impose the property of linearity in the probabilities by assessing their von Neumann–Morgenstern utility function and then using it to calculate their "optimal" (i.e., expected utility maximizing) choice. Under this approach, if clients made choices like those in the Allais Paradox, the common consequence effect, or the common ratio effect of section 3, or their responses to alternative assessment methods yielded different "recovered" utility functions, they would often be told that they had "inconsistent" (translation: not expected utility) preferences, and these would have to be corrected before their optimal action could be determined.

While experimental subjects and real world decision makers sometimes do make mistakes in expressing their preferences, I feel that the widespread and systematic nature of "fanning out" departures from expected utility, and the growing number of models which can simultaneously accommodate this phenomenon along with the more traditional features of stochastic dominance preference and risk aversion, increase both the analyst's ability and obligation to fit and represent clients' risk attitudes within a consistent non-expected utility framework when their expressed risk preferences are pointing in that direction.[53] Why do I feel that departures from the strictures of *probability theory* should be corrected, but (systematic) departures from the strictures of *expected utility theory* should not? Because the former involve the *determination* of the risks involved in an option, which is a matter of accurate representation, whereas the latter involve clients' *attitudes toward bearing* these risks, which is matter of preference. To continue my earlier analogy, reporting a length, a width and an area that are not commensurate implies an internally inconsistent description of a room and is simply wrong, but preferring purple polka dot carpeting is a matter of clients' tastes, to which they have every right if it is their own living room. In the case of health or environmental risks, this would correspond the distinction between *measuring the risks (probabilities) of detrimental effects* of a drug or pollutant, versus determining the individual patient's or society's attitudes toward bearing these risks.

But does this increased respect for clients' preferences mean that the decision analyst should not play *any* guiding role in Steps 3 or 4? No – conscientious decision analysts will still try to elicit and explicitly represent clients' risk attitudes, their underlying properties (such as whether or not they are risk averse, linear in the probabilities, etc.) and their logical implications. Even more important, they will continue to explicitly separate their client's *beliefs* from their *preferences*.[54] For example, say that while Option #1 offers a very high chance of an acceptable but not terrific outcome (e.g., amputation of a gangrenous limb), the client *insists* on "optimism" or "wishful thinking" in connection with Option #2 (e.g., drug therapy), which is not as likely to succeed but does offer a small chance of obtaining the best possible outcome. In that case the decision analysis should take pains to formally represent the client's attitude as a willingness to bear risk (either by a convex utility function as in Figure 1b or by some non-expected utility counterpart) rather than as an exaggerated probability estimate of obtaining the best outcome under Option #2. The job of the decision analyst has hardly become obsolete.

7.2. *Implications for public decision making*

Whereas private sector decision analysts typically act on behalf of an individual client or firm, decision makers in federal, state or local government must act on the behalf of citizens whose preferences and interests generally differ from one another. In the case of decisions under certainty, economists have developed a large body of techniques, collectively termed *welfare economics* or *welfare analysis*, with which to analyze such situations.[55] Not surprisingly, economic theorists have used the expected utility model as a framework for extending such analysis to the world of uncertainty (e.g., Arrow (1953/1964, 1974), Diamond (1967)). But say we wish to respect what the recent evidence implies about individuals' *actual* attitudes toward risk. Can classical welfare analysis, the economist's most important tool for formal policy evaluation, be undertaken with these newer models of non-expected utility phenomena?

The answer to this question depends on the phenomenon. *Fanning-out risk preferences* and the non-expected utility models used to characterize them, as well as the state-payoff model of section 6, are all completely consistent with the assumption of well-defined, transitive individual preference orderings, and hence with traditional welfare analysis along the lines of Pareto (1909), Bergson (1938) and Samuelson (1947/1983, ch. VIII). For example, the classic proof of the Pareto efficiency of a system of complete contingent markets (Arrow (1953/1964), Debreu (1959, ch. 7)) does not require risk preferences to be expected utility or beliefs to be probabilistic. On the other hand, it is clear that the *preference reversal phenomenon* and *framing effects* (and the models that represent them) will prove much more difficult to reconcile with welfare analysis, or at least welfare analysis as currently practiced (see the final two subsections of this paper).

For an example of incorporating fanning out into policy analysis, consider a social decision maker who faces a probability p of a loss L, and is evaluating potential adjustments (tradeoffs) in these two variables by means of their (i.e. "society's") marginal rate of substitution $MRS(p, L)$. We saw in section 2 that with *expected utility* risk preferences, the value of $MRS(p, L)$ varies proportionally to p for any given L. Although it requires a bit of algebra, one can show that with *fanning out* risk preferences, for given L the value of $MRS(p, L)$ varies *less than proportionally* to p (Machina, 1983b, p. 288) Although this is not as strong as expected utility's prediction of exact proportionality, it can at least be used to make one-sided predictions, and in any event is at least more closely tied to what we seem to have observed about individuals' ("citizens'") risk preferences.[56]

Take section 2's question of how to allocate resources between a reactor's early sensing system and its containment system, which respectively determine its p and L. We can summarize and represent the tradeoff in this situation by the standard decreasing relationship $p = f(L)$ (moving resources from sensing to containment lowers L but raises p, and vice versa). Assuming the natural second-order conditions, the *first-order conditions* for both expected utility and non-expected utility risk preferences are the same, namely that the optimal combination (p^*, L^*) satisfies the standard tangency and feasibility conditions

$$MRS(p^*, L^*) = f'(L^*) \qquad \text{and} \qquad p^* = f(L^*)$$

On the other hand, the *comparative statics* of expected utility and fanning out preferences differ. Say there is now a technological breakthrough in sensing which, for any allocation of resources between sensing and containment, halves the reactor's p with no change in its L. This breakthrough has two effects:

(i) the tradeoff function drops to $\hat{f}(\cdot) = f(\cdot)/2$;
(ii) the originally optimal resource allocation now implies the values
     $(\hat{p}, \hat{L}) = (p^*/2, L^*)$.

Under expected utility, proportionality of $MRS\,(p, L)$ in p implies[57]

$$MRS(\hat{p}, \hat{L}) = f'(\hat{L}) \qquad \text{and} \qquad \hat{p} = f(\hat{L})$$

which implies that the original optimal allocation of resources *remains* optimal. Thus under expected utility preferences, the benefits of the breakthrough are taken wholly in the form of a reduction (halving) of the disaster probability, with no change in the disaster magnitude. On the other hand, under fanning out risk preferences $MRS\,(p, L)$ varies *less* than proportionately to p, so at the values $(\hat{p}, \hat{L})$ implied by the original optimal allocation we now have

$$MRS(\hat{p}, \hat{L}) > f'(\hat{L}) \qquad \text{and} \qquad \hat{p} = f(\hat{L})$$

This implies that under fanning out preferences, the optimal response to the breakthrough is to *adjust* the original optimal allocation, by shifting some resources from sensing to containment.[58] Thus with fanning out preferences, the benefits of the breakthrough will be taken in the form of reductions in *both* p and L from (p^*, L^*) (though the reduction in p will no longer be a full halving).

7.3. *Implications of the delayed-resolution nature of policy and environmental uncertainty*

Up to this point we have, if only implicitly, just been considering the types of immediate-resolution risks that one faces in an experimental session or at a gaming table. However, there is another important argument for the use of non-expected utility models in the analysis of policy (e.g., environmental) risks, namely the fact that such risks typically involve a considerable span of time between the time that choices must be made and the time the relevant uncertainty has been realized (or at least, fully realized). The reason this becomes an issue for decision modeling is that even agents whose underlying risk preferences are expected utility will not rank *delayed-resolution* risks in a manner consistent with the expected utility hypothesis.

Although there is a large literature on this phenomenon (Markowitz, 1959, ch. 11; Mossin, 1969; Spence and Zeckhauser 1972; Drèze and Modigliani, 1972; Kreps and Porteus, 1979), it is possible to illustrate it by means of a simple, two-period, example. Consider once again the case of determining an agent's (or society's) preferences over alternative combinations of the probability p and magnitude L of some disaster. However, this time suppose:

(i)   the agent will not know the outcome of the uncertainty (i.e., whether or not the disaster occurs) until the second period, and
(ii) in the meantime, other "interim" decisions (for example, consumption/savings decisions) must be made

Specifically, let $U(C_1, C_2)$ be the agent's von Neumann–Morgenstern utility for two-period consumption streams (C_1, C_2), let (I_1, I_2) be his or her income stream, and let S be the amount of savings (or if negative, borrowing) undertaken in the first period. For simplicity, let the interest rate on saving/borrowing be zero. Thus C_1 will equal first period income I_1 minus savings, and C_2 will equal second period income I_2 plus savings, minus the loss L if the disaster occurs. Given any specific values of the delayed-risk variables p and L, the individual will choose today's level of saving so as to maximize expected utility, as given by

$$(1 - p) \cdot U(I_1 - S, I_2 + S) + p \cdot U(I_1 - S, I_2 + S - L)$$

in other words, they face the maximization problem

$$\max_S (1 - p) \cdot U(I_1 - S, I_2 + S) + p \cdot U(I_1 - S, I_2 + S - L)$$

Given the values of p and L, denote the solution to this maximization problem by $S(p, L)$. Note that while the level of saving S can depend upon both the probability p and potential loss L of the delayed-resolution risk, it *cannot* be a function of whether or not the loss actually occurs, since that won't be known until the second period, well after S must be chosen.

If we substitute this optimal saving function $S(p, L)$ into the first formula above, we get that the optimal level of expected utility achievable under any given (p, L) combination is given by:

$$(1 - p) \cdot U(I_1 - S(p, L), I_2 + S(p, L)) + p \cdot U(I_1 - S(p, L), I_2 + S(p, L) - L)$$

This, then, is the preference function that will be used to evaluate alternative (p, L) combinations, since it incorporates the agent's optimal savings response to whatever values of (p, L) are chosen.

The problem, however, is while the agent's *underlying* preferences (as given by the first formula above) were "linear in the probabilities" or in other words expected utility, their *induced* or *derived* preferences over future risks, as reflected by the last preference function, do not have the expected utility property, as the probability p enters nonlinearly into its formula. This feature is not specific to our example, but rather applies to practically any situation of delayed-resolution risk. In fact, I have elsewhere (Machina, 1984), shown that if $U(c_1, c_2)$ takes the standard discounted form

$$U(c_1, c_2) \equiv v(C_1) + \delta \cdot v(C_2)$$

and the instantaneous utility function $v(\cdot)$ exhibits decreasing absolute risk aversion, then preferences over delayed-resolution risks will exhibit the same type of fanning-out behavior as illustrated in Figures 4b, 5a, 5b and 6.

Of course, real-world environmental risks are much more complicated, last for many "periods," and involve many more interim decisions than as portrayed by this simple example. To the extent that the uncertainty in environmental risk takes time to fully resolve itself, and to the extent that we want to make any interim decisions optimally, our preferences over such delayed-resolution risks will be best modeled by the types of non-expected utility preference functions of Table 1, rather than by the expected utility model itself.

7.4. Implications of response-mode effects

The preference reversal phenomenon and related findings of response-mode effects present substantially greater problems for public policy. Specifically, such findings suggest that questionnaires that elicit the public's "willingness to pay" for alternative environmental and safety programs may yield different results than questionnaires that ask the public to choose among or rank among alternative plans (including, possibly, the plan "take no action"). For example, consider two plans to reduce the probability and/or extent of marine oil spills due to iceberg collisions in a certain northern bay. Say that each plan involves the same total cost, which is known with a high degree of accuracy. The virtue of "Plan A," which uses many small vessels, is that should a spill occur (with probability p_A), it will be relatively small – say, of size L_A. The virtue of "Plan B," which involves a few larger vessels with more sophisticated navigation equipment, is that there is a much lower probability p_B of a spill, but of course, if one occurs, it will be of a larger size L_B. Like our nuclear sensing/nuclear containment example, this is another case of a tradeoff between probability and loss. And except for the replacement of gains by losses, it corresponds to the structure of the "P-bet vs. \$-bet" situation of the Preference Reversal Phenomenon of section 4.

One way to elicit individuals' preferences among these options is to take a simple survey of how they would vote between them. Another way, presumably more useful for cost – benefit analysis, would be to ask each individual their monetary gain equivalent for each option ("What is the least amount of money you would accept *instead of* receiving Plan A?" and similarly for Plan B). Under the classical model of choice these two procedures should yield equivalent results: In the second procedure (eliciting monetary valuations), each individual would assign a greater monetary equivalent to the plan that yielded them the higher level of utility, and in the first procedure (outright choice) they would act similarly.

However, as we have seen from the studies reported in section 4, the cognitive processes of valuation and choice do *not* always yield the same results, even for the simplest of choice situations. In the oil spill example, it could be the case that individuals on average assign a higher monetary equivalent to Plan A, but on average tend to vote for Plan B. Which would be the correct action to take then?

One might argue for the outright choice procedure, on the grounds that the real question is one of choice – namely whether society adopts Plan A or adopts Plan B. A counterargument might be that society should not think of choosing between them at all until we know that each of the options is worth its implementation cost, which means that valuation (determining social monetary benefit) is the more basic issue.

How likely are we to fall into an actual example of "preference reversal" in the real world? After all, the specific examples reported in section 4 were not stumbled upon accidentally – as the Lichtenstein and Slovic quote in that section indicates, these researchers explicitly sought them out. Thus, the probability of reversal between choice and valuation for a given pair is likely to be very low indeed. On the other hand, real world choices are often *not* between specific pairs of options, but rather, lie along some continuum (e.g., "What is the "socially optimal" level of carbon monoxide emissions?"). In that case, the net social valuation of the "optimal" level would be very close to the net social valuation of adjacent levels, and we might expect to obtain such reversals with some regularity if we checked. Thus, the implications of response-mode effects on environmental decision making, and its broader implications or the implementation of social "preferences," seems to be an important open issue.

7.5. Public and corporate obligations regarding the presentation of information

A final issue concerns the public policy implications of framing effects. If individuals' choices actually depend upon the manner in which publicly or privately supplied probabilistic information (such as cancer incidence or flood probabilities) is presented, then the manner of presentation *itself* becomes a public policy issue, over which interest groups may well contend. Say, for example, a projected engineering project is expected to reduce the steady state population of some rare species, whose current population is only imperfectly known. Should its environmental impact report be required to estimate most precisely the expected *reduction* in the population, or the expected *remaining size* of the population?

To take another example, consider two alternative new artifical sweeteners, "Sweetener A" and "Sweetener B." It has been determined that the approval and introduction of Sweetener A would raise the annual death rate from pancreatic cancer from (say) 1 in 1,000,000 to 7 in 1,000,000, whereas the introduction of Sweetener B would raise the death rate from heart disease from 100 in 100,000 to 101 in 100,000. Should we reject Sweetener A in favor of B, on the grounds that the former leads to a 600% increase in death from pancreatic cancer whereas the latter only leads to a 1% increase in death from heart disease? Or should we reject Sweetener B, since it will lead to an extra 10 deaths per million instead of only an extra 6 deaths per million.

More broadly, should "freedom of information" imply that a government or a manufacturer has an obligation to present a broad range of "legitimate" frames when disclosing required information, or would this lead to confusion and waste? Should legal rights of recourse for failures to provide information (e.g., job or product hazards) extend to failures to "properly" frame it? The general issue of public perception of risk is of growing concern to a number of government agencies. To the extent that new products, medical techniques, and environmental hazards continue to appear and the government takes a role their regulation, these issues will become more and more pressing.

Although the issue of the public and private framing of probabilistic information is a comparatively new one, I feel that there are several analogous issues (not all of them fully resolved) from which we can derive useful insights. Previous examples have included the cash discount/credit surcharge issue mentioned above, rotating warning labels on cigarette packages, financial disclosure regulations, bans on certain forms of alcohol advertising, publicity requirements for product recall announcements, and current debates cover issues such as requiring special labels on irradiated produce or on products imported from countries engaging in human and/or animal rights violations. If these issues do not provide us with ready made answers for the case of probabilistic information, they at least allow us to observe how policy makers, interest groups, and the public feel and act toward the general issue of the presentation of information.

Notes

1 E.g., Arrow (1963, 1974), Pratt (1964) and Rothschild and Stiglitz (1970, 1971). For surveys of applications, see Lippman and McCall (1981) and Hey (1979).
2 Bernoulli (1738/1954). For a historical overview of the St. Petersburg Paradox and its impact, see Samuelson (1977).
3 Algebraically, the certainty equivalent of the Petersburg gamble is given by the value ξ that solves $U(W + \xi) = (\frac{1}{2}) \cdot U(W + 1) + (\frac{1}{4}) \cdot U(W + 2) + (\frac{1}{8}) \cdot U(W + 4) + \cdots$,   where W denotes the individual's *initial wealth* (i.e., wealth going into the gamble).
4 Thus, for example, a $\frac{2}{3} : \frac{1}{3}$ chance of $100 or $20 and a $\frac{1}{2} : \frac{1}{2}$ chance of $100 or $30 both stochastically dominate a $\frac{1}{2} : \frac{1}{2}$ chance of $100 or $20.
5 How risk attitudes actually differ over gains versus losses is itself an unsolved problem: evidence consistent with and/or contradictory to the Friedman–Savage observation of risk seeking over gains and risk aversion over losses can be found in Williams (1966), Kahneman and Tversky (1979), Fishburn and Kochenberger (1979), Grether and Plott (1979), Hershey and Schoemaker (1980b), Payne, Laughhunn and Crum (1980, 1981), Hershey, Kunreuther and Schoemaker (1982) and the references cited in these articles. Finally, Feather (1959) and Slovic (1969b) found evidence that subjects' risk attitudes over gains and losses systematically changed when hypothetical situations were replaced by situations involving real money.
6 For example, if $U_c(\cdot)$ and $U_d(\cdot)$ satisfy

$$\frac{-U_c''(x)}{U_c'(x)} \geq \frac{-U_d''(x)}{U_d'(x)}$$

for all x (i.e., if $U_c(\cdot)$ is at least as risk averse as $U_d(\cdot)$), an individual with utility function $U_c(\cdot)$ would always be willing to pay at least as much for (complete) insurance against any risk as an individual with utility function $U_d(\cdot)$. See also the related analyses of Ross (1981) and Kihlstrom, Romer and Williams (1981).
7 Since the utility of ξ_1 will equal the expected utility of the gamble, we have that

$$U(\xi_1) = \frac{1}{2} \cdot U(M) + \frac{1}{2} \cdot U(0)$$

which under the normalization $U(0) = 0$ and $U(M) = 1$ will equal $\frac{1}{2}$.
8 As in the previous note, we have that

$$U(\xi_2) = \frac{1}{2} \cdot U(\xi_1) + \frac{1}{2} \cdot U(0)$$

and

$$U(\xi_3) = \frac{1}{2} \cdot U(M) + \frac{1}{2} \cdot U(\xi_1)$$

which from the normalization $U(0) = 0$, $U(M) = 1$ and the fact that $U(\xi_1) = \frac{1}{2}$, implies $U(\xi_2) = \frac{1}{4}$ and $U(\xi_3) = \frac{3}{4}$.

9   Thus if $x_1 = 20$, $x_2 = 30$ and $x_3 = 100$, the three prospects in note 4 would be represented by the points $(p_1, p_3) = (\frac{1}{3}, \frac{2}{3})$, $(p_1, p_3) = (0, \frac{1}{2})$, and $(p_1, p_3) = (\frac{1}{2}, \frac{1}{2})$ respectively.

10   Modified versions of this triangle diagram appreared as early as Marschak (1950) and Markowitz (1959, Ch. XI).

11   A useful analogy to the concept of indifference curves are the "constant-altitude" curves on a topographic map, which are loci of points having the same altitude. Just as these curves can be used to determine whether a given movement on the map will lead to a greater or lower altitude, indifference curves can be used to determine whether a given movement in the triangle will lead to greater or lower expected utility.

12   This follows since the slope of the indifference curves can be calculated to be

$$\left[\frac{U(x_2) - U(x_1)]}{[U(x_3) - U(x_2)]} \right]$$

the slope of the iso-expected value lines can be calculated to be

$$\frac{[x_2 - x_1]}{[x_3 - x_2]}$$

and a concave shape for $U(\cdot)$ implies

$$\frac{[U(x_2) - U(x_1)]}{[x_2 - x_1]} > \frac{[U(x_3) - U(x_2)]}{[x_3 - x_2]}$$

whenever $x_1 < x_2 < x_3$.

13   Setting his v, w, x and y equal to our x_1, x_2, x_2 and x_3 respectively, this follows from Theorem 1 of Pratt (1964).

14   Algebraically, these two cases are equivalent to the expression

$$[.10 \cdot U(5,000,000) - .11 \cdot U(1,000,000) + .01 \cdot U(0)]$$

being negative or positive, respectively.

15   Let $\mathbf{P}$ be a gain of $\$1,000,000$, let $\mathbf{P}^*$ be a $(\frac{10}{11})$: $(\frac{1}{11})$ chance of $\$5,000,000$ or $\$0$, and let $\alpha = .11$. Then the choice of a_1 vs. a_2 is equivalent to a choice between

$$\alpha \cdot \mathbf{P} + (1-\alpha) \cdot \mathbf{P}^{**}$$

and

$$\alpha \cdot \mathbf{P}^* + (1-\alpha) \cdot \mathbf{P}^{**}$$

when $\mathbf{P}^{**}$ is a gain of $\$1,000,000$, and the choice of a_4 vs. a_3 is a choice between

$$\alpha \cdot \mathbf{P} + (1-\alpha) \cdot \mathbf{P}^{**}$$

and

$$\alpha \cdot \mathbf{P}^* + (1-\alpha) \cdot \mathbf{P}^{**}$$

when $\mathbf{P}^{**}$ is a gain of $\$0$. Thus you should choose a_1 and a_4 if you prefer $\mathbf{P}$ to $\mathbf{P}^*$, or else a_2 and a_3 if you prefer $\mathbf{P}^*$ to $\mathbf{P}$.

16   Reports of this incident can be found in Savage (1954, pp. 101–3) and Allais (1979b, pp. 533–5). In that instance the payoffs {$0; $1,000,000; $5,000,000} were replaced by {$0;$500,000; $2,500,000} (1952 dollars).

17   In each of MacCrimmon's experiments, for example, he obtained approximately 60% conformity with the independence axiom (1968, pp. 7–11). However, when presented with opposing written arguments, the proexpected utility argument was chosen by only 20% of the subjects in the first experiment and 50% of the subjects in the second experiment (subjects in his third experiment were not presented with written arguments). In subsequent interviews with the experimenter, the percentage of subjects conforming to the independence axiom did rise to 75%. Although he did not apply pressure to get the subjects to adopt expected utility and "repeatedly emphasized that there was no right or wrong answer", MacCrimmon did personally believe in "the desirability of using the [expected utility] postulates in training decision makers" (1968, pp. 21–2), a fact which Slovic and Tversky felt "may have influenced the subjects to conform to the axioms" (1974, p. 369)

18   The Allais Paradox choices a_1, a_2, a_3 and a_4 correspond to b_1, b_2, b_4 and b_3, where $\alpha = .11, x = 1,000,000$, $\mathbf{P}$ is a $(\frac{10}{11}) : (\frac{1}{11})$ chance of $5,000,000 or $0, $\mathbf{P}^* = $ is a sure gain of $0, and $\mathbf{P}^{**}$ is a sure gain of $1,000,000.

19   As Bell (1985) notes, "winning the top prize of $10,000 in a lottery may leave one much happier than receiving $10,000 as the lowest prize in a lottery."

20   In a conversation with the author, Kenneth Arrow has offered an alternative phrasing of this argument: The widely maintained hypothesis of decreasing absolute risk aversion asserts that individuals will display more risk aversion in the event of a loss, and less risk aversion in the event of a gain. In the common consequence effect, individuals display more risk aversion in the event of an *opportunity loss*, and less risk aversion in the event of an *opportunity gain*.

21   The former involves setting $p = 1$, and the latter consists of a two-step choice problem where individuals exhibit the effect with $Y = 2X$ and $p = 2q$. Kahneman and Tversky (1979), for example, found that 80% of their subjects preferred a sure gain of 3,000 Israeli pounds to a .80 chance of winning 4,000, but 65% preferred a .20 chance of winning 4,000 to a .25 chance of winning 3,000. The name "common ratio effect" comes from the common value of prob $(X)/$ prob(Y) in the pairs $\{c_1, c_2\}$ and $\{c_3, c_4\}$.

22   Having found the value ξ_1 that solves

$$U(\xi_1) = \frac{1}{2} \cdot U(M) + \frac{1}{2} \cdot U(0)$$

choose $\{\xi_1, \xi_2, \xi_3\} = \{0, \xi_1, M\}$, so that the indifference curve through the point (0, 0) (i.e., a sure gain of ξ_1) also passes through the point $(\frac{1}{2}, \frac{1}{2})$ (i.e., a 50:50 chance of M or 0). The ordering of the values ξ_1, ξ_2, ξ_3, ξ_1^* and ξ_1^{**} in Figure 6a is derived from the individual's preference ordering over the five distributions in Figure 6b for which they are the respective certainty equivalents.

23   More rigorous developments of this approach may be found in Machina (1982, 1983b).

24   As in note 12, this is equivalent to the condition

$$\frac{[U(x_{i+1}) - U(x_i)]}{[x_{i+1} - x_i]} < \frac{[U(x_i) - U(x_{i-1})]}{[x_i - x_{i-1}]}$$

for all i.

25   This is equivalent to the condition that $U^*(x_i) \equiv \rho(U(x_i))$ for some increasing concave function $\rho(\cdot)$.

26 For the appropriate generalizations of the expected utility concepts of "at least as risk averse" in this result, see Machina (1982, 1984).

27 The reader should be warned that the terminology in this literature is not completely uniform – for example, although their criteria are distinct, both Roy (1952) and Telser (1955) use the term "Safety First." Here, we use the terminology proposed by Day, Aigner and Smith (1971) and adopted by Anderson (1979) and others.

28 More specifically, each of these criteria will violate the Independence Axiom.

29 Roughly speaking, the subject states a value for the item, and then the experimenter draws a random price. If the price is above the stated value, the subject forgoes the item and receives the price. If the drawn price is below the stated value, the subject keeps the item. The reader can verify that under such a scheme it will never be in a subject's best interest to report anything other than his or her true value.

30 Economic theory tells us that income effects may well lead an individual to assign a lower *bid* price to the object which, if both were free, would actually be preferred. However, such an effect will *not* apply to either selling prices or the Becker, DeGroot and Marschak procedure. For discussions of the empirical evidence on sell price/bid price disparities, see Knetsch and Sinden (1984) and the references cited there.

31 In addition to the problem with bid prices discussed in the previous note, Grether and Plott (1979) noted that subjects' changing wealth due to the actual play of these gambles during the course of the experiment, or changing *expected* wealth in those experiments in which chosen gambles would be played at the end, could be a source of income effects.

32 Formally, this ordering is represented by the individual's *weak preference relation* $\succeq$, where "$A \succeq B$" is read "A is at least as preferred as B." From this we may derive the individual's *strict preference relation* $\succ$ and *indifference relation* $\sim$, where "$A \sim B$" denotes that $A \succeq B$ but not $B \succeq A$, and "$A \sim B$" denotes that both $A \succeq B$ and $B \succeq A$.

33 See also the discussions of these findings by Edwards (1954b, pp. 404–5), Davis (1958, p. 28) and Weinstein (1968, p. 337).

34 Algebraically, this expected value is given by the two-way sum of all terms of the form $r(x_i, x_j) \cdot p_i^* \cdot p_j$ as the indices i and j both run from 1 to n.

35 This follows since the expected value of $r(x, y) = U(x) - U(y)$ will then reduce to the expected value of $U(\cdot)$ with respect to $\mathbf{P}^*$ minus its expected value with respect to $\mathbf{P}$.

36 In this model, the indifference curves will necessarily all cross at the same point. This (unique) point will accordingly be ranked indifferent to all lotteries in the triangle.

37 Loomes and Sugden, for example, have shown that many of these effects follow if we assume that

$$r(x, y) = Q(x - y)$$

where $Q(\cdot)$ is convex for positive values and concave for negative values.

38 Although we have come to this point in the discussion via an examination of the preference reversal phenomenon over risky prospects, it is important to note that neither the evidence of response mode effects (e.g., Slovic (1975)) nor their implications for economic analysis are confined to the case of choice under uncertainty.

39 A final "twist" on the preference reversal phenomenon: Karni and Safra (1987) and Holt (1986) have shown how the procedures used in most of these studies, namely the Becker, DeGroot and Marschak elicitation technique (see note 29) and the practice of only selecting a few questions to actually play, will only lead to truthful revelation of preferences under the additional assumption that the individual satisfies the independence axiom. Accordingly, it is possible to construct (and they have done so) examples of non–expected utility individuals with *transitive* underlying preferences and no response mode effects, whose optimal responses in such experiments consist

of precisely the typical "preference reversal" responses. How (and whether) experimenters will be able to address this issue remains to be seen.

40   Even though all underlying probabilities were stated explicitly, Slovic found that individuals tended to overestimate the probabilities of these compound events.

41   Subjects were asked to choose either (A) a sure gain of \$240 or (B) a $\frac{1\cdot3}{4\cdot4}$ chance of \$1000 or \$0, and to choose either (C) a sure loss of \$750 or (D) a $\frac{3\cdot1}{4\cdot4}$ chance of $-$ \$1000 or 0. Fully 84% chose A over B and 87% chose D over C, even though $B + C$ dominates $A + D$, and choices over the combined distributions were unanimous when they were presented explicitly.

42   See the discussion and references in Machina (1982, pp. 285–6).

43   This is not to say that well defined reference points never exist. The reference points involved in credit surcharges versus cash discounts, for example, seem unambiguous.

44   Fischhoff (1983, pp. 115–16). Fischhoff notes that "If one can only infer frames from preferences after assuming the truth of the theory, one runs the risk of making the theory itself untestable."

45   A wonderful example, offered by my colleague Joel Sobel, are milk advertisements which make no reference to either price or a particular dairy. What could be a more well-known commodity than *milk?*

46   E.g., Milne (1981). For an application of the theory of induced preferences to choice under uncertainty, see Machina (1984).

47   See also the discussion of Fellner (1961, 1963), Brewer (1963), Ellsberg (1963), Roberts (1963), Brewer and Fellner (1965), MacCrimmon (1968), Smith (1969), Sherman (1974) and Sinn (1980).

48   For an excellent discussion of the history, nature and limitations of such approaches, see Arrow (1951).

49   For a comprehensive overview of this model and its analytics, see Karni (1985).

50   In generating these indifference curves from individuals' preferences over probability distributions we are implicitly assuming that their level of satisfaction from a given amount of money does not depend on the particular state of nature that occurs, i.e., that their preferences are *state-independent*. Beginning with the following sentence, this assumption will no longer be required.

51   A final issue is the lack of a unified model capable of simultaneously handling all of the phenomena described in this chapter: fanning-out, the preference reversal phenomenon, framing effects, probability biases and the Ellsberg paradox. After all, it is presumably the same individuals who are *exhibiting* each of these phenomena – shouldn't there be a single model capable of *generating* them all? Although I am doubtful of our current ability to do this, I also doubt the *need* for a unified model as a prerequisite for further progress. The aspects of behavior considered in this chapter are very diverse, and if (like the wave versus particle properties of light) they cannot be currently unified, this does not mean that we cannot continue to learn by studying and modeling them separately.

52   The classic introductory expositions of the process of decision analysis are Raiffa (1968) and Schlaifer (1969).

53   The components of such models (e.g., the functions $v(\cdot)$, $\pi(\cdot)$, $\tau(\cdot)$ and $g(\cdot)$ in Table 1) can be assessed by procedures similar to the one described in Section 2 for von Neumann–Morgenstern utility functions.

54   Machina and Schmeidler (1992, 1995), written several years after the present chapter, provide a theoretical and axiomatic framework for such "probabilistically sophisticated non–expected utility" preferences.

55   The standard policy techniques of "cost-benefit analysis," "risk-benefit analysis," etc., fall into this category.

56   It also suggests that surveys of the public's willingness to trade off probability against loss should be conducted using the actual range of probabilities involved, rather than be extrapolat-

MARK J. MACHINA ◆

ing from larger, so-called "easier to fathom" probability levels. See Freeman (1990) for additional analytic results along these lines.

57 $MRS(\hat{p}, \hat{L}) = MRS(p^*/2, L^*) = MRS(p^*, L^*)/2 = f'(L^*)/2 = f'(\hat{L})$, and $\hat{p} = p^*/2 = f(L^*)$ $/2 = f(\hat{L})$.

58 The inequality implies that at $(\hat{p}, \hat{L})$ the individual's willingness to accept a gain in p for a small unit drop in L exceeds the gain necessary to achieve that drop. Thus the new optimal allocation uses fewer resources in sensing and more in containment, leading to new optimal values (p^{**}, L^{**}) with $\hat{p} < p^{**} < p^*)$ and $L^{**} < L^*$.

References and Further Reading

Akerlof, G. (1970): "The Market for 'Lemons': Quality Uncertainty and the Market Mechanism," *Quarterly Journal of Economics*, 84, 488–500.

——(1984): *An Economic Theorist's Book of Tales*. Cambridge: Cambridge University Press.

Allais, M. (1952): "Fondements d'une Théorie Positive des Choix Comportant un Risque et Critique des Postulats et Axiomes de l'Ecole Américaine," *Econométrie*, Colloques Internationaux du Centre National de la Recherche Scientifique 40, Paris, 1953.

——(1953): "Le Comportement de l'Homme Rationnel devant le Risque, Critique des Postulats et Axiomes de l'Ecole Américaine," *Econometrica*, 21, 503–46. Summarized version of Allais (1952).

——(1979a). "The Foundations of a Positive Theory of Choice Involving Risk and a Criticism of the Postulates and Axioms of the American School," in Allais and Hagen (1979), English translation of Allais (1952).

——(1979b). "The So-Called Allais Paradox and Rational Decisions Under Uncertainty," in Allais and Hagen (1979).

——(1988): "The General Theory of Random Choices in Relation to the Invariant Cardinal Utility Function and the Specific Probability Function," in Munier (1988).

——and Hagen, O. (eds) (1979): *Expected Utility Hypotheses and the Allais Paradox*. Dordrecht, Holland: D. Reidel Publishing Co.

Allen, B. (1987): "Smooth Preferences and the Local Expected Utility Hypothesis," *Journal of Economic Theory*, 41, 340–55.

Anderson, J. (1979): "Perspective on Models of Uncertain Decision," in Roumasset, Boussard and Singh (1979).

Arkes, H. and Hammond, K. (eds) (1986): *Judgment and Decision Making: An Interdisciplinary Reader*. Cambridge: Cambridge University Press.

Arrow, K. (1951): "Alternative Approaches to the Theory of Choice in Risk-Taking Situations," *Econometrica*, 19, 404–37. Reprinted in Arrow (1983–85, Vol. 3).

——(1953): "Le Rôle des Valeurs Boursières pour la Répartition la Meilleure des Risques," *Econométrie*, Colloques Internationaux du Centre National de la Recherche Scientifique, Paris 40, 41–7.

——(1963): "Comment," *Review of Economics and Statistics*, 45 (Supplement), 24–7. Reprinted in Arrow (1983–85, Vol. 6).

——(1964): "The Role of Securities in the Optimal Allocation of Risk-Bearing," *Review of Economic Studies*, 31, 91–6. English translation of Arrow (1953). Reprinted in Arrow (1983–85, Vol. 2).

——(1974): *Essays in the Theory of Risk-Bearing*. Amsterdam: North-Holland Publishing Company.

——(1982): "Risk Perception in Psychology and Economics," *Economic Inquiry*, 20, 1–9. Reprinted in Arrow (1983–85, Vol. 3).

——(1983–85): *Collected Papers of Kenneth J. Arrow* (6 Volumes). Cambridge, Mass: Harvard University Press.

——and Hurwicz, L. (1972): "An Optimality Criterion for Decision-Making under Ignorance," in Carter and Ford (1972).

——and Intriligator, M. (eds) (1981): *Handbook of Mathematical Economics, I*. Amsterdam: North-Holland Publishing Company.

Bar-Hillel, M. (1973): "On the Subjective Probability of Compound Events," *Organizational Behavior and Human Performance*, 9, 396–406.

——(1974): "Similarity and Probability," *Organizational Behavior and Human Performance*, 11, 277–82.

Battalio, R., Kagel, J. and MacDonald, D. (1985): "Animals' Choices over Uncertain Outcomes," *American Economic Review*, 75, 597–613.

Becker, G., DeGroot, M. and Marschak, J. (1964): "Measuring Utility by a Single-Response Sequential Method," *Behavioral Science*, 9, 226–32. Reprinted in Marschak (1974, Vol I).

Becker, S. and Brownson, F. (1964): "What Price Ambiguity? Or the Role of Ambiguity in Decision-Making," *Journal of Political Economy*, 72, 62–73.

Bell, D. (1982): "Regret in Decision Making Under Uncertainty," *Operations Research*, 30, 961–81.

——(1983): "Risk Premiums for Decision Regret," *Management Science*, 29, 1156–66.

——(1985): "Disappointment in Decision Making Under Uncertainty," *Operations Research*, 33, 1–27.

——and Raiffa, H. (1980): "Decision Regret: A Component of Risk Aversion," manuscript, Harvard University.

Berg, J., Dickhaut, J. and O'Brien, J. (1983): "Preference Reversal and Arbitrage," manuscript, University of Minnesota.

Bergson, A. (1938): "A Reformulation of Certain Aspects of Welfare Economics," *Quarterly Journal of Economics*, 52, 310–34.

Bernoulli, D. (1738): "Specimen Theoriae Novae de Mensura Sortis," *Commentarii Academiae Scientiarum Imperialis Petropolitanae [Papers of the Imperial Academy of Sciences in Petersburg]* V, 175–92. English translation: "Exposition of a New Theory on the Measurement of Risk," *Econometrica*, 22 (1954), 23–36.

Blyth, C. (1972): "Some Probability Paradoxes in Choice from Among Random Alternatives," *Journal of the American Statistical Association*, 67, 366–73.

Borch, K. and Mossin, J. (eds) (1968): *Risk and Uncertainty: Proceedings of a Conference Held by the International Economic Association*. London: Macmillan and Co.

Brewer, K. (1963): "Decisions Under Uncertainty: Comment," *Quarterly Journal of Economics*, 77, 159–61.

——and Fellner, W. (1965): "The Slanting of Subjective Probabilities – Agreement on Some Essentials," *Quarterly Journal of Economics*, 79, 657–63.

Carter, D. and Ford, F. (eds) (1972): *Uncertainty and Expectations in Economics*. Oxford: Basil Blackwell.

Chew, S. (1983): "A Generalization of the Quasilinear Mean with Applications to the Measurement of Income Inequality and Decision Theory Resolving the Allais Paradox," *Econometrica*, 51, 1065–92.

——and MacCrimmon, K. (1979a): "Alpha-Nu Choice Theory: A Generalization of Expected Utility Theory," University of British Columbia Faculty of Commerce and Business Administration working paper 669.

——and——(1979b): "Alpha Utility Theory, Lottery Composition, and the Allais Paradox," University of British Columbia Faculty of Commerce and Business Administration working paper 686.

——and Waller, W. (1986): "Empirical Tests of Weighted Utility Theory," *Journal of Mathematical Psychology*, 30, 55–72.

——Epstein, L. and Segal, U. (1991): "Mixture Symmetry and Quadratic Utility," *Econometrica*, 59, 139–63.

——Karni, E. and Safra, Z. (1987): "Risk Aversion in the Theory of Expected Utility with Rank Dependent Probabilities," *Journal of Economic Theory*, 42, 370–81.

Chipman, J., Hurwicz, L., Richter, M. and Sonnenschein, H. (eds) (1971): *Preferences, Utility and Demand*. New York: Harcourt Brace Jovanovich, Inc.

Cramér, H. (1930): "On the Mathematical Theory of Risk," *Försäkringsakti Skandias Festkrift*, Stockholm: Centraltryckeriet.

Davis, J. (1958): "The Transitivity of Preferences," *Behavioral Science*, 3, 26–33.

Day, R., Aigner, D. and Smith, K. (1971): "Safety Margins and Profit Maximization in the Theory of the Firm," *Journal of Political Economy*, 79, 1293–301.

Debreu, G. (1959): *Theory of Value: An Axiomatic Analysis of General Equilibrium*. New Haven: Yale University Press.

Dekel, E. (1986): "An Axiomatic Characterization of Preferences Under Uncertainty: Weakening the Independence Axiom," *Journal of Economic Theory*, 40, 304–18.

Diamond, P. (1967): "The Role of a Stock Market in a General Equilibrium Model with Techno-logical Uncertainty," *American Economic Review*, 57, 759–73. Reprinted in Diamond and Roths-child (1989).

——and Rothschild, M. (eds) (1989): *Uncertainty in Economics: Readings and Exercises*, 2nd Edn. New York: Academic Press.

——and Yaari, M. (1972): "Implications of the Theory of Rationing for Consumer Choice Under Uncertainty," *American Economic Review*, 62, 333–43.

Drèze, J. and Modigliani, F. (1972): "Consumption Decisions Under Uncertainty," *Journal of Economic Theory* 5, 308–35.

Edwards, W. (1954a): "Probability-Preferences among Bets with Differing Expected Value," *American Journal of Psychology*, 67, 56–67.

——(1954b): "The Theory of Decision Making," *Psychological Bulletin*, 51, 380–417.

——(1955): "The Prediction of Decisions among Bets," *Journal of Experimental Psychology*, 50, 201–14.

——(1962): "Subjective Probabilities inferred from Decisions," *Psychological Review*, 69, 109–35.

——(1971): "Bayesian and Regression Models of Human Information Processing – A Myopic Perspective," *Organizational Behavior and Human Performance*, 6, 639–48.

——Lindman, H. and Savage, L. (1963): "Bayesian Statistical Inference for Psychological Research," *Psychological Review*, 70, 193–242.

Einhorn, H. and Hogarth, R. (1986): "Decision Making under Ambiguity," *Journal of Business*, 59 (Supplement), S225–50. Reprinted in Hogarth and Reder (1987).

Ellsberg, D. (1961): "Risk, Ambiguity, and the Savage Axioms," *Quarterly Journal of Economics*, 75, 643–69.

——(1963): "Risk, Ambiguity, and the Savage Axioms: Reply," *Quarterly Journal of Economics*, 77, 336–42.

Epstein, L. (1985): "Decreasing Risk Aversion and Mean-Variance Analysis," *Econometrica*, 53, 945–61.

——(1987): "The Unimportance of the Intransitivity of Separable Preferences," *International Economic Review*, 28, 315–22.

Feather, N. (1959): "Subjective Probability and Decision Under Uncertainty," *Psychological Review*, 66, 150–64.

Fellner, W. (1961): "Distortion of Subjective Probabilities as a Reaction to Uncertainty," *Quarterly Journal of Economics*, 75, 670–89.

——(1963): "Slanted Subjective Probabilities and Randomization: Reply to Howard Raiffa and K. R. W. Brewer," *Quarterly Journal of Economics*, 77, 676–90.

Fischhoff, B. (1983): "Predicting Frames," *Journal of Experimental Psychology: Learning, Memory and Cognition*, 9, 103–16.

Fishburn, P. (1981): "An Axiomatic Characterization of Skew-Symmetric Bilinear Functionals, with Applications to Utility Theory," *Economics Letters*, 8, 311–13.

——(1982): "Nontransitive Measurable Utility," *Journal of Mathematical Psychology*, 26, 31–67.

——(1983): "Transitive Measurable Utility," *Journal of Economic Theory*, 31, 293–317.

——(1984a): "SSB Utility Theory: An Economic Perspective," *Mathematical Social Sciences*, 8, 63–94.

——(1984b): "SSB Utility Theory and Decision Making under Uncertainty," *Mathematical Social Sciences*, 8, 253–85.

——(1986): "A New Model for Decisions under Uncertainty," *Economics Letters*, 21, 127–30.

——(1988): "Uncertainty Aversion and Separated Effects in Decision Making under Uncertainty," in Kacprzyk and Fedrizzi (1988).

——and Kochenberger G. (1979): "Two-piece Von Neumann-Morgenstern Utility Functions," *Decision Sciences*, 10, 503–18.

Freeman, A. (1990): "Indirect Methods for Valuing Changes in Environmental Risks with Non-Expected Utility Preferences," *Journal of Risk and Uncertainty*, 4, 153–65.

Friedman, M. and Savage, L. (1948): "The Utility Analysis of Choices Involving Risk," *Journal of Political Economy*, 56, 279–304. Reprinted with revision in Stigler and Boulding (1952).

Gardenfors, P. and Sahlin, N. E. (1988): *Decision, Precision and Utility*. New York: Cambridge University Press.

Gilboa, I. (1987): "Expected Utility with Purely Subjective Non-Additive Probabilities," *Journal of Mathematical Economics*, 16, 65–88.

Green, J. and Jullien, B. (1988): "Ordinal Independence in Non-Linear Utility Theory," *Journal of Risk and Uncertainty*, 1, 355–87. ("Erratum", *Journal of Risk and Uncertainty*, 2, 119.)

Grether, D. (1978): "Recent Psychological Studies of Behavior under Uncertainty," *American Economic Review Papers and Proceedings*, 68, 70–4.

——(1980): "Bayes Rule as a Descriptive Model: The Representativeness Heuristic," *Quarterly Journal of Economics*, 95, 537–57.

——and Plott, C. (1979): "Economic Theory of Choice and the Preference Reversal Phenomenon," *American Economic Review*, 69, 623–38.

Grofman, B. and Owen, G. (eds) (1986): *Information Pooling and Group Decision Making*. Greenwich, Conn: JAI Press.

Hagen, O. (1979): "Towards a Positive Theory of Preferences under Risk," in Allais and Hagen (1979).

Hazen, G. (1987): "Subjectively Weighted Linear Utility," *Theory and Decision*, 23, 261–82.

Henderson, J. and Quandt, R. (1980): *Microeconomic Theory: A Mathematical Approach*, 3rd edn. New York: McGraw-Hill.

Hershey, J. and Schoemaker, P. (1980a): "Risk-Taking and Problem Context in the Domain of Losses – An Expected Utility Analysis," *Journal of Risk and Insurance*, 47, 111–32. Reprinted in Schoemaker (1980).

——and——(1980b): "Prospect Theory's Reflection Hypothesis: A Critical Examination," *Organizational Behavior and Human Performance*, 25, 395–418.

——and——(1985): "Probability versus Certainty Equivalence Methods in Utility Measurement: Are they Equivalent?" *Management Science*, 31, 1213–31.

——Kunreuther, H. and Schoemaker, P. (1982): "Sources of Bias in Assessment Procedures for Utility Functions," *Management Science*, 28, 936–54.

Hey, J. (1979): *Uncertainty in Microeconomics*. Oxford: Martin Robinson and Company Ltd.

——(1984): "The Economics of Optimism and Pessimism: A Definition and Some Applications," *Kyklos*, 37, 181–205.

——and Lambert, P. (eds) (1987): *Surveys in the Economics of Uncertainty*. Oxford: Basil Blackwell Ltd.

Hirshleifer, J. (1965): "Investment Decision under Uncertainty: Choice-Theoretic Approaches," *Quarterly Journal of Economics*, 79, 509–36. Reprinted in Hirshleifer (1989).

——(1966): "Investment Decision under Uncertainty: Applications of the State-Preference Approach," *Quarterly Journal of Economics*, 80, 252–77. Reprinted in Hirshleifer (1989).

——(1989): *Time, Uncertainty and Information*. Oxford: Basil Blackwell.

Hogarth, R. (1975): "Cognitive Processes and the Assessment of Subjective Probability Distributions," *Journal of the American Statistical Association*, 70, 271–89.

——(1980): *Judgment and Choice: The Psychology of Decision*. New York: John Wiley and Sons.

——(ed.) (1982): *New Directions for Methodology of Social and Behavioral Science: Question Framing and Response Consistency*. San Francisco: Jossey-Bass.

——and Kunreuther, H. (1985): "Ambiguity and Insurance Decisions," *American Economic Review Papers and Proceedings*, 75, 386–90.

——and——(1989): "Risk, Ambiguity, and Insurance," *Journal of Risk and Uncertainty*, 2, 5–35.

——and Reder, M. (eds) (1987): *Rational Choice: The Contrast between Economics and Psychology*. Chicago: University of Chicago Press.

Holt, C. (1986): "Preference Reversals and the Independence Axiom," *American Economic Review*, 76, 508–15.

Kacprzyk, J. and Fedrizzi, M. (eds) (1988): *Combining Fuzzy Impressions with Probabilistic Uncertainty in Decision Making*. Berlin: Springer Verlag.

Kahneman, D. and Tversky, A. (1973): "On the Psychology of Prediction," *Psychological Review*, 80, 237–51. Reprinted in Kahneman, Slovic and Tversky (1982).

——and——(1979): "Prospect Theory: An Analysis of Decision under Risk," *Econometrica*, 47, 263–91. Reprinted in Gärdenfors and Sahlin (1988).

——and——(1982): "The Psychology of Preferences," *Scientific American*, 246, 160–73.

——and——(1984): "Choices, Values and Frames," *American Psychologist*, 39, 341–50. Reprinted in Arkes and Hammond (1986).

Kahneman, D., Slovic P. and Tversky, A. (eds) (1982): *Judgment under Uncertainty: Heuristics and Biases*. Cambridge: Cambridge University Press.

Karmarkar, U. (1974): "The Effect of Probabilities on the Subjective Evaluation of Lotteries," Massachusetts Institute of Technology Sloan School of Business working paper 698–74.

——(1978): "Subjectively Weighted Utility: A Descriptive Extension of the Expected Utility Model," *Organizational Behavior and Human Performance*, 21, 61–72.

——(1979): "Subjectively Weighted Utility and the Allais Paradox," *Organizational Behavior and Human Performance*, 24, 67–72.

Karni, E. (1985): *Decision Making under Uncertainty: The Case of State Dependent Preferences*. Cambridge, Mass: Harvard University Press.

——and Safra, Z. (1987): " 'Preference Reversal' and the Observability of Preferences by Experimental Methods," *Econometrica*, 55, 675–85.

Kataoka, S. (1963): "A Stochastic Programming Model," *Econometrica*, 31, 181–96.

Keeny, R. and Raiffa, H. (1976): *Decisions with Multiple Objectives: Preferences and Value Tradeoffs* New York: John Wiley and Sons.

Keller, L. (1985): "The Effects of Problem Representation on the Sure-Thing and Substitution Principles," *Management Science*, 31, 738–51.

Kihlstrom, R., Romer, D. and Williams, S. (1981): "Risk Aversion with Random Initial Wealth," *Econometrica*, 49, 911–20.

Kim, T. and Richter, M. (1986): "Nontransitive-Nontotal Consumer Theory," *Journal of Economic Theory*, 38, 324–63.

Knetsch, J. and Sinden, J. (1984): "Willingness to Pay and Compensation Demanded: Experimental Evidence of an Unexpected Disparity in Measures of Value," *Quarterly Journal of Economics*, 99, 507–21.

Knez, M. and Smith, V. (1987): "Hypothetical Valuations and Preference Reversals in the Context of Asset Trading," in Roth (1987).

Kreps, D. and Porteus, E. (1979): "Temporal von Neumann-Morgenstern and Induced Preferences," *Journal of Economic Theory*, 20, 81–109.

Lichtenstein, S. and Slovic, P. (1971): "Reversals of Preferences between Bids and Choices in Gambling Decisions," *Journal of Experimental Psychology*, 89, 46–55.

——and——(1973): "Response-Induced Reversals of Preference in Gambling: An Extended Replication in Las Vegas," *Journal of Experimental Psychology*, 101, 16–20.

Lindman, H. (1971): "Inconsistent Preferences among Gambles," *Journal of Experimental Psychology*, 89, 390–7.

Lippman, S. and McCall, J. (1981): "The Economics of Uncertainty: Selected Topics and Probabilistic Methods," in Arrow and Intriligator (1981).

Loomes, G. and Sugden, R. (1982): "Regret Theory: An Alternative Theory of Rational Choice under Uncertainty," *Economic Journal*, 92, 805–24.

——and——(1983a): "Regret Theory and Measurable Utility," *Economics Letters*, 12, 19–22.

——and——(1983b): "A Rationale for Preference Reversal," *American Economic Review*, 73, 428–32.

MacCrimmon, K. (1965): "An Experimental Study of the Decision Making Behavior of Business Executives," doctoral dissertation, University of California, Los Angeles.

——(1968): "Descriptive and Normative Implications of the Decision-Theory Postulates," in Borch and Mossin (1968).

——and Larsson, S. (1979): "Utility Theory: Axioms versus 'Paradoxes'," in Allais and Hagen (1979).

——and Wehrung D. (1986): *Taking Risks: The Management of Uncertainty*. New York: The Free Press.

Machina, M. (1982): "'Expected Utility' Analysis without the Independence Axiom," *Econometrica*, 50, 277–323.

——(1983a): "Generalized Expected Utility Analysis and the Nature of Observed Violations of the Independence Axiom," in Stigum and Wenstop (1983). Reprinted in Gärdenfors and Sahlin (1988).

——(1983b): "The Economic Theory of Individual Behavior Toward Risk: Theory, Evidence and New Directions," Stanford University Institute for Mathematical Studies in the Social Sciences technical report 443.

——(1984): "Temporal Risk and the Nature of Induced Preferences," *Journal of Economic Theory*, 33, 199–231.

——and Neilson, W. (1987): "The Ross Measure of Risk Aversion: Strengthening and Extension," *Econometrica*, 55, 1139–49.

——and Schmeidler, D. (1992): "A More Robust Definition of Subjective Probability," *Econometrica*, 60, 745–80.

——and——(1995): "Bayes without Bernoulli: Simple Conditions for Probabilistically Sophisticated Choice," *Journal of Economic Theory*, 67, 106–28.

Markowitz, H. (1952): "The Utility of Wealth," *Journal of Political Economy*, 60, 151–8.

——(1959): *Portfolio Selection: Efficient Diversification of Investments*. New Haven: Yale University Press.

Marschak, J. (1950): "Rational Behavior, Uncertain Prospects, and Measurable Utility," *Econometrica*, 18, 111–41 ("Errata," *Econometrica* 18, 312). Reprinted in Marschak (1974, I).

——(1974): *Economic Information, Decision, and Prediction* I–III Dordrecht, Holland: D. Reidel Publishing Co.

Mas-Colell, A. (1974): "An Equilibrium Existence Theorem without Complete or Transitive Preferences," *Journal of Mathematical Economics*, 3, 237–46.

Maskin, E. (1979): "Decision Making under Ignorance with Implications for Social Choice," *Theory and Decision*, 11, 319–37.

May, K. (1954): "Intransitivity, Utility, and the Aggregation of Preference Patterns," *Econometrica*, 22, 1–13.

McCord, M. and de Neufville, R. (1983): "Empirical Demonstration that Expected Utility Analysis is not Operational," in Stigum and Wenstop (1983).

—— and ——(1984): "Utility Dependence on Probability: An Empirical Demonstration," *Large Scale Systems*, 6, 91–103.

McNeil, B., Pauker, S., Sox, H. and Tversky, A. (1982): "On the Elicitation of Preferences for Alternative Therapies," *New England Journal of Medicine*, 306, 1259–62. Reprinted in Arkes and Hammond (1986).

Milne, F. (1981): "Induced Preferences and the Theory of the Consumer," *Journal of Economic Theory*, 24, 205–17.

Mishan, E. (1976): "Choices Involving Risk: Simple Steps toward an Ordinalist Analysis," *Economic Journal*, 86, 759–77.

Morrison, D. (1967): "On the Consistency of Preferences in Allais' Paradox," *Behavioral Science*, 12, 373–83.

Moskowitz, H. (1974): "Effects of Problem Representation and Feedback on Rational Behavior in Allais and Morlat-Type Problems," *Decision Sciences*, 5, 225–42.

Mossin, J. (1969): "A Note on Uncertainty and Preferences in a Temporal Context," *American Economic Review*, 59, 172–4.

Mowen, J. and Gentry, J. (1980): "Investigation of the Preference-Reversal Phenomenon in a New Product Introduction Task," *Journal of Applied Psychology*, 65, 715–22.

Múnera, H. and de Neufville R. (1983): "A Decision Analysis Model when the Substitution Principle is not Acceptable," in Stigum and Wenstop (1983).

Munier, B. (ed.) (1988): *Risk, Decision and Rationality*. Dordrecht: D. Reidel Publishing Co.

Pareto, V. (1909): *Manuel d'Économie Politique*. Paris: V. Giard and E. Brière.

Parkin, M. and Nobay, A. (eds) (1975): *Current Economic Problems*. Cambridge: Cambridge University Press.

Payne, J. and M. Braunstein (1971): "Preferences among Gambles with Equal Underlying Distributions," *Journal of Experimental Psychology*, 87, 13–18.

—— Laughhunn, D. and Crum, R. (1980): "Translation of Gambles and Aspiration Level Effects in Risky Choice Behavior," *Management Science*, 26, 1039–60.

—— and —— (1981): "Further Tests of Aspiration Level Effects in Risky Choice Behavior," *Management Science*, 27, 953–8.

Pommerehne, W., Schneider, F. and Zweifel, P. (1982): "Economic Theory of Choice and the Preference Reversal Phenomenon: A Reexamination," *American Economic Review*, 72, 569–74.

Pratt, J. (1964): "Risk Aversion in the Small and in the Large," *Econometrica*, 32, 122–36. Reprinted in Diamond and Rothschild (1989).

Quiggin, J. (1982): "A Theory of Anticipated Utility," *Journal of Economic Behavior and Organization*, 3, 323–43.

Raiffa, H. (1961): "Risk, Ambiguity, and the Savage Axioms: Comment," *Quarterly Journal of Economics*, 75, 690–4.

——(1968): *Decision Analysis: Introductory Lectures on Choice under Uncertainty*. Reading, Mass.: Addison-Wesley.

Reilly, R. (1982): "Preference Reversal: Further Evidence and Some Suggested Modifications of Experimental Design," *American Economic Review*, 72, 576–84.

Roberts, H. (1963): "Risk, Ambiguity, and the Savage Axioms: Comment," *Quarterly Journal of Economics*, 77, 327–36.

Röell, A. (1987): "Risk Aversion in Quiggin's and Yaari's Rank-Order Model of Choice under Uncertainty," *Economic Journal*, 97 (supplement), 143–59.

Ross, S. (1981): "Some Stronger Measures of Risk Aversion in the Small and in the Large with Applications," *Econometrica*, 49, 621–38.

Roth, A. (ed.) (1987): *Laboratory Experiments in Economics: Six Points of View*. Cambridge: Cambridge University Press.

Rothschild, M. and Stiglitz, J. (1970): "Increasing Risk: I. A Definition," *Journal of Economic Theory*, 2, 225–43. Reprinted in Diamond and Rothschild (1989).

—— and —— (1971): "Increasing Risk: II. Its Economic Consequences," *Journal of Economic Theory*, 3, 66–84.

—— and ——(1972): "Addendum to 'Increasing Risk: I. A Definition'," *Journal of Economic Theory*, 5, 306.

Roumasset, J., Boussard, J.-M. and Singh, I. (1979): *Risk, Uncertainty and Agricultural Development*. New York: Agricultural Development Council.

Roy, A. (1952): "Safety First and the Holding of Assets," *Econometrica*, 20, 431–49.

Russo, J. (1977): "The Value of Unit Price Information," *Journal of Marketing Research*, 14, 193–201.

——Krieser, G. and Miyashita, S. (1975): "An Effective Display of Unit Price Information," *Journal of Marketing*, 39, 11–19.

Samuelson, P. (1947): *Foundations of Economic Analysis*. Cambridge, Mass.: Harvard University Press. Enlarged edn, 1983.

—— (1952): "Probability, Utility, and the Independence Axiom," *Econometrica* 20, 670–78. Reprinted in Stiglitz (1966).

——(1977): "St. Petersburg Paradoxes: Defanged, Dissected, and Historically Described," *Journal of Economic Literature*, 15, 24–55.

Savage, L. (1954): *The Foundations of Statistics*. New York: John Wiley and Sons. Revised and enlarged Edn, New York: Dover Publications, 1972.

Schlaifer, R. (1969): *Analysis of Decisions under Uncertainty*. New York: McGraw-Hill Publishing Co.

Schmeidler, D. (1989): "Subjective Probability and Expected Utility without Additivity," *Econometrica*, 57, 571–87.

Schoemaker, P. (1980): *Experiments on Decisions under Risk: The Expected Utility Hypothesis*. Boston: Martinus Nijhoff Publishing.

—— and H. Kunreuther (1979): "An Experimental Study of Insurance Decisions," *Journal of Risk and Insurance*, 46, 603–18. Reprinted in Schoemaker (1980).

Segal, U. (1984): "Nonlinear Decision Weights with the Independence Axiom," manuscript, University of California, Los Angeles.

——(1987): "The Ellsberg Paradox and Risk Aversion: An Anticipated Utility Approach," *International Economic Review*, 28, 175–202.

——(1990): "Two-Stage Lotteries without the Reduction Axiom," *Econometrica*, 58, 349–77.

Shackle G. (1949): *Expectations in Economics*. Cambridge: Cambridge University Press.

Shafer, W. (1974): "The Nontransitive Consumer," *Econometrica*, 42, 913–19.

——(1976): "Equilibrium in Economies without Ordered Preferences or Free Disposal," *Journal of Mathematical Economics*, 3, 135–7.

Sherman, R. (1974): "The Psychological Difference between Ambiguity and Risk," *Quarterly Journal of Economics*, 88, 166–9.

Sinn, H.-W. (1980): "A Rehabilitation of the Principle of Sufficient Reason," *Quarterly Journal of Economics*, 94, 493–506.

Slovic, P. (1969a). "Manipulating the Attractiveness of a Gamble without Changing its Expected Value," *Journal of Experimental Psychology*, 79, 139–45.

——(1969b): "Differential Effects of Real Versus Hypothetical Payoffs on Choice Among Gambles," *Journal of Experimental Psychology*, 80, 434–7.

—— (1975): "Choice between Equally Valued Alternatives," *Journal of Experimental Psychology: Human Perception and Performance*, 1, 280–7.

—— and Lichtenstein, S. (1968): "Relative Importance of Probabilities and Payoffs in Risk Taking," *Journal of Experimental Psychology*, 78 (2), 1–18.

—— and —— (1971): "Comparison of Bayesian and Regression Approaches to the Study of Information Processing in Judgment," *Organizational Behavior and Human Performance*, 6, 649–744.

—— and —— (1983): "Preference Reversals: A Broader Perspective," *American Economic Review*, 73, 596–605.

—— and Tversky, A. (1974): "Who Accepts Savage's Axiom?" *Behavioral Science*, 19, 368–73.

—— Fischhoff, B. and Lichtenstein, S. (1982): "Response Mode, Framing, and Information Processing Effects in Risk Assessment," in Hogarth (1982).

Smith, V. (1969): "Measuring Nonmonetary Utilities in Uncertain Choices: The Ellsberg Urn," *Quarterly Journal of Economics*, 83, 324–9.

Sonnenschein, H. (1971): "Demand Theory without Transitive Preferences, with Applications to the Theory of Competitive Equilibrium," in Chipman, Hurwicz, Richter and Sonnenschein (1971).

Spence, M. and Zeckhauser, R. (1971): "Insurance, Information, and Individual Action," *American Economic Review Papers and Proceedings*, 61, 380–7.

—— and —— (1972): "The Effects of the Timing of Consumption Decisions and the Resolution of Lotteries on the Choice of Lotteries," *Econometrica*, 40, 401–3.

Stigler, G. and Boulding, K. (eds) (1952): *Readings in Price Theory*. Chicago: Richard D. Irwin.

Stiglitz, J. (ed.) (1966): *Collected Scientific Papers of Paul A. Samuelson, I*, Cambridge, Mass: MIT Press.

—— (1975): "Information and Economic Analysis," in Parkin and Nobay (1975).

—— (1985): "Information and Economic Analysis: A Perspective," *Economic Journal*, 95 (supplement), 21–41.

Stigum, B. and Wenstop, F. (eds) (1983): *Foundations of Utility and Risk Theory with Applications*. Dordrecht, Holland: D. Reidel Publishing Co.

Sugden, R. (1986): "New Developments in the Theory of Choice under Uncertainty," *Bulletin of Economic Research*, 38, 1–24. Reprinted in Hey and Lambert (1987).

Telser, L. (1955): "Safety First and Hedging," *Review of Economic Studies*, 23, 1–16.

Thaler, R. (1980): "Toward a Positive Theory of Consumer Choice," *Journal of Economic Behavior and Organization*, 1, 39–60.

—— (1985): "Mental Accounting and Consumer Choice," *Marketing Science*, 4, 199–214.

Tversky, A. (1969): "Intransitivity of Preferences," *Psychological Review* 76, 31–48.

—— (1975): "A Critique of Expected Utility Theory: Descriptive and Normative Considerations," *Erkenntnis*, 9, 163–73.

—— and D. Kahneman (1971): "Belief in the Law of Small Numbers," *Psychological Bulletin*, 2, 105–10. Reprinted in Kahneman, Slovic and Tversky (1982).

—— and —— (1974): "Judgment under Uncertainty: Heuristics and Biases," *Science*, 185, 1124–31. Reprinted in Diamond and Rothschild (1989), Kahneman, Slovic and Tversky (1982) and Arkes and Hammond (1986).

—— and —— (1981): "The Framing of Decisions and The Psychology of Choice," *Science*, 211, 453–8.

—— and —— (1983): "Extensional vs. Intuitive Reasoning: The Conjunction Fallacy in Probability Judgment," *Psychological Review*, 90, 293–315.

Vanschie, E. C. M. and Vanderpligt, J. (1970): "Problem Representation, Frame Preference, and Risky Choice," *Acta Psychologica*, 75 (3), December, 243–59.

Viscusi, W. (1985a): "A Bayesian Perspective on Biases in Risk Perception," *Economics Letters* 17, 59–62.

—— (1985b): "Are Individuals Bayesian Decision Makers?" *American Economic Review Papers and Proceedings*, 75, 381–5.

—— (1989): "Prospective Reference Theory: Toward an Explanation of the Paradoxes," *Journal of Risk and Uncertainty*, 2, 235–63.

von Neumann, J. and Morgenstern, O. (1944): *Theory of Games and Economic Behavior*. Princeton: Princeton University Press; 2nd edn 1947; 3rd edn 1953.

Weber, M. and Camerer C. (1987): "Recent Developments in Modeling Preferences under Risk," *OR Spektrum*, 9, 129–51.

Weinstein, A. (1968): "Individual Preference Intransitivity," *Southern Economic Journal*, 34, 335–43.

Williams, A. (1966): "Attitudes toward Speculative Risks as an Indicator of Attitudes Toward Pure Risks," *Journal of Risk and Insurance*, 33, 577–86.

Yaari, M. (1969): "Some Remarks on Measures of Risk Aversion and on their Uses," *Journal of Economic Theory*, 1, 315–29. Reprinted in Diamond and Rothschild (1989).

—— (1987): "The Dual Theory of Choice under Risk," *Econometrica*, 55, 95–115.

PART IV

The Market Economy as a Whole

Introduction

This classic article by Radford reproduced as chapter 18 is that rare economic treatise which is both enlightening and entertaining after half a century. It deals with the spontaneous arising of an exchange economy in a World War II German prisoner of war camp, in which the author was an involuntary guest, and with its evolution from a primitive economy to a quite sophisticated economic mechanism. We see the emergence of cigarettes as *numéraire* and medium of exchange, middlemen and arbitrageurs, spot and future markets, speculation, inflation and deflation, changes in the price structure of commodities, a paper money backed by food supplies, well-meant but doomed attempts at price control, and much else. In short, the paper presents a "monetary" exchange economy striving toward a general equilibrium in the face of many exogenous wartime forces. A wry, remarkably detached wit on the part of the author-participant leavens the paper without detracting from its insightful analysis. (*Glossary*: RMks. were German Reichsmarks, the currency of Germany in World War II.)

Social welfare theorists generally assert that when economic externalities arise in situations where property rights are not clearly assigned, the attainment of an efficient allocation of resources requires state imposition of taxes and subsidies or assignment of property rights to bring about equalities of marginal social and private costs. A well-known example cited in such arguments is the externality extended to beekeepers by the orchardist (or vice versa or both). In chapter 19, Cheung takes such writers to task for not examining the institutions that the market economy has established, via contracts between these two parties (and other farmers) to internalize these externalities. The author attempts to show that the payments established by such contracting tend to meet marginal benefit–marginal cost equalities that establish efficient allocations at reasonable transaction costs.

The reader may find that he or she learns a great deal more about bees and beekeeping than desired. Moreover, of necessity, given the paucity and imprecision of the data available to him, the author establishes at best only negative evidence that efficient pricing is established by the market. He does not attempt to extend his example to other externality situations where ownership of resources (farms and bees) is less well defined or is absent or where transaction costs are much more formidable. Nonetheless, the article is an interesting investigation of determining the prices of such evanescent resources as pollination services and nectar collection by the market mechanism. Also interesting is the informal establishment of agreements among farmers and orchardists to equate the densities of beehives hired in order to equalize the spillovers from one farm to another as bees wander outside lessees' areas. Informal designation of "bad neighbor" inflicts sufficient prospective costs to obviate the need for formal contractual agreements. Such agreements extend to limiting bee attrition by specification of common periods for pesticide applications.

And not of least interest is the barely restrained impulse of the dedicated market theorist to demonstrate that government interference in the market's operation is never desirable and seldom required.

Modern economic growth theory, aiming to explain the strong upward trend in productivity over time revealed by market economies, places its emphasis on technological innovation and attempts to endogenize it without disregarding feedbacks from other variables in the economy and the formation of enabling institutions. In chapter 20, Romer, one of the leading exponents of such theory, contrasts the approach of neoclassical growth theory, which was oriented toward validation of growth models, with the newer theory that seeks to explain the historical record. He dichotomizes inputs into *ideas*, which by their nature are nonrival goods (i.e., goods that can be used without depleting the stock of them and restricting use by others), and "*things*", or objects with mass or energy. Using such methodology, he ascribes the strong growth record of the United States economy to (a) interdependent development of adaptive technology, (b) the emergence of institutions that established property rights in many such nonrival goods, (c) the abundance of resources awaiting exploitation, and (d) the existence of large sized markets which permitted scale economies in the production of final goods as well as in the production of capital goods which found usage in many different industries.

The role of innovation in determining the form of the time path of market economies, the contributions of firm and government research and development to its formation and implementation, the influence of market structure in its genesis, the decisions of firms to imitate innovations introduced by other firms or to form their own research departments, its role in reshaping the organization, scale and functions of the firm (see chapter 7), its impact upon functional and personal income distribution, and many other forces it generates to influence market economy dynamics, can only be hinted at in this short an article. Nonetheless, it constitutes a worthy introduction to the field, especially in its effort to establish a methodological groundwork for examining a phenomenon badly neglected until the last quarter century.

IV A

The Integrated Market Mechanism

CHAPTER EIGHTEEN

The Economic Organization of a P.O.W. Camp

R. A. RADFORD

Source: *Economica*, 12 (1945), pp. 189–210. Reprinted with the permission of the London School of Economics & Political Science. © London School of Economics & Political Science.

1. Introduction

AFTER allowance has been made for abnormal circumstances, the social institutions, ideas and habits of groups in the outside world are to be found reflected in a Prisoner of War Camp. It is an unusual but a vital society. Camp organisation and politics are matters of real concern to the inmates, as affecting their present and perhaps their future existences. Nor does this indicate any loss of proportion. No one pretends that camp matters are of any but local importance or of more than transient interest, but their importance there is great. They bulk large in a world of narrow horizons and it is suggested that any distortion of values lies rather in the minimisation than in the exaggeration of their importance. Human affairs are essentially practical matters and the measure of immediate effect on the lives of those directly concerned in them is to a large extent the criterion of their importance at that time and place. A prisoner can hold strong views on such subjects as whether or not all tinned meats shall be issued to individuals cold or be centrally cooked, without losing sight of the significance of the Atlantic Charter.

One aspect of social organisation is to be found in economic activity, and this, along with other manifestations of a group existence, is to be found in any P.O.W. camp. True, a prisoner is not dependent on his exertions for the provision of the necessaries, or even the luxuries of life, but through his economic activity, the exchange of goods and services, his standard of material comfort is considerably enhanced. And this is a serious matter to the prisoner: he is not "playing at shops" even though the small scale of the transactions and the simple expression of comfort and wants in terms of cigarettes and jam, razor blades and writing paper, make the urgency of those needs difficult to appreciate, even by an ex-prisoner of some three months' standing.

Nevertheless, it cannot be too strongly emphasised that economic activities do not bulk so large in prison society as they do in the larger world. There can be little production; as has been said the prisoner is independent of his exertions for the provision of the necessities and luxuries of life; the emphasis lies in exchange and the media of exchange. A prison camp is not to be compared with the seething crowd of higglers in a street market, any more than it is to be compared with the economic inertia of a family dinner table.

Naturally then, entertainment, academic and literary interests, games and discussions of the "other world" bulk larger in everyday life than they do in the life of more normal societies. But it would be wrong to underestimate the importance of economic activity. Everyone receives a roughly equal share of essentials; it is by trade that individual preferences are given expression and comfort increased. All at some time, and most people regularly, make exchanges of one sort or another.

Although a P.O.W. camp provides a living example of a simple economy which might be used as an alternative to the Robinson Crusoe economy beloved by the text books, and its simplicity renders the demonstration of certain economic hypotheses both amusing and instructive, it is suggested that the principal significance is sociological. True, there is interest in observing the growth of economic institutions and customs in a brand new society, small and simple enough to prevent detail from obscuring the basic pattern and disequilibrium from obscuring the working of the system. But the essential interest lies in the universality and the spontaneity of this economic life; it came into existence not by conscious imitation but as a response to the immediate needs and circumstances. Any similarity between prison organisation and outside organisation arises from similar stimuli evoking similar responses.

The following is as brief an account of the essential data as may render the narrative intelligible. The camps of which the writer had experience were Oflags and consequently the economy was not complicated by payments for work by the detaining power. They consisted normally of between 1,200 and 2,500 people, housed in a number of separate but intercommunicating bungalows, one company of 200 or so to a building. Each company formed a group within the main organisation and inside the company the room and the messing syndicate, a voluntary and spontaneous group who fed together, formed the constituent units.

Between individuals there was active trading in all consumer goods and in some services. Most trading was for food against cigarettes or other foodstuffs, but cigarettes rose from the status of a normal commodity to that of currency. RMk.s existed but had no circulation save for gambling debts, as few articles could be purchased with them from the canteen.

Our supplies consisted of rations provided by the detaining power and (principally) the contents of Red Cross food parcels – tinned milk, jam, butter, biscuits, bully [corned beef], chocolate, sugar, etc., and cigarettes. So far the supplies to each person were equal and regular. Private parcels of clothing, toilet requisites and cigarettes were also received, and here equality ceased owing to the different numbers despatched and the vagaries of the post. All these articles were the subject of trade and exchange.

2. The Development and Organisation of the Market

Very soon after capture people realised that it was both undesirable and unnecessary, in view of the limited size and the equality of supplies, to give away or to accept gifts of cigarettes or food. "Goodwill" developed into trading as a more equitable means of maximising individual satisfaction.

We reached a transit camp in Italy about a fortnight after capture and received $\frac{1}{4}$ of a Red Cross food parcel each a week later. At once exchanges, already established, multiplied in volume. Starting with simple direct barter, such as a non-smoker giving a smoker friend his cigarette issue in exchange for a chocolate ration, more complex exchanges soon became an accepted custom. Stories circulated of a padre who started off round the camp with a tin of cheese and five cigarettes and returned to his bed with a complete parcel in addition to his original cheese and cigarettes; the market was not yet perfect. Within a week or two, as the volume of trade grew, rough scales of exchange values came into existence. Sikhs, who had at first exchanged tinned beef for practically any other foodstuff, began to insist on jam and margarine. It was realised that a tin of jam was worth $\frac{1}{2}$ lb. of margarine plus something else; that a cigarette issue was worth several chocolate issues, and a tin of diced carrots was worth practically nothing.

In this camp we did not visit other bungalows very much and prices varied from place to place; hence the germ of truth in the story of the itinerant priest. By the end of a month, when we reached our permanent camp, there was a lively trade in all commodities and their relative values were well known, and expressed not in terms of one another – one didn't quote bully in terms of sugar – but in terms of cigarettes. The cigarette became the standard of value. In the permanent camp people started by wandering through the bungalows calling their offers – "cheese for seven" (cigarettes) – and the hours after parcel issue were Bedlam. The inconveniences of this system soon led to its replacement by an Exchange and Mart notice board in every bungalow, where under the headings "name", "room number", "wanted" and "offered" sales and wants were advertised. When a deal went through, it was crossed off the board. The public and semipermanent records of transactions led to cigarette prices being well known and thus tending to equality throughout the camp, although there were always opportunities for an astute trader to make a profit from arbitrage. With this development everyone, including non-smokers, was willing to sell for cigarettes, using them to buy at another time and place. Cigarettes became the normal currency, though, of course, barter was never extinguished.

The unity of the market and the prevalence of a single price varied directly with the general level of organisation and comfort in the camp. A transit camp was always chaotic and uncomfortable: people were overcrowded, no one knew where anyone else was living, and few took the trouble to find out. Organisation was too slender to include an Exchange and Mart board, and private advertisements were the most that appeared. Consequently a transit camp was not one market but many. The price of a tin of salmon is known to have varied by two cigarettes in 20 between one end of a hut and the other. Despite a high level of organisation in Italy, the market was morcellated in this manner at the first transit camp we reached after our removal to Germany in the autumn of 1943. In this camp – Stalag VIIA at Moosburg in Bavaria – there were up to 50,000 prisoners of all nationalities. French, Russians, Italians and Jugo-Slavs were free to move about within the camp: British and Americans were confined to their compounds, although a few cigarettes given to a sentry would always procure permission for one or two men to visit other compounds. The people who first visited the highly organised French trading centre, with its stalls and known prices, found coffee extract – relatively cheap among the tea-drinking English – commanding a fancy price in biscuits or cigarettes, and some enterprising people made small fortunes that way. (Incidentally we found out later that much of the coffee went "over the wire" and sold for phenomenal prices at black market cafés in Munich: some of the French prisoners were said to have made substantial sums in RMk.s. This was one of the few occasions on which our normally closed economy came into contact with other economic worlds.)

Eventually public opinion grew hostile to these monopoly profits – not everyone could make contact with the French – and trading with them was put on a regulated basis. Each group of beds was given a quota of articles to offer and the transaction was carried out by accredited representatives from the British compound, with monopoly rights. The same method was used for trading with sentries elsewhere, as in this trade secrecy and reason-able prices had a peculiar importance, but as is ever the case with regulated companies, the interloper proved too strong.

The permanent camps in Germany saw the highest level of commercial organisation. In addition to the Exchange and Mart notice boards, a shop was organised as a public utility, controlled by representatives of the Senior British Officer, on a no profit basis. People left their surplus clothing, toilet requisites and food there until they were sold at a fixed price in cigarettes. Only sales in cigarettes were accepted – there was no barter – and there was no higgling. For food at least there were standard prices: clothing is less homogeneous and the price was decided around a norm by the seller and the shop manager in agreement; shirts would average say 80, ranging from 60 to 120 according to quality and age. Of food, the shop carried small stocks for convenience; the capital was provided by a loan from the bulk store of Red Cross cigarettes and repaid by a small commission taken on the first transactions. Thus the cigarette attained its fullest currency status, and the market was almost completely unified.

It is thus to be seen that a market came into existence without labour or production. The B.R.C.S. may be considered as "Nature" of the text-book, and the articles of trade – food, clothing and cigarettes – as free gifts – and or manna. Despite this, and despite a roughly equal distribution of resources, a market came into spontaneous operation, and prices were fixed by the operation of supply and demand. It is difficult to reconcile this fact with the labour theory of value.

Actually there was an embryo labour market. Even when cigarettes were not scarce, there was usually some unlucky person willing to perform services for them. Laundrymen advertised at two cigarettes a garment. Battle-dress was scrubbed and pressed and a pair of trousers lent for the interim period for twelve. A good pastel portrait cost thirty or a tin of "Kam". Odd tailoring and other jobs similarly had their prices.

There were also entrepreneurial services. There was a coffee stall owner who sold tea, coffee or cocoa at two cigarettes a cup, buying his raw materials at market prices and hiring labour to gather fuel and to stoke; he actually enjoyed the services of a chartered accountant at one stage. After a period of great prosperity he overreached himself and failed disastrously for several hundred cigarettes. Such large-scale private enterprise was rare but several middlemen or professional traders existed. The padre in Italy, or the men at Moosburg who opened trading relations with the French, are examples: the more subdivided the market, the less perfect the advertisement of prices, and the less stable the prices, the greater was the scope for these operators. One man capitalised his know-ledge of Urdu by buying meat from the Sikhs and selling butter and jam in return: as his operations became better known more and more people entered this trade, prices in the Indian Wing approximated more nearly to those elsewhere, though to the end a "contact" among the Indians was valuable, as linguistic difficulties prevented the trade from being quite free. Some were specialists in the Indian trade, the food, clothing or even the watch trade. Middlemen traded on their own account or on commission. Price rings and agreements were suspected and the traders certainly co-operated. Nor did they welcome newcomers. Unfortunately the writer knows little of the workings of these people: public opinion was hostile and the professionals were usually of a retiring disposition.

One trader in food and cigarettes, operating in a period of dearth, enjoyed a high reputation. His capital, carefully saved, was originally about 50 cigarettes, with which he bought rations on issue days and held them until the price rose just before the next issue. He also picked up a little by arbitrage; several times a day he visited every Exchange or Mart notice board and took advantage of every discrepancy between prices of goods offered and wanted. His knowledge of prices, markets and names of those who had received cigarette parcels was phenomenal. By these means he kept himself smoking steadily – his profits – while his capital remained intact.

Sugar was issued on Saturday. About Tuesday two of us used to visit Sam and make a deal; as old customers he would advance as much of the price as he could spare then, and entered the transaction in a book. On Saturday morning he left cocoa tins on our beds for the ration, and picked them up on Saturday afternoon. We were hoping for a calendar at Christmas, but Sam failed too. He was left holding a big black treacle issue when the price fell, and in this weakened state was unable to withstand an unexpected arrival of parcels and the consequent price fluctuations. He paid in full, but from his capital. The next Tuesday, when I paid my usual visit he was out of business.

Credit entered into many, perhaps into most, transactions, in one form or another. Sam paid in advance as a rule for his purchases of future deliveries of sugar, but many buyers asked for credit, whether the commodity was sold spot or future. Naturally prices varied according to the terms of sale. A treacle ration might be advertised for four cigarettes now or five next week. And in the future market "bread now" was a vastly different thing from "bread Thursday". Bread was issued on Thursday and Monday, four and three days' rations respectively, and by Wednesday and Sunday night it had risen at least one cigarette per ration, from seven to eight, by supper time. One man always saved a ration to sell then at the peak price: his offer of "bread now" stood out on the board among a number of "bread Monday's" fetching one or two less, or not selling at all – and he always smoked on Sunday night.

3. The Cigarette Currency

Although cigarettes as currency exhibited certain peculiarities, they performed all the functions of a metallic currency as a unit of account, as a measure of value and as a store of value, and shared most of its characteristics. They were homogeneous, reasonably durable, and of convenient size for the smallest or, in packets, for the largest transactions. Incidentally, they could be clipped or sweated by rolling them between the fingers so that tobacco fell out.

Cigarettes were also subject to the working of Gresham's Law. Certain brands were more popular than others as smokes, but for currency purposes a cigarette was a cigarette. Consequently buyers used the poorer qualities and the Shop rarely saw the more popular brands: cigarettes such as Churchman's No. 1 were rarely used for trading. At one time cigarettes hand-rolled from pipe tobacco began to circulate. Pipe tobacco was issued in lieu of cigarettes by the Red Cross at a rate of 25 cigarettes to the ounce and this rate was standard in exchanges, but an ounce would produce 30 home-made cigarettes. Naturally, people with machine-made cigarettes broke them down and re-rolled the tobacco, and the real cigarette virtually disappeared from the market. Hand-rolled cigarettes were not homogeneous and prices could no longer be quoted in them with safety: each cigarette was examined before it was accepted and thin ones were rejected, or extra demanded as a make-weight. For a time we suffered all the inconveniences of a debased currency.

Machine-made cigarettes were always universally acceptable, both for what they would buy and for themselves. It was this intrinsic value which gave rise to their principal disadvantage as currency, a disadvantage which exists, but to a far smaller extent, in the case of metallic currency; – that is, a strong demand for non-monetary purposes. Consequently our economy was repeatedly subject to deflation and to periods of monetary stringency. While the Red Cross issue of 50 or 25 cigarettes per man per week came in regularly, and while there were fair stocks held, the cigarette currency suited its purpose admirably. But when the issue was interrupted, stocks soon ran out, prices fell, trading declined in volume and became increasingly a matter of barter. This deflationary tendency was periodically offset by the sudden injection of new currency. Private cigarette parcels arrived in a trickle throughout the year, but the big numbers came in quarterly when the Red Cross received its allocation of transport. Several hundred thousand cigarettes might arrive in the space of a fortnight. Prices soared, and then began to fall, slowly at first but with increasing rapidity as stocks ran out, until the next big delivery. Most of our economic troubles could be attributed to this fundamental instability.

4. Price Movements

Many factors affected prices, the strongest and most noticeable being the periodical currency inflation and deflation described in the last paragraphs. The periodicity of this price cycle depended on cigarette and, to a far lesser extent on food deliveries. At one time in the early days, before any private parcels had arrived and when there were no individual stocks, the weekly issue of cigarettes and food parcels occurred on a Monday. The non-monetary demand for cigarettes was great, and less elastic than the demand for food: consequently prices fluctuated weekly, falling towards Sunday night and rising sharply on Monday morning. Later, when many people held reserves, the weekly issue had no such effect, being too small a proportion of the total available. Credit allowed people with no reserves to meet their non-monetary demand over the week-end.

The general price level was affected by other factors. An influx of new prisoners, proverbially hungry, raised it. Heavy air raids in the vicinity of the camp probably increased the non-monetary demand for cigarettes and accentuated deflation. Good and bad war news certainly had its effect, and the general waves of optimism and pessimism which swept the camp were reflected in prices. Before breakfast one morning in March of this year, a rumour of the arrival of parcels and cigarettes was circulated. Within ten minutes I sold a treacle ration, for four cigarettes (hitherto offered in vain for three), and many similar deals went through. By 10 o'clock the rumour was denied, and treacle that day found no more buyers even at two cigarettes.

More interesting than changes in the general price level were changes in the price structure. Changes in the supply of a commodity, in the German ration scale or in the make-up of Red Cross parcels, would raise the price of one commodity relative to others. Tins of oatmeal, once a rare and much sought after luxury in the parcels, became a commonplace in 1943, and the price fell. In hot weather the demand for cocoa fell, and that for soap rose. A new recipe would be reflected in the price level: the discovery that raisins and sugar could be turned into an alcoholic liquor of remarkable potency reacted permanently on the dried fruit market. The invention of electric immersion heaters run off the power points made tea, a drug on the market in Italy, a certain seller in Germany.

In August, 1944, the supplies of parcels and cigarettes were both halved. Since both sides of the equation were changed in the same degree, changes in prices were not anticipated. But this was not the case: the non-monetary demand for cigarettes was less elastic than the demand for food, and food prices fell a little. More important however were the changes in the price structure. German margarine and jam, hitherto valueless owing to adequate supplies of Canadian butter and marmalade, acquired a new value. Chocolate, popular and a certain seller, and sugar, fell. Bread rose; several standing contracts of bread for cigarettes were broken, especially when the bread ration was reduced a few weeks later.

In February, 1945, the German soldier who drove the ration waggon was found to be willing to exchange loaves of bread at the rate of one loaf for a bar of chocolate. Those in the know began selling bread and buying chocolate, by then almost unsaleable in a period of serious deflation. Bread, at about 40, fell slightly; chocolate rose from 15; the supply of bread was not enough for the two commodities to reach parity, but the tendency was unmistakable.

The substitution of German margarine for Canadian butter when parcels were halved naturally affected their relative values, margarine appreciating at the expense of butter. Similarly, two brands of dried milk, hitherto differing in quality and therefore in price by five cigarettes a tin, came together in price as the wider substitution of the cheaper raised its relative value.

Enough has been cited to show that any change in conditions affected both the general price level and the price structure. It was this latter phenomenon which wrecked our planned economy.

5. Paper Currency – Bully Marks

Around D-Day, food and cigarettes were plentiful, business was brisk and the camp in an optimistic mood. Consequently the Entertainments Committee felt the moment opportune to launch a restaurant, where food and hot drinks were sold while a band and variety turns performed. Earlier experiments, both public and private, had pointed the way, and the scheme was a great success. Food was bought at market prices to provide the meals and the small profits were devoted to a reserve fund and used to bribe Germans to provide grease-paints and other necessities for the camp theatre. Originally meals were sold for cigarettes but this meant that the whole scheme was vulnerable to the periodic deflationary waves, and furthermore heavy smokers were unlikely to attend much. The whole success of the scheme depended on an adequate amount of food being offered for sale in the normal manner.

To increase and facilitate trade, and to stimulate supplies and customers therefore, and secondarily to avoid the worst effects of deflation when it should come, a paper currency was organised by the Restaurant and the Shop. The Shop bought food on behalf of the Restaurant with paper notes and the paper was accepted equally with the cigarettes in the Restaurant or Shop, and passed back to the Shop to purchase more food. The Shop acted as a bank of issue. The paper money was backed 100 per cent. by food; hence its name, the Bully Mark. The BMk. was backed 100 per cent. by food: there could be no over-issues, as is permissible with a normal bank of issue, since the eventual dispersal of the camp and consequent redemption of all BMk.s was anticipated in the near future.

Originally one BMk. was worth one cigarette and for a short time both circulated freely inside and outside the Restaurant. Prices were quoted in BMk.s and cigarettes with equal freedom – and for a short time the BMk. showed signs of replacing the cigarette as currency. The BMk. was tied to food, but not to cigarettes: as it was issued against food, say 45 for a tin of milk and so on, any reduction in the BMk. prices of food would have meant that there were unbacked BMk.s in circulation. But the price of both food and BMk.s could and did fluctuate with the supply of cigarettes.

While the Restaurant flourished, the scheme was a success: the Restaurant bought heavily, all foods were saleable and prices were stable.

In August parcels and cigarettes were halved and the Camp was bombed. The Restaurant closed for a short while and sales of food became difficult. Even when the Restaurant reopened, the food and cigarette shortage became increasingly acute and people were unwilling to convert such valuable goods into paper and to hold them for luxuries like snacks and tea. Less of the right kinds of food for the Restaurant were sold, and the Shop became glutted with dried fruit, chocolate, sugar, etc., which the Restaurant could not buy. The price level and the price structure changed. The BMk. fell to four-fifths of a cigarette and eventually farther still, and it became unacceptable save in the Restaurant. There was a flight from the BMk., no longer convertible into cigarettes or popular foods. The cigarette re-established itself.

But the BMk. was sound! The Restaurant closed in the New Year with a progressive food shortage and the long evenings without lights due to intensified Allied air raids, and BMk.s could only be spent in the Coffee Bar – relict of the Restaurant – or on the few unpopular foods in the Shop, the owners of which were prepared to accept them. In the end all holders of BMk.s were paid in full, in cups of coffee or in prunes. People who had bought BMk.s for cigarettes or valuable jam or biscuits in their heyday were aggrieved that they should have stood the loss involved by their restricted choice, but they suffered no actual loss of market value.

6. Price Fixing

Along with this scheme came a determined attempt at a planned economy, at price fixing. The Medical Officer had long been anxious to control food sales, for fear of some people selling too much, to the detriment of their health. The deflationary waves and their effects on prices were inconvenient to all and would be dangerous to the Restaurant which had to carry stocks. Furthermore, unless the BMk. was convertible into cigarettes at about par it had little chance of gaining confidence and of succeeding as a currency. As has been explained, the BMk. was tied to food but could not be tied to cigarettes, which fluctuated in value. Hence, while BMk. prices of food were fixed for all time, cigarette prices of food and BMk.s varied.

The Shop, backed by the Senior British Officer, was now in a position to enforce price control both inside and outside its walls. Hitherto a standard price had been fixed for food left for sale in the shop, and prices outside were roughly in conformity with this scale, which was recommended as a "guide" to sellers, but fluctuated a good deal around it. Sales in the Shop at recommended prices were apt to be slow though a good price might be obtained: sales outside could be made more quickly at lower prices. (If sales outside were to be at higher prices, goods were withdrawn from the Shop until the recommended price rose: but the recommended price was sluggish and could not follow the market closely by reason of its very purpose, which was stability.) The Exchange and Mart notice boards came under the control of the Shop: advertisements which exceeded a 5 per cent. departure from the recommended scale were liable to be crossed out by authority: unauthorised sales were discouraged by authority and also by public opinion, strongly in favour of a just and stable price (Recommended prices were fixed partly from market data, partly on the advice of the M.O.)

At first the recommended scale was a success: the Restaurant, a big buyer, kept prices stable around this level: opinion and the 5 per cent tolerance helped. But when the price level fell with the August cuts and the price structure changed, the recommended scale was too rigid. Unchanged at first, as no deflation was expected, the scale was tardily lowered, but the prices of goods on the new scale remained in the same relation to one another, owing to the BMk., while on the market the price structure had changed. And the modifying influence of the Restaurant had gone. The scale was moved up and down several times, slowly following the inflationary and deflationary waves, but it was rarely adjusted to changes in the price structure. More and more advertisements were crossed off the board, and black market sales at unauthorised prices increased: eventually public opinion turned against the recommended scale and authority gave up the struggle. In the last few weeks, with unparalleled deflation, prices fell with alarming rapidity, no scales existed, and supply and demand, alone and unmellowed, determined prices.

7. Public Opinion

Public opinion on the subject of trading was vocal if confused and changeable, and generalisations as to its direction are difficult and dangerous. A tiny minority held that all trading was undesirable as it engendered an unsavoury atmosphere; occasional frauds and sharp practices were cited as proof. Certain forms of trading were more generally condemned; trade with the Germans was criticised by many. Red Cross toilet articles, which were in short supply and only issued in cases of actual need, were excluded from trade by law and opinion working in unshakable harmony. At one time, when there had been several cases of malnutrition reported among the more devoted smokers, no trade in German rations was permitted, as the victims became an additional burden on the depleted food reserves of the Hospital. But while certain activities were condemned as antisocial, trade itself was practised, and its utility appreciated, by almost everyone in the camp.

More interesting was opinion onmiddlemen and prices. Taken as a whole, opinion was hostile to the middleman. His function, and his hard work in bringing buyer and seller together, were ignored; profits were not regarded as a reward for labour, but as the result of sharp practices. Despite the fact that his very existence was proof to the contrary, the middleman was held to be redundant in view of the existence of an official Shop and the Exchange and Mart. Appreciation only came his way when he was willing to advance the price of a sugar ration, or to buy goods spot and carry them against a future sale. In these cases the element of risk was obvious to all, and the convenience of the service was felt to merit some reward. Particularly unpopular was the middleman with an element of monopoly, the man who contacted the ration wagon driver, or the man who utilised his knowledge of Urdu. And middlemen as a group were blamed for reducing prices. Opinion notwithstanding, most people dealt with a middleman, whether consciously or unconsciously, at some time or another.

There was a strong feeling that everything had its "just price" in cigarettes. While the assessment of the just price, which incidentally varied between camps, was impossible of explanation, this price was nevertheless pretty closely known. It can best be defined as the price usually fetched by an article in good times when cigarettes were plentiful. The "just price" changed slowly; it was unaffected by short-term variations in supply, and while opinion might be resigned to departures from the "just price", a strong feeling of resentment persisted. A more satisfactory definition of the "just price" is impossible. Everyone knew what it was, though no one could explain why it should be so.

As soon as prices began to fall with a cigarette shortage, a clamour arose, particularly against those who held reserves and who bought at reduced prices. Sellers at cut prices were criticised and their activities referred to as the black market. In every period of dearth the explosive question of "should non-smokers receive a cigarette ration?" was discussed to profitless length. Unfortunately, it was the non-smoker, or the light smoker with his reserves, along with the hated middleman, who weathered the storm most easily.

The popularity of the price-fixing scheme, and such success as it enjoyed, were undoubtedly the result of this body of opinion. On several occasions the fall of prices was delayed by the general support given to the recommended scale. The onset of deflation was marked by a period of sluggish trade; prices stayed up but no one bought. Then prices fell on the black market, and the volume of trade revived in that quarter. Even when the recommended scale was revised, the volume of trade in the Shop would remain low. Opinion was always overruled by the hard facts of the market.

Curious arguments were advanced to justify price fixing. The recommended prices were in some way related to the calorific values of the foods offered: hence some were overvalued and never sold at these prices. One argument ran as follows: – not everyone has private cigarette parcels: thus, when prices were high and trade good in the summer of 1944, only the lucky rich could buy. This was unfair to the man with few cigarettes. When prices fell in the following winter, prices should be pegged high so that the rich, who had enjoyed life in the summer, should put many cigarettes into circulation. The fact that those who sold to the rich in the summer had also enjoyed life then, and the fact that in the winter there was always someone willing to sell at low prices were ignored. Such arguments were hotly debated each night after the approach of Allied aircraft extinguished all lights at 8 p.m. But prices moved with the supply of cigarettes, and refused to stay fixed in accordance with a theory of ethics.

8. Conclusion

The economic organisation described was both elaborate and smooth-working in the summer of 1944. Then came the August cuts and deflation. Prices fell, rallied with deliveries of cigarette parcels in September and December, and fell again. In January, 1945, supplies of Red Cross cigarettes ran out: and prices slumped still further: in February the supplies of food parcels were exhausted and the depression became a blizzard. Food, itself scarce, was almost given away in order to meet the non-monetary demand for cigarettes. Laundries ceased to operate, or worked for £s or RMk.s: food and cigarettes sold for fancy prices in £s, hitherto unheard of. The Restaurant was a memory and the BMk. a joke. The Shop was empty and the Exchange and Mart notices were full of unaccepted offers for cigarettes. Barter increased in volume, becoming a larger proportion of a smaller volume of trade. This, the first serious and prolonged food shortage in the writer's experience, caused the price structure to change again, partly because German rations were not easily divisible. A margarine ration gradually sank in value until it exchanged directly for a treacle ration. Sugar slumped sadly. Only bread retained its value. Several thousand cigarettes, the capital of the Shop, were distributed without any noticeable effect. A few fractional parcel and cigarette issues, such as one-sixth of a parcel and twelve cigarettes each, led to momentary price recoveries and feverish trade, especially when they coincided with good news from the Western Front, but the general position remained unaltered.

By April, 1945, chaos had replaced order in the economic sphere: sales were difficult, prices lacked stability. Economics has been defined as the science of distributing limited means among unlimited and competing ends. On 12th April, with the arrival of elements of the 30th U.S. Infantry Division, the ushering in of an age of plenty demonstrated the hypothesis that with infinite means economic organisation and activity would be redundant, as every want could be satisfied without effort.

CHAPTER NINETEEN

The Fable of the Bees: An Economic Investigation

STEVEN N. S. CHEUNG

Source: *Journal of Law and Economics*, 16 (1973), pp. 11–33.
Reprinted with the permission of the author and the University of
Chicago. © The University of Chicago.

> Economists possess their full share of the common ability to invent and
> commit errors. . . . Perhaps their most common error is to believe other eco-
> nomists.
>
> GEORGE J. STIGLER

EVER since A. C. Pigou wrote his books on "welfare" (1912, 1920), a divergence between
private and social costs has provided the main argument for instituting government action
to correct allegedly inefficient market activities. The analysis in such cases has been
designed less to aid our understanding of how the economic system operates than to
find flaws in it to justify policy recommendations. Both to illustrate the argument and to
demonstrate the nature of the actual situation, the quest has been for real-world examples
of such defects.

Surprisingly enough, aside from Pigou's polluting factory and Sidgwick's lighthouse,
convincing examples were hard to come by.[1] It was not until 1952, more than thirty years
after Pigou's initial analysis, that J. E. Meade (1952, p. 54) proposed further examples and
revitalized the argument for corrective government actions. Meade's prime example,
which soon became classic, concerned the case of the apple farmer and the beekeeper.
In his own words:

> Suppose that in a given region there is a certain amount of apple-growing and a certain
> amount of bee-keeping and that the bees feed on the apple blossom. If the apple-farmers
> apply 10% more labour, land and capital to apple-farming they will increase the output of
> apples by 10%; but they will also provide more food for the bees. On the other hand, the bee-
> keepers will not increase the output of honey by 10% by increasing the amount of land, labour
> and capital to bee-keeping by 10% unless at the same time the apple-farmers also increase
> their output and so the food of the bees by 10%. . . . We call this a case of an unpaid factor,
> because the situation is due simply and solely to the fact that the apple-farmer cannot charge
> the beekeeper for the bees' food (pp. 56–7).

And Meade applied a similar argument to a reciprocal situation:

While the apples may provide the food of the bees, the bees may fertilize the apples....By a process similar to that adopted in the previous case we can obtain formulae to show what subsidies and taxes must be imposed (p. 58).

In another well-known work, Francis M. Bator used Meade's example to infer "market failure" (Bator, 1958, pp. 351, 364):

It is easy to show that if apple blossoms have a positive effect on honey production...any Pareto-efficient solution...will associate with apple blossoms a positive Lagrangean shadow-price. If, then, apple producers are unable to protect their equity in apple-nectar and markets do not impute to apple blossoms their correct shadow value, profit-maximizing decisions will fail correctly to allocate resources...at the margin. There will be failure "by enforcement." This is what I would call an *ownership* externality.

It is easy to understand why the "apples and bees" example has enjoyed widespread popularity. It has freshness and charm: the pastoral scene, with its elfin image of bees collecting nectar from apple blossoms, has captured the imagination of economists and students alike. However, the universal credence given to the lighthearted fable is surprising; for in the United States, at least, contractual arrangements between farmers and beekeepers have long been routine. This paper investigates the pricing and contractual arrangements of the beekeeping industry in the state of Washington, the location having been selected because the Pacific Northwest is one of the largest apple-growing areas in the world.

Contrary to what most of us have thought, apple blossoms yield little or no honey.[2] But it is true that bees provide valuable pollination services for apples and other plants, and that many other plants do yield lucrative honey crops. In any event, it will be shown that the observed pricing and contractual arrangements governing nectar and pollination services are consistent with efficient allocation of resources.

1. Some Relevant Facts of Beekeeping

Although various types of bees pollinate plants, beekeeping is confined almost exclusively to honeybees.[3] The hive used by beekeepers in the state of Washington is of the Langstroth design which consists of one or two brood chambers, a queen excluder, and from zero to six supers. A brood chamber is a wooden box large enough to contain eight or ten movable frames, each measuring $9 - \frac{1}{8}$ by $17 - \frac{5}{8}$ by $1 - \frac{3}{8}$ inches. Within each frame is a wax honeycomb built by the bees. In the hexagonal cells of this comb the queen lays her eggs and the young bees, or "brood," are raised. It is here also that the bees store the nectar and pollen which they use for food. Honey is not usually extracted from this chamber but from the frames of a shallower box, called a super, placed above the brood chamber. The queen excluder, placed between the super and the brood chamber, prevents the laying of eggs in the upper section.[4]

The bees, and consequently the beekeepers, work according to a yearly cycle. Around the beginning of March, a Washington beekeeper will decide whether he wants to prepare for the pollination season by ordering booster packages of bees from California to strengthen his colonies, depleted and weakened during the winter and early spring.

Alternatively, he may decide to build up the colony by transporting the hives to farms or pastures in warmer areas, such as Oregon and California. The colony hatches continuously from spring to fall, and the growth rate is rapid. Reared on pollen, the infant bees remain in the brood stage for about three weeks before entering the productive life of the colony for five or six weeks. Active workers spend three weeks cleaning and repairing the brood cells and nursing the young, then live out the remainder of their short lives foraging for pollen and nectar.[5]

Because of the bees' quick growth, the working "strength" of a colony includes both brood and workers, and increases from about five frames in early spring to about twelve by late summer. Spring is the primary season for fruit pollination, and beekeepers usually market a standard colony strength of roughly four frames of bees and two to three frames of brood for pollination services. But since empty frames are needed to accommodate the expanding colony, two-story hives, with 16 or 20 frames, are used. The swarming period, beginning in mid-summer and lasting until early fall, is the peak honey season, and the yield per hive will vary positively with the colony strength. Because the maximization of honey yield requires that the colonies be of equal strength, they are usually reassorted in preparation for the major honey season, so that the number of colonies at the "peak" is generally larger than the number in spring.[6]

When pollen fails in late fall, the hives become broodless and the bee population begins to decline. During the idle winter months adult bees live considerably longer than in the active season, and they can survive the winter if about 60 pounds of nectar are left in the hive. But in the northern part of the state and in Canada, where cold weather makes the overwintering of bees more costly, the common practice is to eliminate the bees and extract the remaining honey. It should be noted here that bees can be captured, and that they can be easily eliminated by any of a large number of pesticide sprays.[7] The cost of enforcing property rights in nectar is therefore much lower than economists have been led to believe.

Few agricultural crops, to my knowledge, exhibit a higher year-to-year variance of yield than does the honey crop. Several natural factors contribute. Cold weather and rain discourage the bees from working, and winds alter their direction of flight. Also, the nectar flows of plants are susceptible to shocks of heat and cold.[8] The plants yielding most honey are mint, fire-weed, and the legumes, such as alfalfa and the clovers. Fruit trees usually have low nectar flows, although orange blossoms (in California) are excellent. Indeed, the pollination of fruits, especially the cherry in early spring, may actually detract from the yield of honey: less honey may be in the hive after pollination than was there initially, owing to the bees' own consumption. Another reason for the low honey yield from fruit trees is the relatively short time that the hives are left in the orchards.

Cross-pollination is accidentally effected as the bees forage for nectar and pollen. Pollination services were not marketed before World War I, primarily because small farms had enough flowering plants and trees to attract wild insects. It was not until 1910 and the advent of modern orcharding, with its large acreage and orderly planting, that markets for pollination services began to grow rapidly (Levin, 1971). Today, the services are demanded not only for production of fruits but also for the setting (fertilizing) of seeds for legumes and vegetables. Evidence is incontrovertible that the setting of fruits and seeds increases with the number of hives per acre, that the pollination productivity of bees is subject to diminishing returns, and, despite some bee-keepers' claims to the contrary, beyond some point the marginal productivity may even be negative.[9] There is also strong evidence that pollination yield will improve if the hives are placed strategically throughout the farm rather than set in one spot (Oldershaw, 1970, pp. 171–6; Morse, 1960). The closer a particular area is to a hive, the more effective will be the pollination within that area. Although each individual bee will forage only a few square yards, the bees from one hive will collectively pollinate a large circular area,[10] and this gives rise to a problem: given a high cost to control fully the foraging behavior of bees, if similar orchards are located close to one another, one who hires bees to pollinate his own orchard will in some degree benefit his neighbors. This complication will be further discussed in the next section.

In the state of Washington, about 60 beekeepers each own 100 colonies or more; at the peak season the state's grand total of colonies is about 90,000. My investigation, conducted in the spring of 1972, covered a sample of nine beekeepers and a total of approximately 10,000 spring colonies. (One of these beekeepers specialized in cut-comb honey and he will be treated separately in a footnote.) Table 1 lists the bee-related plants covered by my investigation. As seen from Columns (3) and (4), some plants (such as cherry trees) require

Table 1   Bee-related plants investigated (State of Washington, 1971)

(1) Plants	(2) Number of beekeepers	(3) Pollination services rendered	(4) Surplus honey expected	(5) Approximate season	(6) Number of hives per acre (range)
Fruits & Nuts					
Apple & Soft Fruits[a]	7	Yes	No	Mid-April – Mid-May	0.4 to 2
Blueberry (with maple)	1	Yes	Yes	May	2
Cherry (early)	1	Yes	No	March – Early April	0.5 to 2
Cherry	2	Yes	No	April	0.5 to 2
Cranberry	2	Yes	Negligible	June	1.5
Almond (Calif.)	2	Yes	No	February – March	2
Legumes					
Alfalfa	5	Yes and No[c]	Yes	June – September	0.3 to 3
Red Clover	4	Yes and No	Yes	June – September	0.5 to 5
Sweet Clover	1	No[d]	Yes	June – September	0.5 to 1
Pasture[b]	4	No	Yes	Late May – September	0.3 to 1
Other Plants					
Cabbage	1	Yes	Yes	Early April – May	1
Fireweed	2	No	Yes	July – September	n.a.
Mint	3	No	Yes	July – September	0.4 to 1

[a] Soft fruits include pears, apricots, and peaches.
[b] Pasture includes a mixture of plants, notably the legumes and other wild flowers such as dandelions.
[c] Pollination services are rendered for alfalfa and the clovers if their seeds are intended to be harvested; when they are grown only for hay, hives will still be employed for nectar extraction.
[d] Sweet clover may also require pollination services, but such a case is not covered by this investigation.

pollination services for fruit setting but yield no honey; some (such as mint) yield honey while requiring no pollination service; and some (such as alfalfa) are of a reciprocal nature. Note that when alfalfa and the clovers are grown only for hay, pollination services are not required, although these plants yield honey.

The practice of relocating hives from farm to farm, by truck, enables the beekeeper to obtain multiple crops a year, either in rendering pollination service or in extracting honey. However, while the maximum observed number of crops per hive per year is four and the minimum is two, my estimate is that a hive averages only 2.2 crops a year. More frequent rotation not only involves greater costs of moving and of standardizing hives, but abbreviates the honey yield per crop. In the southern part of the state, where the relatively warm climate permits an early working season, beekeepers usually begin by pollinating either cherry or almond (in California) in early spring. The hives may or may not then be moved northward in late spring, when apple and soft fruits (and some late cherry) begin to bloom.[11]

The lease period for effective pollination during spring bloom is no more than a week. But then, for a month or two between the end of fruit pollination and the beginning of summer nectar flow, the hives have little alternative usage. Since this period is substantially longer than the time needed for the beekeeper to check and standardize his hives for the honey crops, he will generally be in no hurry to move them and will prefer to leave them in the orchards with no extra charge, unless the farmer is planning to spray with insecticide. The appropriate seasons for the various plants listed in Column (5) of Table 1, may not, therefore, match the lengths of hive leases. Lease periods are generally longer for honey crops, for the collection of nectar takes more time.

The sixth column in Table 1 indicates the various hive-densities employed. The number of hives per acre depends upon the size of the area to be serviced, the density of planting, and, in the case of fruit pollination, the age of the orchards. For the pollination of fruits, the hives are scattered throughout the farm, usually with higher densities employed in older orchards because the trees are not strategically placed to facilitate the crossing of pollen. The most popular choices are one hive per acre and one hive per two acres. It is interesting, and easily understood, that farmers demand significantly fewer hives for pollination than the number recommended by entomologists:[12] both are interested in the maximization of yield, but for the farmer such maximization is subject to the constraint of hive rentals. When bees are employed to produce honey only, the hives are placed together in one location, called an apiary, for greater ease of handling (Nye, 1971). The relatively large variation in hive densities required if legumes are, or are not, to be pollinated is discussed in the next section.

Before we turn to an analysis of the pricing and contractual behavior of beekeepers and farmers, I must point out that the two government programs which support the beekeeping industry did not constitute relevant constraints for the period under investigation. The honey price-support program, initiated in 1949, involves purchase of honey at supported prices by the Commodity Credit Corporation (Sullivan, 1971, p. 136). For the period under investigation, however, the supported price was about 20 per cent lower than the market price.[13] Section 804 of the Agricultural Act of 1970, effectuated in 1971 and designed to reimburse beekeepers for any loss due to pesticide sprays, has been largely ignored by beekeepers because of the difficulty of filing effective claims with the federal government.[14]

2. The Observed Pricing and Contractual Behavior

It is easy to find conclusive evidence showing that both nectar and pollination services are transacted in the marketplace: in some cities one need look no further than the yellow pages of the Telephone Directory. But the existence of prices does not in itself imply an efficient allocation of resources. It is, therefore, necessary to demonstrate the effectiveness of the market in dictating the use even of those resources – bees, nectar, and pollen – which, admittedly, are elusive in character and relatively insignificant in value. In doing so, I shall not attempt to estimate the standard sets of marginal values which an efficient market is said to equate: the burden of such a task must rest upon those who believe the government can costlessly and accurately make these estimates for the imposition of the "ideal" tax-subsidy schemes. Rather, I offer below an analysis based on the equimarginal principle. To the extent that the observed pricing and contractual behavior fails to falsify the implications derived from this analysis we conclude that

1   the observed behavior is explained, and
2   the observations are consistent with efficient allocation of resources.

2.1. The analysis

The reciprocal situation in which a beekeeper is able to extract honey from the same farm to which he renders pollination services poses an interesting theoretic riddle. The traditional analysis of such a condition relies on some interdependent production functions, and is, I think, unnecessarily complex.[15] The method employed here simply treats pollination services and honey yield as components of a joint product generated by the hive. That is, the rental price per hive received by a beekeeper for placing his hives on a farm may be paid in terms of honey, of a money fee, or of a combination of both. The money fee or the honey yield may be either positive or negative, but their total measures the rental value of the hive.

The solution is illustrated in Figure 1. We assume that the hives are always strategically placed. In Figure 1a the curve $(\partial N/\partial h)_a$ depicts the value of the marginal nectar product

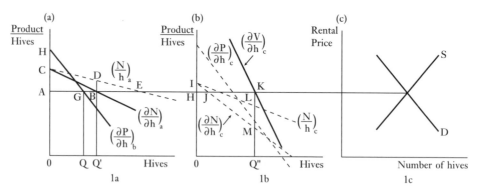

Figure 1

of a farm in which beehives are used *only* for the extraction of nectar (as with fireweed, mint, or alfalfa grown only for hay), with the farming assets held constant. Given the market-determined rental price of OA per hive, constrained wealth maximization implies that OQ' of hives will be employed. In this case, the beekeeper will be remunerated only in honey, and will pay an *apiary rent* equal to area ABC (or DB per hive) to the farmer. The curve $(\partial P/\partial h)_b$, on the other hand, depicts the value of the marginal pollination product for a farm which employes hives for pollination *only* (as with cherry or apple orchards). Here the number of hives employed will be OQ, which again is the result of wealth maximization. With zero honey yield, the money pollination fee per hive is again OA, and the *orchard rent* is represented by the area AGH.

We now turn to the joint product case in Figure 1b, where hives are used both for pollination and for the extraction of nectar (as in the setting of alfalfa and clover seeds). The curves $(\partial P/\partial h)_c$ and $(\partial N/\partial h)_c$ respectively are the values of marginal pollination and of marginal nectar products. Their *vertical* summation, the solid line $(\partial V/\partial h)_c$, is the total marginal value. Wealth maximization implies the employment of OQ'' of hives, the point where the rental price per hive equals the aggregate marginal value. As drawn, area HIJ is smaller than area JKM. This implies that the value of the *average* nectar product, $(N/h)_c$, must pass below point K, as it does here at L. In this case the rental price per hive, KQ'', will consist of LQ'' in honey yield and KL in pollination fee. For this joint product situation, of course, it is possible to construct a case in which $(N/h)_c$ passes above point K, thus yielding an apiary rent. It is also possible to construct cases where the number of hives employed yields zero or negative marginal productivity, in either nectar or pollination. In other words, *zero or negative marginal productivity in one component of the joint product is consistent with efficient allocation of resources.*

Under open competition, there are large numbers of potential participants in each of the cases above. The aggregate total marginal value curve for the market, or the market demand for hives, is therefore the horizontal summation of a large number of the *solid* curves in Figures 1a and 1b. Similarly, the market supply of hives is the horizontal summation of the marginal costs of producing and keeping hives of all actual and potential beekeepers. Both market curves are shown in Figure 1c.[16] Assuming no costs for collating bids and asks or for forming rental contracts among all actual and potential participants, the price per hive, OA, is determined in the market. The Pareto condition is satisfied: the value of the marginal product of a hive is the same on every farm, and in turn equals the rental price and the marginal opportunity cost of producing the hive.

2.2. Tests of implications

Before we derive and test some implications of the above analysis, it is necessary to point out the limitations of the information at hand. Since no attempt is made to estimate the marginal values or the elasticities of the marginal products, we will seek to confirm the marginal equalities with some observed average values. These include apiary rent, pollination fees, honey yields per hive, and the wholesale price of honey. We also have information on the number of hives employed on different farms, and some other numerical data. My choice of data for the honey yield per hive, however, must be qualified. The large fluctuations in yield from year to year and even from farm to farm caused by uncontrollable natural phenomena makes the use of the actual observed yields of a particular year, or even of a few years, irrelevant for our purposes. Take, for example, the exceptionally poor year of 1971 when, in many cases, the yield per hive was just one-third of that in a normal year. This windfall loss is irrelevant for decision making (although the expected variance is relevant), and it cannot be attributed to market "failure." Lacking sufficient data to compute the honey yield per hive extracted from various plants over time, I resort to the expected yields as reported by beekeepers. Fortunately, their estimates for yields under comparable conditions exhibit remarkable consistency.

An overall view of the pricing structure is shown in Table 2. Since a hive has different rental values for different seasons, we divide the time period into three productive seasons: early spring, late spring, and the honey season (summer to fall). Surplus honey is not expected in the early spring season, although nectar may accumulate in the brood chamber and there may be a gain in brood strength. Most beekeepers in the state are idle during this season, and pollination is confined to almond in California or cherry in the southern part of Washington. The rental value of hives is the highest in the major pollination season of late spring (April to June), second highest in the major honey season, and lowest in the early spring (March).

The pollination fees listed in Table 2 are based on 1971 data, but they have remained roughly constant from 1970 to 1972. The wholesale honey prices, however, are based on 1970 and early 1971 data, as the unexpectedly low honey yield throughout the country in 1971 generated a a sharp rise in prices (from 14 cents a pound in April 1971 to 32 cents a pound in March 1972). The apiary rents are paid mostly in refined and bottled honey, and

Table 2   Pricing Schemes and Expected Honey Yields of Bee-Related Plants (State of Washington, 1970–1971)

Seasons	Plants	Surplus honey expected (pounds per hive)	Honey prices per pound (wholesale, 1970)	Pollination fees (range, 1971)	Approximate apiary rent per hive (range, 1970–1)
Early spring	Almond (Calif.)	0	—	$5–$8	0
	Cherry	0	—	$6–$8	0
Late spring (major pollination season)	Apple & Soft Fruits	0	—	$9–10	0
	Blueberry (with maple)	40	14¢	$5	0
	Cabbage	15	13¢	$8	0
	Cherry	0	—	$9–$10	0
	Cranberry	5	13¢	$9	0
Summer and early fall (major honey season)	Alfalfa	60	14.5¢	0	13¢–60¢
	Alfalfa (with pollination)	25–35	14.5¢	$3–$5	0
	Fireweed	60	14.5¢	0	25¢–63¢
	Mint	70–75	11¢	0	15¢–65¢
	Pasture	60	14¢	0	15¢–65¢
	Red Clover	60	14¢	0	65¢
	Red Clover (with pollination)	0–35	14¢	$3–$6	0
	Sweet Clover	60	14¢	0	20¢–25¢

are therefore converted into money values according to 1970 retail honey prices. To maintain consistency with pollination fees, the apiary rents are computed per hive, although in the latter contracts the number of hives is not stipulated.

The following test implications are derived from our analysis:

(1) Our first implication is that, at the same season and with colonies of the same strength, the rental price per hive obtained from different farms or by different beekeepers will be roughly the same whether the hive is employed for pollination, for honey production, or for a combination of both. By "roughly the same" I do not mean that hive rentals are invariable among different beekeepers. Rather, I mean that

(a) any differences which do occur are statistically no more significant than those for most other commodities in the market, and that

(b) there is a strong *negative* correlation between the pollination fee (hive rental in money) and the expected honey yield (hive rental in kind).

Data from the early spring season are not suitable to test this implication because during this period there are great variations in colony strength, in the gains in brood and unextracted nectar, and in distances travelled by beekeepers to deliver the hives.[17] Lacking sufficient information to make appropriate adjustments for these variations in calculating the rental price per hive, we concentrate on data from the late spring and summer seasons.

In contracting for pollination services, beekeepers offer discounts for larger numbers of hives and for less elaborate hive dispersals. Of the four beekeepers from whom detailed records are available, for example, each served from 10 to 14 farms of apples and soft fruits; their mean hive rentals in the major pollination season ranged from $9.20 to $9.68 and their coefficients of variation from 0.025 to 0.053.[18] To reduce the effects on price generated by discounts, we use the mean rentals for the above four beekeepers and the reported means from beekeepers who did not maintain records. Our data thus comprise separate observations of the mean hive rental of each beekeeper, of each different plant, and (for the summer season) of each different expected honey yield for the same plant. The latter separation is requisite because the expectation of honey yield varies greatly depending on whether pollination is, or is not, required in the case of such plants as alfalfa.

The coefficient of variation of the mean hive rentals among beekeepers who engaged in the pollination of apples (including soft fruits) and cherries (9 observations in total) is 0.035. The expected honey yield for these observations is zero. When we extend the computation to include cranberry, blueberry and cabbage pollination (13 observations in total), with expected honey yields converted into monetary terms and added to the pollination fees, the coefficient of variation is 0.042. We may meaningfully compare our coefficients of variations with those cited by George Stigler (1961, p. 213): automobile prices (0.017) and anthracite coal prices (0.068).

Another, and more illuminating, way of testing our implication is through the relationship

$$x_0 = x_1 + x_2 \qquad\qquad (1)$$

where x_0 is the total rent per hive, x_1 is the rent paid in money, and x_2 is the expected rent paid in nectar. During the major pollination season, x_1 is positive for all our observations, but during the summer honey season negative values for x_1 (that is, payments in apiary rents) are common. As noted earlier, x_2 may also be positive or negative, but it is generally either zero or positive for the late spring and summer seasons. In the major pollination season, the mean values of equation (1) are

$9.65 = $9.02 + $0.64

The variance of x_0 can be broken down to

$$\sigma_{x_0}^2 = \sigma_{x_1}^2 + \sigma_{x_2}^2 + 2\,\text{Cov}(x_1, x_2) \tag{2}$$

With a total of 13 observations in late spring, the corresponding values are

$0.166 = 1.620 + 2.317 - 3.771$

The variability in x_1 is almost entirely accounted for by the variability in x_2, as reflected by the large negative covariance term. The coefficient of correlation between x_1 and x_2 is -0.973.

Turning to the summer honey season, we have a total of 23 observations, covering mint (3), fireweed (2), pasture (4), sweet clover (1), red clover (6), and alfalfa (7). The mean values of equation (1) are

$8.07 = $1.30 + $6.77

The values corresponding to equation (2) are

$0.806 = 5.414 + 6.182 - 10.791$

Again, most of the variability in x_1 is strongly and negatively correlated with that of x_2. The remaining variance for x_0 (with a coefficient of variation of 0.111) is larger here than in the major pollination season. This can be explained as follows. First, high risks are associated with the expected honey yields, and beekeepers seem willing to settle for lower, but more certain, incomes. Since x_1 is more certain than x_2 beekeepers seem willing to accept a lower x_0 with a higher ratio of x_1 to x_2,[19] and the variability in this ratio is larger in summer than in spring. Similarly, they will accept a lower expected mean of x_2 for mint than for other honey crops, since mint is generally known to have the smallest variance in expected honey yield of any crop in the state.[20] A second, and more important, factor contributing to the larger variance of x_0 is the premium paid to beekeepers to assume the risk of pollinating crops (notably red clover) where the use of pesticide sprays on neighboring farms poses the danger of loss of bees. Since our information is inadequate to support adjustments for these factors, the resultant distortions must remain. Even so, the coefficient of correlation between x_1 and x_2 computed from the data is -0.933.

(2) The preceding evidence confirms that the rental prices of hives employed in different uses by different beekeepers lie on a roughly horizontal line. However, it does not confirm that these prices are equated to the marginal productivities. Refer to Figure 1,

for example: the employment of hives might be at a point such as E rather than at G, B, or K. We now turn to some testable implications regarding the tendency toward the equalization of price and marginal productivity.

One obvious implication is that, if the employment of hives renders no valuable pollination services, then an apiary rent will always be observed. In the entire body of evidence available to me, there is not a single observation to the contrary,[21] and this means, referring to Figure 1a, that the employment of hives is to the left of point E. It should be noted here that even in the absence of demand for pollination some is effected when bees forage for nectar from alfalfa and the clovers, but this is not to be treated as a service unless the seeds are harvested.

Less obvious implications can be obtained from the case of a farm where hives may be employed for nectar extraction only *or* jointly with pollination services. When we discussed the reciprocal case, as depicted in Figure 1b, it was noted that either an apiary rent or a pollination fee may be paid. With simple manipulation, the following implications are evident:

(a) If an apiary rent is paid in the case of a joint product, and if the marginal pollination product is positive, the number of hives employed per acre is necessarily greater than where bees are used only for nectar extraction on the same or a similar farm.

(b) If a pollination fee is paid in the case of a joint product, the number of hives employed per acre is necessarily greater than where bees are used only for nectar extraction on the same or a similar farm.

While both implications indicate a tendency toward point K (in Figure 1b), we lack sufficient information regarding the marginal pollination product to test (a) above. But since in every available observation involving pollination and nectar extraction a pollination fee is paid, only implication (b) is relevant for our purposes.

The evidence, obtained from red clover and alfalfa farms, strongly confirms the implication. The density of hives employed is at least twice as great when the bees are used for both pollination service and nectar extraction as when used for nectar extraction only. As a rule, this increase in hive density leads to a sharp decrease in the expected honey yield per hive. In the typical case, the density of hives in alfalfa and clover farms for pollination services is about 2.5 times what would be employed for nectar extraction only, and the expected honey yield per hive is reduced by 50 per cent. This indicates the marginal nectar product of a hive is close to zero and possibly negative. In one extreme case, in a red clover farm the hive density with pollination services is reported at about seven or eight times that for nectar extraction only; since the expected honey yield is then reduced to zero, the marginal nectar product of the hive is clearly negative! But, as noted earlier, zero or negative marginal product in one component of a joint product is consistent with efficient allocation of resources.

(3) It remains for us to show that the rental price of a hive is roughly equal to the marginal cost of keeping it. Lacking data on marginal cost, we will show that the price approximates the average cost, as implied by competition. We will make the comparison in terms of some general considerations. The expected annual income of a spring colony under a normal rate of utilization, as of 1970–1971, is about $19.00. This includes rentals

from a pollination crop, a honey crop, an occasional extra crop (for some hives), and a small amount from the sale of beeswax.[22] The costs of delivering or moving a hive and of finding and contracting the farmers for its use are estimated to total about $9.00 per year.[23] This figure is obtained as follows. Some beekeepers lease some of their hives to other beekeepers on a share contract basis; the lessor receives 50 to 55 per cent of whatever income in money and in kind the lessee obtains from the farmers. Since the lessor could have contracted to serve the farmers himself and obtained the entire income of the $19.00, the fact that he has chosen to take 45 to 50 per cent less indicates that $9.00 must approximate such costs. The interest forgone in keeping a hive is about $3.00 per year.[24] The cost of renewing the colony strength in early spring is about $4.50, the price of a standard booster package of bees.[25] This leaves about $2.50 to cover the costs of depreciation of the hive value, the labor involved in checking and standardizing hives, space for keeping hives in the winter, and the equipment used for honey extraction.

2.3. Characteristics of the contractural arrangements

Contracts between beekeepers and farmers may be oral or written. I have at hand two types of written contracts. One is formally printed by an association of beekeepers; another is designed for specific beekeepers, with a few printed headings and space for stipulations to be filled in by hand.[26] Aside from situations where a third party demands documented proof of the contract (as when a beekeeper seeks a business loan), written contracts are used primarily for the initial arrangement between parties; otherwise oral agreements are made. Although a written contract is more easily enforceable in a court of law, extra-legal constraints are present: information travels quickly through the closely knit society of beekeepers and farmers,[27] and the market will penalize any party who does not honor his contracts. Oral contracts are rarely broken.

Pollination contracts usually include stipulations regarding the number and strength of the colonies, the rental fee per hive, the time of delivery and removal of hives, the protection of bees from pesticide sprays, and the strategic placing of hives. Apiary lease contracts differ from pollination contracts in two essential aspects. One is, predictably, that the amount of apiary rent seldom depends on the number of colonies, since the farmer is interested only in obtaining the rent per apiary offered by the highest bidder. Second, the amount of apiary rent is not necessarily fixed. Paid mostly in honey, it may vary according to either the current honey yield or the honey yield of the preceding year.[28]

In general, contractual arrangements between beekeepers and farmers do not materially differ from other lease contracts. However, some peculiar arrangements resulting from certain complications are worth noting. First, because of the foraging behavior of the bees a farmer who hires bees may benefit his neighbors. Second, the use of pesticide sprays by one farmer may cause damage to the bees on an adjacent farm. And third, fireweed, which yields good honey, grows wild in forests. Let us discuss each in turn.

THE CUSTOM OF THE ORCHARDS   As noted earlier, if a number of similar orchards are located close to one another, one who hires bees to pollinate his own orchard will in some degree benefit his neighbors. Of course, the strategic placing of the hives will reduce the spillover of bees. But in the absence of any social constraint on behavior, each farmer will tend to take advantage of what spillover does occur and to employ fewer hives himself. Of course, contractual arrangements could be made among all farmers in an area to determine collectively the number of hives to be employed by each, but no such effort is observed.

Acknowledging the complication, beekeepers and farmers are quick to point out that a social rule, or custom of the orchards, takes the place of explicit contracting: during the pollination period the owner of an orchard either keeps bees himself or hires as many hives per area as are employed in neighboring orchards of the same type. One failing to comply would be rated as a "bad neighbor," it is said, and could expect a number of inconveniences imposed on him by other orchard owners.[29] This customary matching of hive densities involves the exchange of gifts of the same kind, which apparently entails lower transaction costs than would be incurred under explicit contracting, where farmers would have to negotiate and make money payments to one another for the bee spillover.[30]

THE CASE OF PESTICIDE SPRAYS   At the outset, we must remember that to minimize the loss of bees from insecticide usage is not necessarily consistent with efficient allocation of resources. The relevant consideration is whether the gain from using the pesticide is greater than the associated loss of bees, in total and at the margin. Provided that the costs of forming contracts permits, beekeepers and farmers will seek cooperative arrangements such that the expected marginal gain from using the pesticide is equal to the value of the expected marginal bee loss. In the absence of the arrangements, however, the total gain from using the pesticide may still be greater than the associated loss; the greater the expected damage done to bees, the greater will be the gain from the cooperative arrangements.[31]

When a pollination contract is formed, the farmer usually agrees to inform the beekeeper before spraying his crop, but this assurance will not protect the bees from pesticide used on neighboring farms. In areas dominated by orchards which require pollination at roughly the same time, such as the apple-growing disticts, this agreement will suffice, for no farmer will apply the spray during the pollination period. But in regions where adjacent farms require bee pollination at different times, or do not require it at all, a farmer with no present obligation to any beekeeper may spray his fields and inflict damages to the bees rented by other farms. In this situation, only cooperation over a large geographic area can avoid bee loss, and we find just such arrangements in the pollination of cranberries but not of red clover.

Cranberry farms near Seattle are usually found in clusters, and spraying is conducted shortly after the bloom, which may vary by as much as a week or two among neighboring farms. Although each cranberry grower agrees not to spray until the contracted beekeeper removes the bees from his farm, this does not protect bees which may still remain on adjacent farms. Therefore the beekeepers make a further arrangement among themselves to remove all hives on the same date, thus insuring that all the bees are protected.

Red clover presents a different situation. Since the plant is often grown in areas where neighboring farms require no bee pollination, the pesticide danger is reportedly high and beekeepers demand an additional $1.00 to $2.00 per hive to assume the risk. But just as the beekeepers cooperate with one another during cranberry pollination, a clover farmer could make arrangements with his neighbors. Given that neighboring farmers have the legal right to use pesticide, the clover farmer would be willing to pay them an amount not exceeding the beekeeper's risk premium if they would refrain from spraying during the pollination period. Although no such arrangements are observed, it would seem that the costs of reaching an agreement would be no higher than those encountered in the case of the cranberries, and we must infer, pending empirical confirmation, that the gain from using the sprays is greater than the associated loss. This would particularly apply when a single farm requiring pollination is located amidst a large number of farms which require spraying during that same period.

THE CASE OF FIREWOOD   I have at hand two types of apiary contract pertaining to fireweed, a honey plant which grows wild in the forest. The first is between a beekeeper and the Weyerhaeuser Company, owner of private timber land; the second is between a beekeeper and the Water Department of the City of Seattle. Two distinctions between them are worth noting. First, while both contracts stipulate 25 cents per hive, Weyerhaeuser asks a minimum charge of $100, and the Water Department a minimum of $25. In the apiary for fireweed honey, the number of hives used by a beekeeper is more than 100 but less than 400. Thus it happens that in the case of Weyerhauser, the apiary rent is independent of the number of hives, whereas with the Water Department it is dependent. The "underpriced" rent levied by the Water Department would have implied some sort of queuing except that a second unique feature is incorporated in its apiary contracts: no beekeeper is granted the exclusive right to the fireweed nectar in a particular area. The implication is that competition among beekeepers will reduce the honey yield per hive until its apiary rent is no more than 25 cents; while no beekeeper attempts to exclude entrants, the parties do seek a mutual division of the total area to avoid chaotic hive placement. Finally, fireweed also grows wild in the national forests and for this case I have no contract at hand. My information is that apiary rent is measured by the hive, is subject to competitive bidding among beekeepers, and has a reported range of 25 to 63 cents with the winner being granted exclusive right to a particular area.

3. Conclusions

Whether or not Keynes was correct in his claim that policy makers are "distilling their frenzy" from economists, it appears evident that some economists have been distilling their policy implications from fables. In a desire to promote government intervention, they have been prone to advance without the support of careful investigation, the notion of "market failure." Some have dismissed in cavalier fashion the possibility of market operations in matters of environmental degradation, as witnesses the assertion of E. J. Mishan:

> With respect to bodies of land and water, extension of property rights may effectively internalize what would otherwise remain externalities. But the possibilities of protecting the citizen against such common environmental blights as filth, fume, stench, noise, visual distractions, etc. by a market in property right are too remote to be taken seriously.[32]

Similarly, it has been assumed that private property rights cannot be enforced in the case of fisheries, wildlife, and whatever other resources economists have chosen to call "natural." Land tenure contracts are routinely taken as inefficient, and to some the market will fail in the areas of education, medical care, and the like.
   Then, of course, there is the fable of the bees.

In each case, it is true that costs involved in enforcement of property rights and in the formation of contracts will cause the market to function differently than it would without such costs. And few will deny that government does afford economic advantages. But it is equally true that any government action can be justified on efficiency grounds by the simple expedient of hypothesizing high enough transaction costs in the marketplace and low enough costs for government control. Thus to assume the state of the world to be as one sees fit is not even to compare the ideal with the actual but, rather, to compare the ideal with a fable.

I have no grounds for criticizing Meade and other economists who follow the Pigovian tradition for their use of the bee example to illustrate a theoretical point: certainly, resource allocation would in general differ from what is observed if the factors were "unpaid." My main criticism, rather, concerns their approach to economic inquiry in failing to investigate the real-world situation and in arriving at policy implications out of sheer imagination. As a result, their work contributes little to our understanding of the actual economic system.

Notes

1 Pigou had offered other examples. The example of two roads was deleted from later editions of *The Economics of Welfare*, presumably in an attempt to avoid the criticism by F. H. Knight (1924). The railroad example has not enjoyed popularity. Most of Pigou's examples, however, were drawn from land tenure arrangements in agriculture, but an exhaustive check of his source references has revealed no hard evidence at all to support his claim of in efficient tenure arrangements.

2 The presence of apple honey in the market is therefore somewhat mysterious. While occasionally apple orchards in the Northwest do yield negligible amounts of nectar, beekeepers are frank to point out that the dandelion and other wild plants in the orchard are often the sources of "apple" honey, so called. Elsewhere, as in New York, it was reported that apple orchards yielded slightly more nectar. See, for example, Root (1923). The explanation for this divergence of facts, to my mind, lies in the different lengths of time in which the hives are placed in the apple orchards: in Root's day the hives were probably left in the orchards for longer periods than today.

3 See Bohart (1971). Leafcutters, for example, have recently been introduced for the pollination of alfalfa and clover seeds. But these bees yield no honey crop and are seldom kept.

4 For further details see Riedel (1971, pp. 8–9); Root and Root (1923, pp. 440–58); Carl Johansen (1970).

5 For further details see Johansen (1970); Moeller (1971) Oertel (1971).

6 According to a survey conducted by Robert K. Lesser in 1968, based on a sample of 30 out of 60 commercial beekeepers in the state of Washington, the total number of peak colonies is 14.6% higher than that of spring colonies. See Lesser (1969).

7 See, for example, Root and Root (1923, pp. 97–103); Keyarts (1960); U.S. Dep't of Agriculture, (1972); Johansen (1971); Torchio (1971).

8 See Oertel (1971); Ribbands (1953); Morse (1960). Owing to its weather, Washington is not one of the better honey yielding states in the Union. Data made available to me by the U.S. Dep't of Agriculture indicates that over the years (1955–1971) Washington ranks 24th among 48 states in yield per colony and 20th in the total number of colonies. The U.S. Dep't of Agriculture data, like those obtained by Lesser, provide no information on the different honey yields and pollination requirements of various plants and are therefore of little use for our present purpose. It should be noted that the U.S. Dep't of Agriculture overall yield data are significantly lower than those obtained by Lesser and by me. See Lesser (1969).

9   Levin (1971) Oldershaw (1970); Bohart (1960); Free (1960); U.S. Dep't of Agriculture (1968); Wash. St. University (1968, 1970a, 1971a, 1971b).

10 There is, however, little agreement as to how far a bee could fly: estimated range is from one to three miles. For general foraging behavior, see Levin (1971, p. 79); Park (1946); Ribbands (1953).

11 Following the practice of local beekeepers, we use the term "soft fruit" to refer to peaches, pears, and apricots, generally grown in the same area, and often in the same orchard, as apples. (By standard usage, the term refers only to the various berry plants.)

12 See note 9.

13 From 1970 to 1972 the supported prices were near 11.5 cents per pound, whereas the market wholesale price was above 14 cents per pound. Between 1950 and 1965 were seven years in which the CCC purchased no honey, and two years of negligible amounts. See Sullivan (1971, p. 137).

14 See 7 U.S.C. § 135 b, note (1970); Pub. L. No. 91–524 § 804. My judgment is based both on the behavior of beekeepers (see next section) after the initiation of the Act and on the complexity of relevant claim forms which I have at hand. In April 1972 beekeepers associations were still lobbying for easier claiming conditions.

15 In Meade (1952, p. 58), this problem is set up in terms of the interdependent functions $x_1 = H_1(l_1, c_1, x_2)$ and $x_2 = H_2(l_2, c_2, x_1)$. I find Meade's analysis difficult to follow. Elsewhere, Davis and Whinston (1962, p. 241) employ the functions $C_1 = C_1(q_1, q_2)$ and $C_2 = C_2(q_1, q_2)$ in their treatment of certain "externalities." It is not clear, however, that the authors had the bee example in mind.

16 More variables are usually used in the derivation of these curves, but for our present purpose little is gained by incorporating them.

17 In the pollination of almond, for example, $5.00 is charged for a one-story hive and $6.00 to $8.00 for a two-story hive. On the one hand, Washington beekeepers have to travel to California to obtain this amount when they could have earned the same fee locally in the pollination of early cherry. On the other hand, however, the brood gain is greater with almond than with cherry; also, unextracted nectar in the brood chamber gains significantly in the case of almond but is likely to suffer a net loss with early cherry.

18 An analysis of variance performed for these four beekeepers shows no significant difference in their mean rentals in the pollination of apple and soft fruits. However, the coefficient of variation of their means, 0.018, is lower than those computed from a larger body of data. This simply indicates a very low variation among the four who provided detailed records.

19 This statement is drawn only from casual conversations with beekeepers; no attempt was made to seek refuting evidence.

20 Inconclusive evidence indicates that hive rentals (paid in honey) obtained from mint is about 40 cents less than those obtained from other honey-yielding plants. Although available information is insufficient for us to compute the year-to-year variances of the honey yields of different plants, ranges of yields as recalled by beekeepers are larger than most agricultural crops.
    Because honey from mint has an undesirably strong flavor that excludes it from the retail market, it is either sold to bakeries or used to feed bees during the winter. Quite under-standably, onion honey shares the distinction of being much cheaper than any other. Generally rated as the best is orange honey, which commands a wholesale premium of about 1 to 2 cents a pound. Between the extremes, different varieties of honey have roughly the same value and are graded more by clarity than by taste.

21 One beekeeper specializing in cut-comb honey reported that he pays apiary rents even though no surplus honey is expected, provided that gains in brood strength and in unextracted nectar are expected to be substantial, as when the hives are placed in a farm with maples. This beekeeper is excluded from our first test of implication because he did not engage in pollination

and his colonies were of greater strengths. Cut-comb honey is more expensive than ordinary honey because the comb wax, which goes with the honey, is about three times the price of honey per pound. Only honey of top grades (very clear) will be extracted. This observation is implied by the law of demand, since with the comb top-grade honey becomes relatively cheap. Implied by the same law also is that this beekeeper chooses to forgo pollination contracts so that a higher honey yield can be obtained (see evidence in implication test 2). Even during the major pollination season, when little honey can be expected, he prefers to place his hives in farms where the colonies will gain greater strength than would occur if they were used for pollination. For a related discussion on similar implications of the law of demand, see Alchian and Allen (1969, pp. 78–9). These implications are accepted here in spite of the criticisms in Gould and Segall (1969).

22   In Lesser's (1969) investigation the actual mean annual income of a spring colony for the year 1967 was estimated to be $14.71, and the actual honey yields of that year were slightly larger than our expected honey yields. But in 1967 the price of honey was about 16% lower than that in 1970; and Lesser's estimate of pollination income per hive is about 37% lower than mine, owing both to a rise in pollination fees in recent years and to different samplings of beekeepers. According to Lesser's estimate, beeswax constitutes 4.4% of the beekeeper's total income.

23   The moving costs cover labor, truck, and other hive-handling equipment. Depending on the time of the year, a complete hive (with supers) weighs somewhere between 80 and 250 pounds.

24   A complete hive, used but in good condition, sells for about $35.00. The borrowing rate of interest for the beekeepers is around 8%.

25   The nectar left unextracted in the brood chamber, which constitutes the major cost of over-wintering, is not counted as part of income and therefore is not counted as part of the cost.

26   Some beekeepers use just postal cards. The general contractual details reported below are similar to those briefly mentioned in Morse 1970).

27   During my conversations with beekeepers, I was impressed by their personal knowledge of one another, including details such as the number of hives owned, the kinds of farms served, and the rents received.

28   While we may attribute this behavior to the aversion of risks, the apiary contracts are not the same as share contracts. Rather, they resemble fixed-rent contracts with what I have called "escape clauses." For discussion of the "escape clause" and the stipulations of the share contract, see Cheung 1969, ch. 2 & 4). One impression I obtain is that apiary rents generally involve such low values in Washington that elaborate formations and enforcements of apiary contracts are not worthwhile. In further investigations of these contracts, states with higher honey yields are recommended.

29   The distinction between an oral or an implicit contract and a custom is not always clear. A common practice in some areas is that each farmer lets his neighbors know how many hives he employs. Perhaps the absence of a court of law to enforce what could in fact be a highly informal agreement is the reason why farmers deny the existence of any contract among them governing the employment of hives.

30   Since with a sufficiently high reward the notoriety of being a "bad neighbor" will be tolerated, the likelihood of explicit contracting rises with increasing rental values of hives. Alternatively and concurrently, with a high enough rental price of hives the average size of orchards may increase through outright purchases, or the shapes of the orchards may be so tailored as to match the foraging behavior of the bees. By definition, given the gains the least costly arrangement will be chosen.

Some beekeepers reported that there are peculiar situations where the foraging behavior of the bees forces a one-way gift, but these situations are not covered by the present investigation. Even under these rare situations, the absence of both contractual and customary restraints may not result in a different allocation of resources. See Cheung (nd).

31 For a fuller discussion, see Cheung (nd).
32 Mishan (1972) As immediate refutation of Professor Mishan's claim, I refer the reader to a factual example: Professor John McGee has just purchased a house, separated from that of his neighbor by a vacant lot. That the space would remain vacant had been assured by the previous owner who (upon learning that a third party was planning to buy the lot and construct a house there) had negotiated with the neighbor to make a joint purchase of the ground, thus protecting their two households from the "filth, fumes, stench, noise, visual distractions, etc." which would be generated by a new neighbor.

References

Alchian, A. A. and Allen, W. R. (1969): *Exchange and Production: Theory in Use*. Belmont, Ca.: Wadsworth.

Bator, F. M. (1958): "The Anatomy of Market Failure," *Quarterly Journal of Economics*, 72, 351–79.

Bohart, G. E. (1960): "Insect Pollination of Forage Legumes," *Bee World*, 41, 57–64 and 85–97.

—— (1971): "Management of Wild Bees," in Agricultural Research Service's *Beekeeping in the United States*, Agricultural Handbook no. 335, Washington, DC: U.S. Department of Agriculture, 109.

Cheung, S. N. S. (1969): *The Theory of Share Tenancy*. Chicago: University of Chicago Press.

Cheung, —— (nd): *The Theory of Inter-individual Effects and the Demand for Contracts*. University of Washington, Institute of Economic Research.

Davis, O. A. and Whinston, A. (1962): "Externalities, Welfare, and the Theory of Games," *Journal of Political Economy*, 70, 241.

Free, J. B. (1960): "Pollination of Fruit Trees," *Bee World*, 41, 141–51 and 169–86.

Gould, J. P. and Segall, J. (1969): "The Substitution Effects of Transportation Costs," *Journal of Political Economy*, 77, 130.

Johansen, C. (1970): *Beekeeping*, PNW Bulletin 79, revised edn, March.

—— (1971): *How to Reduce Poisoning of Bees from Pesticides*. Pamphlet EM 3473, May. Washington State University, College of Agriculture.

Keyarts, E. (1960): "Bee Hunting," *Gleanings in Bee Culture*, June, 329–33.

Knight, F. H. (1924): "Some Fallacies in the Interpretation of Social Cost," *Quarterly Journal of Economics*, 38, 582.

Lesser, R. K. (1969): "An Investigation of the Elements of Income from Beekeeping in the State of Washington", unpublished thesis, School of Business Administration, Gonzaga University, 74.

Levin, M. D. (1970): *The Indispensable Pollinators*. 9th Pollination Conference, October 12–15, report. Hot Springs, Ark.: Agricultural Extension Service.

—— (1971): "Pollination," in Agricultural Research Service's *Beekeeping in the United States*, Agriculture. Handbook no. 335, Washington, DC: U.S. Department of Agriculture, 77.

Meade, J. E. (1952): "External Economies and Diseconomies in a Competitive Situation," *Economic Journal*, 52.

Mishan, E. J. (1972): "A Reply to Professor Worcester," *Journal of Economic Literature*, 10 (1), 59–62.

Moeller, F. E. (1971): "Managing Colonies for High Honey Yields," in Agricultural Research Service's *Beekeeping in the United States*, Agricultural Handbook no. 335, Washington, DC: U.S. Department of Agriculture, 23.

Morse, G. D. (1970): "How about Pollination," *Gleanings in Bee Culture*, February, 73–8.

Morse, R. A. (1960): "Placing Bees in Apple Orchards," *Gleanings in Bee Culture*, April, 230–3.

Nye, W. P. (1971): "Beekeeping Regions in the United States," in Agricultural Research Service's, *Beekeeping in the United States*, Agricultural Handbook no. 335, Washington, DC: U.S. Department of Agriculture, 17.

Oertel, E. (1971): "Nectar and Pollen Plants," in Agricultural Research Service's *Beekeeping in the United States*, Agricultural Handbook no. 335, Washington, DC: U.S. Department of Agriculture, 10.

Oldershaw, D. (1970): *The Pollination of High Bush Blueberries. The Indispensable Pollinators.* 9th Pollination Conference, October 12–15, report. Hot Springs, Ark.: Agricultural Extension Service.

Park, O. W. (1946): "Activities of Honeybees," in R. A. Grout (ed.), *The Hive and the Honeybee*, 125, Hamilton, Ill.: Dadant, 149–206.

Pigou, A. C. (1912): *Wealth and Welfare*. London: Macmillan.

——(1920): *The Economics of Welfare*. London: Macmillan.

Ribbands, C. R. (1953): *The Behaviour and Social Life of Honeybees*. London: Bee Research Association, 69–75.

Riedel, S. M., Jr. (1971): "Development of American Beehive," in Agricultural Research Service's *Beekeeping in the United States*, Agricultural Handbook no. 335, Washington, D.C: U.S. Department of Agriculture.

Root, A. I. and Root, E. R. (1923): *The ABC and XYZ of Bee Culture 386*. Medina, Ohio: A. I. Root Co.

Stigler, G. J. (1961): "The Economics of Information," *Journal of Political Economy*, 69, 213.

Sullivan, H. A. (1971): "Honey Price Support Program," in Agricultural Research Service's *Beekeeping in the United States*, Agricultural Handbook no. 335, Washington, DC: U.S. Department of Agriculture.

Torchio, P. F. (1971): "Pesticides," in Agricultural Research Service's *Beekeeping in the United States*, 97. (Agricultural Handbook no. 335). Washington, DC: U.S. Department of Agriculture.

U.S. Department of Agriculture (1968): *Using Honey Bees to Pollinate Crops*. Leaflet 549.

U.S. Department of Agriculture (1972): *Protecting Honey Bees from Pesticides*. Leaflet 544.

Washington State University (1968): *Get More Fruit with Honey Bee Pollinators*. Pamphlet EM 2922, March.

Washington State University (1970): *Protect Berry Pollinating Bees*. Pamphlet EM 3341, February.

——(1971a): *Honey Bees Increase Cranberry Production*. Pamphlet EM 3468, April.

——(1971b): *Increase Clover Seed Yields with Adequate Pollination*. Pamphlet EM 3444, April.

Dynamics of the Market Mechanism

CHAPTER TWENTY

Why, Indeed, in America? Theory, History, and the Origins of Modern Economic Growth

Paul M. Romer

Source: *American Economic Review, Papers and Proceedings*, 86 (1996), pp. 202–6. Reprinted with the permission of the author and the American Economic Association. © American Economic Association.

Whether new growth theory and economic history are a good match depends on the kind of question one addresses and the kind of answer one expects. I find that they complement each other when I try to answer questions about the world. Economists who believe that these lines of inquiry can go their separate ways are addressing entirely different kinds of questions or have a different notion of what it means to give a good answer.

1. Growth Without History

Many recent attempts at testing models of growth proceed without making any reference to evidence from economic history. They rely on data series for many countries, typically for the last 30 or so years. They focus on questions about models instead of questions about the world. A representative conclusion is that the right model of economic growth is neoclassical in an extreme sense: it assumes that technology is the same in all countries and concludes that exogenous differences in saving and education cause all of the observed differences in levels of income and rates of growth (N. Gregory Mankiw, 1995).

However, to take a specific case, differences in saving and education do not explain why growth was so much faster in the United States than it was in Britain around the turn of this century. In 1870, per capita income in the United States was 75 percent of per capita income in Britain. By 1929, it had increased to 130 percent. In the intervening decades, years of education per worker increased by a factor of 2.2 in Britain and by a nearly identical factor of 2.3 in the United States. In 1929, this variable remained slightly lower in the United States. (Data are taken from Angus Maddison [1995].)[1]

In addition, differences in rates of investment in the two countries were not the result of exogenous differences in savings rates. The remarkable fact about the British economy during this period is how much of domestic savings was devoted to investment abroad. In the decade prior to 1913, net domestic investment was roughly equal to net foreign investment (A. K. Cairncross, 1953 p. 121). By 1914, net foreign assets were equal to 1.5 times GDP. To understand what happened in Britain, one must explain why investment abroad, especially in the United States, was so attractive to British savers.

It is difficult to look at the data for these two countries without wondering whether the well-documented technological developments in the United States are not part of the story. Nevertheless, the standard model-testing exercise does not even consider this possibility. Nor does it seek out any direct evidence that would help one decide how important any differences in the technology might have been. This would be a glaring flaw if the goal truly were to understand events in the world, but it is as natural as a null hypothesis if all one wants to do is test models.

2. History Without Theory

A second approach recognizes the value of economic history but denies the need for formal theory. It shows up each time someone proposes a new piece of mathematical formalism. Only 30 years ago many economists still objected to a mathematical statement of the relationship between output and capital in terms of an aggregate production function and an aggregate stock of capital, $Y = F(K, L)$. Twenty years ago, a different group of economists objected when labor economists used mathematical equations and a new human-capital variable H to capture the observation that a person's skills could be enhanced by investing in education or experience. Ten years ago, many economists readily acknowledged that output of knowledge must somehow be related to the inputs devoted to the production of knowledge, but they objected nevertheless when growth theorists suggested that economists make another try at capturing these relationships using mathematical expressions of the form $\mathrm{d}A/\mathrm{d}t = G(H, A)$.

Every time a familiar argument is translated for the first time from natural language into mathematics, the same objections arise. "These equations are so simplistic, and the world is so complicated." This reflects a misapprehension of the role of formal theory. Set aside models. The key is to understand what it means to answer a question about the world. In the lead-up to his exposition of evolutionary theory, Richard Dawkins (1986 p. 11) gives a refreshingly straightforward description of what constitutes a good answer to a such a question:

> If I ask an engineer how a steam engine works, I have a pretty fair idea of the general kind of answer that would satisfy me. Like Julian Huxley, I should definitely not be impressed if the engineer said that it was propelled by "*force locomotif.*" And if he started boring on about the whole being greater than the sum of its parts, I would interrupt him: "Never mind about that, tell me how it *works*." What I would want to hear is something about how the parts of an engine interact with each other to produce the behavior of the whole engine. I would initially be prepared to accept an explanation in terms of quite large subcomponents, whose own internal structure and behavior might be quite complicated and, as yet, unexplained. The units of an initially satisfying explanation could have names like fire-box, boiler, cylinder, piston, steam governor.... *Given* that the units each do their particular thing, I can then understand how they interact to make the whole engine move.

Of course I am then at liberty to ask how each part works. Having previously accepted the *fact* that the steam governor regulates the flow of steam, and having used this fact in my understanding of the behavior of the whole engine, I now turn my curiosity on the steam governor itself.

The central element in this account of what Dawkins calls *hierarchical reductionism* is a recognition that explanation operates on many levels that must be consistent with each other. What theories do is take all the available complicated information about the world and organize it into this kind of hierarchical structure.

In building this structure, good theory indicates how to carve a system at the joints. At each level, theory breaks a system down into a simple collection of subsystems that interact in a meaningful way. Dawkins could have used a simple theory that makes a bad split of the engine into its front and back halves. Instead, he uses a simple theory that makes a good split into the fire-box, the boiler, and so on. What growth theory must do is provide a good, simple split of the opportunities available in the physical world.

3. Neoclassical versus New Growth Theory

Neoclassical growth theory explains growth in terms of interactions between two basic types of factors: technology and conventional inputs. At the next level, conventional inputs are subdivided into physical capital, labor, and human capital. The initial split into technology and conventional inputs is promising, because technology does differ from all other inputs. However, for technical reasons, neoclassical theory mapped this split onto the theoretical dichotomy between public and private goods. This means that the theory leads to a dead end when one tries to understand the details about technology in a second-stage analysis analogous to Dawkins's investigation of the steam governor. Technology in the model does not correspond to anything in the world. It is possible to understand capital in terms of things like machine tools that can be observed, but for a description of technology, neoclassical theory only relates to things that live in models – shifting production possibility frontiers and the like.

The obvious real-world candidates for technology simply are not public goods. For example, a promising line of work in the 1960s studied embodied technological change. Implicitly, it modeled technology as designs for machines. This line of work lost its momentum, perhaps because of the difficulty people had in reconciling what is known about machine design with an initial cut that makes technology a public good. In their evolutionary alternative to neoclassical growth theory, Richard Nelson and Sidney Winter (1982) rejected the public-good assumption and represented technology as routines followed within firms. Recent generations of neoclassical growth theorists have not followed up on either approach and have contented themselves with a *force locomotif* explanation: "Technological change causes economic growth."

New growth theory started on the technology-as-public-good path and worried about where technology came from, but it soon backed up and reconsidered the initial split that economists make in the physical world. New growth theorists now start by dividing the world into two fundamentally different types of productive inputs that can be called "ideas" and "things." Ideas are nonrival goods that could be stored in a bit string. Things are rival goods with mass (or energy). With ideas and things, one can explain how economic growth works. Nonrival ideas can be used to rearrange things, for example, when one follows a recipe and transforms noxious olives into tasty and healthful olive oil. Economic growth arises from the discovery of new recipes and the transformation of things from low to high value configurations.

This slightly different initial cut leads to insights that do not follow from the neoclassical model. It emphasizes that ideas are goods that are produced and distributed just as other goods are. It removes the dead end in neoclassical theory and links microeconomic observations on routines, machine designs, and the like with macroeconomic discussions of technology.

In an analysis of American and British growth, the insight that is most relevant concerns scale. By definition, a nonrival idea can be copied and communicated, so its value increases in proportion to the size of the market in which it can be used. For example, if barriers to trade meant that a computer operating system written in the state of Washington could only be used within that state, it would be worth far less than if it could be used all over the world. If there were only a few olive trees, no one would have bothered to figure out how to use the olives. If people can sometimes establish property rights over a nonrival good like an operating system or a recipe (a possibility precluded by the public-good approach) differences in scale will change the rewards for producing new ideas.

4. Why in America?

A great deal of historical analysis has addressed the performance of the British and American economies around the turn of the century. For general discussions, see Nathan Rosenberg (1981), Nelson and Gavin Wright (1992), and Moses Abramovitz and Paul David (1996). From the beginning, observers have pointed to the abundance of natural resources in the United States as an early advantage, especially in agriculture. The surprising conclusion that emerges from recent historical scholarship is that resource abundance also interacted with scale to create a technological lead in manufacturing that persisted well into the 20th century.

The United States started as little more than an importer of European technology, but by the first decades of the 19th century, distinctively American technologies began to emerge. Entrepreneurs and inventors developed specialized machines that economized on human effort and made prolific use of the natural resources and energy that were available (Rosenberg, 1981). Other nations in the new world also faced low prices for natural resources relative to labor. For example, Maddison's (1995) data suggest that Australia had the highest level of GDP per capita from 1870 to 1900 because its stock of resources was so large relative to its population. What made the United States unique was the combination of resource abundance and large markets (Abramovitz and David, 1996). In 1820, the population was 534,000 in Argentina, 33,000 in Australia, and 9.6 million in the United States. Moreover, even at this early date, the United States had a transportation system and a commercial infrastructure that effectively linked most of its citizens into a truly national market. By 1870, the population had grown to 1.8 million in Argentina, 1.6 million in Australia, and 40 million in the United States, a third more than lived in the United Kingdom at that time.

As Rosenberg (1963, 1981) has observed, large markets – which were also populated here by relatively homogeneous consumers – mattered, because they encouraged firms to incur the design and setup costs necessary for long production runs of standardized goods assembled from interchangeable parts. As he emphasizes, they also mattered because they induced large markets for specialized machines. The differences in incentives created by market size were presumably of great consequence when populations differed by a factor of 10 or 20 and flows of goods between nations were still relatively limited. More direct evidence that market size and incentives did matter for invention can be inferred from Kenneth Sokoloff's (1988) evidence on the geographic distribution of patent awards in the United States. His data show that inventive activity was concentrated around locations that had access to cheap transportation, and that it expanded into new areas when the transportation system improved.

Resource abundance and scale effects were therefore key elements in the development of production using specialized machinery, standardized goods, and interchangeable parts. By the middle of the 19th century, when the British first started to take notice, this system was used in only a few industries, gun- making most famously. Other important industries in the United States, such as iron-making, still lagged behind their British counterparts. It took another half century or more for per capita output in the United States to move ahead of Britain's. Scale effects continued to be crucial in this later period as well.

In the beginning, machinery was made in machine shops that were part of large manufacturing enterprises like textile mills. When markets grew, these shops eventually separated from their parent firms and began to operate as suppliers to many firms. However, the growth in potential markets came not just through growth in the industry of the parent firm. Most of it came from growth in other industries because of what Rosenberg (1963) has identified as a process of technological convergence which created an additional scale effect distinct from the one associated with population size. Firms engaged in the production of many different kinds of goods (including machine tools themselves) all used the same kinds of machinery to shape first wood, then metal. Thus, the former machine shop of the textile mill sold not just to other textile firms, but to all manner of manufacturing enterprises. As a result, the proliferation of specialized machine tools was limited only by the extent of what came to be a very large market.

Thus, scale acted through larger markets for both final goods and capital goods. Scale in this sense was determined by a large population, an integrated market, and technological convergence. A large quantity of natural resources was important initially because it changed the price of materials relative to labor, thus encouraging the use of machinery. Over time, abundant quantities of *potential* natural resources created an additional scale effect relating to the supply of *things* that could be transformed by any particular new *idea*. This effect was most obvious in the development of uses for by- products (Rosenberg, 1985). For example, the quantity of animal waste grew with the expansion of the meat-packing industry. Its geographic concentration also increased as refrigeration and the railroad made it possible for meat-packing to be separated from the site of final consumption. This increase in the volume of animal by-products and its concentration created incentives for firms to come up with new nonrival goods – literally, in this case, new recipes – for making use of raw materials that had previously been discarded as waste. This process ultimately led to the development of a by-products industry that was one of the early users of industrial chemistry.

The same motivation led to the investments that were needed to take advantage of other natural resources. Because of the quantities of resources that were available and the large markets for goods, large investments in basic technologies for extracting and processing these resources could be sustained. This enabled the United States to become the world's leading supplier of virtually every industrial raw material, a fact that is reflected in high and increasing intensity of resources in U.S. exports from 1880 to 1930 (Wright, 1990). With the exceptions of wood and land, the United States achieved leadership in most raw materials because of its intensive use of its endowment, not because of the endowment itself (Wright, 1990). Because of the "congruence" (in the terminology adopted by Abramovitz and David [1996]) between the U.S. strength in intensive resource use and its early strength in manufacturing technologies, it developed a technological lead over the rest of the world that expanded throughout the first half of this century (Nelson and Wright, 1992).

5. Conclusion

Scale effects are clearly not the only interesting factor in this story. For example, new institutions like the United States Geological Survey, the private university, the large multidivisional firm, and the specialized research laboratory were important as well. Concerning the scale effects themselves, the arguments presented here will not tell historians anything they did not already know. The relatively modest contribution that new growth theory can make is to move the issue of scale up in the conceptual hierarchy. Scale effects should no longer be treated in the manner of a growth accountant like Edward Dennison, (i.e., as a kind of afterthought that had something to do with plant size). They should be treated in the manner of Adam Smith: as a fundamental aspect of our economic world that follows from the nonrival character of ideas.

If new growth theorists have their way, the first distinction economists will draw when looking at the physical world will be the one that separates rival things from nonrival ideas. Right from the start, this should be the way the physical world is carved up into a small number of interacting elements analogous to pistons and boilers. When the resulting theoretical framework is combined with the evidence and inferences from economic history, economists will be able to give a more convincing answer to the question of how industrial growth works and why it emerged first in America.

Note

1 Note added in proof: Recent work by Claudia Goldin (pers. comm.) suggests that Maddison's data on education in the United States are flawed. Final judgment about the importance of education should be withheld until better evidence becomes available.

References

Abramovitz, Moses and David, Paul A. (1996): "Convergence and Deferred Catch-up: Productivity Leadership and the Waning of American Exceptionalism," in R. Landau, T. Taylor, and G. Wright (eds), *The Mosaic of Economic Growth*, Stanford, CA: Stanford University Press, 21–62.

Cairncross, A.K. (1953): *Home and Foreign Investment 1970–1913*. Cambridge: Cambridge University Press.

Dawkins, R. (1986): *The Blind Watchmaker*. New York: Norton.

Maddison, A. (1995): *Monitoring the World Economy, 1820–1992*. Paris: Organization for Economic Cooperation and Development.

Mankiw, N. G. (1995): "The Growth of Nations," *Brookings Papers on Economic Activity*, 1, 275–326.

Nelson, R. R. and Winter, S. (1984): *An Evolutionary Theory of Economic Change*. Cambridge, MA: Belknap.

Nelson, R. R. and Wright, G. (1992): "The Rise and Fall of American Technological Leadership: The Postwar Era in Historical Perspective," *Journal of Economic Literature*, 30, 4, December, 1931–64.

Rosenberg, N. (1963): "Technological Change in the Machine Tool Industry, 1840–1910," *Journal of Economic History*, 23 (4), December, 414–43: Reprinted in *Perspectives on technology*, Armonk, NY: Sharpe, 9–31.

——(1981): "Why in America?" in O. Mayr and R. C. Post (eds), *Yankee Enterprise, the Rise of the American System of Manufactures*, Washington, DC: Smithsonian Institution Press. Reprinted 1995 in *Exploring the Black Box*, Cambridge: Cambridge University Press.

——(1985): "The Commercial Exploitation of Science by American Industry," in K. B. Clark, R. H. Hayes and C. Lorenz (eds), *The Uneasy Alliance*, Boston: Harvard Business School Press, 18–51.

Sokoloff, K. L. (1988): "Inventive Activity in Early Industrial America: Evidence from Patent Records," *Journal of Economic History*, 48 (4), December, 813–50.

Wright, G. (1990): "The Origins of American Industrial Success, 1879–1940." *American Economic Review*, 80 (4), September, 651–68.

Index